The Microsoft® Office Specialist Study Guide

Joyce Cox
Joan Preppernau
Online Training Solutions, Inc.

PUBLISHED BY
Microsoft Press
A Division of Microsoft Corporation
One Microsoft Way
Redmond, Washington 98052-6399

Copyright © 2008 by Online Training Solutions, Inc.

Library of Congress Control Number: 2010934185

Printed and bound in the United States of America.

1 2 3 4 5 6 7 8 9 QGT 5 4 3 2 1 0

Distributed in Canada by H.B. Fenn and Company Ltd.

A CIP catalogue record for this book is available from the British Library.

Microsoft Press books are available through booksellers and distributors worldwide. For further information about international editions, contact your local Microsoft Corporation office or contact Microsoft Press International directly at fax (425) 936-7329. Visit our Web site at www.microsoft.com/mspress. Send comments mspinput@microsoft.com.

Microsoft, Microsoft Press, Access, Calibri, Excel, Outlook, Pivot Chart, Pivot Table, PowerPoint, SharePoint, SmartArt, SQL Server, Windows, and Windows Vista are either registered trademarks or trademarks of Microsoft Corporation in the United States and/or other countries. Other product and company names mentioned herein may be the trademarks of their respective owners.

The example companies, organizations, products, domain names, e-mail addresses, logos, people, places, and events depicted herein are fictitious. No association with any real company, organization, product, domain name, e-mail address, logo, person, place, or event is intended or should be inferred.

This book expresses the author's views and opinions. The information contained in this book is provided without any express, statutory, or implied warranties. Neither the authors, Microsoft Corporation, nor its resellers, or distributors will be held liable for any damages caused or alleged to be caused either directly or indirectly by this book.

Acquisitions Editor: Juliana Aldous
Developmental Editor: Sandra Haynes
Project Editor: Maria Gargiulo
Editorial Production: Online Training Solutions, Inc.
Technical Reviewers: Rob Carr, Joyce Cox, Barry Preppernau, and Joan Preppernau
Cover: Turnstyle

Body Part No. X14-86383

Contents

What do you think of this book? We want to hear from you!

Microsoft is interested in hearing your feedback so we can continually improve our books and learning
resources for you. To participate in a brief online survey, please visit:

www.microsoft.com/learning/booksurvey/

3   Working with Visual Content   69

4   Organizing Content   97

3 Creating and Modifying Formulas 235

4 Presenting Data Visually 261

2   Creating and Formatting Slide Content   357

3   Working with Visual Content   395

What do you think of this book? We want to hear from you!

Microsoft is interested in hearing your feedback so we can continually improve our books and learning resources for you. To participate in a brief online survey, please visit:

www.microsoft.com/learning/booksurvey/

Taking a Microsoft Office Specialist Exam

Desktop computing proficiency is becoming increasingly important in today's business world. As a result, when screening, hiring, and training employees, more employers are relying on the objectivity and consistency of technology certification to ensure the competence of their workforce. As an employee or job seeker, you can use technology certification to prove that you already have the skills you need to succeed, saving current and future employers the trouble and expense of training you.

The Microsoft Business Certification Program

The Microsoft Business Certification program is designed to assist employees in validating their Windows Vista skills and 2007 Microsoft Office program skills. The following certification paths are available:

- A Microsoft Office Specialist (MOS) is an individual who has demonstrated proficiency in Windows Vista or in a 2007 Office program by passing a certification exam in Windows Vista or in one or more of the 2007 Office programs, including Microsoft Office Word 2007, Microsoft Office Excel 2007, Microsoft Office PowerPoint 2007, Microsoft Office Outlook 2007, and Microsoft Office Access 2007.

- A Microsoft Certified Application Professional (MCAP) is an individual who has taken his or her knowledge of the 2007 Office system and of Microsoft SharePoint Products and Technologies to the next level and has demonstrated by passing a certification exam that he or she can use the collaborative power of the Office system to accomplish job functions such as *Budget Analysis and Forecasting*, or *Content Management and Collaboration*.

Selecting a Certification Path

When deciding which Microsoft Business Certification path you would like to pursue, you should assess the following:

- The program and program version(s) with which you are familiar
- The length of time you have used the program
- Whether you have had formal or informal training in the use of that program

Candidates for MOS-level certification are expected to successfully complete a wide range of standard business tasks, such as formatting a document or worksheet. Successful candidates generally have six or more months of experience with Windows Vista or the specific Office program, including either formal, instructor-led training or self-study using MOS-approved books, guides, or interactive computer-based materials.

Candidates for MCAP-level certification are expected to successfully complete more complex, business-oriented tasks that involve using the advanced functionality of the combined 2007 Office suite of products, as well as SharePoint. Successful candidates generally have at least six months, and may have several years, of experience with the programs, including formal, instructor-led training or self-study using MCAP-approved materials.

Test-Taking Tips

Every MOS and MCAP certification exam is developed from a set of exam skill standards that are derived from studies of how Windows Vista and the 2007 Office programs are used in the workplace. Because these skill standards dictate the scope of each exam, they provide critical information about how to prepare for certification. This book follows the structure of the published exam objectives; see "Using This Book to Study for a Certification Exam" for more information.

The MOS certification exams for the 2007 Office system programs are performance-based and require you to complete business-related tasks in the program for which you are seeking certification. You might be told to adjust program settings or be presented with a file and told to do something specific with it. Your score on the exam reflects how well you perform the requested tasks.

Here is some helpful information about taking the exam:

- Keep track of the time. You have 50 minutes to complete the exam. Your exam time does not officially begin until after you finish reading the instructions provided at the beginning of the exam. During the exam, the amount of time remaining is shown at the bottom of the exam interface. You can't pause the exam after you start it.

- Pace yourself. At the beginning of the exam, you will be told how many questions are included in the exam. Some questions will require that you complete more than one task. During the exam, the number of completed and remaining questions is shown at the bottom of the exam interface.

- Read the exam instructions carefully before beginning. Follow all the instructions provided in each question completely and accurately.

- Enter requested information as it appears in the instructions, but without duplicating the formatting unless you are specifically instructed otherwise. For example, the text and values you are asked to enter might appear in the instructions in bold and underlined (**text**), but you should enter the information without applying these formats.

- Close all dialog boxes before proceeding to the next exam question unless you are specifically instructed otherwise.

- Don't close task panes before proceeding to the next exam question unless you are specifically instructed otherwise.

- If you are asked to print a document, worksheet, chart, report, or slide, perform the task, but be aware that nothing will actually be printed.

- Don't worry about extra keystrokes or mouse clicks. Your work is scored based on its result, not on the method you use to achieve that result (unless a specific method is indicated in the instructions).

- If your computer becomes unstable during the exam (for example, if the exam does not respond or the mouse no longer functions) or if a power outage occurs, contact a testing center administrator immediately. The administrator will restart the computer and return the exam to the point where the interruption occurred, with your score intact.

Strategy This book includes special tips for effectively studying for the Microsoft Office Specialist exams, in Strategy paragraphs such as this one.

Certification Benefits

At the conclusion of the exam, you will receive a score report, which you can print with the assistance of the testing center administrator. If your score meets or exceeds the passing standard (the minimum required score), you will be contacted by e-mail by the Microsoft Certification Program team and mailed a printed certificate within approximately 14 days. The e-mail message you receive will include your Microsoft Certification ID and links to online resources, including the Microsoft Certified Professional site. On this site, you can order a welcome kit and ID card, view and send your certification transcript, build a personalized certification logo, and access other useful and interesting resources, including special offers from Microsoft and affiliated companies.

Using the Logo Builder, you can create a personalized certification logo that includes the MOS logo and the specific programs in which you have achieved certification. If you achieve MOS certification in multiple programs, you can include all of them in one logo, like this:

Microsoft Office Access 2007 Certified
Microsoft Office Excel 2007 Certified
Microsoft Office Outlook 2007 Certified
Microsoft Office Powerpoint 2007 Certified
Microsoft Office Word 2007 Certified
Microsoft Windows Vista Certified

You can include your personalized logo on business cards and other personal promotional materials. This logo attests to the fact that you are proficient in the applications or cross-application skills necessary to achieve the certification.

For More Information

To learn more about the Microsoft Office Specialist exams, the Microsoft Certified Application Professional exams, and related courseware, visit:

www.microsoft.com/learning/mcp/msbc/

In 2007, the Microsoft Certification Application Specialist (MCAS) credential was introduced to support Microsoft Office Suite 2007. While this certification is recognized worldwide as the official credential for Office 2007 applications, it was often confused with the Microsoft Office Specialist (MOS) certification, which is used to validate individuals' skills using previous versions of Office, including Office 2000, Office XP or Office 2003.

To simplify the Microsoft Office certification program, starting on June 1, 2010, MCAS was formally renamed MOS 2007. More details about these changes to the Microsoft Office certification are located at http://www.microsoft.com/learning/en/us/certification/office-cert-update.aspx.

Using This Book to Study for a Certification Exam

The Microsoft Office Specialist (MOS) exams for individual programs in the 2007 Microsoft Office system are practical rather than theoretical. You must demonstrate that you can complete certain tasks rather than simply answering questions about program features. The successful MOS certification candidate will have at least six months of experience using all aspects of the application on a regular basis; for example, using Outlook at work to send messages, track contact information, schedule appointments and meetings, track and assign tasks, and take notes.

This book has been designed to guide you in studying the types of tasks you are likely to be required to demonstrate in the MOS exams for Microsoft Office Word 2007, Microsoft Office Excel 2007, Microsoft Office Access 2007, Microsoft Office PowerPoint 2007, and Microsoft Office Outlook 2007.

Each part of the book covers one exam. The coverage for each exam is divided into chapters representing broad skill sets, and each chapter is divided into sections addressing groups of related skills. Each section includes review information, generic procedures, and practice tasks you can complete on your own while studying. When necessary, we provide practice files you can use to work through the practice tasks. You can practice the procedures in this book by using the practice files supplied or by using your own files. (Keep in mind that functionality in some 2007 Office system programs is limited in files created in or saved for earlier versions of the program. When working in such a file, *Compatibility Mode* appears in the program window title bar.)

As a certification candidate, you probably have a lot of experience with the program you want to become certified in. Many of the procedures we discuss in this book will be familiar to you; others might not be. Read through each study section and ensure that you are familiar with not only the procedures included in the section, but also the concepts and tools discussed in the review information. Graphics depict the tools you will use to perform procedures related to the skill set. Study the graphics and ensure that you are familiar with all the options available for each tool.

Throughout the book, you will find Strategy tips presenting additional methods of study you can pursue on your own to ensure that you achieve mastery of a skill set and are successful in your certification effort.

Features and Conventions of This Book

You can save time when you use this book by understanding how special instructions, keys to press, buttons to click, and other conventions are indicated in this book.

Convention	Meaning
	This icon at the end of a chapter introduction indicates information about the practice files provided on the companion CD for use in the chapter.
1 2	Blue numbered steps guide you through step-by-step procedures.
→	An arrow indicates a procedure that has only one step.
See Also	These paragraphs direct you to more information about a given topic in this book or elsewhere.
Tip	These paragraphs provide a helpful hint or shortcut that makes working through a task easier, or information about other available options.
Important	These paragraphs remind you to install the practice files or to reverse settings when you have completed the practice tasks.
Strategy	These paragraphs provide additional exam study tips.
Interface elements and keyboard keys	In procedures, the names of program elements (such as buttons, and commands) and keyboard keys, are shown in black bold characters.
Ctrl+Enter	A plus sign (+) between two key names means that you must hold down the first key while you press the second key. For example, "press **Ctrl+Home**" means "hold down the **Ctrl** key and press the **Home** key."
User input and *emphasis*	Terms you should become familiar with and anything you are supposed to type appear in italic characters.

Additional Resources

If, after reading the book and completing the practice tasks, you later need help remembering how to perform a procedure, the following features of this book will help you locate specific information:

● **Detailed table of contents.** Scan a listing of the topics covered in each chapter and locate specific topics.

● **Detailed index.** Look up specific tasks and general concepts in the index, which has been carefully crafted with the reader in mind.

● **Companion CD.** Install the practice files needed for the step-by-step exercises and consult a fully searchable electronic version of this book and other useful resources.

Working in the Microsoft Office Fluent User Interface

Many of the programs in the 2007 Microsoft Office system feature a new look and a new way of interacting with the program that is designed to make the commands you need, in the context of the task you are currently performing, easily available. Called the *Microsoft Office Fluent user interface*, this new set of features is available in Microsoft Office Word 2007, Microsoft Office Excel 2007, Microsoft Office Access 2007, Microsoft Office PowerPoint 2007, and Microsoft Office Outlook 2007.

Special features of the Office Fluent user interface include:

- **The Office menu.** This menu, which appears when you click the Microsoft Office Button located in the upper-left corner of the program window, contains commands related to working with entire files (rather than the file content).

- **The Office Fluent Ribbon.** Probably the most visible element of the Office Fluent user interface, the Ribbon replaces the menus and toolbars found in earlier versions of Office programs. Commands are arranged on the Ribbon on task-specific tabs.

- **The Office Fluent Quick Access Toolbar.** This toolbar provides easy access to the commands you use most frequently. You can change its position, add and remove commands, and create custom command groups for specific documents.

- **Contextual commands.** Commands you use for working with specific objects, such as tables, graphics, headers, and footers, appear only when you select one of those objects. A Mini toolbar displaying formatting commands appears when you select text.

- **Office Fluent Live Preview.** This feature displays the effect of a formatting change on the selected text or object without applying the format.

- **Quick Styles, Layouts, and Formats.** These features provide professionally designed color palettes, themes, and graphic effects.

- **SmartArt graphics.** These graphics and new styles and formatting methods greatly simplify the process of creating and formatting a variety of diagrams.

- **Document inspection and finishing tools.** This collection of tools provides a way to safely share information with other people.

See Also For information about the Office Fluent user interface elements in a specific program, refer to the program-specific *Step by Step* book.

If You Are Running Windows XP

The graphics and operating system–related instructions in this book reflect the Windows Vista user interface. However, mastery of Windows Vista is not required for Microsoft Office Specialist exams 77-601, 77-602, 77-603, 77-604, or 77-605.

The differences you will encounter when working through the practice tasks in this book on a computer running the Windows XP operating system center around appearance rather than functionality. Some of the differences are as follows:

- The Windows Vista personal documents folder is the *Documents* folder. The Windows XP equivalent is the *My Document*s folder.

- On a computer running Windows XP, some of the dialog boxes you will work with in the practice tasks not only look different from the graphics shown in this book but also work differently. These dialog boxes are primarily those that act as an interface between Office and the operating system, including any dialog box in which you navigate to a specific location.

For the most part, these differences are small enough that you will have no difficulty completing the procedures in this book on a computer running Windows XP.

Managing the Practice Files

The instructions given in the "Using the Companion CD" section are specific to Windows Vista. On a computer running Windows Vista, the default installation location of the practice files is *Documents\Microsoft Press\MCAS*. On a computer running Windows XP, the default installation location is *My Documents\Microsoft Press\MCAS*. If your computer is running Windows XP, whenever an exercise tells you to navigate to your *Documents* folder, you should instead go to your *My Documents* folder.

Important If you need help installing or uninstalling the practice files, please see the "Using the Companion CD" section later in this book.

Using the Companion CD

The companion CD included with this book contains practice files you can use as you work through the practice tasks at the end of each study section. By using practice files, you won't waste time creating samples and typing large amounts of data. Instead, you can concentrate on testing your knowledge about the programs.

> Digital Content for Digital Book Readers: If you bought a digital-only edition of this book, you can enjoy select content from the print edition's companion CD.
>
> Visit *go.microsoft.com/fwlink/?LinkId=113688* to get your downloadable content. This content is always up-to-date and available to all readers.

In addition to the practice files, the CD contains some exciting resources that will really enhance your ability to get the most out of using this book and the 2007 Microsoft Office system, including the following:

- *Microsoft Certified Application Specialist Study Guide: 2007 Microsoft Office System Edition*
- Sample chapters from *Microsoft Office Word 2007 Step by Step* by Joyce Cox and Joan Preppernau
- Sample chapters from *Microsoft Office Excel 2007 Step by Step* by Curtis Frye
- Sample chapters from *Microsoft Office PowerPoint 2007 Step by Step* by Joyce Cox and Joan Preppernau
- Sample chapters from *Microsoft Office Outlook 2007 Step by Step* by Joan Preppernau and Joyce Cox
- Sample chapters from *Microsoft Office Access 2007 Step by Step* by Steve Lambert, Dow Lambert, and Joan Preppernau
- Sample chapter and poster from *Look Both Ways: Help Protect Your Family on the Internet* (Linda Criddle, 2007)
- *Windows Vista Product Guide*
- *Microsoft Computer Dictionary, Fifth Edition*

Important The companion CD for this book does not contain the 2007 Office system software. You should purchase and install the software before using this book.

CD Contents

The following tables list the practice files supplied on the book's companion CD.

Exam 77-601: Using Microsoft Office Word 2007

Folder\Objective	File
Objective01 Creating and Customizing Documents	AutoCorrect.docx
	Background.docx
	Bookmarks.docx
	Columns.docx
	Contents.docx
	CrossReference.docx
	CustomQATAll.docx
	CustomQATDoc.docx
	CustomTheme.docx
	Header.docx
	Hyperlinks.docx
	Index.docx
	Numbers.docx
	OtherLogos.docx
	Printing.docx
	Properties.docx
	Theme.docx
Objective02 Formatting Content	Changing.docx
	Characters.docx
	Finding.docx
	Pages.docx
	Paragraphs.docx
	Styles.docx
	Tabs.docx
Objective03 Working with Visual Content	AreaChart.docx
	Balloons.docx
	Chart.docx
	ClipArt.docx
	DropCap.docx
	Logo.docx
	Logo.png
	Picture.docx

Folder\Objective	File
Objective03 Working with Visual Content, *continued*	*Process.docx* *Process2.docx* *Shapes.docx* *SmartArt.docx* *TextBoxes.docx* *WordArt.docx*
Objective04 Organizing Content	*Bibiliography1.docx* *Bibliography2.docx* *Calculations.docx* *DataSource.xlsx* *Envelope.docx* *Footnotes.docx* *FormLetter.docx* *Lists.docx* *MergingData.docx* *ModifyTable.docx* *Parts.docx* *PreparingData.docx* *SavedText.docx* *SortTable.docx* *Table.docx* *TabularList.docx*
Objective05 Reviewing Documents	*Combining1.docx* *Combining2.docx* *Comments.docx* *Comparing1.docx* *Comparing2.docx* *TrackChanges1.docx* *TrackChanges2.docx* *Viewing1.docx* *Viewing2.docx*
Objective06 Sharing and Securing Content	*Compatibility.docx* *Finalizing1.docx* *Finalizing2.docx* *Password.docx* *PreventingChanges.docx* *Saving.docx* *Signature.docx*

Exam 77-602: Using Microsoft Office Excel 2007

Folder\Objective	File
Objective01 Creating and Manipulating Data	*AirQualityData.xlsx* *CopyPaste.xlsx* *DataValidation.xlsx* *Duplicates.xlsx* *FillCopies.xlsx* *FillCustom.xlsx* *FillSeries.xlsx* *ListBox.xlsx* *PersonalMonthlyBudget.xlsx* *PopulationData.xlsx* *SalesReport.xlsx*
Objective02 Formatting Data and Content	*FormatCells.xlsx* *FourthCoffee.png* *Gridlines.xlsx* *HeightWidth.xlsx* *Hiding.xlsx* *Hyperlink.xlsx* *InsertingDeleting.xlsx* *Mosaic.jpg* *RowColumnFormatting.xlsx* *Table.xlsx* *TableStyle.xlsx* *Themes.xlsx*
Objective03 Creating and Modifying Formulas	*ConditionalFormula.xlsx* *FormatFormula.xlsx* *LookupFormula.xlsx* *MultiplicationTable.xlsx* *Sales.xlsx* *SalesBySeason.xlsx* *Schedule.xlsx* *SummaryCondition.xlsx* *SummaryFormula.xlsx*

Folder\Objective	File
Objective04 Presenting Data Visually	*ChartElements.xlsx*
	ConditionalFormatting.xlsx
	DataSource.xlsx
	Editing.xlsx
	Filtering.xlsx
	Grouping.xlsx
	Logo2.jpg
	Picture.xlsx
	Plotting.xlsx
	Shapes.xlsx
	SizingMoving.xlsx
	SmartArt.xlsx
	Sorting.xlsx
	Subtotals.xlsx
Objective05 Collaborating and Securing Data	*Comments.xlsx*
	Compatibility.xlsx
	Finalizing.xlsx
	HeaderFooter.xlsx
	Layout.xlsx
	PageBreaks.xlsx
	Password.xlsx
	PrintArea.xlsx
	Properties.xlsx
	Protecting.xlsx
	ResolveChanges.xlsx
	Saving.xlsx
	Sharing.xlsx
	SharingChanges.xlsx
	TrackChanges.xlsx

Exam 77-603: Using Microsoft Office PowerPoint 2007

Folder\Objective	File
Objective01	*DeleteSlide.pptx*
Creating and Formatting Presentations	*Existing.pptx*
	Logo.png
	Mosaic.jpg
	NewSlide.pptx
	NoTransition.pptx
	Outline.docx
	Printing.pptx
	RearrangeSlides.pptx
	Transition.pptx
Objective02	*BulletsNumbers.pptx*
Creating and Formatting Slide Content	*Costs.xlsx*
	CustomAnimation.pptx
	DefaultAnimation.pptx
	Editing.pptx
	Files.pptx
	Formatting.pptx
	HouseHome.wmv
	LinkToSlide.pptx
	Movies.pptx
	Slides1.pptx
	Slides2.pptx
	Sounds.pptx
	TextBox.pptx
	TextShape.pptx
	WordArt.pptx
Objective03	*BulletDiagrams.pptx*
Working with Visual Content	*ChartElements.pptx*
	Charts.pptx
	ChartType.pptx
	ClipArt.pptx
	ClipArtColor.pptx
	DiagramColors.pptx

Folder\Objective	File
Objective03 Working with Visual Content, *continued*	*Diagrams.pptx*
	EditingDiagrams.pptx
	FlipDistribute.pptx
	FormattingDiagrams.pptx
	GuidePosition.pptx
	PictureBorder.pptx
	Pictures1.pptx
	Pictures2.jpg
	Pictures3.jpg
	PictureStyle.pptx
	ShapeFormatting.pptx
	ShapesConnectors.pptx
	ShapesText.pptx
	SizingPictures.pptx
	Tables.pptx
Objective04 Collaborating On and Delivering Presentations	*BigFile.pptx*
	Comments.pptx
	DeleteComments.pptx
	EarlierVersions.pptx
	Finalizing.pptx
	Handouts.pptx
	Loop.pptx
	Notes.pptx
	NotesHandouts.pptx
	Password.pptx
	Pen.pptx
	Printing.pptx
	Rehearsal.pptx
	Subsets.pptx
	Timings.pptx
	Travel.pptx
	ViewingOnly.pptx
	WebPage.pptx
	YinYang.png

Exam 77-604: Using Microsoft Office Outlook 2007

Folder\Objective	File
Objective01 Managing Messages	*Design.pptx*
Objective02 Managing Scheduling	*Agenda.docx*
Objective03 Managing Tasks	none
Objective04 Managing Contacts and Personal Contact Information	*Contacts.xls* *FourthCoffee.png* *Sunset.jpg*
Objective05 Organizing Information	none

Exam 77-605: Using Microsoft Office Access 2007

Folder\Objective	File
Objective01 Structuring a Database	*Changing.accdb* *Design.accdb* *Keys.accdb* *Relationships.accdb* *Report.accdb* *Split.accdb*
Objective02 Creating and Formatting Database Elements	*AddControls.accdb* *AutoFormat.accdb* *CreateFormReport.accdb* *FieldProperty.accdb* *Logo.png* *Manually.accdb* *ModifyTables.accdb* *PivotChart.accdb* *Printing.accdb* *RefineControls.accdb* *Totals.accdb* *Validation.accdb* *Wizard.accdb*

Folder\Objective	File
Objective03 Entering and Modifying Data	*Attachments.accdb*
	DuplicateRecords.accdb
	EnterRecords.accdb
	FindAndReplace.accdb
	FreezeColumns.accdb
	HideColumns.accdb
	ImportAccess.accdb
	Navigate.accdb
	Products.accdb
	Products.xlsx
	YellowRose.jpg
Objective04 Creating and Modifying Queries	*AddTable.accdb*
	Append.accdb
	Calculate.accdb
	CrossTab.accdb
	Delete.accdb
	MakeTable.accdb
	SelectQuery.accdb
	Unmatched.accdb
	Update.accdb
Objective05 Presenting and Sharing Data	*ExportExcel.accdb*
	Filter.accdb
	Objects.accdb
	OtherFileTypes.accdb
	Print.accdb
	Sort.accdb
Objective06 Managing and Maintaining Databases	*Compact.accdb*
	Information.accdb
	Password.accdb
	Routine.accdb
	Startup.accdb

Minimum System Requirements

This book includes discussions of the following programs in the 2007 Office system:

- Microsoft Office Word 2007
- Microsoft Office Excel 2007
- Microsoft Office PowerPoint 2007
- Microsoft Office Outlook 2007
- Microsoft Office Access 2007

To install and run these programs, your computer needs to meet the following minimum requirements:

- 500 megahertz (MHz) processor
- 256 megabytes (MB) RAM
- CD or DVD drive
- 2 gigabytes (GB) available hard disk space; a portion of this disk space will be freed if you select the option to delete the installation files

   Tip Hard disk requirements will vary depending on configuration; custom installation choices might require more or less hard disk space.

- Monitor with 800 × 600 screen resolution; 1024 × 768 or higher recommended
- Keyboard and mouse or compatible pointing device
- Internet connection, 128 kilobits per second (Kbps) or greater, for download and activation of products, accessing Microsoft Office Online and online Help topics, and any other Internet-dependent processes
- Windows Vista or later, Windows XP with Service Pack 2 (SP2), or Windows Server 2003 or later
- Windows Internet Explorer 7 or Microsoft Internet Explorer 6 with service packs

In addition to the hardware, software, and connections required to run the 2007 Office system, you will need the following to successfully complete the practice tasks in this book:

- Word 2007, Excel 2007, PowerPoint 2007, Outlook 2007, and Access 2007, with any available service packs
- Access to a printer
- 91 MB of available hard disk space for the practice files

Installing the Practice Files

You need to install the practice files in the correct location on your hard disk before you can use them in the practice tasks. Follow these steps:

1. Remove the companion CD from the envelope at the back of the book, and insert it into the CD drive of your computer.

   The License Agreement appears. Follow the on-screen directions. To use the practice files, you must accept the terms of the license agreement. After you accept the license agreement, a menu screen appears.

   Important If the menu screen does not appear, click the Start button, and then click Computer. Display the Folders list in the Navigation pane, click the icon for your CD drive, and then in the right pane, double-click the StartCD executable file.

2. Click **Install Practice Files**.

3. Click **Next** on the first screen, and then click **Next** to accept the terms of the license agreement on the next screen.

4. If you want to install the practice files to a location other than the default folder (*Documents\Microsoft Press\MCAS*), click the **Change** button, select the new drive and path, and then click **OK**.

   Important If you install the practice files to a location other than the default, you will need to substitute that path in the practice tasks.

5. Click **Next** on the **Choose Destination Location** screen, and then click **Install** on the **Ready to Install the Program** screen to install the selected practice files.

6. After the practice files have been installed, click **Finish**.

7. Close the Companion CD window.

8. Remove the companion CD from the CD drive, and return it to the envelope at the back of the book.

Using the Practice Files

When you install the practice files from the companion CD that accompanies this book, the files are stored on your hard disk in chapter-specific subfolders under *Documents\ Microsoft Press\MCAS* unless you specify a different location during installation. Each Practice Tasks section begins with a paragraph identifying the location of the practice files provided for the accompanying tasks.

You can display the practice file folder in Windows Explorer by following these steps:

→ On the Windows taskbar, click the **Start** button, click **All Programs**, click **Microsoft Press**, and then click **MCAS Study Guide**.

You can browse to the practice files from a dialog box by following these steps:

1. In the **Favorite Links** pane of the dialog box, click **Documents**.

2. In your *Documents* folder, double-click *Microsoft Press*, double-click *MCAS*, double-click the program folder, and then double-click the specified objective folder.

Removing and Uninstalling the Practice Files

You can free up hard disk space by uninstalling the practice files that were installed from the companion CD. The uninstall process deletes any files that you created in the *Documents\Microsoft Press\MCAS* objective-specific folders while working through the practice tasks. Follow these steps:

1. On the Windows taskbar, click the **Start** button, and then click **Control Panel**.

2. In **Control Panel**, under **Programs**, click the **Uninstall a program** task.

3. In the **Programs and Features** window, click **MCAS Study Guide: 2007 Microsoft Office System Edition**, and then on the toolbar at the top of the window, click the **Uninstall** button.

4. If the **Programs and Features** message box asking you to confirm the deletion appears, click **Yes**.

Important Microsoft Product Support Services does not provide support for this book or its companion CD.

Getting Help

Every effort has been made to ensure the accuracy of this book and the contents of its companion CD. If you do run into problems, please contact the sources listed in the following sections for assistance.

Getting Help with This Book and Its Companion CD

If your question or issue concerns the content of this book or its companion CD, please first search the online Microsoft Press Knowledge Base, which provides support information for known errors in or corrections to this book, at the following Web site:

www.microsoft.com/mspress/support/search.asp

If you do not find your answer at the online Knowledge Base, send your comments or questions to Microsoft Press Technical Support at:

mspinput@microsoft.com

Getting Help with an Office Program

If your question is about a specific 2007 Microsoft Office system application, and not about the content of this book, your first recourse is the Office Help system. This system is a combination of tools and files stored on your computer when you installed the 2007 Office system and, if your computer is connected to the Internet, information available from Microsoft Office Online. You can find general or specific Help information in several ways:

- To find out about an item on the screen, you can display a ScreenTip. For example, to display a ScreenTip for a button, point to the button without clicking it. The ScreenTip gives the button's name, the associated keyboard shortcut if there is one, and unless you specify otherwise, a description of the associated action.

- You can click the Help button in the upper-right corner of the program window to display the Help window.

- In a dialog box, you can click the Help button at the right end of the dialog box title bar to display the Help window with topics related to the functions of that dialog box already identified.

More Information

If your question is about a Microsoft software product and you cannot find the answer in the product's Help system, please search the appropriate product solution center or the Microsoft Knowledge Base at:

support.microsoft.com

In the United States, Microsoft software product support issues not covered by the Microsoft Knowledge Base are addressed by Microsoft Product Support Services. Location-specific software support options are available from:

support.microsoft.com/gp/selfoverview/

Using Microsoft Office
Word 2007

This part of the book covers the skills you need to have for certification as a Microsoft Office Specialist in Microsoft Office Word 2007. Specifically, you need to be able to complete tasks that demonstrate the following skill sets:

1 Creating and Customizing Documents
2 Formatting Content
3 Working with Visual Content
4 Organizing Content
5 Reviewing Documents
6 Sharing and Securing Content

With these skills, you can create and manage the types of documents most commonly used in a business environment.

Prerequisites

We assume that you have been working with Word 2007 for at least six months and that you know how to carry out fundamental tasks that are not specifically mentioned in the Microsoft Office Specialist objectives for Exam 77-601, "Using Microsoft Office Word 2007." Before you begin studying for this exam, you might want to make sure you are familiar with the information in this section.

Selecting Text

Before you can edit or format text, you need to select it. You can select any amount of text by dragging through it. You can select specific units of text as follows:

→ To select a word, double-click it. The word and the space following it are selected. Punctuation following a word is not selected.

→ To select a sentence, click anywhere in the sentence while holding down the Ctrl key. The first character in the sentence through the space following the ending punctuation mark are selected.

→ To select a paragraph, triple-click it. The paragraph and paragraph mark are selected.

You can select adjacent words, lines, or paragraphs by positioning the insertion point at the beginning of the text you want to select, holding down the Shift key, and then pressing an arrow key or clicking at the end of the text that you want to select.

To select non-adjacent blocks of text, select the first block, hold down the Ctrl key, and then select the next block.

To select a block of text quickly, you can use the selection area—the empty area to the left of the document's text column. When the pointer is in the selection area, it changes from an I-beam to a right-pointing arrow. From the selection area, you can select specific units of text as follows:

→ To select a line, click in the selection area to the left of the line.

→ To select a paragraph, double-click in the selection area to the left of the paragraph.

→ To select an entire document, triple-click anywhere in the selection area.

To deselect text, click anywhere in the document window except the selection area.

Moving Around in a Document

You can view various parts of the active document by using the vertical and horizontal scroll bars. Scrolling the document does not move the insertion point—it changes only the part of the document displayed in the window. For example, if you drag the vertical scroll box down to the bottom of the scroll bar, the end of the document comes into view, but the insertion point stays in its original location.

Here are some other ways to use the scroll bars:

→ Click the up or down scroll arrow on the vertical scroll bar to move the document window up or down one line of text.

→ Click above or below the scroll box to move up or down one windowful.

→ Click the left or right scroll arrow on the horizontal scroll bar to move the document window to the left or right several characters at a time.

→ Click to the left or right of the scroll box to move left or right one windowful.

You can also move around in a document by moving the insertion point. You can click to place the insertion point at a particular location, or you can press a key or a key combination to move the insertion point.

The following table shows the keys and key combinations you can use to move the insertion point quickly.

Pressing this key or combination	Moves the insertion point
Left Arrow	Left one character at a time
Right Arrow	Right one character at a time
Down Arrow	Down one line at a time
Up Arrow	Up one line at a time
Ctrl+Left Arrow	Left one word at a time
Ctrl+Right Arrow	Right one word at a time
Home	To the beginning of the current line
End	To the end of the current line
Ctrl+Home	To the start of the document
Ctrl+End	To the end of the document
Ctrl+Page Up	To the beginning of the previous page
Ctrl+Page Down	To the beginning of the next page
Page Up	Up one screen
Page Down	Down one screen

1 Creating and Customizing Documents

The skills tested in this section of the Microsoft Office Specialist exam for Microsoft Office Word 2007 relate to general document-handling processes and management of the Word environment. Specifically, the following objectives are associated with this set of skills:

1.1 Create and format documents.
1.2 Lay out documents.
1.3 Make documents and content easier to find.
1.4 Personalize Word 2007.

Much of the work you do with Word documents involves the document content, but there are also many ways in which you work with the structure and formatting. For example, you can apply a template or theme to the document, change its page orientation, or generate reference materials directly from the content. You can also make changes to the program interface, to personalize it for the types of activities you do most frequently.

This chapter guides you in studying document formatting and layout options, the Word tools that make it easier for readers to find information, and the many options for customizing the Word environment to make your work with Word as efficient as possible.

Important Before you can use the practice files in this chapter, you need to install them from the book's companion CD to their default location. See "Using the Companion CD" at the beginning of this book for more information.

Tip Graphics and operating system–related instructions in this book reflect the Windows Vista user interface. If your computer is running Windows XP and you experience trouble following the instructions as written, refer to the sidebar "If You Are Running Windows XP" in "Working in the Microsoft Office Fluent User Interface" at the beginning of this book.

1.1 Create and format documents

Templates

Every new document you create is based on a *document template*. A Word 2007 document template is a file with a .dotm or .dotx extension that defines information about style sets and color schemes, and can also contain content (words and graphics).

When you create a document from the New Document window, you can choose to base the document on any of the templates installed in the default template location on your computer, or on other templates that you can download from the Microsoft Office Online site. The most common document, a blank document, is based on the Normal document template, which by default is located in the *AppData\Roaming\Microsoft\Templates* folder under your personal folder. Word 2007 also comes with document templates from which you can create a blog post and a variety of faxes, letters, reports, and resumes. From the New Document dialog box, you can download from Office Online design templates for dozens of types of documents including brochures, business cards, calendars, lists, menus, and postcards. Some of these templates were created by Microsoft. Others, known as *Community Templates*, were created and made available by computer users such as yourself.

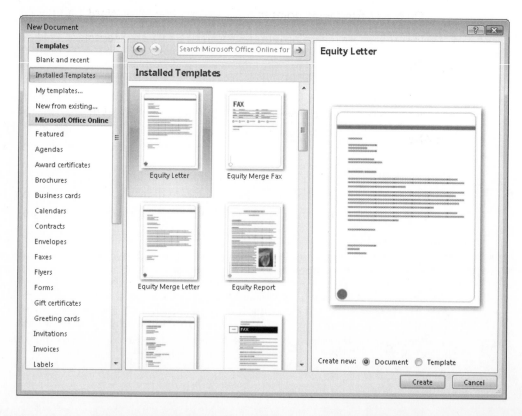

See Also For information about applying styles and using style sets, see section 2.1, "Format text and paragraphs."

If you want to use an existing document as the basis for future documents, you can save the document as a template. The next time you need to create this type of document, you can select your custom template the same way you would select a template supplied by Word.

➤ **To create a document based on an installed template**

1. Click the **Microsoft Office Button**, and then click **New**.

2. In the left pane of the **New Document** dialog box, click **Installed Templates**.

3. In the **Installed Templates** list, click any thumbnail to display a preview in the right pane.

4. In the **Installed Templates** list, double-click the thumbnail of the document template you want.

5. Replace the placeholder text with your own text, and then save the document.

➤ **To save a document as a template**

1. On the **Office** menu, point to **Save As**, and then click **Word Template**.

2. In the **Save As** dialog box, under **Favorite Links**, click **Templates**.

   Tip Word expects templates to be stored in your default Templates folder. If you do not store the templates you create in this folder, Word will not display them in the My Templates list in the New Document dialog box.

3. In the **File name** box, type a name for the template, and then click **Save**.

See Also For information about inserting ready-made cover pages and other document elements, see section 4.1, "Structure content by using Quick Parts."

Borders and Backgrounds

Whether you are creating a document that will be viewed on a printed page, on a computer, or in a Web browser, you can make your document stand out by adding a page border, background color, or pattern. You can also add watermarks—faint words or a graphic that appear behind the text but don't interfere with its readability.

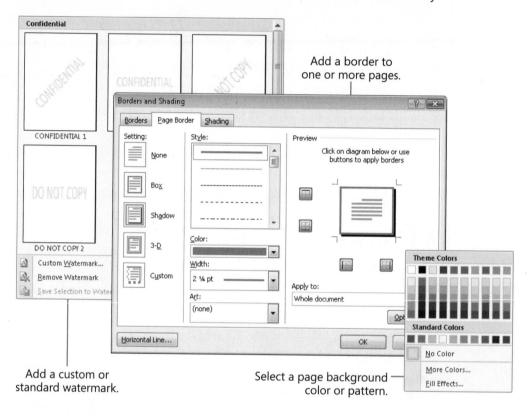

Add a border to one or more pages.

Add a custom or standard watermark.

Select a page background color or pattern.

➤ To add a page border

1. On the **Page Layout** tab, in the **Page Background** group, click the **Page Borders** button.

2. On the **Page Border** tab of the **Borders and Shading** dialog box, under **Setting**, click the type of border you want.

3. To create a line border, make selections in the **Style**, **Color**, and **Width** lists. To create a patterned border, select the pattern you want from the **Art** list.

4. To apply or remove the border from a side of the diagram, in the **Preview** area, click any of the border buttons or any side of the preview diagram.

5. In the **Apply to** list, select the part of the document you want to apply the page border to: the whole document, the current section, or part of the current section.

   See Also For information about creating sections, see section 2.3, "Control pagination."

6. To make adjustments to the border margin or position, click the **Options** button, set the margins, alignment, and positioning, and then click **OK**.

7. In the **Borders and Shading** dialog box, click **OK**.

➤ To add a page background color

1. On the **Page Layout** tab, in the **Page Background** group, click the **Page Color** button.

2. In the **Page Color** palette, click the background color you want.

   Or

1. In the **Page Color** palette, click **More Colors**.

2. On the **Standard** or **Custom** tab of the **Colors** dialog box, make a selection, and then click **OK**.

➤ To add a page background pattern

1. In the **Page Color** palette, click **Fill Effects**.

2. In the **Fill Effects** dialog box, click the tab for the type of fill effect you want.

3. Click the options or thumbnails you want, and then click **OK**.

➤ To add a text watermark

1. On the **Page Layout** tab, in the **Page Background** group, click the **Watermark** button.

2. In the **Watermark** gallery, click the thumbnail for one of the predefined text watermarks.

   Or

1. In the **Watermark** gallery, click **Custom Watermark**.

2. In the **Printed Watermark** dialog box, click **Text watermark**.

3. Either select the watermark text you want from the **Text** list, or type the text in the **Text** box.

4. Format the text by changing the settings in the **Font**, **Size**, and **Color** boxes.

5. Choose a layout, select or clear the **Semitransparent** check box, and then click **OK**.

➤ **To use a picture as a watermark**

1. In the **Watermark** gallery, click **Custom Watermark**.

2. In the **Printed Watermark** dialog box, click **Picture watermark**, and then click **Select Picture**.

3. In the **Insert Picture** dialog box, navigate to the folder where the picture is stored, and double-click the name of the picture.

4. In the **Scale** list, choose how big or small you want the watermark picture to appear in the document.

5. If you want to display a more vibrant picture, clear the **Washout** check box. Then click **OK**.

Themes

You can enhance the look of an entire document by applying one of Word's predefined themes—a combination of colors, fonts, and effects that project a certain feeling or tone. You apply a theme to the entire document from the Themes gallery.

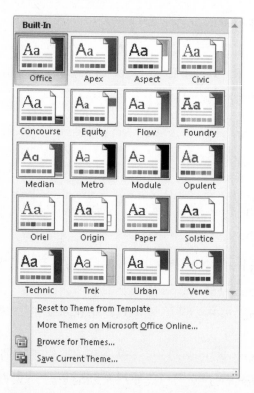

If you like certain aspects of different themes (for example, the colors of one theme and the fonts of another), you can mix and match theme elements.

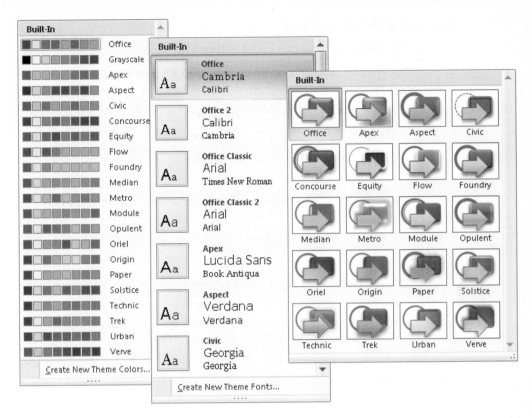

If you create a combination of theme elements that you would like to be able to use with other documents, you can save the combination as a new theme. By saving the theme in the default *Document Themes* folder, you make the theme available in the Themes gallery.

➤ To apply a theme

1. On the **Page Layout** tab, in the **Themes** group, click the **Themes** button.

2. In the **Themes** gallery, click the theme you want.

➤ To modify a theme by mixing color sets, font sets, and effects

1. Select the theme that most closely resembles the look you want.

2. In the **Themes** group, click the **Theme Colors** button, and then in the list, click the color set you want.

3. Click the **Theme Fonts** button, and then in the list, click the font pairing you want.

4. Click the **Theme Effects** button, and then in the list, click the effect you want.

➤ **To create a new color set or font set**

1. In the **Themes** group, click the **Theme Colors** button, and then in the list, click **Create New Theme Colors**.

2. In the **Create New Theme Colors** dialog box, select the colors you want to use for each of the four **Text/Background** colors, the six **Accent** colors, and the two **Hyperlink** colors.

3. Enter a name for the color set in the **Name** box, and then click **Save**.

   Or

1. In the **Themes** group, click the **Theme Fonts** button, and then in the list, click **Create New Theme Fonts**.

2. In the **Create New Theme Fonts** dialog box, select the **Heading** and **Body** fonts you want to use.

3. Enter a name for the font set in the **Name** box, and then click **Save**.

➤ **To save a custom theme**

1. In the **Themes** gallery, click **Save Current Theme**.

2. In the **Save Current Theme** dialog box, enter a name for the theme in the **File name** box, and then click **Save**.

Practice Tasks

The practice files for these tasks are located in the *Documents\Microsoft Press\ MCAS\Word2007\Objective01* folder. If you want, save the task results in the same folder with *My* prepended to the file name.

● Create a new document based on the Median Letter built-in template. Add some text to the new document, and then save it as a new template with the name *MCAS Template*.

● Open the *Theme* document, and apply the Aspect theme to the document.

● Open the *CustomTheme* document, change the color theme to Opulent and the font theme to Apex, and then save the combination as a custom theme with the name *MCAS Design*.

● Open the *Background* document, and change the background color to the second lightest green (Olive Green, Accent 3, Lighter 60%). Then add the Canvas texture to the background. Finally, add the URGENT 1 text watermark.

1.2 **Lay out documents**

Page Settings

Word gives you control of the layout of the pages in a document. You can change the page size, margins, and orientation by clicking the buttons in the Page Setup group on the Page Layout tab. (You can also make the same changes in Print Preview.) All pages of a document have the same margins and are oriented the same way unless you divide the document into sections. Then each section can have independent margin and orientation settings.

See Also For information about creating page and section breaks, see section 2.3, "Control pagination." For information about changing document layout by using Quick Parts or tables, see section 4, "Organizing Content."

➤ **To change the page margins**

1. In the **Page Setup** group, click the **Margins** button.
2. In the **Margins** gallery, click the standard margin set you want or click **Custom Margins**, specify settings on the **Margins** tab of the **Page Setup** dialog box, and then click **OK**.

➤ **To switch the page orientation**

→ In the **Page Setup** group, click the **Page Orientation** button, and then click **Landscape** or **Portrait**.

➤ **To select the paper size**

1. In the **Page Setup** group, click the **Page Size** button.
2. In the **Page Size** gallery, click the standard page size you want, or click **More Paper Sizes**, specify settings on the **Paper** tab of the **Page Setup** dialog box, and then click **OK**.

Headers and Footers

You can display information on every page of your document by creating headers and footers—regions at the top and bottom of the pages that can be created and formatted independently. You can have a different header and footer on the first page of a document, different headers and footers on odd and even pages, or different headers and footers for each section. When you create a header or footer, Word applies the header or footer style specified by the document's template, indicates the header and footer areas by displaying dotted borders, and displays a contextual Design tab on the Ribbon. You can enter information in the header and footer areas the same way you enter ordinary text. You can use the commands on the Design tab to enter and format items such as the date and time, move from one header or footer to another, and establish the location and position of the header and footer.

See Also For information about creating sections, see section 2.3, "Control pagination."

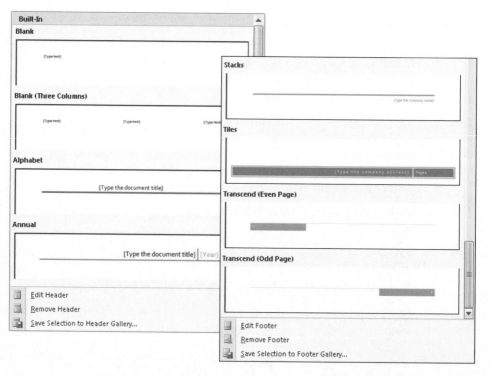

If you want to enter page numbers, you can select the style you want from the Page Number gallery. You can then format the page numbers in a variety of ways in the Page Number Format dialog box.

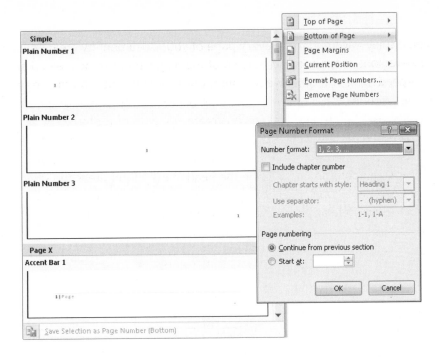

➤ To insert a header or footer

1. On the **Insert** tab, in the **Header & Footer** group, click the **Header** or **Footer** button.

2. In the **Header** or **Footer** gallery, click the style you want to use.

3. In the placeholders, type the text you want.

4. On the **Design** contextual tab, in the **Close** group, click the **Close Header and Footer** button.

➤ To insert a page number in a header or footer

1. In the **Header & Footer** group, click the **Page Number** button.

2. Point to a position option in the list, and then in the gallery, select a page number style.

➤ To change the format of page numbers

1. In the **Header & Footer** group, click the **Page Number** button, and then click **Format Page Numbers**.

2. In the **Page Number Format** dialog box, in the **Number format** list, click the format you want.

3. Select any other options you want, and then click **OK**.

Columns

By default, Word displays text in one column, but you can specify that text be displayed in multiple columns to create layouts like those used in newspapers and magazines. When you format text to flow in columns, the text fills the first column and then moves to the top of the next column. You can insert a column break to force text to move to the next column.

You have the choice of one, two, or three equal columns, or two other two-column formats: one with a narrow left column and the other with a narrow right column. No matter how you set up the columns initially, you can change the layout, the widths of individual columns, and the division between the columns at any time from the Columns dialog box.

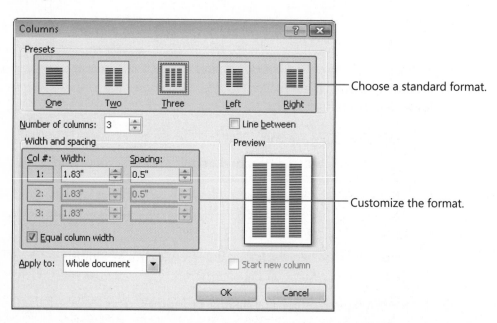

Choose a standard format.

Customize the format.

Tip You can align the text in columns the same way you would any text. If you justify the columns for a neater look, you might want to have Word hyphenate the text to ensure that there are no large gaps between words. For information about hyphenation, see section 2.1, "Format text and paragraphs."

➤ **To format an entire document in multiple columns**

→ With the insertion point anywhere in the text, on the **Page Layout** tab, in the **Page Setup** group, click the **Columns** button, and then click the number of columns you want.

➤ **To format part of a document in multiple columns**

1. Select the text you want to appear in columns.

2. On the **Page Layout** tab, in the **Page Setup** group, click the **Columns** button, and then click the number of columns you want.

➤ **To change the width of columns**

1. Click anywhere in any column. Then on the **Page Layout** tab, in the **Page Setup** group, click the **Columns** button, and click **More Columns**.

2. Clear the **Equal Column Width** check box.

3. In the **Width and spacing area**, change the setting in the **Width** column or the **Spacing** column. Then click **OK**.

Practice Tasks

The practice files for these tasks are located in the *Documents\Microsoft Press\ MCAS\Word2007\Objective01* folder. If you want, save the task results in the same folder with *My* prepended to the file name.

- Open the *Printing* document, and change the orientation to portrait. Then make the margins 1 inch on all sides.

- Open the *Header* document, add a Motion (Even Page) header with the text *The Taguien Cycle*, and specify that the header should not appear on the first page. Then on page 2, add a Motion (Even Page) footer that displays today's date.

- Open the *Numbers* document, add Thin Line page numbers to the bottom of every page, and format the page numbers as uppercase roman numerals.

- Open the *Columns* document, and change all but the first paragraph of the document to three-column layout. Then add a vertical line between the columns.

1.3 Make documents and content easier to find

Properties

If you create a lot of documents, it might become harder and harder to find exactly the one you need. A good way to narrow down the search is to attach properties to all your documents and then display the properties in the Details view of any dialog box in which you browse for files, such as the Open dialog box.

Properties

You can attach properties to a document in the Document Information Panel. Particularly useful are keywords, which appear as keywords in the Properties dialog box and as tags in Windows Vista and in the Details view of browsing dialog boxes. You can enter keywords through the Document Information Panel, or you can insert a Keywords property control into the document to display and modify keywords directly in the document. You can enter multiple keywords, separating them with semicolons.

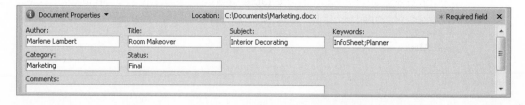

Tip In Windows Vista, the properties of a selected document are displayed in the Windows Explorer window so that you can accurately identify the document without having to open it. You can attach tags directly in Windows Explorer not only to documents but also to workbooks, presentations, and databases. Any tags attached to a document in Windows Explorer show up in Word as keywords in the Document Information Panel.

➤ To enter properties in the Document Information Panel

1. On the **Office** menu, point to **Prepare**, and then click **Properties**.

2. Enter any information that will help you identify the document later.

3. In the upper-right corner of the **Document Information Panel**, click the **Close** button.

➤ To enter properties in a Keywords property control

1. Click where you want to insert the control.

2. On the **Insert** tab, in the **Text** group, click **Quick Parts**. Then point to **Document Property**, and click **Keywords**.

3. Click the control, and type the keywords.

➤ To display properties in a browsing dialog box

1. Display the dialog box in **Details** view.

2. Right-click any column heading, and then click the property you want to display.

   Tip Clearing a property check box removes that property from the display. To add or remove more than one property, click More, and then make adjustments in the Choose Details dialog box.

Tables of Contents

If you create a long document divided into parts by headings (Heading 1, Heading 2, and so on), you can add a table of contents to the beginning of the document to give readers an overview of the document's contents and to help them find specific sections. In a document that will be printed, you can indicate with a page number the starting page of each section; if the document will be distributed electronically, you can link each heading and subheading in the table of contents to the section in the document, so that readers can jump directly there with a click of the mouse.

See Also For information about applying styles, see section 2.1, "Format text and paragraphs."

The Table Of Contents gallery offers three standard table formatting options that use nine levels of built-in TOC styles (TOC 1, TOC 2, and so on). If none of these formats meets your needs, you can choose from several other styles, such as Classic, Fancy, and Simple, in the Table Of Contents dialog box.

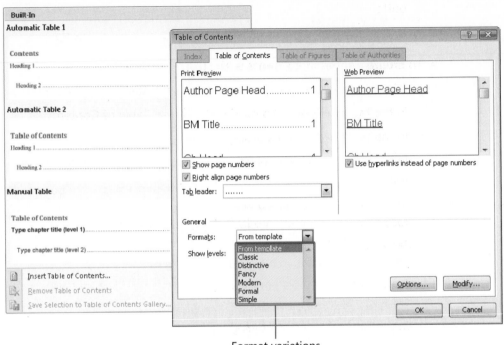

Format variations

After you select the style you want, Word identifies the table of contents entries (based on the document heading levels) and creates the table at the insertion point as one field. You can select text within the table and adjust its formatting in the usual ways; but any individual formatting changes you make will be lost if you update the table of contents. You can edit the text of a table of contents, but it is much easier to have Word update the table for you. You can tell Word to update only the page numbers, or if you have changed, added, or deleted headings, you can have Word update (re-create) the entire table.

➤ **To create a standard table of contents**

1. Assuming that the document has paragraphs styled as headings, click where you want to insert the table of contents.

2. On the **References** tab, in the **Table of Contents** group, click the **Table of Contents** button.

3. In the **Table of Contents** gallery, click the table of contents style you want.

➤ **To create a table of contents with custom TOC styles**

1. Click where you want to insert the table of contents.

2. In the **Tables of Contents** gallery, click **Insert Table of Contents**.

3. In the **Table of Contents** dialog box, click **Modify**.

4. In the **Style** dialog box, select a TOC style you want to modify, and then click **Modify**.

5. In the **Modify Style** dialog box, change the font, paragraph, tabs, border, and other formatting to suit your needs, and then click **OK**.

   See Also For information about modifying styles, see section 2.1, "Format text and paragraphs."

6. Repeat steps 4 and 5 to make additional style modifications. When you finish, click **OK** in the **Style** dialog box.

7. In the **Table of Contents** dialog box, click **OK**.

➤ **To update a table of contents**

1. Position the insertion point in the table of contents.

2. On the **References** tab, in the **Table of Contents** group, click the **Update Table** button.

3. In the **Update Table Of Contents** dialog box, click **Update page numbers only** or **Update entire table**, and then click **OK**.

Indexes

To help readers find specific information that might not be readily located by looking at a table of contents, you can have Word compile an alphabetical listing with page numbers based on index entry fields that you have marked in the document. As with a table of contents, Word creates the index at the insertion point as one field.

Tip You don't need to create indexes for documents that will be distributed electronically because readers can use the Find feature or Windows Desktop Search to go directly to search terms.

To mark an index entry field in the document, you select the text you want to mark and then open the Mark Index Entry dialog box, where you can indicate exactly how the entry should appear.

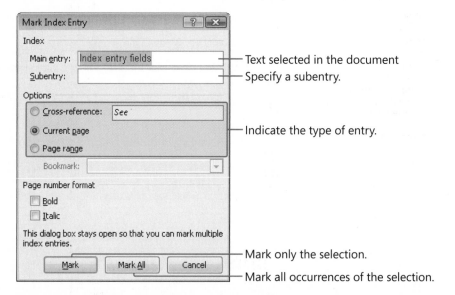

Index entry fields are formatted as hidden text; you cannot see them unless you display hidden text by clicking the Show/Hide ¶ button in the Paragraph group on the Home tab, or by selecting the Hidden Text check box on the Display page of the Word Options dialog box. When the field is visible, it appears in the document enclosed in quotation marks within a set of braces, with the designator *XE* and a dotted underline. You can edit the entry within the quotation marks as you would any other. To delete an entry, you simply select the entire hidden field and then press the Delete key. You can also move and copy index entries by using the techniques you would use for regular text.

See Also For information about hiding text, see section 2.1, "Format text and paragraphs."

To create an index based on the index entries in a document, you position the insertion point where you want the index to appear and then open the Index dialog box, where you can specify the index type, number of columns, and format used, as well as the alignment and leaders of page numbers.

When you click OK in the Index dialog box, Word calculates the page numbers of all the entries and subentries, consolidates them, and inserts the index as one field in the specified format at the specified location in the document. If you make changes to the document that affect its index entries or page numbering, you can have Word update the index.

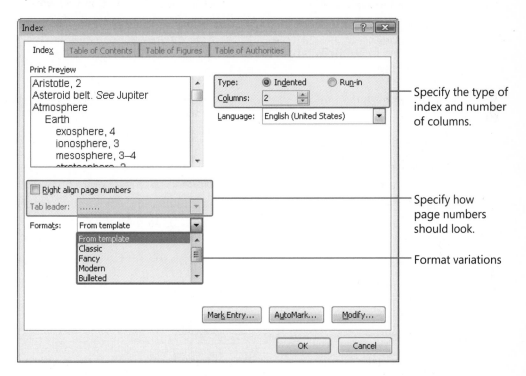

Specify the type of index and number of columns.

Specify how page numbers should look.

Format variations

➤ To mark an index entry

1. Select the word or words you want to mark.

2. On the **References** tab, in the **Index** group, click the **Mark Entry** button.

3. In the **Mark Index Entry** dialog box, format the entry by right-clicking it, clicking **Font**, selecting the options you want in the **Font** dialog box, and clicking **OK**.

4. Enter a subentry, indicate the type of entry, and specify the page number formatting.

5. Click **Mark** or **Mark All**.

➤ **To create an index**

1. Position the insertion point where you want to insert the index.

2. Hide the index entries. (Otherwise, they will affect the pagination.)

3. On the **References** tab, in the **Index** group, click **Insert Index**.

4. In the **Index** dialog box, specify the type of index, the number of columns, the appearance of page numbers, and the index format.

5. Click **OK**.

➤ **To update an index**

1. Position the insertion point anywhere in the index.

2. On the **References** tab, in the **Index** group, click **Update Index**.

   Or

→ Right-click the index, and then click **Update Field**.

Bookmarks

Whether you are creating a document or working in a document created by someone else, you can insert bookmarks to flag information to which you might want to return later. (Word automatically creates bookmarks for headings down to the fourth level by removing articles, spaces, and punctuation and capitalizing the first letter of each word in the heading.) After inserting a bookmark, you can quickly move to that location in the document from the Bookmark dialog box or from the Find And Replace dialog box.

➤ **To insert a bookmark at the insertion point**

1. On the **Insert** tab, in the **Links** group, click **Bookmark**.

2. In the **Bookmark** dialog box, in the **Bookmark name** box, type the bookmark name.

   Tip Bookmark names cannot contain spaces. If you enter a space and then type a character, the Add button becomes inactive. To name bookmarks with multiple words, either run the words together and capitalize each word or replace the spaces with underscores for readability.

3. Click **Add**.

➤ **To move to a bookmark**

1. Display the **Bookmark** dialog box, and click the bookmark you want.

2. Click **Go To**, and then click **Close**.

   Or

1. On the **Home** tab, in the **Editing** group, click **Go To** in the **Find** list.

2. On the **Go To** tab of the **Find and Replace** dialog box, in the **Go to what** list, click **Bookmark**.

3. In the **Enter bookmark name** list, click the bookmark you want.

4. Click **Go To**, and then click **Close**.

Cross-References

If you are developing a long document, you can create cross-references to help readers quickly find associated information elsewhere in the document. You can create cross-references to two types of elements:

- Headings, figures, and tables, for which Word automatically creates pointers
- Manually created bookmarks

If you later delete an item you have designated as the target of a cross-reference, you will also need to update the cross-reference.

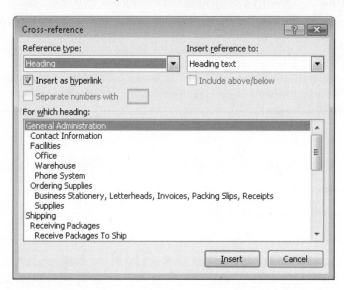

➤ **To insert a cross-reference at the insertion point**

1. In the document, type the introductory text for the cross reference; for example, *For more information, see.*

2. On the **Insert** tab, in the **Links** group, click the **Cross-reference** button.

3. In the **Cross-reference** dialog box, in the **Reference type** list, click the type of reference you want to insert.

4. In the **Insert reference to** list, click the type of item you are referencing.

5. In the **For which** list, click the item you are referencing to, click **Insert**, and then click **Close**.

➤ **To update a cross-reference**

1. Click the cross-reference to select the field.

2. Right-click the selection, and then click **Update Field**.

Hyperlinks

Like Web pages, Word documents can include hyperlinks that provide a quick way to connect to related information, or to perform tasks such as opening another document, downloading a file, or sending an e-mail message. You insert hyperlinks into a Word document from the Insert Hyperlink dialog box, where you specify the type of link you want to create and enter an appropriate target for that type of link. You can specify whether the target information should appear in the same window or frame as the document or in a new window or frame. You can also make a particular setting the default for all hyperlinks.

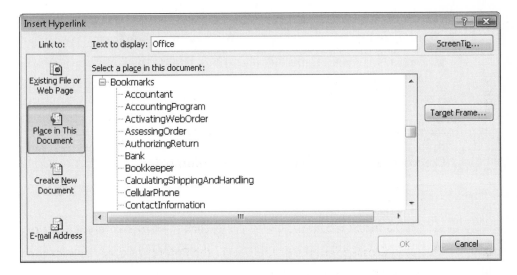

Within the document, the hyperlink appears underlined and in the color specified for hyperlinks by the document's theme. You can jump to the target of the hyperlink by holding down the Ctrl key and clicking the link. After you click the hyperlink, it appears in the color specified for followed hyperlinks.

➤ **To insert a hyperlink**

1. Select the text or item you want to convert to a hyperlink. Then on the **Insert** tab, in the **Links** group, click the **Hyperlink** button.

2. In the **Insert Hyperlink** dialog box, on the **Link to** bar, click the type of location you are linking to.

3. In the **Look in** area, browse to or enter the hyperlink target.

4. Click **Target Frame**. In the **Set Target Frame** dialog box, specify where the hyperlink target will be displayed, and then click **OK**.

5. In the **Insert Hyperlink** dialog box, click **OK**.

➤ **To insert a hyperlink that opens an e-mail message form**

1. Display the **Insert Hyperlink** dialog box, and on the **Link to** bar, click **E-mail Address**.

2. In the **Text to display** box, type the text to which you want to attach the hyperlink; for example, *Click here to contact us*.

3. In the **E-mail address** box, type the address to which the message will be sent, or click an address in the **Recently used e-mail addresses** list.

4. In the **Subject** box, type the subject of the message. Then click **OK**.

➤ **To edit a hyperlink**

1. Right-click the hyperlink, and then click **Edit Hyperlink**.

2. In the **Edit Hyperlink** dialog box, make the necessary changes, and then click **OK**.

➤ **To remove a hyperlink**

→ Right-click the hyperlink, and then click **Remove Hyperlink**.

Practice Tasks

The practice files for these tasks are located in the *Documents\Microsoft Press\ MCAS\Word2007\Objective01* folder. If you want, save the task results in the same folder with *My* prepended to the file name.

- Open the *Properties* document, and use any method to attach the keyword *Planner* to the document.

- Open the *Contents* document, and at the top of the document, create a table of contents based on heading styles that uses the Classic format and dotted line page-number leaders. Then alter the document by inserting page breaks, and update the entire table of contents to reflect your changes.

- Open the *Index* document, scroll to the *Phone System* heading, and mark an index entry that cross-references *intercom* to *phones*. Then on a new page at the end of the document, create a one-column index in the Formal format with the page numbers adjacent to their index entries. (Don't forget to turn off the display of hidden text before creating the index!)

- Open the *Bookmarks* document, and move to page 8. Insert a bookmark named *CreditCheck* to the left of the *Checking the credit of new customers* heading. Move to the beginning of the document, and then jump to the bookmarked location.

- Open the *CrossReference* document, and move to the top of page 7. Type *For more information, see* at the right end of the Step 1 paragraph, and insert a cross-reference to the *Does the customer already have an account?* heading. Click the cross-reference to move to the heading, change *customer* to *client*, move back to the cross-reference, and then update it.

- Open the *Hyperlinks* document, and at the top of the page, create a hyperlink from the logo to the *OtherLogos* document. Set the hyperlink to open the target document in a new window. Then click the hyperlink to jump to the linked file.

1.4   Personalize Word 2007

Common Settings

You can customize the Word environment in various ways by changing settings in the Word Options dialog box. In the dialog box, settings are divided into functional groups on individual *pages*.

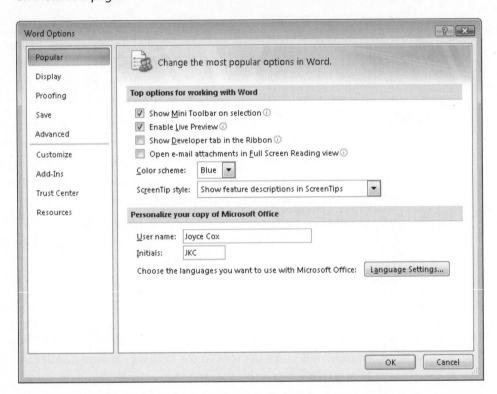

The five pages containing the most common settings are listed above the separator in the page list that appears in the left pane of the dialog box. These include:

- On the Popular page, you can turn off the display of the Mini toolbar that appears when you select text, and change your user name and initials.

- On the Display page, you can shrink the white space representing top and bottom margins in Print Layout view so that you can scroll pages faster.

Strategy You should become familiar with all the program options you can set through the Word Options dialog box and where they are located. Investigate on your own to become familiar with the settings available from each page.

● On the Proofing page, you can click AutoCorrect Options to display the Auto-Correct dialog box, where you can change the autoformatting settings and add words you misspell frequently to the list Word uses to automatically correct typo-graphical errors (typos).

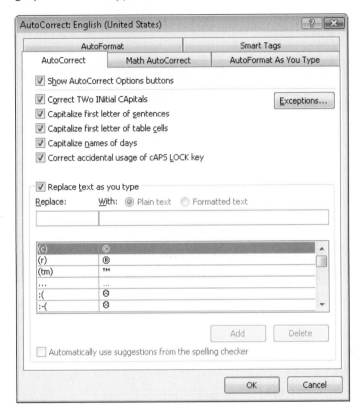

● On the Save page, you can set the default format and location for saving new documents, and you can change how frequently Word saves AutoRecovery infor-mation to enable you to recover files in the event of sudden computer problems.

● On the Advanced page, you can set a variety of editing, display, printing, and saving options not included on other pages.

► **To display the Word Options dialog box**

→ On the **Office** menu, click **Word Options**.

► **To turn off the display of the Mini toolbar**

→ On the **Popular** page of the **Word Options** dialog box, clear the **Show Mini Toolbar on selection** check box, and then click **OK**.

➤ **To make additional editing languages available**

1. On the **Popular** page of the **Word Options** dialog box, click **Language Settings**.

2. In the **Microsoft Office Language Settings 2007** dialog box, choose the languages you want, and then click **OK**.

3. In the **Word Options** dialog box, click **OK**.

➤ **To add a misspelling to the AutoCorrect list**

1. Display the **Proofing** page of the **Word Options** dialog box, and click **AutoCorrect Options**.

2. In the **AutoCorrect** dialog box, type the misspelling in the **Replace** box and the correct spelling in the **With** box. Click **Add**, and then click **OK**.

3. In the **Word Options** dialog box, click **OK**.

➤ **To change the default save location**

1. Display the **Save** page of the **Word Options** dialog box.

2. In the **Save documents** area, to the right of **Default file location**, click **Browse**.

3. Display the folder you want to be the default, and then click **OK**.

4. In the **Word Options** dialog box, click **OK**.

> **Tip** You can change the default location in which Word looks for documents and other types of files by clicking File Locations at the bottom of the Advanced page.

➤ **To change how frequently Word saves AutoRecovery information**

1. Display the **Save** page of the **Word Options** dialog box.

2. In the **Save documents** area, to the right of **Save AutoRecovery information every**, increase or decrease the number of minutes.

3. In the **Word Options** dialog box, click **OK**.

More Specialized Settings

In the Word Options dialog box, the four pages containing more specialized settings are listed below the separator in the page list. These include:

- On the Customize page, you can customize the Quick Access Toolbar to make a set of buttons available for all documents or for a specific document. You might want to add buttons to the Quick Access Toolbar if their commands are not represented on the Ribbon or if you regularly use buttons that are scattered on various tabs.

  Tip You can quickly open the Customize page of the Word Options dialog box by clicking the Customize Quick Access Toolbar button at the right end of the Quick Access Toolbar, and then clicking More Commands.

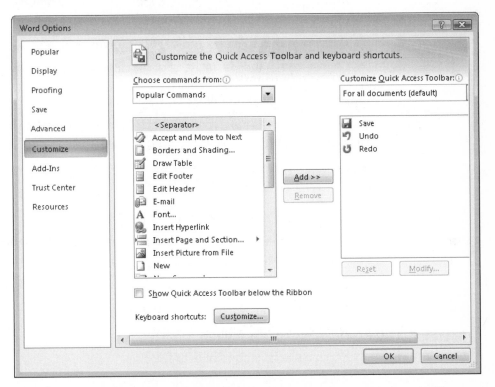

- On the Add-Ins page, you can view and manage six types of add-ins—auxiliary programs and features that extend the Word environment.

- On the Trust page are links to information about privacy and security. You can also access settings that control the response to certain types of documents.

- On the Resources page are links for activating, updating, and maintaining your Office programs. Most of these links require that you have Internet access.

➤ **To add a button to the global Quick Access Toolbar**

1. Display the **Customize** page of the **Word Options** dialog box.

2. In the **Choose commands from** list, click the option containing the command you want to add.

   Tip To list commands that are available in Word but are not included on any standard Ribbon tab, click Commands Not In The Ribbon.

3. In the list on the left, click the command you want, and then click **Add**.

4. In the **Word Options** dialog box, click **OK**.

➤ **To add a button to a document-specific Quick Access Toolbar**

1. Display the **Customize** page of the **Word Options** dialog box.

2. In the **Customize Quick Access Toolbar** list, click **For** *<current document>*.

3. In the **Choose commands from** list, click the option containing the command you want, click the command, and then click **Add**.

4. In the **Word Options** dialog box, click **OK**.

➤ **To restore the default Quick Access Toolbar**

→ Display the **Customize** page of the **Word Options** dialog box, click **Reset**, click **Yes** to confirm the restoration, and then click **OK**.

➤ **To move the Quick Access Toolbar below the Ribbon**

→ Display the **Customize** page of the **Word Options** dialog box, select the **Show Quick Access Toolbar below the Ribbon** check box, and then click **OK**.

→ Click the **Customize Quick Access Toolbar** button, and then click **Show Below the Ribbon**.

➤ **To hide and redisplay the Ribbon**

→ Double-click the active tab to hide the Ribbon.

→ Click any tab title to temporarily display the Ribbon.

→ Double-click any tab title to permanently display the Ribbon.

Research Settings

A few options for personalizing Word don't appear in the Word Options dialog box, including the options to customize the Research, Thesaurus, and Translate tools. Clicking the buttons for these tools displays the Research task pane, from which you can display the Research Options dialog box. There you can add and remove research sources.

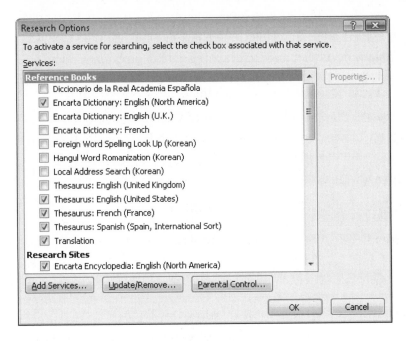

➤ **To add or remove research sources**

1. On the **Review** tab, in the **Proofing** group, click the **Research** button.

2. At the bottom of the **Research** task pane, click **Research Options**.

3. In the **Research Options** dialog box, add or remove a source by selecting or clearing its check box, and then click **OK**.

Practice Tasks

The practice files for these tasks are located in the *Documents\Microsoft Press\ MCAS\Word2007\Objective01* folder. If you want, save the task results in the same folder with *My* prepended to the file name.

- Open the *AutoCorrect* document, and then add the misspelling *avalable* with the correct spelling *available* to the AutoCorrect list.

- With any document open, change the default program window color scheme to Silver and turn off the display of feature descriptions in ScreenTips. Then set the AutoRecover rate to 15 minutes.

- Open the *CustomQATAll* document, and add an AutoText button to the Quick Access Toolbar for all documents. Then insert a separator between the three default buttons and the AutoText button.

- Open the *CustomQATDoc* document, and add a Comments button to the document-specific Quick Access Toolbar. Hide the Ribbon. Then at the end of the paragraph below the numbered list, select *thirsting for more*, and add the comment *Paolini is hard at work on the third book*.

Important After completing the practice tasks, be sure to reset the Word options and the Quick Access Toolbar to those you use for your normal work.

Objective Review

Before finishing this chapter, ensure that you have mastered the following skills:

1.1 Create and format documents.

1.2 Lay out documents.

1.3 Make documents and content easier to find.

1.4 Personalize Word 2007.

2 Formatting Content

The skills tested in this section of the Microsoft Office Specialist exam for Microsoft Office Word 2007 relate to formatting and manipulating text and pages. Specifically, the following objectives are associated with this set of skills:

2.1 Format text and paragraphs.

2.2 Manipulate text.

2.3 Control pagination.

Word 2007 provides you with exacting control over the appearance of a document. You can precisely define the way text looks, the way text looks on a page, and the way a page looks within a document.

Strategy Before taking Microsoft Office Specialist Exam 77-601, "Using Microsoft Office Word 2007," ensure that you are thoroughly familiar with document editing and formatting techniques, especially those that are new to Word 2007.

This chapter guides you in studying the various ways to format characters and paragraphs, both by applying formats directly and by applying styles. You will also study methods of copying and moving text, copying and removing formatting, and finding and replacing both text and formatting. Finally, you will study ways of formatting pages by inserting, changing, and deleting page and section breaks.

 Important Before you can use the practice files in this chapter, you need to install them from the book's companion CD to their default location. See "Using the Companion CD" at the beginning of this book for more information.

Tip Graphics and operating system–related instructions in this book reflect the Windows Vista user interface. If your computer is running Windows XP and you experience trouble following the instructions as written, refer to the sidebar "If You Are Running Windows XP" in "Working in the Microsoft Office Fluent User Interface" at the beginning of this book.

2.1   Format text and paragraphs

Character Formatting

By default, the font used for text in a new Word document is Calibri, but you can change the font at any time. Each font consists of characters, numbers, and/or symbols that share a common design. You can vary the look of the base font by changing the following attributes:

- **Size.** Almost every font comes in a range of sizes, measured in points. A point is approximately 1/72 of an inch.

    Tip You can increase or decrease the size of selected text in set increments by clicking the Grow Font and Shrink Font buttons in the Font group or on the Mini toolbar.

- **Style.** The most common styles are regular (or plain), italic, bold, and bold italic.

- **Color.** The palette includes the colors of the theme applied to the document and a set of standard colors. You can also specify custom colors.

- **Underline.** You can choose from a variety of underline styles as well as change the underline color.

- **Effects.** Various enhancements can be applied, such as strikethrough, shadows, or embossing. You can also hide text by applying the Hidden font effect.

- **Case.** You can specify small capital letters (small caps), all capital letters, or all lowercase. You can mix the case by specifying that the first word in a selection should have an initial capital letter (sentence case) or all words should have initial capital letters (title case). You can also toggle the case of selected text, changing all uppercase letters to lowercase and lowercase letters to uppercase.

    See Also For information about inserting a big capital letter (drop cap) at the beginning of a paragraph, see section 3.3, "Format text graphically."

- **Character spacing.** You can push characters apart or squeeze them together. This is also called *kerning*.

After you select an appropriate font for a document, you can use these attributes to achieve different effects. Although some attributes might cancel each other out, they are usually cumulative. Collectively, the font and its attributes are called *character formatting*. You can change several character formats at once from the Font dialog box.

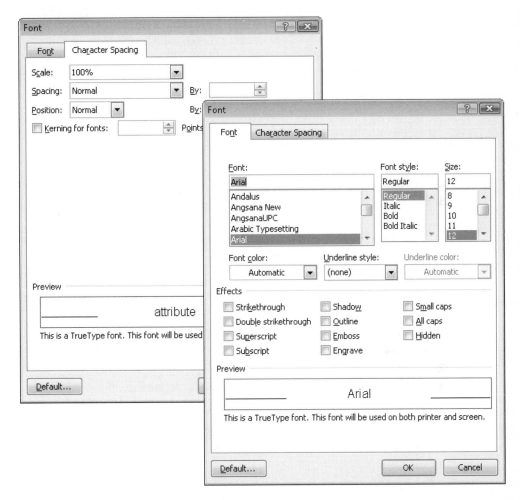

Strategy Word provides so many ways to format text that it would be impossible to detail them all here. Be sure you are conversant with the attributes available from the Font group on the Home tab and from the Font dialog box.

➤ To apply character formatting to text

1. Select the text you want to format.

2. On the **Mini toolbar**, or in the **Font** group on the **Home** tab, click the attribute you want to apply.

   Tip You can format a word by clicking anywhere in the word (other than at the beginning or the end) and then clicking the attribute you want to apply.

➤ To change the font size of selected text

→ On the **Home** tab, in the **Font** group, click the **Grow Font** button to increase the font to the next standard size, or click the **Shrink Font** button to decrease the font to the next standard size.

➤ To change the case of selected text

→ On the **Home** tab, in the **Font** group, click the **Change Case** button, and then click **Sentence case, lowercase, UPPERCASE, Capitalize Each Word**, or **tOGGLE cASE**.

➤ To apply a special effect to selected text

→ In the **Font** group, click the **Strikethrough, Subscript**, or **Superscript** button.

   Or

1. On the **Home** tab, click the **Font** dialog box launcher.

2. In the **Font** dialog box, in the **Effects** area, select the check box for the effect you want to apply. Then click **OK**.

➤ To change the character spacing of selected text

1. In the **Font** dialog box, click the **Character Spacing** tab.

2. Change the **Spacing** setting to **Expanded** or **Condensed**, set the number of points of expansion or contraction, and then click **OK**.

➤ To highlight selected text

→ On the **Mini toolbar**, in the **Highlight** list, click the color you want.

→ On the **Home** tab, in the **Font** group, in the **Text Highlight Color** list, click the color you want.

   Tip If you click the Highlight button without first making a selection, the mouse pointer becomes a highlighter that you can drag across text. Click the Highlight button again or press Esc to turn off the highlighter.

➤ **To clear formatting from selected text**

→ On the **Home** tab, in the **Font** group, click the **Clear Formatting** button.

→ Press **Ctrl+Space**.

Paragraph Formatting

In documents based on the Normal document template, a normal paragraph is aligned at the left margin, has internal line spacing of 1.15 lines, and is followed by 10 points of blank space. You can change the look of a paragraph by changing the following:

● **Alignment.** You can align each line of a paragraph at the left margin (with a ragged right edge) or at the right margin (with a ragged left edge). You can center each line between the left and right margins, with ragged left and right edges. Or you can spread out each line to fill the space between the margins, creating even left and right edges, which is called *justified alignment*.

See Also For information about setting margins, see section 1.2, "Lay out documents."

● **Indentation.** You can vary the position of the text between the margins by indenting paragraphs from the left and right margins, as well as specifying where the first line of a paragraph begins and where the second and subsequent lines begin.

Tip Left and right margin indents are often used to draw attention to special paragraphs, such as quotations.

● **Line spacing.** You can adjust the spacing between the lines in a paragraph proportionally or by specifying an exact amount of space.

● **Paragraph spacing.** To make it obvious where one paragraph ends and another begins, you can add space above or below, or both.

● **Borders.** You can add predefined borders or custom borders of various styles, colors, and thicknesses to a single paragraph or multiple paragraphs.

● **Shading.** Solid colors and patterns can be applied to the background of a single paragraph or multiple paragraphs.

Collectively, the settings you use to vary the look of a paragraph are called *paragraph formatting*. You can change several paragraph formats at once from the Paragraph dialog box.

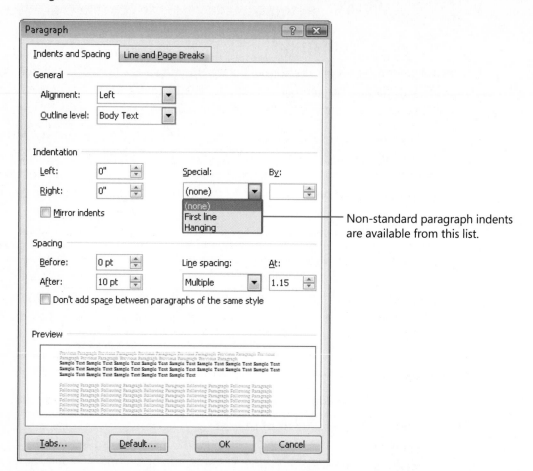

Non-standard paragraph indents are available from this list.

See Also For information about creating bulleted and numbered lists, see section 4.2, "Use tables and lists to organize content."

You can add customized borders, shading, and patterns from the Borders And Shading dialog box.

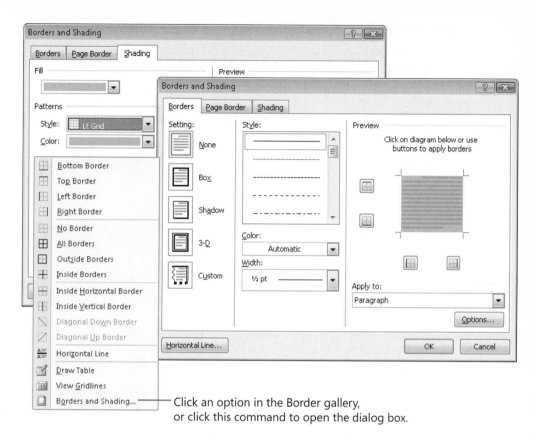

Click an option in the Border gallery,
or click this command to open the dialog box.

Strategy Be sure you are conversant with all the formatting options available from the Paragraph group on the Home tab and from the Paragraph dialog box.

➤ To change the alignment of selected paragraphs

→ On the **Home** tab, in the **Paragraph** group, click the **Align Text Left**, **Center**, **Align Text Right**, or **Justify** button.

Tip When applying paragraph formatting, you don't have to select the entire paragraph.

➤ To change the indentation of selected paragraphs

→ On the **Home** tab, in the **Paragraph** group, click the **Increase Indent** or **Decrease Indent** button.

→ On the **Page Layout** tab, in the **Paragraph** group, in the **Indent** area, increase or decrease the **Left** or **Right** settings.

→ On the horizontal ruler, drag the **First Line Indent**, **Left Indent**, or **Right Indent** marker to the location you want.

➤ **To change the space above or below selected paragraphs**

→ On the **Page Layout** tab, in the **Paragraph** group, under **Spacing**, change the **Before** or **After** setting.

Or

1. On the **Home** tab, click the **Paragraph** dialog box launcher.

2. On the **Indents and Spacing** tab of the **Paragraph** dialog box, in the **Spacing** area, change the **Before** or **After** setting, and then click **OK**.

Or

→ On the **Home** tab, in the **Paragraph** group, click the **Line spacing** button, and then click **Add Space Before Paragraph**, **Remove Space Before Paragraph**, **Add Space After Paragraph**, or **Remove Space After Paragraph**. (Only two options will be visible, depending on the current Before and After settings of the active paragraph.)

➤ **To change the line spacing of selected paragraphs**

1. On the **Home** tab, in the **Paragraph** group, click the **Line spacing** button.

2. In the list, select the standard spacing option you want.

Or

In the list, click **Line Spacing Options**, change the setting under **Line spacing** on the **Indents and Spacing** tab of the **Paragraph** dialog box, and then click **OK**.

➤ **To add a border around selected paragraphs**

→ On the **Home** tab, in the **Paragraph** group, click the **Border** arrow. Then in the list, click the border you want.

Or

1. In the **Paragraph** group, click the **Border** arrow. Then in the list, click **Borders and Shading**.

2. In the **Borders and Shading** dialog box, in the **Setting** area, click a preset border format. Select the **Style**, **Color**, and **Width** you want, and then click **OK**.

   Tip To add and remove borders from specific sides of the paragraph, click the corresponding buttons in the Preview area.

➤ **To add shading to the background of selected paragraphs**

1. Display the **Borders and Shading** dialog box, and then click the **Shading** tab.

2. In the **Fill** area, select the solid color you want; or in the **Patterns** area, select the **Style** and **Color**. Then click **OK**.

➤ **To clear paragraph formatting**

1. Position the insertion point anywhere in the paragraph you want to return to the base style, or select the paragraph(s).

2. In the **Font** group, click the **Clear Formatting** button.

Styles

Styles are named sets of paragraph and/or character formatting that you can use in place of manual formatting to produce a consistent look throughout a document. You can choose from five types of styles: Character, Paragraph, Linked, Table, and List. The most common types of styles you will use are the following:

● **Paragraph styles.** You can use these styles to apply a consistent look to different types of paragraphs, such as headings, body text, captions, quotations, and list paragraphs. Some built-in paragraph styles, such as Heading 1 and Heading 2, are associated with outline levels.

● **Character styles.** You can use these styles to change the appearance of selected words.

You can view the available styles in several locations, including the following:

● In the Styles group on the Home tab of the Ribbon, the Quick Styles gallery displays the styles designated in the active style set as Quick Styles. Part of the Quick Styles gallery is visible at all times in the Styles group—the number of visible styles depends on the width of your program window and screen resolution. You can scroll the gallery or expand it to display all the current Quick Styles. From the Quick Styles gallery, you can apply and manage all Quick Styles.

See Also For information about Quick Styles and Styles Sets, see the topics later in this section.

● At the right side of the program window, the Styles task pane displays all the styles available in the currently active document templates or a subset thereof, such as only those that are currently in use. You can display or hide the Styles task pane, and from it you can apply and manage all styles, including those designated as Quick Styles.

See Also For information about templates, see section 1.1, "Create and format documents."

In the Styles task pane, paragraph styles are identified by a paragraph mark, and character styles are identified by the letter *a*. You can point to any style to display a ScreenTip detailing the formatting included in the style.

● At the left side of a document displayed in Draft view or Outline view, the Style area pane displays the name of the style attached to each paragraph. The Style area pane does not display character styles. You can display or hide the Style area pane.

Tip If you previously used Word 2003, you might be accustomed to working with the Styles list on the toolbar. The Styles list is not available from the Ribbon, but you can add it to the Quick Access Toolbar if you prefer to use it. For information about adding commands to the Quick Access Toolbar, see section 1.4, "Personalize Word 2007."

If you need a style that is not already defined, you can save formatted text as a style that you can easily apply elsewhere, or you can create a new style based on an existing one in the Create New Style From Formatting dialog box. You can modify an existing style in the Modify Style dialog box.

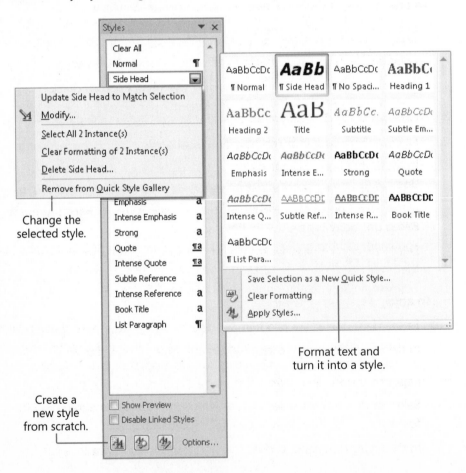

You can tell Word to select all text to which a particular style is applied and then globally switch to a different style. You can also globally clear the formatting of a particular style so that the text reverts to Normal style.

➤ **To display the Style area pane in a document**

1. Display the document in Draft view or Outline view.
2. Click the **Microsoft Office Button**, and then click **Word Options**.
3. Display the **Advanced** page of the **Word Options** dialog box.
4. In the **Display** area, enter a positive number. Then click **OK**.

➤ **To display the Styles task pane in the program window**

→ On the **Home** tab, click the **Styles** dialog box launcher.

➤ **To display visual representations of styles in the Styles task pane**

→ At the bottom of the **Styles** pane, select the **Show Preview** check box.

➤ **To display a specific selection of styles in the Styles task pane**

1. At the bottom of the **Styles** task pane, click **Options**.
2. In the **Style Pane Options** dialog box, click **Recommended, In use, In current document**, or **All styles** in the **Select styles to show** list.
3. In the **Select how list is sorted** list, click **Alphabetical, As Recommended, Font, Based on**, or **By type**.
4. Select the check boxes for the types of formatting you want to show as styles, and then click **OK**.

➤ **To apply a character style**

1. Select the text you want to format.
2. In the **Styles** task pane, click the character style you want to apply.

➤ **To apply a paragraph style**

1. Select or position the insertion point anywhere in the paragraph you want to format.
2. In the **Styles** task pane, click the paragraph style you want to apply.

➤ **To create a style**

1. At the bottom of the **Styles** task pane, click the **New Style** button.

2. In the **Create New Style from Formatting** dialog box, enter a name for the new style in the **Name** box.

3. In the **Style type** list, click **Paragraph**, **Character**, **Linked**, **Table**, or **List**.

4. In the **Style based on** list, select an existing style that closely resembles the style you want to create, or click **(no style)** to build a style from scratch.

   Tip Changes that you make to a base style may also be reflected in other styles based on that style.

5. In the **Formatting** area, make any necessary adjustments to the character and/or paragraph formats to be included in the style.

   Tip You can make more extensive adjustments in the dialog boxes available when you click Format in the lower-left corner of the dialog box.

6. At the bottom of the dialog box, indicate whether the style is to be part of the template or attached only to this document, and then click **OK**.

➤ **To modify an existing style and all text with that style attached**

1. In the **Styles** task pane, point to the style you want to modify, click the arrow that appears, and then click **Modify**.

2. In the **Modify Style** dialog box, in the **Formatting** area, make the necessary adjustments to the character or paragraph formatting of the style. Then click **OK**.

➤ **To clear all instances of a style**

→ In the **Styles** task pane, point to the style you want to clear, click the arrow that appears, and then click **Clear Formatting of Instance(s)**.

Quick Styles

Word 2007 includes Quick Styles: styles that are available from the Quick Styles gallery in the Styles group on the Home tab. You can quickly apply styles from this gallery by clicking the style thumbnail. You can also try out any Quick Style—viewing the effect of the style on text without actually applying it—by using the new Live Preview feature of the Microsoft Office Fluent user interface.

➤ **To display the full Quick Styles gallery**

→ On the **Home** tab, in the **Styles** group, click the **More** button at the bottom of the scroll bar to the right of the style thumbnails.

➤ **To preview the effects of a Quick Style**

1. Select the text you want to preview the style on, or position the insertion point in a word or paragraph.

2. In the **Quick Styles** gallery, point to the thumbnail of the style you want to preview.

➤ **To apply a Quick Style to selected text**

→ In the **Quick Styles** gallery, click the thumbnail of the style you want to apply.

➤ **To create a style and add it to the Quick Styles gallery**

1. Manually format the text or paragraph as you want the Quick Style to apply it. Then select the text or paragraph.

2. Right-click the selection, point to **Styles**, and then click **Save Selection as a New Quick Style**.

   Or

   On the **Home** tab, in the **Styles** group, click the **More** button to display the **Quick Styles** gallery. Then at the bottom of the gallery, click **Save Selection as a New Quick Style**.

3. In the **Create New Style from Formatting** dialog box, enter a name for the style in the **Name** box.

4. To add the style to the template attached to the document instead of to the document itself, click **Modify**. Then at the bottom of the expanded **Create New Style from Formatting** dialog box, click **New documents based on this template**.

5. In the **Create New Style from Formatting** dialog box, click **OK**.

➤ **To add an existing style to the Quick Styles gallery**

→ In the **Styles** task pane, point to the style, click the arrow that appears, and then click **Add to Quick Style Gallery**.

→ In the **Modify Style** dialog box, select the **Add to Quick Style list** check box, and then click **OK**.

➤ **To remove a style from the Quick Styles gallery**

→ In the **Quick Styles** gallery, right-click the style you want to remove, and then click **Remove from Quick Style Gallery**.

→ In the **Styles** pane, point to the style you want to remove, click the arrow that appears, and then click **Remove from Quick Style Gallery**.

Style Sets

Multiple styles can be defined in a Quick Style set—a collection of styles that are saved together and can be applied to any document. (In theory, the formatting of the styles within a style set should define a common look for a specific type of document.) Word 2007 comes with 11 style sets with names such as Elegant, Modern, and Traditional; you can also create your own style sets. You can change the look of an entire document by changing the style set. The Quick Styles gallery changes to display the Quick Styles defined in that style set.

You can also display a live preview of any Quick Style set, to see the changes the style set would apply to an entire document.

➤ To preview the effects of a style set

1. Position the insertion point anywhere in the document.
2. On the **Home** tab, in the **Styles** group, click **Change Styles**, point to **Style Set**, and then point to the style set you want to preview.

➤ To change to a different style set

→ On the **Home** tab, in the **Styles** group, click **Change Styles**, point to **Style Set**, and then click the style set you want.

➤ **To attach a style set to the current document template**

→ In the **Styles** group, click **Change Styles**, and then click **Set as Default for Template**.

➤ **To revert to the style set attached to the document template**

→ In the **Styles** group, click **Change Styles**, point to **Style Set**, and then click **Reset to Quick Styles from Template**.

➤ **To revert to the basic Word 2007 style set**

→ In the **Styles** group, click **Change Styles**, point to **Style Set**, and then click **Reset Document Quick Styles**.

Line Breaks and Hyphenation

You can specify where a line of text within a paragraph should end by inserting a text wrapping break, also called a *line break*. Inserting a line break does not start a new paragraph, so when you apply paragraph formatting to a line of text that ends with a line break, the formatting is applied to the entire paragraph, not just that line. When viewing hidden text, line break characters resemble curved, left-pointing arrows.

If you turn on the automatic hyphenation feature, Word will insert line breaks and hyphens within words to help achieve a more uniform paragraph form. You can control the way Word hyphenates words, from the Hyphenation Options dialog box.

Word makes it easier than ever to add sophisticated visual content to your documents. This visual content can consist of pictures created outside of Word, such as a scanned photograph, a clip art image, or an illustration created with a graphics program. Or it can consist of drawing objects that are created within Word, such as a shape, a diagram, WordArt text, or a text box. You can use the buttons on the Insert tab to insert different kinds of visual content.

After you have inserted a visual object, you can format it many ways. The types of formatting you can apply vary with the type of object and, in the case of pictures, with the type of picture.

Standard left-aligned paragraphs

With automatic hypenation turned on

...sticated visual content to your document. ...ctures created outside of Word, such ...r an illustration created with a graph- ...ects that are created within Word, ...a text box. You can use the buttons on the Insert tab to insert different kinds of visual content.

After you have inserted a visual object, you can format it many ways. The types of formatting you can apply vary with the type of object and, in the case of pictures, with the type of picture.

➤ **To insert a line break**

1. Position the insertion point where you want the break to occur.

2. Press **Shift+Enter**; or on the **Page Layout** tab, in the **Page Setup** group, click the **Breaks** button, and then click **Text Wrapping**.

   See Also For information about page and section breaks, see section 2.3, "Control pagination." For information about column breaks, see section 1.2, "Lay out documents."

➤ **To automatically break lines and hyphenate words**

→ On the **Page Layout** tab, in the **Page Setup** group, click the **Hyphenation** button, and then click **Automatic**.

➤ **To control hyphenation settings**

1. In the **Page Setup** group, click the **Hyphenation** button, and then click **Hyphenation Options**.

2. In the **Hyphenation Options** dialog box, specify whether you want Word to automatically hyphenate the document or to hyphenate uppercase words, the maximum distance of a hyphen from the document margin (the hyphenation zone), and how many consecutive lines of a paragraph may be hyphenated. Then click **OK**.

➤ **To turn off automatic hyphenation**

→ In the **Page Setup** group, click the **Hyphenation** button, and then click **None**.

➤ **To selectively hyphenate words in a document**

1. In the **Page Setup** group, click the **Hyphenation** button, and then click **Manual**.

2. For each hyphenation suggested in the **Manual Hyphenation** dialog box, click **Yes** or **No**.

Tab Stops

You can align text in different locations across the page by using tab stops. By default, Word sets left-aligned tab stops every half inch (or every 0.27 centimeters, if Word is set to display measurements in centimeters). You can set the following types of tabs in any position between the left and right margins:

- **Left tab.** Aligns the left end of the text with the tab stop.
- **Center tab.** Aligns the center of the text with the tab stop.
- **Right tab.** Aligns the right end of the text with the tab stop.
- **Decimal tab.** Aligns the decimal point in the text with the s tab top.
- **Bar tab.** Inserts a vertical bar aligned with the tab stop in the paragraph containing the insertion point.

You can set custom tab stops one at a time or set multiple tab stops at once in the Tabs dialog box. You also use this dialog box to specify tab leaders—visible marks such as dots or dashes connecting the text before the tab with the text after it.

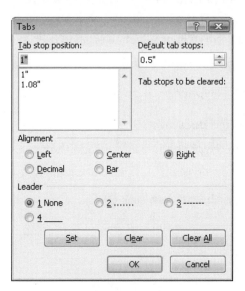

➤ **To set a custom tab stop**

1. Click the **Tab** button located at the left end of the horizontal ruler until the type of tab stop you want appears.

2. Click the horizontal ruler where you want the tab stop to be.

   Or

1. On either the **Home** or **Page Layout** tab, click the **Paragraph** dialog box launcher, and then at the bottom of the **Paragraph** dialog box, click **Tabs**.

2. In the **Tabs** dialog box, type a measurement in the **Tab stop position** box.

3. In the **Alignment** area, click the option you want, click **Set**, and then click **OK**.

➤ **To change the position of an existing custom tab stop**

→ On the ruler, drag the tab stop to the left or right.

→ In the **Tabs** dialog box, select the tab in the list box, type a new measurement in the **Tab stop position** box, click **Set**, and then click **OK**.

➤ **To set a tab stop with a leader**

1. In the **Tabs**, dialog box, set a new tab stop or select an existing one.

2. In the **Leader** area, click the option you want, click **Set**, and then click **OK**.

➤ **To delete a custom tab stop**

→ Drag the tab stop away from the ruler.

→ In the **Tabs** dialog box, select the tab, click **Clear**, and then click **OK**.

➤ **To clear all custom tab stops**

→ In the **Tabs** dialog box, click **Clear All**, and then click **OK**.

Copying, Finding, and Clearing

After you have applied a combination of character and/or paragraph formatting to one text selection, you can easily copy the entire set of formatting to another selection. You can tell Word to select all text with formatting that is identical to a selection and then globally change the formatting. And if you want to get rid of all the formatting and return a selection to the default formats for its style, you can do that with one click of the Clear Formatting button.

See Also For information about styles, see the discussion later in this topic, as well as the discussion about templates in section 1.1, "Create and format documents."

➤ **To copy existing formatting to other text**

1. Select the text that has the formatting you want to copy.

2. On the **Home** tab, in the **Clipboard** group (or on the **Mini toolbar**), click the **Format Painter** button once to copy the formatting for application only once, or twice to copy the formatting for application multiple times.

3. Click the word or select the text to which you want to apply the copied formatting. If you clicked the **Format Painter** button twice, repeat this step as many times as you want.

4. When you finish, click the **Format Painter** button again, or press the **Esc** key, to turn off the Format Painter.

➤ **To find all text with the same formatting**

1. Select the text that has the formatting you want to find.

2. On the **Home** tab, in the **Editing** group, click the **Select** button, and then click **Select Text with Similar Formatting**.

   Tip This command is available only if the Keep Track Of Formatting check box is selected in the Editing Options area of the Advanced page of the Word Options dialog box.

➤ **To select all text formatted with the same style**

1. Display the **Styles** task pane, and scroll the list to the style you want to locate.

2. Point to the style name, click the arrow that appears, and then click **Select All Instance(s)**.

➤ **To replace all instances of one style with another style**

1. In the **Styles** task pane, point to the style you want to replace, click the arrow that appears, and then click **Select All Instance(s)**.

2. In the **Styles** task pane, click the style you want to apply to the selected text.

Practice Tasks

The practice files for these tasks are located in the *Documents\Microsoft Press\ MCAS\Word2007\Objective02* folder. If you want, save the task results in the same folder with *My* prepended to the file name.

- Open the *Characters* document, and format the *Beautiful Bamboo* heading with the Stencil font. Make it bold and 26 points, apply the Outline effect, and expand the character spacing by 2 points. Then change its color to the light green standard color.

- In the *Characters* document, in the paragraph that begins *Because they are so easy to grow*, format the names *chimonobambusa marmorea, indocalamus tessellatus, pleioblastus chino vaginatus, bambusa glaucophylla*, and *otatea acuminata aztectorum* in small caps. Then change all small caps formatting to italic.

- Open the *Paragraphs* document, and display non-printing characters and the rulers. Insert a line break to the left of *Update* in the fourth line, and then center the first four lines of the document. Justify the next two paragraphs, and indent their first lines by a quarter of an inch. Center the *Esther Valle* paragraph. Finally, give all the paragraphs below *Esther Valle* left and right indents of half an inch.

- In the *Paragraphs* document, change the spacing after all paragraphs to 12 points, and then remove the spacing after the *Date, Time, Location*, and *Ticket cost* paragraphs. Change the line spacing of the paragraph that begins *The author of* to 1.5.

- In the *Paragraphs* document, put a Shadow border around the *Book Beat* paragraph, and then make the background of the paragraph light purple (Purple, Accent 4, Lighter 60%).

- Open the *Tabs* document, and for the *Date, Time, Location*, and *Ticket cost* paragraphs, set a left tab at the 2.5-inch mark and a decimal tab at the 4-inch mark.

- Open the *Styles* document, and save the formatting of the *Author Meet and Greet Update* heading as a new style named *Headline*. Make the style part of the attached template, and add it to the Quick Styles list. Then apply the new style to the *Fantasy Author Starts Book Tour* paragraph at the bottom of the document.

2.2   **Manipulate text**

Copying and Moving

Copying and moving text is a familiar process for anyone who has used any Windows program. With the 2007 Microsoft Office programs, copied and cut items are stored on the Clipboard, which can store up to 24 items. When the Clipboard is full, the oldest item is deleted when a new one is added. All items are deleted when you turn off the computer, or you can manually delete individual items or all items.

To paste an item, simply click it.

Specify how and when the Clipboard appears.

Clicking the Paste button pastes the newest item from the Clipboard. To paste an earlier item, or all items simultaneously, you open the Clipboard and paste from there.

Tip When you need to move text only a short distance in the same document, you can use drag and drop editing. To copy the selection instead of moving it, hold down the Ctrl key while you drag. Drag and drop does not involve the Clipboard.

By default, clicking the Paste button pastes the newest item with the formatting specified in the Word Options dialog box. You can change these specifications to suit your needs. To change the formatting of the item you have just pasted, you can click the Paste Options button that appears beside the item and make a selection.

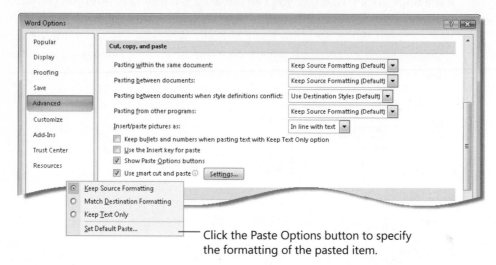

Click the Paste Options button to specify the formatting of the pasted item.

Tip By default the Use Smart Cut And Paste check box is selected on the Advanced page of the Word Options dialog box, so Word inserts and deletes any necessary spaces. To control the spacing yourself, clear this check box.

➤ To cut or copy and paste a selection

1. On the **Home** tab, in the **Clipboard** group, click the **Copy** or **Cut** button.
2. Click where you want to paste the text, and then in the **Clipboard** group, click the **Paste** button.

➤ To paste an earlier cut or copied item

1. On the **Home** tab, click the **Clipboard** dialog box launcher.
2. In the **Clipboard** task pane, click the item you want.

➤ To paste all items from the Clipboard

→ In the **Clipboard** task pane, click **Paste All**.

➤ To delete a cut or copied item

→ In the **Clipboard** task pane, point to the item, click the arrow that appears, and then click **Delete**.

➤ To delete all items from the Clipboard

→ In the **Clipboard** task pane, click **Clear All**.

Paste Special

You can paste the latest cut or copied item into a document in a variety of formats by clicking Paste Special in the Paste list. You can also paste a linked copy of an item, so that if the original item changes, you can update the linked item. And you can paste a hyper-link to the copied item so that you can easily jump to the original from the linked copy.

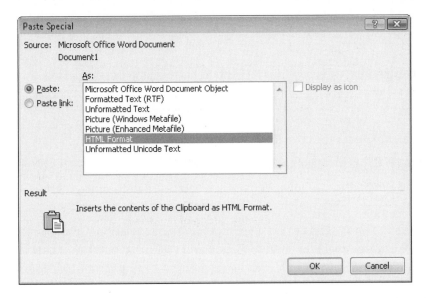

Tip For some formats in both the Paste and Paste Link lists, you can select the Display As Icon check box to paste the item as an icon.

➤ **To paste a cut or copied item in a different format**

1. Cut or copy the item, and then on the **Home** tab, in the **Clipboard** group, in the **Paste** list, click **Paste Special**.

2. In the **Paste Special** dialog box, click the format you want, and then click **OK**.

➤ **To paste a link or hyperlink to a copied item**

1. Copy the item, and in the **Paste Special** dialog box, click the **Paste link** option.

2. Click the format you want, and then click **OK**.

➤ **To update a linked copy to reflect changes to the original**

→ Right-click the copy, and click **Update Link**.

Finding and Replacing

One way to ensure that the text in your documents is accurate and consistent is to search for every instance of a particular word or phrase. In the Find And Replace dialog box, you can highlight all occurrences of the word or phrase, select and count all occurrences, or move from one occurrence to the next.

Tip If you find an error in the document while conducting a search, you can click the document and make editing changes on the fly without closing the Find And Replace dialog box.

You can use other options in the Find And Replace dialog box to carry out more complicated searches. Clicking More expands the box to make these additional options available:

- **Search.** Guides the direction of the search.
- **Match Case.** Matches capitalization.
- **Find Whole Words Only.** Finds only whole-word occurrences of the Find What text.
- **Use Wildcards.** Locates variable information by replacing ? in the Find What text with any one character in this location and * with any number of characters in this location.
- **Sounds Like.** Finds occurrences that sound the same but are spelled differently, such as *there* and *their*.
- **Find All Word Forms.** Finds occurrences in any form, such as *plan*, *planned*, and *planning*.

You can also match a prefix or a suffix, and you can ignore punctuation and spaces.

You can locate or highlight formatting, such as bold, or special characters, such as tabs, by selecting them from the Format or Special list at the bottom of the expanded Find And Replace dialog box. You can also search for styles.

If you want to substitute one word or phrase for another, or one set of formatting for another, you can use options on the Replace tab of the Find And Replace dialog box to replace the selected occurrence and move to the next occurrence, to replace all occurrences, or to leave the selected occurrence as it is and locate the next one.

➤ **To highlight all occurrences of text or formatting**

1. On the **Home** tab, in the **Editing** group, click the **Find** button.

2. On the **Find** tab of the **Find and Replace** dialog box, specify the text or formatting you want to highlight, click **Reading Highlight**, and then click **Highlight All**.

➤ **To select and count all occurrences of text or formatting**

➜ On the **Find** tab of the **Find and Replace** dialog box, specify the text or formatting you want to find, click **Find in**, and then click either **Main Document** or **Comments**.

➤ **To move from one occurrence of text or formatting to the next**

➜ On the **Find** tab of the **Find and Replace** dialog box, specify the text or formatting you want to find, click **Find Next**.

➤ **To find and replace a particular occurrence of text or formatting**

1. On the **Replace** tab of the **Find and Replace** dialog box, specify the text or formatting you want to find and the text or formatting you want to replace it with, and then click **Find Next** until you find the occurrence you are looking for.

2. Click **Replace**.

➤ **To find and replace all occurrences of text or formatting**

➜ On the **Replace** tab of the **Find and Replace** dialog box, specify the text or formatting you want to find and the text or formatting you want to replace it with, and then click **Replace All**.

Practice Tasks

The practice files for these tasks are located in the *Documents\Microsoft Press\ MCAS\Word2007\Objective02* folder. If you want, save the task results in the same folder with *My* prepended to the file name.

● Open the *Changing* document, and copy *A Fantasy Series for Young Adults* from page 1 to the top of page 2 via the Clipboard. Then on page 1, move the *Bartimaeus Trilogy* paragraph above the *Harry Potter series* paragraph, also via the Clipboard. Move the paragraph that begins *Interest in the fantasy genre*, above the preceding paragraph without going via the Clipboard.

● Open the *Finding* document, and highlight all instances of *The Taguien Cycle*. Then change all instances of *The Taguien Cycle* to italic.

2.3   Control pagination

Page Breaks

When you add more content than will fit within the document's top and bottom margins, Word creates a new page by inserting a soft page break. If you want to control how pages break, you can insert a manual page break. You can also control whether related paragraphs stay together or can be separated by a page break, and you can specify that a particular paragraph start on a new page.

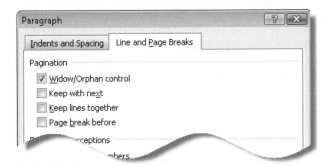

➤ **To insert a page break**

   → On the **Insert** tab, in the **Pages** group, click the **Page Break** button.

   → On the **Page Layout** tab, in the **Page Setup** group, click the **Breaks** button, and then in the list, click **Page**.

   → Press **Ctrl+Enter**.

➤ **To delete a page break**

  1. Switch to **Draft** view, and on the **Home** tab, in the **Paragraph** group, click the **Show/Hide** button to display nonprinting characters.

  2. Select the page break, and then press **Delete**.

➤ **To force a page break before a paragraph**

  1. Right-click anywhere in the paragraph, and click **Paragraph**.

  2. In the **Paragraph** dialog box, click the **Line and Page Breaks** tab.

  3. In the **Pagination** area, select the **Page break before** check box, and then click **OK**.

    Tip If a page break should always appear before a particular type of paragraph, such as a heading, you can incorporate the Page Break Before setting into the paragraph's style.

➤ **To keep related paragraphs together**

→ On the **Line and Page Breaks** tab of the **Paragraph** dialog box, in the **Pagination** area, select the **Keep with next** check box, and then click **OK**.

➤ **To keep all the lines of a paragraph together**

→ On the **Line and Page Breaks** tab of the **Paragraph** dialog box, in the **Pagination** area, select the **Keep lines together** check box, and then click **OK**.

➤ **To avoid one line of a paragraph appearing on the page**

→ On the **Line and Page Breaks** tab of the **Paragraph** dialog box, in the **Pagination** area, select the **Widow/Orphan control** check box, and then click **OK**.

Sections

In addition to controlling pagination with page breaks and paragraph formatting, you can control it with section breaks. A section break identifies a part of the document to which you can apply page settings, such as orientation or margins, that are different from those of the rest of the document. The following types of section breaks are available:

● **Next page.** This break starts the following section on the next page.

● **Continuous.** This break creates a new section without affecting page breaks.

● **Even page.** This break starts the following section on the next even-numbered page.

● **Odd page.** This break starts the following section on the next odd-numbered page.

➤ **To insert a section break**

→ On the **Page Layout** tab, in the **Page Setup** group, click the **Breaks** button, and in the **Section Breaks** area, click the type of section break you want.

➤ **To specify different page settings for part of a document**

1. Select the part of the document that will have different settings.

2. On the **Page Layout** tab, in the **Page Setup** group, click the **Breaks** button, and in the **Section Breaks** area, click the type of section break you want.

3. Click anywhere between the top and bottom section breaks, and change the setting.

   See Also For information about changing page settings, see section 1.1, "Create and format documents" and section 1.2, "Lay out documents."

➤ **To specify a different header or footer for a section**

1. Click anywhere between the top and bottom section breaks, and then on the **Design** tab, in the **Header & Footer** group, click **Header**.

2. In the gallery, click **Edit Header**, and enter your changes.

➤ **To delete a section break**

1. Switch to **Draft** view, and on the **Home** tab, in the **Paragraph** group, click the **Show/Hide** button to display nonprinting characters.

2. Click to the left of the section break, and then press **Delete**.

Practice Tasks

The practice files for these tasks are located in the *Documents\Microsoft Press\MCAS\Word2007\Objective02* folder. If you want, save the task results in the same folder with *My* prepended to the file name.

● Open the *Pages* document, and for the entire document, implement widow and orphan control and ensure that no paragraphs will be broken across pages.

● In the *Pages* document, insert a page break before the *Facilities* heading, and then ensure that the *To use the intercom from the office* heading will always appear on the same page as the following two steps.

● In the *Pages* document, insert a Next Page section break before the *Shipping Quick Reference* heading, set Wide margins for the new section, and change the header of the new section to *Shipping Quick Reference*.

Objective Review

Before finishing this chapter, ensure that you have mastered the following skills:

2.1 Format text and paragraphs.

2.2 Manipulate text.

2.3 Control pagination.

3 Working with Visual Content

The skills tested in this section of the Microsoft Office Specialist exam for Microsoft Office Word 2007 relate to the inserting and formatting of elements that visually enhance documents. Specifically, the following objectives are associated with this set of skills:

3.1 Insert illustrations.
3.2 Format illustrations.
3.3 Format text graphically.
3.4 Insert and modify text boxes.

Word 2007 makes it very easy to add sophisticated visual content to your documents. This visual content can consist of pictures created outside of Word, such as a scanned photograph, a clip art image, or an illustration created with a graphics program. Or it can consist of drawing objects that are created within Word, such as a shape, a diagram, WordArt text, or a text box. You can use the buttons on the Insert tab to insert different kinds of visual content.

After you insert a visual object, you can format it many ways. The types of formatting you can apply vary with the type of object and, in the case of pictures, with the type of picture.

This chapter guides you in studying ways of inserting, positioning, sizing, and formatting pictures, clip art, shapes, SmartArt diagrams, charts, WordArt, and text boxes.

 Important Before you can use the practice files in this chapter, you need to install them from the book's companion CD to their default location. See "Using the Companion CD" at the beginning of this book for more information.

Tip Graphics and operating system–related instructions in this book reflect the Windows Vista user interface. If your computer is running Windows XP and you experience trouble following the instructions as written, refer to the sidebar "If You Are Running Windows XP" in "Working in the Microsoft Office Fluent User Interface" at the beginning of this book.

3.1 Insert illustrations

Pictures

You can insert scanned photographs or pictures created in almost any program into a Word document. To specify the source of the picture, you click one of two buttons in the Illustrations group on the Insert tab:

- **Picture.** Click this button to insert a picture from a file. If you connect a digital camera to your computer, you can also insert a picture directly from the camera.

- **Clip Art.** Click this button to insert one of the hundreds of clip art images that come with Word, such as photos and drawings of people, places, and things.

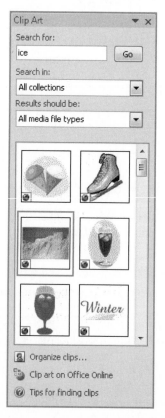

Inserting pictures or clip art images in a document can increase the size of the document file dramatically. By default, Word compresses pictures when you save the file. You can turn off automatic compression and compress only the pictures you want. You can also adjust the compression rate to be appropriate for the way the document will be viewed.

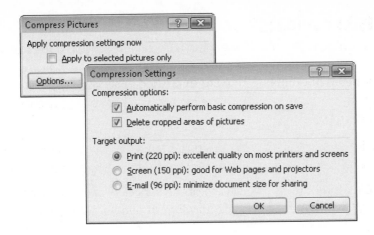

➤ To insert a picture from a file

1. On the **Insert** tab, in the **Illustrations** group, click the **Picture** button.

2. In the **Insert Picture** dialog box, browse to and click the file you want, and then click **Insert**.

   Tip To create a link to the original picture file, click Link To File or Insert And Link in the Insert list.

➤ To replace a selected picture

1. On the **Format** tab, in the **Adjust** group, click **Change Picture**.

2. In the **Insert Picture** dialog box, browse to and click the file you want, and then click **Insert**.

➤ To insert a clip art image

1. On the **Insert** tab, in the **Illustrations** group, click the **Clip Art** button.

2. In the **Clip Art** task pane, enter a keyword in the **Search for** box, and then click **Go**.

3. In the results list, click the thumbnail of the image you want.

➤ To change the picture compression settings

1. On the **Format** tab, in the **Adjust** group, click **Compress Pictures**.

2. In the **Compress Pictures** dialog box, click **Options**.

3. In the **Compression Settings** dialog box, set the options and output you want, and then click **OK** twice.

Shapes

If you want to add visual interest and impact to a document but you don't need a fancy picture or clip art image, you can draw a shape. Shapes can be simple, such as lines, circles, or squares; or more complex, such as stars, hearts, and arrows.

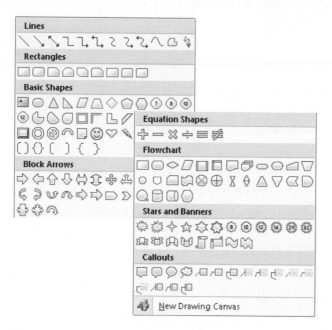

You can draw a shape directly on the page (Word's default setting), or you can draw it on a drawing canvas. Using a drawing canvas is useful if you want to assemble a group of shapes to create a drawing. The drawing canvas keeps the parts of the drawing together, helps you position the drawing, and provides a frame-like boundary between your drawing and the text on the page. Whether you insert shapes directly on the page or on a drawing canvas, you can add text to the shapes.

➤ **To insert a standard shape**

1. On the **Insert** tab, in the **Illustrations** group, click the **Shapes** button.

2. In the **Shapes** gallery, click the shape you want.

3. Move the crosshair to the location in your document where you want to insert the shape, and then click the mouse button.

➤ To insert a custom-size shape

1. In the **Shapes** gallery, click the shape you want.

2. Move the crosshair to the location in your document where you want to insert the shape, and then drag to create a shape the size you want.

    Tip To draw a shape with equal height and width, such as a square or circle, hold down the Shift key while you drag, releasing the mouse button before the Shift key.

➤ To create a drawing on a drawing canvas

1. At the bottom of the **Shapes** gallery, click **New Drawing Canvas**.

2. Draw shapes on the canvas in the usual ways.

    Tip If you always want to use the drawing canvas, select the Automatically Create Drawing Canvas When Inserting AutoShapes check box on the Advanced pane of the Word Options dialog box.

➤ To add text to a selected shape

1. On the **Format** tab, in the **Insert Shapes** group, click the **Edit Text** button.

2. Type the text, and then format it using normal techniques.

SmartArt Diagrams

When you need your document to clearly illustrate a concept such as a process, cycle, hierarchy, or relationship, you can create a dynamic, visually appealing diagram by using SmartArt graphics.

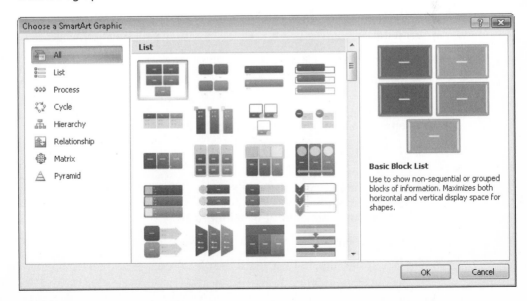

After selecting the type of diagram you want and inserting it into the document, you add text either directly in the diagram's shapes or from its text pane.

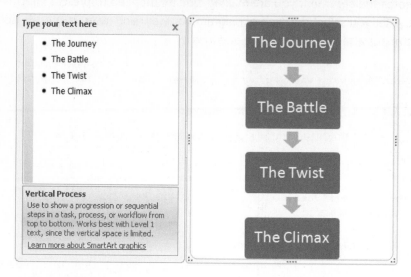

➤ **To insert a diagram**

1. On the **Insert** tab, in the **Illustrations** group, click the **SmartArt** button.

2. In the left pane of the **Choose a SmartArt Graphic** dialog box, click the type of diagram you want.

3. In the center pane, click the layout you want, and then click **OK**.

➤ **To add text to a diagram shape**

→ With the diagram selected, click the shape, and then type the text.

→ In the text pane, click the bullet for the shape, and then type the text.

   Tip If the text pane is not open, click the tab on the left side of the diagram's frame. Or click the Text Pane button in the Create Graphic group on the Design tab.

➤ **To change the layout of a selected diagram**

→ On the **Design** tab, in the **Layouts** group, click a layout in the **Layouts** gallery.

   Tip If you want to switch to a different diagram category, click More Layouts at the bottom of the gallery to display the Choose A SmartArt Graphic dialog box.

➤ **To add a shape to the layout of a diagram**

1. Select the shape adjacent to which you want to add the new shape.

2. On the **Design** tab, in the **Create Graphic** group, click the **Add Shape** button; or select a precise location from the list.

Charts

To reinforce the argument you are making, you might need to present information in a chart. After you select the type of diagram you want and insert it into the document, Word embeds a sample chart in the document.

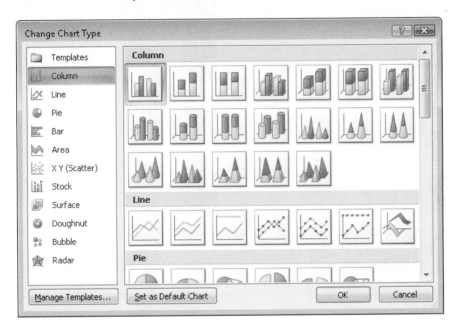

The data used to plot the sample chart is stored in a Microsoft Office Excel 2007 worksheet that is incorporated into the Word file.

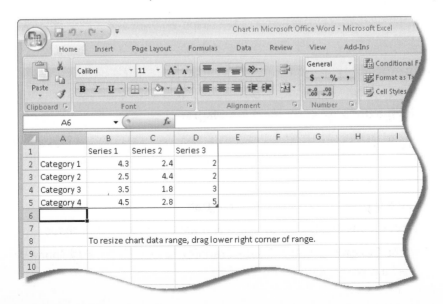

The Excel worksheet is composed of rows and columns of cells that contain values, or *data points*, that make up a data series. To customize the chart, you replace the sample data in the worksheet with your own data. To enter data in an individual cell—the intersection of a row and column—you click the cell to select it, and then start typing. When you have finished, you close the worksheet to see the data plotted in the chart. Because the worksheet is linked to the chart, you can change the values in the worksheet at any time, and the chart changes to reflect the new values.

Strategy Different chart types are useful for plotting different types of data. You can add several elements to a chart, such as titles and labels, and you can manipulate the elements in various ways. You should experiment with different types of charts and chart elements to become familiar with them.

➤ **To insert a chart**

1. On the **Insert** tab, in the **Illustrations** group, click the **Chart** button.

2. In the **Insert Chart** dialog box, click the category of chart you want, click the style you want, and then click **OK**.

➤ **To enter data in a new chart**

→ In the Excel worksheet, replace the sample data by clicking a cell and then typing your own data.

➤ **To edit the data in an existing chart**

1. Click anywhere in the chart to activate it. Then on the **Design** tab, in the **Data** group, click the **Edit Data** button.

2. In the Excel worksheet, click the cell you want to edit, type the new data, and then press **Enter**.

➤ **To change the type of an existing chart**

1. Click anywhere in the chart to activate it. Then on the **Design** tab, in the **Type** group, click the **Change Chart Type** button.

2. In the **Change Chart Type** dialog box, click the category of chart you want, click the style you want, and then click **OK**.

Sizing and Positioning

When you insert an illustration, it is automatically selected. Later, you can select it by clicking it.

While the visual object is selected, you can easily change its size. If you change the height and width proportionally, the object retains its shape; if you change one more than the other, the object changes shape.

You can position a selected object on the page in a variety of ways. Pictures, clip art, diagrams, and charts are inserted in a document in line with the text, meaning that they are associated with a text paragraph. Although you can drag them vertically to a different paragraph, you cannot drag them horizontally. You can align them horizontally by clicking an alignment button in the Paragraph group on the Home tab. Or you can move them to a specific area of the page by making a selection from the Position gallery.

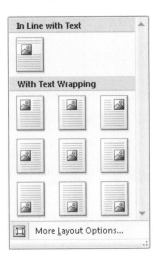

If you want to move a picture, clip art image, diagram or chart to a location other than one of the Position gallery presets, you must make it independent by breaking its association with the surrounding text. (By default, shapes are already independent and can be moved anywhere.)

Tip If you hold down the Ctrl key while you drag an object and release the Ctrl key after you release the mouse button, Word makes a copy of the object in the new location instead of moving it.

➤ **To change the size and/or shape of a selected object**

→ Drag its sizing handles.

→ On the **Format** tab, in the **Size** group, adjust the **Height** and **Width** settings.

→ On the **Format** tab, click the **Size** dialog box launcher to display a dialog box in which you can adjust the size.

Tip You can also use this method to scale the object. This method is not available for diagrams.

➤ **To position a selected object**

→ Drag it vertically to a new location.

→ On the **Format** tab, in the **Arrange** group, click the **Position** button, and then click one of the options in the **Position** gallery.

➤ **To make a selected object independent of the text**

→ On the **Format** tab, in the **Arrange** group, click the **Text Wrapping** button, and then click **In Front of Text**.

See Also For more information about text wrapping, see section 3.2, "Format illustrations."

➤ **To position an independent object**

→ Drag it to a new location.

→ Press the **Arrow** keys to move the object in small increments.

Or

1. On the **Format** tab, in the **Arrange** group, click the **Position** button, and then click **More Layout Options**.

2. On the **Picture Position** tab of the **Advanced Layout** dialog box, set a relative or absolute position for the object, and then click **OK**.

Tip When you draw shapes on a drawing canvas, you can move or size the canvas to move or size the entire drawing.

Practice Tasks

The practice files for these tasks are located in the *Documents\Microsoft Press\ MCAS\Word2007\Objective03* folder. If you want, save the task results in the same folder with *My* prepended to the file name.

- Open the *Picture* document, and at the top, insert the *Logo* graphic. Then size the logo so that it is 0.5" high, maintaining the height to width proportion.

- Open the *ClipArt* document, insert a stylized dollar clip art image at the end of the *Greg Guzik* paragraph, and make it 0.25 inch square. Then insert a copy of the image at the beginning of the paragraph.

- Open the *Shapes* document, and at the end of the document, draw a circle 1.5 inches in diameter in the upper-left corner of a new drawing canvas. Then create a copy of the circle in the upper middle of the drawing canvas and another in the upper-right corner. Draw curved lines resembling strings below each circle.

- Open the *SmartArt* document, and at the end of the document, insert a Vertical Process diagram. In the text pane, type *The Journey, The Battle,* and *The Twist* as bullet points. Then add a new shape containing the words *The Climax.*

- Open the *Chart* document, and at the end of the document, insert a 3-D Clustered Column chart. Then change the headings in row 1 to *January, February,* and *March,* and change the headings in column A to *1st Quarter, 2nd Quarter, 3rd Quarter,* and *4th Quarter.* Then change the chart type to a Stacked Area chart.

3.2   Format illustrations

Strategy Different types of visual objects can be formatted in different ways. We recommend that you create a new, five-page document, insert a different type of object on each page, and then experiment with the objects on your own to understand which types of formatting can be applied to which types of objects.

Text Wrapping

After you insert a visual object in a document, you can specify how the object should relate to the surrounding text. The default setting for all objects except shapes, In Line With Text, embeds the object in the text so that the object moves as the text moves. You have already seen that you need to set text wrapping to In Front Of Text to allow an object to float independently over the text. In addition, you can set the text wrapping so that the text wraps around the object in various ways. On the Text Wrapping tab of the Advanced Layout dialog box, you can specify which side of the object the text appears on and how closely the text hugs the frame of the object.

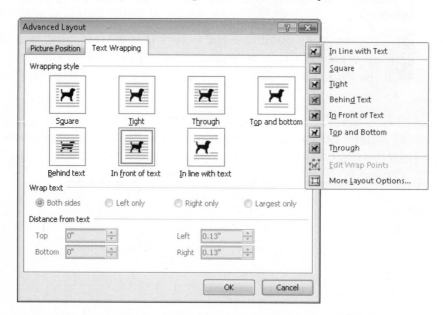

➤ **To specify how text should wrap around a selected object**

→ On the **Format** tab, in the **Arrange** group, click the **Text Wrapping** button, and then click the wrapping style you want.

Cropping

To focus attention on a particular part of a picture or clip art image, you can crop away the parts of the image you don't want. (You cannot crop a shape, diagram, or chart.)

Cropping handles

➤ **To crop a selected image**

1. On the **Format** menu, in the **Size** group, click the **Crop** button.

2. Using the cropping pointer, drag the cropping handles to hide the parts of the image you don't want.

Rotating

You can rotate pictures, clip art images, and shapes in place around their axis. (You do not have to change the text-wrapping setting to rotate an object.) You cannot rotate a chart. You cannot rotate an entire diagram, but you can rotate the shapes within a diagram.

➤ **To rotate a selected object**

→ Drag the green rotate handle in any direction.

→ On the **Format** tab, in the **Arrange** group, click the **Rotate** button, and then select an option.

Or

1. On the **Format** tab, in the **Arrange** group, click the **Rotate** button, and then click **More Rotation Options**.

2. In the **Size** dialog box, in the **Size and Rotate** area, adjust the **Rotation** setting. Then click **Close**.

Stacking Order

To create sophisticated visual effects, you might arrange objects so that they overlap. By default, objects appear in the order in which you insert them. You can change the order, either by pulling an object forward or by pushing it backward.

Front of stack
Back of stack

➤ **To make a selected shape first or last in the stacking order**

→ On the **Format** tab, in the **Arrange** group, click **Bring to Front** or **Send to Back**.

➤ **To bring a selected shape one shape forward in the stacking order**

→ In the **Bring to Front** list, click **Bring Forward**.

➤ **To send a selected shape one shape backward in the stacking order**

→ In the **Send to Back** list, click **Send Backward**.

Grouping

With objects such as shapes, you can simultaneously move or size multiple objects by grouping them so that they act as one object. To break the bond, you ungroup the objects.

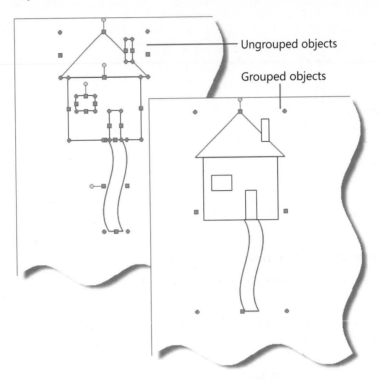

Ungrouped objects

Grouped objects

➤ **To group selected shapes**

→ On the **Format** menu, in the **Arrange** group, click the **Group** button, and then click **Group**.

➤ **To ungroup a selection**

→ On the **Format** menu, in the **Arrange** group, click the **Group** button, and then click **Ungroup**.

Aligning and Distributing

When you want to position shapes evenly on the page, you can display a grid to help you, or you can have Word align and distribute the shapes in various ways.

> ➤ **To align shapes with each other**

1. Select the shape you want to align the other shapes with, and then select the other shapes.

2. On the **Format** tab, in the **Arrange** group, click the **Align** button, and then click the alignment option you want.

> ➤ **To distribute shapes evenly on the page**

1. Select the shapes you want to distribute.

2. On the **Format** tab, in the **Arrange** group, click the **Align** button, and then click the distribution option you want.

Tip You can also use the aligning and distributing techniques with some other types of visual objects.

Styles

Just as you can format text with styles, you can format visual objects with styles. The styles vary depending on the type of object selected and are usually found on the Format tab. In the case of diagrams and charts, there are styles for their component shapes and their text on the Format tab and styles for the object as a whole on the Design tab. Changing the style of an object can have a profound effect, changing such properties as colors, borders, orientation, and dimension (depending on the object) all at the same time.

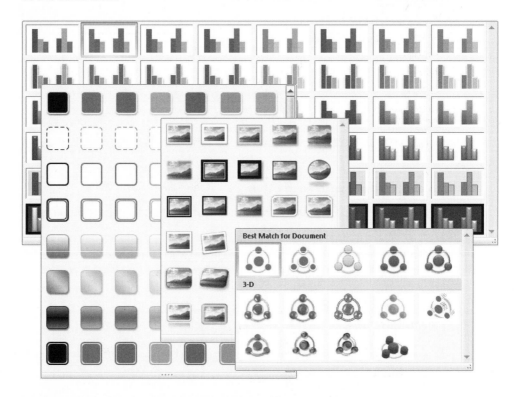

➤ **To apply a style to a selected object or object shape**

→ On the **Format** tab or the **Design** tab, click the style you want in the **Styles** gallery for that type of object.

Tip The SmartArt styles change the look of a diagram but not its colors. To globally change the colors of a diagram, click the color scheme you want in the Change Colors gallery.

Color

You can't change the color of a picture or clip art image by switching styles, but you can adjust the brightness and contrast, and even recolor, some types of pictures and clip art. You can fine-tune the brightness and contrast by clicking Picture Corrections Options at the bottom of either the Brightness or Contrast gallery to display the Format Picture dialog box.

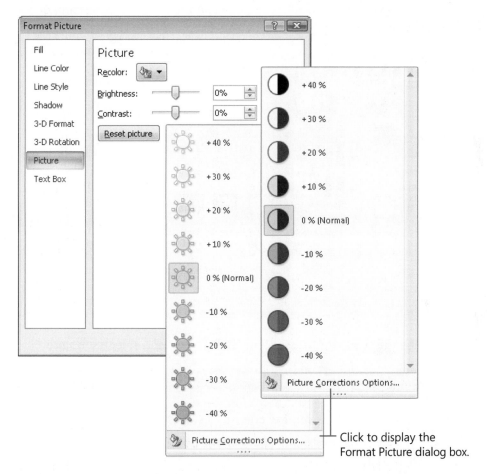

Click to display the
Format Picture dialog box.

Tip To restore the original picture, click Reset Picture in the Format Picture dialog box to discard any changes you made.

You can specify the fill color of shapes, and you can fill shapes with patterns, textures, and even pictures. You can also change the color, weight, and style of the border of an object or of its component shapes.

Tip To make a drawing canvas stand out on the page, you can put a border around it and shade it.

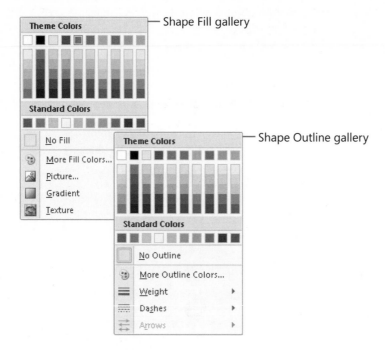

Shape Fill gallery

Shape Outline gallery

➤ **To change the brightness, contrast, or color of a selected image**

→ On the **Format** tab, in the **Adjust** group, click the **Brightness**, **Contrast**, or **Recolor** button, and then make a selection in the corresponding gallery.

➤ **To change the fill or outline color of a selected shape**

→ On the **Format** tab, in the **Shape Styles** group, make a selection in the **Shape Fill** or **Shape Outline** palette.

Tip If you change the attributes of a shape—for example, its fill color and border weight—and you want all the shapes you draw from now on in this document to have those attributes, right-click the shape, and then click Set AutoShape Defaults.

Practice Tasks

The practice files for these tasks are located in the *Documents\Microsoft Press\ MCAS\Word2007\Objective03* folder. If you want, save the task results in the same folder with *My* prepended to the file name.

- Open the *Logo* document, and lighten the color of the logo to Accent Color 1 Light. Then adjust its brightness to +10% and its contrast to -30%. Finally, give the logo a three-dimensional perspective by changing its style to Rounded Diagonal Corner, White.

- Open the *Balloons* document, and at the end of the document, fill the circles with yellow, green, and purple. Then group the right circle and its string, flip them horizontally, and then move them down on the drawing canvas. Finally, shrink the height of the drawing canvas until it fits at the bottom of the first page of the document, and then center it with square text wrapping.

- Open the *Process* document, and make the diagram pane approximately as wide as the shapes within the diagram. Wrap the text tightly on both sides of the diagram. Then position the diagram on the right relative to the document margin and 2 inches from the top of the page.

- Open the *Process2* document, change the style of the diagram to Cartoon, and change the colors to Colorful Range – Accent Colors 2 To 3.

- Open the *AreaChart* document, and change the chart style to Style 48. Then change the color of the plot area to dark red, and put a dark red 6-point border around the chart area.

3.3   Format text graphically

WordArt

When you want a text banner that is fancier than one you can create by applying character formatting, you can use WordArt. WordArt text can swirl, grow bigger from one end to the other or in the middle, take on a three-dimensional shape, and change color from one letter to the next. After you choose the style you want, you type and format the text in the Edit WordArt Text dialog box.

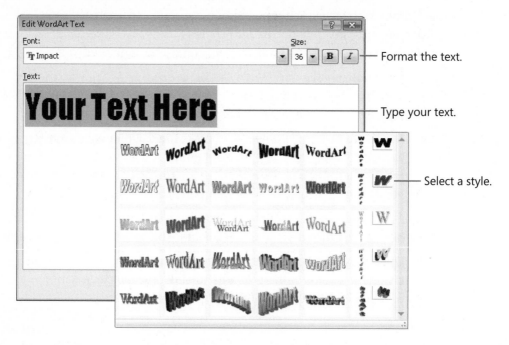

Format the text.

Type your text.

Select a style.

Tip You can also select existing text before clicking the WordArt button to convert that text into a WordArt object.

Selecting a WordArt object displays the Format tab, which you can use to edit and format a WordArt object in many ways, such as the following:

- Change the text spacing, alignment, and orientation.
- Change the style, shape, and fill and outline colors.
- Add special effects such as shadows and 3-D effects.
- Position and size the object.
- Change the text wrapping, alignment, and rotation angle.

➤ **To insert a WordArt object**

1. On the **Insert** tab, in the **Text** group, click the **WordArt** button.

2. In the **WordArt** gallery, click the style you want.

3. In the **Edit WordArt Text** dialog box, type the text.

4. Set the size and other attributes of the text, and then click **OK**.

Drop Caps

Many books, magazines, and reports begin the first paragraph of a section or chapter by using an enlarged, decorative capital letter. Called a *dropped capital*, or simply a *drop cap*, this effect can be an easy way to give a document a finished, professional look.

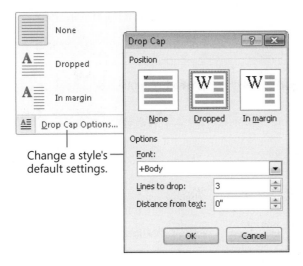

➤ **To change the first character of a paragraph to a drop cap**

1. Position the insertion point in the paragraph. Then on the **Insert** tab, in the **Text** group, click the **Drop Cap** button.

2. In the **Drop Cap** gallery, click the style you want; or click **Drop Cap Options**, click a style, adjust the settings, and then click **OK**.

Practice Tasks

The practice files for these tasks are located in the *Documents\Microsoft Press\ MCAS\Word2007\Objective03* folder. If you want, save the task results in the same folder with *My* prepended to the file name.

- Open the *WordArt* document, and at the top of the document, insert *Welcome Esther Valle!* in WordArt Style 16 and size 44.

- In the *WordArt* document, change the words *Extra! Extra!* into WordArt style 21, and change the color of the letters to orange with a red outline. Next, set the spacing to Very Loose. Make the object two inches wider, and then add perspective with Shadow Style 7.

- Open the *DropCap* document, and replace the first letter in the first paragraph with an In Margin drop cap.

3.4   Insert and modify text boxes

When you want text that is not part of the main flow to appear on a page, you can create a text box in one of several built-in styles. You then type the text, and the box grows vertically to accommodate the number of lines you type.

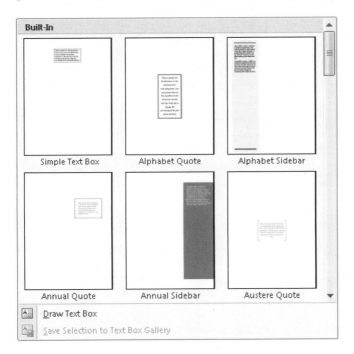

You can also draw a custom text box in one of two ways. You can either click the page where you want the text box to appear, in which case the text box grows vertically to accommodate as much text as you type; or you can drag a text box of a specific size on the page, in which case the text box does not grow and any text that will not fit in the box is hidden until you resize the box.

When you click an existing text box, an insertion point appears, and the box is surrounded by a dashed border. You can then edit the text—for example, you can add, delete, or correct words and punctuation. Clicking the dashed border changes it to a solid border. You can then manipulate the text box as a unit. For example, dragging the solid border is the most efficient way to move a text box on the page, and you can copy the box just as easily by holding down the Ctrl key while you drag it.

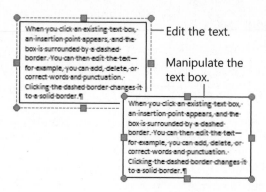

Edit the text.

Manipulate the text box.

You can drag the handles around the solid border to change the box's size and shape, or you can change the Size settings on the Format tab, which you can also use to format the text box in many of the same ways as other visual objects. You can also change the direction of the text in the box, and if you want to continue the text from one text box into another, you can link the boxes.

Tip If you frequently use the same set of formatting for text boxes, you can select a formatted text box, right-click its border, and then click Set AutoShape Defaults. From then on, any text boxes you draw (not those you click in the gallery) will have your preferred formatting.

➤ To insert a ready-made text box

1. On the **Insert** tab, in the **Text** group, click the **Text Box** button.

2. In the **Text Box** gallery, click the built-in format you want.

3. Replace the placeholder text by typing your own text.

➤ To draw a custom text box

1. Display the **Text Box** gallery, and then click **Draw Text Box**.

2. Position the crosshair where you want the box to appear, and click; or drag to create a text box the size you want.

3. Type the text you want to appear in the text box.

➤ **To link text boxes**

1. Select the first text box in the chain.

   Tip It doesn't matter what type of selection border surrounds the box.

2. On the **Format** tab, in the **Text** group, click the **Create Link** button.

3. Point to the next text box, and then click.

➤ **To break the link between text boxes**

1. Select the text box from which you originally created the link.

2. On the **Format** tab, in the **Text** group, click the **Break Link** button.

Practice Tasks

The practice files for these tasks are located in the *Documents\Microsoft Press\ MCAS\Word2007\Objective03* folder. If you want, save the task results in the same folder with *My* prepended to the file name.

● Open the *TextBoxes* document, and insert a Simple Text Box, and then cut and paste the paragraph of the document into the text box.

● Continuing in the *TextBoxes* document, decrease the size of the text box to 1.25 inches high by 2 inches wide, and then draw another text box of the same size below the first one. Link the two text boxes so that the overflow text from the first box is displayed in the second text box.

● Continuing in the *TextBoxes* document, color the first text box light blue with a blue border and the second text box light green with a green border. Then apply Shadow Style 1 to both boxes.

Objective Review

Before finishing this chapter, ensure that you have mastered the following skills:

3.1 Insert illustrations.

3.2 Format illustrations.

3.3 Format text graphically.

3.4 Insert and modify text boxes.

4 Organizing Content

The skills tested in this section of the Microsoft Office Specialist exam for Microsoft Office Word 2007 relate to techniques for structuring, organizing, and referencing document content. Specifically, the following objectives are associated with this set of skills:

4.1 Structure content by using Quick Parts.

4.2 Use tables and lists to organize content.

4.3 Modify tables.

4.4 Insert and format references and captions.

4.5 Merge documents and data sources.

With Word 2007, it is easier than ever to create document elements that make information readily accessible and discoverable. You can draw attention to important information (and simultaneously implement a consistent, professional design) by using elements such as ready-made cover pages, sidebars, and pull quotes. You can quickly create and format complex lists and tables to make data easy to read and understand. You can document sources and have Word gather together resource information. In addition, it is easier than ever to use Word to generate tailored copies of a document for multiple recipients.

This chapter guides you in studying ways of inserting standard text and document parts; organizing content by using tables and lists; referencing content in bibliographies, reference tables, footnotes, and endnotes; and merging content with data sources.

 Important Before you can use the practice files in this chapter, you need to install them from the book's companion CD to their default location. See "Using the Companion CD" at the beginning of this book for more information.

Tip Graphics and operating system–related instructions in this book reflect the Windows Vista user interface. If your computer is running Windows XP and you experience trouble following the instructions as written, refer to the sidebar "If You Are Running Windows XP" in "Working in the Microsoft Office Fluent User Interface" at the beginning of this book.

4.1   Structure content by using Quick Parts

Building Blocks Organizer

Longer documents typically include elements such as a cover page and headers and footers to provide identifying and organizing information. To reinforce key concepts and also alleviate the monotony of page after page of plain text, they might also include elements such as sidebars and quotations pulled from the text. To simplify the creation of professional visual text elements, you can insert ready-made versions of these elements, called *Quick Parts*, from the Insert tab.

All the available Quick Parts are listed in the Building Blocks Organizer. (In fact, the terms *Quick Parts* and *building blocks* seem to be used interchangeably in the Word program.) The Cover Page Quick Parts are also available from the Pages group on the Insert tab. Clicking a Quick Part in the left pane of the Building Blocks Organizer displays a preview in the right pane.

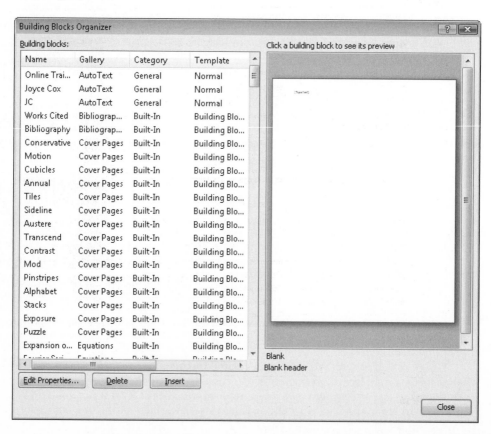

Strategy You might want to insert Quick Parts in a test document and saving modified and new Quick Parts in various ways so that you understand the relationship between the Building Blocks Organizer and the Cover Page, Header, Footer, and Text Box galleries.

The names of some Quick Parts indicate that they belong to a design family, such as Alphabet or Pinstripes. You can sort the list on any column—for example, you might want to sort the list by name to group all the Quick Parts by design family, so that you can preview the entire set before inserting them.

More information about each Quick Part is available by scrolling the Building Blocks list horizontally. The Behavior column indicates whether Word inserts the building block in the existing text, in its own paragraph, or on its own page. The Description column includes information about the Quick Part, and in some cases, recommendations for its use. For an overview of a particular Quick Part, you can click Edit Properties.

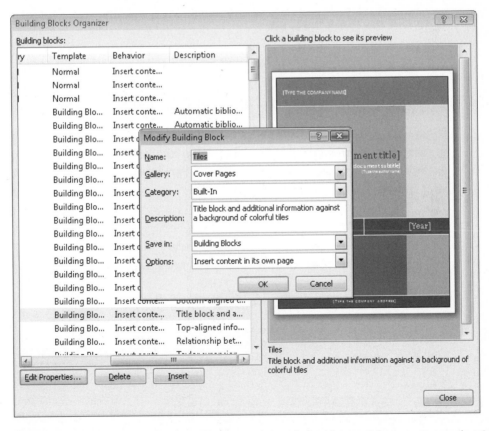

See Also For information about inserting ready-made headers and footers, see section 1.2, "Lay out documents." For information about inserting sidebars and pull quotes, see section 3.4, "Insert and modify text boxes."

➤ **To insert a cover page Quick Part**

1. With the insertion point at the beginning of the document, on the **Insert** tab, in the **Pages** group, click the **Cover Page** button.

2. In the **Cover Page** gallery, click the design you want, and then replace the text placeholders.

➤ **To insert any Quick Part**

1. On the **Insert** tab, in the **Text** group, click the **Quick Parts** button.

2. In the **Building Blocks Organizer**, select the Quick Part you want, and then click **Insert**.

   Tip After you insert a Quick Part, you can reposition it or change its formatting by using normal techniques.

➤ **To sort the Quick Parts list**

→ In the **Building Blocks Organizer**, click the heading of the column on which you want to sort the list.

Custom Quick Parts

If you frequently use the same set of Quick Parts in your documents, you might want to customize them to incorporate changes you routinely make after inserting them. For example, you might want to customize Quick Part cover pages, headers, or footers with your company name, or you might want to incorporate a logo or other graphic element. After you have customized a Quick Part in a document, you can save it with a new name so that it is available in its customized form whenever you need it. By default, custom Quick Parts are displayed in the Quick Parts gallery when you click the Quick Parts button, as well as being listed in the Building Blocks Organizer.

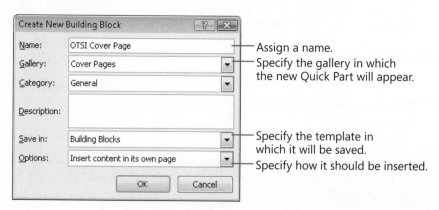

Tip If you customize a field in a Quick Part, that field is customized in all Quick Parts that include the field. Fields are discussed later in this section.

Tip You can save a customized Quick Part directly into the appropriate gallery by clicking Save Selection To at the bottom of the gallery.

To save time and ensure consistency in your documents, you can save any text, graphic, or combination of the two as a Quick Part. For example, you might want to save your company contact information and logo. You can then insert it from the Quick Parts gallery. Alternatively, if you have stored the Quick Part in the AutoText gallery, you can type its name and press the F3 key. Pressing F3 substitutes the Quick Part only if the name you type contains no spaces. There must be a space to its left and a space or a punctuation mark to its right, and the insertion point must immediately follow the name.

Tip When you quit Word, you will be asked whether you want to save the template in which your custom Quick Parts are stored, which by default is the Building Blocks template. If you want to discard the Quick Parts you have created in this Word session, click No. Otherwise, click Yes.

➤ **To save a modified Quick Part**

1. Select the text and/or graphics you want to save.
2. On the **Insert** tab, in the **Text** group, click the **Quick Parts** button, and then click **Save Selection to Quick Part Gallery**.
3. In the **Create New Building Block** dialog box, type a name for the Quick Part; designate the gallery, template, and behavior; and then click **OK**.

➤ **To save selected text as an AutoText Quick Part**

1. On the **Insert** tab, in the **Text** group, click the **Quick Parts** button, and then click **Save Selection to Quick Part Gallery**.
2. In the **Create New Building Block** dialog box, type a name for the Quick Part, set **Gallery** to **AutoText**, and then click **OK**.

➤ **To delete a Quick Part**

1. In the **Text** group, click **Quick Parts**, and then click **Building Blocks Organizer**.
2. In the **Building blocks** list, select the Quick Part you want to delete, and then click **Delete**.

Fields

You can easily insert today's date or the current time in a document in a format of your choosing. Word retrieves the date or time from your computer's internal calendar or clock. You can insert the information as regular text or as a field.

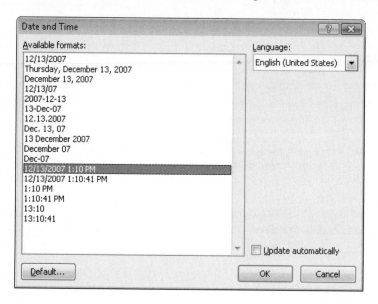

A field is a placeholder that tells Word to supply the specified information in the specified way. The advantage of using a field is that if the information changes, you can have Word update it.

Strategy It is worth exploring the field list, reading the descriptions, and checking the various formats to gain an understanding of the uses for each one.

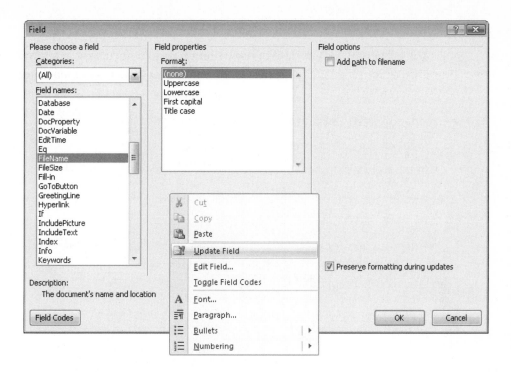

➤ To insert the date or time

1. On the **Insert** tab, in the **Text** group, click the **Date & Time** button.

2. In the **Date and Time** dialog box, in the **Available formats** area, click the format you want.

3. If you want to insert the date or time as a field rather than as text, select the **Update automatically** check box.

4. Click **OK**.

➤ To insert a field

1. On the **Insert** tab, in the **Text** group, click the **Quick Parts** button, and then in the list, click **Field**.

2. In the **Field** dialog box, click the field you want to insert. Then select any properties, formats, or options you want, and click **OK**.

➤ To update a field

→ Right-click the field, and click **Update Field**.

Tip For date and time fields, click the Update button that appears when you click the field.

➤ To change a field or its formatting

1. Right-click the field, and click **Edit Field**.

2. In the **Field** dialog box, make the necessary adjustments, and then click **OK**.

Practice Tasks

The practice files for these tasks are located in the *Documents\Microsoft Press\ MCAS\Word2007\Objective04* folder. If you want, save the task results in the same folder with *My* prepended to the file name.

● Open the *Parts* document, and insert a Pinstripes cover page. Change the subtitle placeholder to *Information Sheet* and the date placeholder to to-day's date.

● Continuing in the *Parts* document, on page 2, insert a Pinstripes Quote, and use Paste Special to insert an unformatted copy of the last sentence of the fourth paragraph (*Go with what you love...*) in the quote box. Then save the customized pull quote as a Quick Part with the name *Inspiration Quote*.

● Open the *SavedText* document, and at the end of the document, select and save *Wide World Importers* as an AutoText Quick Part named *www*. Then in a new paragraph at the end of the document, type *Recommended by* and insert the *www* Quick Part.

● In the *SavedText* document, add a footer that includes only the Author, FileName, and SaveDate fields with their default formats and options.

4.2 Use tables and lists to organize content

Tables

It is often more efficient to present numeric data in a table than to explain it in a paragraph of text. Tables make large amounts or more complex data easier to read and understand because it can be structured in rows and columns, frequently with row and column headings.

See Also For information about Quick Tables, see section 4.3, "Modify tables."

You can create a table in several ways:

● Select the number of rows and columns you want from a grid to create a table that spans the text column with all the cells of equal size.

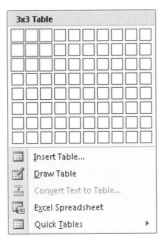

● Display the Insert Table dialog box and specify the number of rows and columns, as well as the size of the columns.

● Draw cells the size you want.

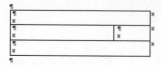

● Convert selected text to a table.

After creating the table, you can enter text, numbers, and graphics into its cells. You can edit the information as you would normal text, and you can sort the information based on any column.

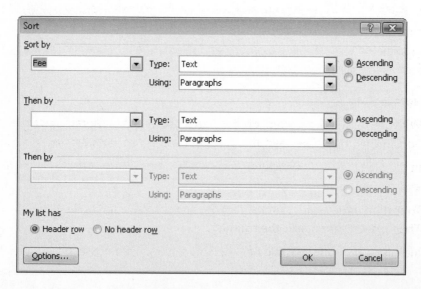

Strategy You should create a table with four or five columns and many rows of data and observe the effect of sorting the table with and without a header row to understand the sorting process.

➤ To insert a table

1. On the **Insert** tab, in the **Tables** group, click the **Table** button.
2. In the grid, move the pointer across and down to select the number of columns and rows you want, and click the lower-right cell in the selection.

➤ To draw a table

1. On the **Insert** tab, in the **Tables** group, click the **Table** button, and then click **Draw Table**.
2. Drag the pointer (which has become a pencil) across and down to create a cell.
3. Point to a corner of the cell, and drag to create another cell, or draw column and row boundaries inside the first cell.
4. Press **Esc** to turn off the table drawing pointer.

   Tip You can adjust an existing table by clicking the Draw Table button in the Draw Borders group on the Design tab. You can also change the style, weight, and color of the borders of drawn tables.

➤ To convert selected text to a table

1. On the **Insert** tab, in the **Tables** group, click the **Table** button, and then click **Convert Text to Table**.
2. In the **Convert Text to Table** dialog box, adjust the **Table size** and **AutoFit behavior** settings, select the type of text separator, and then click **OK**.

   Tip To convert a table to text, click anywhere in the table and then click the Convert To Text button in the Data group on the Layout contextual tab.

➤ To sort a table

1. With any table cell selected, on the **Home** tab, in the **Paragraph** group, click the **Sort** button; or on the **Layout** tab, in the **Data** group, click the **Sort** button.
2. In the **Sort** dialog box, click the first column you want to sort on in the **Sort by** list, and adjust the adjacent settings.
3. To sort on additional columns, click the column you want in the first and second **Then by** lists, and adjust their settings.
4. Indicate whether your table has a row of column headings, and then click **OK**.

Tabular Lists

If you have a relatively small amount of data to present in a table, you might choose to display it in a tabular list, which arranges text in simple columns separated by left, right, centered, or decimal tab stops.

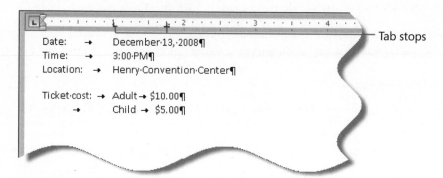

See Also For more information about setting tab stops, see section 2.1, "Format text and paragraphs."

If you press the Tab key multiple times to align the columns of a tabular list, you have no control over the column widths. To be able to fine-tune the columns, you should press Tab only once between the items, apply any necessary formatting, and then set custom tab stops in order from left to right.

Tip In addition to left, right, centered, and decimal tabs, you can set a bar tab to add a vertical line to selected paragraphs, further distinguishing the columns in a tabular list.

> **To create a tabular list**

  1. Type the text of the list, pressing **Tab** between each item on a line and pressing **Enter** at the end of each line.

  2. Select the lines, and set tab stops on the horizontal ruler where you want the items to align in columns.

Bulleted and Numbered Lists

When you want to present a simple list of items in a document, you will usually want to put each item on its own line rather than burying the items in a paragraph. When the order of items is not important, use a bulleted list. When the item order *is* important, use a numbered list.

You can create a multilevel bulleted list, numbered list, or outline by selecting a style from the Multilevel List gallery and then typing the list.

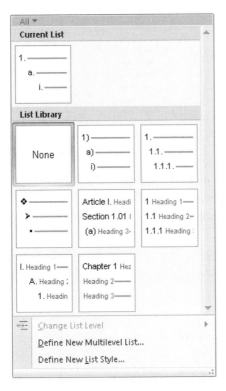

After you create a bulleted or numbered list, you can modify, format, and customize the list as follows:

- Move items up or down, insert new items, or delete unwanted items. If the list is numbered, Word automatically updates the numbers.
- Sort items in a list into ascending or descending order.
- Change the bullet symbol or define a custom bullet.

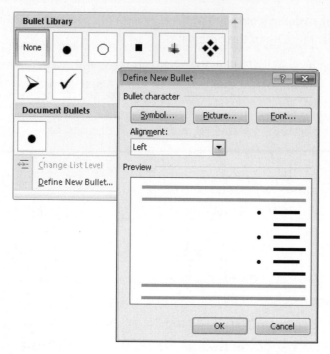

● Change the number style or define a custom style.

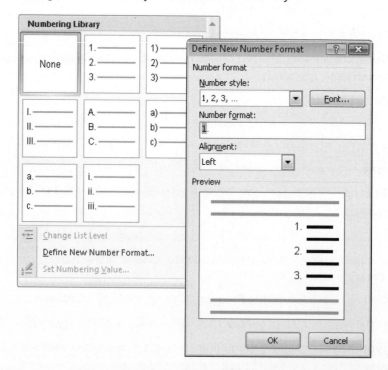

● Change the overall indentation of the entire list or change the relationship of the first "outdented" line to the other lines.

● Change the level of items in a multilevel list.

Strategy The precise formatting of bulleted and numbered lists depends on the interplay of settings in their respective galleries as well as paragraph formatting and the location of tab stops. You should create multiple lists, show paragraph marks, and experiment with various settings, observing their effects.

➤ To create a bulleted list

1. Enter the list items as separate paragraphs.

2. Select the paragraphs, and on the **Home** tab, in the **Paragraph** group, click the **Bullets** button.

   Or

1. Type * (an asterisk) at the beginning of a paragraph, press the **Spacebar** or the **Tab** key, type the first item in the list, and then press **Enter**.

2. Type items and press **Enter** to add subsequent bulleted items.

3. To end the list, press **Enter** twice, or press **Enter** and then **Backspace**.

➤ To create a numbered list

1. Enter the list items as separate paragraphs.

2. Select the paragraphs, and on the **Home** tab, in the **Paragraph** group, click the **Numbering** button.

   Or

1. Type *1.* (the numeral 1 followed by a period) at the beginning of a paragraph, press the **Spacebar** or the **Tab** key, type the first item in the list, and then press **Enter**.

2. Type items and press **Enter** to add subsequent numbered items.

3. To end the list, press **Enter** twice, or press **Enter** and then **Backspace**.

   Tip By default, Word formats lists based on what you type. You can change this default behavior on the AutoFormat As You Type tab of the AutoCorrect dialog box, which you can open from the Proofing page of the Word Options dialog box.

➤ To create a multilevel list

1. On the **Home** tab, in the **Paragraph** group, click the **Multilevel List** button.

2. In the **Multilevel List** gallery, click the thumbnail of the style you want.

3. Type the list items, pressing **Enter** to create a new item at the same level, **Tab** to move down a level, and **Backspace** to move up a level.

➤ **To sort items in a selected list**

1. On the **Home** tab, in the **Paragraph** group, click the **Sort** button.

2. In the **Sort Text** dialog box, in the **Type** list, choose whether to sort by text, number, or date.

3. Select **Ascending** or **Descending**, and then click **OK**.

➤ **To change the style of a selected list**

1. On the **Home** tab, in the **Paragraph** group, click the **Bullets** or **Numbering** arrow.

2. In the **Bullet Library** or **Numbering Library**, click the bullet or number style you want to use.

   Tip If you want to customize the bullet character or number format, click Define New Bullet or Define New Number Format in the library.

➤ **To change the overall indentation of a selected list**

→ On the **Home** tab, in the **Paragraph** group, click the **Decrease Indent** or **Increase Indent** button.

→ On the horizontal ruler, drag the **Left Indent** marker to the left or right.

   Tip You can also adjust the amount by which the first line of each item is outdented by dragging the Hanging Indent marker on the horizontal ruler.

➤ **To change the level of a selected list**

1. On the **Home** tab, in the **Paragraph** group, click the **Bullet** or **Numbering** button, and click **Change List Level**.

2. In the **Change List Level** gallery, click the level you want.

➤ **To change the level of a list item**

→ With the insertion point in the item, on the **Home** tab, in the **Paragraph** group, click the **Increase Indent** button to demote the item or the **Decrease Indent** button to promote the item.

Practice Tasks

The practice files for these tasks are located in the *Documents\Microsoft Press\ MCAS\Word2007\Objective04* folder. If you want, save the task results in the same folder with *My* prepended to the file name.

- Open the *Table* document, and convert the tabular list beginning with *Distance* and ending with *$20.00* into a table with two columns and six rows.

- Open the *SortTable* document, and sort it in ascending order by State, then City, and then Last Name.

- Open the *TabularList* document, and at the end of the document, type the following, pressing Tab where indicated:

  Self Tab *Other People* Tab *Nature*
  Transformation Tab *Life/death* Tab *Weather*
  Time travel Tab *Telepathy* Tab *Oceans*
  Visible/invisible Tab *Mind control* Tab *Animals*

  Make the first line bold, and indent the entire list. Then left-align the second column at the 2-inch mark on the horizontal ruler, and right-align the third column at the 4-inch mark.

- Open the *Lists* document, and convert the paragraphs under each of the bold headings except *The Sequence of Events* to a bulleted list with the four-diamond bullet character. Convert the paragraphs under *The Sequence of Events* heading to a numbered list with the *A. B. C.* number format.

- Continuing in the *Lists* document, convert the bulleted list under *The Teacher* heading to a numbered list with a capital letter as its number format. Then demote the second, third, fourth, and fifth items in the list. Finally, promote the fifth item.

4.3 Modify tables

Table Structure

You can modify a table's structure at any time. To change the structure, you need to know how to select the appropriate parts of the table, as follows:

- **Table.** Click anywhere in the table. Then on the Layout tab, in the Table group, click the Select button, and click Select Table.
- **Column.** Point to the top border of the column. When the pointer changes to a black, down-pointing arrow, click once.
- **Row.** Point to the left border of the row. When the pointer changes to a white, right-pointing arrow, click once.
- **Cell.** Triple-click the cell or click its left border.
- **Multiple cells.** Click the first cell, hold down the Shift key, and press the arrow keys to select adjacent cells in a column or row.

The basic methods for modifying table structure are as follows:

- Size the table, columns, or rows.
- Insert or delete rows, columns, or cells.
- Merge or split cells.

Tip You can move a table by pointing to it and then dragging the move handle that appears in its upper-left corner. Or use the Cut and Paste buttons in the Clipboard group on the Home tab to move the table.

You can control many aspects of a table from the tabs of the Table properties dialog box, each of which provides options for a particular table element.

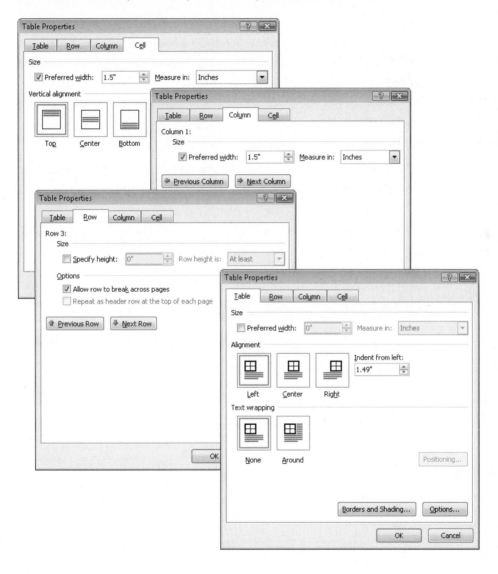

From the Table Properties dialog box, you can control the following:

- Specify the preferred width of the entire table, as well as the way it interacts with the surrounding text.

- Specify the height of each row, whether a row is allowed to break across pages, and whether a row of column headings should be repeated at the top of each page.

    Tip The Repeat As Header Row option is available only if the insertion point is in the top row of the table.

- Set the width of each column.

- Set the preferred width of cells and the vertical alignment of text within them.

    Tip You can also control the widths of selected cells by using the buttons in the Cell Size group on the Layout tab.

- Control the margins of cells (how close text comes to the cell border) by clicking the Options button on either the Table or Cell tab.

    Tip You can also control the margins by clicking the Cell Margins button in the Alignment group on the Layout tab.

➤ To display the Table Properties dialog box

1. Click anywhere in the table, or select the row, a column, or the table.
2. On the **Layout** contextual tab, click the **Cell Size** dialog box launcher.

➤ To change the size of a selected table

→ Drag the table's size handle.

➤ To change the width of a selected column

→ Drag a column's right border to the left or right.

→ Drag the column's **Move Table Column** marker on the horizontal ruler to the left or right.

→ On the **Layout** tab, in the **Cell Size** group, change the **Table Column Width** setting.

➤ To change the height of a selected row

→ Drag a row's bottom border up or down.

→ Drag the row's **Adjust Table Row** marker on the vertical ruler up or down.

→ On the **Layout** tab, in the **Cell Size** group, change the **Table Row Height** setting.

➤ **To insert columns or rows**

1. Click anywhere in the column or row adjacent to which you want to add a single column or row, or select the number of columns or rows you want to insert.

2. On the **Layout** tab, in the **Rows & Columns** group, click an **Insert** button.

➤ **To insert cells**

1. Click the cell adjacent to which you want to add a single cell, or select the number of cells you want to insert.

2. On the **Layout** tab, click the **Rows & Columns** dialog box launcher.

3. In the **Insert Cells** dialog box, specify how adjacent cells should be moved to accommodate the new cell or cells, and then click **OK**.

➤ **To delete a table, columns, or rows**

1. Click anywhere in the table, column, or row you want to delete, or select the number of columns or rows you want to delete.

2. On the **Layout** tab, in the **Rows & Columns** group, click the **Delete** button.

3. Click **Delete Columns**, **Delete Rows**, or **Delete Table**.

➤ **To delete cells**

1. Click the cell, or select the number of cells you want to delete.

2. On the **Layout** tab, in the **Rows & Columns** group, click the **Delete** button, and then click **Delete Cells**.

3. In the **Delete Cells** dialog box, specify how adjacent cells should be moved to replace the deleted cell or cells, and then click **OK**.

➤ **To merge or split selected cells**

→ On the **Layout** tab, in the **Merge** group, click the **Merge Cells** button.

→ On the **Layout** tab, in the **Merge** group, click the **Split Cells** button.

Table Formatting

Formatting a table to best convey its data is often a process of trial and error. You can get started by creating a Quick Table, a preformatted table with sample data that you can customize.

To format an existing table, you can apply one of the table styles available on the Design tab, which include a variety of borders, shading, text colors, and other attributes to give the table a professional look.

If none of the predefined table styles meets your needs, you can create your own styles for tables in much the same way you create styles for regular text.

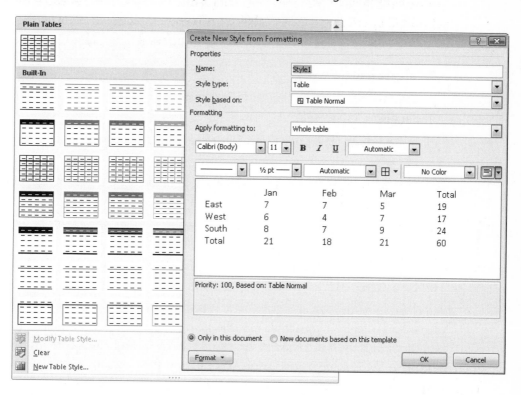

Tip You can click buttons in the Paragraph and Font groups of the Home tab and apply character formatting from the Styles gallery, just as you would to format any text in a Word document.

➤ **To insert a Quick Table**

1. On the **Insert** tab, in the **Tables** group, click the **Table** button, and then point to **Quick Tables**.

2. In the **Quick Tables** gallery, click the table style you want.

➤ **To apply a table style to a selected table**

1. On the **Design** tab in the **Table Style Options** group, select the check boxes of the options you want the table style to include.

2. In the **Table Styles** group, click the style you want in the **Table Styles** gallery.

➤ **To create a table style**

1. On the **Design** tab, in the **Table Styles** group, click the **More** button, and then click **New Table Style**.

2. In the **Create New Style From Formatting** dialog box, type a name for the new style.

3. Select the formatting options you want, until the table shown in the **Preview** area looks the way you want it.

4. If you want the style to be available to tables in other documents based on this template, select that option, and then click **OK**.

Text Alignment

You can change the size and alignment of text within a table cell to fit the available space. For example, if your table includes long headings and short table entries, you can turn the text of the If the first row of your table has several long headings that make it difficult to fit the table on one page, you can turn the headings sideways, going either from top to bottom or from bottom to top.

➤ **To change the direction of text in selected cells**

→ On the **Layout** tab, in the **Alignment** group, click the **Text Direction** button to orient the text the way you want.

Calculations

When you want to perform a calculation on numbers in a Word table, you can construct a formula by using the tools in the Formula dialog box. A formula consists of an equal sign (=), followed by a function name (such as SUM), followed by parentheses containing the addresses of the cells on which you want to perform the calculation. The cell address is a combination of the column letter and the row number—for example, A1. Multiple contiguous cells can be addressed as a range consisting of the upper-left cell and the lower-right cell separated by a colon, such as A1:B4.

Tip If you change a value in a Word table after entering a formula, you must recalculate the formula manually.

> ➤ **To total a column of values in a table**

1. Click the cell in the table where you want the total to appear.

2. On the **Layout** tab, in the **Data** group, click the **Formula** button.

3. In the **Paste function** list, select **SUM**.

4. The insertion point will be between the parentheses after SUM in the **Formula** box. Type the range for the cells you want to total.

5. Click **OK**.

Practice Tasks

The practice files for these tasks are located in the *Documents\Microsoft Press\ MCAS\Word2007\Objective04* folder. If you want, save the task results in the same folder with *My* prepended to the file name.

- Open the *ModifyTable* document, merge the cells in the first row, and then center the cell contents. Add two rows below the last row. Then adjust the size of the entire table until its right edge aligns with the 4-inch mark on the horizontal ruler.

- In a new blank document, create a Matrix Quick Table. Then remove the banded shading from the rows, and apply the Medium Shading 2 – Accent 2 table style. Surround each cell with a border. Finally, fill all the cells containing dashes with the standard red color.

- Open the *Calculations* document, and in the cell below the *Total* column heading, enter the formula =*C2*B2* with the $#,##0.00;($#,##0.00) number format.

4.4   **Insert and format references and captions**

Bibliographies

While conducting research, you can keep track of bibliographic sources in the Source Manager. Word stores the sources in a separate file on your computer's hard disk so that you can cite them in any document you create.

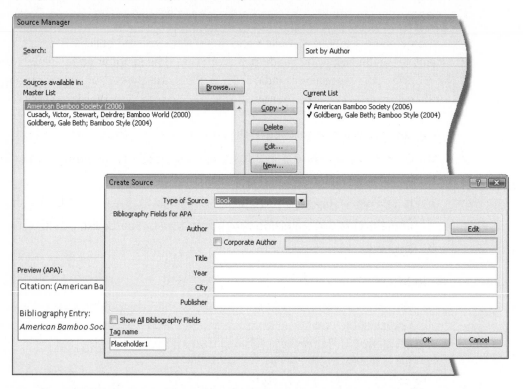

You copy sources from the Master List to the Current List so that they appear in the Insert Citation gallery. You can then cite those sources anywhere in the current document. You can also enter a new source and insert a citation at the same time.

You can select from several style guides, such as the *Chicago Manual of Style*, to have Word compile your sources in a bibliography that reflects that style guide's standard format.

```
APA
Chicago
GB7714
GOST - Name Sort
GOST - Title Sort
ISO 690 - First Element and Date
ISO 690 - Numerical Reference
MLA
SIST02
Turabian
```

When you are ready to compile the bibliography, you can build the list at the insertion point with a Bibliography heading, a Works Cited heading, or no heading. Word inserts the option you choose as a single field. You can edit the text of a bibliography, but if the source information might change, it is much easier to have Word update it.

➤ To add a source to the Source Manager

1. On the **References** tab, in the **Citations & Bibliography** group, click the **Manage Sources** button.

2. In the **Source Manager** dialog box, click **New**.

3. In the **Create Source** dialog box, in the **Type of Source** list, click the source type.

4. Enter the information for the source, and click **OK**.

➤ To insert a citation

1. On the **References** tab, in the **Citations and Bibliography** group, click **Insert Citation**.

2. In the **Insert Citation** gallery, click the citation you want to insert.

➤ To select a bibliography style

→ On the **References** tab, in the **Citations and Bibliography** group, click the style you want in the **Style** list.

➤ To create a bibliography

1. On the **References** tab, in the **Citations & Bibliography** group, click the **Bibliography** button.

2. In the **Bibliography** gallery, click the type of bibliography you want.

➤ To update a bibliography

→ Click anywhere in the bibliography field, and then click the **Update Citations and Bibliography** button.

→ Right-click the bibliography field, and then click **Update Field**.

Reference Tables

If a document includes figures or tables that have captions, you can create a *table of figures* listing the table captions. If a legal document contains items such as regulations, cases, and statutes that are identified as legal citations, you can create a *table of authorities* listing the citations. Word uses the captions or citations to create these types of tables the same way it uses headings to create a table of contents.

See Also For information about tables of contents, see section 1.3, "Make documents and content easier to find."

➤ **To insert a caption**

1. On the **References** tab, in the **Captions** group, click the **Insert Caption** button.

2. To change the designator shown in the **Caption** box (the default is Figure), select either **Equation** or **Table** from the **Label** list, or click **New Label**, type the caption you want, and then click **OK**.

3. In the **Caption** box, click to the right of the default text and number, press the **Spacebar**, type the caption, and then click **OK**.

➤ **To create a table of figures**

1. On the **References** tab, in the **Captions** group, click **Insert Table of Figures**.

2. To change the default caption type, in the **General** area of the **Table of Figures** dialog box, click the type you want in the **Caption label** list.

3. To change the default table format, click the format you want in the **Formats** list.

4. Select any additional options you want, and then click **OK**.

➤ **To mark a legal citation**

1. Select the text you want to mark.

2. On the **References** tab, in the **Table of Authorities** group, click the **Mark Citation** button.

3. In the **Mark Citation** dialog box, edit the citation in the **Selected text** and **Short citation** boxes to reflect the way you want it to appear in the table.

4. To change the category, click the category that applies to the citation in the **Category** list.

5. To mark a single citation, click **Mark**. To mark all citations that match the selected citation, click **Mark All**.

➤ **To create a table of authorities**

1. On the **References** tab, in the **Table of Authorities** group, click the **Insert Table of Authorities** button.

2. In the **Table Of Authorities** dialog box, click the category of citations you want in the **Category** list, or click **All** to include all categories.

3. Select formatting options for the table, and then click **OK**.

Footnotes and Endnotes

When you want to make a comment about a statement in a document—for example, to explain an assumption or cite the source for a different opinion—you can enter the comment as a footnote or as an endnote. Doing so inserts a number or symbol called a *reference mark*, and your associated comment appears with the same number or symbol either as a footnote at the bottom of the page or as an endnote at the end of the document or document section. In most views, footnotes or endnotes are divided from the main text by a note separator line.

Word applies default styles to the reference marks for footnotes and endnotes. You can change the styles in the Footnote And Endnote dialog box.

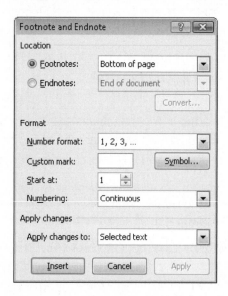

> ➤ **To create a footnote or endnote**

  1. On the **References** tab, in the **Footnotes** group, click **Insert Footnote** or **Insert Endnote**.

  2. In the linked area at the bottom of the page or end of the document or section, type the note text.

➤ **To change the number format of existing footnotes or endnotes**

1. On the **References** tab, click the **Footnotes** dialog box launcher.

2. In the **Footnote and Endnote** dialog box, click **Footnotes** or **Endnotes**.

3. In the **Format** area, in the **Number format** list, click the format you want.

4. With **Whole document** shown in the **Apply changes to** box, click **Apply**.

➤ **To change the formatting of footnote or endnote reference marks**

1. In the document text, select the reference mark for any footnote or endnote.

2. On the **Home** tab, in the **Editing** group, click the **Select** button, and then click **Select Text with Similar Formatting**.

3. On the **Home** tab, apply the character formatting you want the reference marks to have.

Practice Tasks

The practice files for these tasks are located in the *Documents\Microsoft Press\ MCAS\Word2007\Objective04* folder. If you want, save the task results in the same folder with *My* prepended to the file name.

- Open the *Bibliography1* document, and change the bibliography style to Chicago. Then add a new source for a book titled *Bamboo* by Gale Beth Goldberg, published in 2004 by Gibbs Smith.

- Open the *Bibliography2* document, and copy all the sources from the Master List to the Current list so that they will be available to the open document. Then to the right of *Bamboo Style* on the last line of the first paragraph, insert a citation to the Gale Beth Goldberg source.

- Continuing in the *Bibliography2* document, insert a bibliography with the Bibliography heading and the Chicago style at the end of the document. Then change the style to APA.

- Open the *Footnotes* document, and cut the last sentence from the end of the first paragraph to the Clipboard. Then insert a footnote, and paste the cut item as the text of the footnote.

4.5   Merge documents and data sources

Documents

The easiest way to generate a set of documents that are identical except for certain information—such as the name, address, and greeting of a letter—is to use mail merge. The mail merge process replaces placeholders, called *merge fields*, in a main document with information from a structured document called a *data source*. The main document might be a letter, e-mail message, envelope, set of labels, or a directory. The data source can be any document that contains sets, called *records*, of information in a predictable format, such as a Word table, a Microsoft Office Excel worksheet, a Microsoft Office Access database table, or a Microsoft Office Outlook contacts list.

Tip The data source must consist of a matrix of rows and columns, with each row containing one record and each column containing a particular type of information, called a *field*. The first row of the data source identifies the fields with a column heading, called a *field name*. Because the field names are also used as the merge fields in the main document, they cannot contain spaces.

The end result of the mail merge process is one copy of the merged document or, in the case of documents containing labels or directories, a new label or entry for every record in the data source (or you can filter the data source to process only a subset of the records). You can merge the main document and data source into a new document, with each merged document separated from the next by a page break. You can then personalize the merged documents before printing, and you can save the document for later use. If you don't need to edit or save the merged documents, you can merge the main document and data source directly to the printer or to an e-mail message.

Strategy This discussion necessarily skims the surface of mail merge. To understand the process, experiment with using and creating different data sources and then see how you can achieve different results by editing, filtering, and sorting. Also create a variety of main documents to get an idea of the scope of this powerful tool.

➤ **To merge a form letter with an existing data source**

1. Create a document containing the text of the form letter.

2. On the **Mailings** tab, in the **Start Mail Merge** group, click the **Start Mail Merge** button, and then click **Step by Step Mail Merge Wizard**.

3. In the **Mail Merge** task pane, with the **Letters** option selected, at the bottom of the pane, click **Next: Starting document**.

4. With the **Use the current document** option selected, click **Next: Select recipients**.

5. With the **Using an existing list** option selected, click **Browse**. Then in the **Select Data Source** dialog box, identify the data source, and click **Open**.

6. In the **Select Table** dialog box, click the table you want to use as your data source, and then click **OK**.

7. In the **Mail Merge Recipients** dialog box, sort or filter the records as necessary, and then click **OK**.

8. At the bottom of the **Mail Merge** task pane, click **Next: Write your letter**, and then insert the required merge fields in the main document, either by clicking items in the task pane or by clicking buttons in the **Write & Insert Fields** group on the **Mailings** tab.

   Tip Clicking Address Block or Greeting Line opens a dialog box in which you can refine the fields' settings, whereas clicking individual fields inserts them with their default settings.

9. At the bottom of the **Mail Merge** task pane, click **Next: Preview your letters**. Then click the **Next** and **Previous** arrows to preview each document, and edit or exclude recipients as necessary.

10. Click **Next: Complete the merge**.

11. Click **Print** to merge directly to the printer.

   Or

   Click **Edit individual letters** to merge to a document that you can edit and save. In the **Merge to New Document** dialog box, choose to merge all records, only the current record, or a range of records, and then click **OK**.

➤ **To merge an e-mail message with an Outlook contacts list**

1. Create a document containing the text of the e-mail message.

2. On the **Mailings** tab, in the **Start Mail Merge** group, click the **Start Mail Merge** button, and then click **Step by Step Mail Merge Wizard**.

3. In the **Mail Merge** task pane, click **E-mail messages**, and then click **Next: Starting document**.

4. With the **Use the current document** option selected, click **Next: Select recipients**.

5. Click **Select from Outlook contacts**, and then click **Choose Contacts Folder**. In the **Choose Profile** dialog box, select the Outlook profile from which you want to choose your recipients, and then click **OK**. Then in the **Select Contacts** dialog box, identify the data source and click **OK**.

6. In the **Mail Merge Recipients** dialog box, sort or filter the records as necessary, and then click **OK**.

7. In the **Mail Merge** task pane, click **Next: Write your letter**, and insert the necessary merge fields.

8. Preview the e-mail messages, and then click **Next: Complete the merge**.

9. Click **Electronic Mail**, and in the **Merge to E-Mail** dialog box, verify that **Email_ Address** is selected in the **To** box, type a subject in the **Subject line** box, and verify that **HTML** is selected in the **Mail format** box.

10. With the **All** option selected in the **Send records** area, click **OK**.

Labels

Most organizations keep information about their customers or clients in a worksheet or database that can be used for several purposes, including printing sheets of mailing labels that can be attached to items such as packages and catalogs.

Tip You can print a full sheet of the same label or just one label by clicking the Labels button in the Create group on the Mailings tab and completing the Labels tab of the Envelopes And Labels dialog box.

➤ To create sheets of mailing labels

1. Open a new blank document, and display paragraph marks.

2. On the **Mailings** tab, in the **Start Mail Merge** group, click the **Start Mail Merge** button, and then click **Labels**.

3. In the **Label information** area of the **Label Options** dialog box, select the manufacturer and product number of the labels you are using, and then click **OK**.

4. In the **Start Mail Merge** group, click the **Select Recipients** button, and identify the data source.

5. In the **Write & Insert Fields** group, click the **Address Block** button, adjust settings in the **Insert Address Block** dialog box as necessary, and then click **OK**.

6. In the **Write & Insert Fields** group, click the **Update Labels** button.

7. In the **Preview Results** group, click the **Preview Results** button, preview the labels by clicking the **Next** and **Previous** buttons, and then click the **Preview Results** button to turn off preview.

8. Click the **Finish & Merge** button, and then click either **Edit Individual Documents** to merge to a document that you can save, or **Print Documents** to merge directly to the printer.

Envelopes

In addition to creating multiple envelopes by using mail merge, you can create an envelope for only one recipient whose name and address you have selected in a document. In the Envelopes And Labels dialog box, you can edit the address and you can enter a return address in the Return Address box. If you have electronic postage software installed on your computer, you can include electronic postage. You can click Options and then specify the envelope size and the font and font size of both the address and the return address.

Tip You can have Word supply the return address by entering it in the Mailing Address box on the Advanced page of the Word Options dialog box. If you want to use envelopes with a preprinted return address, you must select the Omit check box to avoid over-printing.

➤ To print a set of envelopes from a data source

1. Open a new blank document, and display paragraph marks.

2. On the **Mailings** tab, in the **Start Mail Merge** group, click the **Start Mail Merge** button, and then click **Envelopes**.

3. In the **Envelope Options** dialog box, make any necessary changes to the default settings, and then click **OK**.

4. In the **Start Mail Merge** group, click the **Select Recipients** button, and identify the data source.

5. Type the return address in the upper-left corner of the document, and then click to the left of the paragraph mark in the center of the document.

6. In the **Write & Insert Fields** group, click the **Address Block** button, adjust settings in the **Insert Address Block** dialog box as necessary, and then click **OK**.

7. Click the **Preview Results** button, preview the envelopes by clicking the **Next** and **Previous** buttons, and then click the button to turn off preview.

8. Click the **Finish & Merge** button, and then click either **Edit Individual Documents** to merge to a document that you can save, or **Print Documents** to merge directly to the printer.

➤ To print an envelope from selected data

1. In the document, select the name and address you want to print on the envelope.

2. On the **Mailings** tab, in the **Create** group, click the **Envelopes** button.

3. On the **Envelopes** tab of the **Envelopes and Labels** dialog box, enter or edit the delivery address and the return address, make any other necessary change, and then click **Print**.

Practice Tasks

The practice files for these tasks are located in the *Documents\Microsoft Press\MCAS\Word2007\Objective04* folder. If you want, save the task results in the same folder with *My* prepended to the file name.

- Open the *PreparingData* document, and specify Sheet1 of the *DataSource* workbook as the data source. Sort the records in ascending order based on the PostalCode field, and filter them to show only the records for addresses in the state of Washington (WA).

- Open the *FormLetter* document, attach the *DataSource* workbook, and then adding merge fields for a default inside address and a greeting line consisting of the word *Dear*, a space, the FirstName field, and a comma.

- Open the *MergingData* document, attach the *DataSource* workbook, and preview the merged letters. Then exclude Linda Martin from the merge before merging the letters to a new document called *MyMergedLetters*.

- Open a new blank document, attach the *DataSource* workbook, and then create sheets of Avery 5261 labels, merging them to a new document called *MyMergedLabels*.

- Open the *Envelope* document, and then use the name and address at the top of the letter as the basis for an envelope with a pre-printed return address.

Objective Review

Before finishing this chapter, ensure that you have mastered the following skills:

4.1 Structure content by using Quick Parts.

4.2 Use tables and lists to organize content.

4.3 Modify tables.

4.4 Insert and format references and captions.

4.5 Merge documents and data sources.

5 Reviewing Documents

The skills tested in this section of the Microsoft Office Specialist exam for Microsoft Office Word 2007 relate to ways of efficiently moving around in documents and managing content changes. Specifically, the following objectives are associated with this set of skills:

5.1 Navigate documents.
5.2 Compare and merge document versions.
5.3 Manage tracked changes.
5.4 Insert, modify, and delete comments.

Word 2007 includes a number of tools that enable you to review documents efficiently. You can swiftly move around in a document, locate specific types of content, and display views of a document that simplify visual review so that you can check accuracy and consistency. When conducting a review of document content, you can programmatically compare content, combine multiple versions of the same document, track and resolve revisions, and make notes in the document for yourself or other reviewers.

This chapter guides you in studying efficient navigation methods; ways of viewing a document in multiple windows, comparing and combining document versions, and tracking and resolving changes within a document; and the use of comments.

 Important Before you can use the practice files in this chapter, you need to install them from the book's companion CD to their default location. See "Using the Companion CD" at the beginning of the book for more information.

Tip Graphics and operating system–related instructions in this book reflect the Windows Vista user interface. If your computer is running Windows XP and you experience trouble following the instructions as written, refer to the sidebar "If You Are Running Windows XP" in "Working in the Microsoft Office Fluent User Interface" at the beginning of this book.

5.1   Navigate documents

Navigation Tricks

A common way of navigating in small documents is to simply scroll until you find what you are looking for. You can speed up scrolling in Print Layout view by hiding the white space between pages. You can also adjust the magnification to display more of the document in the window at one time. In Print Layout view, you can speed up scrolling by hiding the white space between pages, and you can display more than one page at a time.

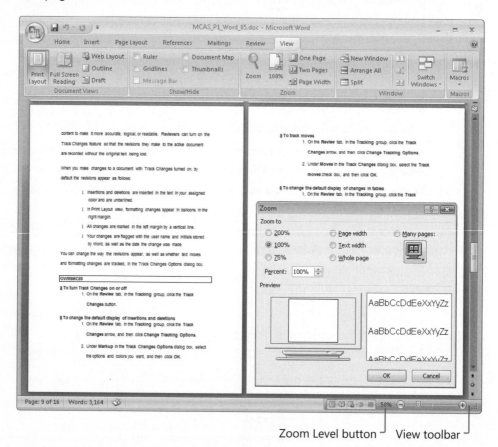

Zoom Level button ⌐   View toolbar ¬

In addition to scrolling in a document, you can move around in the following ways:

- Use commands on the Find tab of the Find And Replace dialog box to jump from one occurrence of the specified text or a particular type of formatting to the next. Use commands on the Go To tab to jump to a specified location. This location can be a page, section, line, bookmark, comment, footnote, endnote, field, table, graphic, equation, object, or heading.

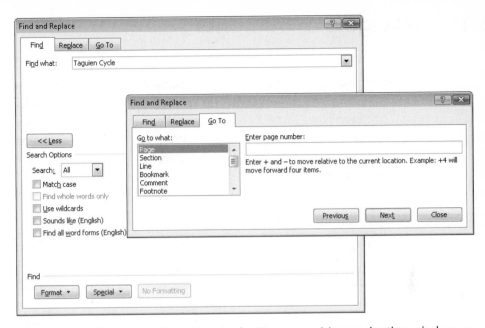

- Display an outline view of headings in the Document Map navigation window, or thumbnails of pages in the Thumbnails navigation window. From the Document Map window, jump to a specific heading, or from the Thumbnails window, jump to a specific page.

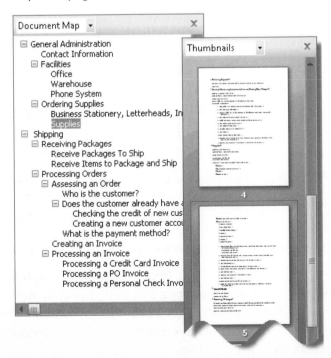

● Choose the type of element you want to move to—table, graphic, edits, heading, page, section, comment, footnote, endnote, or field—from the Select Browse Object menu, and then click the associated Next and Previous buttons to move among the elements.

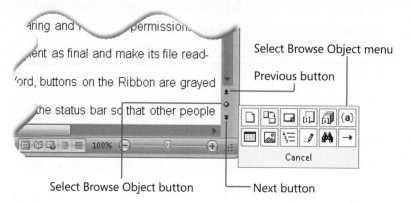

Strategy Spend some time working with the tabs of the Find And Replace dialog box and with the Document Map. Knowing how to quickly move around in a document will save valuable time in the certification exam.

➤ To display a navigation window

→ On the **View** tab, in the **Show/Hide** group, select the **Document Map** check box or the **Thumbnails** check box.

➤ To switch between navigation windows

→ In the **Switch Navigation Window** list at the top of the **Document Map** window, click **Thumbnails**.

→ In the **Switch Navigation Window** list at the top of the **Thumbnails** window, click **Document Map**.

→ On the **View** tab, in the **Show/Hide** group, select the check box for the navigation window you want to switch to.

➤ To move between specific document elements

1. Click the **Select Browse Object** button, and then on the **Select Browse Object** menu, click the document element you want.

2. Click the **Next** or **Previous** button to move forward or backward between the chosen elements.

➤ **To jump to a specific heading**

→ In the **Document Map**, click the heading you want.

Or

1. On the **Home** tab, in the **Editing** group, click the **Find** arrow, and then click **Go To**.

2. On the **Go To** tab of the **Find and Replace** dialog box, click **Heading** in the **Go to what** list.

3. In the **Enter** box, enter the heading number, and then click **Go To**.

   Tip To move between headings, you can enter a plus sign (+) or minus sign (-) followed by the number of headings you want to move.

➤ **To jump to a specific page**

1. On the **View** tab, in the **Show/Hide** group, select the **Thumbnails** check box.

2. In the **Thumbnails** pane, click the page you want.

   Or

1. On the **Select Browse Object** menu, click the **Go To** button; or on the **Home** tab, in the **Editing** group, click the **Find** arrow, and then click **Go To**.

2. On the **Go To** tab of the **Find and Replace** dialog box, click **Page** in the **Go to what** list.

3. In the **Enter** box, type the specific page identifier, and then click **Go To**.

➤ **To jump to specific text or formatting**

1. On the **Select Browse Object** menu, click the **Find** button; or on the **Home** tab, in the **Editing** group, click the **Find** button.

2. On the **Find** tab of the **Find and Replace** dialog box, enter the text you want to find in the **Find what** box; or click the **Format** button, and then select the formatting or style you want to find.

3. Click **Find Next**.

➤ To hide the white space between pages

→ In Print Layout view, point to the gap between any two pages and, when the pointer changes to two opposing arrows, double-click the mouse button.

Tip Restore the white space by pointing to the gray line that separates one page from the next and double-clicking the mouse button.

➤ To zoom in or out

→ On the **View** toolbar, click the **Zoom In** or **Zoom Out** button.

Or

1. On the **View** toolbar, click the **Zoom level** button.

2. In the **Zoom** dialog box, select one of the options under **Zoom to**, and then click **OK**.

Or

→ On the **View** tab, in the **Zoom** group, click the **100%**, **One Page**, **Two Pages**, or **Page Width** button.

Multiple Views

If you have more than one document open, you can switch between them by clicking their taskbar buttons or choosing them from the Window menu. You can visually compare them by arranging their windows so that they are all visible on the screen. You can view different areas of one document by splitting the screen.

➤ To view multiple pages at the same time

1. On the **View** toolbar, click the **Zoom** button.

2. In the **Zoom** dialog box, click the **Many pages** button, drag through the required number of pages in the grid, and then click **OK**.

➤ To see different parts of the same document

1. On the **View** tab, in the **Window** group, click the **Split** button.

2. Drag the split bar up or down until it is where you want it, and then click the mouse button.

➤ **To arrange windows so that you can see all open documents**

→ On the **View** tab, in the **Window** group, click the **View Side by Side** button to arrange two open documents.

→ On the **View** tab, in the **Window** group, click the **Arrange All** button to arrange more than two open documents.

Practice Tasks

The practice files for these tasks are located in the *Documents\Microsoft Press\ MCAS\Word2007\Objective05* folder. If you want, save the task results in the same folder with *My* prepended to the file name.

● Open the *Viewing1* document, and change the magnification so that you can see two pages side by side. Then zoom to 100%, and jump to the *Shipping* heading. Finally, jump to the top of page 5.

● Open the *Viewing1* and *Viewing2* documents, and switch back and forth between the two open windows. Then arrange the two document windows so that they are stacked one above the other.

● Open the *Viewing2* document, and arrange the screen so that you can see the beginning and end of the document at the same time.

5.2   Compare and merge document versions

You can compare the content and formatting of two versions of the same document. After you identify one as the original document and the other as the revised document, Word displays the differences as "legal blackline" in either of the source documents or in a new document. You can also view the original and revised documents in separate windows simultaneously to facilitate the comparison.

Tip If the documents you are comparing contain tracked changes, Word considers the changes as accepted when making the comparison.

If two people have reviewed copies of a document with the change-tracking feature turned on, you can combine their changes into one version of the document with each reviewer's changes identified. Again, you can view the documents in separate windows. If the document has been reviewed by more than two people, repeat the combining process to add the third person's changes to the combined document, repeat again for the fourth person's changes, and so on.

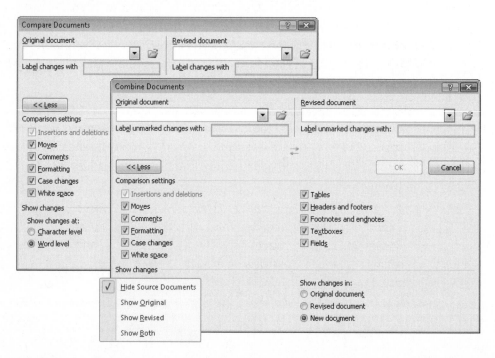

Strategy You should compare documents with various settings and save the legal blackline results in a new document. In particular, try comparing changes in tables, which is a new capability in Word 2007. Similarly, you should combine two documents and then add another version to understand the effects of different combinations of settings.

➤ **To compare document versions**

1. On the **Review** tab, in the **Compare** group, click the **Compare** button, and then click **Compare**.

2. In the **Compare Documents** dialog box, specify the **Original document** and **Revised document**.

3. Adjust the comparison settings as necessary, and then click **OK**.

➤ **To combine document versions**

1. On the **Review** tab, in the **Compare** group, click the **Compare** button, and then click **Combine**.

2. In the **Combine Documents** dialog box, specify the **Original document** and **Revised document**.

3. Adjust the combining settings as necessary, and then click **OK**.

Practice Tasks

The practice files for these taks are located in the *Documents\Microsoft Press\ MCAS\Word2007\Objective05* folder. If you want, save the task results in the same folder with *My* prepended to the file name.

● An original document, *Comparing1*, has been revised and saved as *Comparing2*. Compare the formatting of the *Comparing1* and *Comparing2* documents at the word level in the original document, with all comparison settings selected. Then view the original document and the revised document simultaneously.

● A document has been reviewed by two people who saved their versions as *Combining1* and *Combining2*. Combine the *Combining1* and *Combining2* documents at the character level in a new document, with all comparison settings selected. Then view the new document and the source documents simultaneously.

5.3   Manage tracked changes

Tracking

When two or more people collaborate on a document, one person usually creates and "owns" the document and other people review it, adding or revising content to make it more accurate, logical, or readable. Reviewers can turn on the Track Changes feature so that the revisions they make to the active document are recorded without the original text being lost.

You can change the way the revisions appear, as well as whether text moves and formatting changes are tracked, in the Track Changes Options dialog box.

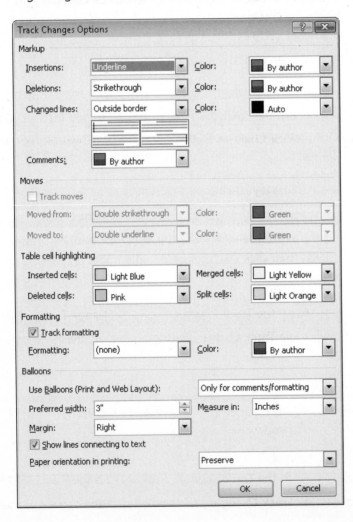

When you make changes to a document with Track Changes turned on, by default insertions and deletions are inserted in the text in your assigned color and are underlined. In Print Layout view, formatting changes appear in balloons in the right margin, and all changes are marked in the left margin by a vertical line. Your changes are flagged with the user name and initials stored by Word, as well as the date the change was made.

➤ **To turn Track Changes on or off**

→ On the **Review** tab, in the **Tracking** group, click the **Track Changes** button.

➤ **To change the default display of insertions and deletions**

1. On the **Review** tab, in the **Tracking** group, click the **Track Changes** arrow, and then in the list, click **Change Tracking Options**.

2. Under **Markup** in the **Track Changes Options** dialog box, select the options and colors you want, and then click **OK**.

➤ **To track the movement of content**

1. In the **Tracking** group, in the **Track Changes** list, click **Change Tracking Options**.

2. Under **Moves** in the **Track Changes** dialog box, select the **Track moves** check box, and then click **OK**.

➤ **To change the default display of changes in tables**

1. In the **Tracking** group, in the **Track Changes** list, click **Change Tracking Options**.

2. Under **Table cell highlighting** in the **Track Changes Options** dialog box, select the colors you want, and then click **OK**.

➤ **To track formatting changes**

1. In the **Tracking** group, in the **Track Changes** list, click **Change Tracking Options**.

2. Under **Formatting** in the **Track Changes** dialog box, select the **Track formatting** check box, and then click **OK**.

➤ **To change which revisions are displayed in balloons**

→ On the **Review** tab, in the **Tracking** group, click the **Balloons** button, and then in the list, click the option you want.

Or

1. In the **Tracking** group, in the **Track Changes** list, click **Change Tracking Options**.

2. Under **Balloons** in the **Track Changes** dialog box, select the options you want, and then click **OK**.

➤ To change the name assigned to your revisions

1. In the **Tracking** group, in the **Track Changes** list, click **Change User Name**; or click the **Microsoft Office Button**, and then click **Word Options**.

2. On the **Popular** page of the **Word Options** window, type the name and initials you want, and then click **OK**.

Reviewing

When you review the revisions made by other people, you can do the following:

● You can view the document in its original state or in its final state, with or without the revisions showing.

● When revisions are visible, you can select the types of revisions displayed—for example, you can display only comments or only insertions and deletions. You can also display or hide the revisions of specific reviewers.

● If revisions are too long or too many to display in balloons in their entirety, you can display them in a vertical or horizontal Reviewing pane.

● You can move forward or backward from one revision mark or comment to another.

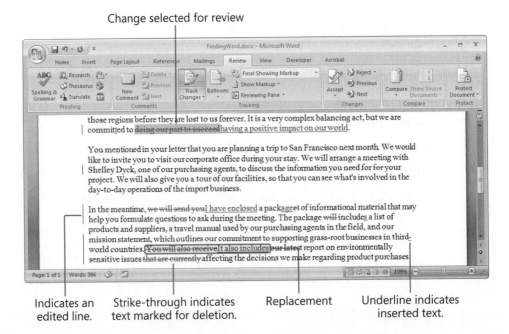

Change selected for review

Indicates an edited line.   Strike-through indicates text marked for deletion.   Replacement   Underline indicates inserted text.

You can process the revisions to a document in the following ways:

- You can accept or reject one change at a time.
- You can highlight text containing changes and then accept or reject all the selected changes.
- You can display specific types of changes or changes from specific reviewers and then accept or reject just those changes.
- You can accept or reject all the changes in the document at once.

➤ **To display the document as it will appear with changes incorporated**

→ On the **Review** tab, in the **Tracking** group, click **Final** in the **Display for Review** list.

➤ **To turn off the display of a particular type of change**

1. In the **Tracking** group, click the **Show Markup** button.
2. In the list, click the type of change you want to turn off.

➤ **To hide the revisions and comments of a particular reviewer**

1. In the **Tracking** group, click the **Show Markup** button.
2. Point to **Reviewers**, and then in the list, select the reviewer whose markup you want to hide.

➤ **To move from one revision mark or comment to another**

→ On the **Review** tab, in the **Changes** group, click the **Next** or **Previous** button.

➤ **To accept or reject one change at a time**

1. In the **Changes** group, click the **Next** button.
2. For the change displayed, click the **Accept** or **Reject** button.

   Or

→ Right-click a change, and then click **Accept Change** or **Reject Change**.

➤ **To accept or reject an entire set of changes**

1. On the **Review** tab, in the **Tracking** group, click the **Show Markup** button, and then hide the changes you don't want to accept or reject.

2. In the **Changes** group, click the **Accept** or **Reject** arrow, and then click **Accept All Changes Shown** or **Reject All Changes Shown**.

➤ **To accept or reject all the changes in the document**

→ On the **Review** tab, in the **Changes** group, click the **Accept** or **Reject** arrow, and then click **Accept All Changes in Document** or **Reject All Changes in Document**.

Practice Tasks

The practice files for these tasks are located in the *Documents\Microsoft Press\ MCAS\Word2007\Objective05* folder. If you want, save the task results in the same folder with *My* prepended to the file name.

● Open the *TrackChanges1* document, turn on Track Changes, and in the table at the end of the document, delete *much* from *Some much lower* in the third column. Then in the fourth column of the same row, type *but slow* to the right of *Adequate*.

● Continuing in the *TrackChanges1* document, display revisions in balloons, turn off the tracking of formatting, and then display the final version of the document.

● Open the *TrackChanges2* document, accept all the formatting changes, and reject all the changes made by Florian Stiller.

5.4 Insert, modify, and delete comments

In addition to tracking the changes made to a document, you can insert comments to ask questions, make suggestions, or explain changes. The comment includes the text you enter, your username, and the date and time you created the comment. Each comment is identified by your initials followed by a number representing the ordinal of the comment in the document. In any view, comments and changes are visible in the Reviewing Pane, which you can display vertically at the left side or horizontally at the bottom of the program window. A summary of the tracked changes and comments in the document is visible at the top of the Reviewing Pane, followed by sections detailing changes in the main document, header and footer, text boxes (such as those inserted from the Building Blocks Organizer), header and footer text boxes, footnotes, and endnotes. In Print Layout view, Full Screen Reading view, and Web Layout view, comments are shown in balloons in the page margin. In other views, the commented text is highlighted in a color assigned to your username, and followed by your initials in square brackets. In these views, you display the comment text by pointing to the highlighted text.

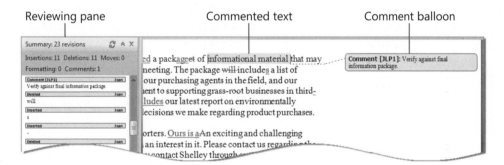

You can work with comments in the following ways:

- You can jump from comment to comment.
- To edit a comment, you can simply click the balloon and use normal editing techniques.
- To respond to a comment, you can add text to an existing balloon or attach a new balloon to the existing one.
- You can view hidden parts of comments in a vertical or horizontal Reviewing pane.

  Tip To change the size of the Reviewing pane, point to its border, and when the pointer changes to a double-headed arrow, drag the border.

- You can hide the comments of a specific person or hide all comments to reduce screen clutter.

➤ To insert a comment about selected text

1. On the **Review** tab, in the **Comments** group, click the **New Comment** button.

2. In the comment balloon, type the comment.

➤ To edit a comment

→ Click the comment, and then change the text by using normal editing techniques.

➤ To respond to a comment

1. Click the comment, and then on the **Review** tab, in the **Comments** group, click the **New Comment** button.

2. Type your comment as usual.

➤ To delete a comment

→ Click the comment balloon. Then on the **Review** tab, in the **Comments** group, click the **Delete** button.

→ Right-click the comment, and then click **Delete Comment**.

Practice Tasks

The practice file for these tasks is located in the *Documents\Microsoft Press\MCAS\ Word2007\Objective05* folder. If you want, save the task results in the same folder with *My* prepended to the file name.

- Open the *Comments* document, and in the fifth column of the table, add the comment *They carry the new Ultra line* to the words *some good*. Then delete the comment associated with the word *competitors*.

- Continuing in the *Comments* document, add *These are special order* in a new paragraph at the end of the second comment. Then respond to the comment associated with *Adequate* with a new comment balloon containing the text *If I were a real customer, I would have left.*

Objective Review

Before finishing this chapter, ensure that you have mastered the following skills:

5.1 Navigate documents.

5.2 Compare and merge document versions.

5.3 Manage tracked changes.

5.4 Insert, modify, and delete comments.

6 Sharing and Securing Content

The skills tested in this section of the Microsoft Office Specialist exam for Microsoft Office Word 2007 relate to the things you can do to protect your documents and their content. Specifically, the following objectives are associated with this set of skills:

6.1 Prepare documents for sharing.
6.2 Control document access.
6.3 Attach digital signatures.

With printed documents, what you see is exactly what you get. You don't have to be concerned when you distribute them that recipients will have access to hidden information or be able to make unauthorized changes. That is not the case with electronic documents. More than ever, Word users need to be concerned about the condition of the files they share with others and about protecting them from inadvertent or malicious changes.

This chapter guides you in studying the various techniques for finalizing documents, including locking them down with passwords and permissions. You will set options for controlling who can do what to documents, and will attach signatures to certify authenticity.

 Important Before you can use the practice files in this chapter, you need to install them from the book's companion CD to their default location. See "Using the Companion CD" at the beginning of this book for more information.

Tip Graphics and operating system–related instructions in this book reflect the Windows Vista user interface. If your computer is running Windows XP and you experience trouble following the instructions as written, refer to the sidebar "If You Are Running Windows XP" in "Working in the Microsoft Office Fluent User Interface" at the beginning of this book.

6.1   Prepare documents for sharing

File Formats

The 2007 Microsoft Office system introduced a new file format based on XML, called *Microsoft Office Open XML Formats*. By default, Word 2007 files are saved in the .docx format, which is the Word variation of this new file format. The .docx format provides the following benefits:

- Files are compressed when saved, so the file size is smaller.
- Recovering at least some of the content of damaged files is possible because XML files can be opened in a text program such as Notepad.
- Security is greater because .docx files cannot contain macros, and personal data can be detected and removed from the file.

Tip Word 2007 provides a separate file format—.docm—for files that contain macros.

If you want to share a Word document with users of an earlier version of Word (Word 97–2003), you can save it in the .doc file format. If you don't know what program will be used to open the file, you can use one of the formats that can be opened by a wide variety of programs:

- **Rich Text Format (*.rtf).** Preserves text and formatting.
- **Text Only (*.txt).** Preserves only text.

Tip If you want someone to be able to view a document but not change it, you can download a free add-in from the Microsoft Downloads Web site and then save the document in XML Paper Specification (XPS) format or Portable Document Format (PDF) format.

Strategy You should be familiar with the types of file formats in which you can save Word documents and when it is appropriate to use each one.

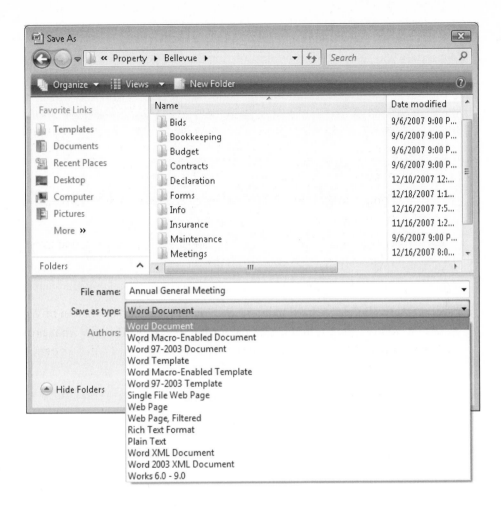

➤ **To save a document in a different format**

1. Click the **Microsoft Office Button**, point to **Save As**, and then click **Other Formats**.

2. In the **Save As** dialog box, select the format you want in the **Save as type** list, and then click **OK**.

Compatibility Checker

Whenever you save a document in the .doc file format so that it can be opened in a previous version of Word, Word runs the Microsoft Office Word Compatibility Checker. If the document uses any feature that is not supported in previous versions of Word, the Compatibility Checker displays a summary of the feature and the number of times it occurs in the document.

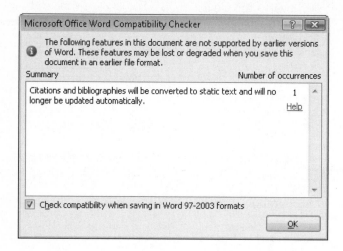

You then have three choices:

- Click Cancel, and then save the document in the .docx format.
- Click Cancel, and then modify the document to implement the feature in a different way. (For example, you could enter a bibliography by hand instead of having Word compile it for you.)
- Click Continue to allow Word to save the document without the feature.

If you want to know ahead of time whether a feature is supported in the .doc format, you can run the Compatibility Checker manually at any time.

➤ To check for unsupported features

1. On the **Office** menu, point to **Prepare**, and then click **Run Compatibility Checker**.

2. Make a note of any issues reported in the **Compatibility Checker** dialog box, and then click **OK**.

Document Inspector

Many documents go through several revisions, and some are scrutinized by multiple reviewers. During this development process, documents can accumulate information you might not want in the final version, such as the names of people who worked on the document, comments reviewers have added to the file, or hidden text about status and assumptions. This extraneous information is not a concern if the final version is to be delivered as a printout. However, if the file is to be delivered electronically, you might not want this information to be available with the file. You can use the Document Inspector to find and remove comments, revisions, annotations, personal information, and hidden text.

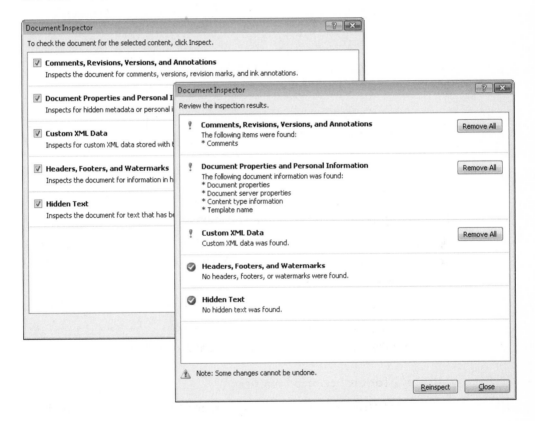

➤ **To remove unwanted or personal information**

1. On the **Office** menu, point to **Prepare**, and then click **Inspect Document**.

2. In the **Document Inspector** dialog box, clear the check boxes for types of information you don't want to locate, and then click **Inspect**.

3. When the **Document Inspector** reports its findings, click **Remove All** for any type of information you want to remove.

4. Click **Close** to close the **Document Inspector** dialog box.

Practice Tasks

The practice files for these tasks are located in the *Documents\Microsoft Press\ MCAS\Word2007\Objective06* folder. If you want, save the task results in the same folder with *My* prepended to the file name.

● Open the *Saving* document, and save it so that it can be viewed and worked on by a colleague who has not yet upgraded to Word 2007.

● Open the *Compatibility* document, and determine whether it is compatible with earlier versions of Word.

● Open the *Finalizing1* document, and remove the document properties, personal information, and custom XML data.

6.2   **Control document access**

Editing and Formatting Restrictions

Sometimes you want people to be able to open and view a document but not make changes to it, or you want to allow access with restrictions, such as the following:

- Comments are allowed in the document but not changes.

- Changes must be tracked.

- Only the specific styles you select can be applied.

- Only a recommended minimum set of styles consisting of all the styles needed by Word can be applied. (This set doesn't necessarily include all the styles used in the document.)

You implement these restrictions in the Restrict Formatting And Editing task pane.

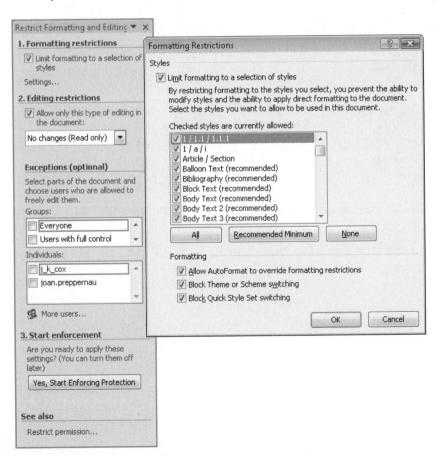

➤ **To restrict formatting**

1. On the **Review** tab, in the **Protect** group, click the **Protect Document** button, and then click **Restrict Formatting and Editing**.

2. In the **Restrict Formatting and Editing** task pane, under **Formatting restrictions**, select the **Limit formatting to a selection of styles** check box, and then click **Settings**.

3. In the **Formatting Restrictions** dialog box, click **Recommended Minimum**. Then in the **Checked styles are currently allowed** list, select the check boxes for other styles you want to include.

4. In the **Formatting** area, select the check boxes for any other restrictions you want to set on the document. Then click **OK**.

5. If a message box asks if you want to remove any styles in the document that aren't allowed, click **Yes**.

6. Under **Start enforcement** in the task pane, click **Yes, Start Enforcing Protection**.

7. In the **Start Enforcing Protection** dialog box, enter a password if you want. Then click **OK**.

➤ **To restrict editing**

1. Display the **Restrict Formatting and Editing** task pane, and in the **Editing restrictions** area, select the **Allow only this type of editing in the document** check box.

2. In the list, select the type of editing you want to allow.

3. In the **Start enforcement** area in the task pane, click **Yes, Start Enforcing Protection**.

4. In the **Start Enforcing Protection** dialog box, enter a password if you want. Then click **OK**.

Passwords

If you want only certain people to be able to open and change a document, you can assign a password to protect the document. Word then requires that the password be entered correctly before it will allow the document to be opened and changed. Anyone who doesn't know the password has no choice but to open a read-only version.

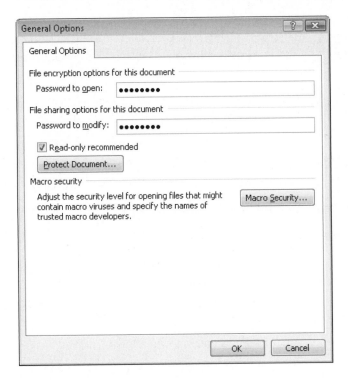

► **To set a password**

1. Display the **Save As** dialog box, and specify a location and name for the document.

2. At the bottom of the dialog box, click **Tools**, and then click **General Options**.

3. In the **General Options** dialog box, in the **Password to open** or **Password to modify** box, type a password.

   Tip Instead of setting a password, you can select the Read-Only Recommended check box to tell Word to display a message suggesting that the document be opened as read-only.

4. Click **OK** to close the **General Options** dialog box.

5. In the **Confirm Password** dialog box, in the **Reenter password to modify** box, type the password again, and then click **OK**.

6. In the **Save As** dialog box, click **Save**.

Rights Management

If you have access to a server that is running Windows Rights Management Services (RMS) and have RMS Client Service Pack 1 (SP1) installed on your computer, you can restrict who can do what for how long with a document.

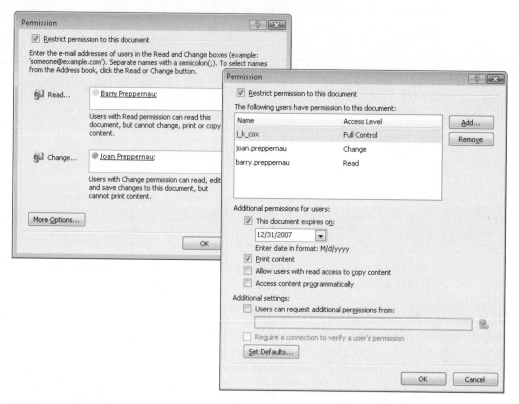

Strategy To practice working with document permissions if you do not have access to an RMS server, you should sign up for the free Microsoft Information Rights Management service by using the wizard that appears the first time you try to restrict access to a document.

➤ To restrict permissions to documents

1. On the **Review** tab, in the **Protect** group, click the **Protect Document** button, and then in the list, click **Restricted Access**.

   Tip You can also point to Prepare on the Office menu, point to Restrict Permission, and then click Restricted Access.

2. In the **Permission** dialog box, click **Restrict permission to this document**, and type the names of the people to whom you want to assign **Read** or **Change** permission.

3. To refine the permissions, click **More Options**, and then adjust the settings in the **Additional permissions for users** and **Additional settings** areas.

4. Click **OK** to close the **Permission** dialog box.

Finalizing

After you have prepared a document for sharing and restricted permissions as necessary, you might want to mark a document as final and make its file read-only. When the document is opened in Word, buttons on the Ribbon are unavailable and the Marked As Final Icon appears in the status bar so that other people know that they should not make changes to the document.

➤ **To mark a document as final**

1. On the **Office** menu, point to **Prepare**, and then click **Mark as Final**.

2. Click **OK** in the message box that tells you the file will be marked as final and saved, and then click **OK** in the finalization message box.

   Tip To make additional changes to the document, point to Prepare on the Office menu, and then click Mark As Final to reverse the final status.

Practice Tasks

The practice files for these tasks are located in the *Documents\Microsoft Press\ MCAS\Word2007\Objective06* folder. If you want, save the task results in the same folder with *My* prepended to the file name.

- Open the *PreventingChanges* document, and restrict formatting to the recommended minimum set of styles. Also block theme or scheme switching. Then require that all editing be carried out in Track Changes. Finally, enforce document protection without a password.

- Open the *Password* document, set a password of *P@ssword* for the file, and save the document as *MyPassword*. Then close and reopen the document.

- Open the *Finalizing2* document, and mark it as final.

6.3 Attach digital signatures

When you create a document that will be circulated to other people via e-mail or the Web, you might want to attach a *digital signature*, which is an electronic stamp of authentication. The digital signature confirms the origin of the document and indicates that no one has tampered with the document since it was digitally signed.

To add a digital signature to a Word document, you must first create or obtain a *digital certificate*, also called a *digital ID*. You can create a local digital certificate on your computer (although its use is limited—it will authenticate documents only on your computer) or obtain one online from a commercial certificate authority (CA). Some companies can also issue their own digital certificates internally. Different types of digital certificates connote varying degrees of identity certification. For example, you can relatively easily obtain a digital ID specifically for documents or e-mail messages, but a digital ID for the purpose of certifying programmatic code can be costly and may require that you submit detailed information to verify that you are who you claim to be.

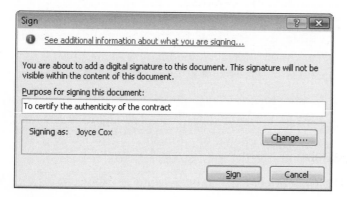

Strategy For purposes of studying for the certification exam, follow the instructions for creating your own digital ID so that you can practice attaching it to documents.

When you create a document with the intent of digitally signing it, or if you create it for someone else to digitally sign, you can insert a digital *signature line* that allows the document to be digitally signed from within the document. The digital signature line resembles a standard signature line, so in a printed document it can also be used as a signature location.

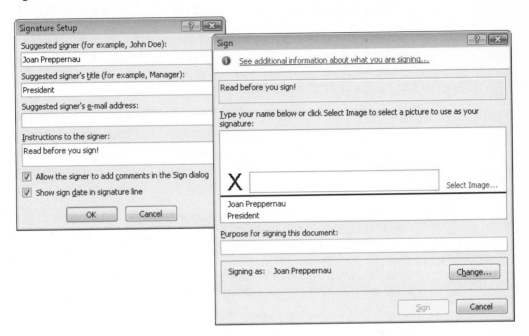

➤ **To obtain a digital ID**

1. On the **Office** menu, point to **Prepare**, and then click **Add a Digital Signature**.

2. In the message box, click **OK**.

3. In the **Get a Digital ID** dialog box, click the option you want, and then click **OK**.

4. If you clicked **Get a digital ID from a Microsoft partner**, follow the instructions to get an ID from the vendor of your choice.

   Or

   If you clicked **Create your own digital ID**, enter your information in the **Create a Digital ID** box, and then click **Create**. Click **Cancel** in the **Sign** dialog box if you do not want to sign the open document.

➤ To attach your digital signature to a document

1. On the **Office** menu, point to **Prepare**, and then click **Add a Digital Signature**.
2. If a message box opens, click **OK**.
3. In the **Sign** dialog box, click **Sign**.
4. In the **Signature Confirmation** message box, click **OK**.
5. In the **Signatures** task pane, verify that the correct signature has been attached to the document.

➤ To remove your digital signature from a document

1. In the **Signatures** task pane, point to your signature, click the arrow that appears, and then click **Remove Signature**.
2. Click **Yes** in the **Remove Signature** message box, and then click **OK** in the **Signature Removed** message box.

➤ To insert a digital signature line

1. On the **Insert** tab, in the **Text** group, click the **Signature Line** arrow, and then click **Microsoft Office Signature Line**.
2. In the four text boxes of the **Signature Setup** dialog box, type the text you want to appear directly beneath the signature line.
3. Set any other options you want. Then click **OK**.

➤ To sign a document with a signature line

1. Double-click the signature line, and in the message box, click **OK**.
2. In the **Sign** dialog box, type your name in the text box, or click **Select Image** to locate and insert your picture.
3. Click **Sign**.

   Tip If you want, you can click the link at the top of the dialog box to see what information will be stored with your signature.

Practice Tasks

The practice file for these tasks is located in the *Documents\Microsoft Press\MCAS\ Word2007\Objective06* folder. If you want, save the task results in the same folder with *My* prepended to the file name.

- Open the *Signature* document and add a digital signature to it by creating a local digital ID if you do not have one of your own. Verify that you can't make changes to the digitally signed document, and then remove the digital signature.

- Continuing in the *Signature* document, insert a digital signature line at the end of the document. Then sign the document with your typed name or picture.

Objective Review

Before finishing this chapter, ensure that you have mastered the following skills:

6.1 Prepare documents for sharing.

6.2 Control document access.

6.3 Attach digital signatures.

Using Microsoft Office
Excel 2007

This part of the book covers the skills you need to have for certification as a Microsoft Office Specialist in Microsoft Office Excel 2007. Specifically, you need to be able to complete tasks that demonstrate the following skill sets:

1 Creating and Manipulating Data

2 Formatting Data and Content

3 Creating and Modifying Formulas

4 Presenting Data Visually

5 Collaborating and Securing Data

With these skills, you can create and manage the types of workbooks most commonly used in a business environment.

Prerequisites

We assume that you have been working with Excel 2007 for at least six months and that you know how to carry out fundamental tasks that are not specifically mentioned in the Microsoft Office Specialist objectives for Exam 77-602, "Using Microsoft Office Excel 2007." Before you begin studying for this exam, you might want to make sure you are familiar with the information in this section.

Managing Worksheets

➤ **To insert a new worksheet**

→ Click the **Insert Worksheet** button at the right end of the worksheet tab section. Or

1. Right-click the worksheet tab before which you want to insert a new worksheet, and then click **Insert**.

2. On the **General** tab of the **Insert** dialog box, click **Worksheet**, and then click **OK**.

➤ **To delete a worksheet**

→ Right-click the worksheet tab, and then click **Delete**.

➤ **To rename a worksheet**

1. Right-click the worksheet tab, and then click **Rename**.

2. Type the new worksheet name, and then press **Enter**.

Managing Worksheet Content

➤ **To select all content on a worksheet**

→ At the junction of the row and column headings (above row 1 and to the left of column A), click the **Select All** button.

➤ **To select an individual column or row**

→ Click the column heading (labeled with the column letter) or the row heading (labeled with the row number).

➤ **To size a column or row to fit its contents**

→ Select the column or row, and then double-click its right or bottom edge.

Managing Excel Tables

➤ **To select the data in a table, table column, or table row**

→ Point to the upper-left corner of the table. When the pointer changes to a diagonal arrow, click once.

→ Point to the top edge of the table column. When the pointer changes to a downward-pointing arrow, click once.

→ Point to the left edge of the table row. When the pointer changes to a right-pointing arrow, click once.

➤ **To select the data and headers of a table, table column, or table row**

→ Point to the upper-left corner of the table. When the pointer changes to a diagonal arrow, click twice.

→ Point to the top edge of the table column. When the pointer changes to a downward-pointing arrow, click twice.

→ Point to the left edge of the table row. When the pointer changes to a right-pointing arrow, click twice.

Managing Data Entries

You enter text or a number in a cell simply by clicking the cell and typing the entry. A Cancel (X) button and an Enter (check mark) button appear between the formula bar and name box, and the indicator at the left end of the status bar changes from *Ready* to *Enter,* because what you have typed will not be recorded in the cell until you "enter" it.

Excel allows a long text entry to overflow into an adjacent empty cell and truncates the entry only if the adjacent cell also contains an entry. However, unless you tell it otherwise, Excel displays long numbers in their simplest form, as follows:

- If you enter a number with fewer than 12 digits in a standard-width cell (which holds 8.43 characters), Excel adjusts the width of the column to accommodate the entry.

- If you enter a number with 12 or more digits, Excel displays it in scientific notation. For example, if you enter 12345678912345 in a standard-width cell, Excel displays 1.23457E+13 (1.23457 times 10 to the 13th power).

- If you enter a value with many decimal places, Excel might round it. For example, if you enter 123456.789 in a standard-width cell, Excel displays 123456.8.

- If you manually set the width of a column and then enter a currency value that is too large to be displayed in its entirety, Excel displays pound signs (#) instead of the value.

➤ **To complete a data entry**

→ Press the **Enter** key to complete the entry and stay in the same cell.

→ Press the **Enter** or **Down Arrow** key to complete the entry and move to the next cell in the same column.

→ Press the **Tab** or **Right Arrow** key to complete the entry and move to the next cell in the same row.

→ Press **Shift+Enter** or the **Up Arrow** key to complete the entry and move to the previous cell in the same column.

→ Press **Shift+Tab** or the **Left Arrow** key to complete the entry and move to the previous cell in the same row.

1 Creating and Manipulating Data

The skills tested in this section of the Microsoft Office Specialist exam for Microsoft Office Excel 2007 relate to working with data in worksheets, and working with multiple worksheets. Specifically, the following objectives are associated with this set of skills:

1.1 Insert data by using Auto Fill.

1.2 Ensure data integrity.

1.3 Modify cell contents and formats.

1.4 Change worksheet views.

1.5 Manage worksheets.

Simply entering and working with data in an Excel worksheet are basic skills that certification candidates should already be familiar with. This section of the exam covers some of the more advanced skills that may not be used by the casual Excel worker.

You can easily create functional workbooks by using basic Excel features. Many users never have need of the more advanced features of Excel, but to create complex, powerful workbooks and become certified as an Excel specialist, it is necessary to master advanced skills.

This chapter guides you in studying how to automatically fill in a series of cells with patterns of data, create data validation checks, move data within a worksheet and between worksheets, and how to manage multiple worksheets.

Important Before you can use the practice files in this chapter, you need to install them from the book's companion CD to their default location. See "Using the Companion CD" at the beginning of this book for more information.

Tip Graphics and operating system–related instructions in this book reflect the Windows Vista user interface. If your computer is running Windows XP and you experience trouble following the instructions as written, refer to the sidebar "If You Are Running Windows XP" in "Working in the Microsoft Office Fluent User Interface" at the beginning of this book.

1.1   Insert data by using Auto Fill

Filling Series

You can quickly fill adjacent cells with data that continues a series of numbers, days, or dates, either manually from the Fill menu, or automatically by dragging the fill handle. When copying or filling data by using the Fill menu commands, you can set specific options for the pattern of the data sequence you want to create.

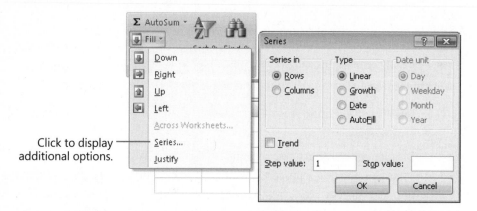

Click to display additional options.

When creating a series based on one or more selected cells (called *filling a series*), you can select from the following series types:

- **Linear.** Excel calculates the series values by adding the value you enter in the Step Value box to each cell in the series.

- **Growth.** Excel calculates the series values by multiplying each cell in the series by the step value.

- **Date.** Excel calculates the series values by incrementing each cell in the series of dates, designated by the Date Unit you select, by the step value.

- **AutoFill.** Creates a series that produces the same results as dragging the fill handle.

When using the Auto Fill feature, either by dragging the fill handle or from the Fill menu, the Auto Fill Options button appears in the lower-right corner of the fill range. Clicking the button displays a menu of context-specific fill options.

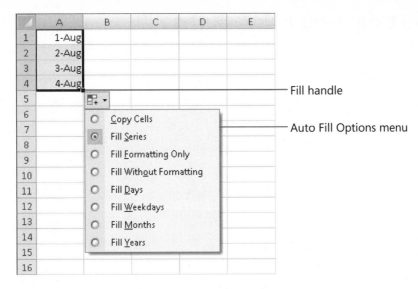

Fill handle

Auto Fill Options menu

Tip The Auto Fill Options button does not appear when copying data to adjacent cells.

You can use the Auto Fill feature to create sequences of numbers, days, and dates; to apply formatting from one cell to adjacent cells; or, if you use Excel for more sophisticated purposes, to create sequences of data generated by formulas, or custom sequences based on information you specify.

If you want to fill a series of information that does not match the available series type or unit, you can create a custom fill series consisting of a specific list of data you want your series to conform to. For example, this could be a list of names, regions, or industry-specific reference points.

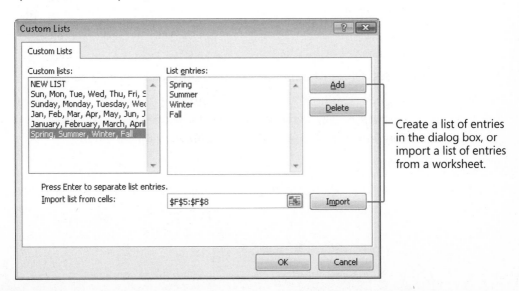

Create a list of entries in the dialog box, or import a list of entries from a worksheet.

➤ To fill a simple numeric, day, or date series

1. In the upper-left cell of the range you want to fill, enter the first number or date of the series you want to create.

   Or

   To create a series in which numbers or dates increment by more than one, enter the first two or more values of the series in the first cells of the range you want to fill.

   Tip Enter as many numbers or dates as are necessary to establish the series.

2. Select the cell or cells beginning the series.

3. Drag the fill handle down or to the right to create an increasing series.

   Or

   Drag the fill handle up or to the left to create a decreasing series.

   Tip When using the fill handle, you can drag in only one direction; you can't define a cell range of multiple columns and rows.

➤ To fill a selective day or date series

1. Fill the series. Immediately after you release the mouse button, click the **Auto Fill Options** button that appears in the lower-right corner of the cell range.

2. On the **Auto Fill Options** menu, click **Fill Days**, **Fill Weekdays**, **Fill Months**, or **Fill Years**.

➤ To fill a formatted numeric series

1. Enter the amount or amounts beginning the series.

2. On the **Home** tab, use the commands in the **Number** group to format the amount or amounts as currency, percentage, fraction, or whatever number format you want.

3. Select the cell or cells beginning the series.

4. Drag the fill handle down or to the right to create an increasing series, or up or to the left to create a decreasing series.

5. Click the **Auto Fill Options** button that appears in the lower-right corner of the cell range. Then on the **Auto Fill Options** menu, click **Fill Series**.

➤ **To set advanced options for a numeric, day, or date series**

   1. Enter the number or date beginning the series, and then select the cell range you want to fill.

   2. On the **Home** tab, in the **Editing** group, click the **Fill** button, and then in the list, click **Series**.

   3. In the **Series** dialog box, select the options you want, and then click **OK**.

➤ **To exclude formatting when filling a series**

   1. Fill the series, and then click the **Auto Fill Options** button that appears in the lower-right corner of the cell range.

   2. On the **Auto Fill Options** menu, click **Fill Without Formatting**.

➤ **To create a custom fill series**

   1. In a series of cells, enter the items you want to use in your custom series, and then select the cells.

   2. Click the **Microsoft Office Button**, and then click **Excel Options**.

   3. On the **Popular** page of the **Excel Options** dialog box, to the right of **Create lists for use in sorts and fill sequences**, click **Edit Custom Lists**.

   4. In the **Custom Lists** dialog box, with the selected cell range shown in the **Import list from cells** box, click **Import**.

   5. In the **List entries** list, verify or edit the entries.

   6. Click **OK** in the **Custom Lists** dialog box and in the **Excel Options** dialog box.

➤ **To apply a custom fill series**

   → Select a cell containing any entry from the custom list, and then drag the fill handle to create a series.

     Tip Excel fills the series with either lowercase or capitalized entries to match the cell you start with.

Copying Data

You can use the fill functionality to copy text data, numeric data, or cell formatting (such as text color, background color, and alignment) to adjacent cells.

➤ **To copy text or currency amounts to adjacent cells**

1. In the upper-left cell of the range you want to fill, enter the text or currency amount (formatted as currency) you want to duplicate, and then select the cell.

2. Drag the fill handle up, down, to the left, or to the right to encompass the cell range you want to fill.

➤ **To copy numeric data to adjacent cells**

1. In the upper-left cell of the range you want to fill, enter the value you want to duplicate, and then select the cell.

2. Drag the fill handle up, down, to the left, or to the right to encompass the cell range you want to fill.

3. Click the **Auto Fill Options** button, and then click **Copy Cells**.

   Or

1. In the upper-left cell of the range you want to fill, enter the value you want to duplicate.

2. Select the entire cell range you want to duplicate the value into.

3. On the **Home** tab, in the **Editing** group, click the **Fill** button, and then in the list, click the first direction in which you want to duplicate the value (**Down** or **Right**).

4. To fill a cell range that includes multiple rows and columns, repeat step 3, selecting the other direction.

   Tip You can also fill a cell range up or to the left; if you do so, make sure that the value you want to duplicate is in the lower-right cell of the range you want to fill.

➤ **To copy formatting to adjacent cells without changing the cell content**

1. Select the cell that has the formatting you want to copy.

2. Drag the fill handle up, down, to the left, or to the right to copy the formatting to the adjacent cells.

3. Click the **Auto Fill Options** button, and then click **Fill Formatting Only**.

Practice Tasks

The practice files for these tasks are located in the *Documents\Microsoft Press\ MCAS\Excel2007\Objective01* folder. If you want, save the task results in the same folder with *My* prepended to the file name.

- Open the *FillSeries* workbook. Using the fill handle, fill cells A2:A21 with *Item 1, Item 2*, *Item 3*, and so on through *Item 20*. Fill cells B2:B21 with *10, 20, 30*, and so on through *200*. Then fill cells C2:C21 with *$3.00, $2.95, $2.90*, and so on through *$2.05*.

- In the *FillSeries* workbook, copy the background and font formatting from cell A1 to cells A2:A21.

- Open the *FillCustom* workbook. Using the fill handle and AutoFill Options button, fill cells B1:K1 with the days *Monday* through *Friday*, repeated twice.

- In the *FillCustom* workbook, create a custom series using the names entered in cells B2:B7. Fill the series in each row to create a rotating duty roster for the two weeks.

- Open the *FillCopies* workbook. Select cells A2:F14. Using the fill functionality, create a duplicate of the selected term schedule and empty rows immediately below the original. Ensure that the Period column in the copy of the schedule displays 1st through 8th periods.

1.2   Ensure data integrity

Data Entry Restrictions

A simple way to ensure that worksheets produce the expected results is to take measures to ensure that the data being entered meets necessary criteria. This is especially important in workbooks that you will be distributing for other people to populate with data. You can do this in two ways:

- By limiting entries to those the user chooses from a list that you provide.
- By checking the data against specific criteria as it is entered. This is referred to as *validating the data*.

You can validate data in several ways. For any numeric, date, or time validation check, you can specify if you want to allow the entry to be between two values, not between two values, greater than, less than, equal to, or not equal to a value. Any of the values to be used for validation are entered into criteria boxes and can either be a specific value, or can be a reference to a cell on the worksheet or a cell on another worksheet, or be calculated with a formula referencing cells. With this, very complex validation rules can be created. For example, you could create a rule in a budget worksheet specifying that the budget item for charitable contributions should be at least as large as the previous year, but no more than 10 percent of the net pre-tax profit.

You can restrict cell content to the following types of data:

- **Any Value.** This is the default value.
- **Whole Number.** An integer, either positive or negative.
- **Decimal.** Any type of number, whole or otherwise, positive or negative.
- **List.** An input list from which the user can select only a specific value.
- **Date.** Any recognized date format.
- **Time.** Any recognized time format.
- **Text Length.** Used to validate the number of characters being entered. The same options are available as for any numeric validation check.
- **Custom.** Any valid Excel formula that equates to True or False can be used. To use the value that is being entered, simply use the cell reference. For example, to find out whether the value in C3 contains text, use the formula =ISTEXT(C3).

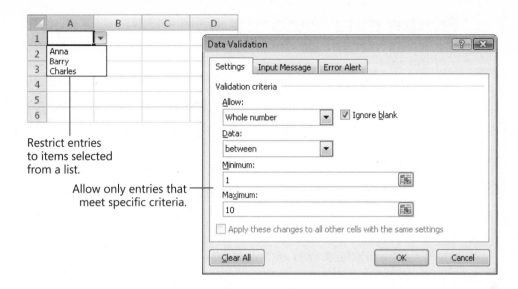

Restrict entries
to items selected
from a list.

Allow only entries that
meet specific criteria.

➤ **To restrict entries to those chosen from a list**

1. On the worksheet on which you will create the input list, enter the items you want to make available from the list into a range of cells. Choose a location that will not interfere with data entry.

    Or

    On a worksheet other than the one on which you will create the input list, enter the list items in a range of cells. Then select and name the range.

    See Also For information about naming ranges, see section 3.1, "Reference data in formulas."

2. Select the cell or range of cells for which you want to create the input list.

3. On the **Data** tab, in the **Data Tools** group, click the **Data Validation** button.

4. On the **Settings** tab of the **Data Validation** dialog box, in the **Allow** list, click **List**.

5. Position the insertion point in the **Source** box, and then select the list items you created in step 1, or enter the cell range.

6. In the **Data Validation** dialog box, click **OK**.

> ➤ **To restrict entries to those meeting specific criteria**

1. Select the cell or range of cells for which you want to enforce data validation criteria.

2. On the **Data** tab, in the **Data Tools** group, click the **Data Validation** button.

3. On the **Settings** tab of the **Data Validation** dialog box, click the **Allow** arrow, and then in the list, click the type of data you want to allow.

4. In the data type–specific criteria boxes that appear, select or enter the criteria data that the selected cells must meet. Then click **OK**.

   Tip Take care when setting up data validation checks that you don't inadvertently disallow valid data. Test your data validation criteria by entering both valid and invalid data and verifying that you get the expected results.

> ➤ **To locate worksheet cells with data validation functionality**

→ On the **Home** tab, in the **Editing** group, click **Find & Select**, and then in the list, click **Data Validation**.

> ➤ **To cancel data validation**

1. Select the cells (or the entire worksheet) from which you want to remove data validation.

2. On any tab of the **Data Validation** dialog box, click **Clear All**, and then click **OK**.

Input and Error Messages

You can display two types of messages for each cell that uses the data validation functionality: an input message that displays when the user selects the cell, and an error alert that displays if the user enters data that does not match the validation criteria.

Input messages appear in tooltip-like boxes that disappear when the user clicks another cell. Error alerts appear in message windows that require the user to click a button to exit.

You can choose from three styles of error alerts, each represented by a different symbol and allowing a different level of input control. The styles are:

- **Stop.** An error message appears, labeled with the letter *X* in a red circle; the user may either retry or cancel the data entry. Invalid data is not entered. Use this severity level for critical cells, when entering the wrong data could yield very incorrect or unexpected results.

- **Warning.** A warning message appears, labeled with an exclamation point in a yellow triangle; the user may enter the data and continue data entry, enter the data and keep the cell active, or cancel the data entry.

- **Information.** An informational message appears, labeled with the letter *i* in a blue circle; the user may either enter the data or cancel the data entry.

For each input or error message, you can use the default language supplied by Excel or customize the message text to be more specific to the selected cell.

➤ To display a message when a cell is selected

1. Select the cell or range of cells for which you want to display the message.
2. Display the **Data Validation** dialog box, and click the **Input Message** tab.
3. Select the **Show input message when cell is selected** check box, if it isn't already selected.
4. In the **Title** box, enter the text you want to appear in bold at the top of the input message. This could be a message title or an actual message. (This field is limited to 32 characters.)
5. In the **Input Message** box, enter the message you want to appear beneath the bold text; for example, *How many of this item would you like to purchase?*
6. In the **Data Validation** dialog box, click **OK**.

   Tip You can display an input message for any cell, regardless of whether data validation is enforced. To do so, set the validation criteria to Any Value.

➤ **To display an error message when invalid data is entered**

1. Select the cell or range of cells for which you want to display the message.

2. Display the **Data Validation** dialog box, and click the **Error Alert** tab.

3. Select the **Show error alert after invalid data is entered** check box, if it isn't already selected.

4. In the **Style** list, select the icon you want to appear in the message box: **Stop** (the letter *X* in a red circle), **Warning** (an exclamation point in a yellow triangle), or **Information** (the letter *i* in a blue circle).

5. In the **Title** box, enter the text you want to appear in bold at the top of the input message. This could be a message title or an actual message. (This field is limited to 32 characters.)

6. In the **Error Message** box, enter the message you want to appear beneath the bold text; for example, *This field may contain no more than 16 characters.*

7. In the **Data Validation** dialog box, click **OK**.

Duplicate Rows

It is not uncommon in worksheets that are used for data collection for duplicate entries to occur. This is a likely scenario when multiple people are entering data, or if the data is coming from a data feed. It can be tedious to manually locate and remove duplicate entries; instead, you can have Excel do it for you.

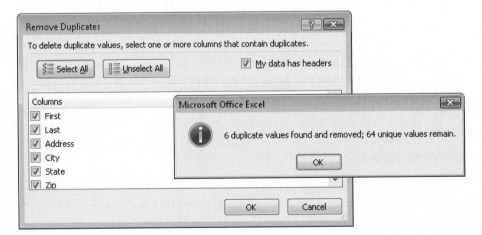

➤ **To remove duplicate rows from a worksheet**

1. Select the table or range of cells from which you want to remove duplicate entries.

2. On the **Data** tab, in the **Data Tools** group, click the **Remove Duplicates** button.

   Tip If the cells adjacent to your selection contain data, Excel asks whether you want to select more cells or continue with only the current selection.

3. In the **Remove Duplicates** dialog box, if the selected range includes a header row, select the **My data has headers** check box.

4. Select the columns that you want to use to determine if a data row is duplicated.

5. Click **OK** in the **Remove Duplicates** dialog box and again in the message box displaying the number of duplicate values found and removed and the number of unique values remaining.

Practice Tasks

The practice files for these tasks are located in the *Documents\Microsoft Press\ MCAS\Excel2007\Objective01* folder. If you want, save the task results in the same folder with *My* prepended to the file name.

- Open the *DataValidation* workbook, and add a data validation check to the Discount column to ensure that the value is between 0 and .2 (in other words, that the discount does not exceed 20 percent). Include an input message and display a warning if an incorrect value is entered.

- Open the *Duplicates* workbook, and remove each entry that contains the same last name and phone number as another entry.

- Open the *ListBox* workbook, and add a data validation check to the Employee column to limit the value to one of the three existing employee names.

1.3   Modify cell contents and formats

The cut, copy, and paste features are used by virtually everyone who uses Excel. You can do some advanced things when pasting that a great many Excel users are unaware of or rarely use although they allow the user to do some very powerful things.

Using the Paste Special feature, you can perform mathematical operations when you paste data onto existing data that already exists, you can transpose columns to rows and rows to columns, and you can be selective about what you want to paste from the source cells. You have the option to paste only values, formulas, formatting, data validation, comments, or column widths. You can choose to exclude borders when you paste. You can also link data that you've copied, so that if the source data changes, the copied data will also change.

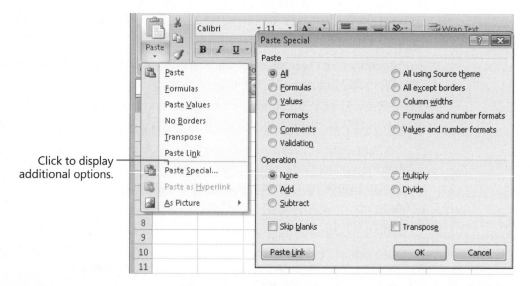

Click to display
additional options.

Strategy In this section, we discuss some of the most common advanced paste techniques. You should experiment with all the options in the Paste Special dialog box.

➤ To transpose rows and columns

1. Select the row(s) or column(s) you want to transpose.

2. On the **Home** tab, in the **Clipboard** group, click the **Copy** button; or press **Ctrl+C**.

3. Select the cell into which you want to copy the first value of the transposed data.

4. On the **Home** tab, in the **Clipboard** group, click the **Paste** arrow, and then in the list, click **Transpose**.

➤ **To paste formula results from one cell range to another**

1. Select and copy the cell range containing the formulas you want to copy the values from.

2. Select the cell into which you want to copy the first value.

3. In the **Clipboard** group, click the **Paste** arrow, and then in the list, click **Paste Values**.

➤ **To add, subtract, multiply, or divide values in two data ranges**

1. Select and copy the first data range—the numbers you want to add to, subtract from, or multiply by the numbers in the second range, or the numbers you want to divide the second range by.

2. Select the first cell of the second data range—the numbers you want to add to, multiply by, or divide by the numbers in the first range, or subtract the first range from.

3. In the **Clipboard** group, click the **Paste** arrow, and then in the list, click **Paste Special**.

4. In the **Paste Special** dialog box, in the **Operation** area, click **Add**, **Subtract**, **Multiply**, or **Divide**. Then click **OK**.

Practice Tasks

The practice file for these tasks is located in the *Documents\Microsoft Press\MCAS\ Excel2007\Objective01* folder. If you want, save the task results in the same folder with *My* prepended to the file name.

● Open the *CopyPaste* workbook and transpose the CategoryName column values to the first row of a new worksheet.

● In the *CopyPaste* workbook, practice pasting only the values (with and without borders) and formatting of cell ranges.

1.4 Change worksheet views

Views

From the View toolbar at the bottom of the program window, or from the View tab, you can switch among three views of a worksheet:

- **Normal.** The worksheet is displayed in the window at 100 percent magnification or at whatever zoom level you select. Page breaks are indicated by black dashed lines.

- **Page Layout.** Each worksheet page appears as it will when printed, with space between the individual pages. A ruler appears at the left edge of the window next to the optional row headings. The page header and footer are visible and you can select them for editing.

- **Page Break Preview.** The entire worksheet is displayed in the window, with page breaks indicated by bold blue dashed lines and page numbers displayed in the center of each page. You can change the page breaks by dragging the blue lines.

➤ **To change the way a worksheet is displayed**

→ On the **Zoom** toolbar, click the **Normal**, **Page Layout**, or **Page Break Preview** button.

→ On the **View** tab, in the **Workbook Views** group, click the **Normal**, **Page Layout**, or **Page Break Preview** button.

Zoom Level

From the Zoom toolbar at the bottom of the program window, or from the Zoom group on the View tab, you can change the zoom level of a worksheet in any range from 10 percent to 400 percent. You can zoom the entire worksheet or select a range of cells and have Excel determine the zoom level necessary to fit the selection in the program window.

➤ **To change the Zoom level in 10 percent increments**

→ On the **Zoom** toolbar, click the **Zoom Out** button (labeled with a minus sign) or the **Zoom In** button (labeled with a plus sign).

➤ **To change the Zoom level dynamically**

→ On the **Zoom** toolbar, move the **Zoom** slider to the left to zoom out or to the right to zoom in.

➤ **To set the Zoom level to a specific percentage**

1. On the **View** tab, in the **Zoom** group, click the **Zoom** button.

   Or

   On the **Zoom** toolbar, click the **Zoom level** button.

2. In the **Zoom** dialog box, click a specific magnification level, or click **Custom** and then enter a value from *10* to *400*. Then click **OK**.

➤ **To zoom in on selected cells**

1. Select the cell or cell range you want to zoom in on.

2. On the **View** tab, in the **Zoom** group, click **Zoom to Selection**.

   Or

1. On the **Zoom** toolbar, click the **Zoom level** button.

2. In the **Zoom** dialog box, click **Fit selection**, and then click **OK**.

Program Window Area

To maximize your work area, you can display a worksheet in full-screen mode, so that only the title bar is visible. To increase the vertical space of the work area but still have easy access to commands, you can hide the Ribbon so that only its tabs are visible, and hide the Formula Bar.

See Also For information about hiding column and row headings, see section 2.1, "Format worksheets."

➤ **To hide all program window elements other than the title bar**

→ On the **View** tab, in the **Workbook Views** group, click the **Toggle Full Screen** button.

➤ **To redisplay all program window elements**

→ Right-click the worksheet, and then click **Close Full Screen**.

➤ **To hide the Ribbon**

→ Double-click any Ribbon tab.

➤ **To temporarily redisplay the Ribbon**

→ Click the tab you want to display.

➤ **To permanently redisplay the Ribbon**

→ Double-click any tab.

➤ **To hide or display the Formula Bar**

→ On the **View** tab, in the **Show/Hide** group, select or clear the **Formula Bar** check box.

Freezing and Splitting

It is cumbersome to work in a worksheet that is too long or wide to display legibly in the program window, to scroll up and down or back and forth to view data elsewhere in the worksheet, or to switch back and forth between multiple worksheets in the same workbook if you frequently need to access information on both of them.

You can view multiple parts of a worksheet at one time by freezing rows or columns so they stay in view while you scroll the rest of the worksheet, or by splitting the window so you can independently scroll and work in two views of the worksheet at one time.

See Also Another way to bring disparate rows or columns together on one screen is to hide the rows or columns between them. For information about hiding rows and columns, see section 2.2, "Insert and modify rows and columns."

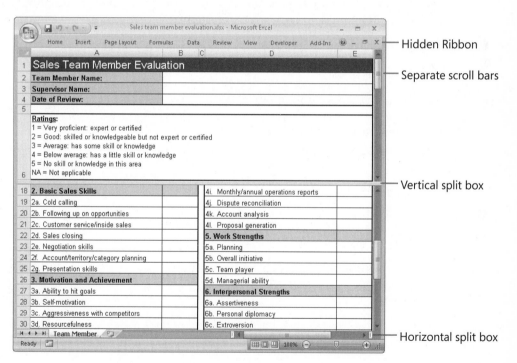

➤ To freeze the first row or first column

→ On the **View** tab, in the **Window** group, click the **Freeze Panes** button, and then click **Freeze Top Row** or **Freeze First Column**.

➤ To freeze multiple rows or columns

1. Select the row or column following those you want to freeze, by clicking the row selector or column selector.

2. On the **View** tab, in the **Window** group, click the **Freeze Panes** button, and then click **Freeze Panes**.

➤ To simultaneously freeze columns and rows

1. Select the cell that is below and to the right of the intersection of the row and column you want to freeze.

2. On the **View** tab, in the **Window** group, click the **Freeze Panes** button, and then click **Freeze Panes**.

   Tip You can freeze as many columns and rows as you like depending on what cell is selected when you execute the Freeze Panes command. Selecting a cell in row 1 freezes only columns. Selecting a cell in column A freezes only rows.

➤ To unfreeze all rows and columns

→ On the **View** tab, in the **Window** group, click the **Freeze Panes** button, and then click **Freeze Panes**.

➤ To split the window vertically or horizontally

→ Drag the vertical or horizontal split box to the row or column where you want to split the window.

➤ To remove a split

→ Drag the vertical or horizontal split box to its original location at the top or right end of the scroll bar.

Multiple Windows

You can open multiple windows with a view of the current worksheet and then arrange those windows in a variety of ways.

➤ **To open a second instance of a workbook in a separate window**

→ On the **View** tab, in the **Window** group, click the **New Window** button.

➤ **To arrange multiple program windows**

1. In the **Window** group, click the **Arrange All** button.

2. In the **Arrange Windows** dialog box, click **Tiled**, **Horizontal**, **Vertical**, or **Cascade**.

3. To include only windows displaying views of the current workbook, select the **Windows of active workbook** check box.

4. In the **Arrange Windows** dialog box, click **OK**.

Practice Tasks

The practice files for these tasks are located in the *Documents\Microsoft Press\ MCAS\Excel2007\Objective01* folder. If you want, save the task results in the same folder with *My* prepended to the file name.

● Open the *PersonalMonthlyBudget* workbook and freeze rows 1 through 9, so that when you scroll the rest of the workbook, those rows are always visible. Then unfreeze the panes.

● Continuing from the previous task, open the *AirQualityData* and *PopulationData* workbooks. Using the commands in the Window group on the View menu, tile the windows, and then arrange them in an overlapping pattern.

● Continuing from the previous task, use the New Window command to open a second instance of one of the workbooks. Then arrange only the two windows of the active workbook horizontally.

1.5   Manage worksheets

Hiding and Displaying

It is common for a workbook to include multiple worksheets for one project or purpose. For example, the first worksheet might display a simple summary of more complex data presented on other, purpose-specific worksheets. You can hide worksheets you don't need to use or don't want other people to see.

➤ To hide a worksheet

→ Right-click the worksheet tab, and then click **Hide**.

➤ To display a hidden worksheet

1. Right-click the worksheet tab, and then click **Unhide**.

2. In the **Unhide** dialog box, select the worksheet you want to display, and then click **OK**.

Moving and Copying

You can move and copy worksheets within and between workbooks.

➤ To copy a worksheet within a workbook or to another workbook

1. Right-click the worksheet tab, and then click **Move or Copy**.

2. In the **Move or Copy** dialog box, if you want to copy the worksheet to another workbook, select that workbook in the **To book** list.

3. In the **Before sheet** list, click the worksheet you want to position the copy before.

4. Select the **Create a copy** check box, and then click **OK**.

➤ To reposition a worksheet within a workbook

→ In the **Move or Copy** dialog box, click the worksheet that you want to move the current worksheet in front of, and then click **OK**.

→ Drag the worksheet tab to reposition it.

Practice Tasks

The practice file for these tasks is located in the *Documents\Microsoft Press\MCAS\ Excel2007\Objective01* folder. If you want, save the task results in the same folder with *My* prepended to the file name.

● Open the *SalesReport* workbook, and make a copy of the By Product worksheet.

● In the *SalesReport* workbook, move the Source Data worksheet so that it is the last worksheet in the workbook.

Objective Review

Before finishing this chapter, ensure that you have mastered the following skills:

1.1 Insert data by using Auto Fill.

1.2 Ensure data integrity.

1.3 Modify cell contents and formats.

1.4 Change worksheet views.

1.5 Manage worksheets.

2 Formatting Data and Content

The skills tested in this section of the Microsoft Office Specialist exam for Microsoft Office Excel 2007 relate to visually formatting worksheets, optimizing rows and columns on a worksheet, formatting cell contents, and creating and working with Excel tables. Specifically, the following objectives are associated with this set of skills:

2.1 Format worksheets.
2.2 Insert and modify rows and columns.
2.3 Format cells and cell content.
2.4 Format data as a table.

Worksheets can contain just a few columns and rows of data or complex calculations involving hundreds of cells. The goal of formatting is to structure the data in such a way that no matter what the size of the worksheet, key information is readily identifiable. With Excel, you can format the information in an ordinary worksheet on three levels: you can manipulate the worksheet as a whole; you can work with entire columns or rows; and you can change individual cells to achieve precisely the results you want. If you define a range of cells as a table, you have additional formatting options available.

This chapter guides you in studying ways of formatting worksheets by using themes and backgrounds; changing the name and color of worksheet tabs; and hiding, displaying, and printing gridlines and headings. You also study ways of formatting cells to display numeric content in a specific format

 Important Before you can use the practice files in this chapter, you need to install them from the book's companion CD to their default location. See "Using the Companion CD" at the beginning of this book for more information.

Tip Graphics and operating system–related instructions in this book reflect the Windows Vista user interface. If your computer is running Windows XP and you experience trouble following the instructions as written, refer to the sidebar "If You Are Running Windows XP" in "Working in the Microsoft Office Fluent User Interface" at the beginning of this book.

2.1   Format worksheets

Themes

You can enhance the look of an entire worksheet by applying a pre-defined theme—a combination of colors, fonts, and effects. In the Themes gallery, you can point to a theme to preview its effect on the worksheet before you apply it.

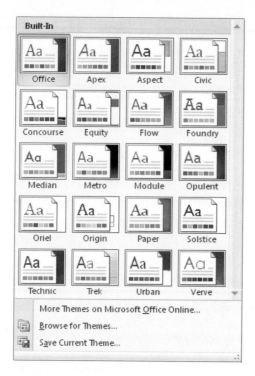

If you like certain aspects of different themes (for example, the colors of one theme and the fonts of another), you can mix and match theme elements. First find the theme that most closely resembles the look you want, and then in the Themes group, change the colors by clicking the Theme Colors button, the fonts by clicking the Theme Fonts button, or the effects by clicking the Theme Effects button.

If you create a combination of theme elements that you would like to be able to use with other worksheets, you can save the combination as a new theme. By saving the theme in the default Document Themes folder, you make the theme available in the Themes gallery in a new Custom section.

➤ **To apply a theme to a worksheet**

1. On the **Page Layout** tab, in the **Themes** group, click the **Themes** button.

2. In the **Themes** gallery, click the theme you want.

➤ **To modify a theme**

1. In the **Themes** group, click the **Colors**, **Fonts**, or **Effects** button.

2. In the gallery, click the theme element you want.

➤ **To save a custom theme**

1. In the **Themes** gallery, click **Save Current Theme**.

2. In the **Save Current Theme** dialog box, in the **File name** box, type a name for the theme, and then click **Save**.

Gridlines and Headings

While you are developing a worksheet, you want to see gridlines and row and column headings to efficiently move among cells. But when you distribute the final worksheet, you might want to turn off gridlines and headings for a cleaner look.

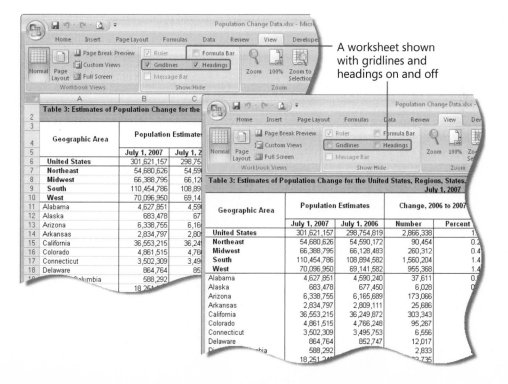

A worksheet shown with gridlines and headings on and off

When you print a worksheet, by default gridlines and row and column headings are not printed. If you want to include these elements, you can turn them on for printing.

➤ **To hide or show gridlines**

→ On the **Page Layout** tab, in the **Sheet Options** group, in the **Gridlines** area, clear or select the **View** check box.

→ On the **View** tab, in the **Show/Hide** group, clear or select the **Gridlines** check box.

➤ **To hide or show column and row headings**

→ On the **Page Layout** tab, in the **Sheet Options** group, in the **Headings** area, clear or select the **View** check box.

→ On the **View** tab, in the **Show/Hide** group, clear or select the **Headings** check box.

➤ **To print gridlines or headings**

→ On the **Page Layout** tab, in the **Sheet Options** group, in the **Gridlines** or **Headings** area, select the **Print** check box.

Tip Selecting the Print check box in the Sheet Options group selects the corresponding check box on the Sheet tab of the Page Setup dialog box. You can make this adjustment in either place.

Worksheet Tabs

When a workbook contains several sheets, it is helpful to change the names on the sheet tabs to reflect the worksheet contents. You can also assign different colors to the tabs to categorize them or to make them easily distinguishable.

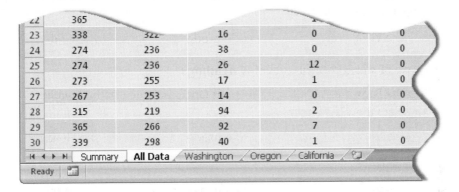

➤ **To change the name of a worksheet tab**

→ Double-click the tab, and then type the name you want.

→ Right-click the tab, click **Rename**, and then type the name you want.

➤ **To assign a color to a worksheet tab**

→ Right-click the tab, click **Tab Color**, and then in the color palette, click the color you want.

Worksheet Background

Excel has no command to apply a background color to a worksheet, but you can accomplish this effect by applying a color fill to all the worksheets cells. This effect will be part of a printed worksheet.

For something a little more dramatic, you can add a picture to the worksheet background. This effect is for display purposes only; the picture will not be printed with the worksheet.

Alabama	4,627,851	4,590,240	37,611	0.8	23
Alaska	683,478	677,450	6,028	0.9	47
Arizona	6,338,755	6,165,689	173,066	2.8	16
Arkansas	2,834,797	2,809,111	25,686	0.9	32
California	36,553,215	36,249,872	303,343	0.8	1
Colorado	4,861,515	4,766,248	95,267	2.0	22
Connecticut	3,502,309	3,495,753	6,556	0.2	29
Delaware	864,764	852,747	12,017	1.4	45
District of Columbia	588,292	585,459	2,833	0.5	50
Florida	18,251,243	18,057,508	193,735	1.1	4
Georgia	9,544,750	9,342,080	202,670	2.2	9
Hawaii	1,283,388	1,278,635	4,753	0.4	42
Idaho	1,499,402	1,463,878	35,524	2.4	39
Illinois	12,852,548	12,777,042	75,506	0.6	5
Indiana	6,345,289	6,302,646	42,643	0.7	15
Iowa	2,988,046	2,972,566	15,480	0.5	30

If you want to display or print text behind the worksheet to denote draft or confidential information or to indicate copyright ownership, you can simulate a watermark either by inserting an appropriate image in the header or footer or by adding a WordArt object to the sheet.

	A	B	C	D	E
1	Employee	Title	E-mail Address	Start Date	Salary
2	Adams, Terry	Human Resources Director	terry@consolidatedmessenger.com	4/1/1997	$ 75,000.00
3	Carey, Richard	Personnel Manager	richard@consolidatedmessenger.com	2/16/2004	$ 75,000.00
4	Carter, Adam	President	adam@consolidatedmessenger.com	3/1/1998	$220,000.00
5	Chow, Ray	Administrative Assistant	ray@consolidatedmessenger.com	3/1/1998	$ 30,000.00
6	Ciccu, Alice	Accountant	alice@consolidatedmessenger.com	8/16/2001	$ 60,000.00
7	Coleman, Pat	Sales Representative	pat@consolidatedmessenger.com	7/1/2006	$ 30,000.00
8	Counts, Robin	Retail Manager	robin@consolidatedmessenger.com	1/1/1996	$ 40,000.00
9	Dickson, Holly	Sales Representative	holly@consolidatedmessenger.com	9/1/2005	$ 32,000.00
10	Freehafer, Nancy	Sales & Marketing Manager	nancy@consolidatedmessenger.com	7/1/2006	$ 80,000.00
11	Gabel, Ron	Warehouse Manager	ron@consolidatedmessenger.com	8/16/2001	$ 40,000.00
12	Hance, Jim	Packager	jim@consolidatedmessenger.com	9/1/2005	$ 22,000.00
13	Kelly, Bob	Delivery Driver	bob@consolidatedmessenger.com	12/1/2007	$ 30,000.00
14	Kotas, Jan	Administrative Assistant	jan@consolidatedmessenger.com	4/1/1997	$ 30,000.00
15	Krieger, Doris	Controller	doris@consolidatedmessenger.com	2/16/2004	$ 80,000.00
16	Lan, Andrew	Loading Dock Specialist	andrew@conolidatedmessenger.com	11/16/2003	$ 27,000.00
17	Langhorn, Carl	Sanitation Engineer	carl@consolidatedmessenger.com	12/1/2007	$ 25,000.00
18	Lysaker, Jenny	Delivery Driver	jenny@consolidatedmessenger.com	1/1/1996	$ 30,000.00
19	Moore, Bobby	Warehouse Clerk	bobby@consolidatedmessenger.com	11/16/2003	$ 27,000.00

➤ To add a colored background to a worksheet

1. Click the **Select All** button at the upper-left junction of the row and column headings to select the entire worksheet.

2. On the **Home** tab, in the **Font** group, click the **Fill Color** button, and then in the palette, click the color you want.

   Tip Filling all the cells obscures the gridlines. You can change the color of gridlines to make them visible by changing the Gridline Color setting in the Display Options For This Worksheet area on the Advanced page of the Excel Options dialog box.

➤ To add a picture to the worksheet background

1. On the **Page Layout** tab, in the **Page Setup** group, click the **Background** button.

2. In the **Sheet Background** dialog box, locate and double-click the graphic file you want.

➤ To simulate a picture watermark

1. Switch to Page Layout view, and then click the worksheet header.

2. On the **Design** tab, in the **Header & Footer Elements** group, click the **Picture** button.

3. In the **Insert Picture** dialog box, locate and double-click the picture file you want to use.

4. In the **Header & Footer Elements** group, click the **Format Picture** button.

5. On the **Size** tab of the **Format Picture** dialog box, adjust the size or scale of the picture.

6. On the **Picture** tab, in the **Image control** area, click **Washout** in the **Color** list, and then adjust the **Brightness** and **Contrast** settings the way you want them.

7. Click **OK**, and then click away from the header to see the results.

➤ To simulate a text watermark

1. On the **Insert** tab, in the **Text** group, click the **WordArt** button.

2. In the **WordArt** gallery, click a transparent text style.

3. Type the text of the watermark, and then click away from the WordArt object.

4. On the **Format** tab, in the **Arrange** group, click the **Rotate** button.

5. On the **Size** tab of the **Size and Properties** dialog box, adjust the size or scale of the picture, and set the **Rotation** angle as necessary. Then click **Close**.

Practice Tasks

The practice files for these tasks are located in the *Documents\Microsoft Press\ MCAS\Excel2007\Objective02* folder. If you want, save the task results in the same folder with *My* prepended to the file name.

- Open the *Themes* workbook, and apply the Apex theme to the Last24Hours worksheet. Then change the theme colors to Flow.

- Open the *Gridlines* workbook, and on the Expenses worksheet, hide the gridlines and row and column headings.

- Open a blank workbook, and change the tabs to a pale shade of green, blue, and purple, in that order. Then use the *Mosaic* graphic as a background for the Sheet1 worksheet.

- Continuing in the same workbook, insert the *FourthCoffee* graphic as a watermark on Sheet2. Then on Sheet3, insert the word *Confidential* diagonally across the entire visible part of the worksheet, and make it faint to simulate a watermark.

2.2   Insert and modify rows and columns

Inserting and Deleting

Inserting and deleting rows and columns is a natural part of worksheet development, and in Excel 2007, it couldn't be easier. You can insert an entire row above the selected cell or an entire column to the left of it. If you want to insert a cell instead of a row or column, you are given the option of making room by moving cells down or to the right. Similarly you can delete a selected row or column, or you can delete just the selected cells, optionally specifying how the remaining cells should fill the space.

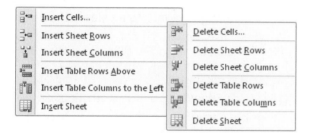

After making an insertion, you can choose whether to format the inserted cell or cells by duplicating the formatting above or below the insertion or to apply no formatting at all.

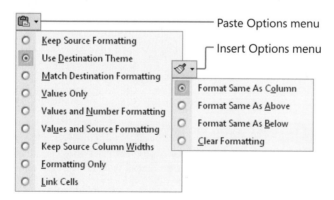

In addition to inserting empty rows, columns, or cells, you can paste cut or copied cell contents directly into newly inserted cells with one command. If you cut a row, this technique inserts a row; if you copy a column, this technique inserts a column; and if you cut just a range of cells, this technique requests instructions for making room before inserting a similarly shaped range.

Tip Always select a single cell when inserting cut or copied cells. If you select a range that is a different size and shape from the one you want to insert, you will get an error message.

➤ To insert rows or columns

1. Select the number of rows you want to insert, starting with the row above which you want the inserted rows to appear.

   Or

   Select the number of columns you want to insert, starting with the column to the left of which you want the inserted columns to appear.

2. On the **Home** tab, in the **Cells** group, click the **Insert** button.

➤ To insert cells

1. Select the number of cells you want to insert.

2. On the **Home** tab, in the **Cells** group, click the **Insert** button.

   Tip If your selection is one cell or a horizontal range, Excel inserts the new cells above the selection. If your selection is a vertical range, Excel inserts the new cells to the left of the selection.

   Or

   On the **Home** tab, in the **Cells** group, click the **Insert** arrow, and click **Insert Cells**. Then in the **Insert** dialog box, indicate the direction in which the existing cells should be moved, and click **OK**.

   Tip You can also insert an entire row or column from the Insert dialog box.

➤ To control the formatting of a new insertion

→ Immediately after inserting the rows, columns, or cells that contain formatting or values, click the **Insert Options** buttons, and click an option in the list.

➤ To paste copied or cut cells into inserted cells

1. Click a cell at the beginning of the range you want to insert.

2. On the **Home** tab, in the **Cells** group, click the **Insert** arrow, and then click **Insert Cut Cells** or **Insert Copied Cells**.

➤ To delete selected rows or columns

→ On the **Home** tab, in the **Cells** group, click the **Delete** button.

➤ To delete selected cells

→ On the **Home** tab, in the **Cells** group, click the **Delete** button.

Or

1. On the **Home** tab, in the **Cells** group, click the **Delete** arrow, and then click **Delete Cells**.

2. In the **Delete** dialog box, indicate the direction in which the existing cells should be moved, and then click **OK**.

   Tip You can also delete an entire row or column from the Delete dialog box.

Formatting

Text formatting can be applied to one cell, an entire row, and entire column, or the entire worksheet. However, some kinds of formatting can detract from the readability of a worksheet if they are applied haphazardly. The kinds of formatting you will probably want to apply to a row or column include the following:

- **Text wrapping.** By default, Excel does not wrap text in a cell. Instead it allows the entry to overflow into the cell to the right if that cell is empty, or hides the part that won't fit if the cell to the right contains its own entry. To make the entire entry visible, you can tell Excel to increase the height of the row to allow the cell entry to wrap to multiple lines.

  Tip Increasing the height of one cell increases the height of the entire row.

- **Alignment.** By default, text is left aligned and numbers are right aligned. You can specify a particular horizontal alignment, and you can specify whether multiline entries should start at the top of their cells and grow down, be centered, or start at the bottom of their cells and go up.

- **Orientation.** By default, entries are horizontal and read from left to right. You can rotate entries for special effect or to allow you to display more information on the screen or a printed page. This capability is particularly useful when you have long column headings above columns of short entries.

	A	B	C	D
		Scenario 1 (Best case)	Scenario 2 (Average case)	Scenario 3 (Worst case)
1	**Budget Drivers**			
2	Probability of shipping on time	98%	95%	90%
3	Number of building permits released within last 6 months	25,000	30,000	35,000
4	Regional economic growth	3.50%	3.20%	2.00%
5	Competitive strength (products, pricing, promotion, placement)	7	8	9
6	Probability of key supplier performance	99%	95%	90%

See Also For information about text formatting, see section 2.3, "Format cells and cell content."

> ➤ **To allow the entries in a selected column to wrap**

→ On the **Home** tab, in the **Alignment** group, click the **Wrap Text** button.

> ➤ **To align the entries of a selected column**

→ On the **Home** tab, in the **Alignment** group, click the **Align Text Left**, **Center**, or **Align Text Right** button to specify horizontal alignment, or click the **Top Align**, **Middle Align**, or **Bottom Align** button to specify vertical alignment.

> ➤ **To change the orientation of a selected row of headings**

→ On the **Home** tab, in the **Alignment** group, click the **Orientation** button, and then click the angle you want in the list.

Tip You can also change all three settings on the Alignment tab of the Format Cells dialog box.

Hiding

If parts of a worksheet contain sensitive information, you can hide the rows or columns containing the data. Anyone who notices that column letters or row numbers are missing can unhide the information unless you protect the workbook. If you don't want to go to the trouble of enforcing protection, you can hide the column and row headings to make the hidden information harder to detect.

Columns D and E are hidden.

	A	B	C	F	G
4	Days with AQI data	Days AQI was Good	Days AQI was Moderate	Maximum AQI value	90th percentile AQI value
5	365	93	150	237	147
6	323	98	163	166	122
7	365	168	152	182	106
8	345	182	116	173	114
9	365	181	123	161	112
10		287	65	152	69
		284			68

See Also For information about protecting a workbook, see section 5.2, "Protect and share workbooks." For information about hiding headings, see section 2.1, "Format worksheets."

➤ **To hide a selected row or column**

→ Right-click the selection, and click **Hide**.

Or

1. On the **Home** tab, in the **Cells** group, click the **Format** button.
2. Below **Visibility**, point to **Hide & Unhide**, and then click the option you want in the list.

➤ **To unhide a row or column**

1. Select the columns or rows flanking the hidden column(s) or row(s).
2. Right-click the selection, and then click **Unhide**.

Or

1. Select the rows or columns on either side of the hidden row(s) or column(s).
2. On the **Home** tab, in the **Cells** group, click the **Format** button.
3. Below **Visibility**, point to **Hide & Unhide**, and then click the option you want in the list.

Tip To find hidden cells in a worksheet, click the Find & Select button, click Go To Special, select Visible Cells Only, and then click OK. Cells adjacent to hidden cells are identified by a white border.

Height and Width

By default, worksheet rows have a standard height of 15 points (1 point equals approximately 1/72 inch), and their height increases and decreases to accommodate the number of lines in their longest entry. You can manually change the height of a row, but it is best to leave it automatic unless you have a good reason to specify a particular height. For example, you might want to specify a skinny row to create a visual break between blocks of data. (You can restore dynamic height adjustment if you need to.)

By default, worksheet columns have a standard width of 8.43 characters, and their width is not dynamic. You are more likely to want to change column width than row height, usually to accommodate long cell entries. You can have Excel adjust a column to fit its longest entry, or you can adjust it manually. In conjunction with text wrapping, adjusting column widths is a key technique for making as much data as possible visible on the screen or page.

	A	B	C	D	E	F
1	ID	Project Name	Owner	Days	Start	End
2	1.0	Marketing Research Tactical Plan	R. Ihrig	70	9-Jul	17-Sep
4	1.1	Scope Definition Phase	R. Ihrig	10	9-Jul	19-Jul
5	1.1.1	Define research objectives	R. Ihrig	3	9-Jul	12-Jul
6	1.1.2	Define research requirements	S. Abbas	7	10-Jul	17-Jul
7	1.1.3	Determine in-house resource or hire vendor	R. Ihrig	2	15-Jul	17-Jul
9	1.2	Vendor Selection Phase	R. Ihrig	19	19-Jul	7-Aug
10	1.2.1	Define vendor selection criteria	R. Ihrig	3	19-Jul	22-Jul
11	1.2.2	Develop vendor selection questionnaire	S. Abbas, T. Wang	2	22-Jul	24-Jul
12	1.2.3	Develop Statement of Work	S. Abbas	4	26-Jul	30-Jul
13	1.2.4	Evaluate proposal	R. Ihrig, S. Abbas	4	2-Aug	6-Aug
14	1.2.5	Select vendor	R. Ihrig	1	6-Aug	7-Aug
16	1.3	Research Phase	Y. Li	47	9-Aug	25-Sep
17	1.3.1	Develop market research information needs questionnaire	Y. Li	2	9-Aug	11-Aug

See Also For information about text wrapping, see "Formatting" earlier in this section.

To adjust rows and columns manually, you can use two methods:

● Drag a selector border. As you drag, a ScreenTip shows you the new dimension of the row or column.

● Adjust the settings in a dialog box.

For the purposes of height and width adjustments, selecting a single cell in a row or column is the same as selecting the entire row or column. You can select multiple rows or columns to change all their heights or widths at the same time.

➤ To change the height of a selected row

→ Drag the bottom border of the row selector up or down.

Or

1. On the **Home** tab, in the **Cells** group, click **Row Height** in the **Format** list.
2. In the **Row Height** dialog box, specify the height you want, and then click **OK**.

➤ To return a selected row to autofitting

→ On the **Home** tab, in the **Cells** group, click **AutoFit Row Height** in the **Format** list.

➤ To change the width of a selected column

→ Drag the right border of the column selector to the left or right.

Or

1. On the **Home** tab, in the **Cells** group, click **Column Width** in the **Format** list.
2. In the **Column Width** dialog box, specify the width you want, and then click **OK**.

➤ To make the width of a column fit its longest entry

→ Double-click the right border of the column heading.

→ On the **Home** tab, in the **Cells** group, click **AutoFit Column Width** in the **Format** list.

> **Tip** You can adjust the width of all the columns in a worksheet at the same time. Click the Select All button to select the entire worksheet, then double-click the border between any two columns. Every column resizes to fit its contents. Empty columns remain unchanged.

Practice Tasks

The practice files for these tasks are located in the *Documents\Microsoft Press\ MCAS\Excel2007\Objective02* folder. If you want, save the task results in the same folder with *My* prepended to the file name.

- Open the *InsertingDeleting* workbook. Delete rows to move the headings to row 1. Delete columns to move the Magazine column to column A. Cut the data from the Mag3 row (B4:F4) and insert it into the Mag2 row (B3:F3). Move the Cost Per Ad data to the left of the Total Cost cells. Finally, insert two cells in positions B8:B9, shifting any existing data down.

- Open the *RowColumnFormatting* workbook, and set the entire worksheet so that all entries wrap in their cells. Right-align the entries in column A, and bottom-align the headings in row 9. Finally, turn off text wrapping in rows 4, 5 and 9, and turn the headings in row 9 sideways at a 45-degree angle.

- Open the *Hiding* workbook. Hide the column containing the Inventory ID and the row containing the data's source notes. Then unhide the row but not the column.

- Open the *HeightWidth* workbook. Set row 4 to a height of 6.00, and then drag row 3 to a height of 45.00. Then simultaneously set the width of columns F, G, and H to 10. Finally, use the quickest method to reset the width of column B to fit its longest entry.

2.3   Format cells and cell content

Built-In Number Formats

Strategy Knowing which number format is appropriate for which type of data is important for efficient worksheet construction. Take the time to explore the formats so that you understand which one to apply when.

By default, all the cells in a new worksheet are assigned the General format. When setting up a worksheet, you assign cells the format that is most appropriate for the type of information you expect them to contain. The format determines not only how the information looks but also how Excel can work with it.

You can assign the format before or after you type an entry in the cell. You can also just start typing and have Excel intuit the format from what you type. If you choose the format from the list or allow Excel to assign it for you, the format is applied with its default settings. For number and currency formats, you can change those settings in limited ways by clicking buttons on the Home tab. For all formats, you can change them in more precise ways in the Format Cells dialog box.

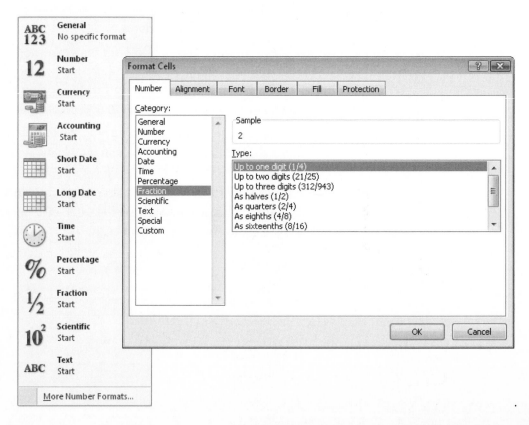

> ➤ **To apply a default data format to a selected cell**

  → On the **Home** tab, in the **Number** group, click a format in the **Number Format** list.

    Tip If you want a number to be treated as text, apply the text format.

> ➤ **To refine a number or currency format**

  → On the **Home** tab, in the **Number** group, click buttons to add a currency symbol, percent sign, or comma; or to increase or decrease the number of decimal places.

  Or

  1. On the **Home** tab, click the **Number** dialog box launcher.
  2. In the **Format Cells** dialog box, with the format selected in the **Category** list, adjust the settings, and then click **OK**.

Custom Formats

Strategy The rules for constructing custom formats are complex. For the exam, you might be asked to modify a format in simple ways, so you should become familiar with the characters used in a format and how to represent different types of data, as well as color.

If none of the number formats is exactly what you want, you can modify an existing format to define your own. Your format then appears in a list of custom formats so that you can reuse it elsewhere in the workbook.

Tip A custom format is saved in the workbook in which it is created and is not available for other workbooks unless you save the workbook containing the custom format as an Excel template.

A number format can include up to four sections that correspond to positive numbers, negative numbers, zero values, and text, separated by semicolons, such as

<POSITIVE>;<NEGATIVE>;<ZERO>;<TEXT>

You don't have to include all the sections in the format, but you must include semicolons if you leave a section blank. For example, the custom formatting

[Blue]#,##0.00_);[Red](#,##0.00);0.00;"Test "@

would result in the following display based on the value entered:

Value entered	Value displayed
123 (<positive>)	123.00 (blue text, right aligned, stepped one space left)
-123 (<negative>)	(123.00) (red text, right aligned)
0 (<zero>)	0.00 (default font color, right aligned)
One (<text>)	Test One (default font color, left aligned)

See Also For more information, refer to the Excel Help topic "Create or delete a custom number format."

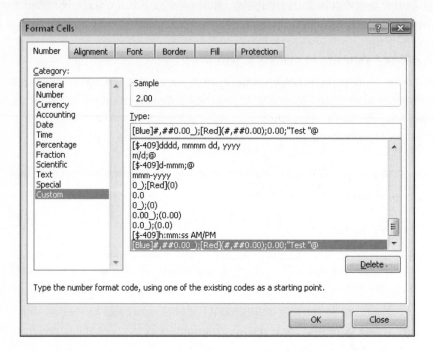

➤ **To create a custom format**

1. On the **Home** tab, click the **Number** dialog box launcher.

2. In the **Format Cells** dialog box, in the **Categories** list, click **Custom**.

3. In the **Type** list, select a format that is close to the one you want, and then in the **Type** box, modify the format to meet your needs.

4. Click **OK** to apply the custom format to the selected cell(s).

➤ **To delete a custom format**

1. Display the Number tab of the **Format Cells** dialog box, and then in the **Categories** list, click **Custom**.

2. In the **Type** list, select the custom format, and click **Delete**.

   Tip You cannot delete a built-in format from the Type list.

3. Click **OK**.

Hyperlinks

Excel worksheets can include hyperlinks that provide a quick way to connect to related information or to perform tasks such as opening an e-mail message window. If you copy and paste a hyperlink into a cell in a worksheet, it is pasted as regular text. Excel recognizes simple URL structures and automatically formats such a structure as a hyperlink when you enter one as the only content in a cell. You can style other cell content as a hyperlink through the Insert Hyperlink dialog box, in which you specify the type of link you want to create, the text you want to display in the worksheet, and the link target. You cannot style only a portion of the content in a cell as a hyperlink.

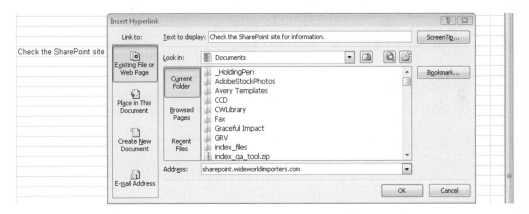

Within the worksheet, the hyperlink appears underlined and in the color specified for hyperlinks by the applied theme. Clicking the cell takes you to the link's target. After you click the hyperlink, it appears in the theme color specified for followed hyperlinks.

Tip To select a cell containing a hyperlink for formatting, point to the cell and hold down the mouse button until the cell is surrounded by the active cell border.

➤ **To insert a hyperlink**

1. On the **Insert** tab, in the **Links** group, click the **Hyperlink** button.

2. In the **Insert Hyperlink** dialog box, in the **Link to** list, click the type of link you want to create.

3. In the **Look in** area, click the type of target, and then either click an option in the list or enter a URL in the **Address** box.

4. If you want the cell to show an entry that represents the link rather than the link itself, type the entry in the **Text to display** box.

5. Click **OK**.

➤ **To edit a hyperlink**

1. Select the cell containing the link, and then on the **Insert** tab, in the **Links** group, click the **Hyperlink** button.

2. In the **Edit Hyperlink** dialog box, make your changes, and then click **OK**.

➤ **To remove a hyperlink**

1. Select the cell containing the link.

2. To delete the hyperlink completely, press the **Delete** key.

Or

To remove the hyperlink formatting, display the **Edit Hyperlink** dialog box, click **Remove Link**, and then click **OK**.

Merged Cells

Worksheets that involve data at multiple hierarchical levels often use horizontal and vertical merged cells to clearly delineate relationships. With Excel, you have the following three merge options:

● **Merge & Center.** Merges the cells across the selected rows and columns, and centers the data from the first selected cell in the merged cell.

● **Merge Across.** Creates a separate merged cell for each row in the selection area, and maintains default alignment for the data type of the first cell of each row of the merged cells.

● **Merge Cells.** Merges the cells across the selected rows and columns, and maintains default alignment for the data type of the first cell of the merged cells.

In the case of Merge & Center and Merge Cells, data in selected cells other than the first is deleted. In the case of Merge Across, data in selected cells other than the first cell of each row is deleted.

Merged horizontal cells   Merged vertical cells

	Sunday		Monday		Tuesday		Wednesday		Thursday		Friday		Saturday	
	5/29/2005		5/30/2005		5/31/2005		6/1/2005		6/2/2005		6/3/2005		6/4/2005	
Time In		Total		Total		Total		Total		Total		Total		Total	
Time Out		0.00		0.00		0.00		0.00		0.00		0.00		0.00	
Meal Break															
Time In		Total		Total		Total		Total		Total		Total		Total	Total Hours Scheduled
Time Out		0.00		0.00		0.00		0.00		0.00		0.00		0.00	
Total	0.00		0.00		0.00		0.00		0.00		0.00		0.00		0.00

➤ To merge selected cells

→ On the **Home** tab, in the **Alignment** group, click the **Merge & Center** button to center and bottom-align the entry from the first cell.

→ On the **Home** tab, in the **Alignment** group, click **Merge Across** in the **Merge & Center** list to create a separate merged cell on each selected row, maintaining the horizontal alignment of the data type in the first cell of each row.

→ On the **Home** tab, in the **Alignment** group, click **Merge Cells** in the **Merge & Center** list to merge the entire selection, maintaining the horizontal alignment of the data type in the first cell.

➤ To split a selected merged cell

→ On the **Home** tab, in the **Alignment** group, click the **Merge & Center** button.

→ On the **Home** tab, in the **Alignment** group, click **Unmerge Cells** in the **Merge & Center** list.

Formatting

By default, the font used for text in a new Excel worksheet is Calibri, but you can use the same techniques you would use with Microsoft Office Word 2007 to change the font and the following font attributes:

- Size
- Style
- Color
- Underline

You can change several attributes at once in the Format Cells dialog box.

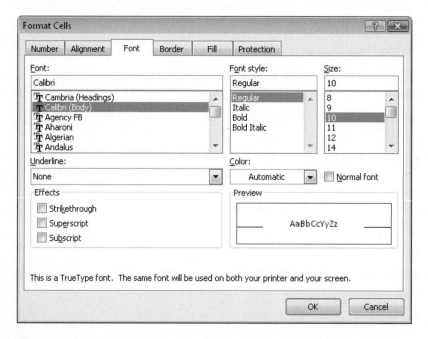

Tip By default, row height is dynamic and grows to fit the size of the text in its cells. If you manually change the height of a row, you might have to adjust it if you change the font size of cells in that row. See section 2.2, "Insert and modify rows and columns."

In addition, you can format cells by using borders and shading to make them stand out. You can add predefined borders or custom borders of various styles, colors, and thicknesses to a single cells or multiple cells. You can apply solid colors, gradients, and patterns to the background of one or more cells as creative ways of delineating structure and drawing attention to key information.

See Also For information about aligning and wrapping cell entries, see section 2.2, "Insert and modify rows and columns."

➤ **To format all the text in a selected cell**

→ On the **Home** tab, in the **Font** group, click buttons to make the text in the cell look the way you want it.

➤ **To format some of the text in a cell**

1. In the formula bar or in the cell, select the text you want to format.

2. On the **Home** tab, click buttons in the **Font** group.

   Or

   Click buttons on the **Mini toolbar** that appears.

➤ **To change the color of a selected cell**

→ On the **Home** tab, in the **Font** group, click the **Fill Color** button to apply the active color.

▫ In the **Font** group, click the **Fill Color** arrow, and then click a theme color or a standard color in the palette.

   Tip Clicking More Colors at the bottom of the palette displays the Colors dialog box, where you have a wider range of choices (more than 16 million).

➤ **To add a border to a selected cell**

→ On the **Home** tab, in the **Font** group, click the **Border** button to apply the active border.

→ In the **Font** group, click the **Border** arrow, and then click the border you want.

   Tip Clicking More Borders at the bottom of the list displays the Border tab of the Format Cells dialog box, where you can change the style and color of a border or define a custom border.

➤ **To remove the border from a selected cell**

→ On the **Home** tab, in the **Font** group, click **No Borders** in the **Border** list.

See Also For information about conditional formatting, see section 4.3, "Apply conditional formatting."

Cell Styles

You don't have to apply cell formats one at a time. You can quickly apply several formats at once by clicking a style in the Cell Styles gallery. Some of the categories of styles in this gallery are static, while others are dynamic and change according to the theme applied to the worksheet.

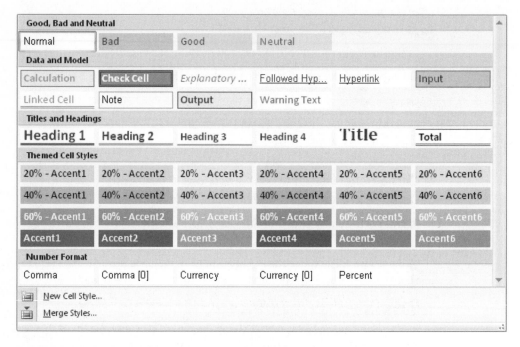

See Also For information about themes, see section 2.1, "Format worksheets."

If you need a style that is not already defined, you can manually format a cell and then save the combination of formatting as a cell style that you can easily apply elsewhere.

> ➤ **To apply a style to a selected cell**

1. On the **Home** tab, in the **Styles** group, click **Cell Styles**.

2. In the **Cell Styles** gallery, click the style you want.

> ➤ **To create a cell style**

1. Select a cell that has the combination of formatting you want to save as a style.

2. Display the **Cell Styles** gallery, and then click **New Cell Style**.

3. In the **Style** dialog box, name the style, clear the check boxes of any elements you don't want to include in the style, and then click **OK**.

   Tip You can click Format to display the Format Cells dialog box, where you can adjust the formatting that will be saved.

Practice Tasks

The practice files for these tasks are located in the *Documents\Microsoft Press\ MCAS\Excel2007\Objective02* folder. If you want, save the task results in the same folder with *My* prepended to the file name.

- Open the *FormatCells* workbook, and select cell K10. Format the cell to display its contents in either of the currency formats (Currency or Accounting) with no decimal places. Then apply the same formatting to cells K11:K23.

- In the *FormatCells* workbook, apply custom number formatting to the TOTAL value in cell K23 (2,643) that will cause it to be displayed in green if it is a positive number and red if it is a negative number. Do not add formatting for zero or text values. Place a value of 3,000 into the Advances field (K22) to verify the formatting of negative numbers.

- In the *FormatCells* workbook, change the font weight of the labels in A4:A6, D4:D5, and J4:J5 to bold. Select cells A9:K19 and apply one of the 20% - Accent cell styles. Select cells A9:K9 and K10:K19 and apply a background color that is two shades darker than the current one. Lastly, place a thick box border around the merged cells in row 2.

- Open the *Hyperlink* workbook. In cell A12 of the Employees worksheet, enter a hyperlink to the Web site located at *www.otsi.com*. Instead of the URL, display *Please visit our Web site* in the cell.

- In the *Hyperlink* workbook, merge cells A12:C13 so that the hyperlink is centered across the bottom of the three columns.

2.4 Format data as a table

Tables

A table is a discrete block of data in an Excel worksheet. (Tables resemble the lists available in earlier versions of Excel.) When you create a table, Excel associates a name with the range you specify, and you can then work with the table independently of other data in the worksheet. The range can contain data, or you can enter the data after creating the table. You enter and edit data in the usual ways. You can change the defined range, as well as insert or delete rows or columns, without disturbing the other cells in the worksheet.

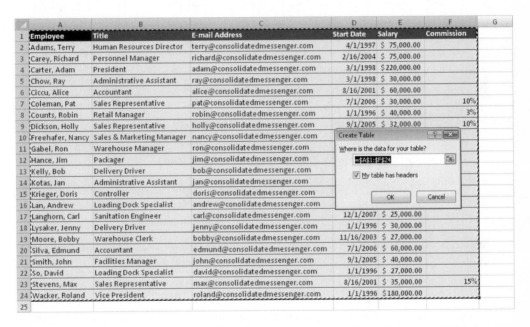

Excel tables have built-in sort and filter functionality. By clicking the arrow that appears at the right end of each column header, you can quickly display the content you want in the order you want it.

➤ To convert a range of cells to a table without applying a style

1. Select the range of cells you want to define as a table. (These can either be empty or can contain data.)

2. On the **Insert** tab in the **Tables** group, click the **Table** button.

3. In the **Create Table** dialog box, ensure that the correct range is selected. If the first row of the selected range contains column headers, select the **My table has headers** check box.

4. Click **OK**.

➤ To convert a range of cells to a table and apply a style

1. Select the range of cells you want to convert to a table.

2. On the **Home** tab, in the **Styles** group, click **Format as Table**, and then click the table style you want.

3. In the **Format As Table** dialog box, verify the cell range and whether it includes headers, and then click **OK**.

   See also For more information about table styles, see the next topic.

➤ To change the range of a table

→ In the lower-right corner of the table, drag the resize handle until the dotted rectangle encloses the new range.

   Or

1. Click anywhere in the table, and then on the **Design** tab, in the **Properties** group, click the **Resize Table** button.

2. In the **Resize Table** dialog box, adjust the range in the **Select the new data range for your table** box, and then click **OK**.

   Tip You can click the Collapse button to collapse the dialog box so that you can select the new range and then click the button again to restore the dialog box.

➤ To insert a table column

→ Click one or more cells in the column to the left of which you want to make the insertion. Then on the **Home** tab, in the **Cells** group, click the **Insert** button.

→ Click a cell in the column to the left of which you want to insert another. Then in the **Cells** group, click the **Insert** button and in the list, click **Insert Table Columns to the Left**.

> **To insert multiple table columns**

→ Select the same number of columns as you want to insert, in the location you want to insert them. Then in the **Cells** group, click **Insert Sheet Columns** in the **Insert** list.

> **To insert a table row**

→ Click two or more cells in the row above which you want to insert another. Then on the **Home** tab, in the **Cells** group, click the **Insert** button.

→ Click a cell in the row above which you want to insert another. Then in the **Cells** group, click **Insert Table Rows Above** in the **Insert** list.

> **To insert multiple table columns**

→ Select the same number of rows as you want to insert, in the location you want to insert them. Then in the **Cells** group, click **Insert Sheet Rows** in the **Insert** list.

> **To add rows or columns after the existing table rows or columns**

→ Click a cell in the last row or the last column of the table. On the **Home** tab, in the **Cells** group, click the **Insert** arrow and then click **Insert Table Rows Below** or **Insert Table Columns to the Right** in the **Insert** list. (These choices are available only when the selection is in the last row or column.)

Tip Typing an entry in any cell in the row below or the column to the right of a table automatically expands the table to include that row or column.

> **To delete a table row or table column**

1. Click a cell in the row or column you want to delete.
2. On the **Home** tab, in the **Cells** group, click **Delete Table Rows** or **Delete Table Columns** in the **Delete** list.

> **To convert a table into a data range**

1. Click any cell in the table, and then on the **Design** tab, in the **Tools** group, click the **Convert to Range** button.
2. Confirm that you want to convert the table by clicking **Yes**.

Tip When you convert a table to a range, the cells retain the formatting applied to the table.

Table Styles

Formatting a worksheet to visually support its data is often a process of trial and error. Formatting a table is much easier. A default combination of formatting called a *table style* is applied to a table when you create it. The style includes a variety of borders, shading, text colors, and other attributes to give the table a professional look. If that style doesn't suit the data, you can change it at any time by choosing a new one from the Table Styles gallery.

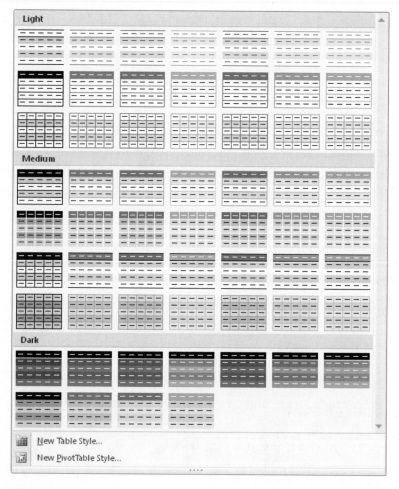

Each style can be varied by selecting options that apply different formatting to the first or last row of the table, the first or last column, and every other row or column.

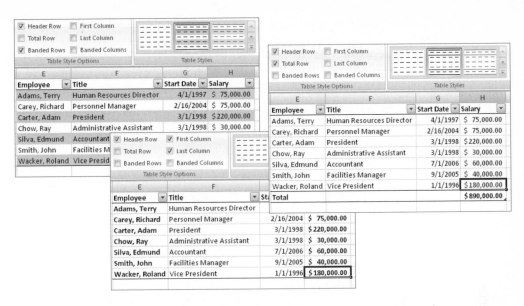

If, even with all these possible variations, none of the predefined table styles meets your needs, you can create your own styles for tables in much the same way that you create styles for regular text.

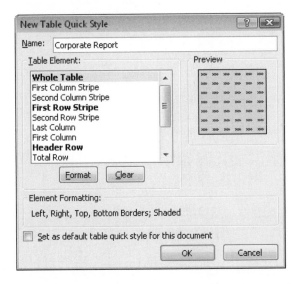

➤ **To apply a table style**

1. On the **Design** tab, in the **Table Styles** group, click the **More** button.

2. In the **Table Styles** gallery, click the style you want.

➤ **To make table header rows stand out**

→ On the **Design** tab, in the **Table Style Options** group, select the **Header Row** check box.

➤ **To make the first or last column of a table stand out**

→ On the **Design** tab, in the **Table Style Options** group, select the **First Column** or **Last Column** check box.

➤ **To shade table rows or columns**

→ On the **Design** tab, in the **Table Style Options** group, select the **Banded Rows** or **Banded Columns** check box.

Total Row

If a table contains numeric data, you can add a Total row to the end of the table. By default, Excel inserts a Sum function to total the values in the rightmost column of the table. You can easily change this function or insert a summary function for any other numeric column. The following functions are available for selection in a list:

● Sum and Average

● Count and Count Numbers

● Max and Min

● StdDev and Var

	Days with AQI d	Days AQI was G	Days AQI was M	Maximum AQI	90th percentile	Median AQI va
36	335	281	48	129	59	34
37	342	302	35	124	54	34
38	335	281	50	111	58	32
39	365	337	26	116	46	32
40	340	330	10	83	41	30
41	365	361	4	64	38	30
42	365	362	3	61	38	29
43	Total		2430			
44				None		
45				Average		
46				Count		
				Count Numbers		
47				Max		
				Min		
48				Sum		
				StdDev		
49				Var		
50				More Functions...		

See Also You can insert additional functions by clicking More Functions to display the Insert Function dialog box. For information about using this dialog box, see section 3.3, "Summarize data by using subtotals."

➤ **To add a Total row to a table**

→ On the **Design** tab, in the **Table Style Options** group, select the **Total Row** check box.

➤ **To change the summary function in a Total row**

→ Click the cell, click its arrow, and then click a summary function in the list.

Practice Tasks

The practice files for these tasks are located in the *Documents\Microsoft Press\ MCAS\Excel2007\Objective02* folder. If you want, save the task results in the same folder with *My* prepended to the file name.

● Open the *Table* workbook, and convert cells A1:D30 into a table formatted with the default table style. Add a table row above row 9, using the correct Insert Options menu option to incorporate the row into the table formatting. Then enter *Garden Hardware Mfg., Sprinkler hose 100', 1 ea., $25.35.*

● In the *Table* workbook, convert the existing table in cells A1:D31 to an ordinary data range.

● Open the *TableStyle* workbook, and change the style of the table in cells B3:D30 to Table Style Medium 10. Then turn off banded rows, and shade the first and last columns in the table.

● In the *TableStyle* workbook, add a Total row that computes the number of items in the Product column and the average price from the Unit Price column.

Objective Review

Before finishing this chapter, ensure that you have mastered the following skills:

2.1 Format worksheets.

2.2 Insert and modify rows and columns.

2.3 Format cells and cell content.

2.4 Format data as a table.

3 Creating and Modifying Formulas

The skills tested in this section of the Microsoft Office Specialist exam for Microsoft Office Excel 2007 relate to working with formulas. Specifically, the following objectives are associated with this set of skills:

3.1 Reference data in formulas.

3.2 Summarize data by using a formula.

3.3 Summarize data by using subtotals.

3.4 Conditionally summarize data by using a formula.

3.5 Look up data by using a formula.

3.6 Use conditional logic in a formula.

3.7 Format or modify text by using formulas.

3.8 Display and print formulas.

Formulas are what make Excel a truly powerful application. Excel 2007 includes an amazing array of built-in functions with which you can perform statistical analysis, sophisticated financial calculations, and conditional calculations. You can also use functions to look up data, manipulate text, and work with date and time calculations.

This chapter guides you in studying the basics of formulas and how to reference cells within formulas, use formulas to summarize your data, create conditional formulas, create formulas that format cells based on a calculation, and display and print formulas so you can more easily work with them.

 Important Before you can use the practice files in this chapter, you need to install them from the book's companion CD to their default location. See "Using the Companion CD" at the beginning of this book for more information.

Tip Graphics and operating system–related instructions in this book reflect the Windows Vista user interface. If your computer is running Windows XP and you experience trouble following the instructions as written, refer to the sidebar "If You Are Running Windows XP" in "Working in the Microsoft Office Fluent User Interface" at the beginning of this book.

3.1   Reference data in formulas

An Excel worksheet without a calculation is merely electronic accounting paper. Most worksheets contain at least simple calculations, such as adding the values of two cells together. Other Excel worksheets contain mathematic or date-driven formulas so daunting that it might seem as though only a computer scientist or mathematician could understand them. While it is helpful to have some knowledge of the types of function-driven operations you are performing, Excel greatly simplifies the process of creating formulas by providing specific guidelines as you create any formula.

Cell References

Formulas in an Excel worksheet most often involve functions performed on the values contained in one or more other cells on the worksheet (or on another worksheet). A reference that you make in a formula to the contents of a worksheet cell is either a relative reference, an absolute reference, or a mixed reference. It is important to understand the difference and know which to use when creating a formula.

A relative reference to a cell takes the form *A1*. When you copy or fill a formula from the original cell to other cells, a relative reference will change to indicate the cell having the same relationship to the formula cell that A1 did to the original formula cell.

An absolute reference takes the form *A1*; the dollar sign indicates an absolute reference to column A and an absolute reference to row 1. When you copy or fill a formula from the original cell to other cells, an absolute reference will not change—regardless of the relationship to the referenced cell, the reference will stay the same.

A mixed reference refers absolutely to either the column or row and relatively to the other. The mixed reference *A$1* will always refer to row 1, and *$A1* will always refer to column A.

	A	B	C	D	E	F
1		Customer	Wingtip Toys			
2		Discount	20%			
3						
4	Quantity	Price Each	Subtotal	Discount	Total	
5	100	$ 5.00	$ 500.00	$ 100.00	$ 400.00	
6	200	$ 10.00	$ 2,000.00	$ 400.00	$ 1,600.00	
7	300	$ 15.00	$ 4,500.00	$ 900.00	$ 3,600.00	
8	400	$ 20				
9	500	$ 25				
10						

Relative reference   Absolute reference

	A	B	C	D	E
1		Customer	Wingtip Toys		
2		Discount	0.2		
3					
4		Quantity	Price Each	Subtotal	Discount	Total
5	100	5	=A5*B5	=C5*C2	=C5-D5
6	200	10	=A6*D6	=C6*C2	=C6-D6
7	300	15	=A7*B7	=C7*C2	=C7-D7
8	400	20	=A8*B8	=C8*C2	=C8-D8
9	500	25	=A9*B9	=C9*C2	=C9-D9
10					

➤ **To relatively reference the contents of a cell**

→ Enter the column letter followed by the row number, like this:

A1

➤ **To absolutely reference the contents of a cell**

→ Precede the column letter and row number by dollar signs, like this:

A1

➤ **To absolutely reference a column or row**

→ Precede the column letter or row number by a dollar sign.

Cell Ranges

You can refer to the content of a range of adjacent cells. For example, you might use a formula to return the maximum value of all the cells in a row. When you are referencing a range of cells in a formula, the cell references can be relative, absolute, or mixed.

➤ **To reference the contents of a range of cells**

→ Enter the upper-left cell of the range and the lower-right cell of the range, separated by a colon, like this:

A1:B3

Worksheet References

You can reference cells in other worksheets of your workbook. For example, you might prepare a Summary worksheet that displays results based on data tracked on other worksheets. References to cells on other worksheets can be relative, absolute, or mixed.

Tip You can reference a worksheet by whatever name appears on the worksheet tab.

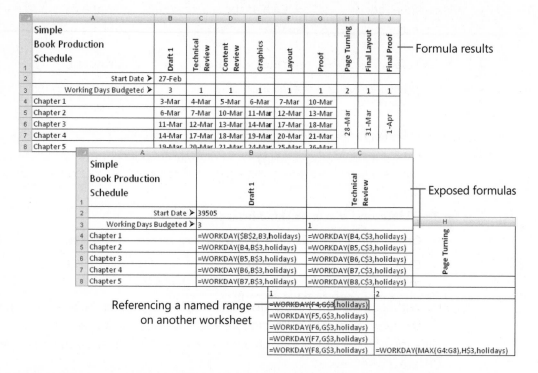

Formula results

Exposed formulas

Referencing a named range on another worksheet

> ## To reference a cell on a different worksheet in the same workbook

→ Enter the worksheet name and the cell reference, separated by an exclamation point, like this:

Data!C2

Or

1. Click the worksheet tab of the worksheet containing the cell you want to reference.

2. Click the cell or select the range of cells you want to reference, and then press **Enter** to enter the cell reference into the formula and return to the original worksheet.

Workbook References

You can reference cells in other workbooks. For example, you might prepare a report that collates data from workbooks submitted by multiple regional managers.

When referencing a workbook located in a folder other than the one your active workbook is in, enter the path to the file along with the file name. If the path includes a non-alphabetical character (such as the backslash in "C:\") in the file name, enclose the path in single quotation marks

➤ To reference a cell in another workbook in the same folder

→ Enter the workbook name in square brackets followed by the worksheet name and cell reference, separated by an exclamation point, like this:

[Sales.xlsx]Data!C2

→ Enter the path to the workbook and the workbook name in square brackets followed by the worksheet name and cell reference, separated by an exclamation point, like this:

'[C:\Example.xlsx]Sheet1'!A1.

Or

1. Open the workbook that contains the cell you want to reference, and then switch to the workbook you want to create the formula in.

2. With the insertion point active where you want to insert the reference, switch to the second workbook, click the worksheet containing the cell you want to reference, click the cell or select the range you want to reference, and then press **Enter**.

Named Ranges

To simplify the process of creating formulas that refer to a specific range of data, and to make your formulas easier to read and create, you can refer to a cell or range of cells by a name that you define. For example, you might name a cell containing an interest rate *Interest*, or a range of cells containing non-work days *Holidays*. In a formula, you refer to a named range by name. Thus you might end up with a formula like this:

=WORKDAY(StartDate,DaysOfWork,Holidays)

A formula using named ranges is simpler to understand than its standard equivalent, which could look like this:

=WORKDAY(B2,B$3,Data!B2:B16)

Each range name has a scope, which is the context in which the name is recognized. The scope can be the entire workbook, or it can be specific to a worksheet. This allows you to use the same name on multiple worksheets. You can include a comment with each name to provide more information about the range. (The comment is visible only in the Name Manager.)

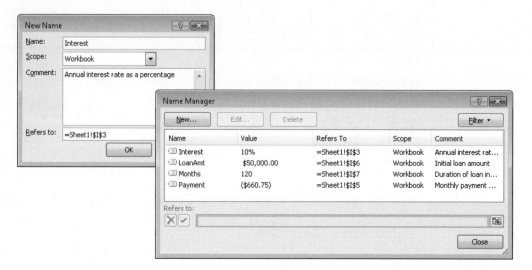

After defining a named range, you can change the range name or the cells included in the named range. You can delete a range name definition from the Name Manager. Note that deleting a cell from a worksheet does not delete any associated range name. Invalid range names are indicated in the Name Manager by #REF! in the Value column.

▶ **To define a selected cell or range of cells as a named range**

→ In the **Name Box** at the right end of the **Formula Bar**, type the range name, and then press **Enter**.

Or

1. On the **Formulas** tab, in the **Defined Names** group, click the **Define Name** button.

2. In the **New Name** dialog box, enter the range name in the **Name** box.

   Tip The New Name dialog box does not indicate any named ranges the selected cell or cells are already part of.

3. In the **Scope** list, click **Workbook** to define the named range for the entire work-book, or click a specific worksheet name.

4. In the **Comment** box, enter any notes you want to make for your own reference.

5. Verify that the cell or range of cells in the **Refers to** box is correct, and then click **OK**.

Tip If a cell is part of multiple named ranges, only the first name is shown in the Name Box. The Name Box displays the name of a multiple-cell named range only when all cells in the range are selected.

➤ To change the name of, or redefine the cells in, a named range

1. On the **Formulas** tab, in the **Defined Names** group, click the **Name Manager** button.

2. In the **Name Manager** window, click the named range you want to change, and then click **Edit**.

3. In the **Edit Name** dialog box, change the range name, the cell or cells the range refers to, or the comment. Then click **OK**.

➤ To delete a named range definition

1. On the **Formulas** tab, in the **Defined Names** group, click the **Name Manager** button.

2. In the **Name Manager** window, click the named range you want to delete, and click **Delete**. Then click **OK** to confirm the deletion.

Practice Tasks

The practice files for these tasks are located in the *Documents\Microsoft Press\ MCAS\Excel2007\Objective03* folder. If you want, save the task results in the same folder with *My* prepended to the file name.

● Open the *MultiplicationTable* workbook. On the Practice worksheet, create a formula in cells B2:T20 to complete the multiplication table of the numbers 1 through 20. (Challenge: Create the table in six or fewer steps.) Compare the formulas in your multiplication table to those on the Results worksheet.

● In the *MultiplicationTable* workbook, define cells A1:T1 as a range named *FirstRow,* and cells A1:A20 as a range named *ColumnA*. Then change the formulas in cells B2:T20 to reference the named ranges.

● Open the *SalesBySeason* workbook. On the Summary worksheet, display the total sales for each period in cells B2, B3, B4, and B5 by referencing the corresponding worksheets.

3.2   Summarize data by using a formula

Formulas in Excel can be made up of values that you enter, cell references, names, mathematical operators, and functions. A function can be thought of as a service provided by Excel to do a specific task. That task might be to perform some math operation, it could be to make a decision based on information you give it, or it could be to perform an action on some text. A function is always indicated by the function name followed by a set of parentheses. For most functions, arguments inside the parentheses either tell the function what to do or indicate the values that the function is to work with. An argument can be a value that you type, a cell reference, a range reference, a name, or even another function. The number and type of arguments vary depending on which function you're using. It is important to understand the syntax of common functions and be able to correctly enter the function arguments. Fortunately, you don't have to memorize anything—Excel 2007 does an excellent job of walking you through the process of using a function within your formulas. You can type a function's syntax yourself if you wish, but it's almost always easier to let Excel guide you through the process.

Probably the most common formula used in Excel is one that totals the values in a set of cells. Rather than individually adding the values of all the cells you want to total, you can use the SUM function to perform this common task. The following table describes other functions that allow you to summarize information from sets of cells:

Function	Purpose	Arguments
SUM()	Total a set of numbers	*number1,number2,…,number255*
COUNT()	Count the number of cells that have numbers	*value1,value2,…,value255*
COUNTA()	Count the number of cells that are not empty	*value1,value2,…,value255*
AVERAGE()	Average a set of numbers	*number1,number2,…,number255*
MIN()	Find the minimum value in a set of numbers	*number1,number2,…,number255*
MAX()	Find the maximum value in a set of numbers	*number1,number2,…,number255*

Each of these functions takes up to 255 arguments; each argument can be a range or named reference and can refer to thousands of values.

In the preceding table, any argument specified as a number can be a number that is entered directly, a text representation of a number (a number inside quotation marks), a cell reference, a range reference, or a named reference. Any cells that contain text that can't be translated to a number, that are empty, or that have an error are simply ignored by the function.

In the preceding table, any argument specified as a value can be any type of value. In the case of COUNT, the function will simply ignore anything that it can't interpret as a number. In the case of COUNTA, the function will count everything that isn't empty.

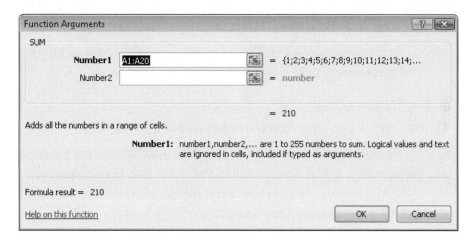

➤ To sum values in a cell range

1. Select the cell immediately below or to the right of the values you want to sum.

2. On the **Home** tab, in the **Editing** group, click the **AutoSum** button.

   Or

   On the **Formulas** tab, in the **Function Library** group, click the **AutoSum** button.

3. Verify that the cell range displayed in the formula is correct, and then press **Enter**.

   Or

1. Select the cell in which you want to place the total.

2. On the **Formulas** tab, in the **Function Library** group, click the **Math & Trig** button, and then in the list, click **SUM**.

3. In the **Function Arguments** box, enter the cell range you want to sum, and then click **OK**.

➤ **To count cells containing values**

1. Select the cell immediately below or to the right of the values you want to total.

2. On the **Formulas** tab, in the **Function Library** group, click the **AutoSum** arrow, and then in the list, click **Count Numbers**.

3. Verify that the cell range displayed in the formula is correct, and then press **Enter**.

Or

1. Select the cell in which you want to place the count.

2. On the **Formulas** tab, in the **Function Library** group, click the **More Functions** button, point to **Statistical**, and then in the list, click **COUNT**.

3. In the **Function Arguments** box, enter the cell range within which you want to count non-empty cells, and then click **OK**.

➤ **To count empty cells**

1. Select the cell in which you want to place the count.

2. On the **Formulas** tab, in the **Function Library** group, click the **More Functions** button, point to **Statistical**, and then in the list, click **COUNTA**.

3. In the **Function Arguments** box, enter the cell range within which you want to count empty cells, and then click **OK**.

➤ **To average values in a data range**

1. Select the cell immediately below or to the right of the values you want to average.

2. On the **Formulas** tab, in the **Function Library** group, click the **AutoSum** arrow, and then in the list, click **Average**.

3. Verify that the cell range displayed in the formula is correct, and then press **Enter**.

Or

1. Select the cell in which you want to place the average.

2. On the **Formulas** tab, in the **Function Library** group, click the **More Functions** button, point to **Statistical**, and then in the list, click **AVERAGE**.

3. In the **Function Arguments** box, enter the cell range that you want to average, and then click **OK**.

➤ **To return the lowest value in a data range**

1. Select the cell immediately below or to the right of the values you want to evaluate.

2. On the **Formulas** tab, in the **Function Library** group, click the **AutoSum** arrow, and then in the list, click **Min**.

3. Verify that the cell range displayed in the formula is correct, and then press **Enter**.

   Or

1. Select the cell in which you want to place the minimum value.

2. On the **Formulas** tab, in the **Function Library** group, click the **More Functions** button, point to **Statistical**, and then in the list, click **MIN**.

3. In the **Function Arguments** box, enter the cell range you want to evaluate, and then click **OK**.

➤ **To return the highest value in a data range**

1. Select the cell immediately below or to the right of the values you want to evaluate.

2. On the **Formulas** tab, in the **Function Library** group, click the **AutoSum** arrow, and then in the list, click **Max**.

3. Verify that the cell range displayed in the formula is correct, and then press **Enter**.

   Or

1. Select the cell in which you want to place the maximum value.

2. On the **Formulas** tab, in the **Function Library** group, click the **More Functions** button, point to **Statistical**, and then in the list, click **MAX**.

3. In the **Function Arguments** box, enter the cell range you want to evaluate, and then click **OK**.

Practice Tasks

The practice file for these tasks is located in the *Documents\Microsoft Press\MCAS\ Excel2007\Objective03* folder. If you want, save the task results in the same folder with *My* prepended to the file name.

● Open the *SummaryFormula* workbook, and in cell B18, create a formula that returns the number of non-empty cells in the Period range. Then in cell B19, create a formula that returns the number of empty cells in the same range.

● In the *SummaryFormula* workbook, in cell C18, create a formula that returns the average value in the Sales range. Then in cell D5, create a formula that returns the lowest Sales value for the Fall period.

3.3   Summarize data by using subtotals

Another mechanism you can use to quickly summarize data is the subtotal feature, with which you can efficiently perform operations on subsets of data within a data range. The data range must include column headers, because Excel uses these to identify data subsets. You can use the SUM, COUNT, AVERAGE, MAX, MIN, PRODUCT, COUNT NUMBERS, STDDEV, STDDEVP, VAR, or VARP function to summarize the data of each subset of cells.

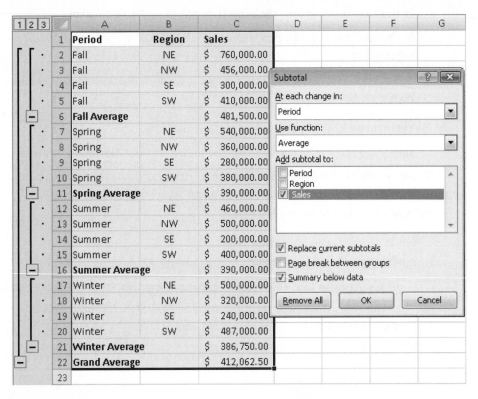

After creating subtotals, you can use the controls that appear in the bar to the left of the row headings to collapse and expand subsets of data.

➤ **To create subtotals within a data range**

1. Select the data range and sort it by the column containing the category of data you want to base the subset on.

2. On the **Data** tab, in the **Outline** group, click the **Subtotal** button.

3. In the **Subtotal** dialog box, verify that the correct subtotal category is shown in the **At each change in** list.

4. In the **Use function** list, click the summary function you want to use.

5. In the **Add subtotal to** box, select the check box of each column you want to add subtotals to.

6. Select the check boxes to replace current subtotals, present each data subset on its own page, or summarize the subtotals, and then click **OK**.

Practice Tasks

The practice file for these tasks is located in the *Documents\Microsoft Press\MCAS\ Excel2007\Objective03* folder. If you want, save the task results in the same folder with *My* prepended to the file name.

● Open the *Sales* workbook, and create subtotals of sales amounts first by Period and then by Region.

│ In the *Sales* workbook, find the average sales by Period and then by Region.

│ In the *Sales* workbook, find the maximum and minimum sales by Period and then by Region.

3.4 Conditionally summarize data by using a formula

Excel provides a set of functions that allow you to summarize data based whether certain criteria are met. The cells that are examined against the criteria don't have to be the same cells that are summarized. For example, in a budget worksheet, you could create a formula that counts all expenditures that are over a certain dollar amount, or you could total all expenditures in the Entertainment category that are over $75.

Use the AVERAGEIF, COUNTIF, and SUMIF conditional functions to evaluate one condition, or the AVERAGEIFS, COUNTIFS, and SUMIFS conditional functions to evaluate multiple conditions (up to 127). The following table summarizes the uses of these functions.

Function	Purpose	Arguments
AVERAGEIF()	Average values that meet one condition	*range,criteria,average_range*
COUNTIF()	Count cells that meet one condition	*range,criteria*
SUMIF()	Sum values that meet one condition	*range,criteria,sum_range*
AVERAGEIFS()	Average values that meet multiple criteria	*average_range,criteria_range1,criteria1, criteria_range2,criteria2,...*
COUNTIFS()	Count cells that meet multiple criteria	*criteria_range1,criteria1,criteria_range2, criteria2,criteria_range3,...*
SUMIFS()	Sum values that meet multiple criteria	*sum_range,criteria_range1,criteria1, criteria_range2,criteria2,...*

In the preceding table, the *range* arguments are references to the set of cells that will be evaluated against the criteria. A *criteria* argument can be a number, an expression enclosed in quotation marks, or text enclosed in quotation marks. The *average_range* and *sum_range* arguments are references to the set of cells whose values will be averaged or summed. In the single criteria versions, if the *average_range* or *sum_range* argument is omitted, the function uses the values from the range. The *average_range* and *sum_range* arguments are not optional for the multi-criteria functions.

Strategy Take the time to experiment with conditional functions using both cell ranges and named ranges.

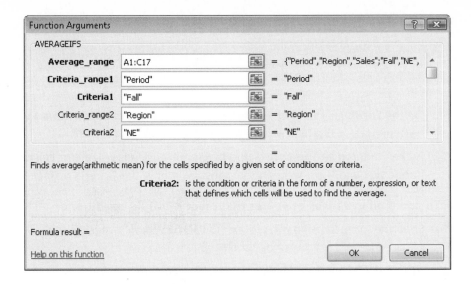

➤ To sum values that meet a specific condition

→ Enter the formula using the syntax =SUMIF(*range,criteria*) like this:

=SUMIF(Amount,">100")

Or

1. On the **Formulas** tab, in the **Function Library** group, click the **Math & Trig** button, and then in the list, click **SUMIF**.

2. In the **Function Arguments** dialog box, enter the range name or cell range in the **Range** box and the condition that must be met in the **Criteria** box. Then click **OK**.

➤ To sum values that meet multiple conditions

→ Enter the formula using the syntax =SUMIFS(*sum_range,criteria_range1,criteria1, criteria_range2,criteria2*) like this:

=SUMIFS(A1:C21,Region,"North",Sales,">100000")

Or

1. On the **Formulas** tab, in the **Function Library** group, click the **Math & Trig** button, and then in the list, click **SUMIFS**.

2. In the **Function Arguments** dialog box, enter the range name or cell range containing the values you want to sum in the **Sum_range** box.

3. Enter the range name or cell range for the first conditional evaluation in the **Criteria_range1** box, and the condition that must be met in the **Criteria1** box.

4. Repeat step 3 for each additional range/condition you want to evaluate. Then click **OK**.

➤ **To count all instances of a specific value**

→ Enter the formula using the syntax =COUNTIF(*range,criteria*) like this:

=COUNTIF(C2:C22,">300")

Or

1. On the **Formulas** tab, in the **Function Library** group, click the **More Functions** button, point to **Statistical**, and then in the list, click **COUNTIF**.

2. In the **Function Arguments** dialog box, enter the range name or cell range in the **Range** box and the condition that must be met in the **Criteria** box. Then click **OK**.

➤ **To count all instances of values that meet multiple conditions**

→ Enter the formula using the syntax =COUNTIFS(*count_range,criteria_range1,criteria1,criteria_range2,criteria2*) like this:

=COUNTIFS(Fruit,Fruit,"Apples",Type,"Granny Smith")

Or

1. On the **Formulas** tab, in the **Function Library** group, click the **More Functions** button, point to **Statistical**, and then in the list, click **COUNTIFS**.

2. In the **Function Arguments** dialog box, enter the range name or cell range containing the values you want to count in the **Count_range** box.

3. Enter the range name or cell range for the first conditional evaluation in the **Criteria_range1** box, and the condition that must be met in the **Criteria1** box.

4. Repeat step 3 for each additional range/condition you want to evaluate. Then click **OK**.

➤ **To average values that meet a specific condition**

→ Enter the formula using the syntax =AVERAGEIF(*range,criteria*) like this:

=AVERAGEIF(Fruit,"Oranges",Quantity)

Or

1. On the **Formulas** tab, in the **Function Library** group, click the **More Functions** button, point to **Statistical**, and then in the list, click **AVERAGEIF**.

2. In the **Function Arguments** dialog box, enter the range name or cell range in the **Range** box and the condition that must be met in the **Criteria** box. Then click **OK**.

➤ **To average values that meet multiple conditions**

→   Enter the formula using the syntax =AVERAGEIFS(*average_range,criteria_range1, criteria1,criteria_range2,criteria2*) like this:

=AVERAGEIFS(Amount,Fruit,"Oranges",Type,"Navel")

Or

1. On the **Formulas** tab, in the **Function Library** group, click the **More Functions** button, point to **Statistical**, and then in the list, click **AVERAGEIFS**.

2. In the **Function Arguments** dialog box, enter the range name or cell range containing the values you want to average in the **Average_range** box.

3. Enter the range name or cell range for the first conditional evaluation in the **Criteria_range1** box, and the condition that must be met in the **Criteria1** box.

4. Repeat step 3 for each additional range/condition you want to evaluate. Then click **OK**.

Practice Tasks

The practice file for these tasks is located in the *Documents\Microsoft Press\MCAS\ Excel2007\Objective03* folder. If you want, save the task results in the same folder with *My* prepended to the file name.

● Open the *SummaryCondition* workbook, and in cell F2, create a formula to count the number of Berry Bushes products in the cell range A2:A38, which has been defined as the named range Category. Then in cell F8, count the number of Flowers products in the Category range that are more than $20.00.

● In cell F4 of the *SummaryCondition* workbook, sum the value of all Flowers products in the Category range. Then in cell F12, add up the cost of all Carnivorous products in the Category range that are less than $7.00.

● In cell F6 of the *SummaryCondition* workbook, average the price of all Herbs products in the Category range. Then in cell F10, calculate the average cost of Carnivorous products in the Category range that are named *Bladderwort*.

3.5   Look up data by using a formula

Although Excel is not a database program, many people use it for database-like purposes. Typically each column in a table is the equivalent of a field in a database and each row is a record. There isn't anything stopping you from using rows as fields and columns as records, it's just less conventional. In a spreadsheet that is being used like a database, you will often need to find a value in a record that matches or comes close to matching a criterion. Excel provides two functions that enable looking up values in tables, HLOOKUP and VLOOKUP. The H and the V stand for horizontal and vertical, the difference being whether the formula searches horizontally in a row or vertically in a column for the value being looked up, respectively. For these two functions to work properly, the table must be sorted on the row or column being used for the lookup, in ascending order, especially if you're not looking for an exact match. The following table summarizes the uses of these functions.

Function	Purpose	Arguments
HLOOKUP()	Return a value from the column in which a value in the first row matches the criteria	*lookup_value,table_array, row_index_num,range_lookup*
VLOOKUP()	Return a value from the row in which a value in the first column matches the criteria	*lookup_value,table_array, column_index_num,range_lookup*

In the preceding table, the *lookup_value* argument is the value to be looked up. This argument can be a number, text, or a cell reference. The *table_array* argument is a reference to a range that has one or more rows, in the case of HLOOKUP, or one or more columns, in the case of VLOOKUP. Excel evaluates the first row or column of this range for the lookup value. The *row_index_num* and *column_index_num* arguments specify which row or column to return the value from. For example, in an HLOOKUP function, a *row_index_num* value of 1 would return the value from the first row, the same one being used for the look up. A *row_index_num* value of 2 would return the value from the second row, and so on. The *range_lookup* argument is either TRUE or FALSE. If it is TRUE or omitted and an exact match is not found, the largest value that is less than the *lookup_value* argument is used as a match. If the *lookup_value* argument is smaller than any number in the first row (HLOOKUP) or column (VLOOKUP), a #N/A error occurs. If the *range_lookup* argument is FALSE, only an exact match is allowed. If an exact match isn't found, a #N/A error occurs.

Tip Text lookups are not case sensitive. The value "Apples" would match "Apples", "apples", or "APPLES".

Don't get confused thinking you can only look up values based on the first column or row of your table. For example, if a table is in A1:T900 and you want to look up a value based on column C, you would use C1:T900 as the *table_array* argument.

➤ **To return the value in the fifth column of a table called Products, where the first column contains product names, for the product called "2% Milk"**

→ Use your preferred formula entry method to enter the formula

=VLOOKUP("2% Milk",Products,5,FALSE)

Practice Tasks

The practice file for these tasks is located in the *Documents\Microsoft Press\MCAS\ Excel2007\Objective03* folder. If you want, save the task results in the same folder with *My* prepended to the file name.

● Open the *LookupFormula* workbook, and create a formula in cell C12 to find the last name of employee number 5.

● In the *LookupFormula* workbook, create a formula in cell C14 that finds the street address of the employee named *Kirk*.

3.6   Use conditional logic in a formula

Excel provides a set of logic functions. The most common of these is the IF function. This function gives you one of two values based on a logical test. If the test is TRUE, the formula returns the first value. If the test is FALSE, the formula returns the second value.

Another pair of logical functions is AND and OR. These are used to combine multiple logical tests and give a value of TRUE or FALSE. The AND function gives a value of TRUE only if every logical test within it is TRUE. The OR function gives a value of TRUE if any of the logical tests within it are TRUE.

The NOT function reverses the logical outcome of a logical test, so if the test is TRUE, NOT will give you FALSE. You would use this when you want to check whether a cell is not equal to a certain value. For example, NOT(A1=3), returns TRUE as long as the value in cell A1 is not equal to 3.

The IFERROR function is a special-purpose function whose main purpose is to make your worksheets more user friendly. You use it by "wrapping it around" another function that might return an error. The errors that Excel displays in the cells are pretty cryptic, especially for someone not used to Excel. You can use the IFERROR function to display text that is more understandable to your users and that will help them figure out how to correct the error. The following table summarizes the use of these functions.

Function	Purpose	Arguments
IF()	Return one value if a test is TRUE, and another if the test is FALSE	*logical_test,value_if_true,value_if_false*
AND()	Return TRUE if all arguments are true	*logical1,logical2,...*
OR()	Return TRUE if any arguments are true	*logical1,logical2,...*
NOT()	Reverse the logical value of the argument	*logical*
IFERROR()	Return a user-friendly message if a formula has an error due to user input	*value,value_if_error*

Conditional logic functions are even more useful when you nest them. For example, you could create a formula that returns "Leap Year" if a year is divisible by 4 but not by 400, or "Not Leap Year" otherwise, like this:

=IF(OR(MOD(Year,400)=0,AND(MOD(Year,4)=0,NOT(MOD(Year,100)=0))),"Leap Year","Not Leap Year")

Tip The MOD function is used to return the remainder after a division operation; the first argument is the number to be divided and the second argument is the divisor. By testing to see if the remainder is equal to zero, we're testing to see if the year is evenly divisible by 400, 4, or 100.

Practice Tasks

The practice file for these tasks is located in the *Documents\Microsoft Press\MCAS\ Excel2007\Objective03* folder. If you want, save the task results in the same folder with *My* prepended to the file name.

- Open the *ConditionalFormula* workbook, and in cell C25, use the AND function to determine if the Entertainment total is less than $200.00 and the Misc. total is less than $100.00. Then in cell C27, use the IF function to display the text "Expenses OK" if the function in C25 evaluates to TRUE and "Expenses too high" if it evaluates to FALSE.

- In cell C26 of the *ConditionalFormula* workbook, use the OR function to determine if the Entertainment total is more than $200.00 or the Misc. total is more than $100.00. Then in cell C28, use the IF function to display the text "Expenses OK" if the function in C26 evaluates to NOT TRUE and "Expenses too high" if it evaluates to NOT FALSE.

- In the *ConditionalFormula* workbook, add 60.00 to either the Entertainment column or the Misc. column to check your work.

3.7   Format or modify text by using formulas

Excel provides several ways to work with text. The simplest text operation is concatenation—adding one text value to the end of another. This is useful where one part of the text value is the result of a calculation and another part is fixed or the result of a different calculation.

Some text functions help you to manage the capitalization of text. You can use the following functions on one cell at a time:

- LOWER returns a text value in all lowercase letters.
- PROPER returns a text value with an uppercase letter followed by lowercase letters.
- UPPER returns a text value in all uppercase letters.

Tip Changing the case of text for more than one cell requires an array formula. See the Excel Help topic "Guidelines and examples of array formulas" for more information.

Two functions are available to replace parts of a text value:

- REPLACE replaces a specific number of characters in a text value.
- SUBSTITUTE replaces one part of a text value with another (which could include an empty string, in order to delete part of a text value).

Excel provides a way to separate the text in one column into multiple columns. For example, if a column contains both first and last names, you can separate its entries into a first name column and a last name column.

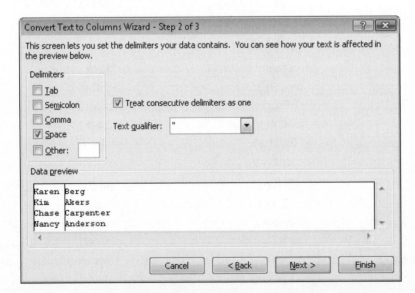

Tip The Convert Text To Columns Wizard does not insert blank columns to capture the split data; it overwrites the contents of the column to the right. If you know how many columns will be created by the conversion, manually insert them before starting the wizard.

➤ To return a text value in a specific case

→ Create a formula by using the following syntax:

=UPPER(A1)

=PROPER(A1)

=LOWER(A1)

➤ To convert one column of space-delimited text to multiple columns

1. Select the column or columns of text you want to separate into multiple columns.

2. On the **Data** tab, in the **Data Tools** group, click the **Text to Columns** button.

3. On the first page of the **Convert Text to Columns Wizard**, click **Delimited**, and then click **Next**.

4. On the second page of the wizard, select **Space** as the delimiter, and click **Next**.

5. On the last page of the wizard, select how you want the data formatted and the destination, and then click **Finish**.

Practice Tasks

The practice file for these tasks is located in the *Documents\Microsoft Press\MCAS\ Excel2007\Objective03* folder. If you want, save the task results in the same folder with *My* prepended to the file name.

● Open the *FormatFormula* workbook, and insert two blank columns to the right of the Names column. Select the Names column, and start the Convert Text To Columns Wizard. Proceed through the wizard to select the appropriate file type for the data source, to select the delimiter that best fits your text, and to set the data format for the proposed column(s). After the wizard finishes, make any corrections necessary to account for irregularities in the data or columns.

● In the *FormatFormula* workbook, use a function in cell B12 to change Karen to Kathren. In cell C12, use a function to change the value in cell B12 to lowercase. In cell D12, use a function to change the value in C12 to uppercase. Lastly, in cell E12, use a function to change the value in cell D12 back to proper case.

3.8 Display and print formulas

You can create a formula in the Formula Bar or directly in a cell. When you click a cell that contains a formula, the formula is visible in the Formula Bar.

See Also You can hide the Formula Bar to increase the available vertical workspace. For information, see section 1.4, "Change worksheet views."

When you're creating a worksheet and working on the formulas, it is sometimes useful to see all of the formulas at once. You can easily tell Excel to display the formulas or to print them.

➤ **To display formulas rather than their values**

→ On the **Formulas** tab, in the **Formula Auditing** group, click the **Show Formulas** button.

➤ **To print formulas**

→ Display formulas in the worksheet, and then print the worksheet.

Practice Tasks

The practice file for this task is located in the *Documents\Microsoft Press\MCAS\Excel2007\Objective03* folder. If you want, save the task results in the same folder with *My* prepended to the file name.

● Open the *Schedule* workbook, and then display and print the formulas.

Objective Review

Before finishing this chapter, ensure that you have mastered the following skills:

3.1 Reference data in formulas.

3.2 Summarize data by using a formula.

3.3 Summarize data by using subtotals.

3.4 Conditionally summarize data by using a formula.

3.5 Look up data by using a formula.

3.6 Use conditional logic in a formula.

3.7 Format or modify text by using formulas.

3.8 Display and print formulas.

4 Presenting Data Visually

The skills tested in this section of the Microsoft Office Specialist exam for Microsoft Office Excel 2007 relate to the presentation of data, to make it easy to analyze and understand. Specifically, the following objectives are associated with this set of skills:

4.1 Create and format charts.

4.2 Modify charts.

4.3 Apply conditional formatting.

4.4 Insert and modify illustrations.

4.5 Outline data.

4.6 Sort and filter data.

Although Excel worksheets are usually all about numbers, you can enhance them in visual ways to make those numbers easier to interpret. You can also use visual techniques to identify or extract key information. And sometimes it is appropriate to use visual elements to present additional information that has a bearing on the worksheet content.

This chapter guides you in studying the creation of charts, SmartArt business graphics, shapes, and outlines, and the use of conditional formatting and pictures. You also study ways of sorting and filtering data to ensure that you are presenting information in a way that effectively supports your message.

 Important Before you can use the practice files in this chapter, you need to install them from the book's companion CD to their default location. See "Using the Companion CD" at the beginning of this book for more information.

Tip Graphics and operating system–related instructions in this book reflect the Windows Vista user interface. If your computer is running Windows XP and you experience trouble following the instructions as written, refer to the sidebar "If You Are Running Windows XP" in "Working in the Microsoft Office Fluent User Interface" at the beginning of this book.

4.1 Create and format charts

Plotting Charts

Charts are an important tool for data analysis and are therefore a common component of certain types of worksheets. You can easily plot selected data as a chart to identify trends and relationships that might not be obvious from the data itself.

Tip You must select only the data you want to appear in the chart. If the data is not in a contiguous range of rows or columns, either rearrange the data or hold down the Ctrl key while you select noncontiguous ranges.

Different types of data are best suited for different types of charts. The following table shows the available chart types and the type of data they are particularly useful for plotting.

Chart type	Typically used to show
Column	Variations in value over time or comparisons
Line	Multiple data trends over evenly spaced intervals
Pie	Percentages assigned to different components of one item (non-negative, non-zero, no more than seven values)
Bar	Variations in value over time or the comparative values of several items at one point in time
Area	Multiple data series as cumulative layers showing change over time
Scatter (XY)	Correlations between independent items
Stock	Stock market or similar activity
Surface	Trends in values across two different dimensions in a continuous curve, such as a topographic map
Bubble	Correlations between three or more independent items
Doughnut	Percentages assigned to different components of more than one item
Radar	Percentages assigned to different components of an item, radiating from a center point

See Also For more information on chart types see the Excel Help topic "Available chart types."

To plot selected data as a chart, all you have to do is specify the chart type. If the type of chart you initially select doesn't adequately depict your data, you can change the type at any time. The 11 chart types each have several two-dimensional and three-dimensional variations, and you can customize each aspect of each variation.

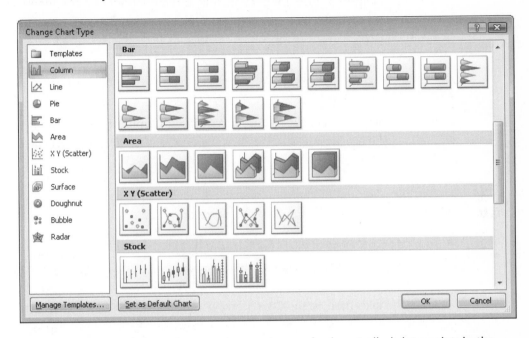

When you plot worksheet data, a row or column of values (called *data points* in the charting world) constitutes a set of data called a *data series*. Each data point in a data series is represented graphically in the chart by a data marker and in the chart legend by a unique color or pattern. The data is plotted against an x-axis (or *category axis*) and a y-axis (or *value axis*). Three-dimensional charts also have a z-axis (or *series axis*). Sometimes a chart does not produce the results you expect because the data series are plotted against the wrong axes; that is, Excel is plotting the data by row when it should be plotting by column, or vice versa. You can quickly switch the rows and columns to see whether that produces the desired effect. To see what Excel is doing behind the scenes, you can display the Select Data Source dialog box, which shows you exactly what is plotted where.

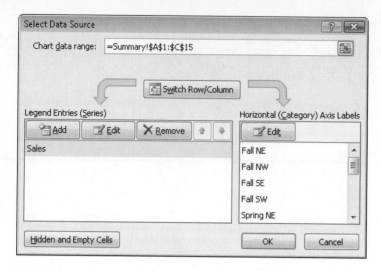

Strategy Practice plotting the same data in different ways. In particular, understand the effects of plotting data by column or by row.

➤ To plot selected data as a chart on the data worksheet

> **Tip** Before plotting the data, ensure that it is correctly set up for the type of chart you want to create. For example, a pie chart can display only one data series.

→ On the **Insert** tab, in the **Charts** group, click the button of the chart type you want, and then click a sub-type.

➤ To change the type of a selected chart

1. On the **Design** contextual tab, in the **Type** group, click the **Change Chart Type** button.

2. In the **Change Chart Type** dialog box, click a new type and sub-type, and then click **OK**.

➤ To switch rows and columns in a selected chart

→ On the **Design** contextual tab, in the **Data** group, click the **Switch Row/Column** button.

Or

1. On the **Design** contextual tab, in the **Data** group, click the **Select Data** button.

2. In the **Select Data Source** dialog box, click **Switch Row/Column**, and then click **OK**.

Layouts and Styles

You can apply predefined combinations of layouts and styles to quickly format a chart. You can also apply a shape style to the chart area to set it off from the rest of the sheet.

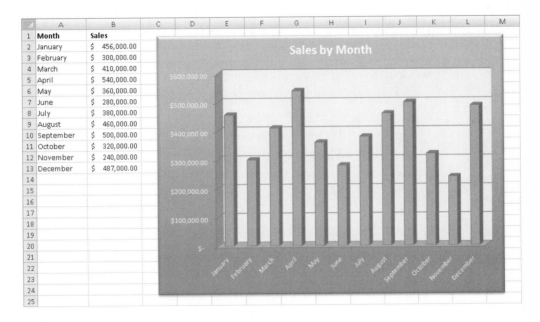

> ➤ **To change the layout of a selected chart**

   → On the **Design** contextual tab, in the **Chart Layouts** gallery, click the layout you want.

> ➤ **To apply a style to a selected chart**

   → On the **Design** contextual tab, in the **Chart Styles** gallery, click the style you want.

> ➤ **To apply a shape style to a selected chart**

   → On the **Format** contextual tab, in the **Shape Styles** gallery, click the style you want.

Practice Tasks

The practice files for these tasks are located in the *Documents\Microsoft Press\ MCAS\Excel2007\Objective04* folder. If you want, save the task results in the same folder with *My* prepended to the file name.

- Open the *DataSource* workbook, and use the data on the Seattle worksheet to plot a simple pie chart.

- Open the *Plotting* workbook, and on the Sales worksheet, plot the data as a simple 2-D Clustered Column chart. Then switch the rows and columns.

- Continuing on the Sales worksheet of the *Plotting* workbook, change the chart to a 3-D Clustered Column chart. Then apply Layout 1, Style 34, and the Subtle Effect – Accent 3 shape style.

4.2 Modify charts

Moving and Sizing

The charts you create often don't appear where you want them on a worksheet, and their default size might be too big or too small to adequately show their data. You can move and size a chart by using simple dragging techniques.

Tip You can change the size of only one chart at a time. Simultaneous resizing of multiple charts is not supported by Excel 2007.

If you prefer to display a chart on its own sheet instead of embedded in the worksheet containing its data, you can easily move it. You can also move it to any other existing worksheet in the workbook.

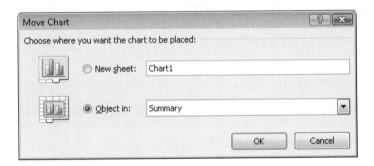

➤ **To move a selected chart to a chart sheet**

1. On the **Design** tab, in the **Location** group, click the **Move Chart** button.

2. In the **Move Chart** dialog box, click **New sheet**, and then if you want, type a name for the sheet.

3. Click **OK**.

➤ **To move a selected chart to a different sheet in the same workbook**

1. Display the **Move Chart** dialog box, click **Object in**, and then select the worksheet you want from the list.

2. Click **OK**.

➤ **To change the size of a selected chart**

→ Point to a handle (set of dots) on the chart's frame, and then drag in the direction you want the chart to grow or shrink.

→ Point to a handle in a corner of the chart's frame, hold down the Shift key, and then drag in the direction you want the chart to grow or shrink proportionally.

→ On the **Format** tab, in the **Size** group, change the **Shape Height** and **Shape Width** settings.

Or

1. On the **Format** tab, click the **Size** dialog box launcher.

2. In the **Size and Properties** dialog box, change the settings in the **Size and rotate** or **Scale** area, and then click **OK**.

Tip Select the Lock Aspect Ratio check box before changing the settings if you want to size the chart proportionally.

Editing Data

A chart is linked to its worksheet data, so any changes you make to the plotted data are immediately reflected in the chart. If you want to add or delete values in a data series or add or remove an entire series, you need to increase or decrease the range of the plotted data in the worksheet.

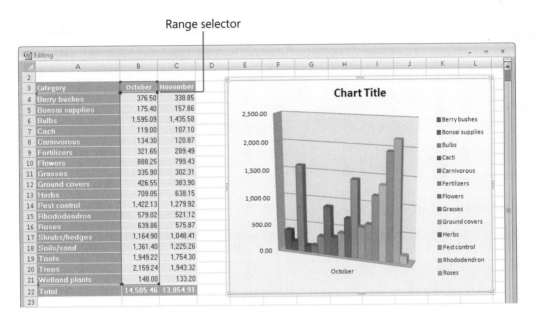

Range selector

➤ To edit the data in a chart

→ In the linked Excel worksheet, change the plotted values.

➤ To change the range of plotted data in a selected chart

→ In the linked Excel worksheet, drag the range selectors until they enclose the series you want to plot.

Chart Elements

To augment the usefulness or the attractiveness of a chart, you can add elements such as a title, axis labels, data labels, a data table, and gridlines. You can format each element in appropriate ways. You can also format the plot area (the area defined by the axes) and the chart area (the entire chart object).

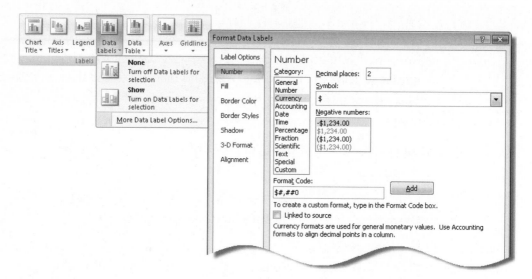

Strategy You can tailor chart elements in too many ways for us to cover them in detail here. In addition to choosing options from galleries, you can open a Format dialog box for each type of element. Make sure you are familiar with the chart elements and how to use them to enhance a chart.

➤ **To add a chart title**

1. On the **Layout** tab, in the **Labels** group, click the **Chart Title** button.

2. In the **Title** gallery, click the option you want.

3. Select the title placeholder, and replace it with the one you want.

➤ To add or remove axis titles

1. On the **Layout** tab, in the **Labels** group, click the **Axis Titles** button.

2. In the list, point to **Primary Horizontal Axis Title**, and then click **None** or **Title Below Axis**; or click **More Primary Horizontal Axis Title Options**, make specific selections in the **Format Axis Title** dialog box, and then click **Close**.

   Or

   In the list, point to **Primary Vertical Axis Title**, and then click **None**, **Rotated**, **Horizontal**, or **Vertical**; or click **More Primary Vertical Axis Title Options**, make specific selections in the **Format Axis Title** dialog box, and then click **Close**.

3. Select the placeholder axis title, and enter the text you want to appear as the axis title.

➤ To add, remove, or move the legend

1. On the **Layout** tab, in the **Labels** group, click the **Legend** button.

2. In the **Legend** gallery, click the **Show Legend** (**Right**, **Top**, **Left**, or **Bottom**) or **Overlay Legend** (**Right** or **Left**) option you want.

   Or

   Click **More Legend Options**, make specific selections in the **Format Legend** dialog box, and then click **Close**.

➤ To display data labels

1. On the **Layout** tab, in the **Labels** group, click the **Data Labels** button.

2. In the **Data Labels** gallery, click **Show** to display the value of each data point on its marker.

   Or

   Click **More Data Label Options**, make specific selections (including the number format and decimal places) in the **Format Legend** dialog box, and then click **Close**.

   Tip Data labels can clutter up all but the simplest charts. If you need to show the data for a chart on a separate chart sheet, consider using a data table instead.

➤ **To display the chart data under the axis titles**

1. On the **Layout** tab, in the **Labels** group, click the **Data Table** button.

2. In the **Data Table** gallery, click **Show Data Table** or **Show Data Table with Legend Keys**.

   Or

   Click **More Data Table Options**, make specific selections in the **Format Data Table** dialog box, and then click **Close**.

➤ **To display or hide axes**

1. On the **Layout** tab, in the **Axes** group, click the **Axes** button.

2. In the list, point to **Primary Horizontal Axis**, and then click **None, Show Left to Right Axis, Show Axis without labeling**, or **Show Right to Left Axis**; or click **More Primary Horizontal Axis Options**, make specific selections in the **Format Axis** dialog box, and then click **Close**.

   Or

   In the list, point to **Primary Vertical Axis**, and then click **None, Show Default Axis, Show Axis in Thousands, Show Axis in Millions, Show Axis in Billions**, or **Show Axis with Log Scale**; or click **More Primary Vertical Axis Options**, make specific selections in the **Format Axis** dialog box, and then click **Close**.

➤ **To display or hide gridlines**

1. On the **Layout** tab, in the **Axes** group, click the **Gridlines** button.

2. In the list, point to **Primary Horizontal Gridlines**, and then click **None, Major Gridlines, Minor Gridlines**, or **Major & Minor Gridlines**; or click **More Primary Horizontal Gridlines Options**, make specific selections in the **Format Gridlines** dialog box, and then click **Close**.

   Or

   In the list, point to **Primary Vertical Gridlines**, and then click **None, Major Gridlines, Minor Gridlines**, or **Major & Minor Gridlines**; or click **More Primary Vertical Gridlines Options**, make specific selections in the **Format Gridlines** dialog box, and then click **Close**.

➤ **To select a chart element for formatting**

→ On the **Layout** tab, in the **Current Selection** area, click the element you want in the **Chart Elements** list, and then click the **Format Selection** button to open the corresponding **Format** dialog box.

Tip An element does not appear in the Chart Elements list unless it is present in the chart.

Practice Tasks

The practice files for these tasks are located in the *Documents\Microsoft Press\ MCAS\Excel2007\Objective04* folder. If you want, save the task results in the same folder with *My* prepended to the file name.

● Open the *SizingMoving* workbook, and on the Sales worksheet, increase the size of the chart until it occupies cells A1:L23. Then move it to a new chart sheet named *Sales Chart*.

● Open the *Editing* workbook, and change the October sales amount for the Flowers category to *888.25*. Then add the November data series to the chart, and change the way the data is plotted so that you can compare sales for the two months.

● Open the *ChartElements* workbook, and add the title *Air Quality Index Report* to the chart. Then add data labels that show the percentage relationship of each data marker to the whole, with no decimal places.

4.3 Apply conditional formatting

You can make worksheet data easier to interpret by using conditional formatting to format cells based on their values. If a value meets a particular condition, Excel applies the formatting; if it doesn't, the formatting is not applied.

You set up conditional formatting by specifying the condition, which is called a *rule*. You can select from the following types of rules:

- Highlight cells or top/bottom
- Data bars, color scales, or icon sets

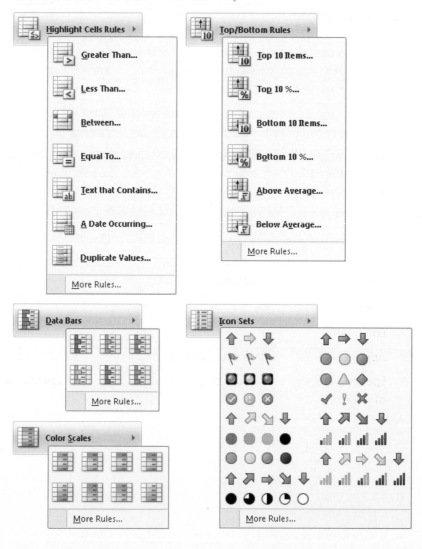

You can also define a rule from scratch in the New Formatting Rule dialog box.

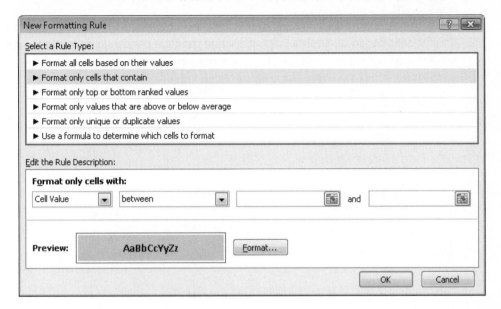

The options available in the Edit The Rule Description area vary depending on the selection in the Select A Rule Type list. You can define multiple conditions for the same range of cells or table.

Strategy Familiarize yourself with all the types of rules and their variations so that you know how to quickly apply any condition that might be requested on the exam.

All the rules you create are listed in the Conditional Formatting Rules Manager dialog box, where you can do the following:

● Create and delete rules.

● Edit a selected rule.

● Adjust the order in which Excel processes rules.

● Specify whether Excel should stop processing rules after a cell meets the conditions of a specific rule.

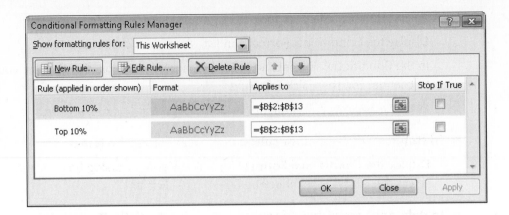

➤ To apply cell fill and font color based on cell value

1. On the **Home** tab, in the **Styles** group, click the **Conditional Formatting** button.

2. In the list, point to **Highlight Cell Rules** or **Top/Bottom Rules**, and then click the type of condition you want.

3. In the dialog box, complete the condition if necessary for the selected type. Then click one of the available fill, font, or border color options in the list.

   Tip You can click Custom Format and then click style, underline, color, and effects on the Font tab of the Format Cells dialog box.

4. Click **OK**.

➤ To display data bars, a color scale, or icons based on cell value

→ Display the **Conditional Formatting** list, point to **Data Bars**, **Color Scales**, or **Icon Sets**, and then click the option you want.

➤ To create a rule from scratch

1. Display the **Conditional Formatting** list, and then click **New Rule**.

2. In the **New Formatting Rule** dialog box, in the **Select a Rule Type** list, click the type you want.

3. In the **Edit the Rule Description** area, specify the condition. Then click **Format**.

4. On the **Font** tab of the **Format Cells** dialog box, specify the formatting to apply if the condition is met.

5. Click **OK** in the **Format Cells** dialog box, and again in the **New Formatting Rule** dialog box.

➤ To modify the conditional format applied to selected cells

1. Display the **Conditional Formatting** list, and then click **Manage Rules**.

2. In the **Conditional Formatting Rules Manager** dialog box, click the rule you want to change, and then click **Edit Rule**.

3. In the **Edit Formatting Rule** dialog box, make your changes, and then click **OK**.

➤ To stop testing the cell for subsequent rules if this rule is met

→ Display the **Conditional Formatting Rules Manager** dialog box, click the rule, select the **Stop If True** check box, and then click **OK**.

➤ To delete the conditional format applied to selected cells

→ Display the **Conditional Formatting** list, point to **Clear Rules**, and then click **Clear Rules from Selected Cells** or **Clear Rules from Entire Sheet**.

→ Display the **Conditional Formatting Rules Manager** dialog box, click the rule, click **Delete Rule**, and then click **OK**.

Practice Tasks

The practice file for these tasks is located in the *Documents\Microsoft Press\ MCAS\Excel2007\Objective04* folder. If you want, save the task results in the same folder with *My* prepended to the file name.

- Open the *ConditionalFormatting* workbook, and on the Orders worksheet, format Seattle in the City column with red text.

- On the Details worksheet of the *ConditionalFormatting* workbook, display the Three Arrows (Colored) icon set for all the values in the Extended Price column. Then show blue data bars for the same values. Finally, in the same column, fill all cells containing values over $100 with bright yellow.

- Continuing on the Details worksheet of the *ConditionalFormatting* workbook, tell Excel to first process the rule that makes the cells fill with yellow, and not to process any more rules for cells that meet this condition.

4.4 Insert and modify illustrations

Pictures

You might want to add pictures created and saved in other programs or scanned photographs and illustrations to a worksheet such as a catalog of products or a list of employees. If a worksheet might be viewed by people outside your company, you might want to add your logo to the worksheet's header or footer to establish worksheet ownership and reinforce your business identity.

Graphic inserted in header

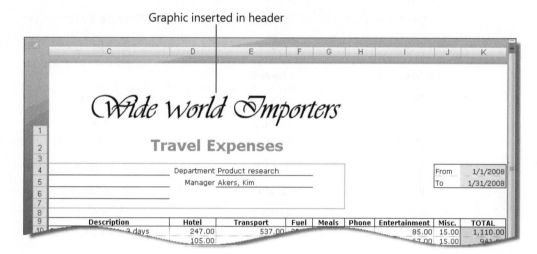

➤ **To insert a picture on a worksheet**

1. On the **Insert** tab, in the **Illustrations** group, click the **Picture** button.

2. In the **Insert Picture** dialog box, locate and double-click the picture you want.

   See Also If the picture is large or if it might change, you might want to insert a hyperlink to the picture instead. For information about hyperlinks, see section 2.3, "Format cells and cell content." For more information about modifying pictures, see section 3.2, "Format illustrations," in Exam 77-601, "Using Microsoft Office Word 2007."

➤ **To replace a selected picture**

1. On the **Format** tab, in the **Adjust** group, click the **Change Picture** button.

2. In the **Insert Picture** dialog box, locate and double-click the replacement picture.

➤ **To insert a picture in the header or footer**

1. On the **Insert** tab, in the **Text** group, click the **Header & Footer** button.

2. Click the left, center, or right section of the header or footer, and then on the **Design** tab, in the **Header & Footer Elements** group, click the **Picture** button.

3. In the **Insert Picture** dialog box, locate and double-click the picture you want.

4. In the **Header & Footer Elements** group, click the **Format Picture** button.

5. In the **Format Picture** dialog box, change settings in the **Size and rotate** area or the **Scale** area to make the picture fit in the header or footer.

6. Click **OK**, and then click away from the header or footer to view the picture in Page Layout view.

SmartArt Diagrams

When you create a worksheet that details a process such as a project schedule, you might want to include a diagram to illustrate the process visually. You can use the same SmartArt graphics feature in Excel that you use in Microsoft Office PowerPoint 2007. By using predefined sets of formatting, you can easily create the type of diagram best suited to the worksheet's information.

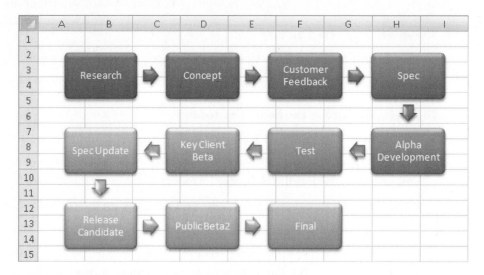

Strategy To become proficient with SmartArt diagrams, review section 3.1, "Create SmartArt diagrams," and section 3.2, "Modify SmartArt diagrams," in Exam 77-603, "Using Microsoft Office PowerPoint 2007."

After you insert the diagram, you add text either directly to its shapes or to the bulleted list in the text pane that opens to the left of the diagram. You can add shapes, delete shapes, and rearrange them by dragging the shapes or editing the bulleted list.

You can customize a diagram as a whole by changing its shape and color and adding shading and three-dimensional effects. You can modify all the shapes simultaneously or individual shapes.

See Also You can format one shape by using the same formatting techniques you would use for text boxes. For information about formatting text boxes, see section 2.1, "Insert and format text boxes," in Exam 77-603, "Using Microsoft Office PowerPoint 2007."

➤ To create a SmartArt diagram

1. On the **Insert** tab, in the **Illustrations** group, click the **SmartArt** button.

2. In the left pane of the **Choose a SmartArt Graphic** dialog box, click the category you want.

3. In the center pane, click the desired layout. Then click **OK**.

➤ To add text to a SmartArt diagram

→ Open the **Text** pane by clicking the arrow on the left edge of the diagram frame, and then replace the bullet point placeholders with your own text.

→ Click a shape, and then type the text.

   Tip Double-clicking a SmartArt shape displays the Mini toolbar.

➤ To delete a shape

→ Click the shape, and then press the **Delete** key.

➤ To modify a selected SmartArt diagram

→ Click buttons on the **Design** tab to add or change the level of shapes, change the diagram layout, and adjust its colors and style.

Shapes

To emphasize an important area of a worksheet, you can draw shapes (such as arrows) to which you can add text (such as assumptions, warnings, or notes). You can format a shape by changing its style, color, or outline. You can format its text in the usual ways or by applying a WordArt style to it.

➤ **To draw a shape**

1. On the **Insert** tab, in the **Illustrations** group, click the **Shapes** button.

2. In the **Shapes** gallery, click the shape you want.

3. Move the crosshair pointer to the position on the slide where you want the upper-left corner of the shape to be, and drag down and to the right to draw a shape the size you want.

➤ **To change to a different shape**

1. With the shape selected, on the **Format** tab, in the **Insert Shapes** group, click the **Edit Shape** button.

2. Point to **Change Shape**, and then in the **Shapes** gallery, click the shape you want.

➤ **To add text to a selected shape**

1. On the **Format** tab, in the **Insert Shapes** group, click the **Text Box** button.

2. Click the shape, and then type the text.

➤ **To modify a selected shape**

→ Click buttons on the **Format** tab to adjust the shape's colors and style or to adjust the text formatting or style.

Practice Tasks

The practice files for these tasks are located in the *Documents\Microsoft Press\ MCAS\Excel2007\Objective04* folder. If you want, save the task results in the same folder with *My* prepended to the file name.

- Open the *Picture* workbook, and insert the *Logo2* graphic in the upper-left corner of the Employees worksheet header. Scale the logo so that it does not obscure cell A1 of the worksheet.

- Open the *SmartArt* workbook, and on the Diagram worksheet, insert a Basic Bending Process diagram. Add the following text to the shapes: *Take order, Create invoice, Fulfill order, Ship order, Order received*. Then apply the Powdered style and one of the Colorful color schemes.

- Open the *Shapes* workbook, and to the right of the Tools Total amount, draw a large, red, left-pointing arrow containing the words *Successful weekend sale*.

4.5   Outline data

You can designate specific rows or columns of data within a data range as groups. When you do so, Excel inserts a control, to the left of the row headings or above the column headings, with which you can contract and expand the data group. You can have column groups and row groups on the same worksheet; you cannot have two consecutive groups of rows or columns; they must be separated by one row. (The row may contain data.) The grouping feature is particularly useful when you're working with a data range or table that is larger than your display, because you can use it to easily display and hide groups of columns and rows.

If your data range contains groups of data that are summarized or subtotaled, you can tell Excel to group the data in up to eight groups corresponding to outline levels. In effect, Excel outlines the data, making it possible to hide or display as much detail as you want.

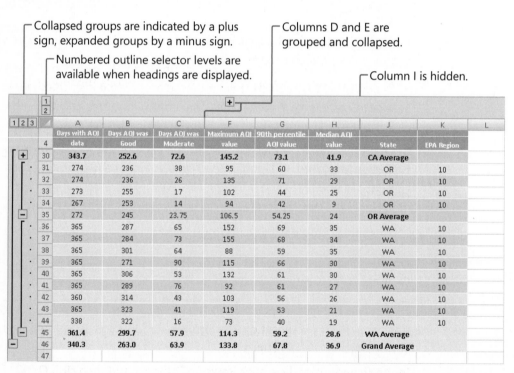

Collapsed groups are indicated by a plus sign, expanded groups by a minus sign.

Numbered outline selector levels are available when headings are displayed.

Columns D and E are grouped and collapsed.

Column I is hidden.

	Days with AQI data	Days AQI was Good	Days AQI was Moderate	Maximum AQI value	90th percentile AQI value	Median AQI value	State	EPA Region
30	343.7	252.6	72.6	145.2	73.1	41.9	CA Average	
31	274	236	38	95	60	33	OR	10
32	274	236	26	135	71	29	OR	10
33	273	255	17	102	44	25	OR	10
34	267	253	14	94	42	9	OR	10
35	272	245	23.75	106.5	54.25	24	OR Average	
36	365	287	65	152	69	35	WA	10
37	365	284	73	155	68	34	WA	10
38	365	301	64	88	59	35	WA	10
39	365	271	90	115	66	30	WA	10
40	365	306	53	132	61	30	WA	10
41	365	289	76	92	61	27	WA	10
42	360	314	43	103	56	26	WA	10
43	365	323	41	119	53	21	WA	10
44	338	322	16	73	40	19	WA	10
45	361.4	299.7	57.9	114.3	59.2	28.6	WA Average	
46	340.3	263.0	63.9	133.8	67.8	36.9	Grand Average	
47								

Tip To outline by rows, each column must have a heading in the first row. To outline by columns, each row must have a heading in the first column. In either case, no row or column should be blank.

If your worksheet does not already have summary rows or columns, you can have Excel calculate the summary rows and outline the data in one operation, using the Subtotal feature. For example, you might calculate the total sales for each product in a particular category. You specify the way the data should be summarized in the Subtotal dialog box. Note that Excel cannot add summary rows to the data in a worksheet unless at least one column is sorted into ascending or descending order.

See Also For more information about using functions with the Subtotal feature, see section 3.3, "Summarize data by using subtotals." For information about sorting data, see section 4.6, "Sort and filter data."

After grouping or outlining data, you can expand and collapse groups or levels by clicking either the plus and minus signs or the outline level buttons.

➤ **To add summary rows and group worksheet data**

1. Click any cell in the data, and on the **Data** tab, in the **Outline** group, click the **Subtotal** button.

2. In the **Subtotal** dialog box, click the column containing the values you want to group in the **At each change in** list.

3. Click the summary function you want to use in the **Use function** list.

4. Select the check box of the column containing the values on which Excel should calculate the summary function in the **Add subtotal to** list.

5. Select or clear the check boxes of the other options at the bottom of the dialog box. Then click **OK**.

   See Also For information about using the Subtotal feature to perform mathematical functions on subgroups of data, see section 3.3, "Summarize data by using subtotals."

➤ **To group worksheet data that contains summary rows or columns**

→ Click any cell in the data. Then on the **Data** tab, in the **Outline** group, click **Auto Outline** in the **Group** list.

   Or

1. Click any cell in the subset of data you want to group, and on the **Data** tab, in the **Outline** group, click **Group**.

2. In the **Group** dialog box, click **Rows** or **Columns**, and then click **OK**.

➤ **To hide or display grouped data**

→ In the headings area, click the button representing the outline level you want to display.

    Tip Each button displays that level and all those above it.

→ Click a visible group's **Hide Detail** button to hide its rows or columns.

→ Click a hidden group's **Show Detail** button to redisplay its rows or columns.

→ On the **Data** tab, in the **Outline** group, click the **Hide Detail** or **Show Detail** button.

➤ **To ungroup worksheet data**

→ To ungroup a specific group, click any cell in the group, and then on the **Data** tab, in the **Outline** group, click the **Ungroup** button.

→ To ungroup all groups but leave Excel-generated summary rows intact, click any cell in the outline, and then on the **Data** tab, in the **Outline** group, click **Clear Outline** in the **Ungroup** list.

Or

1. To ungroup all groups and remove Excel-generated summary rows, click any cell in the outline, and then on the **Data** tab, in the **Outline** group, click the **Subtotal** button.

2. In the **Subtotal** dialog box, click **Remove All**.

Practice Tasks

The practice files for these tasks are located in the *Documents\Microsoft Press\ MCAS\Excel2007\Objective04* folder. If you want, save the task results in the same folder with *My* prepended to the file name.

● Open the *Grouping* workbook, and outline the data on the SalesByCategory worksheet based on its summary rows. Then hide all rows except those containing subtotals.

● Open the *Subtotals* workbook, and tell Excel to outline the SalesByCategory worksheet by adding summary rows that calculate total product sales by category. Next, add a grouping to hide column A. Then hide all rows other than those containing subtotals. Finally, remove the outline without removing the summary rows.

4.6   Sort and filter data

Sorting

You can sort the values in one or more columns in a worksheet or table in either ascending or descending order. To sort on multiple columns, you specify in the Sort dialog box the order in which you want them to be sorted.

By default, Excel assumes that the first row in the worksheet contains column headings and does not include it in the sort. It also assumes that you want to sort on the cell's values, but if the worksheet or table is formatted, you can specify that you want to sort on any of the following:

- Cell color
- Font color
- Cell icon

See Also For information about cell icons, see section 4.3, "Apply conditional formatting."

You can also specify whether entries starting with uppercase and lowercase letters should be sorted separately and the orientation of the sort (whether you want to sort columns or rows).

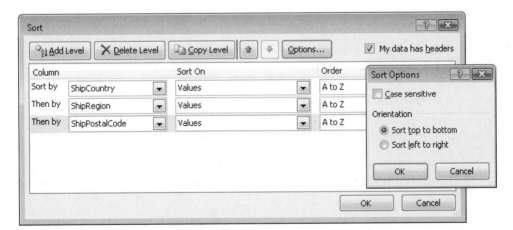

➤ To sort a worksheet or table on one column

→ Click any cell in the column. Then on the **Home** tab, in the **Editing** group, click the **Sort & Filter** button, and click the sorting option you want.

Tip The sorting options vary depending on the number format of the data in the column.

→ Click any cell in the column. Then on the **Data** tab, in the **Sort & Filter** group, click the **Sort A to Z** or **Sort Z to A** button.

➤ To sort a worksheet or table on more than one column

1. Click any cell in the range to be sorted. Then on the **Home** tab, in the **Editing** group, click the **Sort & Filter** button, and click **Custom Sort**.

   Or

   Click any cell in the range to be sorted, and then on the **Data** tab, in the **Sort & Filter** group, click the **Sort** button.

2. In the **Sort** dialog box, click the first column you want in the **Sort by** list. Then click the criteria by which you want to sort in the **Sort on** list. Finally, click the order you want in the **Order** list.

   Tip The options in the Sort dialog box change if you click Cell Color, Font Color, or Cell Icon in the Sort On list.

3. Click **Add Level**, and repeat step 2 for the second column. Repeat this step for additional columns.

4. Click **OK**.

➤ To remove a sort level

1. Display the **Sort** dialog box, and click the level you want to remove.

2. Click **Delete Level**, and then click **OK**.

Filtering

Sorting organizes data in a logical manner, but does not locate specific entries. To locate a specific value, you can apply a filter. To filter by multiple criteria, you can apply additional filters to the results of the first one.

Filters applied

	A	B	C	D	E	F
1	Orderl ▼	Customerl ▼	OrderDat ▼	ShippedDat ▼	Freig ▼	ShipName ▼
7	11084	COXBR	1/12/2008	1/14/2008	8.50	Arlette Cox
8	11085	RAMLU	1/12/2008	1/13/2008	3.00	Cynthia Randall
9	11086	OVESC	1/12/2008	1/13/2008	6.95	Lani Ota
10	11087	THIRA	1/12/2008	1/13/2008	20.00	John Thorson
63						
64						

Rows that don't meet the filter conditions are hidden.

In addition to filtering on entire values, you can use ready-made filters to locate values that meet certain criteria. The criteria vary depending on the number format. If the worksheet or table is formatted, you can filter for the cell color, font color, or cell icon.

Strategy Take the time to familiarize yourself with the wide range of ready-made filters and the kinds of criteria you can create with them. Experiment with criteria that include and don't include a specific value.

If none of the ready-made criteria meets your needs, you can create a criterion from scratch.

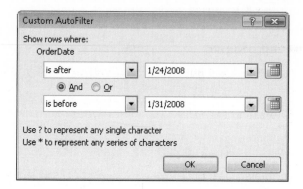

The location of the selected cell determines which columns in the range are filtered. If you select a cell, filter buttons appear in the column headers for all columns in the range. If you select a row, filter buttons appear in that row, with which you can filter only the cells that follow. If you select a column, a filter button appears for only that column.

➤ To display rows containing a specific column value

1. Click any cell in the range to be sorted. Then on the **Home** tab, in the **Editing** group, click the **Sort & Filter** button, and click **Filter**.

   Or

   Click any cell in the range to be sorted. Then on the **Data** tab, in the **Sort & Filter** group, click the **Filter** button.

2. Click the filter arrow for the column by which you want to filter the worksheet, and then click **Select All** to clear all the check boxes.

3. Select the check box(es) of the field value(s) you want to display, and then click **OK**.

➤ To remove a filter

→ On the **Home** tab, in the **Editing** group, click the **Sort & Filter** button, and then click **Clear**.

→ On the **Data** tab, in the **Sort & Filter** group, click the **Clear** button.

Tip If you have finished filtering, you can turn off the filtering arrows by clicking the Sort & Filter button and then Filter on the Editing tab or the Filter button on the Data tab.

➤ To apply a common filtering criterion

1. Display the filter arrows, and click the arrow of the column on which you want to filter.

2. Point to *<data type>* **Filters**, and then click the criterion you want to filter by.

   Tip In a column containing date values, you can click All Dates In Period to display all date values in a particular quarter or month.

3. In the **Custom AutoFilter** dialog box, enter the value that completes the criterion. Then if you want, add a second criterion.

4. Click **OK**.

➤ To filter on formatting

1. Display the filter arrows, and click the arrow of the column on which you want to filter.

2. Point to **Filter by Color**, and then click the formatting you want to filter by.

   Tip You can quickly filter a worksheet to display all the rows containing the value or formatting of the active cell. Right-click the cell, point to Filter, and then click the filtering option you want.

➤ To create a custom filter

1. Display the filter arrows, and click the arrow of the column on which you want to filter.

2. Point to *<data type>* **Filters**, and then click **Custom Filter**.

3. In the **Custom AutoFilter** dialog box, construct the criterion by which you want to filter, using **And** to specify two criteria or **Or** to specify alternatives.

   See Also You can use wildcards when filtering text, but not when filtering numbers. For information about wildcards, see section 3.3, "Find and replace data," in Exam 77-605, "Using Microsoft Office Access 2007."

4. Click **OK**.

   Tip Pointing to the filter arrow displays the current filter criteria for the column.

Practice Tasks

The practice files for these tasks are located in the *Documents\Microsoft Press\ MCAS\Excel2007\Objective04* folder. If you want, save the task results in the same folder with *My* prepended to the file name.

- Open the *Sorting* workbook. Sort the SalesByCategory worksheet first by Category and then by Category and Price.

- Open the *Filtering* workbook. In the OrdersJan worksheet, display only those rows containing WA (Washington state) in the ShipRegion column. Then re-display all the rows.

- On the OrdersJan worksheet of the *Filtering* workbook, display only the orders that were shipped on January 23, 24, and 25. Then display only the orders that were shipped to states other than Washington (WA) during that time.

- On the OrdersFeb worksheet of the *Filtering* workbook, display only the rows for which the value in the Freight column has a colored fill, and then display only the rows for which the cell in the Freight column has no fill color. Lastly, redisplay all the rows.

Objective Review

Before finishing this chapter, ensure that you have mastered the following skills:

4.1 Create and format charts.

4.2 Modify charts.

4.3 Apply conditional formatting.

4.4 Insert and modify illustrations.

4.5 Outline data.

4.6 Sort and filter data.

5 Collaborating and Securing Data

The skills tested in this section of the Microsoft Office Specialist exam for Microsoft Office Excel 2007 relate to the tasks involved with sharing and working on workbooks with others. Specifically, the following objectives are associated with this set of skills:

5.1 Manage changes to workbooks.

5.2 Protect and share workbooks.

5.3 Prepare workbooks for distribution.

5.4 Save workbooks.

5.5 Set print options for printing data, worksheets, and workbooks.

If you collaborate with other people on the development of workbooks, or if you create workbooks that will be used by more than one person, you need to know how to protect those workbooks from inadvertent changes by authorized users as well as malicious changes by unauthorized people. You also need to know how to finalize workbooks and how to deliver them in the format most appropriate for your purpose.

This chapter guides you in studying how to manage changes made by different people, how to make comments without making actual changes, how to protect a workbook before sharing it with other people, how to save a workbook in a different format, and how set up workbooks for printing.

 Important Before you can use the practice files in this chapter, you need to install them from the book's companion CD to their default location. See "Using the Companion CD" at the beginning of this book for more information.

Tip Graphics and operating system–related instructions in this book reflect the Windows Vista user interface. If your computer is running Windows XP and you experience trouble following the instructions as written, refer to the sidebar "If You Are Running Windows XP" in "Working in the Microsoft Office Fluent User Interface" at the beginning of this book.

5.1   Manage changes to workbooks

Change Tracking

When two or more people collaborate on the development of a workbook, it helps to turn on the Track Changes feature so that the revisions are recorded without the original cell entries being overwritten. Implementing Track Changes saves and shares the workbook. You can specify that changes be tracked for a particular time period, for everyone but you, or in a particular range of cells.

After sharing a workbook for the purpose of tracking changes, you can further specify how long the change history will be retained within the workbook and how frequently changes made in each user's personal view of the shared workbook are saved and made available to other users. You can also specify whether you want to have the option of resolving conflicting changes if two people make changes to one cell.

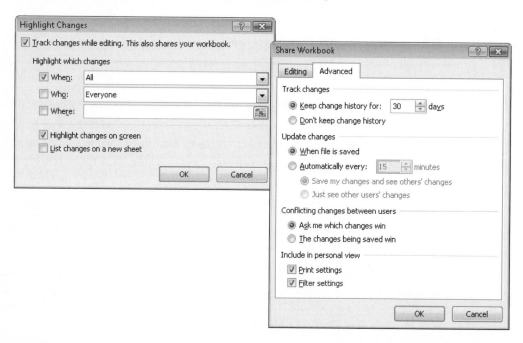

See Also For information about sharing workbooks, see section 5.2, "Protect and share workbooks."

When someone makes a change to a worksheet with Track Changes turned on, the change is implemented in the cell, and the cell is flagged with a triangle in the upper-left corner and a border in the color assigned to that person. Pointing to the cell displays a ScreenTip identifying the author and the date and describing the change.

See Also You can enable protection that prevents other users from turning off Track Changes. For information about protecting workbooks, see section 5.2, "Protect and share workbooks."

G	H	J	K	L
90th percentile AQI value	Median AQI value	State	EPA Region	
73.1	41.9	CA Average		
60	33	OR	10	
71	29	OR	10	
44	25	OR	10	
42	15			
54.25	25.5			
69	35			
68	34	WA	10	
59	35	WA	10	

Joan, 3/15/2008 4:43 PM:
Changed cell H34 from '8' to '15'.

Tip You can change the name shown with your revisions by changing your user name on the Popular page of the Excel Options dialog box.

You can review and accept or reject changes to the worksheet for a particular time period, for particular reviewers, or in a particular range of cells. You can accept or reject each change or all changes in the worksheet.

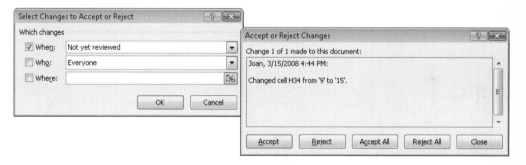

If you accept a change, the change history is stored with the worksheet and you can review it at any time as long as the workbook continues to be shared. If you reject a change, all record of the change is erased.

See Also For information about starting and stopping workbook sharing, see section 5.2, "Protect and share workbooks."

➤ To turn Track Changes on or off

1. On the **Review** tab, in the **Changes** group, click the **Track Changes** button, and then click **Highlight Changes**.

2. In the **Highlight Changes** dialog box, select or clear the **Track changes while editing** check box.

3. Make any appropriate changes to the other settings, and then click **OK**.

4. Click **OK** to save the workbook.

> **Tip** After you share a workbook, you can tell Excel to keep track of changes on a separate worksheet by displaying the Highlight Changes dialog box and selecting the List Changes On A New Sheet check box.

➤ To track changes on a separate worksheet

→ In the **Highlight Changes** dialog box, select the **Track changes while editing** check box, and the **List changes on a new sheet** check box. Then click **OK**.

➤ To accept or reject changes

1. On the **Review** tab, in the **Changes** group, click the **Track Changes** button, and then click **Accept/Reject Changes**.

2. Click **OK** to save the workbook.

3. In the **Select Changes to Accept or Reject** dialog box, specify the **When**, **Who**, and **Where** settings of the changes you want to review, and then click **OK**.

4. For each change displayed in the **Accept or Reject Changes** dialog box, click **Accept** or **Reject** for this change or **Accept All** or **Reject All** for all changes.

5. If you are asked to confirm the action, click **OK**.

➤ To hide changes you have already accepted

1. Save the workbook and display the **Highlight Changes** dialog box.

2. In the **When** list, click **Since I last saved**.

3. Click **OK** in the **Highlight Changes** dialog box and again in the message box saying that no changes were found that match this specification.

Comments

In addition to tracking the changes made to a worksheet, you can attach comments to cells without affecting the worksheet's functionality. A cell with an attached comment is identified by a red triangle in its upper-right corner. The comment itself appears in a box attached to the red triangle by an arrow. The text of the comment is preceded by the name of the person who added it. By default, the comment is visible only when you point to or select the cell to which it is attached.

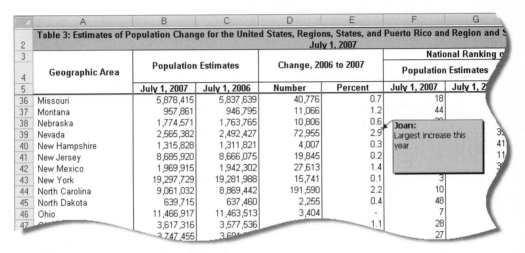

You can work with comments in the following ways:

- Permanently display one comment or all comments.
- Move from comment to comment.
- Edit a displayed comment by using normal editing techniques.
- Size and reposition a comment so that it does not obscure important information.

➤ **To insert a comment about a selected cell**

1. On the **Review** tab, in the **Comments** group, click the **New Comment** button.

   Or

   Right-click the cell and then click **Insert Comment**.

2. In the comment box, type the comment.

➤ **To permanently display one or all comments**

→ Click the cell to which the comment you want to display is attached, and then on the **Review** tab, in the **Comments** group, click the **Show/Hide Comment** button.

→ Right-click the cell to which the comment you want to display is attached, and then click **Show/Hide Comments**.

→ On the **Review** tab, in the **Comments** group, click the **Show All Comments** button.

➤ **To move among comments**

→ On the **Review** tab, in the **Comments** group, click the **Previous** or **Next** button.

➤ **To edit a comment**

1. Click the cell to which the comment is attached, and then on the **Review** tab, in the **Comments** group, click the **Edit Comment** button.

   Or

   Right-click the cell to which the comment is attached, and then click **Edit Comment**.

2. Change the text by using normal editing techniques.

➤ **To size or reposition a comment**

1. Display the comment, and then click its border.

2. Drag its sizing handles to increase or decrease its size.

   Or

   Drag its frame to reposition it.

➤ **To delete a comment**

→ Click the cell to which the comment is attached, and then on the **Review** tab, in the **Comments** group, click the **Delete** button.

→ Right-click the cell to which the comment is attached, and then click **Delete Comment**.

Practice Tasks

The practice files for these tasks are located in the *Documents\Microsoft Press\ MCAS\Excel2007\Objective05* folder. If you want, save the task results in the same folder with *My* prepended to the file name.

● Open the *TrackChanges* workbook, and turn on Track Changes for everyone. Then change the entry in the Category column from Roses to *Rose bushes* and its entry in the Price column from $139.86 to *$145.95*.

● Continuing in the *TrackChanges* workbook, save the workbook and then turn off the display of revisions.

● Open the *ResolveChanges* workbook, accept all the changes made by Shelley, and reject all the changes made by Florian.

● Open the *Comments* workbook, and in cell A59, add the comment *What happened to the common name?* Then delete the comment attached to cell E108.

● Continuing in the *Comments* workbook, add *These are special-order items* to the end of the comment attached to cell A103. Size the comment box so that the entire comment is visible, and move the box to an empty area of the worksheet. Then turn off the display of comments.

5.2   Protect and share workbooks

Passwords

If you want only certain people to be able to open and change a workbook, you can assign a password to protect it. Excel then requires that the password be entered correctly before it will allow the workbook to be opened and changed. Anyone who doesn't know the password can open a read-only version.

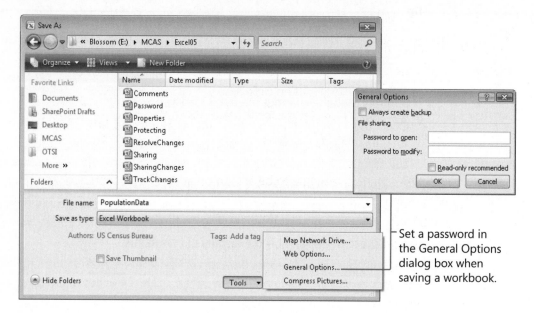

Set a password in the General Options dialog box when saving a workbook.

Tip You can also protect a workbook by using the Information Rights Management (IRM) feature. This requires access to an IRM server.

➤ To set a password

1. Click the **Microsoft Office Button**, click **Save As**, and select the file format you want.

2. In the **Save As** dialog box, specify a location and name for the workbook.

3. At the bottom of the **Save As** dialog box, click **Tools**, and then click **General Options**.

4. In the **General Options** dialog box, enter a password in the **Password to open** box, and optionally in the **Password to modify** box.

   Tip Instead of setting a password, you can select the Read-Only Recommended check box to tell Excel to display a message suggesting that the workbook be opened as read-only.

5. Click **OK** to close the **General Options** dialog box.

6. In the **Confirm Password** dialog box, in the **Reenter password** box, type the password again, and then click **OK**.

7. In the **Save As** dialog box, click **Save**.

Workbook Protection

Sometimes you want people to be able to open and view a workbook but not make changes to it, or you might want to allow only specific people to make particular types of changes. You can protect the information in your workbooks on the following levels:

- **Workbooks.** In the Protect Structure And Windows dialog box, you can prevent users from inserting, deleting, or renaming worksheets or from displaying hidden worksheets. You can also control the moving, closing, or resizing of the workbook windows.

- **Worksheet.** In the Protect Sheet dialog box, you can allow or prevent changes such as the formatting of cells, columns, and rows; the insertion or deletion of columns and rows; sorting or filtering; or the editing of objects or scenarios.

  Tip You cannot protect a worksheet while a workbook is shared; the option remains unavailable until sharing is turned off.

- **Cell.** On the Protection tab of the Format Cells dialog box, you can lock cells or hide formulas. By default, all cells in a protected workbook are locked so they can't be selected; this prevents an unauthorized user not only from changing cell contents but also from viewing a formula that generates cell contents. You can lock or unlock specific cells and cell ranges, and hide formulas in specific cells or cell ranges.

See Also For more information about workbook and worksheet protection, see the Excel Help topic "Protect worksheet or workbook elements".

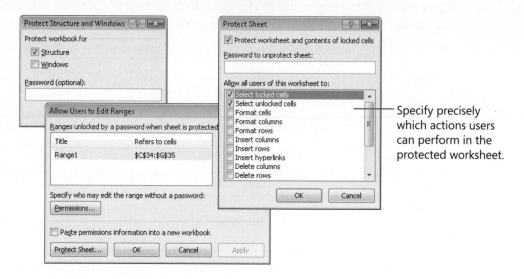

Specify precisely which actions users can perform in the protected worksheet.

➤ To protect workbook structure

1. On the **Review** tab, in the **Changes** group, click the **Protect Workbook** button, and then click **Protect Structure and Windows**.

2. In the **Protect Structure and Windows** dialog box, select the **Structure** check box.

3. If you want, specify a password that can be entered to turn off this protection. Then click **OK**.

➤ To protect workbook windows

1. In the **Protect Structure and Windows** dialog box, select the **Windows** check box.

2. If you want, specify a password that can be entered to turn off this protection. Then click **OK**.

➤ To turn off workbook protection

→ On the **Review** tab, in the **Changes** group, click the **Protect Workbook** button, and then click **Protect Structure and Windows** to remove the check mark.

Worksheet Protection

If you want to prevent changes to all cells other than a particular range in a worksheet, you can apply the desired protection to the entire sheet and then specify the changeable range and which users or groups of users may change it.

➤ **To prevent changes to the active worksheet**

1. On the **Review** tab, in the **Changes** group, click the **Protect Sheet** button.

2. In the **Protect Sheet** dialog box, select or clear check boxes in the **Allow all users of this worksheet to** list.

3. If you want, specify a password that can be entered to turn off this protection. Then click **OK**.

   Tip This step is a prerequisite for enabling the Locked or Hidden cell attributes.

➤ **To turn off worksheet protection**

→ On the **Review** tab, in the **Changes** group, click the **Unprotect Sheet** button.

➤ **To prevent changes to specific worksheet cells of an unprotected worksheet**

1. Start with an unprotected worksheet.

2. Select the cells you want to prevent changes to. On the **Home** tab, in the **Cells** group, click the **Format** button, and then click **Lock Cell**.

3. On the **Home** tab, in the **Cells** group, click the **Format** button, and then click **Protect Sheet**.

   Or

   On the **Review** tab, in the **Changes** group, click the **Protect Sheet** button.

4. In the **Protect Sheet** dialog box, in the **Allow all users of this worksheet to** list, clear the **Select locked cells** check box.

5. If you want, enter a password that must be entered before this protection can be turned off. Then click **OK**.

➤ **To allow changes to specific worksheet cells of a protected worksheet**

1. Start with an unprotected worksheet.

2. On the **Review** tab, in the **Changes** group, click the **Allow Users to Edit Ranges** button.

3. In the **Allow Users to Edit Ranges** dialog box, click the **New** button.

4. In the **New Range** dialog box, enter a range name (or accept the default range number) and cell or cell range you want to allow changes to. (If you have preselected the range, it will be populated in the **Refers to cells** field.) Specify the password a user must enter to edit the cell or cell range, and then click **OK**.

5. To allow specific users to edit the cell or cell range without entering a password, click the **Permissions** button. Then in the **Permissions** dialog box, assign permissions to specific users or groups, and click **OK**.

6. Click **OK** to close the **Allow Users to Edit Ranges** dialog box. If the **Confirm Password** dialog box appears, enter the password so you can continue working, and then click **OK**.

Workbook Sharing

To allow more than one person to access and edit a workbook at the same time, you must first share the workbook.

See Also You must also share the workbook before turning on the change-tracking feature. For information about change tracking, see section 5.1, "Manage changes to workbooks."

After setting up sharing in the Share Workbook dialog box, you can specify the following:

● Whether to keep a history of changes and if so, for how long.

● Whether the file should be updated to reflect changes when it is saved or after a specified period of time. If it is saved after a specified time, you can also indicate which changes you want to see after a save.

● How changes to the same cell by different users should be resolved. If changes are implemented as they are saved, the first person to save is allowed to do so with no warnings; subsequently, for any new modifications to a changed cell, users are prompted to either keep the change that was already saved or save their own change.

● Which settings are set individually in each user's view of the worksheet.

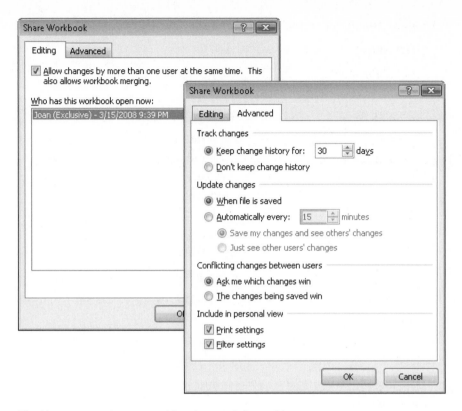

Tip You cannot share a workbook containing tables.

After a workbook is shared, *[Shared]* appears after its title in the title bar. Some Excel features are not available in a shared workbook—for example, the ability to add or change data validation, the ability to group or outline data, and the ability to protect a worksheet.

If you want to share a workbook and prevent users from making changes without you knowing what those changes are, you don't have to share the workbook first. You can share it with the Track Changes feature in effect, so that you can accept or reject all changes.

See Also For information about tracking changes, see section 5.1, "Manage changes to workbooks."

You can stop sharing a workbook at any time. Doing so erases the history of changes and prevents more than one user from making changes at the same time.

➤ To share a workbook for multiuser editing

1. On the **Review** tab, in the **Changes** group, click the **Share Workbook** button.

2. On the **Editing** tab of the **Share Workbook** dialog box, select the **Allow changes by more than one user at the same time** check box.

3. On the **Advanced** tab, make any changes you want to the settings that control track changes, updating, conflicts, and views.

4. Click **OK** in the **Share Workbook** dialog box, and then click **OK** in the message box to save and share the workbook.

➤ To turn off workbook sharing

1. On the **Review** tab, in the **Changes** group, click the **Share Workbook** button.

2. On the **Editing** tab of the **Share Workbook** dialog box, if anyone other than you is listed in the **Who has this workbook open now** box, select that user, and then click **Remove User**.

   Tip As a courtesy, you should contact other users before removing them.

3. Clear the **Allow changes by more than one user at the same time** check box, and then click **OK**.

4. In the message box, click **Yes** to stop sharing the workbook.

> **To require users to track changes in a shared workbook**

1. On the **Review** tab, in the **Changes** group, click the **Protect and Share Workbook** button.

2. In the **Protect Shared Workbook** dialog box, select the **Sharing with track changes** check box.

3. If you want only people with a password to be able to turn off the Track Changes requirement, type the password in the **Password (optional)** box. Then click **OK**.

   Tip If you do not enter a password, anyone can click Unprotect Shared Workbook in the Changes group of the Review tab to turn off Track Changes.

4. If you entered a password, reenter it in the **Confirm Password** dialog box, and click **OK**. Then in the message box, click **OK** to save and share the workbook.

Practice Tasks

The practice files for these tasks are located in the *Documents\Microsoft Press\ MCAS\Excel2007\Objective05* folder. If you want, save the task results in the same folder with *My* prepended to the file name.

- Open the *Password* workbook, set the password to *W0rkB00k* (using a zero in place of each letter *o*) for the file, and save it as *MyPassword*. Then close and reopen the workbook.

- Open the *Protecting* workbook, and restrict all changes in the active worksheet. Then enforce worksheet protection without a password.

- Continuing in the *Protecting* workbook, allow users to edit the range C2:C32 if they enter the password *Super^User*.

- Open the *Sharing* workbook, and share it with a change history of 15 days, automatic saving every 10 minutes, and all other default settings.

- Open the *SharingChanges* workbook, and require that all editing be carried out in Track Changes.

5.3 Prepare workbooks for distribution

Properties

Before distributing a workbook, you might want to attach properties to it so that the file is readily identifiable in the Details view of any browsing dialog box, such as the Open dialog box. You can attach properties to a workbook in the Document Information Panel. Particularly useful are properties called *keywords* in the Document Information Panel, which are identified as *tags* in Windows Vista and in the Details view of browsing dialog boxes.

Document Properties ▼		Location: E:\MCAS\Excel05\Properties.xlsx		✳ Required field ✕
Author:	Title:	Subject:	Keywords:	
Joyce Cox	2009Advertising	2009 budget proposal	magazine advertising cost	
Category:	Status:			
Financial	Draft			
Comments:				
Based on previous year costs + 10 percent				

You enter keywords in the Document Information Panel, separating multiple keywords with semicolons.

Tip In Windows Vista, the properties of a selected workbook are displayed in the Windows Explorer window so that you can accurately identify the workbook without having to open it.

➤ **To display or edit workbook properties from an Excel workbook**

1. On the **Office** menu, point to **Prepare**, and then click **Properties**.

2. In the **Document Information Panel**, click the **Property Views and Options** button, and then click **Document Properties – Server** to display properties associated with a server version of the document (for example, properties used in the document workspace), **Document Properties** to display the common properties stored with the document, or **Advanced Properties** to display the **Properties** dialog box.

3. Enter any properties you want to associate with the document. Fields marked with a red asterisk are required; you must provide information in these fields before saving the document.

➤ **To display properties in a browsing dialog box**

1. Display the dialog box contents in **Details** view.

2. If the Tags property is not displayed, right-click any column heading, and then click **Tags**.

Tip Clicking a property with a check mark removes it from the display. To add or remove more than one property or a property that is not displayed in the basic list, click More, make selections in the Choose Details dialog box, and then click OK.

Document Inspector

Many workbooks go through several revisions. During this development process, information such as the names of people who worked on the workbook, time spent editing the workbook, and comments from reviewers can become attached to the workbook. If the final version will be delivered electronically, you might want to use the Document Inspector to find and remove document properties and personal information as well as any comments, revisions, or hidden content in the workbook.

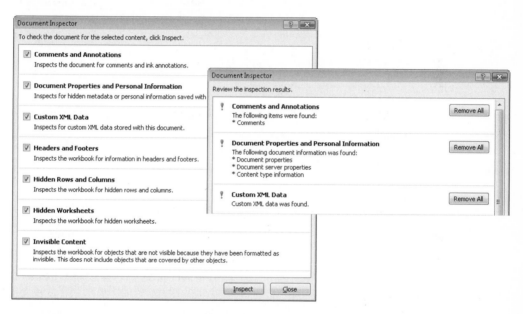

➤ **To inspect a document for properties, editorial marks, and hidden content**

1. On the **Office** menu, point to **Prepare**, and then click **Inspect Document**.

2. In the **Document Inspector** dialog box, clear the check boxes for types of information you don't want to locate, and then click **Inspect**.

➤ **To remove classes of information located by the Document Inspector**

1. When the **Document Inspector** reports its findings, click **Remove All** for any type of information you want to remove.

2. In the **Document Inspector** dialog box, click **Close**.

Permissions

When you are ready to distribute a final workbook, you might want to restrict who can do what, and for how long, with the workbook. If you have access to a server that is running Windows Rights Management Services (RMS) and have RMS Client Service Pack 1 (SP1) installed on your computer, you can assign Read or Change permissions to individual users.

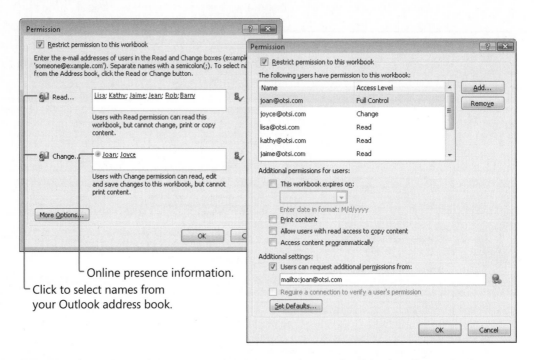

Online presence information.

Click to select names from
your Outlook address book.

Strategy If you do not have access to an RMS server, you should subscribe to the free Microsoft Information Rights Management service by using the wizard that appears the first time you try to restrict permissions for a workbook.

➤ **To restrict permissions for a workbook**

1. On the **Office** menu, point to **Prepare**, click **Restrict Permission**, and then click **Restricted Access**.

2. In the **Permission** dialog box, select the **Restrict permission to this workbook** check box.

3. In the **Read** or **Change** box, type the names of the people to whom you want to assign permission.

   Or

   Click **Read** or **Change** to open your Microsoft Office Outlook address book, double-click users' names in the list, and then click **OK**.

4. To refine the permissions, click **More Options**, adjust the settings in the **Additional permissions for users** and **Additional settings** areas, and click **OK**.

Digital Signatures

When you distribute a workbook, you want the people viewing it to know that it is authentic. You can attach a digital signature—an electronic stamp of authentication—to confirm the origin of the workbook and verify that no one has tampered with the workbook since it was signed.

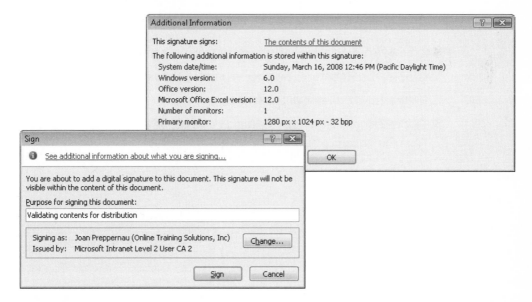

Strategy For purposes of studying for this objective of the certification exam, you need a digital ID. If you do not already have one, follow the instructions for creating your own digital signature in section 6.3, "Attach digital signatures," in Exam 77-601, "Using Microsoft Office Word 2007."

➤ To attach your digital signature to a workbook

1. On the **Office** menu, point to **Prepare**, and then click **Add a Digital Signature**.

2. If a message box opens, displaying information about legal enforceability and a link to the Office Marketplace site, click **OK**.

3. In the **Sign** dialog box, enter the purpose for signing the workbook if you want to record one.

4. If you have multiple digital certificates on this computer, click **Change**, click the certificate you want to use, and then click **OK**.

5. In the **Sign** dialog box, click **Sign**. Then in the **Signature Confirmation** message box, click **OK**.

6. In the **Signatures** task pane, verify that the correct signature has been attached to the workbook.

➤ To view an attached digital signature

→ On the **Office** menu, point to **Prepare**, and then click **View Signatures** to display the **Signatures** task pane.

➤ To remove a digital signature so that you can change a workbook

1. Display the **Signatures** task pane, point to the signature, and click its arrow.

2. In the list, click **Remove Signature**.

3. In the **Remove Signature** message box, click **Yes**. Then click **OK** to acknowledge that the signature has been removed.

Finalizing

To complete preparations for delivery, you might want to mark a workbook as final, which makes its file read-only. When users open a final workbook in Excel, they cannot make changes to the workbook, and the Marked As Final icon appears in the status bar.

➤ **To mark a workbook as final**

1. On the **Office** menu, point to **Prepare**, and then click **Mark as Final**.

2. Click **OK** in the message box that tells you the file will be marked as final and saved, and then click **OK** in the finalization message box.

   Tip To make additional changes to the workbook, point to Prepare on the Office menu and click Mark As Final to reverse the final status.

Practice Tasks

The practice files for these tasks are located in the *Documents\Microsoft Press\ MCAS\Excel2007\Objective05* folder. If you want, save the task results in the same folder with *My* prepended to the file name.

- Open the *Properties* workbook, and attach the keywords *magazine* and *advertising* to the workbook.

- Open the *Finalizing* workbook, and use the quickest method to remove the properties, personal information, headers and footers, and hidden rows and columns.

- Mark the *Finalizing* workbook as final.

5.4 Save workbooks

File Formats

Strategy You should become familiar with the types of file formats in which you can save Excel workbooks and when it is appropriate to use each one.

By default, Excel 2007 files are saved in the .xlsx format, which is the Excel variation of the new Microsoft Office Open XML Formats. Like the other Open XML Formats, the .xlsx format allows for compressed files, improved data recovery, and greater security.

In addition to saving a workbook for use with Excel 2007, you can save it in other formats, including the following:

- **Excel Macro-Enabled Workbook.** If you want to be able to store VBA macro code or Excel 4.0 macro sheets, use the XML-based .xlsm format.

- **Excel 97–2003.** If you want to share an Excel workbook with users of an earlier version of Excel, you can save it in the .xls file format.

- **Single File Web Page or Web Page.** If you want a workbook to be viewable in a Web browser, you can convert it into HTML. Single File Web Pages have the supporting files embedded in the Web page (.mht and .mhl), whereas Web pages have the supporting files in Excel-created folders (.htm and .html).

- **Excel Template.** If you want to be able to use a workbook as the starting point for other workbooks, you can save the file as a template.

- **Text (Tab Delimited) or CSV (Comma Delimited).** If you don't know what program will be used to open the file, you can save it as a delimited text file that can be opened by many programs.

  Tip When you save a workbook in one of the text formats you lose all formatting.

See Also For more information about supported and unsupported file formats, see the Excel Help topic "File formats that are supported in Excel."

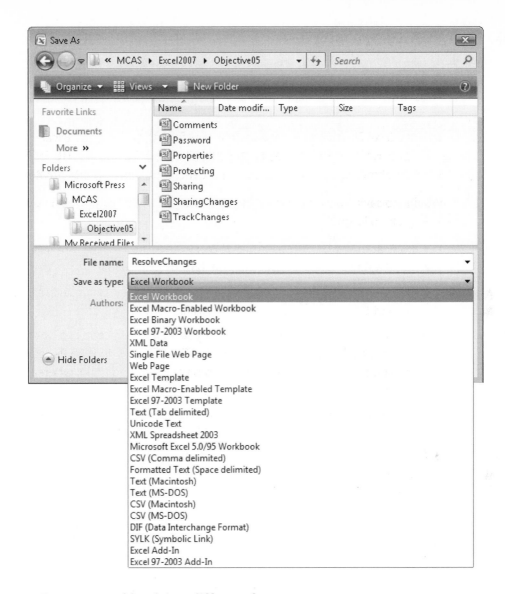

➤ To save a workbook in a different format

1. On the **Office** menu, click **Save As**.

2. In the **Save As** dialog box, select the format you want in the **Save as type** list, and then click **OK**.

Tip If you want someone to be able to view a workbook but not change it, you can download a free add-in from the Microsoft Downloads Web site and then save the workbook in XML Paper Specification (XPS) format or Portable Document Format (PDF) format.

Compatibility Checker

Before saving a workbook in the .xls file format, you can use the Compatibility Checker to check whether the workbook uses features that are not supported in previous versions of Excel. You can then decide how to handle any reported issues.

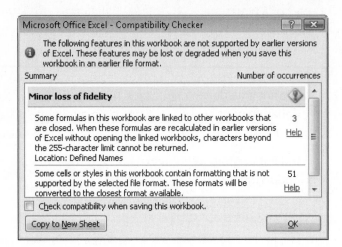

➤ **To check for unsupported features**

1. On the **Office** menu, point to **Prepare**, and then click **Run Compatibility Checker**.

2. Make a note of any issues reported in the **Compatibility Checker** dialog box, and then click **OK**.

Practice Tasks

The practice files for these tasks are located in the *Documents\Microsoft Press\ MCAS\Excel2007\Objective05* folder. If you want, save the task results in the same folder with *My* prepended to the file name.

- Open the *Saving* workbook, and save it so that it can be viewed and worked on by a colleague who has not yet upgraded to Excel 2007.

- Save the *Saving* workbook so that it can be used as the basis for other similar workbooks in the future.

- Save the *Saving* workbook so that the user will be able to run the attached macro.

- Open the *Compatibility* workbook, and check whether it is compatible with Excel 2002.

5.5 Set print options for printing data, worksheets, and workbooks

Print Area

If you want to print only part of a worksheet, you can select the range you want to print and then, in the Print What area of the Print dialog box, click Selection. If you will often print the same portion of the worksheet, you can define that portion as the print area.

After defining the print area, you can add selected ranges to it. A contiguous range becomes part of the original print area definition; a range that is non-contiguous or a different shape becomes a separate print area and is printed on a separate page. You can also remove ranges from the print area.

When you no longer want to limit printing to the print area, you can simply clear it, or check the Print dialog box option Ignore Print Areas.

➤ **To define a selected range as the print area**

→ On the **Page Layout** tab, in the **Page Setup** group, click the **Print Area** button, and then click **Set Print Area**.

➤ **To add a selected range to the print area**

→ On the **Page Layout** tab, in the **Page Setup** group, click the **Print Area** button, and then click **Add to Print Area**.

Tip The Add To Print Area option will not display if the area of the worksheet designated as the print area is currently selected.

➤ **To remove a range from the print area**

1. On the **Page Layout** tab, click the **Page Setup** dialog box launcher.

2. On the **Sheet** tab of the **Page Setup** dialog box, change the range reference in the **Print area** box, and then click **OK**.

➤ **To clear the print area**

→ On the **Page Layout** tab, in the **Page Setup** group, click the **Print Area** button, and then click **Clear Print Area**.

Page Breaks

When the cell entries in a worksheet will not fit within the margins of one printed page, Excel indicates which cells will print on which page by inserting a soft page break. If you want to control how pages break, you can insert manual page breaks. Before printing a worksheet, you can preview the page breaks and fine-tune their placement.

	A	B	C	D	E	F	G	H	I	J
2	Table 3: Estimates of Population Change for the United States, Regions, States, and Puerto Rico and Region and State Rankings: July 1, 2006 to July 1, 2007									
3						National Ranking of Regions and States				
4	Geographic Area	Population Estimates		Change, 2006 to 2007		Population Estimates		Change, 2006 to 2007		
5		########	########	Number	Percent	########	########	Number	Percent	
15	California	36,553,215	36,249,872	303,343	0.8	1	1	2	25	
16	Colorado	4,861,515	4,766,248	95,267	2.0	22	22	7	8	
17	Connecticut	3,502,309	3,495,753	6,556	0.2	29	29	40	44	
18	Delaware	864,764	852,747	12,017	1.4	45	45	35	14	
19	District of Columbia	588,292	585,459	2,833	0.5	50	50	46	36	
20	Florida	18,251,243	18,057,508	193,735	1.1	4	4	4	19	
21	Georgia	9,544,750	9,342,080	202,670	2.2	9	9	3	5	
22	Hawaii	1,283,388	1,278,635	4,753	0.4	42	42	42	37	
23	Idaho	1,499,402	1,463,878	35,524	2.4	39	39	23	4	
24	Illinois	12,852,548	12,777,042	75,506	0.6	5	5	11	33	
25	Indiana	6,345,289	6,302,646	42,643	0.7	15	15	18	31	
26	Iowa	2,988,046	2,972,566	15,480	0.5	30	30	33	34	
27	Kansas	2,775,397	2,755,817	20,180	0.7	33	33	28	28	
28	Kentucky	4,241,474	4,204,444	37,030	0.9	26	26	22	24	
29	Louisiana	4,293,204	4,243,288	49,916	1.2	25	25	16	16	
30	Maine	1,317,207	1,314,910	2,297	0.2	40	40	47	46	
31	Maryland	5,618,344	5,602,017	16,327	0.3	19	19	31	40	
32	Massachusetts	6,449,755	6,434,389	15,366	0.2	14	13	34	42	
33	Michigan	10,071,822	10,102,322	-30,500	-0.3	8	8	51	50	
34	Minnesota	5,197,621	5,154,586	43,035	0.8	21	21	17	26	
35	Mississippi	2,918,785	2,899,112	19,673	0.7	31	31	30	30	
36	Missouri	5,878,415	5,837,633	40,776	0.7	18	18	19	29	
37	Montana	957,861	946,795	11,066	1.2	44	44	36	17	
38	Nebraska	1,774,571	1,763,765	10,806	0.6		38	37	32	
39	Nevada	2,565,382	2,492,427	72,955	2.9		35	12	1	
40	New Hampshire	1,315,828	1,311,821	4,007	0.3		41	43	39	
41	New Jersey	8,685,920	8,666,075	19,845	0.2		11	29	43	
42	New Mexico	1,969,915	1,942,302	27,613	1.4		36	26	13	
43	New York	19,297,729	19,281,988	15,741	0.1	3	3	32	47	
44	North Carolina	9,061,032	8,869,442	191,590	2.2	10	10	5	6	
45	North Dakota	639,715	637,460	2,255	0.4	48	48	48	38	
46	Ohio	11,466,917	11,463,513	3,404	-	7	7	4	49	
47	Oklahoma	3,617,316	3,577,536	39,780	1.1	28	28	4	18	
48	Oregon	3,747,455	3,691,084	56,371	1.5	27	27	66	11	
49	Pennsylvania	12,432,792	12,402,817	29,975	0.2	6	6	24	41	
50	Rhode Island	1,057,832	1,061,641	-3,809	-0.4	43	43	50	51	
51	South Carolina	4,407,709	4,330,108	77,601	1.8	24	24	10	10	
52	South Dakota	796,214	788,467	7,747	1.0	46	46	39	20	
53	Tennessee	6,156,719	6,074,913	81,806	1.3	17	17	9	15	
54	Texas	23,904,380	23,407,629	496,751	2.1	2	2	1	7	
55	Utah	2,645,330	2,579,535	65,795	2.6	34	34	14	3	
56	Vermont	621,254	620,778	476	0.1	43	43	49	48	
57	Virginia	7,712,091	7,640,249	71,842	0.9	12	12	13	21	
58	Washington	6,468,424	6,374,910	93,514	1.5	13	14	8	12	
59	West Virginia	1,812,035	1,808,693	3,336	0.2	37	37	45	45	
60	Wisconsin	5,601,640	5,572,660	28,980	0.5	20	20	25	35	
61	Wyoming	522,830	512,757	10,073	2.0	51	51	38	9	
62										
63	Puerto Rico	3,941,459	3,925,971	15,488	0.4	(X)	(X)	(X)	(X)	
64	Note: Dash (-) represents zero or rounds to zero. (X) Not applicable. See Geographic Terms and Definitions at http://www.census.gov/popest/geographic/ for a list of the states that are included in each region.									
65	Suggested Citation:									
66	Table 3: Estimates of Population Change for the United States, Regions, States, and Puerto Rico and Region and State Rankings: July 1, 2006 to July 1, 2007									
67	Source: Population Division, U.S. Census Bureau									

Joan: Largest increase this year

NST03

➤ **To insert a page break**

1. Click the cell in column A above which you want to insert a horizontal page break.

   Or

   Click the cell in row 1 to the left of which you want to insert a vertical page break.

   Or

   Click a cell anywhere in the worksheet above and to the left of which you want to insert both horizontal and vertical page breaks.

2. On the **Page Layout** tab, in the **Page Setup** group, click the **Breaks** button, and then click **Insert Page Break**.

➤ **To delete a manual page break**

1. Click any cell below or to the right of the page break you want to remove.

2. On the **Page Layout** tab, in the **Page Setup** group, click the **Breaks** button, and then click **Remove Page Break**.

➤ **To delete all manual page breaks**

→ On the **Page Layout** tab, in the **Page Setup** group, click the **Breaks** button, and then click **Reset All Page Breaks**.

➤ **To preview and adjust page breaks**

1. On the **View** toolbar, click the **Page Break Preview** button, and if a message box appears, click **OK**.

2. To adjust an existing page break, point to it, and then drag it in the direction of either of its arrows.

Worksheet Layout

You can control the layout of printed worksheets not only by inserting page breaks but also by changing the margins, orientation, and page size.

If none of these methods enables you to fit the required amount of information on a printed page, you can avoid having to adjust the font size and the width and height of columns and rows by scaling the worksheet to less than 100 percent. This option achieves the effect you want at print time but does not change the worksheet layout for people who will be viewing it onscreen. You can scale the worksheet manually or allow Excel to scale it for you by specifying the number of pages you want the printed worksheet to be.

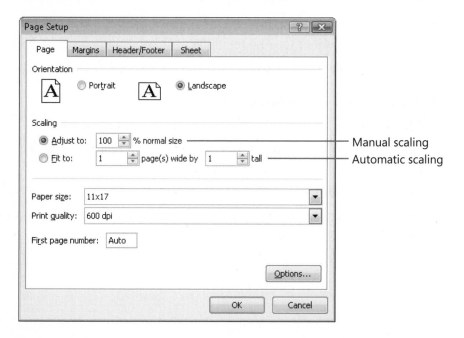

➤ To change the page margins

1. On the **Page Layout** tab, in the **Page Setup** group, click the **Margins** button.

2. In the **Margins** gallery, click the setting you want.

   Or

   Click **Custom Margins**, and then on the **Margins** tab of the **Page Setup** dialog box, specify the settings you want, and click **OK**.

➤ To change the orientation

→ On the **Page Layout** tab, in the **Page Setup** group, click the **Orientation** button, and then click **Landscape** or **Portrait**.

➤ To change the page size

→ On the **Page Layout** tab, in the **Page Setup** group, click the **Size** button, and then make a selection from the **Paper Size** gallery.

➤ To scale the worksheet when printing

1. On the **Page Layout** tab, click the **Page Setup** dialog box launcher.

2. On the **Page** tab of the **Page Setup** dialog box, with **Adjust to** selected in the **Scaling** area, adjust the **% normal size** setting.

   Or

   Click **Fit to**, and then specify the number of pages horizontally and vertically on which you want to print the worksheet.

3. Click **OK**.

Headers and Footers

You can display information on every page of a printed worksheet by creating and formatting headers and footers. You can have a different header and footer on the first page or different headers and footers on odd and even pages. When you create a header or footer, Excel opens header and footer areas and displays a contextual Design tab on the Ribbon. You can enter information in the header and footer areas in the following ways:

- Select ready-made information, such as the company name or the name of the workbook, from a list.
- Type the information the same way you would enter ordinary text.
- Use commands on the Design tab to enter and format items such as the page number or the date and time.

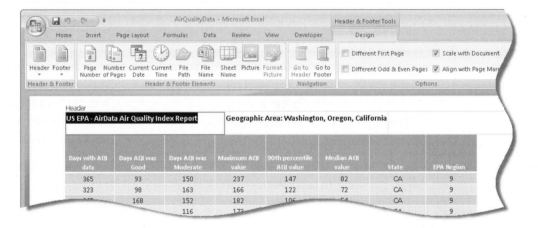

> ➤ **To insert a header or footer**

1. On the **Insert** tab, in the **Text** group, click the **Header & Footer** button.
2. Click the left, center, or right area of the header, and use a combination of typing and the commands on the contextual **Design** tab to create the header you want.
3. On the **Design** tab, in the **Navigation** group, click the **Go to Footer** button.
4. Repeat step 2 to create the footer.
5. Click away from the footer area to review the header and footer in Page Layout view.

> ➤ **To change the header or footer**

→ On the **Insert** tab, in the **Text** group, click the **Header & Footer** button, and then make your changes.

Practice Tasks

The practice files for these tasks are located in the *Documents\Microsoft Press\ MCAS\Excel2007\Objective05* folder. If you want, save the task results in the same folder with *My* prepended to the file name.

● Open the *PrintArea* workbook, and configure the worksheet so that clicking Quick Print prints only columns B and C.

● Open the *PageBreaks* workbook, and insert a page break before row 31. Then review the page breaks, and ensure that only columns A through D will appear on the first page.

● In the *Layout* workbook, display the JanFeb worksheet. By changing only the orientation, ensure that all the contents will print horizontally on two pages of letter-size paper.

● Continuing in the *Layout* workbook, by changing only the margins, ensure that all the contents of the JanFeb worksheet will print on two pages.

● Open the *HeaderFooter* workbook, and create a header that will print on all the pages of the Orders worksheet except the first. On the left, enter today's date; in the center, enter the name of the workbook; and on the right, enter the page number. Return to Normal view, and then change the center section of the header to reflect the name of the worksheet instead of the workbook.

● Continuing in the *HeaderFooter* workbook, remove the page numbers from the header and add them so they print at the bottom of each page.

Objective Review

Before finishing this chapter, ensure that you have mastered the following skills:

5.1 Manage changes to workbooks.

5.2 Protect and share workbooks.

5.3 Prepare workbooks for distribution.

5.4 Save workbooks.

5.5 Set print options for printing data, worksheets, and workbooks.

Using Microsoft Office
PowerPoint 2007

This part of the book covers the skills you need to have for certification as a Microsoft Office Specialist in Microsoft Office PowerPoint 2007. Specifically, you need to be able to complete tasks that demonstrate the following skill sets:

1 Creating and Formatting Presentations
2 Creating and Formatting Slide Content
3 Working with Visual Content
4 Collaborating On and Delivering Presentations

With these skills, you can create the types of presentations you will most commonly use in a business environment.

Prerequisites

We assume that you have been working with PowerPoint 2007 for at least six months and that you know how to carry out fundamental tasks that are not specifically mentioned in the Microsoft Office Specialist objectives for Exam 77-603, "Using Microsoft Office PowerPoint 2007." Before you begin studying for this exam, you might want to make sure you are familiar with the information in this section.

Understanding PowerPoint Views

You work in a PowerPoint presentation in one of four views:

- **Normal view.** You do most presentation and slide content development work in this view, where the program window is divided into three panes.

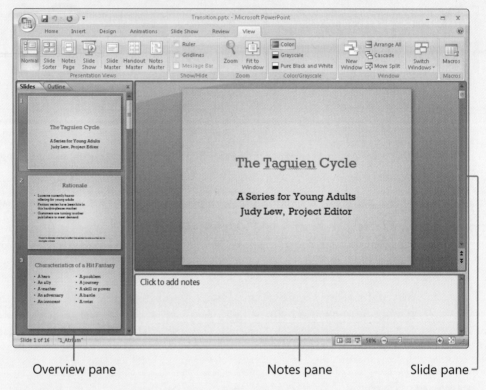

Overview pane   Notes pane   Slide pane

Tip We use the names shown in the graphic to make it easier to refer to the Normal view panes in procedures.

- **Slide Sorter view.** You work with the presentation and its slides as a whole in this view. You cannot edit the slide contents, but you can move, insert, and delete slides within the presentation.

- **Slide Show view.** You deliver a presentation in this view. You also use it throughout development to see the effect of changes from your audience's perspective.

- **Notes Page view.** You work with the presenter notes in this view. You cannot edit the slide contents.

When making changes to the base templates on which slides, handouts, and notes are built, you work in the corresponding Master view.

See Also For information about the Master views, see section 1.2, "Customize slide masters" and section 4.4 "Prepare printed materials."

Entering Slide Text

When you add a new slide to a presentation, the layout you select indicates the type and position of the objects on the slide with placeholders. Most slides have a placeholder for a title and either a bulleted list with one or more levels of bullet points (and subordinate levels called *subpoints*) or an illustration such as a table, chart, graphic, or movie clip. You can enter text directly into a placeholder on a slide in the Slide pane, or you can enter text on the Outline tab of the Overview pane, where the entire presentation is displayed in outline form. As you type, the text appears both on the slide and on the Outline tab.

See Also If you want to add text to a slide that has no text placeholder, you do so in an independent text box. For information about creating text boxes, see section 2.1, "Insert and format text boxes."

From the Slide pane or the Outline tab, you can use the keyboard to quickly create slide text, as follows:

- Pressing Enter creates a new item at the same level as the current one. On the Outline tab, you can quickly create a new slide by pressing Enter while a slide title is active.

- Pressing Tab demotes the current item to the next lower level. For example, a bullet point becomes a subpoint. On the Outline tab, you can also demote slide titles to bullet points.

- Pressing Shift+Tab promotes the current item to the next higher level. For example, a subpoint becomes a bullet point. On the Outline tab, you can promote a bullet point to a slide title.

Tip You can use the Increase List Level and Decrease List Level buttons to promote and demote text items. However, it is often quicker to use keys—Tab and Shift+Tab—to perform these functions than it is to take your hands off the keyboard to use your mouse.

Selecting Text

Before you can edit or format existing text, you have to select it. Selected text appears highlighted on the screen. You can select specific items as follows:

- **A word.** Double-click it. The word and the space following it are selected. Punctuation following a word is not selected.

- **A bullet point or subpoint.** Click its bullet on either the Outline tab or in the Slide pane.

- **All the text in a placeholder.** Click inside the placeholder, click Select in the Editing group on the Home tab, and then click Select All.

- **All the text on a slide.** Click its slide icon on the Outline tab.

  Tip You can select adjacent words, lines, or paragraphs by dragging through them.

Selected text appears highlighted in the location where you made the selection—that is, on either the slide or the Outline tab.

Moving Around in a Presentation

When developing a presentation in Normal view, you can move around in several ways:

➤ **To display a specific slide in the Slides pane**

→ On the **Outline** tab or the **Slides** tab of the **Overview** pane, click the slide's icon.

➤ **To move backward or forward one slide at a time**

→ At the bottom of the vertical scroll bar to the right of the **Slides** pane, click the **Previous Slide** or **Next Slide** button.

  Tip Clicking the up or down scroll arrow has the same effect.

➤ **To move to a different slide in a presentation**

→ On the vertical scroll bar, drag the scroll box until the adjacent ScreenTip indicates that the slide you want will be displayed if you release the mouse button.

1 Creating and Formatting Presentations

The skills tested in this section of the Microsoft Office Specialist exam for Microsoft Office PowerPoint 2007 relate to presentations as a whole rather than to individual slides or slide content. Specifically, the following objectives are associated with this set of skills:

1.1 Create new presentations.

1.2 Customize slide masters.

1.3 Add elements to slide masters.

1.4 Create and change presentation elements.

1.5 Arrange slides.

Using templates simplifies the creation of consistent presentations, both for yourself and across your organization. Knowing how to manipulate a presentation as a whole is important for efficient presentation development, and being able to work skillfully with slide masters helps you create unique slide shows tailored to your needs.

This chapter guides you in studying ways of creating presentations and customizing masters by applying themes, adding backgrounds, changing the master elements, and creating custom master layouts. You will also study ways of changing the size, orientation, number, and arrangement of slides, and the transition between them.

Important Before you can use the practice files in this chapter, you need to install them from the book's companion CD to their default location. See "Using the Companion CD" at the beginning of this book for more information.

Tip Graphics and operating system–related instructions in this book reflect the Windows Vista user interface. If your computer is running Windows XP and you experience trouble following the instructions as written, refer to the sidebar "If You Are Running Windows XP" in "Working in the Microsoft Office Fluent User Interface" at the beginning of this book.

1.1 Create new presentations

Blank Presentations

When you first start PowerPoint, the program window displays a temporary presentation consisting of one blank title slide. You can develop a new presentation from scratch from this blank presentation, and create new blank presentations at any time.

➤ **To create a blank presentation**

1. Click the **Microsoft Office Button**, and then click **New**.
2. In the **New Presentation** dialog box, double-click **Blank Presentation**.

Templates

Creating presentations from scratch is time-consuming. In the New Presentation dialog box, you can create a presentation based on one of several templates installed on your computer with the PowerPoint program. You can also preview and download templates from Microsoft Office Online. Some templates come complete with content you can customize to meet your needs; others are design templates—blank presentations with formatting, a color scheme, and sometimes graphics already applied to them.

Also from the New Presentation dialog box, you can create a new presentation based on any existing presentation, even if it hasn't been saved as a template.

➤ To create a presentation based on a template

1. On the **Office** menu, click **New**.

2. In the left pane of the **New Presentation** dialog box, under **Microsoft Office Online**, click the type of template you want.

3. In the middle pane, if a category list appears, click the category you want. Then click the template you want, and click **Download**.

➤ To create a presentation based on an existing presentation

1. Display the **New Presentation** dialog box. In the left pane, under **Templates**, click **New from existing**.

2. In the **New from Existing Presentation** dialog box, navigate to the folder containing the presentation on which you want to base the new one, and then double-click that presentation.

Outlines

You can easily create a presentation based on an outline saved as a Microsoft Office Word document (*.doc* or *.docx*) or a Rich Text Format (RTF) file (*.rtf*). PowerPoint creates a slide for each. When you open the outline in PowerPoint, the heading styles in the outline become slide titles and bullet points.

➤ **To create a presentation based on a Word 2007 outline**

1. On the **Office** menu, click **Open**.

2. In the **Open** dialog box, click **All PowerPoint Presentations**, and in the list of file types, click **All Files**.

3. Navigate to the outline document you want to use, and then double-click it.

Practice Tasks

The practice files for these tasks are located in the *Documents\Microsoft Press\ MCAS\PowerPoint2007\Objective01* folder. If you want, save the task results in the same folder with *My* appended to the file name.

- Create a new blank presentation, and save it with the name *MyBlank*.

- Create a new presentation based on the *Company Meeting Presentation* template in the Presentations/Business category of Office Online, and save it with the name *MyTemplate*.

- Create a new presentation based on the *Existing* presentation, and save it with the name *MyExisting*.

- Create a new presentation based on the *Outline* document, and save it with the name *MyOutline*.

1.2 Customize slide masters

Slide Masters

By default, PowerPoint presentations have three masters:

- **Slide master.** This master controls the look of all the slides in a presentation, such as the theme, text placement, and background graphics. The master includes designs for most of the layouts you are likely to want to use.

- **Handout master.** This master controls the look of student handouts.

- **Notes master.** This master controls the look of speaker notes.

  See Also For information about the masters for notes and handouts, see section 4.4, "Prepare printed materials."

When you create a new presentation, its slides assume the design of its slide master, which by default contains placeholders for a title, bullet points, the date, the slide number, and footer information. The placeholders control the position of the corresponding elements on the slide. Text placeholders also control the formatting of their text.

On an individual slide, you can make changes to the design elements provided by the master, but you can change the basic design only on the master. When you change a design element on the master, all the slides reflect the change.

See Also For information about overriding the master design for a particular slide, see section 2, "Creating and Formatting Slide Content."

To make changes to a presentation's master, you switch to Slide Master view, which adds a Slide Master tab to the Ribbon and hides the tabs that aren't needed. In this view, the slide master thumbnail is displayed at the top of the Overview pane, followed by thumbnails of its associated layouts.

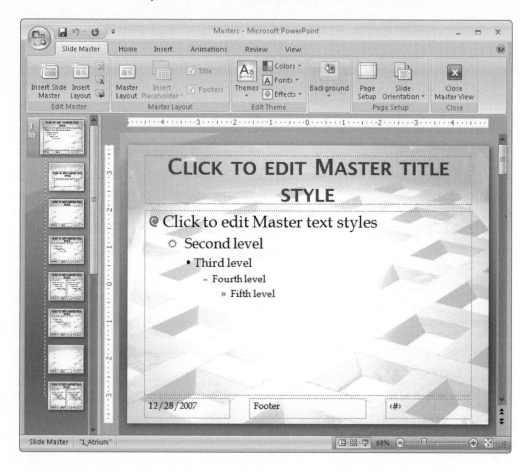

By displaying the slide master and clicking buttons on the Slide Master tab, you can make the following adjustments, which are applied to all the layouts:

● Add a new layout with the same background, title, and footer style to which you can add your own placeholders.

See Also For information about adding and customizing a master layout, see section 1.3, "Add elements to slide masters."

● Delete or rename a selected layout.

● Apply a theme; or change the colors, fonts, or effects associated with the current theme.

● Control the background color, texture, and graphics.

● Change the default page setup for the presentation.

You can also make another slide master available to the presentation and preserve that master so that it remains available even if it is not currently used in the presentation.

➤ **To switch to Slide Master view**

→ On the **View** tab, in the **Presentation Views** group, click the **Slide Master** button.

➤ **To close Slide Master view**

→ On the **Slide Master** tab, in the **Close** group, click the **Close Master View** button.

→ On the **View** toolbar at the right end of the status bar, click any view button.

See Also While working in Slide Master view, you can format text placeholders, insert graphic objects, and add animations and transitions to the slide master or its layouts. For information, see section 2, "Creating and Formatting Slide Content," and section 3, "Working with Visual Content."

Themes

The primary formatting of the slide master is dictated by a theme—a combination of colors, fonts, formatting, graphics, and other elements that gives the presentation a coherent look. Even a presentation developed from scratch has a theme, albeit one that consists of only a white background and a basic set of font styles and sizes. You can change the theme applied to the slide master at any time by making a selection from the Themes gallery.

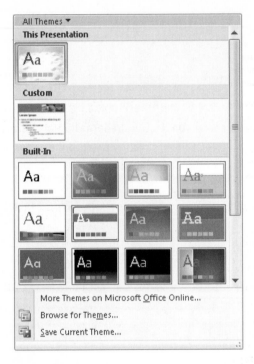

If you like some components of the theme but not others, you can change the following:

- **Colors.** Every presentation, even a blank one, has an associated set of 12 complementary colors: four Text/Background colors for dark or light text on a dark or light background; Accent 1 through Accent 6 for the colors of objects other than text; Hyperlink to draw attention to hyperlinks; and Followed Hyperlink to indicate visited hyperlinks. Ten of these colors appear with light to dark gradients in the various color palettes. (The two background colors are not represented in these palettes.)

- **Fonts.** Every presentation, even a blank one, has an associated set of two fonts. The Fonts gallery lists the combination of fonts that is used by each of the themes, in alphabetical order by theme. The top font in each combination is used for titles, and the bottom font is used for other slide text.

- **Effects.** Like the Fonts gallery, the Effects gallery displays the combination of effects that is applied to shapes on the slides by each of the themes.

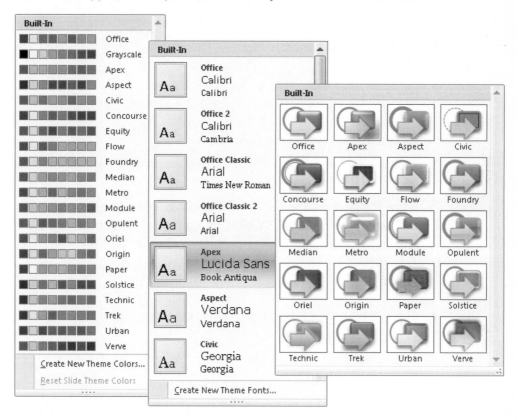

Changes made to a component of a theme are stored with the presentation and do not affect the default theme.

➤ **To apply a theme to the slide master**

1. Display **Slide Master** view, and in the **Overview** pane, click the slide master.

2. On the **Slide Master** tab, in the **Edit Theme** group, click the **Themes** button.

3. In the **Themes** gallery, click the theme you want.

➤ **To change the theme colors, fonts, or effects**

1. Display **Slide Master** view, and in the **Overview** pane, click the slide master.

2. On the **Slide Master** tab, in the **Edit Theme** group, click the **Colors**, **Fonts**, or **Effects** button.

3. In the corresponding gallery, click the color scheme, font set, or combination of effects you want.

➤ **To create a new color set or font set**

1. On the **Slide Master** tab, in the **Edit Themes** group, click the **Theme Colors** button, and then in the list, click **Create New Theme Colors**.

2. In the **Create New Theme Colors** dialog box, select the colors you want to use for each of the four **Text/Background** colors, the six **Accent** colors, and the two **Hyperlink** colors.

3. Enter a name for the color set in the **Name** box, and then click **Save**.

   Or

1. In the **Edit Themes** group, click the **Theme Fonts** button, and then in the list, click **Create New Theme Fonts**.

2. In the **Create New Theme Fonts** dialog box, select the **Heading** and **Body** fonts you want to use.

3. Enter a name for the font set in the **Name** box, and then click **Save**.

➤ **To save a custom theme**

1. In the **Themes** gallery, click **Save Current Theme**.

2. In the **Save Current Theme** dialog box, enter a name for the theme in the **File name** box, and then click **Save**.

Background

You can customize the background of all the slides in a presentation by applying the following to the slide master:

- **Background style.** These ready-made choices include solid colors and gradients reflecting the color scheme applied to the presentation.
- **Solid fill.** This simple effect can be customized with varying degrees of transparency.
- **Color gradient.** In these visual effects, a solid color gradually changes from light to dark or dark to light. PowerPoint offers several gradient patterns, each with several variations. You can also choose a preset arrangement of colors from professionally designed backgrounds in which the different colors gradually merge.
- **Texture.** PowerPoint comes with several preset textures that you can easily apply to the background of slides.
- **Picture.** You can also add a picture to the background as a single object or as a tiled image that fills the entire slide.

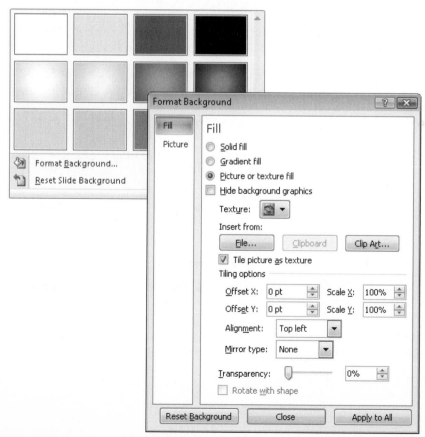

➤ **To apply a background style to the slide master**

1. Display **Slide Master** view, and in the **Overview** pane, click the slide master.

2. On the **Slide Master** tab, in the **Background** group, click the **Background Styles** button.

3. In the **Background Styles** gallery, click the style you want.

➤ **To fill the background with a color, gradient, or texture**

1. Display **Slide Master** view, and in the **Overview** pane, click the slide master.

2. On the **Slide Master** tab, click the **Background** dialog box launcher.

3. On the **Fill** page of the **Format Background** dialog box, click the option you want.

4. Choose the color or texture, and fine-tune the effect as necessary.

5. Click **Apply to All**, and then click **OK**.

➤ **To fill the background with a picture**

1. Display **Slide Master** view, and in the **Overview** pane, click the slide master.

2. On the **Slide Master** tab, click the **Background** dialog box launcher.

3. On the **Fill** page of the **Format Background** dialog box, click **Picture or texture fill**, and then click **File**.

4. In the **Insert Picture** dialog box, navigate to the folder containing the picture, and double-click it.

5. Fine-tune the effect as necessary.

    Tip You can adjust the color, brightness, and contrast of the picture on the Picture page of the Format Background dialog box.

6. Click **Apply to All**, and then click **OK**.

Practice Tasks

The practice file for these tasks is located in the *Documents\Microsoft Press\ MCAS\PowerPoint2007\Objective01* folder. If you want, save the task results in the same folder with *My* appended to the file name.

- Open a new blank presentation, and ensure that the Apex theme will be automatically applied to any slides you create. Then change the color scheme that will be used for all slides to Verve.

- Open another blank presentation, and ensure that any slides you create will be formatted with the Style 8 background. Then change the background for all slides to the Denim texture.

- In the blank presentation, change the background so that any slides you create will be filled with the *Mosaic* graphic.

1.3 Add elements to slide masters

Layouts

If a slide master does not include a layout you need for a presentation, you can insert a new layout and then add the desired elements and formatting. You can also modify an existing layout. If you might want to use the existing layout, you can duplicate it and then save it with a new name.

Pointing to a layout in the Overview pane in Slide Master view displays the name of the layout and the number of slides that use it in the presentation. If a layout is not used by any slide, you can delete it.

➤ **To insert a new master layout**

1. In the **Overview** pane of **Slide Master** view, click the layout after which you want to insert the new layout.

2. On the **Slide Master** tab, in the **Edit Master** group, click the **Insert Layout** button.

➤ **To duplicate a selected master layout**

→ In the **Overview** pane of **Slide Master** view, right-click the layout you want to duplicate, and then click **Duplicate Layout**.

➤ **To rename a selected master layout**

1. On the **Slide Master** tab, in the **Edit Master** group, click the **Rename** button.

2. In the **Rename Layout** dialog box, type a name, and then click **Rename**.

➤ **To delete a selected master layout**

→ On the **Slide Master** tab, in the **Edit Master** group, click the **Delete** button.

Content Placeholders

By default, the slide master includes ready-made placeholders for a title, bullet points, the date, a footer, and the slide number. You can delete any of these placeholders from the slide master the same way you would delete an ordinary text box. If you later want to restore a placeholder, you can select it from the Master Layout dialog box.

See Also For information about deleting text boxes, see section 2.1, "Insert and format text boxes."

You can add ready-made placeholders for content such as text, tables, and charts to any layout. After selecting the type of placeholder you want, you drag to create a place-holder of the size and in the location you want. You can also turn the title placeholder on or off. If you have not deleted the ready-made placeholders for the date, footer, and slide number (collectively known as the *footers*) on the slide master, you can turn those placeholders on and off.

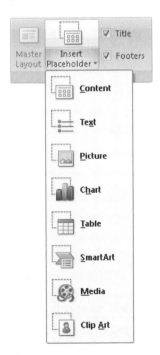

Strategy The way the standard repeating information on the slide master, its layouts, and individual slides interact is not very intuitive. You should experiment with slide master changes, observing their effects on the layouts and slides. That way, you will know where to make different types of changes for maximum efficiency.

➤ **To restore a placeholder to the slide master**

1. In the **Overview** pane in **Slide Master** view, click the slide master.

2. On the **Slide Master** tab, in the **Master Layout** group, click the **Master Layout** button.

3. In the **Master Layout** dialog box, select the check box of the type of placeholder you want to restore, and then click **OK**.

➤ **To change the date and time format on the slide master**

1. With the slide master displayed, in the **Slide** pane, click the date in the **Date** placeholder to select the entire field.

2. On the **Insert** tab, in the **Text** group, click **Date & Time**.

3. In the **Date and Time** dialog box, click the format you want.

4. If you want PowerPoint to update the date each time the presentation is opened, select the **Update automatically** check box. Then click **OK**.

5. To apply the new format to all the layouts, click the date, and then on the **Insert** tab, in the **Text** group, click **Header & Footer**.

6. Without changing the settings in the **Header and Footer** dialog box, click **Apply to All**.

Tip To hide the date and other repeating information on the title slide, select the Don't Show On Title Slide check box before clicking Apply To All.

➤ **To add a content placeholder to a selected master layout**

1. On the **Slide Master** tab, in the **Master Layout** group, click the **Insert Placeholder** arrow.

2. In the **Placeholder** gallery, click the type of placeholder you want to add.

3. In the **Slide** pane, position the crosshair pointer, and drag down and to the right to draw a placeholder of the size and in the location you want.

See Also For information about sizing and repositioning existing placeholders, see section 2.1, "Insert and format text boxes."

➤ **To display or hide the title placeholder on a selected master layout**

→ On the **Slide Master** tab, in the **Master Layout** group, select or clear the **Title** check box.

➤ **To display or hide repeating information on a selected master layout**

→ On the **Slide Master** tab, in the **Master Layout** group, select or clear the **Footers** check box.

Custom Elements

In addition to adding ready-made placeholders to the slide master and its layouts, you can add custom elements, including most objects that can be placed on individual slides. Likely candidates are graphics such as logos and repeating text such as slogans.

➤ **To add a graphic to the slide master**

1. In the **Overview** pane in **Slide Master** view, click the slide master.

2. On the **Insert** tab, in the **Illustrations** group, click the **Picture** button.

3. In the **Insert Picture** dialog box, locate and double-click the graphic you want to insert.

   See Also For information about sizing and moving graphics, see section 3.5, "Arrange illustrations and other content."

Practice Tasks

The practice file for these tasks is located in the *Documents\Microsoft Press\ MCAS\PowerPoint2007\Objective01* folder. If you want, save the task results in the same folder with *My* appended to the file name.

- Open a new blank presentation, insert a new master layout after the Title Slide Layout, and then delete the Blank Layout.

- In the blank presentation, insert a copy of the Two Content Layout. Then change the name of the copy to *My Two Content*.

- Open another blank presentation, and add a Table placeholder to the Title Only Layout. Then rename the layout as *My Table*.

- In the blank presentation, turn off the footer placeholders on the Title Slide Layout.

- In the blank presentation, insert the *Logo* graphic in the lower-right corner of all the slides.

1.4   Create and change presentation elements

Slide Orientation and Size

By default, slides are sized for an on-screen slide show, oriented horizontally, with slides numbered starting at 1. If you need to print a presentation, you can set the size and orientation of your slides to fit the paper. The size and orientation can be controlled from the Slide Master tab in Slide Master view or without displaying the slide master.

In the Page Setup dialog box, you can select from Portrait and Landscape orientation, and from the following slide sizes:

- **On-screen Show.** For an electronic slide show on screens of various aspects (4:3, 16:9, or 16:10)
- **Letter Paper.** For a presentation printed on 8.5 by 11 inch U.S. letter-size paper
- **Ledger Paper.** For a presentation printed on 11 by 17 inch legal-size paper
- **A3 Paper, A4 Paper, B4 (ISO) Paper, B5 (ISO) Paper.** For a presentation printed on paper of various international sizes
- **35mm Slides.** For 35mm slides to be used in a carousel with a projector
- **Overhead.** For transparencies for an overhead projector
- **Banner.** For a banner for a Web page
- **Custom.** For slides that are a non-standard size

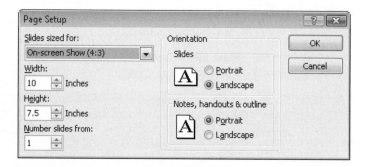

➤ **To change the orientation of slides**

1. On the **Design** or **Slide Master** tab, in the **Page Setup** group, click **Slide Orientation**.

2. Click either **Portrait** or **Landscape**.

➤ **To set the size of slides**

1. On the **Design** or **Slide Master** tab, in the **Page Setup** group, click **Page Setup**.

2. In the **Page Setup** dialog box, set the width and height of the slides, and click **OK**.

Transitions

Transitions control the way successive slides move into view. They include such effects as sliding in, dissolving in from the outer edges or the center, and opening like a vertical blind.

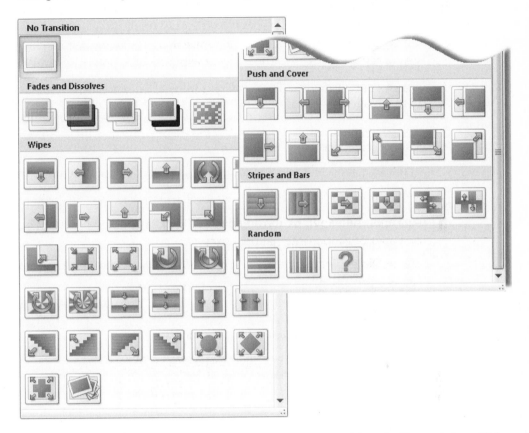

Each slide can have only one transition. You can set transitions in Normal view, Slide Sorter view, or Slide Master view, and you can set them for one slide at a time, for a group of slides, or for an entire presentation. In addition to selecting the type of transition, you can specify the following:

- The sound
- The speed
- When the transition occurs

➤ **To add transitions between slides**

→ On the **Animations** tab, in the **Transition to This Slide** group, display the **Transitions** gallery, and then click the transition you want.

➤ **To incorporate a sound into a transition**

→ In the **Transition to This Slide** group, click the sound you want in the **Transition Sound** list.

Tip To associate a sound file of your own with a slide transition, click Other Sound at the bottom of the Transition Sound list. Then in the Add Sound dialog box, find and select the sound file you want to use, and click Open.

➤ **To change the speed of a transition**

→ In the **Transition to This Slide** group, click the speed you want in the **Transition Speed** list.

➤ **To apply the same transition to all slides**

→ In the **Transition to This Slide** group, click the **Apply To All** button.

➤ **To remove transitions between slides**

1. In the **Transition to This Slide** group, display the **Transitions** gallery, and then click **No Transition**.

2. In the **Transition to This Slide** group, click the **Apply To All** button.

Practice Tasks

The practice files for these tasks are located in the *Documents\Microsoft Press\MCAS\PowerPoint2007\Objective01* folder. If you want, save the task results in the same folder with *My* appended to the file name.

● Open the *Printing* presentation, change the slide orientation to Portrait, and then size the slides to fit Letter Paper.

● Open the *Transition* presentation, and apply the Cover Left-Up transition to all the slides in the presentation. Add the Wind sound to the transition, and then set the transition speed to Slow.

● Open the *NoTransition* presentation, and remove the transition effect from all the slides.

1.5 Arrange slides

Adding and Deleting

No matter how you create a presentation, you will probably need to add new slides and delete ones you no longer need. When you add a slide, PowerPoint inserts it with the default layout immediately after the current slide. If you want to add a slide with a different layout, you can select the layout you want from the New Slide list. You can also duplicate one or more existing slides as the basis for new slides, create new slides by inserting an existing outline, and reuse slides stored in existing presentations on your hard disk or in a Microsoft SharePoint slide library.

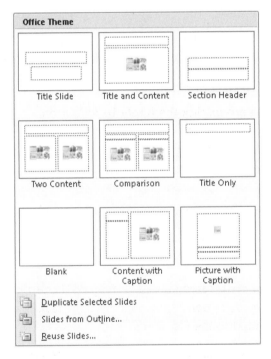

See Also For information about reusing slides, see section 2.3, "Add and link existing content to presentations."

➤ **To insert a new slide after the current slide**

→ On the **Home** tab, in the **Slides** group, click the **New Slide** button to insert a slide with the default layout.

Or

1. On the **Home** tab, in the **Slides** group, click the **New Slide** arrow.

2. In the **New Slide** gallery, click the layout you want.

➤ **To duplicate a slide**

→ On the **Slides** tab in the **Overview** pane, right-click the slide, and then click **Duplicate Slide**.

➤ **To insert slides from an outline**

1. On the **Home** tab, in the **Slides** group, click the **New Slide** arrow.

2. At the bottom of the **New Slide** gallery, click **Slides from Outline**.

3. In the **Insert Outline** dialog box, locate and double-click the outline file.

See Also For information about creating a new presentation from an outline, see section 1.1, "Create new presentations."

➤ **To delete the current slide**

→ On the **Home** tab, in the **Slides** group, click the **Delete** button.

Slide Order

After you have created several slides, you might need to rearrange them so that they effectively communicate your message. You can rearrange a presentation in three ways:

● In Slide Sorter view, you can drag slide thumbnails into the correct order.

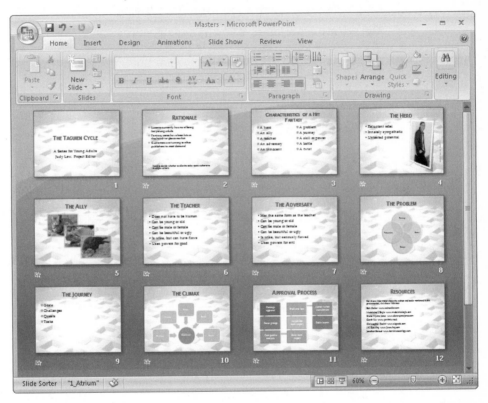

● In Normal view, you can drag slides up and down in the Overview pane to change their order.

● You can also cut and paste slides in the Overview pane.

Tip On the Outline tab of the Overview pane, you can hide bullet points under slide titles to make it easier to rearrange slides. Double-click the icon of the slide whose bullet points you want to hide. Double-click again to redisplay the bullet points. To expand or collapse the entire outline at once, right-click the title of any slide, point to Expand or Collapse, and then click Expand All or Collapse All.

➤ To reorganize slides in Slide Sorter view

1. On the **View** toolbar, click the **Slide Sorter** button.

2. Adjust the size of the thumbnails as necessary to see all the slide thumbnails, by clicking the **Zoom In** or **Zoom Out** button on the **View** toolbar.

3. Drag the slide thumbnails to their new positions.

   Tip You can move slides from one open presentation to another in Slide Sorter view. Display both presentations in Slide Sorter view, and then on the View tab, in the Window group, click the Arrange All button. You can then drag slides from one presentation window to another.

➤ To move a slide in Normal view

→ On the **Slides** tab of the **Overview** pane, click the slide's thumbnail, and then drag it up or down.

Or

1. On the **Slides** tab, click the slide's thumbnail, and then cut it.

2. Click the thumbnail of the slide after which you want the cut slide to appear, and then paste the slide.

Or

→ On the **Outline** tab of the **Overview** pane, click the icon of the slide, and then drag it up or down.

Or

1. On the **Outline** tab of the **Overview** pane, click the slide's icon, and then cut the selection, clicking **Yes** to confirm the command.

2. Click the icon of the slide after which you want the cut slide to appear, and then paste the slide.

Practice Tasks

The practice files for these tasks are located in the *Documents\Microsoft Press\ MCAS\PowerPoint2007\Objective01* folder. If you want, save the task results in the same folder with *My* appended to the file name.

- Open the *NewSlide* presentation, and add a new slide with the default layout after the title slide. Then add a slide with two content placeholders.

- Open the *DeleteSlide* presentation, and delete Slide 6.

- Open the *RearrangeSlides* presentation, and reorder the slides so that Slide 8 (*The Teacher*) appears before Slide 6 (*The Problem*). Then make Slide 9 (*The Adversary*) appear before Slide 7 (*The Problem*).

Objective Review

Before finishing this chapter, ensure that you have mastered the following skills:

1.1 Create new presentations.
1.2 Customize slide masters.
1.3 Add elements to slide masters.
1.4 Create and change presentation elements.
1.5 Arrange slides.

2 Creating and Formatting Slide Content

The skills tested in this section of the Microsoft Office Specialist exam for Microsoft Office PowerPoint 2007 relate to inserting and formatting text-based content. Specifically, the following objectives are associated with this set of skills:

2.1 Insert and format text boxes.
2.2 Manipulate text.
2.3 Add and link existing content to presentations.
2.4 Apply, customize, modify, and remove animations.

For each slide to accomplish its purpose, it needs to present its content in the most effective way. For most presentations, text is the foundation on which you build everything else, and knowing how to work with text in text boxes is a basic skill for PowerPoint. But other types of content play an important role, whether they are inserted directly or as links on slides.

This chapter guides you in studying various ways of working with text, WordArt, sounds, movies, and links on slides, and animating the transition between slides.

 Important Before you can use the practice files in this chapter, you need to install them from the book's companion CD to their default location. See "Using the Companion CD" at the beginning of this book for more information.

Tip Graphics and operating system–related instructions in this book reflect the Windows Vista user interface. If your computer is running Windows XP and you experience trouble following the instructions as written, refer to the sidebar "If You Are Running Windows XP" in "Working in the Microsoft Office Fluent User Interface" at the beginning of this book.

2.1   Insert and format text boxes

Text Boxes

The size and position of the placeholders on a slide are dictated by the slide's design. Every slide you create with a particular layout has the same placeholders in the same locations, and the text you type in them has the same format.

See Also For information about the master layouts that control slide designs, see section 1.2, "Customize slide masters."

When you want additional text to appear on the slide, such as annotations or minor points that do not belong in a bulleted list, you can create two types of text boxes:

- **Fixed height.** The box grows horizontally to fit what you type, even expanding beyond the border of the slide if necessary.
- **Fixed width.** The box grows vertically to fit what you type.

When you click in a text box, an insertion point appears, and the box is surrounded by a dashed border. You can then edit the text—for example, you can add, delete, or correct words and punctuation. Clicking the dashed border changes it to a solid border, indicating that the box itself is selected. You can then manipulate the text box as a unit—for example, you can size, move, or copy it as a whole.

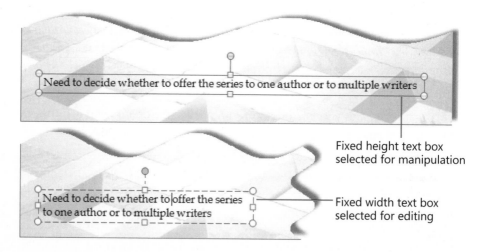

Fixed height text box
selected for manipulation

Fixed width text box
selected for editing

➤ **To insert a text box**

1. On the **Insert** tab, in the **Text** group, click the **Text Box** button.

2. Click the slide where you want the upper-left corner of the text box to appear, and then type the text.

Size and Position

PowerPoint adjusts the size of a text box you create to fit the text within it. (It does not adjust the size of content placeholders.) You can drag the handles around the border of either type of text box to change its size and shape manually, or you can specify precise dimensions. Similarly, you can manually move a text box, or you can set precise coordinates.

Tip To change the size or position of the same placeholder on every slide, make the adjustments on the slide's master layout; see section 1.2, "Customize slide masters."

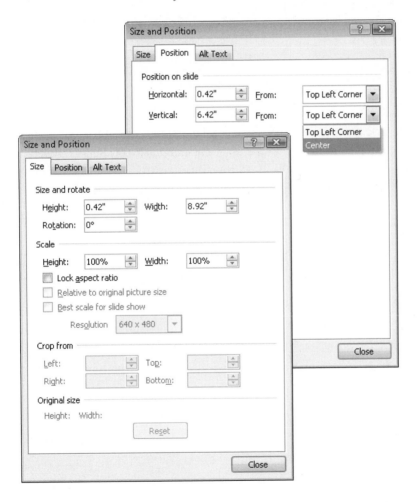

Strategy You should also be familiar with the commands in the Arrange group on the Format tab, which enable you to control the stacking order, alignment, and rotational angle of text boxes.

➤ **To size a selected text box**

→ Drag a round text box handle to change the size of the box and maintain the aspect ratio.

→ Drag a square text box handle to change the height or width only.

→ On the **Format** tab, in the **Size** group, adjust the **Shape Height** and **Shape Width** settings to change the height and width individually.

Or

1. On the **Format** tab, click the **Size** dialog box launcher.

2. In the **Size and Position** dialog box, change the **Height** and **Width** settings, and then click **Close**.

Tip Select the Lock Aspect Ratio check box if you want the relationship between the height and width to remain constant no matter what the size of the box.

➤ **To move a selected text box**

→ Drag the border until the box is positioned where you want it.

Or

1. On the **Format** tab, click the **Size** dialog box launcher.

2. In the **Size and Position** dialog box, click the **Position** tab.

3. Adjust the **Horizontal** and **Vertical** settings.

4. If you want to measure the settings from the center of the slide instead of the upper-left corner, click **Center** in the appropriate **From** list.

5. Click **Close**.

Shape Formatting

By default, text boxes appear with transparent backgrounds, no border, and no special effects. You can format text boxes in the following ways:

- **Styles.** Apply a ready-made combination of fill, outline, and shape effects, such as shadows or bevels.

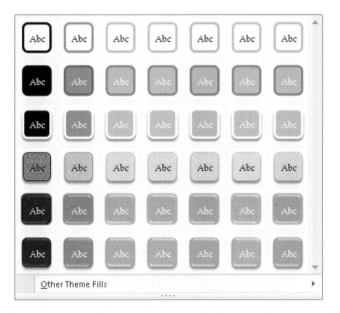

- **Fills.** Format the background of the box with a solid color in various shades, a color gradient, a texture, or a picture.

- **Outlines.** Specify the color, weight, and style.

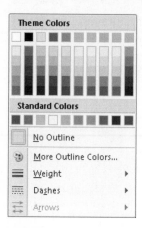

- **Effects.** Apply a preset combination of effects, or choose from among six categories of effects.

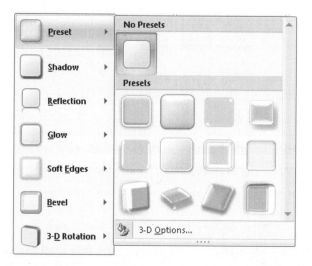

You can refine the formatting of the box in the Format Shape dialog box. When you finish formatting a text box that you have created to your liking, you can specify that all text boxes you create in the future should have that formatting.

Refine the formatting on these pages.

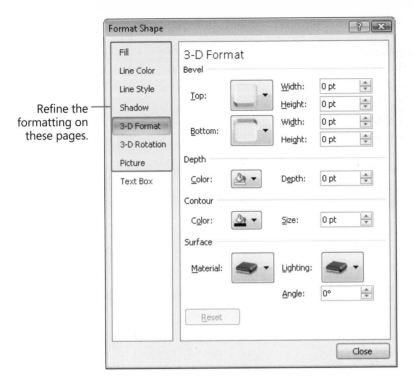

Strategy You should explore the pages of the Format Shape dialog box to understand the many ways you can control text box formatting.

➤ To apply a ready-made style to a selected text box

1. On the **Format** tab, in the **Shape Styles** group, click the **More** button.

2. In the **Shape Styles** gallery, click the style you want.

➤ To change the fill, outline, or effect of a selected text box

1. On the **Format** tab, in the **Shape Styles** group, click the **Shape Fill**, **Shape Outline**, or **Shape Effects** button.

2. In the gallery that appears, click the formatting you want.

➤ **To display the Format Shape dialog box for a selected text box**

→ On the **Format** tab, click the **Shape Styles** dialog box launcher.

▫ Right-click the box's border, and then click **Format Shape**.

Tip This command is available only if you right-click the placeholder's border while the pointer is a four-headed arrow.

➤ **To make the formatting of the selected text box the default**

→ Right-click the border of the text box, and then click **Set as Default Text Box**.

Text Layout

You can apply character and paragraph formatting to the text in text boxes in standard ways. In addition, you can specify the following on the Text Box page of the Format Shape dialog box:

● **Text layout.** You can specify the alignment and direction of text within the text box.

Tip You can also change the direction of text by rotating the entire text box. Click the Rotate button in the Arrange group on the Format tab, or drag the green rotating handle attached to the upper-middle handle of the selected text box.

● **AutoFit.** When you type more text than will fit in a text box, you can specify whether PowerPoint should adjust the size of text to fit the box, adjust the size of the box to fit the text, or leave both the same size and hide any text that does not fit.

● **Margins.** You can set whether text should wrap within the text box and the wrapping distance from the four sides of the box.

● **Columns.** You can set the number of columns and the spacing between them.

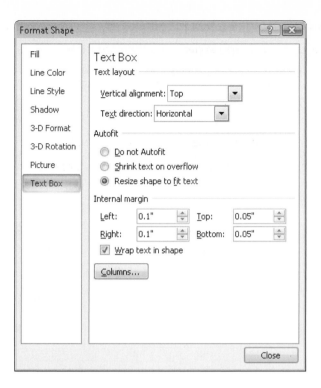

➤ **To set the text alignment and direction in a selected text box**

→ On the **Home** tab, in the **Paragraph** group, click an alignment button.

▫ On the **Home** tab, in the **Paragraph** group, click the **Text Direction** button, and then click the direction you want.

Or

1. Display the **Text Box** page of the **Format Shape** dialog box.

2. In the **Text layout** area, click the alignment option you want in the **Vertical alignment** list.

3. Click the direction option you want in the **Text Direction** list.

4. Click **Close**.

➤ **To set the autofit behavior of the selected text box**

1. Display the **Text Box** page of the **Format Shape** dialog box.

2. In the **Autofit** area, click the option you want, and then click **Close**.

➤ **To set margins in the selected text box**

1. Display the **Text Box** page of the **Format Shape** dialog box.

2. In the **Internal margin** area, adjust **Left**, **Right**, **Top**, and **Bottom** settings, and then click **Close**.

➤ **To flow text in columns in the selected text box**

1. Display the **Text Box** page of the **Format Shape** dialog box, and then click **Columns**.

2. In the **Columns** dialog box, adjust the **Number** and **Spacing** settings, click **OK**, and then click **Close**.

See Also For information about character and paragraph formatting, see section 2.2, "Manipulate text." See also Exam 77-601, section 2.1, "Format text and paragraphs."

Practice Tasks

The practice files for these tasks are located in the *Documents\Microsoft Press\ MCAS\PowerPoint2007\Objective02* folder. If you want, save the task results in the same folder with *My* prepended to the file name.

● Open the *TextBox* presentation, and on Slide 3, create a text box that will hold multiple lines of text. Cut and paste the last bullet point into the text box. Then position it exactly 1.5 inches from the top and left edges of the slide.

● Open the *TextShape* presentation, and apply the Intense Effect – Accent 1 style to the text box on Slide 2. Then change the fill color to dark red.

● In the *TextShape* presentation, on Slide 3, rotate the text and the text box so that the letters appear stacked from top to bottom. Then move the text box so that it sits on the brown bar at the bottom of the slide.

2.2   Manipulate text

Basic Editing

You can use standard editing techniques to ensure that the text on your slides is exactly the way you want it. It helps to know where to perform certain operations most efficiently. For example, to move or copy a selection to a new location on the same slide, you can simply drag it in the Slide pane. To move or copy a selection to a different slide, you can either drag it on the Outline tab of the Overview pane, or you can cut or copy and paste the selection. The advantage of cutting or copying and pasting is that the item is stored temporarily on the Clipboard and can be pasted between presentations or multiple times in different locations.

Strategy Make sure you know how to quickly select different units of text. For information about selecting text, see "Prerequisites" at the beginning of this exam.

When you want to control the format of the pasted text, you can use the Paste Special command.

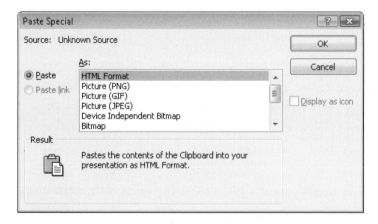

See Also For information about pasting links and displaying linked information as an icon, see section 2.3, "Add and link existing content to presentations."

➤ **To move selected text by dragging**

→ On the slide in the **Slide** pane or on the **Outline** tab of the **Overview** pane, drag the selection to the desired location.

Or

1. On the slide in the **Slide** pane or on the **Outline** tab of the **Overview** pane, use the right mouse button to drag the selection to the desired location.

2. When you release the mouse button, click **Move Here**.

Tip Using the second method gives you the options of moving or copying the text or of cancelling the operation.

➤ **To copy selected text by dragging**

→ On the slide in the **Slide** pane or on the **Outline** tab of the **Overview** pane, hold down the **Ctrl** key and drag the selection to the desired location, releasing the mouse button and then the **Ctrl** key.

Or

1. On the slide in the **Slide** pane or on the **Outline** tab of the **Overview** pane, use the right mouse button to drag the selection to the desired location.

2. When you release the mouse button, click **Copy Here**.

➤ **To move or copy selected text via the Clipboard**

1. On the **Home** tab, in the **Clipboard** group, click the **Cut** button or the **Copy** button.

2. Click where you want to insert the text, and then click the **Paste** button.

Strategy You should be thoroughly familiar with how to use the Clipboard to copy and move information from one place to another. For information about the Clipboard, see Exam 77-601, "Using Microsoft Office Word 2007," section 2.2, "Manipulate text."

➤ **To control formatting while pasting an item**

1. On the **Home** tab, in the **Clipboard** group, click the **Paste** arrow, and then click **Paste Special**.

2. In the **Paste Special** dialog box, select the **Paste** option, and in the list, select the type of file you want to paste.

3. Click **OK**.

Tip You can use the same techniques to move and copy other types of elements, such as text boxes and graphics, on a slide, between slides, or between presentations.

Bulleted and Numbered Lists

Bulleted lists form the foundation of most presentations. You can enter up to five levels of bullets on any slide with a content placeholder. By default, the bullet points you type are all first-level points, but you can easily demote bullet points to subpoints and promote subpoints to bullet points, both on the slide in the Slide pane and on the Outline tab of the Overview pane. (On the Outline tab, you can also change slide titles to bullet points and vice versa.)

If you have typed regular text in a placeholder or a text box you have created, you can convert the text to a bulleted list or a numbered list. (Numbers are appropriate for items that must appear in a specific order.) You can also convert a bulleted list or numbered list to regular text.

The basic look of the bullet points and subpoints is determined by the formatting prescribed on the slide master. However, you can customize a bulleted list by using basic formatting techniques. You can also change the size, color, and symbol of the bullets.

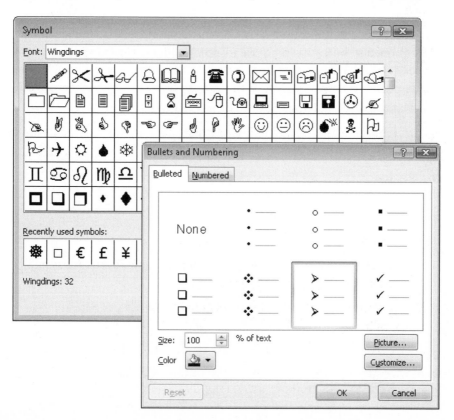

For a numbered list, you can change the number scheme and the size and color of the numbers.

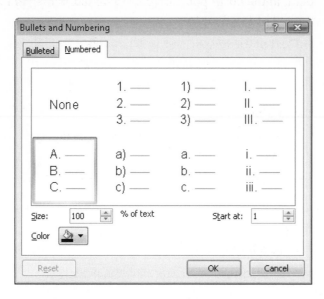

For both types of lists, you can specify the indenting of each level. If you want to adjust the indenting of multiple levels, it is best to start with the lowest level and work your way up, using equal increments. Otherwise it is easy to create a list that looks uneven and unprofessional.

Move the markers on the ruler
to adjust the indentation.

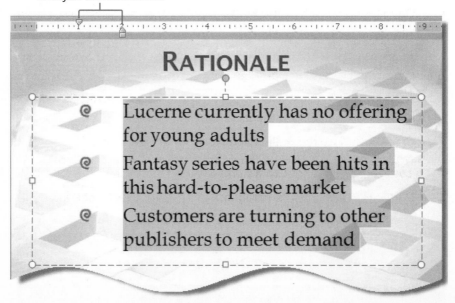

➤ **To demote a bullet point to a subpoint**

→ With the insertion point in the bullet point, on the **Home** tab, in the **Paragraph** group, click the **Increase List Level** button.

→ Click to the left of the text of the bullet point, and then press the **Tab** key.

Tip You can also use these techniques to change a slide title to a bullet point or a numbered item to a lower level.

➤ **To promote a subpoint to a bullet point**

→ With the insertion point in the subpoint, on the **Home** tab, in the **Paragraph** group, click the **Decrease List Level** button.

→ Click to the left of the text of the bullet point, hold down **Shift**, and then press **Tab**.

Tip You can also use these techniques to change a bullet point to a slide title or a numbered item to a higher level.

➤ **To convert selected text to a bulleted list**

→ On the **Home** tab, in the **Paragraph** group, click the **Bullets** button.

➤ **To change the bullets in a selected bulleted list**

1. On the **Home** tab, in the **Paragraph** group, click the **Bullets** arrow.

2. In the **Bullets** gallery, select the bullet style you want.

   Or

1. Display the **Bullets** gallery, and click **Bullets and Numbering**.

2. On the **Bulleted** tab of the **Bullets and Numbering** dialog box, change the size and color of the existing bullet.

3. To change the bullet symbol, click **Customize**, and in the **Symbol** dialog box, choose a font and symbol. Then click **OK**.

4. To use a picture as a bullet, click **Picture**, and in the **Insert Picture** dialog box, locate and double-click the picture file you want.

5. Click **OK** to close the **Bullets and Numbering** dialog box.

➤ **To convert selected text to a numbered list**

→ On the **Home** tab, in the **Paragraph** group, click the **Numbering** button.

➤ To change the numbers in a selected numbered list

1. On the **Home** tab, in the **Paragraph** group, click the **Numbering** arrow.
2. In the **Numbering** gallery, select the number scheme you want.

Or

1. In the **Numbering** gallery, click **Bullets and Numbering**.
2. On the **Numbered** tab of the **Bullets and Numbering** dialog box, change the size and color of the numbers.
3. Click **OK**.

➤ To adjust the hanging indent of a list

→ Drag the **First Line Indent** and **Hanging Indent** markers on the ruler.

Tip To display the ruler, select the Ruler check box in the Show/Hide group on the View tab.

Basic Formatting

You can use standard character and paragraph formatting techniques to change the following:

- **Font and size.** You can pick a different font or size for any selection.
- **Color.** You can pick a color from the applied color scheme to create a pleasing design impact. You can also add colors that are not part of the color scheme, including colors from the standard palette or from the almost infinite spectrum of colors available in the Colors dialog box.

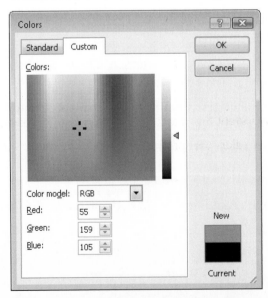

- **Style and effects.** You can apply simple styles such as bold and italic, or you can choose more dramatic effects such as colored underlining or small caps.

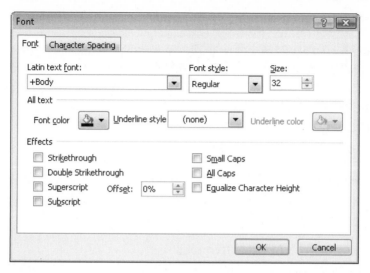

- **Alignment.** You can align the text horizontally to the left, right, or center; or you can justify it to span the text box. You can align the text vertically at the top of the text box, in the middle, or at the bottom.

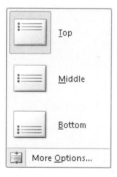

- **Indentation.** You can indent the text from the left side of the text box.
- **Line spacing.** You can adjust the spacing within and between paragraphs.

After you have formatted one text selection to suit your needs, you can quickly apply the same combination of formatting to another selection by using the Format Painter.

➤ **To change the font of selected text**

→ Either on the **Mini toolbar** or in the **Font** group of the **Home** tab, click the font you want in the **Font** list.

➤ **To increase or decrease the size of selected text**

→ Either on the **Mini toolbar** or in the **Font** group of the **Home** tab, click the **Increase Font Size** or **Decrease Font Size** button.

➤ **To precisely size selected text**

→ Either on the **Mini toolbar** or in the **Font** group of the **Home** tab, click the size you want on the **Font Size** list.

➤ **To change the color of selected text**

→ Either on the **Mini toolbar** or in the **Font** group of the **Home** tab, click the color you want in the **Font Color** palette.

Or

1. Display the **Font Color** palette, and then click **More Colors**.
2. On either the **Standard** or **Custom** tab of the **Colors** dialog box, specify the color you want, and then click **OK**.

➤ **To change the style or effect of selected text**

→ Either on the **Mini toolbar** or in the **Font** group of the **Home** tab, click the button for the style you want.

Or

1. On the **Home** tab, click the **Font** dialog box launcher.
2. In the **Font** dialog box, specify the style or effect you want, and then click **OK**.

➤ **To change the alignment of selected text**

→ Either on the **Mini toolbar** or in the **Paragraph** group of the **Home** tab, click the **Left**, **Center**, or **Right** button.

Tip To justify text, click the Justify button in the Paragraph group.

→ On the **Home** tab, in the **Paragraph** group, click the **Align Text** button, and then click the vertical alignment you want.

➤ **To change the indentation of selected text**

→ Either on the **Mini toolbar** or in the **Paragraph** group of the Home tab, click the **Increase List Level** or **Decrease List Level** button.

Tip You can use these buttons to increase and decrease the left indent of regular text paragraphs as well as lists.

Or

1. On the **Home** tab, click the **Paragraph** dialog box launcher.

2. In the **Paragraph** dialog box, in the **Indentation** area, change the **Before text** setting, and then click **OK**.

➤ **To change the spacing of selected text**

→ On the **Home** tab, in the **Paragraph** group, click the **Line Spacing** button, and then click the spacing you want.

Tip Clicking Line Spacing Options displays the Paragraph dialog box.

Or

1. On the **Home** tab, click the **Paragraph** dialog box launcher.

2. In the **Paragraph** dialog box, in the **Spacing** area, change the **Before** or the **After** setting, or the **Line Spacing** option, and then click **OK**.

➤ **To copy the formatting of selected text**

1. Either on the **Mini toolbar** or in the **Clipboard** group of the **Home** tab, click the **Format Painter** button.

2. Select the text to which you want to apply the formatting.

WordArt

If you want to add a fancy title to a slide and you can't achieve the effect you want with regular text formatting, you can use WordArt to create stylized text in various shapes. WordArt text can be stretched horizontally, vertically, or diagonally to shape it in fantastic ways. You can also apply additional formatting to achieve unique effects.

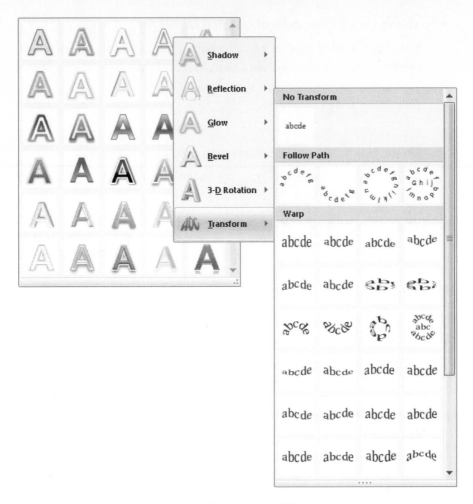

Strategy WordArt on a PowerPoint slide behaves differently than WordArt in a text document. In PowerPoint, WordArt styles and effects can be applied to any text in a text box. Experiment with WordArt in the two programs so that you understand the differences.

➤ To create WordArt text

1. On the **Insert** tab, in the **Text** group, click the **WordArt** button.

2. In the **WordArt** gallery, click the style you want, and then type the text.

➤ To apply a different style to selected WordArt text

1. On the **Format** tab, in the **WordArt Styles** group, click the **More** button.

2. In the **WordArt Styles** gallery, click the style you want to apply.

   Tip You can apply WordArt styles to any text.

➤ **To add special effects to selected WordArt text**

1. On the **Format** tab, in the **WordArt Styles** group, click the **Text Effects** button.

2. In the **Text Effects** gallery, click an effect category, and then choose the one you want.

➤ **To change the shape of selected WordArt text**

1. On the **Format** tab, in the **WordArt Styles** group, click the **Text Effects** button, and then click **Transform**.

2. In the **Transform** gallery, click the shape you want.

3. Size and position the WordArt object the same way you would size and position any other text box.

4. To exaggerate the shape, drag the purple diamond handle to achieve the effect you want.

Practice Tasks

The practice files for these tasks are located in the *Documents\Microsoft Press\ MCAS\PowerPoint2007\Objective02* folder. If you want, save the task results in the same folder with *My* prepended to the file name.

● Open the *Editing* presentation, and on Slide 3, move the *Reluctant rebel* subpoint above the *Innately sympathetic* subpoint. Then move *A hero* above *A teacher*.

● Open the *BulletsNumbers* presentation, and on Slide 2, change the first-level and second-level bullets to dark red dollar signs. Then increase the hanging indent of the subpoints bullets to 1 inch.

● In the *BulletsNumbers* presentation, and on Slide 7, change the first-level bullet points to a numbered list. Then set the numbering scheme to use purple capital letters.

● Open the *Formatting* presentation, and on Slide 2, make the title bold, yellow, and small caps. Then apply the same formatting to the title of the last slide.

● Open the *WordArt* presentation, and on Slide 1, insert *Organization 101* as a WordArt object with the Fill - White, Outline - Accent 1 style. Move the object so that it spans the middle of the top half of the slide, and then make the text the standard dark red color with an Indigo, Accent 6 outline.

2.3 Add and link existing content to presentations

Ready-Made Slides

You can copy and paste existing slide elements within a presentation or between presentations by using the same techniques you would use for copying and pasting text. However, if your presentations often include the same slides, you don't have to recreate the slides for each presentation. You can easily tell PowerPoint to copy an entire slide and insert it in a specific location in a different presentation. By default, the slide assumes the formatting of its new presentation.

Tip If you have access to a Microsoft SharePoint slide library, you and your coworkers can share slides or entire presentations stored in the library.

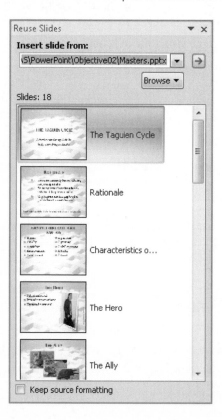

➤ **To reuse a slide from an existing presentation**

1. Click the slide after which you want to insert the slide.

2. On the **Home** tab, in the **Slides** group, click **Reuse Slides** in the **New Slide** list.

3. In the **Reuse Slides** task pane, click **Browse**, and then click **Browse File**.

4. In the **Browse** dialog box, locate and double-click the presentation containing the slide you want to use.

5. If you want to keep the formatting of the original presentation, at the bottom of the task pane, select the **Keep source formatting** check box.

6. Click the slide you want to insert in the current presentation.

Sounds

You can insert the following types of sounds:

- **Audio files.** You can insert an audio file such as a speech or an interview.

  Tip You can record a sound or narration and attach it to a slide, all from within PowerPoint.

- **Sound clips.** The sound clips that ship with PowerPoint, which include applause and a phone ring, are available from the Clip Art task pane. You can also download hundreds of sounds from Microsoft Office Online.

See Also For information about using the Clip Art task pane, see section 3.3, "Insert illustrations and shapes."

● **CD tracks.** You can insert music tracks or other audio tracks from a CD into a slide. If you want to play the tracks during a slide show, the CD must be in the CD drive.

The sound object appears on the slide represented by an icon indicating the type of sound. You can adjust the size and position and format the icon in much the same way that you would format a picture. You can also adjust its volume and specify whether it is displayed on the slide and whether the sound plays automatically or when you click its icon.

Audio clip icon

CD track icon

➤ To insert an audio file

1. On the **Insert** tab, in the **Media Clips** group, click **Sound from File** in the **Sound** list.

2. In the **Insert Sound** dialog box, locate and double-click the sound file you want.

3. When a message box asks how you want the sound to start, click **Automatically** or **When Clicked**.

➤ To insert a sound clip

1. On the **Insert** tab, in the **Media Clips** group, click **Sound from Clip Organizer** in the **Sound** list.

2. In the **Clip Art** task pane, click the sound you want.

3. When a message box asks how you want the sound to start, click **Automatically** or **When Clicked**.

➤ To insert a CD track

1. On the **Insert** tab, in the **Media Clips** group, click **Play CD Audio Track** in the **Sound** list.

2. In the **Insert CD Audio** dialog box, choose the settings you want, and then click **OK**.

3. When a message box asks how you want the sound to start, click **Automatically** or **When Clicked**.

➤ **To change the settings for a selected sound object**

→ On the **Options** tab, in the **Sound Options** group, adjust the volume and then specify whether the sound icon should be visible, how the sound should start playing, and whether it should play continuously.

Movies

Sometimes the best way to ensure that your audience understands your message is to show a movie. You can insert the following types of movies in slides:

● **Video clips.** You can insert a digital video that has been saved as a file.

● **Animated clips.** PowerPoint comes with several animated clips, also known as animated GIFs. (GIF stands for Graphics Interchange Format.) You can insert these clips from the Clip Art task pane or download many others from Office Online.

See Also For information about using the Clip Art task pane, see section 3.3, "Insert illustrations and shapes."

Both videos and animated clips appear on the slide as objects represented by icons that you can size and move to meet your needs. In Slide Show view, a video plays either automatically or when you click its icon, depending on your specifications, whereas an animated clip always plays automatically. You can also adjust the volume of a video clip and specify whether it is displayed on the slide and whether it plays continuously.

➤ To insert a video clip

1. On the **Insert** tab, in the **Media Clips** group, click **Movie from File** in the **Movie** list.

2. In the **Insert Movie** dialog box, locate and double-click the video file you want.

3. When a message box asks how you want the video clip to play, click **Automatically** or **When Clicked**.

➤ To insert an animated clip

1. On the **Insert** tab, in the **Media Clips** group, click **Movie from Clip Organizer** in the **Movie** list.

2. In the **Clip Art** task pane, click the animated clip you want.

➤ To change the settings for a selected video clip

→ On the **Options** tab, in the **Movie Options** group, adjust the volume, and specify whether the object should be visible, how the video should start playing, whether it should play continuously, and whether it should be rewound upon completion.

Other Types of Files

You can insert a file created in another Microsoft Office application instead of having to recreate its content in PowerPoint. The file is inserted as an object that you can double-click to activate the file in the source program.

Cost of Mismanagement

Weekly Cost of Disorganization

	Time Wasted (minutes)	Average Cost
Locating documents	120	$80.00
Time management issues	240	$160.00
Locating e-mails	60	$40.00
Locating reference information	180	$120.00
TOTAL		$400.00

Double-clicking a worksheet object opens it for editing in Microsoft Office Excel.

> ➤ **To insert a file as an object**

1. On the **Insert** tab, in the **Text** group, click the **Object** button.

2. In the **Insert Object** dialog box, click **Create from file**, and then click **Browse**.

3. In the **Browse** dialog box, locate and double-click the file you want.

   Tip You can link the inserted object to its source file by selecting the Link check box. You can display an icon for the object instead of the object itself by selecting the Display As Icon check box.

4. Click **OK**.

Links

Presentations that are intended to be delivered on a computer or viewed on the Web often include links that provide access to supporting information. You can add links to slides in three ways:

● When pasting information copied from another file, you can use the Paste Special command to create a link to the information. Then if the information in the source file changes, you can tell PowerPoint to update the information in the presentation to reflect the change. You can also insert the linked information as an icon that you can click to open the source file.

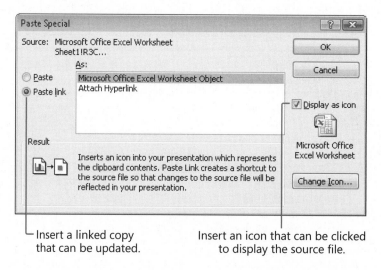

Insert a linked copy that can be updated.   Insert an icon that can be clicked to display the source file.

● When pasting information copied from another file, you can use the Paste As Hyperlink command to paste a link to the information rather than the information itself. Clicking the link opens the source file.

● You can attach a hyperlink to any selected object, such as text or a graphic, that displays a different slide in the same presentation, opens another presentation or a file on your computer or your organization's network, displays a Web page, or opens an e-mail message form with the recipient address and subject already filled in.

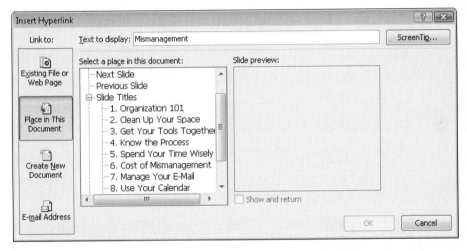

Tip To have a hyperlink appear on every slide, you can insert the link on the slide master. However, you cannot attach a hyperlink to the default placeholders on the slide master or its layouts. You must create a text box to which you can attach the link. For information about slide masters, see section 1.2, "Customize slide masters" and section 1.3, "Add elements to slide masters."

➤ To insert copied information that is linked to its source file

1. On the **Home** tab, in the **Clipboard** group, click **Paste Special** in the **Paste** list.

2. In the **Paste Special** dialog box, click **Paste Link**.

3. In the **As** list, click the format you want.

4. If you want to be able to click an icon to view the information rather than having it incorporated into the slide, select the **Display as icon** check box.

5. Click **OK**.

➤ To insert a hyperlink to copied information at the insertion point

→ On the **Home** tab, in the **Clipboard** group, click **Paste as Hyperlink** in the **Paste** list.

➤ To link a selection to another slide

1. On the **Insert** tab, in the **Links** group, click the **Hyperlink** button.

2. In the **Insert Hyperlink** dialog box, under **Link to**, click **Place in This Document**.

3. In the **Select a place in this document** list, click the slide you want, and then click **OK**.

➤ To link a selection to a file

1. Display the **Insert Hyperlink** dialog box, and under **Link to**, click **Existing File or Web Page**.

2. With **Current Folder** selected, locate and click the file you want. Or click **Recent Files**, and then click the file you want in the list.

3. Click **OK**.

➤ To link a selection to a Web page

1. Display the **Insert Hyperlink** dialog box, and under **Link to**, click **Existing File or Web Page**.

2. In the **Address** box, type the URL of the Web page, or click **Browsed Pages**, and in the list, click the URL you want.

3. Click **OK**.

➤ **To insert a hyperlink that opens an e-mail message form**

1. Click where you want the hyperlink to appear, display the **Insert Hyperlink** dialog box, and under **Link to**, click **E-mail Address**.

2. In the **Text to display** box, type text to which you want to attach the hyperlink; for example, *Contact us*.

3. Enter the recipient's **E-mail address** and the **Subject**, and then click **OK**.

Practice Tasks

The practice files for these tasks are located in the *Documents\Microsoft Press\ MCAS\PowerPoint2007\Objective02* folder. If you want, save the task results in the same folder with *My* prepended to the file name.

- Open the *Slides1* presentation, and move to Slide 3. Then insert the seventh thumbnail, titled *Bamboo Product Line*, from the *Slides2* presentation.

- Open the *Sounds* presentation, and on Slide 7, insert the Claps Cheers sound clip, formatted so that its icon is hidden and it starts automatically when the slide is displayed.

- Open the *Movies* presentation, and on Slide 3, insert the *HouseHome* video clip, formatted so that it starts playing when it is clicked.

- Open the *Files* presentation, and on Slide 6, insert the *Costs* workbook.

- Open the *LinkToSlide* presentation, and on Slide 2, attach a hyperlink to the word *once* that displays Slide 5.

- In the *LinkToSlide* presentation, on Slide 6, attach a hyperlink to the words *Web Resources* that opens the Web site at *www.microsoft.com*.

2.4   Apply, customize, modify, and remove animations

Built-In Animations

If you are delivering a presentation from your computer, you keep your audience focused and reinforce your message by applying built-in animations to the text and graphics on your slides. In the case of bullet points, you can animate them as a set or one by one.

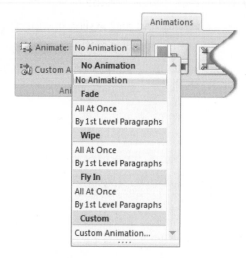

> ➤ **To apply a built-in animation to a selected object**
>
>   → On the **Animations** tab, in the **Animations** group, click the **Animate** arrow, and then in the list, click the animation you want.

> ➤ **To remove the animation from a selected object**
>
>   → In the **Animate** list, click **No Animation**.

Custom Animations

You can create your own animations in the Custom Animation task pane by applying the following types of effects:

- **Entrance.** You can animate the way that the element appears on the slide.
- **Emphasis.** You can increase or decrease the importance of the element by changing its font, size, or style; by making it grow or shrink; or by making it spin.
- **Exit.** You can animate the way that the element leaves the slide.
- **Motion Path.** You can move the element around on the slide in various ways, such as diagonally to the upper-right corner or in a circular motion.

If none of the lists of predefined effects meets your needs, you can display galleries of professionally designed animations in four categories: Basic, Subtle, Moderate, and Exciting.

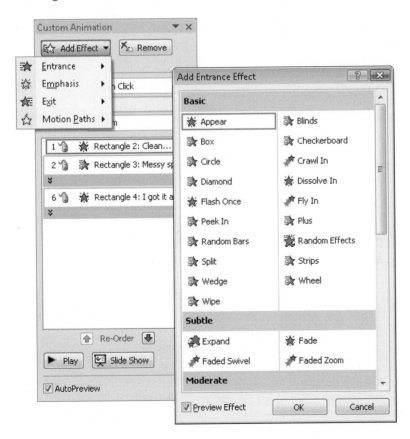

After you apply an animation effect, you can fine-tune its action. For example:

- You can specify whether the animation should be accompanied by a sound.

- You can dim or hide the element after the animation, or you can have it change to a specific color.

- If the animation is applied to text, you can animate all the text at once or animate it word by word or letter by letter.

- You can set the exact timing of the animation.

- If a slide has more than one level of bullet points, you can animate different levels separately.

- If an object has text, you can animate the object and the text together (the default) or separately, or you can animate one but not the other.

- You can specify the order of appearance of text or objects.

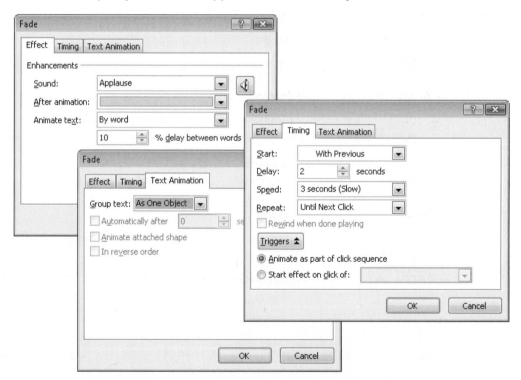

Strategy You can build sophisticated animation effects involving sequences of multiple settings. Be sure you know where to find various settings and how to change their order.

➤ **To apply an entrance, emphasis, exit, or motion-path animation to a selected element**

1. On the **Animations** tab, in the **Animations** group, click **Custom Animation**.

2. In the **Custom Animation** task pane, click **Add Effect**, and then click the animation category you want.

3. In the list, click the animation you want.

➤ **To change when an animation starts**

1. In the **Custom Animation** task pane, click the animation.

2. Click **On Click**, **With Previous**, or **After Previous** in the **Start** list.

➤ **To change the speed of an animation**

1. Display the **Custom Animation** task pane, and click the animation.

2. Click the speed you want in the **Speed** list.

➤ **To add sound to an animation**

1. Display the **Custom Animation** task pane, click the animation, click its arrow, and then click **Effect Options**.

2. In the **Enhancements** area of the dialog box, click the sound you want in the **Sound** list, and then click **OK**.

➤ **To change the animation order**

1. Display the **Custom Animation** task pane, and click the animation whose order you want to change.

2. Click the **Re-Order Up** or **Re-Order Down** arrow.

Practice Tasks

The practice files for these tasks are located in the *Documents\Microsoft Press\ MCAS\PowerPoint2007\Objective02* folder. If you want, save the task results in the same folder with *My* prepended to the file name.

- Open the *DefaultAnimation* presentation, and on Slide 3, apply the Fly In animation to the title. Then apply the Checkerboard animation to the bulleted list.

- Open the *CustomAnimation* presentation, and on Slide 3, apply the Teeter emphasis effect to the picture. Reorder the animations on this slide so that the picture animation occurs before those of the bullet points, and make the animations occur automatically one after the other.

- Continuing in the *CustomAnimation* presentation, on Slide 3, set the speed of the animations to Medium. Then add the Voltage sound to all the animations. Finally, make the bullet points turn orange after they appear.

Objective Review

Before finishing this chapter, ensure that you have mastered the following skills:

2.1 Insert and format text boxes.

2.2 Manipulate text.

2.3 Add and link existing content to presentations.

2.4 Apply, customize, modify, and remove animations.

3 Working with Visual Content

The skills tested in this section of the Microsoft Office Specialist exam for Microsoft Office PowerPoint 2007 relate to creating business diagrams within PowerPoint. Specifically, the following objectives are associated with this set of skills:

3.1 Create SmartArt diagrams.

3.2 Modify SmartArt diagrams.

3.3 Insert illustrations and shapes.

3.4 Modify illustrations.

3.5 Arrange illustrations and other content.

3.6 Insert and modify charts.

3.7 Insert and modify tables.

When presenting information in a PowerPoint presentation, you can provide visual impact and effectively illustrate processes, relationships, and business information by using various types of graphic components.

This chapter guides you in studying ways of creating and modifying SmartArt diagrams that illustrate business processes, using pictures, clip art, and shapes to illustrate and enhance a presentation, and presenting data in charts and tables.

 Important Before you can use the practice files in this chapter, you need to install them from the book's companion CD to their default location. See "Using the Companion CD" at the beginning of this book for more information.

Tip Graphics and operating system–related instructions in this book reflect the Windows Vista user interface. If your computer is running Windows XP and you experience trouble following the instructions as written, refer to the sidebar "If You Are Running Windows XP" in "Working in the Microsoft Office Fluent User Interface" at the beginning of this book.

3.1   Create SmartArt diagrams

Independent Diagrams

When you want to illustrate a process or the relationship between hierarchical elements, you can create a dynamic, visually appealing diagram by using SmartArt graphics. By using predefined sets of formatting, you can almost effortlessly put together the type and style of diagram that best conveys your information, such as the following:

- **List.** Shows groups of multilevel sequential or non-sequential information.
- **Process.** Visually describes the ordered set of steps required to complete a task or workflow.
- **Cycle.** Represents a circular sequence of steps, tasks, or events; or the relationship of a set of steps, tasks, or events to a central, core element.
- **Hierarchy.** Illustrates the structure of an organization or entity.
- **Relationship.** Shows convergent, divergent, overlapping, merging, or containing elements.
- **Matrix.** Shows items or concepts as they relate to the whole.
- **Pyramid.** Shows proportion, interconnected, or hierarchical relationships in a triangle.

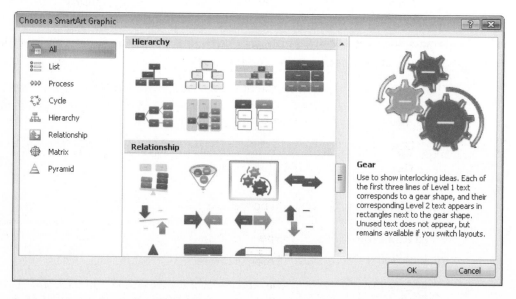

Strategy Get to know the kinds of diagrams you can create so that you can quickly pinpoint a specific type in the Choose A SmartArt Graphic dialog box.

After you insert the diagram, you add text either directly to its shapes or as a bulleted list in the text pane that opens to the left of the diagram. You can add shapes, delete shapes, and rearrange them by dragging them.

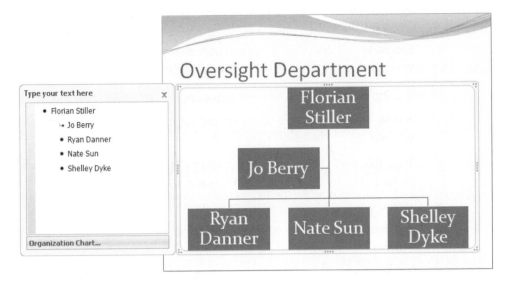

➤ To create a SmartArt diagram

1. On a slide that contains a content placeholder, click the **Insert SmartArt Graphic** button. Or on the **Insert** tab, in the **Illustrations** group, click the **SmartArt** button.

2. In the left pane of the **Choose a SmartArt Graphic** dialog box, click the category you want.

3. In the center pane, click the desired layout. Then click **OK**.

➤ To add text to a SmartArt diagram

→ Open the **Text** pane, and replace the bullet point placeholders with your own text.

Tip You can quickly open the Text pane by clicking the button on the left side of the diagram's frame.

→ Click a shape, and then type the text.

➤ To add a subordinate shape

→ In the **Text** pane, press **Enter**, and then press **Tab**.

→ Click the supervisor shape, and then on the **Design** tab, in the **Create Graphic** group, click **Add Shape Below** in the **Add Shape** list.

➤ **To promote or demote an existing shape**

→ Click the shape, and then on the **Design** tab, in the **Create Graphic** group, click the **Promote** or **Demote** button.

➤ **To delete a shape**

→ Click the shape, and then press the **Delete** key.

Diagrams from Bulleted Lists

After creating an ordinary bulleted list on a slide, you can easily convert it to a SmartArt diagram that retains the relationship of the bullet levels.

➤ **To create a SmartArt diagram from a bulleted list**

→ Right-click any item in the list, point to **Convert to SmartArt**, and then in the gallery, click the diagram you want.

Practice Tasks

The practice files for these tasks are located in the *Documents\Microsoft Press\ MCAS\PowerPoint2007\Objective03* folder. If you want, save the task results in the same folder with *My* prepended to the file name.

● Open the *Diagrams* presentation, and in the content placeholder on Slide 5, insert an Organization Chart diagram. Then enter *Florian Stiller* as the boss, *Jo Berry* as his assistant, and *Ryan Danner, Nate Sun,* and *Shelley Dyke* as his subordinates.

● Open the *EditingDiagrams* presentation, and on Slide 5, delete the shape for Florian Stiller's assistant. Then assign him another subordinate called *Lukas Keller.* Finally, move and size the organization chart so that it fits neatly in the lower-right corner of the slide.

● Open the *BulletDiagrams* presentation, and on Slide 9, convert the bulleted list to a Basic Venn diagram. Then change the word *Choices* to *Temptation.*

3.2   Modify SmartArt diagrams

Design Changes

You can customize a diagram as a whole by making changes such as the following:

- Switch to a different layout of the same type or a different type.

  Tip If the text in the original diagram doesn't fit in the new layout, the text is not shown, but is retained so that you don't have to retype it if you switch again.

- Add shading and three-dimensional effects to all the shapes in a diagram.

- Select a different combination of colors that coordinates with the presentation's color scheme.

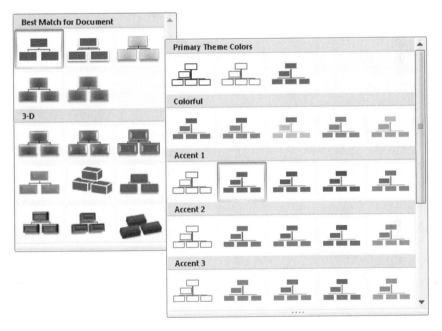

- Change an individual shape.

➤ To change the layout of a selected diagram

1. On the contextual **Design** tab, in the **Layouts** group, click the **More** button.

2. In the **Layouts** gallery, click the layout you want.

➤ **To apply a style to all the shapes in a selected diagram**

1. On the contextual **Design** tab, in the **SmartArt Styles** group, click the **More** button.

2. In the **SmartArt Styles** gallery, click the style you want.

➤ **To change the color of shapes**

1. On the contextual **Design** tab, in the **SmartArt Styles** group, click the **Change Colors** button.

2. In the **Colors** gallery, click the color scheme you want.

Shape Changes

You can select an individual shape in a diagram and change it in various ways. In addition to assigning it a different shape, you can format the shape and the text within it by using the same formatting techniques you would use for text boxes.

See Also For information about formatting text boxes and their text, see section 2.1, "Insert and format text boxes."

➤ **To change a selected shape**

1. On the **Format** tab, in the **Shapes** group, click the **Change Shape** button.

2. In the **Shape** gallery, click the shape you want.

Tip After customizing a diagram, you can revert to the original by clicking the Reset Graphic button in the Reset group on the Design contextual tab.

Practice Tasks

The practice files for these tasks are located in the *Documents\Microsoft Press\ MCAS\PowerPoint2007\Objective03* folder. If you want, save the task results in the same folder with *My* prepended to the file name.

- Open the *FormattingDiagrams* presentation, and change the layout of the diagram on Slide 5 to a Radial Cycle. Then change the style of the diagram to 3-D Bird's Eye Scene.

- Open the *DiagramColors* presentation, and change the color scheme to Colorful – Accent Colors. Then change the center shape to a 7-Point Star.

3.3   Insert illustrations and shapes

Pictures

Pictures make slides more attractive and visually interesting and can convey information in a way that words cannot. You can add pictures created and saved in other programs or scanned photographs and illustrations to your slides.

You can also use a special-purpose presentation to distribute photographs as a photo album or catalog.

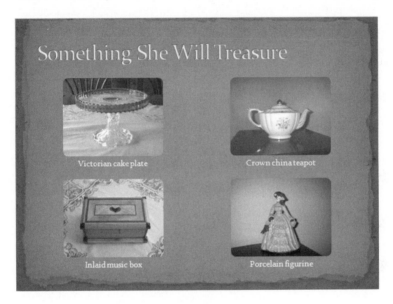

➤ **To insert a picture from a file**

1. In a content placeholder, click the **Insert Picture from File** button.

   Or

   On the **Insert** tab, in the **Illustrations** group, click the **Picture** button.

2. In the **Insert Picture** dialog box, locate and double-click the picture you want.

   Tip If the picture might change, you can ensure that the picture on the slide is always up to date by linking it to its source file. With the picture selected in the Insert Picture dialog box, click Link To File or Insert And Link in the Insert list.

➤ To replace a selected picture

1. On the **Format** tab, in the **Adjust** group, click the **Change Picture** button.

2. In the **Insert Picture** dialog box, locate and double-click the replacement picture.

➤ To create a photo album

1. Open a new blank presentation, and on the **Insert** tab, in the **Illustrations** group, click **New Photo Album** in the **Photo Album** list.

2. In the **Photo Album** dialog box, click **File/Disk**, and in the **Insert New Pictures** dialog box, locate and select the pictures you want. Then click **Insert**.

3. In the **Pictures in album** box in the **Photo Album** dialog box, adjust the order of the pictures by clicking the **Move Down** or **Move Up** button.

4. Below **Picture Options**, specify whether the pictures should have captions and whether they should appear in black and white.

5. In the **Album Layout** area, select the options you want in the **Picture layout** and **Frame shape** lists.

6. To the right of **Theme**, click **Browse**, and then in the **Choose Theme** dialog box, double-click the theme you want.

7. Click **Create**.

Clip Art

PowerPoint includes hundreds of professionally designed pieces of clip art—license-free graphics that often take the form of cartoons, sketches, or symbolic images, but can also include photographs, videos, and audio clips. In a PowerPoint presentation, you can use clip art to illustrate a point you are making, as interesting bullet characters, or to mark pauses in a presentation such as discussion periods.

You search for clip art and add images to slides from the Clip Art task pane. You can search for clip art by keyword, search a specific collection, or search for files of a specific format, such as GIFs. If you can't locate a suitable image from those on your computer, you can search for additional images by clicking the Clip Art On Office Online link at the bottom of the Clip Art task pane.

> ## To insert a clip art image

1. In a content placeholder, click the **Clip Art** button. Or on the **Insert** tab, in the **Illustrations** group, click the **Clip Art** button.

2. In the **Search for** box at the top of the **Clip Art** task pane, type a keyword for the type of image you are looking for.

3. Make any changes to the **Search in** and **Results should be** settings that will narrow the search criteria, and then click **Go**.

4. Click the clip art image you want.

Shapes

To emphasize key points in a presentation, you can draw shapes, including stars, banners, boxes, lines, circles, and squares. You can also combine shapes to create simple illustrations.

You can add text to any shape. PowerPoint centers the text as you type, and the text becomes part of the shape. You can then format the text with a WordArt Style or by clicking buttons in the Font group on the Home tab.

If you want to show a relationship between two shapes, you can connect them with a line by joining special handles called *connection points*. Moving a connected shape also moves the line, maintaining the relationship between the connected shapes.

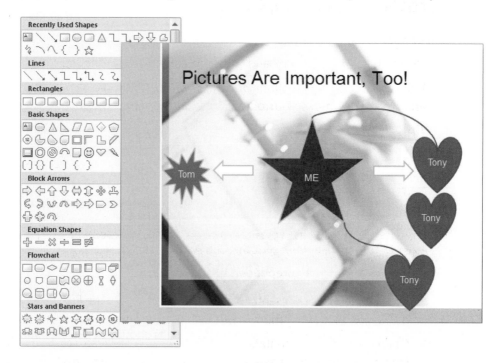

> ➤ **To draw a shape**

    1. On the **Insert** tab, in the **Illustrations** group, click the **Shapes** button.

    2. In the **Shapes** gallery, click the shape you want.

       Tip If you click a shape button and then change your mind about drawing the shape, you can release the shape by pressing the Esc key.

    3. Move the crosshair pointer to the position on the slide where you want the upper-left corner of the shape to be, and drag down and to the right to draw a shape the size you want.

Tip To draw a circle or a square, click the Oval or a Rectangle shape, and hold down the Shift key while you drag.

➤ **To change to a different shape**

1. With the shape selected, on the **Format** tab, in the **Insert Shapes** group, click the **Edit Shape** button.

2. Point to **Change Shape**, and then in the **Shapes** gallery, click the shape you want.

➤ **To add text to a selected shape**

1. On the **Format** tab, in the **Insert Shapes** group, click the **Text Box** button.

2. Click the shape, and then type the text.

➤ **To connect two shapes**

1. Display the **Shapes** gallery, and below **Lines**, click one of the connector shapes.

2. Point to the first shape, point to a connection point, drag to the second shape, and release the mouse button over one of its connection points.

Tip Connection points are red. If a blue handle appears instead of a red one, the shapes are not connected. Click the Undo button on the Quick Access Toolbar to remove the connection line, and then redraw it.

Practice Tasks

The practice files for these tasks are located in the *Documents\Microsoft Press\ MCAS\PowerPoint2007\Objective03* folder. If you want, save the task results in the same folder with *My* prepended to the file name.

● Open the *Pictures1* presentation, and on Slide 5, insert the *Pictures2* image in the left content pane. Then insert the *Pictures3* image in the right content pane.

● Open the *ClipArt* presentation, and with Slide 7 displayed, search for clip art images that have been assigned the keyword *ideas*. Then insert the light bulb that floats in the sky like a balloon.

● Open the *ShapesText* presentation, and in the center of Slide 5, insert a 5-Point Star. Insert the word *ME* in the star, and make it dark red.

● Open the *ShapesConnectors* presentation, and change the star to a Sun shape. Then draw a dark red Curved Connector between the sun's right-middle connection point and the diamond's top connection point.

3.4 Modify illustrations

Picture and Clip Art Formatting

After you insert a picture or clip art image into your presentation, you can modify it in the following ways:

- Adjust the brightness and contrast.

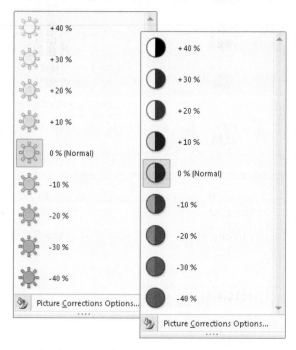

- Tint the image with various shades of a color, or make parts of an image transparent.

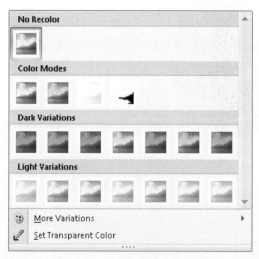

● Apply ready-made styles that include shadows, reflections, and borders, or apply custom borders and effects.

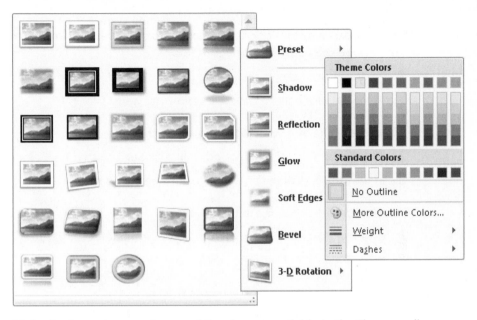

● Make the image appear in any of the shapes available in the Shapes gallery.

➤ To modify the brightness or contrast of a selected image

1. On the **Format** tab, in the **Adjust** group, click the **Brightness** or **Contrast** button.

2. In the corresponding gallery, click the option you want.

➤ To change the color of a selected image

1. On the **Format** tab, in the **Adjust** group, click the **Recolor** button.

2. In the **Recolor** gallery, click the option you want.

➤ To make areas of a selected image transparent

1. Display the **Recolor** gallery, and then click **Set Transparent Color**.

2. In the image, click the area you want to be transparent.

➤ To change the style of a selected image

1. On the **Format** tab, in the **Picture Styles** group, click the **More** button.

2. In the **Picture Styles** gallery, click the style you want.

➤ To change the border of a selected image

1. On the **Format** tab, in the **Picture Styles** group, click the **Picture Border** button.

2. In the **Colors** palette, click the color, weight, and style you want.

➤ To apply special effects to a selected image

1. On the **Format** tab, in the **Picture Styles** group, click the **Picture Effects** button.

2. Point to the category you want, and then in the gallery, click the desired effect.

➤ To change the shape of a selected image

1. On the **Format** tab, in the **Picture Styles** group, click the **Picture Shape** button.

2. In the **Shape** gallery, click the shape you want.

Tip If you don't like the changes made to an image, you can restore the original image by clicking the Reset Picture button in the Adjust group on the Format tab.

Shape Formatting

After drawing a shape, you can format it by using the same techniques you would use for formatting a text box. The quickest way to apply an eye-catching combination of formatting is to use a style.

See Also For information about formatting text boxes, see section 2.1, "Insert and format text boxes."

➤ **To apply a style to a selected shape**

1. On the **Format** tab, in the **Shape Styles** group, click the **More** button.

2. In the **Shape Styles** gallery, click the style you want.

Practice Tasks

The practice files for these tasks are located in the *Documents\Microsoft Press\ MCAS\PowerPoint2007\Objective03* folder. If you want, save the task results in the same folder with *My* prepended to the file name.

● Open the *PictureBorder* presentation, and on Slide 5, make the borders of both pictures orange and 3 points wide. Then increase the contrast of the pictures by 20 percent.

● Open the *PictureStyle* presentation, and change the style of the picture on Slide 4 to Rotated, White. Then change the 3-D Rotation effect to Perspective Contrasting Left.

● Open the *ClipArtColor* presentation, and on Slide 5, recolor the image to Accent color 2 Light. Then make all the white areas of the image transparent so that the background of the slide shows through.

● Open the *ShapeFormatting* presentation, and on Slide 6, make the image fit in a hexagonal shape. Then on Slide 4, fill the shape with the Purple Mesh texture.

3.5   Arrange illustrations and other content

Size and Position

After you insert a picture, clip art image, or shape, you can change its size by dragging handles, by specifying the height and width, or by scaling it in proportion to its original size. For pictures and clip art images, you can focus attention on a particular part of an image by cropping away the parts you don't need.

You can change the orientation of an image on the slide by rotating or flipping it. Rotating turns the image 90 degrees to the right or left; flipping turns it 180 degrees horizontally or vertically. You can also rotate a shape to any degree by dragging its green rotating handle.

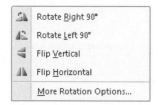

Tip If a shape has a yellow diamond handle, you can drag this handle to alter the appearance of the shape without changing its size or angle of rotation.

When the image is the size you want, you can position it roughly by dragging it, position it exactly by setting coordinates in the Size And Position dialog box, or position it visually by using a grid and guides.

The grid is a fixed matrix of horizontal and vertical dotted lines for which you can specify the spacing. The guides are movable pair of horizontal and vertical lines. As you drag a guide, a ScreenTip shows in inches how far the guide is from the center of the slide. (As you drag, numbers are skipped because the Snap Objects To Grid check box is selected in the Grid And Guides dialog box. When turned on, this option snaps guidelines and graphics to the grid whether or not it is visible.)

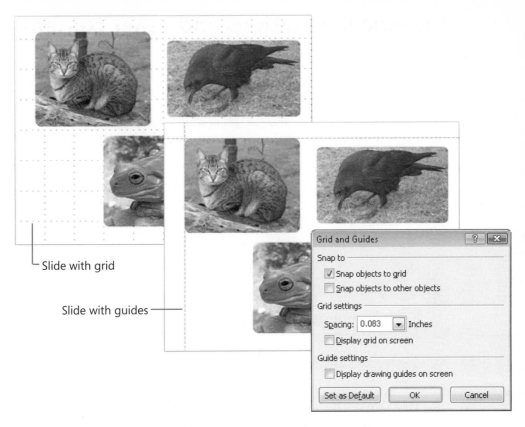

Slide with grid

Slide with guides

Tip You can create a copy of a selected shape by dragging it while holding down the Ctrl key or by clicking Duplicate in the Paste list in the Clipboard group on the Home tab.

➤ To change the size of a selected image

→ Drag a sizing handle until the image is the shape and size you want.

→ On the **Format** tab, in the **Size** group, change the **Shape Height** or **Shape Width** setting.

Or

1. On the **Format** tab, click the **Size** dialog box launcher.

2. On the **Size** tab of the **Size and Position** dialog box, change the **Height** or **Width** setting, and then click **Close**.

   Tip You cannot change the height and the weight of an image disproportionately unless the Lock Aspect Ratio check box is cleared.

➤ **To change the scale of a selected image**

→ Display the **Size** tab of the **Size and Position** dialog box, change the **Height** or **Width** setting, and then click **Close**.

➤ **To crop a selected image**

1. On the **Format** tab, in the **Size** group, click the **Crop** button.

2. Move the cropping pointer over one of the cropping handles surrounding the image, and drag to crop away the parts of the image you don't want.

3. Turn off the cropping pointer by clicking the **Crop** button a second time.

➤ **To rotate a selected image**

→ Drag the green rotating handle until the image sits at the angle you want.

Or

1. On the **Format** tab, in the **Arrange** group, click the **Rotate** button.

2. In the **Rotate** gallery, click the option you want.

Or

1. Display the **Size** tab of the **Size and Position** dialog box, and in the **Size and rotate** area, change the **Rotation** setting.

2. Click **Close**.

➤ **To position a selected image**

→ Drag the image to the position you want.

→ Display the **Position** tab of the **Size and Position** dialog box, change the **Horizontal** or **Vertical** settings, and then click **Close**.

➤ **To display gridlines and guides to assist in arranging images**

1. Right-click a blank area of the slide, and then click **Grid and Guides**.

2. In the **Grid and Guides** dialog box, select the options you want, and then click **OK**.

Stacking Order

When graphics overlap each other, they are *stacked*. The stacking order is determined by the order in which you inserted the graphics, but you can change it by moving graphics in the stack.

Tip If you can't select a graphic because it is covered by others in the stack, click the Selection Pane button in the Arrange group on the Format tab to display the Selection And Visibility task pane, and then select the graphic you want from the Shapes On This Slide list.

➤ **To bring a selected image forward in the stack**

→ On the **Format** tab, in the **Arrange** group, click the **Bring to Front** button.

→ On the **Format** tab, in the **Arrange** group, click **Bring Forward** in the **Bring to Front** list to move forward one image at a time.

➤ **To send a selected image backward in the stack**

→ On the **Format** tab, in the **Arrange** group, click the **Send to Back** button.

→ On the **Format** tab, in the **Arrange** group, click **Send Backward** in the **Send to Back** list to move backward one image at a time.

Grouping

When you have multiple images on a slide, you can group them so that you can format, copy, and move them as a unit. You can change the attributes of an individual shape—for example, its color, size, or location—without ungrouping the shapes. If you do ungroup the graphics, you can regroup the same shapes by selecting one of them and then clicking Regroup in the Group list.

Tip If you add pictures to a slide by clicking the Picture button in the Illustrations group on the Insert tab, you can group them. However, if you add them by clicking the Insert Picture From File button in a content placeholder, you cannot group them.

➤ **To group or ungroup selected images**

→ On the **Format** tab, in the **Arrange** group, click **Group**, and then in the list, click **Group** or **Ungroup**.

Alignment

After inserting pictures, clip art images, or shapes in approximate locations, you can align them precisely in several ways. For example, you can:

- Align graphics vertically or horizontally.
- Distribute graphics evenly within their current space, either horizontally or vertically.
- Align graphics relative to the slide that contains them or to other selected objects.
- Align graphics relative to a position on the slide.
- Align graphics against adjustable horizontal and vertical guidelines.

Strategy The alignment options can produce unexpected results when multiple images are selected, depending on whether Align To Slide or Align Selected Objects is turned on. Practice selecting the same images in different orders and then using various commands in the Align list to become familiar with the results.

➤ **To align a selected image relative to the slide**

→ On the **Format** tab, in the **Arrange** group, click the type of alignment you want in the **Align** list.

➤ **To align selected images relative to each other**

1. On the **Format** tab, in the **Arrange** group, click **Align to Slide** or **Align Selected Objects** in the **Align** list.

2. In the **Align** list, click the type of alignment you want.

Practice Tasks

The practice files for these tasks are located in the *Documents\Microsoft Press\ MCAS\PowerPoint2007\Objective03* folder. If you want, save the task results in the same folder with *My* prepended to the file name.

- Open the *SizingPictures* presentation, and on Slide 2, make the three pictures all 2.5 inches high by 3.5 inches wide. Then bring the bottom picture to the top of the stack.

- Open the *FlipDistribute* presentation, and on Slide 5, flip the arrow on the right horizontally. Then distribute all the shapes evenly across the slide.

- Open the *GuidePosition* presentation, and group the pictures on Slide 2. Then use the guides to position the upper-left corner of the top picture at the 2-inch mark on the vertical ruler and the 4-inch mark on the horizontal ruler.

3.6   Insert and modify charts

Basic Charts

You can easily add a chart to a slide to make it easy to see trends that might not be obvious from looking at numbers. When you create a chart in PowerPoint, you specify the chart type and then use a linked Microsoft Office Excel worksheet to enter the information you want to plot.

You can enter the data into the linked worksheet by typing it directly, or you can copy and paste it from an existing Excel worksheet, Microsoft Office Access table, or Microsoft Office Word table. You then identify the chart data range in the linked worksheet to ensure that only the data you want appears in the chart, and close the worksheet to plot the data.

If you decide that the type of chart you initially selected doesn't adequately depict your data, you can change the type at any time. You can choose from 11 chart types, each with two-dimensional and three-dimensional variations, and you can customize each aspect of each variation.

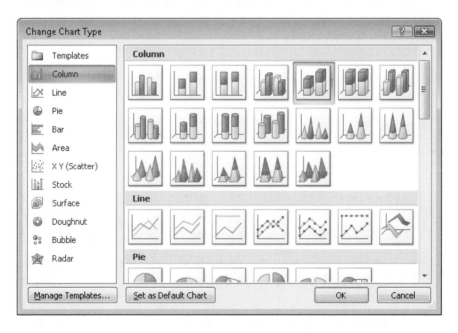

➤ **To insert a chart**

1. In a content placeholder, click the **Insert Chart** button.

2. In the **Insert Chart** dialog box, click a chart category in the left pane, click the chart type in the right pane, and then click **OK**.

3. In the linked Excel worksheet, enter the values to be plotted.

4. Ensure that the blue border delineating the chart data range encompasses only the data you want to be included in the chart, by dragging the blue triangle in the lower-right corner of the range.

5. Close the Excel window.

➤ **To change the type of a selected chart**

1. On the contextual **Design** tab, in the **Type** group, click the **Change Chart Type** button.

2. In the **Change Chart Type** dialog box, in the left pane, click a new type of chart.

3. In the right pane, click the specific chart sub-type you want, and then click **OK**.

➤ **To move a selected chart**

➜ Point to a blank part of the chart area, and drag the chart to its new position.

➤ **To size a selected chart**

➜ Point to one of the sets of dots on the chart's frame, and drag to change the chart size.

Chart Elements

The linked Excel worksheet is composed of rows and columns of cells that contain values, or data points, that make up a data series. Each data point in a data series is represented graphically in the chart by a data marker. The data is plotted against an x-axis—also called the *category axis*—and a y-axis—also called the *value axis*. (Three-dimensional charts also have a z-axis—also called the *series axis*.) Tick-mark labels along each axis identify the categories, values, or series in the chart. A legend provides a key for identifying the data series. The chart might also have a title, axis labels, data labels, a data table, and gridlines. Each element can be adjusted in appropriate ways, as can the plot area (the area defined by the axes) and the chart area (the entire chart object).

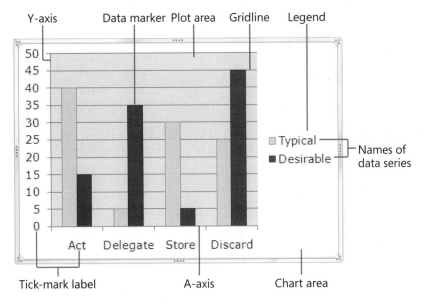

Strategy There are too many possible permutations of chart elements for us to cover them in detail here. Make sure you are familiar with the elements and how to work with them to best convey different types of data.

➤ **To add, remove, or adjust the position of the legend**

1. On the **Layout** tab, in the **Labels** group, click the **Legend** button.

2. In the **Legend** gallery, click the option you want.

➤ **To add a title**

1. On the **Layout** tab, in the **Labels** group, click the **Chart Title** button.

2. In the **Title** gallery, click the option you want.

Chart Formatting

You can modify and format a chart to get the effect you want. If you don't want to spend a lot of time on individual chart elements, you can apply predefined combinations of layouts and styles to create sophisticated charts with a minimum of effort. You can also apply a shape style to the chart area.

➤ **To change the layout of a selected chart**

1. On the contextual **Design** tab, in the **Chart Layouts** group, click the **Quick Layout** button.

2. In the **Chart Layouts** gallery, click the layout you want.

➤ **To apply a style to a selected chart**

1. On the contextual **Design** tab, in the **Chart Styles** group, click the **Quick Styles** button.

2. In the **Chart Styles** gallery, click the style you want.

➤ **To apply a shape style to a selected chart**

1. On the **Format** tab, in the **Shape Styles** group, click the **More** button.

2. In the **Shape Styles** gallery, click the style you want.

Practice Tasks

The practice files for these tasks are located in the *Documents\Microsoft Press\ MCAS\PowerPoint2007\Objective03* folder. If you want, save the task results in the same folder with *My* prepended to the file name.

● Open the *Charts* presentation, and on Slide 7, insert a Clustered Column chart. Then cut and paste the data from the text box on Slide 6 into cells A1:C5 of the chart's linked worksheet. (Don't worry about the data formatting.) Resize the chart data range to include only A1:C5, and close the Excel window.

● Open the *ChartElements* presentation, and on Slide 7, remove the vertical axis. Also turn off the horizontal gridlines. Finally, move the legend to the left side of the chart, and add the title *How Do You Spend Your Time?* above the chart.

● Open the *ChartType* presentation, and on Slide 7, change the chart type to Stacked Column in 3-D. Format the chart by applying Style 35 and Layout 8. Then apply the Colored Outline – Accent 2 shape style.

3.7   Insert and modify tables

Basic Tables

When you want to present a lot of data in an organized and easy-to-read format, a table is often your best choice. After you specify the number of columns and rows you want in the table, PowerPoint creates the table object, ready for you to enter your data.

To enter information in the table, you click a cell and then type. You can move the insertion point from cell to cell by pressing the Tab key. If the information you want to use already exists in an Excel worksheet or a Word or Access table, you can copy and paste the information, rather than re-creating it.

➤ **To insert a table**

1. In a content placeholder, click the **Insert Table** button.

2. In the **Insert Table** dialog box, specify the number of columns and rows, and then click **OK**.

3. Enter or copy and paste the information into the table structure.

    Or

1. On the **Insert** tab, in the **Tables** group, click the **Table** button.

2. In the grid, point to the upper-left cell, move the pointer across and down to select the number of columns and rows you want, and click the lower-right cell in the selection.

3. Enter or copy and paste the information into the table structure.

Table Editing and Formatting

After you create a table on a PowerPoint slide, you can work with it in much the same way as you work with tables in Word.

Strategy Review the information about working with tables in Exam 77-601, "Using Microsoft Office Word 2007," section 4.3, "Modify tables."

Practice Tasks

The practice file for these tasks is located in the *Documents\Microsoft Press\ MCAS\PowerPoint2007\Objective03* folder. If you want, save the task results in the same folder with *My* prepended to the file name.

- Open the *Tables* presentation, and on Slide 5, insert a table with three columns and four rows. If you want, copy and paste the information from the text box on Slide 4 into the table on Slide 5. (You will have to copy each cell separately.)

- Continuing in the *Tables* presentation, turn off Banded Rows formatting, and turn on First Column formatting. Then apply the Medium Style 2 - Accent 2 style to the table.

- Continuing in the *Tables* presentation, insert a row at the top of the table, and merge its cells. In the merged cell, enter and center the title *Effect of Focused Activity*.

- Continuing in the *Tables* presentation, apply a border around the entire table.

Objective Review

Before finishing this chapter, ensure that you have mastered the following skills:

3.1 Create SmartArt diagrams.

3.2 Modify SmartArt diagrams.

3.3 Insert illustrations and shapes.

3.4 Modify illustrations.

3.5 Arrange illustrations and other content.

3.6 Insert and modify charts.

3.7 Insert and modify tables.

4 Collaborating On and Delivering Presentations

The skills tested in this section of the Microsoft Office Specialist exam for Microsoft Office PowerPoint 2007 relate to finalizing presentations and related materials. Specifically, the following objectives are associated with this set of skills:

4.1 Review presentations.

4.2 Protect presentations.

4.3 Secure and share presentations.

4.4 Prepare printed materials.

4.5 Prepare for and rehearse presentation delivery.

A presentation is often a collaborative effort. Even if you develop a presentation by yourself, you might want to have other people review it to ensure that it has the impact you intend on an audience. When all the development work is over, you still need to finalize the presentation before you are ready to show it to the world.

This chapter guides you in studying the use of comments to aid in reviewing a presentation, attaching a digital signature or password to a presentation to prevent other people from changing it, removing personal information, and saving a presentation in an appropriate format. You also study printing a presentation or the accompanying audience notes, selecting a subset of slides, setting up slide delivery timing, and packaging the presentation for delivery.

 Important Before you can use the practice files in this chapter, you need to install them from the book's companion CD to their default location. See "Using the Companion CD" at the beginning of this book for more information.

Tip Graphics and operating system–related instructions in this book reflect the Windows Vista user interface. If your computer is running Windows XP and you experience trouble following the instructions as written, refer to the sidebar "If You Are Running Windows XP" in "Working in the Microsoft Office Fluent User Interface" at the beginning of this book.

4.1   Review presentations

Comments

The development of a presentation, especially one that will be delivered to clients, shareholders, or other important people, is often a collaborative effort, with several people contributing ideas and feedback. If you are asked to review a presentation, you can give feedback about a slide without disrupting its text and layout by inserting a comment in a comment box.

After you type your comment, clicking away from the comment box hides the comment but leaves a small comment icon with your initials and a number. If you add a comment without first selecting an object on the slide, the comment icon appears in the upper-left corner of the slide. If you select an object such as the title or a graphic before adding the comment, the comment icon appears in the upper-right corner of the object. In either case, pointing to the icon displays the comment temporarily, and clicking the icon displays the comment until you click somewhere else.

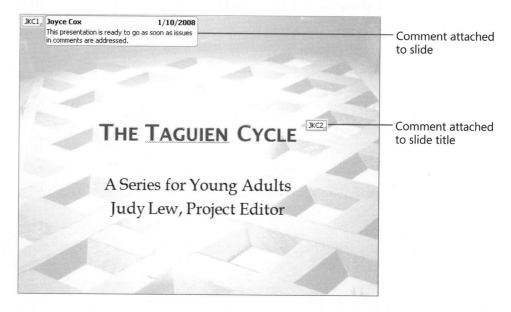

Comment attached to slide

Comment attached to slide title

Tip Comment boxes include the user name and initials you specified the first time you started any program in the 2007 Microsoft Office system. To change this information, click PowerPoint Options at the bottom of the Office menu, and then change the entries in the User Name and Initials boxes on the Popular page of the PowerPoint Options dialog box.

➤ To insert a comment

1. Click the slide or object on the slide to which you want to attach a comment.

2. On the **Review** tab, in the **Comments** group, click the **New Comment** button.

3. In the comment box, type the comment, and then click away from the comment box to close it.

Comment Review

You can turn the display of comments on and off and move quickly back and forth among them.

➤ To show and hide comments and other markup

→ On the **Review** tab, in the **Comments** group, click the **Show Markup** button.

➤ To move among comments

→ On the **Review** tab, in the **Comments** group, click the **Previous** or **Next** button.

Comment Management

You can respond to a displayed comment by inserting a new one or by activating the comment box for editing so that you can make additions or changes. When issues raised in comments have been resolved, you can delete each comment individually, delete all the comments on the current slide, or delete all the comments in the entire presentation.

See Also For information about circling or underlining important points and drawing arrows and diagrams on slides while reviewing a presentation, see section 4.5, "Prepare for and rehearse presentation delivery."

➤ To edit a comment

→ Quickly activate the comment for editing by double-clicking it, and then make your changes or additions.

→ Right-click the comment icon, click **Edit Comment**, and then make your changes or additions.

Or

1. Click the comment icon, and then on the **Review** tab, in the **Comments** group, click the **Edit Comment** button.

2. In the comment box, make your changes.

➤ To delete a specific comment

→ Right-click the comment icon, and click **Delete Comment**.

→ Click the comment icon, and then on the **Review** tab, in the **Comments** group, click the **Delete** button.

➤ To delete all the comments on a slide

→ On the **Review** tab, in the **Comments** group, click **Delete All Markup on the Current Slide** in the **Delete** list.

➤ To delete all the comments in the presentation

1. On the **Review** tab, in the **Comments** group, click **Delete All Markup in this Presentation** in the **Delete** list.

2. To confirm the deletion, click **Yes**.

Tip When you delete a comment, subsequent comments are not renumbered.

Practice Tasks

The practice files for these tasks are located in the *Documents\Microsoft Press\ MCAS\PowerPoint2007\Objective04* folder. If you want, save the task results in the same folder with *My* prepended to the file name.

● Open the *Comments* presentation, and attach the comment *Feng shui not mentioned. Good or bad?* to Slide 1. Then attach the comment *Do we need the word "Ancient"?* to the title.

● In the *Comments* presentation, attach the comment *A graphic would add interest here* to the bulleted list on Slide 2. Click away from the comment to close the box, and then edit the comment to add the word *tasteful* to the left of the word *graphic*.

● Open the *DeleteComments* presentation, and delete all the comments attached to the title slide. Review the remaining comments in the presentation, and then using only one command, delete them all.

4.2 Protect presentations

Digital Signatures

When you create a presentation that will be distributed to other people via e-mail or the Web, you might want to attach a digital signature to it to authenticate its origin. Attaching a digital signature should be the last task you perform on a presentation, because changing the presentation after signing it invalidates the signature.

Certified digital IDs can be obtained from Microsoft partner companies and other independent certification authorities. You can also create your own ID, but other people will not be able to verify its authenticity. After you have obtained or created a digital ID for one Microsoft Office program, you can use it with any program.

See Also For more information about obtaining or creating a digital ID, see Exam 77-601, "Using Microsoft Office Word 2007," section 6.3, "Attach digital signatures."

➤ **To attach a digital signature to a presentation**

1. On the **Office** menu, point to **Prepare**, and then click **Add a Digital Signature**.

2. If a message box opens, click **OK**.

3. In the **Sign** dialog box, enter a purpose if desired, and then click **Sign**.

4. In the **Signature Confirmation** message box, click **OK**.

5. In the **Signatures** task pane, verify that the correct signature has been attached to the document.

Tip To remove the signature so that you can make further changes to the presentation, click the signature in the Signatures task pane, click the arrow, and then click Remove Signature, confirming the action.

Passwords

Sometimes you might want only specified people to be able to view a presentation. Or you might want some people to be able to view it and others to be able to change it. The simplest way to control access to the presentation is to assign a password to it. You can assign two types of passwords:

● **Password to open.** When you assign a password that must be entered to open the presentation, the presentation is encrypted so that only people with the password can view the presentation.

● **Password to modify.** When you assign a password that must be entered to modify the presentation, people who don't have the password can open a read-only version but they cannot make changes or save a copy with a different name.

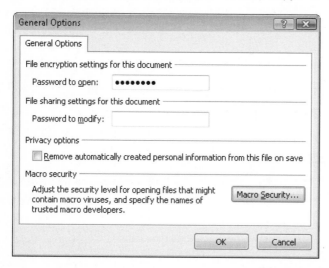

Tip In the General Options dialog box, you can tell PowerPoint to remove personal information every time you save the file, or you can remove it all at once before distributing the presentation; see section 4.3, "Secure and share presentations." Clicking Macro Security displays the Trust Center, which is also accessible from the PowerPoint Options dialog box.

When you try to open a presentation to which a password has been assigned, the Password dialog box opens. If the password must be entered to open the presentation, you must enter the exact password—including capitalization, numbers, spaces, and symbols. If the password must be entered to modify the presentation, you can either enter the exact password to open it or click Read-Only to open a version that you can view but not modify.

➤ **To set a password for a presentation**

1. On the **Office** menu, click **Save As**.

2. At the bottom of the **Save As** dialog box, click **General Options** in the **Tools** list.

3. In the **Password to open** or **Password to modify** box of the **General Options** dialog box, type the password you want, and then click **OK**.

4. In the **Reenter password to open** or **Reenter password to modify** box of the **Confirm Password** dialog box, retype the password you previously entered, and then click **OK**.

   Tip In the General Options dialog box, you can enter both passwords. In that case, you will be asked to confirm each in turn.

5. In the **Save As** dialog box, click **Save**.

Tip To remove the password from a password-protected presentation, open it using the password, and display first the Save As dialog box and then the General Options dialog box. Remove the password from the password box(es), and then save the presentation.

Practice Tasks

The practice file for these tasks is located in the *Documents\Microsoft Press\ MCAS\PowerPoint2007\Objective04* folder. If you want, save the task results in the same folder with *My* prepended to the file name.

● Open the *Password* presentation, assign the password *P@ssword* for modifying the file, and save the presentation with the name *MyPassword*. Then close the presentation.

❙ Continuing with the password-protected *Password* presentation, open a read-only version, try to make a change, and then close the presentation.

❙ Continuing with the *Password* presentation, use the password to open a version that you can edit, and delete the word *The* in the presentation title.

4.3   Secure and share presentations

Document Inspector

As you develop a presentation, PowerPoint attaches identifying and tracking information to it as properties. These properties include the name of the author, the title, when the file was created and updated, and so on. You might want to enter other properties, such as keywords, to help you easily find the presentation or to keep track of its status.

See Also For information about entering properties, see Exam 77-601, "Using Microsoft Office Word 2007," section 1.3, "Make documents and content easier to find."

These days, most presentations are delivered electronically, either in person, by e-mail, or from a Web site. If the presentation will never leave your computer, you don't have to worry that these properties might contain something that you would rather other people did not see. However, if the presentation file is going to be shared with other people, you will want to remove this identifying and tracking information before you distribute the presentation. This is known as *scrubbing* a file.

The scrubbing process is carried out by the Document Inspector, a 2007 Office system feature that checks for behind-the-scenes and hidden information, as well as leftover comments and ink annotations. When you run the Document Inspector, you can have it inspect the presentation for any of six categories of information, including the presence of document properties that you might not want others to be able to view. When it reports its findings, you can choose whether to have the Document Inspector remove the information you specify or to track down and remove the information yourself.

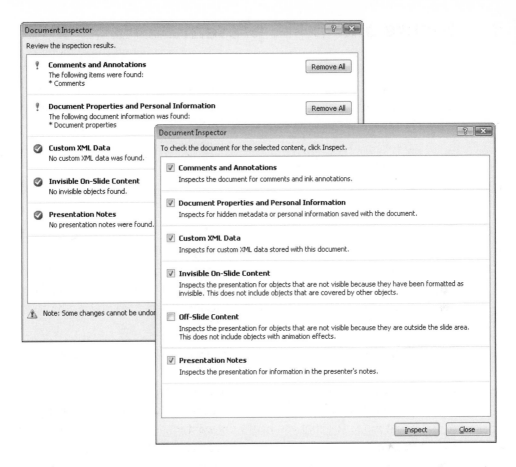

➤ To remove information before distributing a presentation

1. On the **Office** menu, point to **Prepare**, and then click **Inspect Document**.

2. In the **Document Inspector** dialog box, clear the check boxes for types of information you don't want to locate, and then click **Inspect**.

3. When the **Document Inspector** reports its findings, click **Remove All** for any type of information you want to remove.

4. Click **Close** to close the **Document Inspector** dialog box.

Permissions

If your organization has implemented Information Rights Management (IRM) or if you sign up for the free IRM trial service from Microsoft, you can restrict who can change, print, or copy a presentation, and you can limit these permissions for a specified period of time.

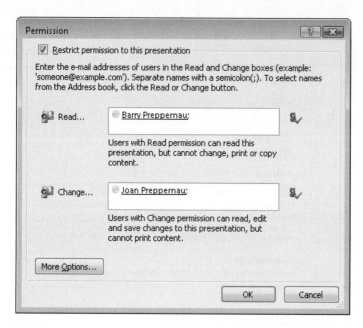

Tip To sign up for the free Microsoft Information Rights Management service, use the wizard that appears the first time you try to restrict access to a presentation.

➤ To restrict permissions to a presentation

1. On the **Review** tab, in the **Protect** group, click the **Protect Presentation** button, and then in the list, click **Restricted Access**. Or point to **Prepare** on the **Office** menu, point to **Restrict Permission**, and then click **Restricted Access**.

2. In the **Permission** dialog box, select the **Restrict Permission to this presentation** check box.

3. Type the names of the people to whom you want to assign **Read** or **Change** permission.

4. To refine the permissions, click **More Options**, and then adjust the settings in the **Additional permissions for users** and **Additional settings** areas.

5. Click **OK** to close the **Permission** dialog box.

Compression

The file size of a presentation that contains pictures can become quite large. You can shrink the size of a picture (without affecting the displayed image) to minimize the file size. Depending on the resolution you set for the compression, you might lose some visual quality. You choose the resolution based on where or how the presentation will be viewed—for example, on the Web or printed. You can also set other options, such as deleting cropped areas of a picture, to achieve the best balance between visual quality and file size.

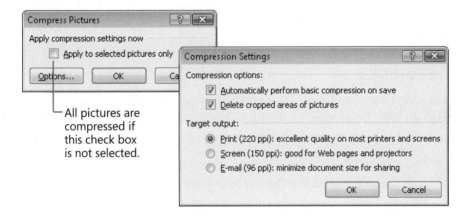

All pictures are compressed if this check box is not selected.

➤ **To compress all the pictures in a presentation**

1. On the **Format** tab, in the **Adjust** group, click the **Compress Pictures** button.

   Tip To compress only the selected picture, select the Apply To Selected Pictures Only check box.

2. In the **Compress Pictures** dialog box, click **Options**.

3. In the **Compression Settings** dialog box, in the **Target output** area, select the delivery option you want, and then click **OK**.

4. In the **Compress Pictures** dialog box, click **OK**.

Finalizing

Before distributing a presentation, you should mark it as final. This feature saves the file, deactivates most PowerPoint tools, and displays an icon in the status bar to indicate that no further changes should be made to the presentation.

➤ To mark a presentation as final

1. On the **Office** menu, point to **Prepare**, and then click **Mark as Final**.

2. In the message box, click **OK**, and then click **OK** in the confirmation box.

Tip If you want to make additional changes to the presentation, you can turn off the final status by choosing Mark As Final again.

File Formats

By default, PowerPoint 2007 presentations are saved in PPTX format, a new file format based on XML. Depending on how you intend to distribute the presentation, you can also save it in a variety of other formats, such as the following:

● **PowerPoint 97–2003 Presentation.** If you want to share a PowerPoint presentation with users of an earlier version of PowerPoint, you can save it in the PPT file format. Before saving a presentation in this format, you can use the Compatibility Checker to check whether the presentation includes features that are not supported in previous versions of PowerPoint. You can then decide how to handle any reported issues.

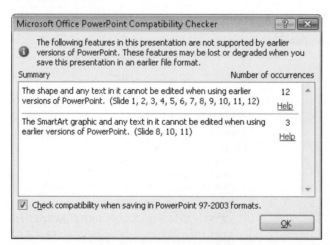

● **PowerPoint Show.** Provided PowerPoint 2007 or Microsoft Office PowerPoint Viewer is installed on the computer, double-clicking a presentation file saved in the PPSX format opens the presentation in Slide Show view instead of Normal view. Pressing Esc closes the presentation.

- **GIF, JPEG, PNG, TIFF, or other graphic format.** You can save slides as images that can be inserted in documents or displayed on Web pages. When you select an image format and click Save, PowerPoint asks whether you want to save only the current slide or every slide in the presentation as an image.

You can also save a presentation as a Web page, in two formats:

- **Single File Web Page.** If you select this format, PowerPoint saves everything that is necessary to display the Web presentation in a single file in the MHTML format.

- **Web Page.** If you select this format, PowerPoint saves the presentation file in the HTML format, creates a folder with the same name as the Web presentation, and stores in the folder all the other files necessary to display the presentation in a Web browser.

In both cases, PowerPoint expands the Save As dialog box so that you can change the title that will appear in the Web browser's title bar and publish the Web page. You can also specify other options to control the navigation frame, the target browser, and the way graphics and fonts are handled.

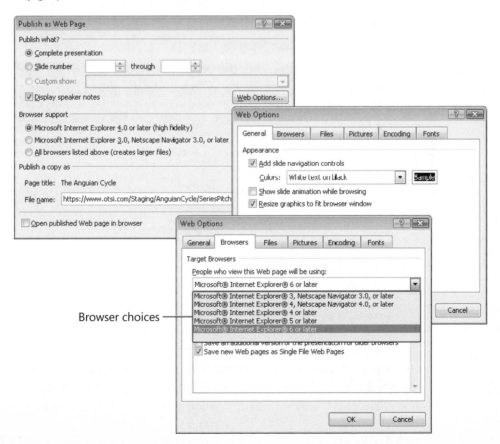

Browser choices

➤ **To save a presentation for use in an earlier PowerPoint version**

1. On the **Office** menu, point to **Save As**, and then click **PowerPoint 97-2003 Presentation**.

2. In the **Save As** dialog box, specify the file name and storage location, and then click **Save**.

➤ **To check for features unsupported in earlier PowerPoint versions**

1. On the **Office** menu, point to **Prepare**, and then click **Run Compatibility Checker**.

2. Make a note of any issues reported in the **Compatibility Checker** dialog box, and then click **OK**.

➤ **To save a presentation that can be displayed only in Slide Show view**

1. On the **Office** menu, point to **Save As**, and then click **PowerPoint Show**.

2. In the **Save As** dialog box, specify the file name and storage location, and then click **Save**.

➤ **To save slides as images**

1. On the **Office** menu, click **Save As**.

2. In the **Save As** dialog box, click the image format you want in the **Save as type** list.

3. Specify a file name and storage location for the file, and then click **Save**.

4. In the message box, click **Every Slide**, and then click **OK** to acknowledge the creation of the folder.

   Or

   Click **Current Slide Only**.

➤ **To save a presentation as a Web page on your hard disk**

1. Display the **Save As** dialog box, and then click either **Single File Web Page** or **Web Page** in the **Save as type** list.

2. Specify the file name and storage location, and then click **Save**.

Practice Tasks

The practice files for these tasks are located in the *Documents\Microsoft Press\ MCAS\PowerPoint2007\Objective04* folder. If you want, save the task results in the same folder with *My* prepended to the file name.

● Open the *Finalizing* presentation, and remove all identifying and tracking information and comments from the file. Then mark the presentation as final.

● Open the *BigFile* presentation, and then shrink the file size as much as possible so that you can share the presentation as an e-mail attachment.

● Open the *EarlierVersions* presentation, check it for compatibility with Microsoft PowerPoint 2002, and then save it in a format that allows the presentation to be opened and edited in that program.

● Open the *ViewingOnly* presentation, and save it as a presentation that can be opened and viewed only in Slide Show view.

● Open the *WebPage* presentation, and save the entire presentation as a single file Web page that will be displayed with navigation controls in the presentation's accent color and with the title *New Young Adults Series*. Make the Web presentation compatible with most common browsers.

4.4   Prepare printed materials

Handouts and Notes

As a courtesy for your audience, you might want to supply handouts showing the presentation's slides so that people can take notes. You don't need to do anything special to create handouts.

If you will be delivering your presentation before a live audience, you will probably need some speaker notes to guide you. Each slide in a PowerPoint presentation has a corresponding notes page. As you create each slide in Normal view, you can enter notes that relate to the slide's content by simply clicking the Notes pane and typing. If you want to include anything other than text in your speaker notes, you must switch to Notes Page view.

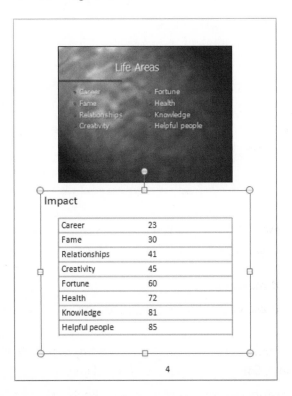

Handouts and notes have their own masters, and you can customize them by using the same techniques you use to customize slide masters. Usually, you will find that the default masters are more than adequate.

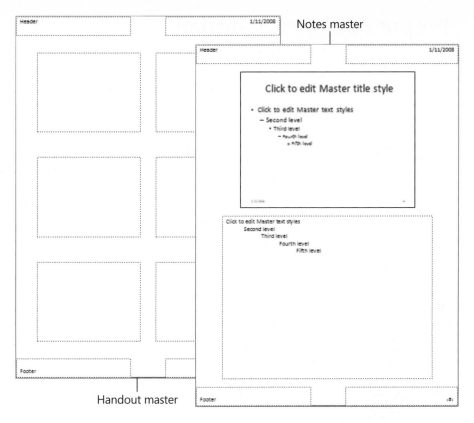

Notes master

Handout master

See Also For information about customizing masters, see section 1.2, "Customize slide masters."

➤ **To display Notes Page view**

→   On the **View** tab, in the **Presentation Views** group, click the **Notes Page** button.

➤ **To customize the handout master**

1. On the **View** tab, in the **Presentation Views** group, click the **Handout Master** button.

2. On the **Handout Master** tab, make the changes you want by clicking buttons in the **Page Setup**, **Placeholders**, **Edit Theme**, and **Background** groups.

3. On the preview page, customize the text in the **Header**, **Footer**, **Date**, and **Page Number** placeholders.

4. Click the **Close Master View** button to return to the previous view.

➤ **To customize the notes master**

1. On the **View** tab, in the **Presentation Views** group, click the **Notes Master** button.

2. On the **Notes Master** tab, make the changes you want by clicking buttons in the **Page Setup**, **Placeholders**, **Edit Theme**, and **Background** groups.

3. On the preview page, customize the text in the **Header**, **Footer**, **Date**, and **Page Number** placeholders. Also make any necessary adjustments to the **Notes** placeholder in the bottom half of the page.

4. Click the **Close Master View** button to return to the previous view.

Printing

If you will deliver a presentation by using transparencies on an overhead projector, you will need to print your presentation on special sheets of acetate. Even if you plan to deliver your presentation electronically, you might want to print your presentation to proof it for typographical errors and stylistic inconsistencies.

Assuming that you have already set the slide size and orientation, you can preview your presentation to see how the slides will look when printed. If you will be printing a color presentation on a monochrome (usually black ink) printer, it's a good idea to preview in pure black and white or grayscale (shades of gray) to verify that the text is legible against the background.

Tip In Normal view, you can see how your slides will look when they are printed on a monochrome printer by clicking either the Grayscale or the Pure Black And White button in the Color/Grayscale group on the View tab.

When you are ready to print, you can use Quick Print to print one copy of each slide on the default printer. If you want to adjust any print settings, you need to display the Print dialog box, in which you can make the following changes:

● Specify the printer you want to use and set its properties.

● Print to a file instead of printing a physical copy of the presentation.

● Specify which slides to print.

● Print and collate multiple copies.

● Specify whether to print slides (one per page), handouts (multiple slides per page), notes pages (one half-size slide per page with space for notes), or an outline.

Tip If you use two monitors and Presenter view to deliver the presentation, you don't need to print speaker's notes. You can see the notes on one monitor while the audience sees the presentation in Slide Show view through the other monitor.

● Print your presentation in color, grayscale, or pure black and white.

● Scale slides to fit the paper.

● Put a frame around slides.

● Print electronic or handwritten notes attached to the presentation so that you can review them along with the slides.

● Print slides that will be hidden in the electronic presentation.

● Print in high quality.

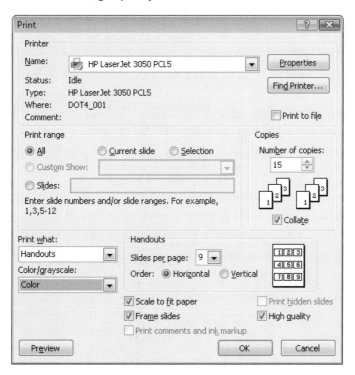

➤ **To preview a presentation**

→ On the **Office** menu, point to **Print**, and then click **Print Preview**.

→ Click **Preview** in the lower-left corner of the **Print** dialog box.

➤ **To print slides, handouts, notes, or an outline**

1. On the **Office** menu, click **Print**.

2. In the **Print** dialog box, click the presentation component you want to print in the **Print what** list.

3. Change other settings as necessary, and then click **OK**.

Practice Tasks

The practice files for these tasks are located in the *Documents\Microsoft Press\ MCAS\PowerPoint2007\Objective04* folder. If you want, save the task results in the same folder with *My* prepended to the file name.

● Open the *Notes* presentation, and attach the note *Welcome and introductions* to Slide 1. Then insert the *YinYang* graphic file in a note attached to Slide 3.

● Open the *Handouts* presentation, and customize the handout master to show three slides per page. Then enter *The Ancient Art of Placement* as the header and *Wide World Importers* as the footer for all handouts.

● Open the *Printing* presentation, and print slides 1, 2, 3, and 5 in grayscale with frames to a file named *MySlides*.

● Open the *NotesHandouts* presentation, and print one set of handouts with three slides per page in color to a file named *MyHandouts*. Then print a set of speaker's notes in grayscale to a file named *MyNotes*.

4.5   **Prepare for and rehearse presentation delivery**

Slide Subsets

Sometimes you might want to be able to make an on-the-spot decision during a presentation about whether to display a particular slide. You can give yourself this flexibility by hiding slides so that you can skip over them if their information doesn't seem useful to a particular audience. If you decide to include a slide's information while delivering the presentation, you can easily display it at that time.

If you plan to deliver variations of the same presentation to different audiences, you can start by preparing a single presentation containing all the slides you are likely to need for all the audiences. Then you can select slides from the presentation that are appropriate for a particular audience and group them as a custom slide show. When you need to deliver the presentation for that audience, you open the main presentation and show the subset of slides by choosing the custom slide show from a list.

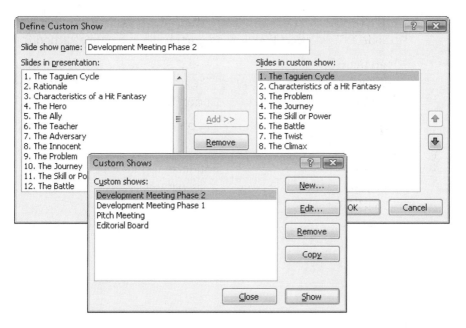

➤ **To hide a selected slide**

→ On the **Slide Show** tab, in the **Set Up** group, click the **Hide Slide** button.

Tip On the Slides tab of the Overview pane, or in Slide Sorter view, you can right-click a slide and then click Hide Slide.

➤ **To display a hidden slide while delivering a presentation**

→ Right-click the screen, point to **Go to Slide**, and then click the hidden slide.

➤ **To create a custom slide show**

1. On the **Slide Show** tab, in the **Start Slide Show** group, click the **Custom Slide Show** button, and then click **Custom Shows**.

2. In the **Custom Shows** dialog box, click **New**.

3. In the **Slide show name** box of the **Define Custom Show** dialog box, type a name for the custom show.

4. In the **Slides in presentation** list, click the slides you want, click **Add**, and then click **OK**.

Tip To change an existing custom show, click Edit in the Custom Shows dialog box.

➤ **To deliver a custom show**

→ On the **Slide Show** tab, in the **Start Slide Show** group, click the **Custom Slide Show** button, and then click the custom show you want.

Or

1. In **Slide Show** view, move the mouse to display the navigation toolbar.

2. On the navigation toolbar, click the **Navigation** button, click **Custom Show**, and then click the show you want.

Rehearsals

When delivering a presentation, you can move from slide to slide in the following ways:

- **Manually.** You control when you move by clicking the mouse button, pressing keys, or clicking commands.
- **Automatically.** PowerPoint displays each slide for a predefined length of time and then displays the next slide.

For automatic slide shows, the length of time a slide appears on the screen is controlled by its slide timing. You can apply timings to a single slide, to a group of slides, or to an entire presentation, either by allocating the same amount of time to each slide or by rehearsing the presentation while PowerPoint automatically tracks and sets the timings for you.

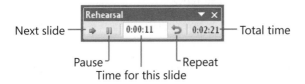

Rehearsing a presentation gives you the opportunity to practice moving smoothly among slides. The simplest way to move linearly from one slide to the next is to click the mouse button without moving the mouse, but you can also move around by using the keyboard. If you need to move to a slide other than the next one or the previous one, you can click buttons on an inconspicuous toolbar that appears in the lower-left corner of the slide when you move the mouse.

During a presentation, you might want to reinforce your message by drawing on the slides with an electronic "pen" or changing the background behind text with a highlighter. These techniques take practice, so you might want to rehearse them ahead of time. You might also want to test the pen or highlighter color and change it as necessary to make it stand out on the slide.

Tip If you don't erase the markup on a presentation while you are in Slide Show view, you are asked whether you want to keep the markup when you switch to a different view. If you click Keep, you can save the markup with the presentation. You can then toggle the markup on and off by clicking the Show Markup button in the Comments group on the Review tab.

➤ To apply the same timing to all slides

1. On the **Animations** tab, in the **Transition to This Slide** group, click the **Automatically After** check box. Then specify the timing in the adjacent box.

> **Tip** To apply the same timing to a group of slides, switch to Slide Sorter view, select the slides, and then set the timing.

2. In the **Transition to This Slide** group, click the **Apply To All** button.

> **Tip** When you click Apply To All, all the transition effects applied to the current slide are transferred to the other slides. If you have applied different transitions to different slides, those individually specified transitions are overwritten. So it's a good idea to apply all the effects that you want the slides to have in common first. Then you can select individual slides and customize their effects.

➤ To time the delivery of a presentation

1. With Slide 1 displayed, on the **Slide Show** tab, in the **Set Up** group, click the **Rehearse Timings** button.

2. Rehearse the presentation. To repeat the rehearsal for a particular slide, on the **Rehearsal** toolbar, click the **Repeat** button to reset the time for that slide to 0:00:00.

> **Tip** If you want to start the entire rehearsal over again, click the Rehearsal toolbar's Close button, and when a message asks whether you want to keep the existing timings, click No.

3. At the end of the slide show, click **Yes** to apply the recorded slide timings to the slides.

➤ To move to the next slide

→ Press the **Spacebar**, the **Page Down** key, the **Down Arrow** key, the **Right Arrow** key, or the **Enter** key.

→ On the navigation toolbar, click the **Next** button.

➤ **To move to the previous slide**

→ Press the **Page Up** key, the **Up Arrow** key, or the **Left Arrow** key.

→ On the navigation toolbar, click the **Previous** button.

➤ **To jump to a slide out of sequence (even if it is hidden)**

→ On the navigation toolbar, click the **Navigation** button, click **Go To Slide**, and then click the slide you want.

Tip You can also display the Navigation button's menu by right-clicking the slide.

➤ **To use a pen or highlighter to mark up slides**

1. On the navigation toolbar, click the **Pen** button, and then click the tool you want to use.

   Tip To change the color, click the Pen button, point to Ink Color, and then click a color in the palette.

2. Use the tool to annotate the slide.

3. To remove the annotations, click the **Pen** button on the navigation toolbar, click **Eraser**, and then move the eraser over the annotation you want to remove.

   Or

   Click the **Pen** button, and then click **Erase All Ink on Slide**.

4. Turn off the pen or highlighter by clicking the **Pen** button on the navigation toolbar and clicking **Arrow**.

Tip To display a list of keyboard shortcuts for carrying out slide show tasks, click the Navigation button, and then click Help.

Delivery Preparation

The final preparations for delivering a presentation depend on the delivery method. In the Set Up Show dialog box, you can specify the following:

● How the presentation will be delivered

● Whether all slides will be shown, or just a slide subset

● Whether an automatic slide show will loop continuously, be shown without narration, and be shown without animation

● Whether slide timings will be used

● Whether your hardware setup includes multiple monitors, and if so, whether you want to use Presenter view

● What monitor resolution should be used

If you will deliver your presentation from a computer other than the one on which you developed it, you need to make sure the fonts, linked objects, and any other necessary items are available. The Package for CD feature helps you gather all the presentation components and save them to a CD or other type of removable media. By default, the presentation is set up to run automatically in the Microsoft Office PowerPoint Viewer so that you can send the presentation to people who do not have PowerPoint installed on their computers.

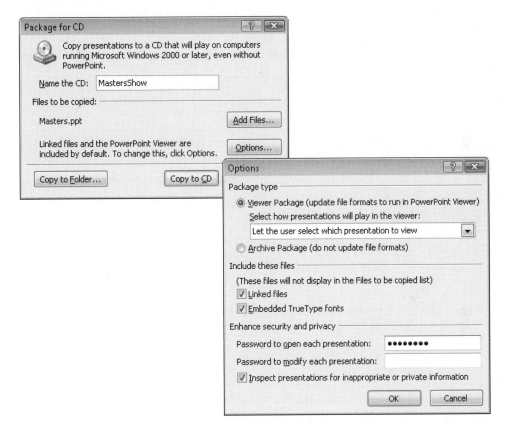

► **To set presentation delivery options**

1. On the **Slide Show** tab, in the **Set Up** group, click the **Set Up Slide Show** button.

2. In the **Set Up Show** dialog box, select the options you want, and then click **OK**.

➤ To package a presentation for delivery on a different computer

1. On the **Office** menu, point to **Publish**, and then click **Package for CD**.

2. When a message tells you that to be compatible with PowerPoint Viewer, the file format will be changed, click **OK**.

3. In the **Package for CD** dialog box, type the name you want in the **Name the CD** box. Then click **Options**.

4. In the **Package type** area, specify how the presentation will play in PowerPoint Viewer.

5. To include embedded fonts, in the **Include these files** area of the **Options** dialog box, select the **Embedded TrueType fonts** check box.

   Tip You can also embed fonts when you first save the presentation. In the Save As dialog box, click Tools, click Save Options, and on the Save page, select the Embed Fonts In The File check box. Then select the Embed Only The Characters Used In The Presentation option to embed only the characters in the font set that are actually used, or select the Embed All Characters option to embed the entire font set.

6. In the **Enhance security and privacy** area, enter passwords if needed, and select the **Inspect Presentations** check box to check for information that is inappropriate for distribution. Then click **OK**.

7. If necessary, reenter the password in the **Confirm Password** dialog box and click **OK**.

8. Insert a blank CD in your CD writer, and then click **Copy to CD**.

   Or

   Click **Copy to Folder**, and then in the **Copy to Folder** dialog box, specify the drive and folder in which you want to store the package, and click **OK**.

9. When PowerPoint asks you to verify that you want to include linked content, click **Yes**.

10. If PowerPoint indicates that the presentation contains inappropriate information, click **Continue**, and then use the **Document Inspector** to remove the information.

    See Also For information about the Document Inspector, see section 4.3, "Secure and share presentations."

11. When the process is complete, click **Close** to close the **Package for CD** dialog box.

Practice Tasks

The practice files for these tasks are located in the *Documents\Microsoft Press\MCAS\PowerPoint2007\Objective04* folder. If you want, save the task results in the same folder with *My* prepended to the file name.

- Open the *Subsets* presentation, and create a custom show named *Project Editors* that includes Slides 1, 3, and 14 through 16. Then edit the custom show to remove Slide 14.

- In the *Subsets* presentation, hide Slide 12.

- Open the *Timings* presentation, and set a timing of 01:00 for Slides 1, 2, and 3. Then apply the timing to all the slides in the presentation.

- Open the *Rehearsal* presentation, rehearse delivery of the first three slides of the presentation, and apply the rehearsed timings to the slides.

- Open the *Pen* presentation, switch to Slide Show view, and change the pen color to light purple. Then on Slide 5, underline the word *Colorizing*, and on Slide 6, draw circles around *color wheel* and *swatches*.

- Open the *Loop* presentation, and set it up to loop continuously without narration or animation.

- Open the *Travel* presentation, and create a presentation package named *MyTravel* with embedded fonts in the *Documents\Microsoft Press\MCAS\PowerPoint2007\Objective4* folder.

Objective Review

Before finishing this chapter, ensure that you have mastered the following skills:

4.1 Review presentations.

4.2 Protect presentations.

4.3 Secure and share presentations.

4.4 Prepare printed materials.

4.5 Prepare for and rehearse presentation delivery.

Using Microsoft Office
Outlook 2007

This part of the book covers the skills you need to have for certification as a Microsoft Office Specialist in Microsoft Office Outlook 2007. Specifically, you need to be able to complete tasks that demonstrate the following skill sets:

1 Managing Messages
2 Managing Scheduling
3 Managing Tasks
4 Managing Contacts and Personal Contact Information
5 Organizing Information

With these skills, you can communicate with colleagues and perform the scheduling and tracking tasks that are important to working efficiently in a business environment.

Prerequisites

We assume that you have been working with Outlook 2007 for at least six months and that you know how to carry out fundamental tasks that are not specifically mentioned in the Microsoft Office Specialist objectives for Exam 77-604, "Using Microsoft Office Outlook 2007." Before you begin studying for this exam, you might want to make sure you are familiar with the information in this section.

Program Window Panes

The Navigation Pane on the left side of the Outlook window changes depending on which Outlook module you are working in: Mail, Calendar, Contacts, Tasks, or Notes.

Like many aspects of the Outlook window, you can customize the Navigation Pane to suit the way you work. Most of the customization options are grouped on the View menu.

You switch between Outlook program modules by clicking the corresponding button at the bottom of the pane. Additional buttons provide access to the Folder List and to your saved Shortcuts. Depending on the space allocated to the buttons, they may be pane-width or iconic.

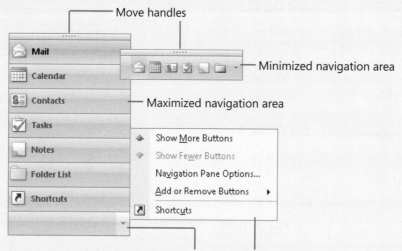

You can minimize the Navigation Pane to a vertical bar on the left side of the window. In the Mail module, information about unread messages in your Inbox and items flagged for follow-up appears on the bar. In any module, you can temporarily expand the Navigation Pane for that module by clicking the bar.

The To-Do Bar, which displays the Date Navigator, upcoming appointments, and your Task List, is open by default on the right side of the program window in all modules other than Calendar. You can display or close the To-Do Bar, or minimize it to a vertical bar displaying only your next appointment and the number of tasks remaining to do today. You can temporarily expand the To-Do Bar by clicking it.

The Reading Pane, which displays a preview of the selected Outlook item and commands for working with it, is open by default in the Mail module. You can display or close the Reading Pane in any module, on the right side or at the bottom of the program window.

➤ **To display or close the Navigation Pane**

→ On the **View** menu, point to **Navigation Pane**, and then click **Normal** to display the pane or **Off** to hide it.

➤ **To change the width of the Navigation Pane**

→ Drag the divider between the **Navigation Pane** and the content pane to the right or left.

➤ **To change the space allocated to the navigation buttons**

→ Drag the move handle at the top of the navigation button space up or down.

➤ **To minimize or expand the Navigation Pane**

→ On the **View** menu, point to **Navigation Pane**, and then click **Minimize**.

→ At the top of the **Navigation Pane**, click the **Minimize the Navigation Pane** button or the **Expand the Navigation Pane** button.

→ Click the minimized **Navigation Pane** to temporarily expand it.

➤ **To display or close the To-Do Bar**

→ On the **View** menu, point to **To-Do Bar**, and then click **Normal** to display the pane or **Off** to hide it.

→ In the upper-right corner of the **To-Do Bar**, click the **Close** button.

➤ **To minimize or expand the To-Do Bar**

→ On the **View** menu, point to **Navigation Pane**, and then click **Minimize**.

→ At the top of the To-Do Bar, click the **Minimize the To-Do Bar** button or the **Expand the To-Do Bar** button.

➤ **To display or close the Reading Pane**

→ On the **View** menu, click **Reading Pane**, and then click **Bottom**, **Right**, or **Off**.

Module-Specific Behavior

Mail

Each time you start Outlook and connect to your e-mail server, any new messages received since the last time you connected appear in your Inbox. Depending on your settings, Outlook downloads either the entire message to your computer or only the message header. The headers, which are listed in the Content pane to the right of the Navigation Pane, provide basic information about the message, such as:

- The item type (such as message, meeting request, or task assignment)
- Who sent it
- When you received it
- The subject
- If you forwarded or replied to it
- If it contains attachments
- If it has been digitally signed or encrypted
- If it has been marked as being of high or low importance

Messages you haven't yet read are indicated by closed envelope icons and bold headers. You can view the text of a message in the following ways:

- You can open a message in its own window by double-clicking its header in the message list.
- You can read a message without opening it by clicking its header in the message list to display the message in the Reading Pane.

Calendar

When you display the Calendar module, the Navigation Pane changes to include the Date Navigator, areas for the various calendars you can display, and links to various calendar-related tasks. By default, the Date Navigator displays a six-week date range. The days of the selected month are black; days of the previous and next months are gray, but you can still select them in the Date Navigator. Dates with scheduled appointments are bold.

▶ **To change the date range displayed in the Date Navigator**

→ Click the left arrow to display the previous month or the right arrow to display the next month.

→ Click the month heading, and then in the drop-down list, click the month you want to display.

➤ **To select dates for display in the Content pane**

→ In the **Date Navigator**, click the specific date.

→ In the **Date Navigator**, click in the margin to the left of a week to display that week in Week view.

Contacts, Tasks, and Notes

When you display these modules, the Navigation Pane changes to include areas for the various contact, task, or note lists you can display, view options, and links to various tasks you might want to perform. To the right of the Content pane in the Contacts Module, you can click alphabetic buttons to quickly jump to contact names starting with a particular letter.

Switching Views

In addition to switching views by clicking options in the Navigation Pane, you can use commands on the View menu. If none of the standard views meets your needs, you can click Current View and then click Customize Current View or Define Views to create your own view of your Outlook information.

Creating Outlook Items

You can create a new message, appointment, contact record, task, or note from within the appropriate module by clicking the New button on the Standard toolbar. You can also create any type of item from any module.

You can create a new folder to contain mail messages, calendar information, contact records, and other items. You must specify the folder type when you create it.

➤ **To create an item from any module**

→ On the toolbar, click the **New** arrow, and then in the list, click the type of item you want to create.

➤ **To create a folder**

1. On the toolbar, click the **New** arrow, and then in the list, click **Folder**.

2. In the **Create New Folder** dialog box, enter a name for the folder in the **Name** box, and then in the **Folder contains** list, click **Calendar Items**, **Contact Items**, **InfoPath Form Items**, **Journal Items**, **Mail and Post Items**, **Note Items**, or **Task Items**.

3. In the **Select where to place the folder** list, click the location you want to create the folder. Then click **OK**.

Addressing Messages

Addressing an e-mail message is as simple as typing the intended recipient's e-mail address into the To box. If you want to send a message to more than one person, separate the addresses with semicolons.

As you type in the To, Cc, or Bcc box, Outlook might display matching addresses in a list below the box. Select a name or e-mail address from the list, and then press Tab or Enter to insert the entire name or address in the box.

If your e-mail account is part of a Microsoft Exchange Server network, you can send messages to another person on the same network by typing only his or her e-mail alias (for example, *joan*)—the at symbol (@) and domain name aren't required.

If a message recipient's address is in your address book, you can type the person's name and Outlook will look for the corresponding e-mail address. (You can either wait for Outlook to validate the name or press Ctrl+K to immediately validate the names and addresses you type.) By default, Outlook searches your Global Address List and main address book, but you can instruct the program to search other address books as well. If no address book contains an entry for the name you typed, when you send the message, Outlook prompts you to select an address book entry or provide a full e-mail address.

➤ **To have Outlook search additional address books**

1. On the **Tools** menu, click **Address Book**.

2. In the **Address Book** window, on the **Tools** menu, click **Options**.

3. In the **Addressing** dialog box, click **Add**.

4. In the **Add Address List** dialog box, click the address list you want to add, click **Add**, and then click **Close**.

5. In the **Addressing** dialog box, click **OK**, and then close the **Address Book** window.

Editing and Formatting Messages

The certification exam is likely to focus on using Outlook 2007 to manage and organize information. Nevertheless, you should be familiar with the 2007 Office techniques for editing and formatting text, applying themes and page backgrounds, and inserting lists, tables, charts, and graphics. All of these functions work in the same way as they do in Word 2007, which is the default Outlook 2007 mail editor.

1 Managing Messages

The skills tested in this section of the Microsoft Office Specialist exam for Microsoft Office Outlook 2007 relate to creating, sending, and receiving full-featured e-mail messages. Specifically, the following objectives are associated with this set of skills:

1.1 Create and send an e-mail message.

1.2 Create and manage your signature and automated messages.

1.3 Manage e-mail message attachments.

1.4 Configure e-mail message sensitivity and importance settings.

1.5 Configure e-mail message security settings.

1.6 Configure e-mail message delivery options.

1.7 View e-mail messages.

Although Outlook is a full-featured information-management program, most people use the program primarily for e-mail. Outlook provides a broad range of e-mail messaging functionality that you can use to efficiently manage incoming and outgoing messages.

This chapter guides you in studying basic and advanced e-mail practices, including sending, viewing, and responding to messages; setting message options such as priority, sensitivity, and delivery time; sending, previewing, and opening attachments; setting up electronic signatures for manual or automatic insertion; setting up auto-reply messages by using the Microsoft Exchange Server 2007–specific functionality of Outlook 2007; restricting permission to, encrypting, and digitally signing messages; and adding messages to your task list for follow-up.

Important Before you can use the practice files in this chapter, you need to install them from the book's companion CD to their default location. See "Using the Companion CD" at the beginning of this book for more information.

Tip Graphics and operating system–related instructions in this book reflect the Windows Vista user interface. If your computer is running Windows XP and you experience trouble following the instructions as written, refer to the sidebar "If You Are Running Windows XP" in "Working in the Microsoft Office Fluent User Interface" at the beginning of this book.

1.1   Create and send an e-mail message

Sending

Regardless of the type of e-mail account you have, as long as you have an Internet connection you can send e-mail messages to people within your organization and around the world.

Strategy We assume you know how to create and send an e-mail message. This section primarily reviews techniques for efficiently addressing messages.

You can send a message to one person or to multiple people by entering e-mail addresses in the To box of the message window. By default, Outlook requires that you separate multiple e-mail addresses with semicolons.

You can send courtesy copies of a message by entering e-mail addresses in the Cc box of the message window. All recipients can see the addresses of To and Cc recipients. To send "blind" courtesy copies without making their recipients' addresses known to the To and Cc recipients, you can display the Bcc box and enter the addresses there. (Outlook does not display this box by default.)

If you frequently send messages to the same people, you can create distribution lists and then enter the name of the list instead of the individual addresses in the To, Cc, or Bcc box. Each list member receives a copy of the message. If you want to send a message to most, but not all, members of a distribution list, you can remove people from the list for a specific message before you send it.

Tip When sending a message to a distribution list, enter the distribution list name in the To or Cc box if you want recipients to be able to respond to all members of the distribution list, or in the Bcc box if you want recipients to respond only to you.

See Also For information about creating distribution lists, see section 4.3, "Create and modify distribution lists."

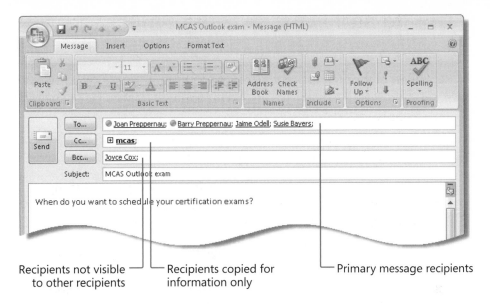

Recipients not visible to other recipients — Recipients copied for information only — Primary message recipients

If you want to send a new version of a message you've already sent, you can resend the message. Outlook creates a new message identical to the original. You can change the recipient addresses, subject, attachments, or content before you send the message.

➤ To display the Bcc box

→ In the message window, on the **Options** tab, in the **Fields** group, click the **Show Bcc** button.

➤ To send a message to a subset of a distribution list

1. In the message window, enter the name of the distribution list in the **To**, **Cc**, or **Bcc** box.

2. Click the **Expand** button (the plus sign) to the left of the distribution list name, or right-click the name and then click **Expand DL**. If the **Expand List** message box opens, click **OK** to acknowledge that you will not be able to collapse the list again.

3. Add or remove addresses as necessary.

➤ To resend a message

1. In the **Inbox** or the **Sent Items** folder, open the message you want to resend.

2. On the **Message** tab, in the **Actions** group, click **Resend This Message** in the **Other Actions** list.

Replying and Forwarding

You can reply to or forward most e-mail messages that you receive, as follows:

- **Reply.** Outlook fills in the To box, addressing the response to the original message sender only. You can add, change, and delete recipients from the reply before sending it.

- **Reply To All.** Outlook fills in the To box with the addresses of the original message sender and any recipients in the To box of the original message. Outlook also fills in the Cc box with the addresses of any recipients in the Cc box of the original message.

  Tip You can not include recipients of blind courtesy copies in message replies.

- **Forward.** Outlook does not fill in the To or Cc boxes for you. After you enter the recipients' addresses, a copy of the original message is sent, including any attached files and sensitivity and importance settings.

  See Also For information about message attachments, see section 1.3, "Manage e-mail message attachments." For information about sensitivity and importance, see section 1.4, "Configure e-mail message sensitivity and importance settings."

You might also need to respond to specific types of messages, such polling messages, meeting requests, and task delegations. These types of messages are covered in their respective sections of this exam.

➤ **To reply only to the sender of a message**

→ On the **Standard** toolbar, click the **Reply** button.

→ In the message window, on the **Message** tab, in the **Respond** group, click the **Reply** button.

➤ **To reply to all recipients of a message**

→ On the **Standard** toolbar, click the **Reply to All** button.

→ In the message window, on the **Message** tab, in the **Respond** group, click the **Reply to All** button.

➤ **To forward a message**

→ On the **Standard** toolbar, click the **Forward** button.

→ In the message window, on the **Message** tab, in the **Respond** group, click the **Forward** button.

  See Also For information about restricting recipients from forwarding messages, see section 1.5, "Configure e-mail message security settings."

Recalling

If you inadvertently send a message that you don't want the recipient to receive, you can try to recall the message by instructing Outlook to delete or replace any unread copies of the message. Message recall is available only for Exchange Server accounts. Just remember that with the speed of networks today, it is very possible for a recipient to have read your e-mail message, no matter how quickly you try to recall it.

➤ To recall a message

1. In the **Sent Items** folder, open the message you want to recall.

2. On the **Message** tab, in the **Actions** group, click **Recall This Message** in the **Other Actions** list.

3. In the **Recall This Message** dialog box, select the option to delete or replace unread copies of the message, and then click **OK**.

Practice Tasks

You need to be online and have a working e-mail account to complete these tasks. There are no practice files for these tasks.

- Open a new message window, address a message with the subject *MCAS Schedule* to yourself, and then send it.

- Without opening the *MCAS Schedule* message, send a reply to yourself. Then open the message, send another response, and close the message window.

- Open any message with an attachment in your Inbox, change the subject to *MCAS Forward*, and forward it to yourself.

- Resend the *MCAS Forward* message to yourself as *MCAS Resend*.

1.2   Create and manage your signature and automated messages

Signatures

You can save specific text and/or images as an e-mail signature (so named because it usually includes your name and goes at the end of the message, although you can insert it anywhere) that you can manually or automatically insert into outgoing e-mail messages. You can format the text of your signature in the same ways that you can format message text. You can also use your electronic business card as all or part of your e-mail signature.

See Also For information about electronic business cards, see section 4.2, "Edit and use an electronic business card."

You can create multiple signatures and then select the one you want for a particular message before sending it. You can have Outlook automatically add a signature to all outgoing messages, or attach one signature to all new messages and a different signature to all replies and forwarded messages.

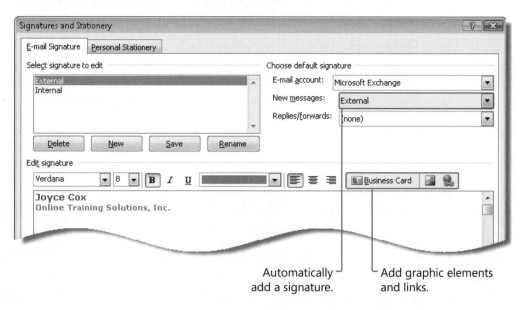

Automatically add a signature.

Add graphic elements and links.

➤ **To create a signature**

1. On the **Tools** menu, click **Options**. Then on the **Mail Format** tab of the **Options** dialog box, click **Signatures**.

2. On the **E-mail Signature** tab of the **Signatures and Stationery** dialog box, click **New**.

3. In the **New Signature** dialog box, type a name for the signature, and then click **OK**.

4. In the **Edit signature** area, enter and format the text of the signature, and if you want, insert your business card, images, or hyperlinks.

5. Click **OK** twice.

➤ **To set up an automatic signature**

1. Display the **E-mail Signature** tab of the **Signatures and Stationery** dialog box.

2. In the **Choose default signature** area, in the **New messages** list, click the name of the signature you want to automatically attach to new messages.

3. In the **Replies/forwards** list, click the name of the signature you want to automatically attach to replies and forwarded messages.

4. Click **OK** twice.

➤ **To manually insert a signature**

1. On the **Message** tab, in the **Include** group, click the **Signature** button.

2. Click the signature you want in the list.

Automated Messages

If your organization is running Exchange Server, you can turn on the Out Of Office Assistant to automatically send a reply in response to messages received when you are unavailable to respond yourself. (You don't have to be physically out of the office.) This feature works differently depending on which version of Exchange Server your organization is using:

- **Microsoft Exchange Server 2003.** You can create one auto-reply message, and you cannot format the text of the message. From the time you turn on the Out Of Office Assistant until the time you turn it off, Outlook sends the message in response to the first message received from each person.

- **Microsoft Exchange Server 2007.** You can create two auto-reply messages: one sent only to people in your organization (on the same domain); and another sent either to everyone else, or to only the people in your primary address book. You can apply limited character and paragraph formatting to the messages. You can specify start and end dates and times for the automated messages so that you don't have to remember to turn the Out Of Office Assistant on and off.

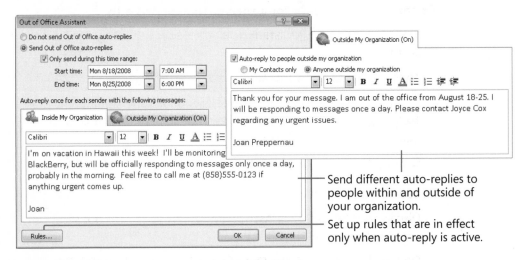

Send different auto-replies to people within and outside of your organization.

Set up rules that are in effect only when auto-reply is active.

Strategy This section covers functionality that is specific to an Exchange Server 2007 environment. In the exam environment, Outlook 2007 runs against a simulated Exchange Server 2007 back end. If you have access only to Exchange Server 2003 or a non-Exchange Server account, study this section carefully.

In addition to sending auto-replies, you can have Outlook process messages that arrive while you are unavailable by using rules that are in effect only when the Out Of Office Assistant is active.

See Also For information about using rules to process incoming messages, see section 5.5, "Create, modify, and remove rules to manage e-mail messages."

➤ **To set up auto-replies**

1. On the **Tools** menu, click **Out Of Office Assistant**.
2. In the **Out of Office Assistant** dialog box, click **Send Out of Office auto-replies**.
3. On the **Inside My Organization** tab, enter and format the text of the message you want your colleagues to receive.
4. Click the **Outside My Organization** tab, and then click **My Contacts Only** or **Anyone outside my organization**.
5. Enter and format the text of the message you want external people to receive.
6. Click **OK**.

➤ **To create an auto-reply for a specific time period only**

1. In the **Out of Office Assistant** dialog box, select the **Only send during this time range** check box.
2. To the right of **Start time**, set the date and time you want Outlook to begin automatically replying to messages.
3. To the right of **End time**, set the date and time you want Outlook to stop automatically replying to messages.
4. Create your internal and external out of office messages, and then click **OK**.

➤ **To turn off auto-replies**

→ Display the **Out of Office Assistant** dialog box, click **Do not send Out of Office auto-replies**, and then click **OK**.

→ On the status bar, click the **Out of Office** icon, and then click **Turn off Out of Office auto-replies**.

Practice Tasks

You need to be online and have a working e-mail account to complete these tasks. (The automatic messaging tasks require an Exchange account.) There are no practice files for these tasks.

- Create an e-mail signature named *Internal* that includes your cell phone number, a personal picture, and a favorite slogan.

- Create a more formal e-mail signature named *External*, with three lines of information. Format the first line in bold, blue, 10-point Verdana, and format the remaining text in 8-point Verdana of a lighter shade of blue.

- Create a new message addressed to yourself with *MCAS Signature* as the subject. Insert the External signature at the bottom of the message, and then send it.

- Turn on automatic messages, enter the message *MCAS Testing one two three*. Then turn the messages off again.

- If your organization is running Exchange Server 2007, set an internal message of *MCAS Testing one two three* formatted in bold, purple, 12-point Verdana, and an external message of *MCAS Testing two four six* formatted in the same text font as your usual messages. Send the external message only to recipients in your Contacts list.

- Continuing with the previous exercise, set both messages to be sent from to-morrow at midnight through the coming Sunday at one minute before mid-night. Then turn the messages off again.

1.3   Manage e-mail message attachments

Attachments

A convenient way to distribute a file (such as a Microsoft Office Word document, a Microsoft Office Excel workbook, or a Microsoft Office PowerPoint presentation) to other people is to attach the file to an e-mail message.

You can also attach Outlook items to messages, including other messages, appointments, and contact information.

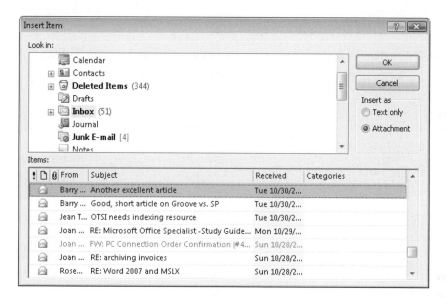

➤ **To attach a file to a message**

1. On the **Message** tab of the message window, in the **Include** group, click the **Attach File** button.

2. In the **Insert File** dialog box, locate and click the file you want to attach, and then click **Insert**.

   Tip You can also drag a file from the Windows Explorer window into the message area of a message window to attach it to the message.

➤ **To attach an Outlook item to a message**

1. On the **Message** tab of the message window, in the **Include** group, click the **Attach Item** button.

2. In the **Insert Item** dialog box, locate and click the item you want to attach.

3. With **Attachment** selected in the **Insert as** area, click **OK**.

Opening and Previewing

You can open an attached file in its source program directly from the message in Outlook. You can also preview some file formats (including Excel workbooks, PowerPoint slideshows, Word documents, and Portable Document Format (PDF) files) directly in the Reading Pane without opening the attached file. If you install add-ins provided by companies other than Microsoft (called *third-party add-ins*), you can preview other types of files as well.

You can open and preview an attached Outlook item just like any other attachment.

➤ **To open a file attached to a message**

1. In the header in the **Reading Pane**, double-click the attachment.
2. In the **Opening Mail Attachment** dialog box, click **Open**.

    Or

1. In the message list, right click the message, click **View Attachments**, and then click the attachment you want.
2. In the **Opening Mail Attachment** dialog box, click **Open**.

➤ **To open an Outlook item attached to a message**

→ In the header in the **Reading Pane**, double-click the attachment.

→ In the message list, right click the message, click **View Attachments**, and then click the attachment you want.

➤ **To preview a file attached to a message**

1. In the header in the **Reading Pane**, click the attachment.
2. In the **Reading Pane**, click **Preview file**.

➤ **To preview an Outlook item attached to a message**

→ In the header in the **Reading Pane**, click the attachment.

See Also For information about the Reading Pane, see section 1.7, "View e-mail messages."

Saving

You can save an attached file to your hard disk. This strategy is recommended if you suspect an attachment might contain a virus, because you can scan the attachment for viruses before opening it (provided that you have a virus scanning program installed).

You can save an attached Outlook item by dragging it into a folder in your mailbox so that it is available from Outlook.

➤ **To save a file attached to a message**

1. In the header in the **Reading Pane**, right-click the attachment, and click **Save As**.

2. In the **Save Attachment** dialog box, specify the storage location and file name, and then click **Save**.

➤ **To save an Outlook item attached to a message**

1. In the **Navigation Pane**, expand the display of folders in your Mailbox so that you can see the one in which you want to store the item.

2. In the header in the **Reading Pane**, click the attachment, and then drag it to the desired folder.

Practice Tasks

You need to be online and have a working e-mail account to complete these tasks. The practice file for these tasks is located in the *Documents\Microsoft Press\MCAS\ Outlook2007\Objective01* folder.

- Open a new message window, address a message with the subject *MCAS File* to yourself, attach the *Design* presentation, and then send the message.

- Send another message to yourself with the subject *MCAS Item* and with the *MCAS Schedule* message (or any other message) attached to it.

- When the *MCAS File* message arrives, preview the attachment in the Reading Pane. Then open the attachment in PowerPoint.

- When the *MCAS Item* message arrives, store its attached message in your Inbox.

1.4   Configure e-mail message sensitivity and importance settings

Sensitivity

When sending a message, you can indicate that a message should be kept private by setting its sensitivity to Confidential, Personal, or Private.

Sensitivity options

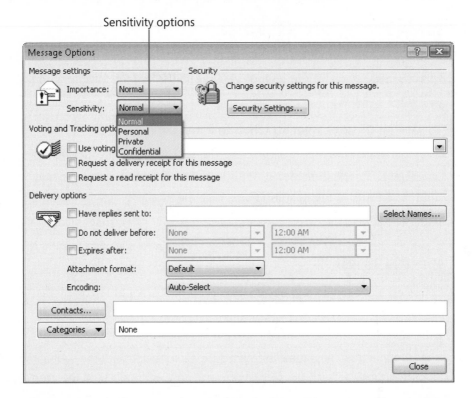

When you receive a message with a sensitivity setting, no indicator appears in the message list. However, in the message window and the Reading Pane, a banner appears in the message header to indicate a sensitivity other than Normal.

➤ **To set the sensitivity of a message**

1. On the **Message** tab of the message window, click the **Options** dialog box launcher.

2. In the **Message Options** dialog box, click the option you want in the **Sensitivity** list, and then click **Close**.

Importance

You can indicate the priority of a message you are sending by indicating that it has High Importance or Low Importance.

When you receive a message with a priority setting, a banner appears in the message header in the message window and the Reading Pane to indicate a priority other than Normal. If the Importance field is included in the view, an importance icon appears in the message list.

➤ **To designate a message as high priority**

→ On the **Message** tab of the message window, in the **Options** group, click the **High Importance** button.

➤ **To designate a message as low priority**

→ On the **Message** tab of the message window, in the **Options** group, click the **Low Importance** button.

➤ **To remove the priority setting from a message before forwarding**

→ With the message window open, on the **Message** tab, in the **Options** group, click the **High Importance** or **Low Importance** button to turn it off.

➤ **To sort messages based on priority**

→ In the **Arranged By** list at the top of the message list, click **Importance**.

Practice Tasks

You need to be online and have a working e-mail account to complete these tasks. There are no practice files for these tasks.

- Send a message to yourself with the subject *MCAS Sensitivity*, and flag it as personal.

- Send a message to yourself with the subject *MCAS Urgent* and with a high priority setting.

- When you receive the message, forward it to yourself with a normal priority setting.

- Send a message to yourself with the subject *MCAS Secret*, and flag it as both high priority and confidential.

1.5 Configure e-mail message security settings

Permissions

If you don't want a message recipient to forward, print, or copy a message, you can send it with restricted permissions. You use Information Rights Management (IRM) to set these permissions. If the restricted message includes an attachment, such as a Word document, an Excel workbook, or a PowerPoint presentation, the recipient can't edit, copy, or print the attachment (unless you have set individual permissions within the document).

When permissions are restricted for a received message, an icon appears in the message list, and a banner explaining the restriction spans the header in the Reading Pane and the message window.

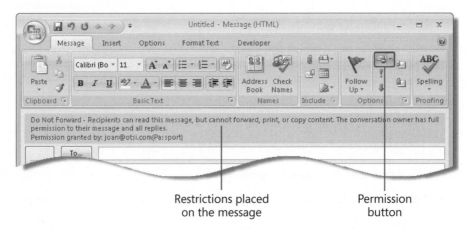

                    Restrictions placed   Permission
                      on the message   button

Strategy To use IRM, you need access to an IRM server. To practice working with permissions if you do not have access to an IRM server, you can sign up for the free Microsoft Information Rights Management service by using the wizard that appears the first time you try to place restrictions on a message.

➤ To prevent a message from being forwarded, printed, or copied

1. On the **Message** tab, in the **Options** group, click **Do Not Forward** in the **Permission** list.

    Or

    On the **Office** menu, point to **Permission**, and then click **Do Not Forward**.

2. In the **Select User** dialog box, click the user account used to restrict access, and then click **OK**.

Digital Signatures

When sending a message, you can reassure the recipients that the message came from you by using a digital signature that validates the identity of the e-mail account and computer from which the message originates.

When a received message is digitally signed, an icon appears in the message list, the Reading Pane, and the message window. When you receive a signed message, you can view the signature details.

You must have a digital certificate (also called a *digital ID*) installed on your computer and associated with your Outlook profile to digitally sign a message and for the digital signature options to be available in the Options group on the Message tab and in the Security Properties dialog box.

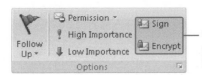 When a digital certificate is associated with your Outlook profile, these buttons appear in the Options group on the Message tab.

You can obtain a digital ID from a third-party provider or, if your Exchange Server setup supports it, from your Exchange administrator. The Set Up Security For Me On The Exchange option is available only on Exchange Server networks with this feature enabled.

Strategy You will not be tested on the process of obtaining a digital ID, but we provide you with instructions for obtaining and associating a digital ID so that you can practice digitally signing and encrypting messages.

➤ **To obtain a digital ID from your Exchange administrator**

1. Obtain a password, called a *token*, from your Exchange administrator.

2. On the **E-mail Security** page of the **Trust Center** dialog box, click **Get a Digital ID**.

3. Click **Set up Security for me on the Exchange**, and then click **OK**.

4. In the **Digital ID Name** box, type your name.

5. In the **Token** box, type the special password that your Exchange administrator assigned to you.

6. In the **Microsoft Office Outlook Security Password** dialog box, type a different password for the digital ID, and then type the password again in the **Confirm** box.

   Tip You will receive a message in your Inbox from your Exchange administrator that will require you to enter the password you created in this step.

7. In the dialog box that appears, enter your password, click the **Remember password for** check box, and then enter the number of minutes for which you want Outlook to remember your password.

8. In the **Root Certificate Store** message that appears, click **Yes**.

➤ **To obtain a digital ID from a third-party provider**

1. On the **Tools** menu, click **Trust Center**.

2. On the **E-mail Security** page of the **Trust Center** dialog box, click **Get a Digital ID**.

3. On the **Digital ID** page of **Microsoft Office Online**, click the link to the Web site of the third-party provider you want to obtain your digital ID from.

4. Follow the instructions on the provider's Web site to obtain the digital ID, and then follow the instructions in the e-mail message sent to you by the provider to install the digital ID on your computer.

➤ **To associate a third-party digital ID before first use**

1. On the **Tools** menu, click **Trust Center**.

2. On the **E-mail Security** page of the **Trust Center** dialog box, click **Settings**.

3. In the **Change Security Settings** dialog box, confirm that entries appear in the **Signing Certificate** and **Encryption Certificate** boxes. If not, click the **Choose** button to the right of each box, click the certificate you want to use, and then click **OK**.

4. Click **OK** in the **Change Security Settings** dialog box.

5. On the **E-mail Security** page of the **Trust Center** dialog box, confirm that the information in the Default Setting box is active, and then click **OK**.

➤ **To digitally sign an outgoing message**

→ On the **Message** tab, in the **Options** group, click the **Digitally Sign Message** button.

Tip The Digitally Sign Message button appears in the Options group only if a digital ID is installed on your computer and associated with your Outlook account.

Or

1. On the **Message** tab, click the **Options** dialog box launcher.

2. In the **Message Options** dialog box, click **Security Settings**.

3. In the **Security Properties** dialog box, select the **Add digital signature to this message** check box.

Tip The Add Digital Signature To This Message check box appears in the Security Properties dialog box regardless of whether a digital ID is installed on your computer and associated with your Outlook account. When you sign a message by using this method, a message box appears when you send the message if the digital ID is not set up as required.

4. If you want to sign the message by using a certificate other than the default, click **Change Settings** in the **Security Settings** area. In the **Change Security Settings** dialog box, click the **Choose** button to the right of **Signing Certificate**. Then in the **Select Certificate** dialog box, click the certificate you want to use, and click **OK**.

5. Click **OK** in the **Security Properties** dialog box, and then click **OK** in the **Message Options** dialog box.

➤ **To digitally sign all outgoing messages**

1. On the **Tools** menu, click **Trust Center**.

2. On the **E-mail Security** page of the **Trust Center** dialog box, select the **Add digital signature to outgoing messages** check box.

3. Click **OK** in the **Trust Center** dialog box.

➤ **To view details of a digital signature attached to a message**

1. In the **Reading Pane** or message window, click the digital signature icon.

2. In the **Digital Signature** dialog box, click **Details**.

3. View the information in the **Message Security Properties** dialog box, and then click **Close** twice.

Encryption

You can secure the contents of outgoing messages by using encryption. Encryption ensures that only the intended recipients can read the messages you send. The message recipient's e-mail program must have corresponding decryption capabilities in order to read the message. You must have a digital certificate installed on your computer to encrypt a message and for the encryption options to be available in the Options group on the Message tab and in the Security Properties dialog box.

Tip For information about obtaining and installing a digital ID for the purpose of encrypting a message, see the "Digital Signatures" topic earlier in this section.

An encrypted message has a blue lock on its icon in the message list and an encryption icon (also a blue lock) in the header in the Reading Pane and the message window. When you receive an encrypted message, you can view the layers of security applied to the message.

Tip If you try to send an encrypted message from Outlook to a recipient whose setup doesn't support encryption, Outlook notifies you and gives you the option of sending the message in an unencrypted format.

➤ **To encrypt an outgoing message**

→ On the **Message** tab, in the **Options** group, click the **Encrypt** button.

   Tip The Encrypt button appears in the Options group only if a digital ID is installed on your computer and associated with your Outlook account.

   Or

1. On the **Message** tab, click the **Options** dialog box launcher.

2. In the **Message Options** dialog box, and click **Security Settings**.

3. In the **Security Properties** dialog box, select the **Encrypt message contents and attachments** check box.

4. If you want to sign the message by using a certificate other than the default, click **Change Settings** in the **Security Settings** area. In the **Change Security Settings** dialog box, click the **Choose** button to the right of **Signing Certificate**. Then in the **Select Certificate** dialog box, click the certificate you want to use, and click **OK**.

5. Click **OK** in the **Security Properties** dialog box, and then click **OK** in the **Message Options** dialog box.

Tip The Encrypt Message Contents And Attachments check box appears in the Security Properties dialog box regardless of whether a digital ID is installed on your computer and associated with your Outlook account. When you encrypt a message by using this method, a message box appears when you send the message if the digital ID is not set up as required.

➤ To encrypt all outgoing messages

1. On the **Tools** menu, click **Trust Center**.

2. On the **E-mail Security** page of the **Trust Center** dialog box, in the **Encrypted e-mail** area, select the **Encrypt contents and attachments for outgoing messages** check box.

3. Click the **Settings** button.

4. In the **Change Security Settings** dialog box, click the **Choose** button to the right of **Encryption Certificate**.

5. In the **Select Certificate** dialog box, click the certificate you want to use, and then click **OK**.

6. Click **OK** in the **Change Security Settings** dialog box, and then click **OK** in the **Trust Center** dialog box.

Practice Tasks

You need to be online and have a working e-mail account to complete these tasks. There are no practice files for these tasks.

- Sign up for the Microsoft IRM service if necessary, and then send a message with restricted permissions.

- Obtain a digital ID, if you don't already have one, and associate it with your Outlook profile.

- Send a digitally signed message.

- Send an encrypted message.

1.6   Configure e-mail message delivery options

Flags

Frequently, you need to take some type of action by a particular date based on the information you receive from another person in an e-mail message. By flagging an e-mail message, you can quickly add a task with a deadline to your task list. Similarly, you can flag a message you are sending to create a task in your task list. For both received and sent messages, you can attach a reminder to the flag.

You can also flag a message you are sending for follow up by the recipient.

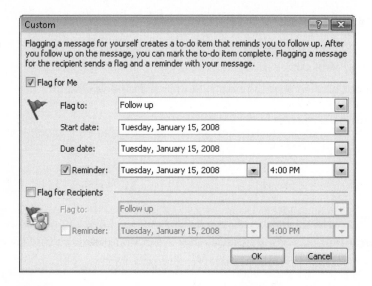

See Also   For information about the task list, which you can view from the To-Do Bar or the Tasks module, see section 3, "Managing Tasks."

When you have completed a task associated with a message, you can mark it as complete. Doing so removes the message from the task list and changes the flag to a check mark. Deleting the message deletes the task from the task list, as does clearing the flag.

➤ **To flag a received message for follow up**

→ In the message list, click the flag icon to the right of the message header to insert a default flag for follow up today.

→ Click the message in the message list, and then on the **Standard** toolbar, click the **Follow Up** button, and then click the deadline you want.

→ Right-click the message in the message list, point to **Follow Up**, and then click the deadline you want.

Tip You can click Custom in the deadline list and then set specific start and due dates in the Custom dialog box.

➤ **To attach a different type of flag**

1. Display the flag list, and click **Custom**.

2. In the **Flag for Me** area of the **Custom** dialog box, select the type of flag you want to attach to the message in the **Flag to** list, and then click **OK**.

➤ **To set a deadline reminder**

1. Display the flag list, and click **Custom**.

2. In the **Flag for Me** area of the **Custom** dialog box, select the **Reminder** check box, adjust the reminder date and time as necessary, and then click **OK**.

➤ **To flag an outgoing message for your follow up**

→ On the **Message** tab of the message window, in the **Options** group, click the **Follow Up** button, and then click the deadline you want.

➤ **To flag an outgoing message for the recipient's follow up**

1. Display the flag list, and click **Custom**.

2. In the **Custom** dialog box, select the **Flag for Recipients** check box, and then select the type of flag you want.

3. If you want, select the **Reminder** check box, and adjust the reminder date and time as necessary.

4. Click **OK**.

➤ **To remove an existing flag**

→ Display the flag list, and click **Clear Flag**.

➤ **To mark a task as complete**

→ Display the flag list, and click **Mark Complete**.

Scheduled Deliveries and Expirations

You can schedule the delivery of a message by setting the date and time before which a message should not be delivered. You can indicate that a message is no longer relevant by setting an expiry date and time. Expired messages have a banner in the header in the Reading Pane and message window announcing when the message expired.

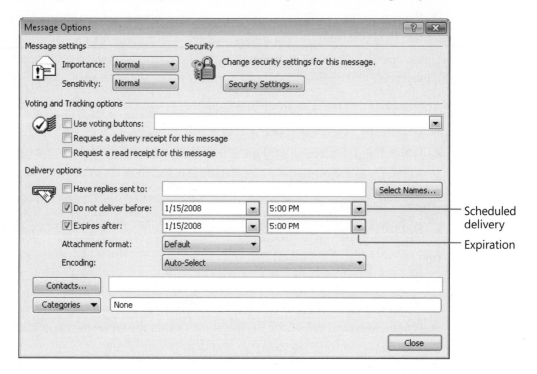

> ➤ **To schedule the delivery of a message**

1. Display the **Message Options** dialog box, and in the **Delivery options** area, select the **Do not deliver before** check box.

2. Set the date and time, and then click **Close**.

➤ To set an expiration for a message

1. Display the **Message Options** dialog box, and in the **Delivery options** area, select the **Expires after** check box.

2. Set the date and time, and then click **Close**.

Receipts

You can track messages by requesting delivery receipts and read receipts. These receipts are messages automatically generated by the recipient's e-mail server when it delivers the message to the recipient and when the recipient reads the message.

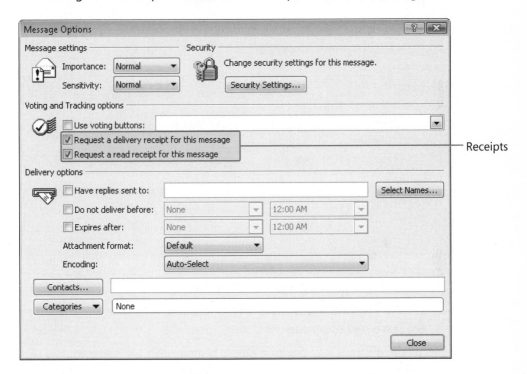

➤ To request a delivery or read receipt

1. Display the **Message Options** dialog box, and in the **Voting and Tracking options** area, select the **Request a delivery receipt for this message** or **Request a read receipt for this message** check box.

2. Click **Close**.

Reply Rerouting

You can specify that replies to a message should be sent to an e-mail address other than the one from which you are sending the message. Clicking Reply or Reply to All then displays a message window with the specified e-mail address entered in the To box.

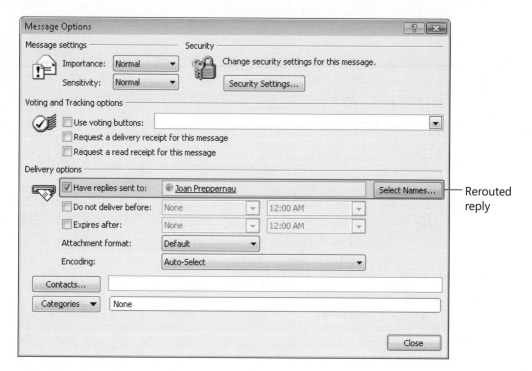
Rerouted reply

➤ To specify a different reply e-mail address

1. Display the **Message Options** dialog box, and in the **Delivery options** area, select the **Have replies sent to** check box.

2. Type the e-mail address, or multiple e-mail addresses separated by semicolons, in the adjacent box.

   Or

   Click **Select Names**, and then click the address(es) you want.

3. Click **Close**.

E-Mail Polls

If you and your message recipients have Exchange Server accounts, you can conduct e-mail polls by adding voting buttons to a message to enable recipients to quickly select from multiple-choice response options. If you receive an e-mail poll, you can send a blank response containing your vote in the message header, or you can edit the response to include additional text.

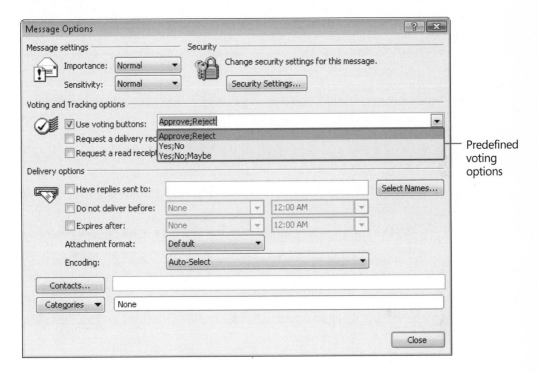

Predefined voting options

> **To create an e-mail poll**

1. Display the **Message Options** dialog box, and in the **Voting and Tracking options** area, select the **Use voting buttons** check box.

2. In the adjacent box, click the voting buttons you want in the list.

   Or

   Type the button labels you want, separated by semicolons.

3. Click **Close**.

➤ **To respond to an e-mail poll**

1. In the **Reading Pane**, click the **Click here to vote** banner, and then click the option you want.

2. In the message box, click **OK** to send your vote without a message.

   Or

   Click **Edit the response before sending**, and click **OK**. Then in the message window, type a message, and send it.

Practice Tasks

You need to be online and have a working e-mail account to complete these tasks. There are no practice files for these tasks.

● Send a message to yourself with the subject *MCAS Flag* and a flag that creates a task with a deadline of tomorrow.

● When the *MCAS Flag* message arrives, set a reminder for its follow-up deadline.

● Send a message to yourself with the subject *MCAS Delivery* that is scheduled to be delivered after noon tomorrow and to expire at midnight tomorrow.

● Send a message to yourself with the subject *MCAS Receipt* and a request for a read receipt. When the message arrives, open it, and then close it.

● Send a message to yourself with the subject *MCAS Vote* that has Yes, No, and Maybe voting buttons.

● When you receive the *MCAS Vote* message, vote Maybe, and then send the response with no message.

1.7 View e-mail messages

Strategy To be able to move quickly around the Mail component of Outlook, you should be familiar with its panes and folders, and with the different ways of viewing messages.

Reading Pane

You can double-click any message header in the message list to open the message in its own window, but it is often more efficient to display the Reading Pane at the right side or bottom of the screen so that you can read messages without actually opening them. You can scroll through messages in the Reading Pane, or if Single Key Reading Using Space Bar is turned on, you can page through them by pressing the Spacebar. When you reach the end of a message, the first page of the next message is displayed.

➤ **To display the Reading Pane**

→ On the **View** menu, point to **Reading Pane**, and then click **Right** or **Bottom**.

➤ **To hide the Reading Pane**

→ On the **View** menu, point to **Reading Pane**, and then click **Off**.

➤ **To be able to page through messages by pressing the Spacebar**

1. On the **Tools** menu, click **Options**.
2. On the **Other** tab of the **Options** dialog box, in the **Outlook Panes** area, click **Reading Pane**.
3. In the **Reading Pane** dialog box, select the **Single key reading using space bar** check box, and then click **OK** twice.

Message Preview

If you don't want to allocate space on your screen to the Reading Pane, you can display the first three lines of each message under the header in the message list by using the AutoPreview feature. Scanning the first three lines of a message frequently gives you enough information to make basic decisions about how to manage it. The only drawback is that fewer messages are visible on your screen at one time.

➤ **To display a preview of message text in the mail pane**

→ On the **View** menu, click **AutoPreview**.

Header Fields

If you turn off the Reading Pane, you have more space to display information about each message in the columns, or *fields*, in its header. You can customize the header by adding and removing fields. You can then sort the message on any field by clicking its field name at the top of the message list.

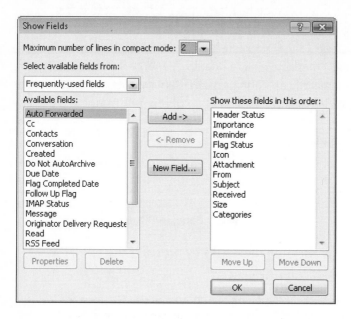

> ## To specify the fields that appear in the header

1. On the **View** menu, point to **Current View**, and then click **Customize Current View**.

2. In the **Customize View: Messages** dialog box, click **Fields**.

3. In the **Select available fields from** list in the **Show Fields** dialog box, click the field category you want.

4. In the **Available fields** list, click any field you want to show in the header, and then click **Add**.

5. In the **Show these fields in this order** list, click any field you don't want to show in the header, and then click **Remove**.

6. To adjust the order of a field, click it in the **Show these fields in this order** list, and then click **Move Up** or **Move Down**.

7. Click **OK** twice.

   Tip To restore the original Messages view, click Reset Current View at the bottom of the Customize Views: Messages dialog box.

Practice Tasks

You need to have a working e-mail account to complete these tasks. There are no practice files for these tasks.

● If the Reading Pane is not open, open it on the right side of the Outlook window. Then move it to the bottom of the window.

● If you cannot use the Spacebar to scroll messages in the Reading Pane, change your setup so that you can scroll with the Spacebar now.

● Close the Reading Pane. Then without changing the message list view, display the first three lines of the messages in your Inbox.

● Add the Cc field to the message header. Then move the Cc field so that it appears after the From field.

Objective Review

Before finishing this chapter, ensure that you have mastered the following skills:

1.1 Create and send an e-mail message.

1.2 Create and manage your signature and automated messages.

1.3 Manage e-mail message attachments.

1.4 Configure e-mail message sensitivity and importance settings.

1.5 Configure e-mail message security settings.

1.6 Configure e-mail message delivery options.

1.7 View e-mail messages.

2 Managing Scheduling

The skills tested in this section of the Microsoft Office Specialist exam for Microsoft Office Outlook 2007 relate to creating and managing appointments, meetings, and events, and managing aspects of the Outlook Calendar. Specifically, the following objectives are associated with this set of skills:

2.1 Create appointments, meetings, and events.

2.2 Send meeting requests.

2.3 Update, cancel, and respond to meeting requests.

2.4 Customize calendar settings.

2.5 Share your calendar with other people.

2.6 View other calendars.

Outlook 2007 provides full calendar and scheduling functionality to help you manage a schedule of business and personal appointments, meetings, and events.

This chapter guides you in studying ways of creating and customizing Outlook Calendar items, inviting people to meetings by using the Microsoft Exchange Server 2007–specific functionality of Outlook 2007, customizing your Calendar settings to fit the way you work, and displaying different views of multiple calendars.

Important Before you can use the practice files in this chapter, you need to install them from the book's companion CD to their default location. See "Using the Companion CD" at the beginning of this book for more information.

Tip Graphics and operating system–related instructions in this book reflect the Windows Vista user interface. If your computer is running Windows XP and you experience trouble following the instructions as written, refer to the sidebar "If You Are Running Windows XP" in "Working in the Microsoft Office Fluent User Interface" at the beginning of this book.

2.1   Create appointments, meetings, and events

Appointments

Appointments are blocks of time you enter on only your calendar. You can enter an appointment directly in the Calendar pane, in which case the time is shown on your calendar as Busy and the appointment reminder is set to 15 minutes. If you want to change those default settings, or if you want to schedule an appointment for something other than the default half-hour increments shown in the Calendar pane, you can enter the appointment in an appointment window.

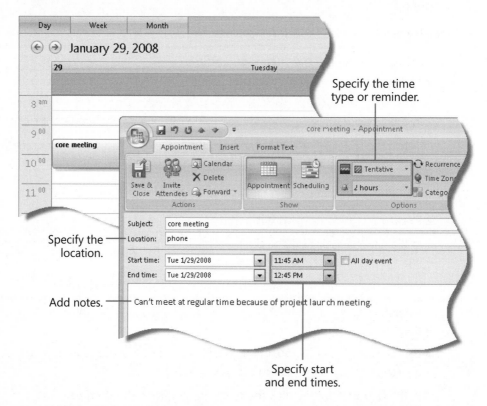

Time scheduled for an appointment can be shown as Free, Tentative, Busy, or Out Of Office. You can change the reminder time or turn it off completely. You can also include information such as driving directions or Web site links in the content pane, and attach related files so that they are easily available to you at the time of the appointment.

Tip If you synchronize your Outlook installation with a mobile device such as a BlackBerry or a mobile phone running Microsoft Windows Mobile, you can also receive reminders on your device.

You can also create an appointment based on an e-mail message or task simply by dragging it to the Calendar button in the Navigation Pane. When you release the mouse button, an appointment window opens with the message or task subject as the appointment subject and the message or task details in the appointment window's content pane. The start and end times are set to the next half-hour increment following the current time. You can then make any necessary adjustments before saving the appointment.

See Also You can convert an appointment to a meeting by opening its window and clicking the Scheduling button in the Show group on the Appointment tab. For more information, see section 2.2, "Send meeting requests."

➤ To create an appointment with default settings

1. In the Calendar, display the date on which you want to schedule the appointment.
2. In the **Calendar** pane, click the desired time slot, or drag through consecutive time slots.
3. Type the appointment subject, and then press **Enter**.

➤ To create an appointment with custom settings

1. In the Calendar, display the date on which you want to schedule the appointment, and then click the **New Appointment** button.
2. In the appointment window, type the appointment subject and location.
3. Click the desired start time in the right **Start time** list and the desired end time in the right **End time** list.
4. On the **Appointment** tab, in the **Options** group, click the type of time you want displayed in your calendar in the **Show As** list.
5. In the **Options** group, click the reminder period in the **Reminder** list.

    Tip You can also specify the sound to play for reminders by clicking Sound at the bottom of the list.

6. Add notes about the appointment in the content pane.
7. On the **Appointment** tab, in the **Actions** group, click the **Save & Close** button.

    Tip To attach a file to the appointment, click Attach File in the Include group on the Insert tab, and locate and double-click the file.

➤ **To change the appointment time**

→ Drag the appointment to a new time slot.

→ Drag the bottom border of the time slot up or down to change the end time.

→ Double-click the appointment to open its appointment window, adjust the **Start time** and **End time** settings, and then on the **Appointment** tab, in the **Actions** group, click the **Save & Close** button.

➤ **To create an appointment from an e-mail message or task**

1. In the message list or task list, drag the message to the **Calendar** button at the bottom of the **Navigation Pane**.

2. When the appointment window opens, make any necessary adjustments.

3. On the **Appointment** tab, in the **Actions** group, click the **Save & Close** button.

Events

Events are day-long blocks of time that you schedule on your calendar. In all other respects, events are identical to appointments. You can enter an event directly in the Calendar pane, in which case the time is shown on your calendar as Free and the event reminder is set to 15 minutes. You can change those settings by opening the event window.

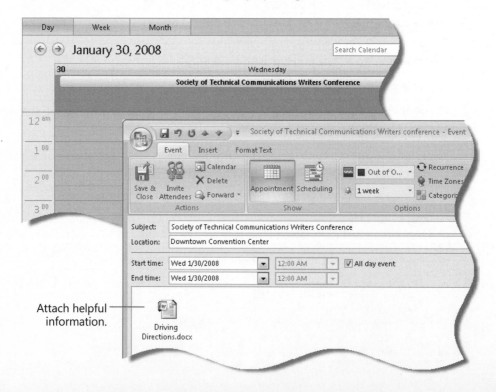

Attach helpful information.

You can create an event from an e-mail message or task by first creating an appointment and then converting it.

➤ **To create an event with default settings**

1. In the Calendar, display the date on which you want to schedule the event.

2. At the top of the **Calendar** pane, click the bottom of the blank space between the header and the first time slot.

   Tip *Click to add event* appears in the space when you point to the right spot.

3. Type the event subject, and then press **Enter**.

➤ **To create an event with custom settings**

1. In the Calendar, display the date on which you want to schedule the appointment.

2. Click the space between the header and the first time slot, and then click the **New Appointment** button.

   Tip You can also click New All Day Event on the Actions menu without first clicking the space above the time slots.

3. In the appointment window, with the **All day event** check box selected, fill in the other event details and adjust the **Show As** and **Reminder** settings in the usual way.

4. On the **Event** tab, in the **Actions** group, click the **Save & Close** button.

➤ **To convert an appointment into an event**

1. In the Calendar, double-click the appointment.

2. In the appointment window, select the **All Day Event** check box.

3. Save and close the event.

Recurring Appointments and Events

If an appointment or event happens more than once at specific intervals, such as every Tuesday or every month, you can set it up as a recurring appointment or event. Outlook then creates multiple instances of the appointment in your calendar at the time interval you specify.

Recurring appointments are linked, and if you need to make changes, you can choose to update a specific occurrence or all occurrences.

➤ **To create a recurring appointment or event**

1. Open the appointment window, and then on the **Appointment** or **Event** tab, in the **Options** group, click the **Recurrence** button.

2. In the **Recurrence pattern** area of the **Appointment Recurrence** dialog box, click a frequency option.

3. In the adjacent area, which changes according to the frequency option you select, adjust the settings to reflect the desired recurrence.

4. In the **Range of recurrence** area, select the appropriate end date for the series of appointments or events.

5. Click **OK**, and then click **Save & Close**.

Private Appointments and Events

You can mark any item in your calendar as Private. Then when other people look at your calendar, they can see that you are busy but not see why.

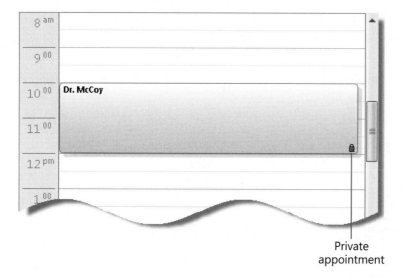

Private
appointment

➤ **To mark a Calendar item as private**

1. Open the appointment window, and on the **Appointment** tab, in the **Options** group, click **Private**.

2. Click **Save & Close**.

Practice Tasks

You need to be online and have a working Outlook account to complete these tasks. The practice file for the last task is located in the *Documents\Microsoft Press\ MCAS\Outlook2007\Objective02* folder.

- Display tomorrow's date in the Calendar pane. Create a half-hour appointment from 11:30 to 12:00, with the subject *MCAS Lunch with Jane*. Accept all other default settings.

- Continuing with the previous task, without opening the appointment window, start the *MCAS Lunch with Jane* appointment one hour earlier, and make it a one-hour appointment.

- Continuing with the previous task, indicate that the *MCAS Lunch with Jane* appointment is at *Fourth Coffee*, and set a one-hour reminder. Show the time on your calendar as Out of Office, and mark the appointment as private.

- Create a recurring one-hour appointment with the subject *MCAS Book Club* on the first Monday of the month at 6:00 PM. Set the series to end after six occurrences.

- Create a two-day event on Tuesday and Wednesday two weeks from now in Portland, Oregon, with the subject *MCAS Annual General Meeting*. Attach the *Agenda* document to the event.

2.2   **Send meeting requests**

Meeting Requests

You can send a meeting invitation (referred to as a *meeting request*) to any person who has an e-mail account (even to people who don't use Outlook). You can let people who don't have to attend the meeting know that it is taking place by marking their attendance as optional. You can invite entire groups of people by using a distribution list. The meeting request can include text and Web links, as well as file attachments to ensure that attendees have specific information available to them.

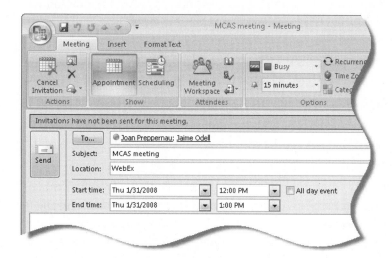

Just as you can create recurring appointments and events, you can create recurring meetings by adjusting the settings in the Appointment Recurrence dialog box.

➤ **To invite required attendees to a meeting**

1. In the Calendar, display the date on which you want to schedule the meeting.

2. On the **Standard** toolbar, in the **New** list, click **Meeting Request**.

   Or

   On the **Actions** menu, click **New Meeting Request**.

3. In the meeting window, type the e-mail addresses of the attendees in the **To** box.

4. In the **Subject** box, type the name of the meeting; and in the **Location** box, indicate where the meeting will take place.

5. Adjust the **Start time** and **End time** settings, and then click **Send**.

➤ **To invite an optional attendee to a meeting**

1. After entering the attendee's e-mail address in step 3 of the previous procedure, click the **Scheduling** button in the **Show** group on the **Meeting** tab.

2. Click the icon immediately to the left of the attendee's name, and in the list, click **Optional Attendee**.

3. On the **Meeting** tab, in the **Show** group, click the **Appointment** button, and then proceed with step 4 of the previous procedure.

➤ **To create a recurring meeting**

1. On the **Meeting** tab of the meeting window, in the **Options** group, click the **Recurrence** button.

2. In the **Recurrence pattern** area of the **Appointment Recurrence** dialog box, click a frequency option, and adjust settings to reflect the desired recurrence.

3. In the **Range of recurrence** area, select the appropriate end date for the series of meetings. Then click **OK**.

Scheduling

A primary difficulty when scheduling a meeting is finding a time that works for everyone. The Scheduling Assistant page of a meeting request window displays the schedules of people within your own organization and of people outside of your organization who have published their availability to the Internet. If free/busy information is available for meeting invitees, their time is shown as white (Available), blue (Busy), or purple (Out of Office). Tentative bookings are indicated by light-blue diagonal stripes. If no information is available (either because Outlook can't connect to a person's calendar or because the proposed meeting is further out than the scheduling information stored on the server), Outlook indicates this by gray diagonal stripes. The gray row at the top of the schedule indicates the collective schedule of all the invitees. Outlook indicates the selected meeting time with green (start time) and red (end time) vertical bars.

If your organization is running Exchange Server 2007, Outlook simplifies even further the process of selecting a suitable meeting time by displaying a list of suggested meeting times on the right side of the Scheduling Assistant page. The Suggested Times list displays meeting times of any duration you specify in the Duration list and indicates for each time the number of required and optional attendees who are available.

Strategy This section covers functionality that is specific to an Exchange Server 2007 environment. In the exam environment, Outlook 2007 runs against a simulated Exchange Server 2007 back end. If you have access only to Exchange Server 2003 or a non-Exchange Server account, study this section carefully.

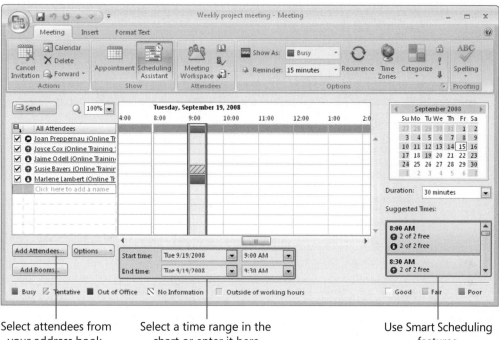

Select attendees from
your address book.

Select a time range in the
chart or enter it here.

Use Smart Scheduling
features.

The calendar in the upper-right corner of the Scheduling Assistant page indicates the collective availability of the group by color, as follows:

- Days when all attendees are available are white (Good).

- Days when most attendees are available are light blue (Fair).

- Days when most attendees are not available are medium blue (Poor).

- Days that occur in the past and non-working days are gray; scheduling suggestions are not provided for those days.

Selecting a date in the calendar displays suggested meeting times for that day. The availability of required attendees is shown separately from that of optional attendees and resources.

See Also For information about publishing calendars, see section 2.5, "Share your calendar with other people."

If your organization is running Microsoft Exchange Server and the Exchange Server directory includes shared resources such as conference rooms or presentation equipment, you can include these resources when scheduling a meeting.

If you meet frequently with the same people, instead of adding them individually when you schedule a meeting, you can create a group schedule. Then any time you need to schedule a meeting with that group, you can view the group schedule and then send a meeting request for the time when everyone is available.

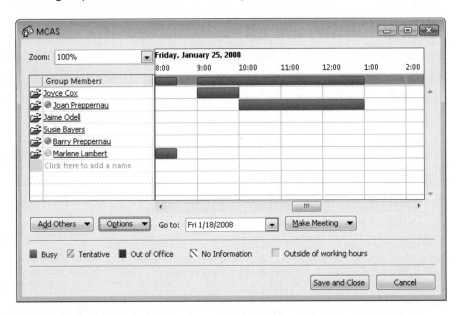

➤ To schedule a meeting

1. In the Calendar, display the date on which you want to schedule the meeting.

2. On the **Standard** toolbar, in the **New** list, click **Meeting Request**.

   Or

   On the **Actions** menu, click **New Meeting Request**.

   Tip If you prefer, you can organize a meeting directly from a Scheduling page-like interface by clicking Plan A Meeting on the Actions menu.

3. On the **Meeting** tab, in the **Show** group, click **Scheduling Assistant**.

4. Click **Add Attendees**. Then in the **Select Attendees and Resources** dialog box, double-click each required attendee name. Click each optional attendee name, and then click **Optional** and select any resources and click **Resources**. When the list is complete, click **OK**.

   Tip To add an attendee from outside your organization, enter the attendee's e-mail address directly in the All Attendees list on the Scheduling Assistant page, or in the To box on the Appointment page.

5. Select a time when all the required attendees are available from the **Suggested Times** list on the right.

6. On the **Meeting** tab, in the **Show** group, click **Appointment**.

7. Complete the details of the meeting, and then click **Send**.

➤ To create a group schedule

1. Display your calendar, and then on the **Actions** menu, click **View Group Schedules**.

2. In the **Group Schedules** dialog box, click **New**.

3. In the **Create New Group Schedule** dialog box, type a name for the schedule, and then click **OK**.

4. In the group's window, add members by clicking in the **Group Members** list and then typing a name or an e-mail address, or by clicking **Add Others** and then selecting group members from your address book.

5. Select a time for the meeting, click **Make Meeting**, and then send the meeting request.

   Tip You can view an up-to-date group schedule at any time by clicking View Group Schedules on the Actions menu and double-clicking the schedule name.

➤ **To use Smart Scheduling to schedule a meeting**

1. In the Calendar, display the date on which you want to schedule the meeting.

2. On the **Standard** toolbar, in the **New** list, click **Meeting Request**.

   Or

   On the **Actions** menu, click **New Meeting Request**.

3. On the **Meeting** tab, in the **Show** group, click **Scheduling Assistant**.

4. Specify the required and optional attendees, as well as any necessary resources.

5. In the **Duration** list on the right, specify the duration of the meeting.

6. In the **Suggested Times** list, click a meeting time when all or most of the required attendees are available.

7. On the **Meeting** tab, in the **Show** group, click **Appointment**.

8. Complete the details of the meeting, and then click **Send**.

Response Tracking

When someone responds to a meeting request, you receive an e-mail message. You can open the message to see who has accepted, tentatively accepted, or declined your invitation. In addition, you can open the meeting window, where Outlook automatically tracks responses from attendees in a banner below the Ribbon. Either way, you always have an up-to-date report of how many people will be attending your meeting.

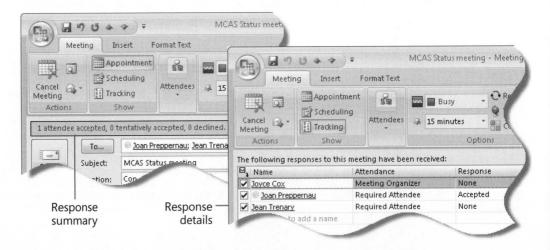

Response summary

Response details

If you set up a meeting that includes resources, such as a conference room, the meeting request might be automatically approved, or the person assigned responsibility for the resources might approve the request.

➤ **To track responses to a meeting request**

→ Open the meeting window to view the tally of attendees who have accepted, tentatively accepted, or declined.

→ On the **Meeting** tab, in the **Show** group, click the **Tracking** button to see response details.

Tip To send an e-mail message to everyone you've invited to a meeting, open the meeting window, and then on the Meeting tab, in the Attendees group, click the Message To Attendees button.

Practice Tasks

You need to be online and have a working Outlook account to complete these tasks. There are no practice files for these tasks. You should alert two colleagues that you are going to practice scheduling meetings before getting started.

● Create a request for a half-hour meeting with the subject *MCAS Status Meeting* at 3:00 P.M. tomorrow. Type *Test – please accept* as the location, and send the request to one person.

● Schedule a one-hour *MCAS Budget Meeting* with two colleagues at the first available time next week. Set up this meeting to occur at the same time every month for three months.

● Create a group schedule for yourself and two colleagues, and then schedule a half-hour *MCAS Lunch* meeting for the first day on which the entire group is available for lunch.

2.3   Update, cancel, and respond to meeting requests

Rescheduling and Canceling

If it is necessary to change the date, time, or location of a meeting, you can easily do so in the meeting window. You can also cancel the meeting entirely. If the meeting you want to change is recurring, Outlook asks whether you want to change the series or just that occurrence. After you make changes, Outlook sends an updated meeting request to the invited attendees to keep them informed.

If one of the invitees cannot attend the meeting at the scheduled time and proposes a new meeting time, as the organizer of the meeting, you can accept or decline the proposal. If you accept, Outlook updates the entry in your calendar and opens up a meeting request for you to send an updated meeting request to the other attendees. If the proposed time doesn't work for you, reply to the message or delete it and go back into the meeting and try and find another time that works.

Tip You can specify that attendees cannot propose new meeting times. To do this for all meetings, display the Options dialog box, click Calendar Options, and then clear the Allow Attendees To Propose New Times check box. To do it for the current meeting request, click Responses in the Attendees group on the Meeting tab, and then clear the Allow New Time Proposals check box.

➤ To update a meeting request

1. Double-click the meeting in the **Calendar** pane.
2. In the meeting window, make any necessary changes, and then click **Send Update**.

➤ To update a recurring meeting request

1. Double-click the meeting in the **Calendar** pane.
2. In the **Open Recurring Item** dialog box, click either **Open this occurrence** or **Open the series**, and then click **OK**.
3. In the meeting window, make any necessary changes, and then click **Send Update**.

➤ To cancel a meeting

1. Open the meeting window, and then on the **Meeting** tab, in the **Actions** group, click the **Cancel Meeting** button.

2. If the meeting is a recurring one, in the **Confirm Delete** dialog box, click either **Delete this occurrence** or **Delete the series**.

3. Click **Send Cancellation**.

➤ To accept a proposed meeting time

→ In the response message, click **Accept Proposal**, and then click **Send Update**.

➤ To decline a proposed meeting time

1. Reply to the **New Time Proposed** e-mail message to let the attendee know that you are not accepting the proposed time.

2. Delete the **New Time Proposed** message.

Additional Attendees

You can add an attendee to a meeting at any time. If this is the only change you make to the attendee list, Outlook gives you the option of sending an update only to the new attendee.

➤ To add a meeting attendee

1. Open the meeting window, and on the **Meeting** tab, in the **Attendees** group, click the **Add or Remove Attendees** button.

2. In the **Select Attendees and Resources** dialog box, double-click the name of a required attendee, or click the name and then click **Optional**. Then click **OK**.

3. Click **Send Update**.

4. In the **Send Update to Attendees** dialog box, click **Send updates only to added or deleted attendees** or **Send updates to all attendees**, and then click **OK**.

Responding

You receive a meeting request as a message in your Inbox, and Outlook automatically schedules the meeting on your calendar as Tentative. You can respond in one of four ways:

- **Accept.** Outlook deletes the meeting request and shows the scheduled time on your calendar as the meeting organizer indicated in the meeting request.

- **Tentatively accept.** Outlook deletes the meeting request and shows the time on your calendar as tentatively scheduled.

- **Propose a new time.** Outlook sends your proposal to the meeting organizer for confirmation and shows the original time on your calendar as tentatively scheduled.

- **Decline.** Outlook deletes the meeting request and removes the meeting from your calendar.

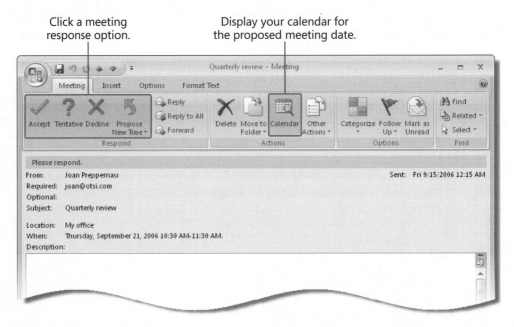

> Click a meeting response option.

> Display your calendar for the proposed meeting date.

➤ **To propose a new meeting time**

   1. In the **Reading Pane** of the meeting request window, click **Propose New Time**.

2. In the schedule area of the **Propose New Time** dialog box, set the proposed meeting start and end times, and then click **Propose Time**.

3. In the meeting response window that opens, enter a message to the meeting organizer, and then click **Send**.

Practice Tasks

You need to be online and have a working e-mail account to complete these tasks. There are no practice files for these tasks. You should alert two colleagues that you are going to practice scheduling meetings before getting started.

- Reschedule the *MCAS Budget Meeting* from the previous practice tasks to the week after next, and then send the updated meeting request.

- Add an optional attendee to the meeting request for the *MCAS Status Meeting* from the previous practice tasks, and then send the meeting request only to the new attendee.

- Ask a colleague to send you a meeting request for a meeting with the subject *MCAS Project Update*. When the request arrives, suggest that the meeting be held at the same time on the following day.

2.4   Customize calendar settings

Work Week

By default, Outlook defines the work week as Monday through Friday from 8:00 A.M. to 5:00 P.M. If you work a different schedule, you can change your work week so that other people can make appointments with you only during the times that you plan to be available. Your work week is colored differently in your calendar and by default is the only time displayed to other people on your network who look at your calendar.

See Also For information about looking at other people's calendars, see section 2.6, "View other calendars."

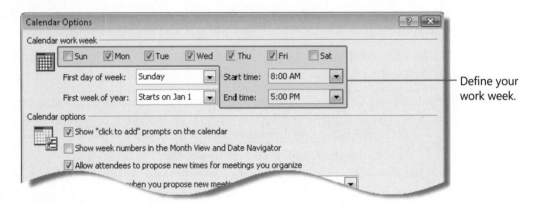

Define your work week.

> ➤ **To view your work week**

1. Display your calendar in **Week** view.

2. At the top of the **Calendar** pane, click **Show work week**.

> ➤ **To define your work week**

1. On the **Tools** menu, click **Options**.

2. On the **Preferences** tab of the **Options** dialog box, click **Calendar Options**.

3. In the **Calendar work week** area of the **Calendar Options** dialog box, select or clear the check boxes of the days of the week.

4. Set the start and end times for your work day.

   Tip You cannot define a work day that crosses midnight or define different start and end times for different days.

5. Click **OK** twice.

Time Zones

If you travel to a location outside of your usual time zone, you might want to change the time zone on your computer so that information such as the receipt time of e-mail messages, appointment times, and the time on the clock in the Windows taskbar notification area reflects your current location. If you have appointments in both time zones, you can display both time zones on the left side of the calendar pane, and swap between zones when you travel. That way, for example, if you live and work in California, you can be sure to correctly enter an appointment that occurs at 4:00 P.M. in Texas, and then receive an appointment reminder at the correct time after you arrive there.

If you frequently work with colleagues or clients in another time zone, you might want to display that time zone in your calendar in addition to your own, even if you don't travel there.

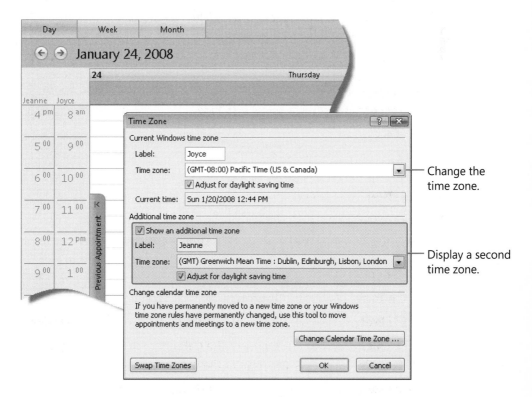

➤ To change the time zone

1. On the **Tools** menu, click **Options**. On the **Preferences** tab of the **Options** dialog box, click **Calendar Options**.

2. In the **Calendar Options** dialog box, click **Time Zone**.

3. In the **Time Zone** dialog box, click the time zone you want in the **Time zone** list.

4. Click **OK** in each of the open dialog boxes.

➤ To display multiple time zones

1. Display the **Time Zone** dialog box, and then select the **Show an additional time zone** check box.

2. In the second **Time zone** list, click the additional time zone you want to display.

3. Enter a label for each time zone in its corresponding **Label** box.

4. Click **OK** in each of the open dialog boxes.

➤ To swap time zones

1. Display the **Time Zone** dialog box, and then click **Swap Time Zones**.

2. Click **OK** in each of the open dialog boxes.

Holidays

You can add the national holidays of any country to your calendar. You can also remove all holidays from your calendar.

Tip Outlook assigns a color category named *Holiday* to all holidays in your calendar, and you can view them by displaying the calendar in By Category view and then scrolling to the Holiday category.

➤ **To add national holidays to your calendar**

1. Display the **Calendar Options** dialog box, and click **Add Holidays**.

2. In the **Add Holidays to Calendar** dialog box, select the check boxes of the countries whose holidays you want to add.

3. Click **OK** in each open dialog box.

➤ **To delete national holidays from your calendar**

1. Display your calendar in **Events** view.

2. Click the **Location** column header to sort all events by location.

3. Select all the events with the region you want to delete in the **Location** column and **Holiday** in the **Category** column.

4. Press the **Delete** key, and then restore the original view.

Practice Tasks

You need to be online and have a working e-mail account to complete these tasks. There are no practice files for these tasks.

- Display your work week, and then change it to show that you work a Friday-through-Monday schedule from 3:00 P.M. through 11:00 P.M.

- Add the time zone for a colleague who works in Sidney, Australia to your calendar.

- Display the Australian national holidays in your calendar.

Important Be sure to reverse the changes made for these tasks when you finish preparing for the certification exam.

2.5   Share your calendar with other people

Free/Busy Information

For other people to be able to see whether you are available for a meeting, you need to make information about your calendar available to them. You can make this information available on your Exchange server for people who are on your network, or on the Internet for colleagues outside your network.

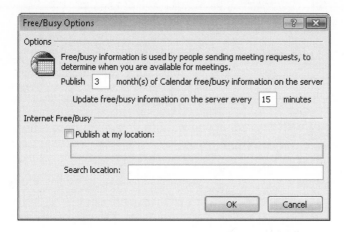

> **To make your free/busy information available on your network and/or the Internet**

1. Display the **Calendar Options** dialog box, click **Free/Busy Options**, and then click **Other Free/Busy**.

2. In the **Free/Busy Options** dialog box, set the number of months of calendar information you want to be available, and how often you want Outlook to update the server.

3. If you want to make your free/busy times available on the Internet, select the **Publish at my location** check box and type a valid URL into the textbox.

4. Click **OK** in each open dialog box.

Sharing

You can share your calendar with another person by sending a sharing invitation. You can convert an invitation message to a sharing request by asking the other person to share his or her calendar.

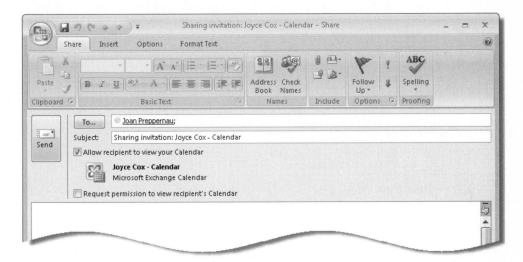

➤ To share a calendar with other people

1. In the **Navigation Pane**, click **Share My Calendar**.

2. In the **To** box of the message window, enter the e-mail address of the person with whom you want to share calendar information.

3. Select or clear the **Allow recipient to view your Calendar** or **Request permission to view recipient's Calendar** check boxes.

    Tip The subject of the message changes if you select the Request Permission check box.

4. Write any message you want in the content pane, and then click **Send**.

5. Click **Yes** to confirm that you want to share your calendar, and then click **OK**.

➤ To stop sharing a calendar

1. In the **Navigation Pane**, right-click the shared calendar (designated with a hand symbol), and click **Change Sharing Permissions**.

2. On the **Permissions** tab of the **Calendar Properties** dialog box, click the name of the person with whom you no longer want to share the calendar.

3. Click **Remove**, and then click **OK**.

E-Mailing

To share your schedule with someone who uses an HTML-capable e-mail program, you can embed selected calendar information as a static image in the body of an e-mail message and attach it as an iCalendar (.ics) file that can be opened in Outlook 2007. You can choose the period of time and the level of detail you want to share, as follows:

● **Availability only.** Includes only your availability (Free, Busy, Tentative, or Out Of Office) during scheduled time periods.

● **Limited details.** Includes only your availability and the subjects of calendar items.

● **Full details.** Includes your availability and the full details of calendar items.

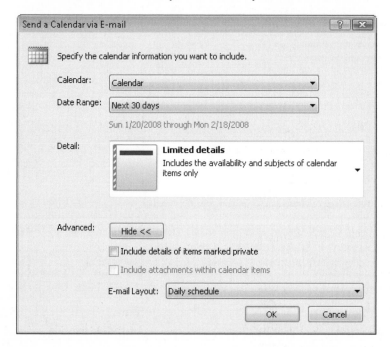

> ➤ **To send calendar information in an e-mail message**

1. In the **Navigation Pane**, click **Send a Calendar via E-mail**.

2. In the **Send a Calendar via E-mail** dialog box, in the **Date Range** list, click the dates you want.

3. In the **Detail** list, click the option you want.

4. To the right of **Advanced**, click **Show**, and set any options. Then click **OK**.

5. In the message header, fill in the header, type a message, and then click **Send**.

Delegating

You can delegate control of your calendar to a co-worker so that meeting requests sent to you are instead delivered to your delegate. You receive copies of the meeting requests and copies of your delegate's responses, but you don't have to respond. Your delegate can also create meeting requests on your behalf (that is, they appear to come from you).

➤ **To delegate control of your calendar**

1. On the **Delegates** tab of the **Options** dialog box, click **Add**.

2. In the **Add Users** dialog box, click the person you want to delegate control to, click **Add**, and then click **OK**.

3. In the **Delegate Permissions** dialog box, in the **Calendar** list, click the level of permission you want to delegate.

4. Select the **Automatically send a message to delegate summarizing these permissions** check box.

5. Click **OK** in each of the open dialog boxes.

   Tip You can cancel the delegation by removing your delegate from the Delegates list.

Publishing

If you need to share your calendar with people who are not on your network, you can publish it to Microsoft Office Online. After registering for the Microsoft Office Outlook Calendar Sharing Service, you can specify the period of time covered by the published calendar, the level of detail, the people with permission to view it, and how often it is updated (Advanced settings).

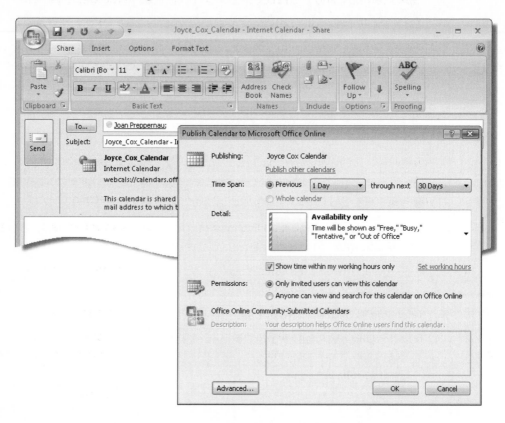

➤ **To publish your calendar to Office Online**

1. In the **Navigation Pane**, click **Publish My Calendar**.

2. If necessary, follow the instructions for registering for the Microsoft Office Outlook Calendar Sharing Service.

3. In the **Publish Calendar to Microsoft Office Online** dialog box, adjust the **Time Span** settings, and then click the option you want in the **Detail** list.

4. Click the **Permissions** option you want, and then click **OK**.

5. In the **Send a Sharing Invitation** dialog box, click **Yes**. Then in the message window, enter the address of the person with whom you want to share the published calendar, and click **Send**.

Practice Tasks

You need to be online and have a working e-mail account to complete these tasks. There are no practice files for these tasks. You should alert a colleague that you are going to practice sharing your calendar before getting started.

- If you are working on an Exchange server, change your free/busy settings to publish four months of information every 30 minutes.

- Send an invitation to a colleague to view your calendar, and include a request that you be allowed to view his or her calendar.

- E-mail a snapshot of your calendar for the next month to a colleague.

- Delegate responsibility for your calendar to a colleague for the next two weeks, without informing him or her of these new responsibilities. Then cancel the delegation.

2.6 View other calendars

Multiple Calendars

You can create a secondary calendar and view it either individually or at the same time as your primary calendar. You can view multiple calendars next to each other, or you can overlay them to display a composite view. When you view and click a date in the Date Navigator or scroll one calendar, all the calendars display the same date or time period.

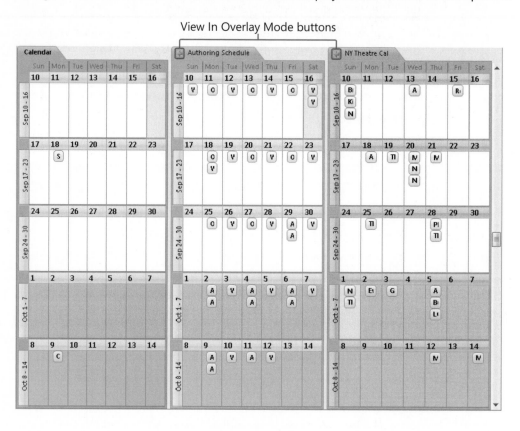

➤ **To create a secondary calendar**

1. On the **File** menu, point to **New**, and then click **Calendar**.

2. In the **Create New Folder** dialog box, name the calendar, select its location, and then click **OK**.

➤ **To view multiple calendars**

➜ In either the **My Calendars** or **Other Calendars** list in the **Navigation Pane**, select the check boxes of the calendars you want to view.

➤ **To switch between Overlay Mode and Side-By-Side Mode**

➜ On the title bar tab of any secondary calendar, click the **View in Overlay Mode** button. In Overlay Mode, click either calendar tab to display that calendar on top of the other calendar.

➜ On either of the overlaid calendars, click the **View in Side-By-Side Mode** button to return to the standard display.

Other People's Calendars

When someone on your network sends you an invitation to share his or her calendar, you can click a button in the message to open the calendar beside your own in a separate instance of Outlook, or you can display the calendar in the existing Outlook window.

See Also For information about sharing calendars, see section 2.5, "Share your calendar with other people."

➤ **To view a calendar you have permission to share**

➜ In the **Navigation Pane**, select the check box to the left of the name of the person whose calendar you want to view.

Or

1. In the **Navigation Pane**, click **Open a Shared Calendar**.

2. In the **Open a Shared Calendar** dialog box, enter the e-mail address of the person whose calendar you want to view, and then click **OK**.

Internet Calendars

A variety of specialized calendars that track professional sports schedules, holidays, entertainment, scientific data, and so on are available from the Microsoft Office Online Web site. You can link to these Internet calendars from your calendar so that you have up-to-date information conveniently available, in the same place as your own scheduling information. You can display Internet calendars as you would any other, viewing them independently, next to another calendar, or in overlay view.

➤ **To subscribe to an Internet Calendar**

1. In the **Navigation Pane**, click **Search Calendars Online**.

2. On the **Internet Calendars** page of Office Online, locate and click the Internet calendar you want.

3. If an **Internet Explorer Security** message box prompts you to allow Outlook to open Web content, click the **Allow** button.

4. In the **Microsoft Office Outlook** message box asking whether you want to add the calendar to Outlook and subscribe to updates, click **Yes**.

Tip You can remove an Internet calendar from your list of available calendars by right-clicking it and then clicking Delete.

Practice Tasks

You need to be online and have a working e-mail account to complete these tasks. There are no practice files for these tasks.

- Create a secondary calendar, and display it beside your primary calendar. Turn off the secondary calendar.

- If you asked a colleague to share his or her calendar with you in the previous practice tasks, display that calendar with your own in overlay view.

- Search for Internet calendars on the Office Online Web site, and subscribe to a calendar with information that interests you.

Objective Review

Before finishing this chapter, ensure that you have mastered the following skills:

2.1 Create appointments, meetings, and events.

2.2 Send meeting requests.

2.3 Update, cancel, and respond to meeting requests.

2.4 Customize calendar settings.

2.5 Share your calendar with other people.

2.6 View other calendars.

3 Managing Tasks

The skills tested in this section of the Microsoft Office Specialist exam for Microsoft Office Outlook 2007 relate to tracking and managing tasks in the Outlook task list. Specifically, the following objectives are associated with this set of skills:

3.1 Create and modify tasks, and mark tasks as complete.

3.2 Accept, decline, assign, update, and respond to tasks.

Outlook 2007 provides new functionality for adding tasks related to other Outlook items to your task list. You can view your tasks for each day at the bottom of the Calendar pane displaying that day, work week, or week, as well as in the To-Do Bar. You manage tasks from the To-Do Bar in the same way that you do from the Tasks module.

This chapter guides you in studying ways of creating tasks, marking tasks as complete or private, assigning tasks to other people, accepting and declining tasks, and sending status reports about assigned tasks.

Important No practice files are required to complete the exercises in this chapter. See "Using the Companion CD" at the beginning of this book for more information.

Tip Graphics and operating system–related instructions in this book reflect the Windows Vista user interface. If your computer is running Windows XP and you experience trouble following the instructions as written, refer to the sidebar "If You Are Running Windows XP" in "Working in the Microsoft Office Fluent User Interface" at the beginning of this book.

3.1 Create and modify tasks, and mark tasks as complete

Tasks

If you use your task list diligently, you will frequently want to add tasks to it. You can create tasks in several ways:

- In the Tasks module, add a task to the task list.
- In other modules, add a task to the To-Do Bar task list.
- Create a new task in the task window.
- Base a task on an existing Outlook item (such as a message).

The only information you must include when creating a task is the subject. You can also specify the following:

- Start date
- Due date
- Status (Not Started, In Progress, Completed, Waiting On Someone, or Deferred)
- Priority (Normal, Low, or High)
- Reminder (date and time)
- Category

You can attach files to tasks, and you can include text, tables, charts, illustrations, hyperlinks, and other content in the task window content pane.

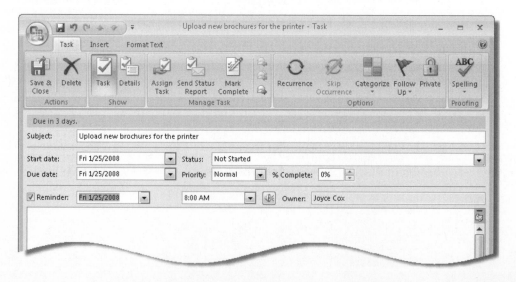

Just as you can create recurring appointments, events, and meetings, you can create recurring tasks. You can set the task to occur every day, week, month, or year; or you can specify that a new task should be generated a certain amount of time after the last task is complete.

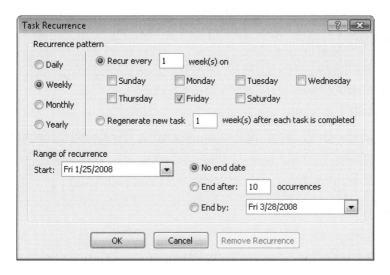

➤ **To create a task in the task list**

1. At the top of the task list in either the **Tasks** module or on the **To-Do Bar**, click the **Type a new task** box.

2. Type the subject of the task, and then press **Enter**.

3. To assign the task to a category, right-click the category icon to the right of the task subject in the task list, and then click the category you want.

4. To assign a due date, right-click the flag icon, and then click the option you want.

➤ **To create a task in the task window**

1. On the **Standard** toolbar, click **New**, and in the list, click **Task**.

2. Enter details about the task in the task header.

3. If you want, set a reminder to ensure that you complete the task on time.

4. On the **Task** tab, in the **Actions** group, click the **Save & Close** button.

Tip To automatically set task reminders, display the Options dialog box, click Task Options, select the Set Reminders On Tasks With Due Dates check box, and click OK. Set the default reminder time in the Tasks area of the Options dialog box, and then click OK.

➤ **To create a task from an e-mail message**

→ In the message list, right-click the flag icon to the right of the message subject, and then click a follow-up due date.

See Also For more information about flagging messages to create tasks, see section 1.6, "Configure e-mail message delivery options."

Or

1. From the message list, drag the e-mail message to the **Tasks** button at the bottom of the **Navigation Pane**.

2. In the task window that opens, set the options you want.

3. Click **Save & Close**.

➤ **To create a recurring task**

1. On the **Task** tab of the task window, in the **Options** group, click the **Recurrence** button.

2. In the **Task Recurrence** dialog box, select the **Recurrence Pattern** and **Range of Recurrence** options you want, and then click **OK**.

Tip When you mark an instance of a recurring task as complete, Outlook generates a new instance of the task at whatever interval you specified when creating the task.

Task Management

To effectively manage your tasks, you can open the task window and change any setting in the header at any time. You can also click the buttons in the Options group on the Task tab to change the task's category or due date, or mark the task as private.

To track tasks to completion, you can update the Status and % Complete information in the task window.

➤ **To mark a task as private**

→ On the **Task** tab of the task window, in the **Options** group, click the **Private** button.

➤ **To mark a task as complete**

→ In the message list, click the flag icon to the right of the message subject.

→ In the task window, set **% Complete** to **100%**.

→ On the **Task** tab of the task window, in the **Manage Task** group, click the **Mark Complete** button.

Tip If you delete a task, it moves to the Deleted Items folder and is permanently deleted when you empty that folder. No record of it remains on your task list.

Practice Tasks

You need to be online and have a working Outlook account to complete these tasks. There are no practice files for these tasks.

● From the To-Do Bar, create a task with the subject *MCAS Dinner Reservations*, flag it for completion this week, and assign it to the Business category.

● Open a new task window, and create a task with the subject *MCAS Send Dinner Invitations*. Set a due date of next Tuesday with a reminder at 5:00 P.M., and then set the status to Waiting On Someone Else.

● Open the *MCAS Dinner Reservations* task, and mark it as private and high priority. Then set it to 25 percent complete.

● Create a new task with the subject *MCAS Status Report* that must be carried out on the first Monday of every month for six months.

3.2 Accept, decline, assign, update, and respond to tasks

Task Assignments

You can assign tasks from your Outlook task list to other people within your organization, and other people can assign tasks to you. You can't assign tasks you have created from other Outlook items; you can assign only those you create from scratch as tasks.

When you assign a task, you can choose whether to keep a copy of the task on your own task list or transfer it entirely to the assignee's task list. (Either way, the task remains on your own task list until accepted, so you won't lose track of it.)

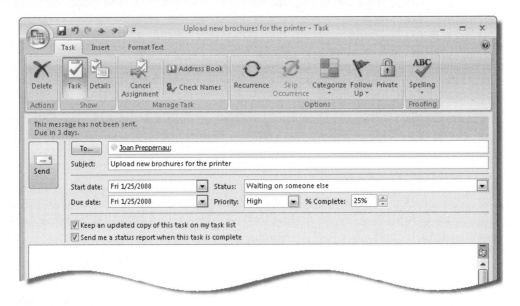

Tip Outlook indicates assigned tasks in your task list by an outstretched hand on the task icon, similar to that of a shared folder in Windows Explorer.

When you send the assignment, Outlook sends a task request, similar to a meeting request, to the assignee. If the assignee declines the task, you can return it to your task list or reassign it. If the assignee accepts the task, ownership of the task transfers to that person, and you can no longer update the information in the task window.

If you keep a copy of the task on your task list, you can follow the task's progress as the assignee updates its status and details. Unless you choose otherwise, Outlook automatically sends you a status report on an assigned task when the assignee marks the task as complete.

➤ **To assign a task to someone else**

1. On the **Task** tab of the task window, in the **Manage Task** group, click the **Assign Task** button.

2. In the **To** box that appears, type the e-mail address of the assignee.

3. If you don't want to keep the task on your task list or receive a report when the task is complete, clear the corresponding check box.

4. Click **Send**.

5. If a message notifies you that the task reminder has been turned off, click **OK**.

Assignment Responses

If you are assigned a task, you receive an e-mail message with the assignment in your Inbox. You can accept or decline the task assignment by clicking the corresponding button in the Reading Pane or in the task window.

➤ **To accept an assigned task**

1. Open the message with the task assignment, and click **Accept**.

2. In the **Accepting Task** dialog box, click the option you want, and then click **OK**.

3. If you chose to send a message with your acceptance, type the message, and then click **Send**.

➤ **To decline an assigned task**

1. Open the message with the task assignment, and click **Decline**.

2. In the **Declining Task** dialog box, click the option you want, and then click **OK**.

3. If you chose to send a message explaining your rejection of the assignment, type the message, and then click **Send**.

➤ **To send a status report to the person who assigned the task**

1. On the **Task** tab of the task window, in the **Manage Task** group, click the **Send Status Report** button.

2. Enter the e-mail address of the person to whom you want to send the report, type any message you want, and then click **Send**.

Practice Tasks

You need to be online and have a working Outlook account to complete these tasks. There are no practice files for these tasks. You should alert a colleague that you are going to practice assigning tasks before getting started.

- Assign the *MCAS Dinner Reservations* task you created in the previous practice tasks to a colleague, without retaining the task on your task list.

- Ask your colleague to assign two tasks to you. When you receive the first task assignment, accept it. When you receive the second assignment, reject it with a polite message explaining why.

- Open the task you accepted in the previous practice task, mark it 50 percent complete, and set its status to In Progress. Then send a task status report to the colleague who assigned the task.

Objective Review

Before finishing this chapter, ensure that you have mastered the following skills:

3.1 Create and modify tasks, and mark tasks as complete.

3.2 Accept, decline, assign, update, and respond to tasks.

4 Managing Contacts and Personal Contact Information

The skills tested in this section of the Microsoft Office Specialist exam for Microsoft Office Outlook 2007 relate to populating and managing address books. Specifically, the following objectives are associated with this set of skills:

4.1 Create and modify contacts.
4.2 Edit and use an electronic business card.
4.3 Create and modify distribution lists.
4.4 Create a secondary address book.

Having immediate access to current, accurate contact information for the people you need to interact with—by e-mail, telephone, mail, or otherwise—is important for timely and effective communication. You can easily build and maintain a detailed contact list, or address book, in Microsoft Office Outlook 2007. From your address book, you can look up information, generate messages, and share contact information with other people.

This chapter guides you in studying ways of creating contact records, distribution lists, and address books, and designing, sending, and receiving electronic business cards.

 Important Before you can use the practice files in this chapter, you need to install them from the book's companion CD to their default location. See "Using the Companion CD" at the beginning of this book for more information.

Tip Graphics and operating system–related instructions in this book reflect the Windows Vista user interface. If your computer is running Windows XP and you experience trouble following the instructions as written, refer to the sidebar "If You Are Running Windows XP" in "Working in the Microsoft Office Fluent User Interface" at the beginning of this book.

4.1   Create and modify contacts

Contact Address Lists

Outlook stores contact information from different sources in separate address lists:

- **Global Address List (GAL).** If you're using Outlook to connect to a Microsoft Exchange Server account, your organization's contact information is stored in the GAL. The GAL is administered as part of Exchange Server. Outlook users can view the GAL but cannot change its contents.

- **Outlook Address Books.** The Contacts address book automatically created by Outlook is your main address book. This address book does not appear in the folder structure within the Navigation Pane—you display it by clicking the Contacts button.

- **Mobile Address Book.** A Mobile Address Book containing all the contacts in your main address book for whom you have mobile phone numbers listed is created automatically if you have an Outlook Mobile Service account.

You can view all your address lists and address books in the Contacts module.

➤ To view an address list

1. On the **Standard** toolbar, click the **Address Book** button.

2. In the **Address Book** list, click the name of the Outlook address book or address list you want to display.

Contact Records

For each person whose information you record in an address book, you can store the following types of general information:

- Name, company name, and job title
- Business, home, and alternate addresses
- Business, home, mobile, pager, and other telephone numbers
- Business, home, and alternate fax numbers
- Web page address (URL), instant messaging (IM) address, and up to three e-mail addresses
- Photo or other identifying image
- General notes, which can include text and illustrations such as photos, clip art images, SmartArt diagrams, charts, and shapes

You can also store personal and organization-specific details for each contact:

● Professional information, including department, office location, profession, manager's name, and assistant's name

● Personal information, including nickname, spouse or partner's name, birthday, anniversary, and the title (such as Miss, Mrs., or Ms.) and suffix (such as Jr. or Sr.) to use in correspondence

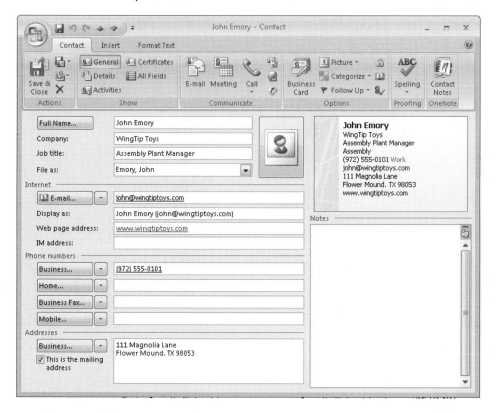

In addition to creating contact records from scratch, you can quickly clone information from an existing record to create contact records for several people who work for the same company. You can also create new contact records from e-mail messages. If someone sends you a contact record or an electronic business card, you can easily turn it into a contact record in your own Outlook address book.

See Also   For information about creating and sending electronic business cards, see section 4.2, "Edit and use an electronic business card."

You can add to or change the information stored in a contact record at any time.

By default, Outlook files contacts by last name (Last, First order). You can change the default File As setting for new contacts to any of the following:

- First Last
- Company
- Last, First (Company)
- Company (Last, First)

Tip The first time you enter a phone number for a contact, the Location Information dialog box opens, prompting you to enter your own country, area code, and any necessary dialing information such as a carrier code. Outlook sets up dialing rules based on the information you enter. You must enter at least your country and area code in the dialog box and then click OK; you can't close the dialog box without entering the requested information. When you finish entering information in the Addresses area, Outlook verifies that the address conforms to a standard pattern. If Outlook detects irregularities in the address you enter, the Check Address dialog box opens, prompting you to enter the street address, city, state or province, postal code, and country in separate fields from which it reassembles the address. If the information in the Check Address dialog box is correct, you can click Cancel to close the dialog box without making changes.

➤ **To create a new contact**

1. With the **Contacts** pane displayed, on the **Standard** toolbar, click the **New Contact** button.

   Or

   In any Outlook module, on the **Standard** toolbar, click the **New** arrow, and then click **Contact**.

2. In the contact window, enter the new contact information. To make multiple entries in the same box, click the arrow, click an appropriate description, and then enter the corresponding information.

3. On the **Contact** tab, in the **Show** group, click the **Details** button, and then enter additional information.

4. On the **Contact** tab, in the **Actions** group, click the **Save & Close** button.

➤ **To create a new contact with the same company information**

1. In the contact list, double-click the contact on which you want to base a new contact from the same company.

2. On the **Contact** tab, in the **Actions** group, click the **Save & New** arrow, and then click **New Contact from Same Company**.

3. In the contact window, enter the contact information.

4. Save and close the record.

➤ **To create a new contact based on another contact**

1. In the contact list, click the contact on which you want to base a new contact.

2. Press **Ctrl+C** and then **Ctrl+V**.

3. In the **Duplicate Contact Detected** dialog box, select **Add new contact**, and then click **Add**.

4. In the contact list, double-click the duplicate contact, and in the contact window, change the contact information.

5. Save and close the record.

➤ **To create a contact from a message header**

1. Open the message, right-click the name in the **From** field, and then click **Add to Outlook Contacts**.

2. In the contact window, edit the contact information as required.

3. Save and close the record.

➤ **To save contact information received as an electronic business card**

1. In the message, right-click the business card, and then click **Add to Outlook Contacts**.

2. Edit the contact record if required, and then save and close the record.

➤ **To save contact information received as a contact record**

1. In the message, double-click the contact record to open it in a contact window.

2. Edit the contact record if required, and then save and close the record.

➤ **To change the default filing order**

1. On the **Tools** menu, click **Options**.

2. In the **Contacts and Notes** area of the **Options** dialog box, click **Contact Options**.

3. In the **Contact Options** dialog box, in the **Name and filing options for new contacts** area, change the **Default "File As" order** setting to the one you want.

4. Click **OK** twice.

   Tip You can change the File As order for an individual contact by selecting the order you want in the File As list in the contact record.

➤ **To change the default mailing address**

1. In the **Addresses** list, click the type of address you want to designate as the default, and then select the **This is the mailing address** check box.

2. Save and close the record.

➤ **To attach a document, message, or other information to a contact record**

1. Open the contact, and on the **Insert** tab, in the **Include** group, click the **Attach File** or **Attach Item** button.

2. In the **Insert File** or **Insert Item** dialog box, locate and then double-click the file or item you want to attach to the record.

3. Save and close the record.

Practice Tasks

You need to have a working Outlook account to complete these tasks. The practice file for the first task is located in the *Documents\Microsoft Press\MCAS\ Outlook2007\Objective04* folder.

- Create a new contact record for yourself, filling in as much information as you can. Attach the *Sunset* image to the record (or any image you want).

- Create a new contact for John Emory, the assembly plant manager of Wingtip Toys, which is located at 111 Magnolia Lane, Flower Mound, TX 98053. John's e-mail address is *john@wingtiptoys.com*, and the company Web site's URL is *www.wingtiptoys.com*.

- Using the quickest method, create a new contact record for Andrea Dunker. Andrea is a sales associate for WingTip Toys, and her e-mail address is *andrea@wingtiptoys.com*.

- Edit the John Emory contact record so that it is filed as *John Emory* instead of *Emory, John*. Then note that John's nickname is Jack, his spouse's name is Barbara, and his birthday is July 31.

4.2   Edit and use an electronic business card

When you enter information in a contact record, the first 10 lines of information appear in the business card in the upper-right corner of the contact window. If the contact record includes an image, the image appears on the left side. You can change the types of information that appear, rearrange the information fields, format the text and background, and add, change, or remove images such as a logo or photograph.

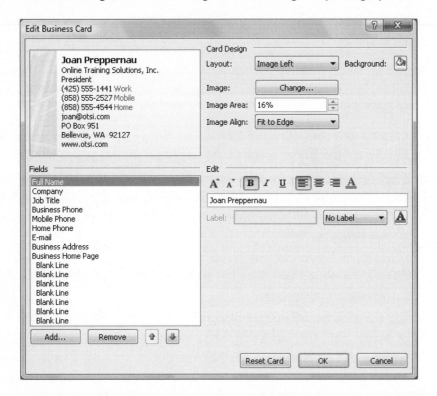

Creating a business card for yourself provides you with an attractive way of presenting your contact information to people you correspond with in e-mail. You can send your business card to someone else by attaching the card to an e-mail message. The recipient can then save the contact information in his or her own address book.

You can also use your business card as your e-mail message signature. Then Outlook not only displays the business card at the bottom of your messages but also attaches it to the message.

See Also For information about automatic e-mail signatures, see section 1.2, "Create and manage your signature and automated messages."

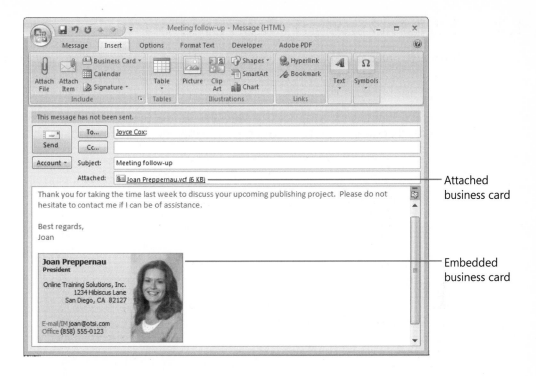

Attached business card

Embedded business card

➤ To modify the information that appears in a business card

1. Display the contact record, and then on the **Contact** tab, in the **Options** group, click the **Business Card** button.

2. In the **Edit Business Card** dialog box, below the **Fields** box, click **Add**, point to the type of field you want, and then click the specific field.

    Tip Use custom user fields to add text that is not part of the contact record to the business card.

3. Use the arrows below the **Fields** box to move the field to where you want it to appear on the business card.

4. In the **Edit** area, type the field's value in the box and format it the way you want. If necessary, select a label location from the list, and then type the field's label.

5. In the **Fields** box, click any field you want to remove, and then click **Remove**.

6. Click **OK** to save the modified business card.

➤ To format the appearance of a business card

1. Display the **Edit Business Card** dialog box.

2. To change the background color, in the **Card Design** area, click the **Background** button. Then in the **Color** dialog box, click a color you like, and click **OK**.

3. To add or change the picture attached to the card, to the right of **Image** in the **Card Design** area, click **Change**. Then browse to the folder containing the image, click the image, and click **OK**.

4. In the **Image Area** box, type or select the image area size.

5. In the **Image Align** list, click a type of alignment.

6. Click **OK** to save the business card.

➤ To send an electronic business card to others

1. Open a new message window, and address the message to the recipient.

2. On the **Message** tab, in the **Include** group, click the **Insert Business Card** button, and then in the list, click **Other Business Cards**.

   Tip Business cards that you've previously sent appear in the Insert Business Card list. You can insert a card in a message by selecting it from the list.

3. In the **Insert Business Card** dialog box, select the card or cards you want to send, and then click **OK**.

➤ To use an electronic business card as a signature in messages

1. Display the message window.

2. On the **Message** tab, in the **Include** group, click the **Signature** button, and in the list, click **Signatures**.

3. In the **Signatures and Stationery** dialog box, on the **E-mail Signature** tab, select the signature to edit.

   Or

   Click **New**, type a name for the signature, and click **OK** to create a new signature.

4. In the **Edit signature** area, click **Business Card**.

5. In the **Insert Business Card** dialog box, locate and double-click the card you want, and then click **OK**.

6. In the message window on the **Message** tab, in the **Include** group, click the **Signature** button, and then click the business card signature.

Practice Tasks

You need to have a working Outlook account to complete these tasks. The practice file for the fourth task is located in the *Documents\Microsoft Press\MCAS\Outlook2007\Objective04* folder.

- If you haven't already done so, create a contact record for yourself. Include your name, company, job title, business and mobile phone numbers, fax number, one or more e-mail addresses, and one or more addresses.

- From your contact record, create a business card that includes only your name, company name, business phone number, and business e-mail address. Then add the slogan *We'll take it from here* to the bottom of the card.

- Format the information on the business card, so that your name appears below and is smaller than your company name. Make the slogan italic.

- Add the *FourthCoffee* logo graphic to the upper-left corner of your business card, allowing it to occupy 20 percent of the card. Then change the background color to beige.

- Create a new e-mail message to a friend, and attach your business card both as a file and as a signature.

4.3   Create and modify distribution lists

If you frequently send messages to a specific group of people, such as employees in a department, clients in a particular region, or players on a sports team, you can create a distribution list containing the e-mail addresses of all the people in the group. Then when you send a message to the distribution list, each member of the group receives a copy of the message.

You can add people to a distribution list by selecting them from an address book or by manually entering their e-mail addresses.

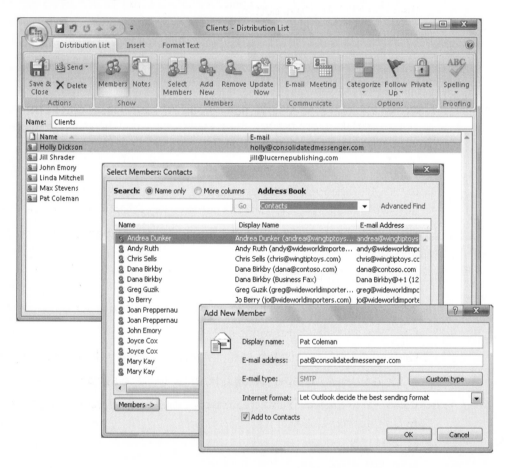

➤ **To create a new distribution list from contact records**

1. On the **Standard** toolbar, click the **New** arrow, and then click **Distribution List**.

2. In the **Name** box, type a name for the list.

3. On the **Distribution List** tab, in the **Members** group, click the **Select Members** button.

4. In the **Select Members** dialog box, in the **Address Book** list, click the address book from which you want to add contacts.

5. In the **Name** list, click the name of someone you want to include in the list, and then click the **Members** button.

   Tip You can add multiple names to a distribution list by double-clicking each name to insert it in the Members box, or by holding down the Ctrl key while selecting multiple names and then clicking the Members button.

6. Click **OK**.

7. On the **Contact** tab, in the **Actions** group, click the **Save & Close** button.

➤ **To modify an existing distribution list**

1. On the **Standard** toolbar, click the **Address Book** button.

2. In the **Address Book** dialog box, display the address book containing the distribution list, and then double-click the name of the distribution list to open its window.

3. On the **Distribution List** tab, click buttons in the **Members** group to add or remove members.

4. Save and close the distribution list.

➤ **To add someone who does not have a contact record to a new distribution list**

1. Open the distribution list window.

2. On the **Distribution List** tab, in the **Members** group, click the **Add New** button.

3. In the **Add New Member** dialog box, enter the **Display name** and **E-mail address**.

4. If you want Outlook to also create a contact record for this person, select the **Add to Contacts** check box.

5. Click **OK**.

➤ **To update a distribution list with new contact information**

1. Open the distribution list window.

2. On the **Distribution List** tab, in the **Members** group, click the **Update Now** button.

Practice Tasks

You need to have a working Outlook account to complete these tasks. There are no practice files for these tasks.

- Create a new distribution list named *MCAS Clients*, and select the John Emory contact record you created in the previous tasks as a member. Then add Pat Coleman, whose e-mail address is *pat@consolidatedmessenger.com*, as a new member, and save and close the distribution list.

- Add the following people to the MCAS Clients distribution list and to your contact list:

Holly Dickson	*holly@consolidatedmessenger.com*
Max Stevens	*max@consolidatedmessenger.com*
Linda Mitchell	*linda@lucernepublishing.com*
Jill Shrader	*jill@lucernepublishing.com*

- Open the contact record for Jill Shrader, and change her e-mail address to *jill@wingtiptoys.com*. Then update the MCAS Clients distribution list.

4.4   Create a secondary address book

You can track all your contacts in one address book and then locate specific contacts or groups of contacts by categorizing, sorting, and filtering. Or you can create separate address books for specific groups of people. You create an additional address book by creating a contacts folder; that is, a folder designated as containing contact items.

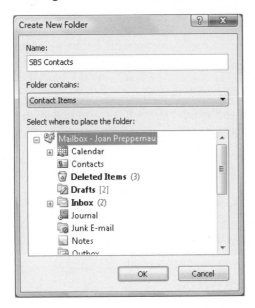

You can also create a secondary address book by importing address information into a contacts folder.

Tip Outlook 2007 will not import a file created in Microsoft Office Excel 2007. To import worksheet information, save the file in the Excel 97-2003 format.

In the Contacts module, any contacts folders you create appear under My Contacts in the Navigation Pane. You can display all your Outlook folders, including any contacts folders you have created, by displaying the Folder List in the Navigation Pane. You can then organize your contacts folders as you want.

➤ To create a contacts folder

1. On the **Standard** toolbar, click the **New** arrow, and then click **Folder**.

2. In the **Name** box of the **Create New Folder** dialog box, type a name by which you want to identify the folder.

3. In the **Folder contains** list, click **Contact Items**.

4. In the **Select where to place the folder** list, click a location for the folder, and then click **OK**.

➤ To import contacts from a file into a contacts folder

1. On the **File** menu, click **Import and Export**.

2. On the first page of the **Import and Export Wizard**, in the **Choose an action to perform list**, click **Import from another program or file**, and then click **Next**.

3. In the **Select file type to import from** list, click the option you want, and then click **Next**.

4. Click **Browse**, and locate and double-click the file you want to use. Then click **Next**.

5. Click the contacts folder into which you want to import the contacts, and click **Next**. Then click **Finish**.

➤ To move a contacts folder

1. At the bottom of the **Navigation Pane**, click the **Folder List** button.

2. In the **Folder List**, drag the contacts folder where you want it.

Practice Tasks

You need to have a working Outlook account to complete these tasks. The practice file for the third task is located in the *Documents\Microsoft Press\MCAS\Outlook2007\Objective04* folder.

● Create a contacts folder named *MCAS Contacts*, as a subfolder of your main Contacts folder.

● Move the MCAS Contacts folder so that it is a top-level folder within your Mailbox above Sent Items.

● Import the contact information saved in the *Contacts* workbook into the MCAS Contacts folder.

Objective Review

Before finishing this chapter, ensure that you have mastered the following skills:

4.1   Create and modify contacts.

4.2   Edit and use an electronic business card.

4.3   Create and modify distribution lists.

4.4   Create a secondary address book.

5 Organizing Information

The skills tested in this section of the Microsoft Office Specialist exam for Microsoft Office Outlook 2007 relate to organizing and locating messages within Outlook, managing second-tier messages, and customizing the Outlook program environment beyond the coverage in "Prerequisites" at the beginning of this exam. Specifically, the following objectives are associated with this set of skills:

5.1 Categorize Outlook 2007 items by color.

5.2 Create and manage Outlook 2007 data files.

5.3 Organize mail folders.

5.4 Locate Outlook 2007 items by using the search feature.

5.5 Create, modify, and remove rules to manage e-mail messages.

5.6 Customize your Outlook 2007 experience.

This chapter guides you in studying the categorization and sorting by category of Outlook items, creating and managing data files, managing folders, archiving mes-sages, managing sent and deleted messages, and managing junk e-mail. You will study the various search features, ways in which you can manage messages by using rules, and ways of customizing the Outlook environment.

 Important No practice files are required to complete the exercises in this chapter. See "Using the Companion CD" at the beginning of this book for more information.

Tip Graphics and operating system–related instructions in this book reflect the Windows Vista user interface. If your computer is running Windows XP and you experience trouble following the instructions as written, refer to the sidebar "If You Are Running Windows XP" in "Working in the Microsoft Office Fluent User Interface" at the beginning of this book.

5.1   Categorize Outlook 2007 items by color

Color Categories

Assigning messages, appointments, contacts, and tasks to color categories can help you more easily locate information. You can apply color categories several ways. If you frequently use a particular category, you can assign it as your Quick Click category. You can also assign keyboard shortcuts to up to 11 color categories.

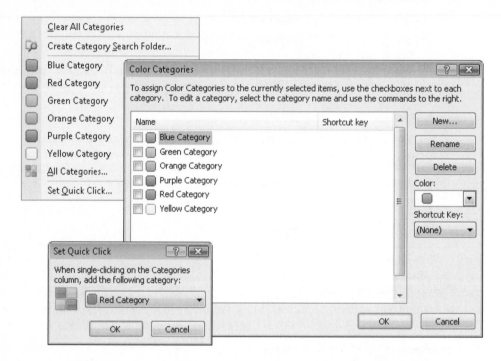

An item that has been assigned to a color category appears as follows:

- Messages have colored boxes to the right of the message header in the message list. In the Reading Pane, colored bars appear above the header. Up to three categories can be displayed in one row; additional categories are displayed in additional rows.

- Appointments, events, and meetings are shaded in the calendar pane with the color of the category.

- Contacts have colored boxes in Phone List view.

► **To assign an item to a color category**

→ In any folder, select the item, click the **Categorize** button on the **Standard** toolbar, and then click the category you want.

Tip If you haven't renamed a color category, Outlook gives you the option of renaming the category the first time you use it.

→ In any folder, right-click the item, point to **Categorize**, and then click the category you want.

→ In any mail folder or in the task list on the **To-Do Bar**, apply the Quick Click category to a message or task by clicking its **Category** box.

→ In any mail folder or in the task list on the **To-Do Bar**, right-click the **Category** box to the right of the message or task header, and then click the category you want.

► **To assign an item to multiple categories**

1. In any folder, select the item, display the category list, and then click **All Categories**.

2. In the **Color Categories** dialog box, select the check boxes of the categories you want, and then click **OK**.

► **To designate the Quick Click category**

1. With any item selected in any folder, display the categories list, and then click **Set Quick Click**.

2. In the **Set Quick Click** dialog box, click the color you want in the category list, and then click **OK**.

► **To assign a keyboard shortcut to a category**

1. With any item selected in any folder, display the categories list, and then click **All Categories**.

2. In the **Color Categories** dialog box, click the category, and then in the **Shortcut Key** list, click the key combination you want.

3. Click **OK**.

Custom Categories

You can rename a default color category and change its color to create a new category. Twenty-five colors are available, but if that's not sufficient, you can assign the same color to multiple categories. You can also create new categories from scratch.

> ➤ **To create a custom category**

1. Display the categories list, and click **All Categories**.

2. In the **Color Categories** dialog box, click **New**.

3. In the **Name** box of the **Add New Category** dialog box, type a name for the category.

4. Click the **Color** arrow, and click the color you want to associate with the new category.

5. Click the **Shortcut Key** arrow, and click the keyboard shortcut you want.

6. Click **OK** twice.

> ➤ **To rename a color category**

1. Display the categories list, and click **All Categories**.

2. In the **Color Categories** dialog box, click the name of a color category (not the check box), and then click **Rename**.

3. With the category name selected for editing, type the name you want, and then press **Enter**.

4. Click **OK**.

Automatic Color Display

To help you easily distinguish messages received from certain people, you can have Outlook display the message headers in different colors when they are received in your Inbox. You can also choose to have messages that were sent only to you displayed in a different color than messages sent to multiple people or a distribution list. This method does not assign the messages to a color category, but it does make it easy to visually identify them.

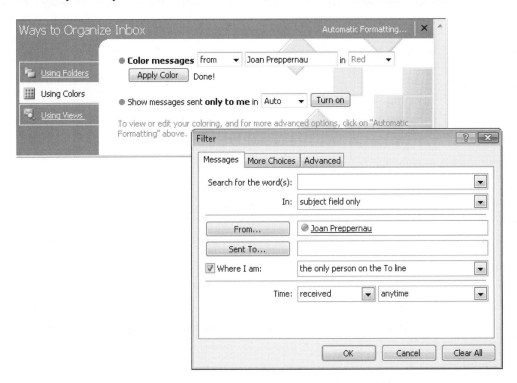

➤ **To display the headers of messages from a specific person in color**

1. In your **Inbox**, click a message from the person whose message headers you want to display in color.

2. On the **Tools** menu, click **Organize**.

3. In the **Ways to Organize Inbox** pane, click **Using Colors**.

4. In the color list, click the color you want, and then click **Apply Color**.

5. To refine the color rule, click **Automatic Formatting**. Then in the **Automatic Formatting** dialog box, in the **Rules for this view** list, click the **Mail received from** rule you just created, and click **Condition**. In the **Filter** dialog box, change settings as necessary, and then click **OK** twice.

6. Close the **Ways to Organize Inbox** pane.

Sorting

To quickly view the messages and tasks belonging to a category, you can sort them. By default, the uncategorized items are shown at the top of the list. You can also sort contacts by their categories.

➤ **To sort messages or tasks by category**

1. At the top of the message list or task list, click **Arranged By**, and then click **Categories**.

2. To display the categorized messages at the top of the message list, to the right of the **Arranged By** bar, click **A on top**.

➤ **To sort calendar items by category**

→ In the **Calendar** module, point to **Current View** on the **View** menu, and then click **By Category**.

➤ **To sort contacts by category**

→ In the **Contacts** module, in the **Current View** area of the **Navigation Pane**, click **By Category**.

Practice Tasks

You need to have a working Outlook account to complete these tasks. There are no practice files for these tasks.

● In your Inbox, assign two messages to the blue category and two to the green category.

● Create a new category named *Management* with the assigned color of orange and the assigned shortcut key of Ctrl+F2. Then assign one blue message and one green message to the Management category.

● Arrange your Inbox by category.

● Assign two contacts to the Management category. Then sort your contacts list by category.

5.2 Create and manage Outlook 2007 data files

The items you create and receive in Outlook—including messages, appointments, contacts, tasks, notes, and journal entries—are kept in a data file in one of the following locations:

- **On a network server.** If your Outlook items are stored on a server, which is usually the case when you are working on a network that uses Exchange Server, they are stored in a data file called a *private store*. You can access this store only when you are connected to your server. This is the most common storage configuration.

- **On your computer.** If your Outlook items are stored on your computer, they are stored in a data file called a *Personal Folders file*, which has a .pst file extension.

Whether your Outlook items are stored on a server or on your computer, you can create a Personal Folders file at any time. You can name the file to reflect its contents and store it anywhere on your hard disk. By default, a newly created Personal Folders file contains only a Deleted Items folder and a Search Folders folder, but you can create subfolders within the Personal Folders file in the same way you would within your Inbox.

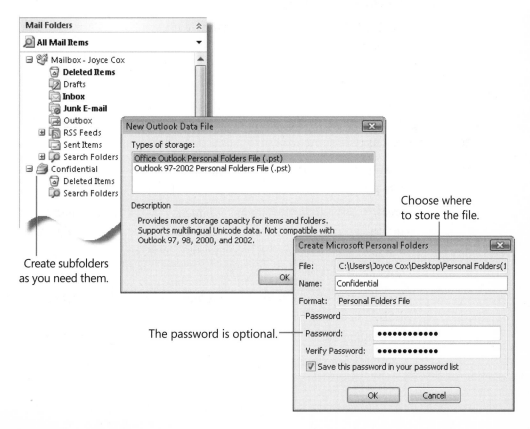

Create subfolders as you need them.

Choose where to store the file.

The password is optional.

➤ **To create a new Personal Folders file**

1. On the **File** menu, point to **New**, and then click **Outlook Data File**.

2. With **Office Outlook Personal Folders File (.pst)** selected in the **New Outlook Data File** dialog box, click **OK**.

   Tip If you want to use the Personal Folders file on a computer running an older version of Outlook, you must export the file in the Outlook 97-2002 Personal Folders File format. Both file formats have the same extension (.pst).

3. In the **Create or Open Outlook Data File** dialog box, navigate to the location where you want to save the file, and then click **OK**.

4. In the **Create Microsoft Personal Folders** dialog box, assign a display name and a password (optional), and then click **OK**.

➤ **To export Outlook items as a .pst file**

1. On the **File** menu, click **Import and Export**.

2. In the **Choose an action to perform** list on the first page of the **Import and Export Wizard**, click **Export to a file**, and then click **Next**.

3. In the **Create a file of type** list, click **Personal Folder File (.pst)**, and then click **Next**.

4. In the **Select the folder to export from** list, click the folder you want to export as a .pst file, and then click **Next**.

5. Click **Browse** to the right of the **Save exported file as** box. Then in the **Open Personal Folders** dialog box, navigate to the location where you want to save the file, type a name for the file, and click **OK**.

6. Click **Finish**.

7. In the **Create Microsoft Personal Folders** dialog box, assign a display name and a password (optional), and then click **OK**.

➤ **To open a data file**

1. On the **File** menu, point to **Open**, and then click **Outlook Data File**.

2. In the **Open Outlook Data File** dialog box, locate and double-click the file you want to open.

➤ **To close a data file**

→ In the **Navigation Pane**, right-click the data file, and then click **Close "*<file>*"**.

➤ **To change the display name of a data file**

1. In the **Navigation Pane**, right-click the data file, and then click **Properties for "<*file*>"**.

2. In the **Properties** dialog box, click **Advanced**.

3. In the **Name** box, type the display name you want.

4. Click **OK** twice.

➤ **To add a data file created on a different computer to your Outlook profile**

1. On the **Tools** menu, click **Account Settings**.

2. On the **Data Files** tab of the **Account Settings** dialog box, click **Add**.

3. In the **New Outlook Data File** dialog box, select **Office Outlook Personal Folders File (.pst)**, and click **OK**.

4. In the **Create or Open Outlook Data File** window, locate and double-click the data file you want to add.

5. In the **Personal Folders** dialog box, change the display name and assign a password if necessary, and then click **OK**.

6. Close the **Account Settings** dialog box.

➤ **To remove a data file from your Outlook profile**

1. On the **Tools** menu, click **Account Settings**.

2. On the **Data Files** tab of the **Account Settings** dialog box, select the file that you want to delete, and click **Remove**.

3. Close the **Account Settings** dialog box.

Practice Tasks

You need to have a working Outlook account to complete these tasks. There are no practice files for these tasks.

- Create a new Personal Folders file named *MCAS Confidential*, and save it on your desktop. Then close the data file.

- Export the contents of your Contacts folder as *MCAS Contacts.pst*, and save it on your desktop so that it is available in the Navigation Pane.

- Open the *MCAS Confidential* data file by adding it to your Outlook profile.

- Change the display name of the *MCAS Confidential* data file to *MCAS Private*.

5.3   Organize mail folders

Folder Structure

If you keep messages for future reference, the number of messages in your Inbox can increase to hundreds and even thousands. To avoid an accumulation of unrelated messages, you can create folders in which to organize messages.

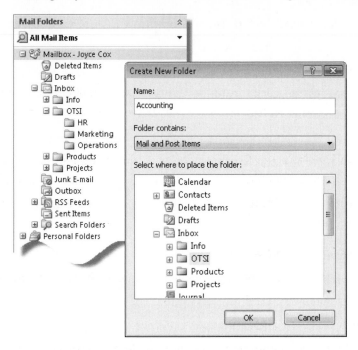

You can move messages to folders manually, or you can create rules that tell Outlook which messages to move where.

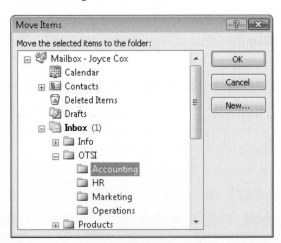

See Also   For information about rules, see section 5.5, "Create, modify, and remove rules to manage e-mail messages."

If your Outlook items are stored on a server in a private store and your administrator restricts the amount of storage space available for your account, you can create a Personal Folders file on your local computer and use the same techniques to move messages from your private store to folders created within your Personal Folders file.

See Also   For information about Personal Folders files, see section 5.2, "Create and manage Outlook 2007 data files."

➤ **To create a new mail folder**

1. In the **Navigation Pane**, click the folder in which you want to create a subfolder, and then on the **Standard** toolbar, in the **New** list, click **Folder**.

   Or

   In the **Navigation Pane**, right-click the folder in which you want to create a subfolder, and click **New Folder**.

2. In the **Name** box of the **Create New Folder** dialog box, type the folder name, and then click **OK**.

➤ **To move a message to a different folder**

→ Drag the message from the message list to the folder in the **Navigation Pane**.

   Or

1. Right-click the message, and click **Move to Folder**.

2. In the **Move Items** dialog box, in the **Move the selected items to the folder** list, click the folder where you want to move the message, and then click **OK**.

➤ **To move a folder to another location**

→ In the **Navigation Pane**, drag the folder to its new location.

   Or

1. In the **Navigation Pane**, right-click the folder, and click **Move "*<folder name>*"**.

2. In the **Move Folder** dialog box, click the destination folder, and then click **OK**.

Archiving

Archiving messages helps control clutter and the size of your primary data file, while still allowing easy access to the archived messages from within Outlook. By default, Outlook automatically archives messages in all your folders at regular intervals to a location determined by your operating system—usually an archive data file you can access from the Navigation Pane. The data file contents are organized in the same folder structure as the original contents.

You can change the following settings in the AutoArchive dialog box:

- Archive frequency and location
- Whether Outlook requests approval to run the autoarchive process
- How old an item is before it is archived
- Whether old items are permanently deleted
- Whether the archive data file is displayed in the Folder List

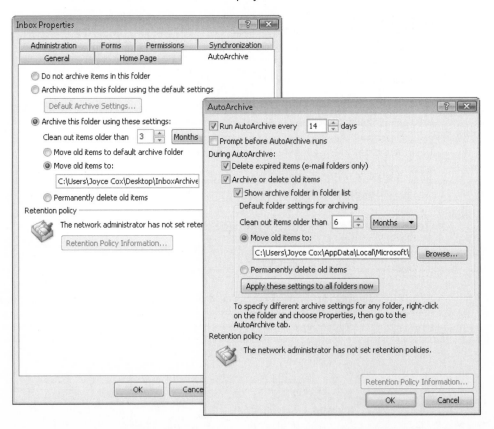

(If you are working on an Exchange Server network, your archival options might be limited by retention policies set by your network administrator.)

You can set the archive options for each folder individually from the AutoArchive tab of the folder's Properties dialog box, as follows:

● If you select the Archive Items In This Folder Using The Default Settings option, you can view and modify the default settings in the AutoArchive dialog box by clicking the Default Archive Settings button.

● If you select the Archive This Folder Using These Settings option, you can specify a unique archival age and location for the items in this folder.

If you turn off autoarchiving, you can manually archive your entire mailbox or selected folders from the Archive dialog box. When you click OK, Outlook displays archiving progress on the status bar in the lower-right corner of the program window. You can cancel an archive process by clicking the Archiving button on the status bar and then, in the list, clicking Cancel Archiving.

Tip You can restore archived Outlook items from the Archive Folders data file by dragging or moving them to mailbox folders.

➤ **To change the global autoarchive settings**

1. On the **Tools** menu, click **Options**.

2. On the **Other** tab of the **Options** dialog box, click **AutoArchive**.

3. In the **AutoArchive** dialog box, adjust the settings as you want them.

4. To apply the changes to all the folders in your mailbox, click **Apply these settings to all folders now**.

5. Click **OK** twice.

➤ **To change the autoarchive settings for one folder**

1. In the **Navigation Pane**, right-click the folder, and then click **Properties**.

2. On the **AutoArchive** tab of the **Properties** dialog box, click **Archive this folder using these settings**.

3. Make changes to the folder's autoarchive settings, and then click **OK**.

➤ **To manually archive messages**

1. On the **Tools** menu, click **Options**.

2. On the **Other** tab of the **Options** dialog box, click **AutoArchive**.

3. In the **AutoArchive** dialog box, adjust the settings, and then click **OK** twice.

Tip You can click Mailbox Cleanup on the Tools menu to see the size of your mailbox, find and delete old items or items that are larger than a certain size, manually archive your mail, empty your Deleted Items folder, and delete conflicting versions of items stored on your computer or on the server.

Sent Messages

By default, a copy of each message you send is saved in the Sent Items folder, and this folder can quickly become bloated with copies you don't need. If you delete the copies in the normal way, you can end up with a hefty Deleted Items folder. For efficiency, you can purge your Sent Items folder while bypassing the Deleted Items folder.

If you want to keep copies of only important messages, or if you want to choose where copies are saved, you can override the default option for individual messages by instructing Outlook not to save a copy or to save a copy in a different folder.

➤ **To empty the Sent Items folder**

1. In your Sent Items folder, select the items you want to delete.

2. Press **Delete** to move the selected items to the Deleted Items folder, or press **Shift+Delete** to permanently delete the selected items.

➤ **To tell Outlook not to save a copy of a sent message**

1. On the **Options** tab of the message window, in the **More Options** group, click the **Save Sent Item** button.

2. In the list, click **Do Not Save**.

➤ **To save a copy of a sent message in a different folder**

1. On the **Options** tab of the message window, in the **More Options** group, click the **Save Sent Item** button.

2. In the list, click **Other Folder**.

3. In the **Select Folder** dialog box, click the folder you want, and then click **OK**.

➤ **To stop saving sent messages in the Sent Items folder**

1. On the **Tools** menu, click **Options**.

2. On the **Preferences** tab of the **Options** dialog box, click **E-mail Options**.

3. In the **E-mail Options** dialog box, in the **Message handling** area, clear the **Save copies of messages in the Sent Items folder** check box, and then click **OK** twice.

Deleted Items

When you delete a message, contact record, or any other item, Outlook temporarily moves it to the Deleted Items folder. You can open the folder from the Navigation Pane, view items that have been deleted but not purged, and restore items (undelete them) by moving them to other folders.

Outlook does not permanently delete an item unless you do one of the following:

- Delete the item while bypassing the Deleted Items folder.
- Delete the item from the Deleted Items folder.
- Empty the Deleted Items folder manually or automatically.

➤ **To bypass the Deleted Items folder**

→ Click the item you want to delete, and then press **Shift+Delete**.

➤ **To empty the Deleted Items folder**

1. In the **Navigation Pane**, right-click **Deleted Items**, and click **Empty "Deleted Items" Folder**.

2. In the message box asking you to confirm the deletion, click **Yes**.

➤ **To empty the Deleted Items folder when exiting Outlook**

1. On the **Tools** menu, click **Options**.

2. On the **Other** tab of the **Options** dialog box, select the **Empty the Deleted Items folder upon exiting** check box, and then click **OK**.

Junk Mail

Outlook offers levels of protection for managing junk e-mail messages, also called *spam*. In the Junk E-mail Options dialog box, you can change settings such as the following:

- Turn on the Junk E-Mail Filter, with varying degrees of protection. If you don't have additional filters in place, such as those that might be supplied by your organization, you might prefer to select the High option. Otherwise, select Low.

- Specify whether suspected junk e-mail should be deleted rather than moved to a special folder. Do not select this check box if you set the protection level to High or to Safe Lists Only. With these settings, it is likely that the Junk E-Mail Filter will catch quite a few valid messages that you don't want deleted.

- Clear the Disable Links And Other Functionality In Phishing Messages check box. Unless you are very confident that you have another protective system in place, leave this option selected.

- Add a specific person's e-mail address to the Safe Senders List, or specify that e-mail received from any sender at a particular domain is safe by adding only the domain.

- Ensure that messages from your legitimate contacts aren't held by the Junk E-Mail Filter by selecting the Also Trust E-mail From My Contacts and Automatically Add People I E-mail To The Safe Senders List check boxes.

- Add distribution lists or mailing lists to which you belong to your Safe Recipients List to ensure that messages sent to them won't be treated as junk e-mail.

- Manually add e-mail addresses and domain names to the Blocked Senders List. Outlook will add these for you when you identify a received message as junk e-mail.

- Block all messages from a country-specific, top-level domain (click Blocked Top-Level Domain List to see them all), or all messages containing specific non-English text encoding (click Blocked Encodings List to see them all).

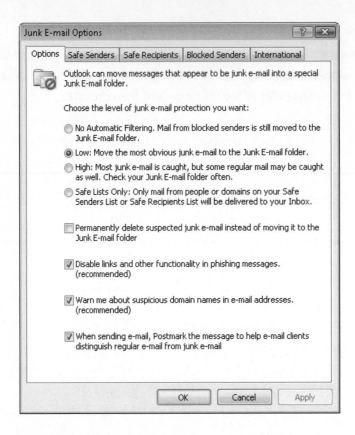

➤ **To add a user or domain to the Safe Senders, Safe Recipients, or Blocked Senders list**

→ In the message list, right-click a message header, point to **Junk E-Mail**, and then click **Add Sender to Blocked Senders List**, **Add Sender to Safe Senders List**, **Add Sender's Domain to Safe Senders List**, or **Add Recipient to Safe Recipients List**.

Or

1. On the **Actions** menu, point to **Junk E-mail**, and then click **Junk E-mail Options**.

2. In the **Junk E-mail Options** dialog box, click the tab for the category you want.

3. Click **Add**. Then in the **Add address or domain** dialog box, enter the address or domain, and click **OK**.

4. Adjust any other junk e-mail settings, and then click **OK**.

➤ **To tell Outlook that a message in the Junk E-mail folder is not junk**

1. Right-click the message, point to **Junk E-mail**, then click **Mark as Not Junk**.

2. In the **Mark as Not Junk** dialog box, select the check box if you want to always trust e-mail from the sender of the message, and then click **OK**.

➤ **To empty the Junk E-mail folder**

1. In the **Navigation Pane**, right-click the **Junk E-mail** folder, and click **Empty "Junk E-mail" Folder**.

2. Click **Yes** when asked to confirm that you want to permanently delete the items in the folder.

Practice Tasks

You need to have a working Outlook account to complete these tasks. There are no practice files for these tasks.

● Create a folder named *MCAS Practice Messages* as a subfolder of your Inbox, and drag a message you have created in previous practice tasks from the message list to the new subfolder. Then use the Move To Folder command to move a different practice message to the new folder.

● Change the autoarchive settings of the MCAS Practice Messages folder so that Outlook will run the archival process every three months and will store old items in a data file stored on your desktop.

● Create a message addressed to yourself with the subject *MCAS Copy*. Before sending the message, specify that a copy be saved in the MCAS Practice Messages folder.

● Set the Deleted Items folder to be emptied when you exit Outlook.

● In your Inbox, use a message from someone you trust to add that person's e-mail address to your Safe Senders list. Then if your Junk E-mail folder contains no messages you want to keep, empty it.

Important Be sure reset your autoarchive and Deleted Items settings the way you want them.

5.4   Locate Outlook 2007 items by using the search feature

Instant Search

The Instant Search feature is based on the same technology that drives the search functionality in Windows Vista. With this very powerful search engine, you can find any file on your computer containing a specified search term—including in an e-mail message header, in the message itself, or in a message attachment.

Although you can use Instant Search to locate calendar items, contact records, and tasks, you will most often use it to locate messages in your Inbox and other mail folders. You can search a particular mail folder or search all mail folders. As you type the search term, Outlook filters out all messages that don't match, displays only those items containing the characters you enter, and highlights the search term in the displayed messages, making it easy to find exactly what you're looking for. In the lower-left corner of the program window, the status bar displays the number of messages included in the search results.

Unless you specify otherwise, the search results include only the contents of the displayed folder, not any of its subfolders or any other folders. However, you can choose to search all mail folders or all Outlook items. If you search more than one folder, Outlook displays the search results grouped by the folder in which they appear.

You can open, delete, and process a message from the Search Results pane as you would from any other folder. However, if you change a message so that it no longer fits the search criteria, the message is removed from the Search Results pane.

➤ **To search a specific e-mail folder**

1. In the **Mail** module, click the folder in the **Navigation Pane**.
2. In the **Search** box at the top of the message list, type the search term.
3. To clear the filter, click the **Clear Search** button to the right of the **Search** box.

➤ **To search all e-mail folders**

1. In the **Mail** module, click the **Show Instant Search Pane Menu** arrow to the right of the **Search** box, and then click **Search All Mail Items**.

2. In the **Search** box at the top of the message pane, type the search term.

3. To clear the filter, click the **Clear Search** button to the right of the **Search** box or any folder in the **Navigation Pane**.

   Or

   → If you have already searched one folder and you want to expand the search to include all the folders in your mailbox, at the bottom of the **Search Results** pane, click **Try Searching Again In All Mail Items**.

➤ **To find a calendar item, contact, or task**

   → In the corresponding module, type a search term in the **Search** box at the top of the **Content** pane.

   → To clear the filter, click the **Clear Search** button to the right of the **Search** box.

➤ **To find all items related to a specific person**

1. Display the **Folder List**, and then click **All Outlook Items**.

2. Type a search term in the **Search** box at the top of the **Content** pane.

3. To clear the filter, click the **Clear Search** button to the right of the **Search** box.

➤ **To quickly return to previous search results**

   → Click the **Show Instant Search Pane Menu** arrow at the right end of the **Search** box, point to **Recent Searches**, and then click the search term you want.

Query Builder

If the search term you enter produces more than 200 results, the Search Results pane displays this information bar:

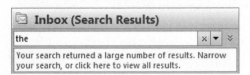

You can display all the results for the current search term by clicking the message bar, or you can narrow the results by using the Query Builder to specify additional search criteria, such as the name of the sender, the recipient (whether the message was addressed or only copied to you), whether the message contains attachments, and so on.

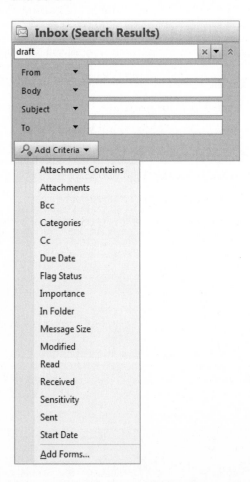

➤ **To refine a search**

1. Click the **Expand the Query Builder** button to the right of the **Search** box.

2. To add a field, click **Add Criteria**, and click the field in the list.

3. Type additional search terms in any appropriate field.

➤ **To search for all items in a category**

1. Display the **Folder List**, and then click **All Outlook Items**.

2. Click the **Expand the Query Builder** button to the right of the **Search** box.

3. Click **Add Criteria**, and then click **Categories** in the list.

4. In the **Categories** list, click the category you want.

Search Folders

The Search Folders module is part of your mailbox. A Search Folder is a virtual folder that contains pointers to all the messages in your mailbox that match a specific set of search criteria, no matter which folders the messages are actually stored in. Depending on the contents of your Inbox and your previous use of Outlook, you might have any of the following four folders within the Search Folders folder:

- The Categorized Mail folder displays messages assigned to a category.
- The For Follow Up folder displays messages flagged for future action.
- The Large Mail folder displays messages larger than 100 kilobytes (KB).
- The Unread Mail folder displays messages that are marked as unread.

In addition to taking advantage of the default Search Folders, you can create your own to conveniently gather together related messages. When you create a Search Folder, it becomes part of your mailbox and is kept up to date.

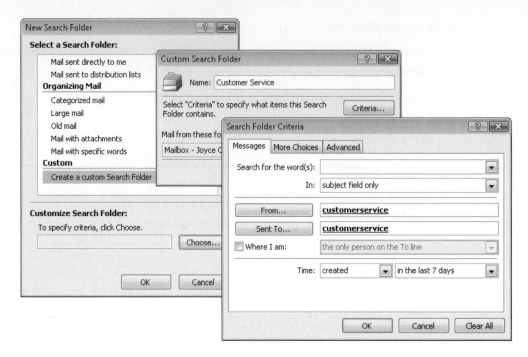

Tip The names of folders whose contents are not up to date are italic. To update a Search Folder, click the folder name.

Each message in your mailbox is stored in only one folder, but it might appear in several Search Folders. Changing or deleting a message in a Search Folder changes or deletes the message in the folder where it is stored.

➤ To create a new Search Folder

1. In the **Navigation Pane**, right-click the **Search Folders** folder, and click **New Search Folder**.

2. In the **New Search Folder** dialog box, select the type of Search Folder you want to create.

3. If you need to set additional criteria, click **Choose** in the **Customize Search Folder** area, enter the criteria, and then click **OK**.

   Tip If you are creating a custom Search Folder, you will need to enter a name for the folder before clicking Criteria to enter the criteria for the search.

4. Click **OK** to close any open dialog boxes.

➤ **To change the contents of an existing Search Folder**

1. In the **Navigation Pane**, right-click the folder, and click **Customize this Search Folder**.

2. In the **Customize "*<folder>*"** dialog box, make the changes you want, and then click **OK**.

Practice Tasks

You need to have a working Outlook account to complete these tasks. There are no practice files for these tasks.

- Use the Instant Search feature to locate a specific message in your Inbox. For example, if you completed the previous tasks, you could enter the search term *schedule* or *signature*. Then without changing the query, expand it to include all Outlook items.

- Search all Outlook items for anything related to a specific person, such as your manager.

- Search all Outlook items for anything you have assigned to a specific category, such as the Management category. Then search for all items that have attachments.

- Create a new Search Folder containing all the messages in your Inbox (not your mailbox) from a specific person, such as your boss.

5.5 Create, modify, and remove rules to manage e-mail messages

You can have Outlook evaluate your incoming or outgoing e-mail messages and make decisions about what to do with them based on instructions called *rules*. You can create rules based on senders, recipients, words, attachments, categories, or other message criteria, and have Outlook automatically move, copy, delete, forward, redirect, reply to, or otherwise process messages based on those criteria.

Any Outlook user can set up client rules that are applied to messages stored on the computer. If you have a Microsoft Exchange Server account, you can set up server rules that are applied to messages as they are received or processed by your Exchange server.

You can base a rule on one of the ten rule templates provided by Outlook. Clicking a template on the first page of the Rules Wizard displays an example in the Edit The Rule Description box. If none of the templates meets your needs, you can start from a blank rule, or you can copy and modify an existing rule. All the rules you specify are summarized in the Rules And Alerts dialog box, from which you can modify, copy, delete, and run them. (Rules whose check boxes are selected will be run automatically.)

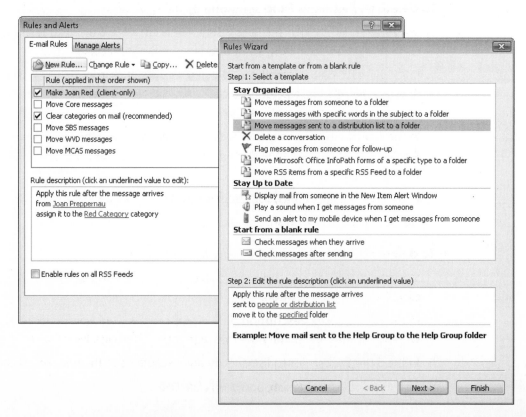

➤ **To move messages by using a rule**

1. On the **Tools** menu, click **Rules and Alerts**. Then in the **Rules and Alerts** window, on the **E-mail Rules** tab, click **New Rule**.

2. On the first page of the **Rules Wizard**, below **Stay Organized** in the **Select a template** list, click one of the first three **Move** rules, and then click **Next**.

3. In the **Select condition(s)** list, select the conditions you want to apply to your new rule. Then in the **Edit the rule description** area, click the underlined words or phrases, and replace them with criteria that will select the target messages. Click **Next**.

4. In the **Select action(s)** list, select the move action you want Outlook to perform. Then in the **Edit the rule description** area, click the underlined words or phrases, and replace them with the specific action. Click **Next**.

5. Select any exceptions to the rule, and make them specific. Then click **Next**.

6. Specify a name for the new rule, select the **Turn on this rule** check box, and click **Finish**.

7. Click **OK** to close the **Rules and Alerts** dialog box.

➤ **To delete all messages from someone by using a rule**

1. Start the **Rules Wizard**, and in the **Select a template** list, under **Stay Organized**, click **Move messages from someone to a folder**. Then click **Next**.

2. In the **Edit the rule description** box, click **people or distribution list**, and in the **Rule Address** dialog box, double-click a name in an address book or type an e-mail address in the **From** box. Click **OK**.

3. In the **Edit the rule description** area, click **specified**, and then in the **Rules and Alerts** dialog box, click the **Deleted Items** folder. Click **OK**, and then click **Next** three times.

4. In the **Select exception(s)** list, specify any exceptions to the rule, and click **Next**.

5. Name the rule, click **Finish**, and then click **OK**.

➤ **To delete all messages about a topic by using a rule**

1. Start the **Rules Wizard**, and in the **Select a template** list, below **Stay Organized**, click **Delete a conversation**.

2. In the **Edit the rule description** box, click the underlined words, and replace them with words that will identify the message topic. Then click **Next** three times.

3. In the **Select exception(s)** list, specify any exceptions to the rule, and click **Next**.

4. Name the rule, click **Finish**, and then click **OK**.

➤ **To categorize messages by using a rule**

1. Start the **Rules Wizard**, and in the **Select a template** list, below **Start from a blank rule**, click **Check messages when they arrive**. Click **Next**.

2. Select the condition under which you want a message to be assigned to a category, and click **Next**.

3. Select **assign it to the category**, and in the rule description area, click the under-lined **category**.

4. In the **Color Categories** dialog box, select a category check box, and click **OK**. Then click **Next**.

5. In the **Select exception(s)** list, specify any exceptions to the rule, and click **Next**.

6. Name the rule, click **Finish**, and then click **OK**.

➤ **To forward messages by using a rule**

1. Start the **Rules Wizard**, and then in the **Select a template** list, below **Start from a blank rule**, click **Check messages when they arrive**. Click **Next**.

2. In the **Select condition(s)** list, select the conditions you want to apply to your new rule. Then in the **Edit the rule description** box, click the underlined word(s), and replace them with rule-specific text. Click **Next**.

3. In the **Select action(s)** list, select the **forward it to people or distribution list** check box. Then in the **Edit the rule description** box, click **people or distribution list**, and replace the underlined text with a specific e-mail address. Click **Next**.

4. In the **Select exception(s)** list, specify any exceptions to the rule, and click **Next**.

5. Name the rule, click **Finish**, and then click **OK**.

➤ **To create a new rule based on an existing rule**

1. Display the **Rules and Alerts** dialog box, and on the **E-mail Rules** tab, click the rule you want to use as the basis for the new rule. Then click **Copy**.

2. In the **Copy rule to** dialog box, click **OK**.

3. With the copy selected, click **Change Rule**, and then click **Edit Rule Settings** to start the Rules Wizard.

4. Adapt the rule by changing it as necessary.

5. Name the rule, click **Finish**, and then click **OK**.

➤ **To run a rule on existing messages**

1. Display the **Rules and Alerts** dialog box, and on the **E-mail Rules** tab, click **Run Rules Now**.

2. In the **Run Rules Now** dialog box, select the check box of the rule you want to run, change the remaining settings as necessary, and then click **Run Now**.

3. Click **Close**, and then click **OK**.

➤ **To delete a rule**

1. Display the **Rules and Alerts** window, and on the **E-mail Rules** tab, click the rule you want to delete.

2. Click **Delete**, and then confirm the deletion by clicking **Yes**.

Tip If you are using Exchange Server, you can create rules to filter messages differently when you are away from the office by using the Out of Office Assistant. To find out how, click Out Of Office Assistant on the Tools menu.

Practice Tasks

You need to have a working Outlook account to complete these tasks. There are no practice files for these tasks.

- Create a subfolder of your Inbox named *High*, and then flag a few messages in your Inbox for follow up today. Create a rule that moves all the messages flagged for follow up to the High folder, and run the rule on your Inbox.

- Create a rule that assigns all incoming messages from your manager to the Red Category or another category of your choosing. Run the rule on your Inbox.

- Create a distribution list that includes only your own e-mail address, and then create a rule that forwards all messages from a specific colleague or friend to the distribution list. Run the rule on your Inbox.

- Delete the three rules you just created.

Important Be sure to move messages back into your Inbox and delete any flags and category assignments you don't want to keep.

5.6   Customize your Outlook 2007 experience

To-Do Bar

On the right side of the Outlook window, the To-Do Bar displays a monthly calendar, your upcoming appointments, and your task list. You can minimize, maximize, or turn off the bar; change the number of calendar months and appointments shown; and arrange the task list in different ways. When minimized, the To-Do Bar displays your next appointment and the number of active and completed tasks due today.

See Also For more information about managing the To-Do Bar, see "Prerequisites" at the beginning of this exam.

➤ To customize the To-Do Bar

1. On the **View** menu, point to **To-Do Bar**, and then click **Options**.
2. Select the options you want, and then click **OK**.

Default Message Format

Outlook can send and receive e-mail messages in three message formats:

● **Hypertext Markup Language (HTML).** Supports paragraph styles (including numbered and bulleted lists), character styles (such as fonts, sizes, colors, weight), and backgrounds (such as colors and pictures). Most (but not all) e-mail programs—those that don't display HTML messages as Plain Text—support the HTML format.

● **Rich Text Format (RTF).** Supports more paragraph formatting options than HTML, including borders and shading, but is compatible with only Outlook and Microsoft Exchange Server. Outlook converts RTF messages to HTML when sending them outside of your Exchange network.

● **Plain Text.** Does not support the formatting features available in HTML and RTF messages, but is supported by all e-mail programs.

Depending on who you communicate with most often, you might want to change your default message format to one that is compatible with the e-mail programs used by likely message recipients.

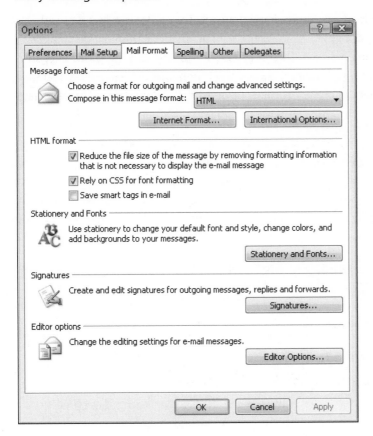

➤ **To set the default message format**

1. On the **Tools** menu, click **Options**.

2. On the **Mail Format** tab of the **Options** dialog box, in the **Message format** area, click one of the formats in the **Compose in this message format** list, and then click **OK**.

Default Message Look

By default, the content of an Outlook message appears in black, 10-point Calibri (a very readable sans serif font that is new in this release of the Office system), arranged in left-aligned paragraphs on a white background. You can change the appearance of individual messages either by applying local formatting or global formatting. The local formatting options are largely the same text and paragraph attributes as those available in Word and other programs in the 2007 Office system. The global formatting options use themes to apply a pre-selected combination of formatting options to the entire message and styles to apply sets of formatting options to individual elements of a message.

In addition to formatting messages on a case-by-case basis, you can change the default look of all new messages. You can choose a theme or a combination of effects called *stationery* that controls the background and fonts used in all your messages. If you don't choose a theme or stationery, you can separately specify the font, size, style, and color of the text of new messages, responses and forwarded messages, and messages sent in Plain Text format.

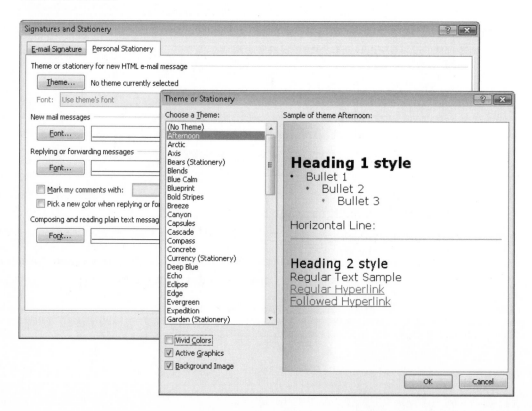

See Also For information about themes, see section 1.1, "Create and format documents" in Exam 77-601, "Using Microsoft Office Word 2007." For information about styles, see section 2.1, "Format text and paragraphs," in the same exam.

➤ **To set a default theme or stationery for all new messages**

1. On the **Tools** menu, click **Options**.

2. On the **Mail Format** tab of the **Options** dialog box, click **Stationery and Fonts**.

3. On the **Personal Stationery** tab of the **Signatures and Stationery** dialog box, click **Theme**.

4. In the **Theme or Stationery** dialog box, in the **Choose a Theme** list, click a theme, and then click **OK** three times.

➤ **To set a default font for new messages**

1. Display the **Mail Format** tab of the **Options** dialog box, and then click **Stationery and Fonts**.

2. On the **Personal Stationery** tab of the **Signatures and Stationery** dialog box, in the **New mail messages** area, click **Font**.

3. In the **Font** dialog box, set the options you want, and then click **OK**.

Outlook Anywhere

If you work on a network domain, Outlook communicates with your organization's Exchange server by using remote procedure calls (RPC). If your organization is running Microsoft Exchange Server 2003 or later on Microsoft Windows Server 2003, your Exchange administrator can configure the server to permit connections that use the RPC communication path. You can then connect to your Exchange account over the Internet by using the Outlook Anywhere feature (formerly called *RPC over HTTP*). No special connection is required. This is by far the simplest method of remotely accessing Exchange resources.

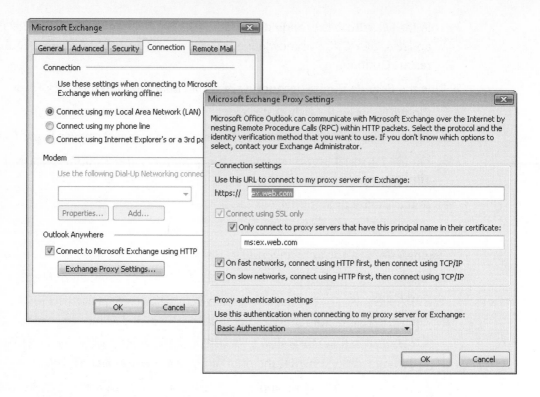

➤ To configure Outlook Anywhere

1. On the **Tools** menu, click **Account Settings**.

2. On the **E-mail** tab of the **Account Settings** dialog box, in the **Name** list, click your **Microsoft Exchange** account, and then click **Change**.

3. In the **Change E-mail Account** dialog box, click **More Settings**.

4. In the **Microsoft Exchange** dialog box, click the **Connection** tab.

5. In the **Outlook Anywhere** area, select the **Connect to Microsoft Exchange using HTTP** check box.

6. Click **Exchange Proxy Settings**.

7. In the **Microsoft Exchange Proxy Settings** dialog box, in the **Connection settings** area, type your organization's secure Exchange proxy address in the **https://** box. Then click **OK**.

    Tip You can choose to have Outlook connect first through Outlook Anywhere and then transfer the connection to TCP/IP, by selecting either or both of the check boxes at the bottom of the Connection Settings area. Your organization might require an authentication method other than the default; check with your network administrator.

8. In the **Microsoft Exchange** dialog box, click **OK**. Then in the message box that appears, click **OK** to acknowledge that the change will not take effect until you restart Outlook.

9. In the **Change E-mail Account** dialog box, click **Next**, and then click **Finish**.

10. Close the **Account Settings** dialog box, and then quit and restart Outlook.

11. In the **Connect to** dialog box, enter your user name and password, and then click **OK**.

Tip Be sure to repeat these steps to turn off Outlook Anywhere if you don't want to use it.

Practice Tasks

You need to have a working Outlook account to complete these tasks. There are no practice files for these tasks.

● Minimize the To-Do Bar, and then remove it from the program window completely.

● Change the To-Do Bar options to display two months in the Date Navigator and two appointments, and then redisplay the bar in Normal view.

● With no default theme applied, change the font for all new messages to dark blue, 10-point Verdana. Then send yourself a message.

● Change the theme applied to all new messages to Network. Then send yourself a new message.

Important Be sure to reset the message format and theme or font to those you prefer.

Objective Review

Before finishing this chapter, ensure that you have mastered the following skills:

5.1 Categorize Outlook 2007 items by color.

5.2 Create and manage Outlook 2007 data files.

5.3 Organize mail folders.

5.4 Locate Outlook 2007 items by using the search feature.

5.5 Create, modify, and remove rules to manage e-mail messages.

5.6 Customize your Outlook 2007 experience.

Using Microsoft Office
Access 2007

This part of the book covers the skills you need to have for certification as a Microsoft Office Specialist in Microsoft Office Access 2007. Specifically, you need to be able to complete tasks that demonstrate the following skill sets:

1 Structuring a Database

2 Creating and Formatting Database Elements

3 Entering and Modifying Data

4 Creating and Modifying Queries

5 Presenting and Sharing Data

6 Managing and Maintaining Databases

With these skills, you can create and manage the types of databases most commonly used in a business environment.

Prerequisites

We assume that you have been working with Access 2007 for at least six months and that you know how to carry out fundamental tasks that are not specifically mentioned in the Microsoft Office Specialist objectives for Exam 77-605, "Using Microsoft Office Access 2007." Before you begin studying for this exam, you might want to make sure you are familiar with the information in this section.

Working with Databases

Some databases contain macros that can run code on your computer. In most cases, the code is there to perform a database-related task, but hackers can also use macros to spread a virus to your computer. When you open a database containing one or more macros, if the database is not stored in a Trusted Location or signed by a Trusted Publisher, Access displays a security warning just below the Ribbon.

You can enable macros for the current database only, or change the way Access handles macros for all databases. The macro options are:

- **Disable all macros without notification.** If a database contains macros, Access disables them and doesn't display the security warning to give you the option of enabling them.

- **Disable all macros with notification.** Access disables all macros and displays the security warning. This is the default setting.

- **Disable all macros except digitally signed macros.** Access automatically enables digitally signed macros.

- **Enable all macros.** Access automatically enables all macros.

➤ **To display the Getting Started page**

➙ Start Access without opening a database.

➙ In the Access program window, click the **Microsoft Office Button**, and then click **New** or **Close Database**.

➤ **To create a new blank database**

1. On the **Getting Started with Microsoft Access** page, click **Blank Database**.

2. In the **File Name** box, enter a name for the database.

3. Click the **Browse for a location** button, navigate to the folder in which you want to store the database, and then click **OK**.

4. On the **Getting Started with Microsoft Access** page, click **Create**.

➤ **To open an existing database from Access**

1. On the **Office** menu, click **Open**.

2. In the **Open** dialog box, navigate to the folder where the database you want to open is stored, click the database file, and then click **Open**.

➤ **To enable macros in the current database**

1. In the **Security Warning** area, click **Options**.

2. In the **Microsoft Office Security Options** dialog box, select the **Enable this content** option, and then click **OK**.

➤ **To change the way Access handles macros in all databases**

1. On the **Office** menu, click **Access Options**.

2. In the page list on the left side of the **Access Options** dialog box, click **Trust Center**.

3. On the **Trust Center** page, click **Trust Center Settings**.

4. In the **Trust Center** dialog box, display the **Macro Settings** page.

5. Click the option for the way you want Access to handle macros.

6. Click **OK** in the **Trust Center** dialog box and in the **Access Options** dialog box.

➤ **To close a database**

→ On the **Office** menu, click **Close Database**.

Displaying Database Objects

You open database objects from the Navigation Pane that appears on the left side of the database window. You can change the category and grouping of objects displayed in the Navigation Pane by making selections on the Navigation Pane menu at the top of the Navigation Pane.

By default, Access 2007 displays database objects as tabbed documents in the document window. If you prefer, you can display each object in a separate window rather
than on a separate tab. When you are displaying tabbed documents, a Close button for
the active database object appears to the right of the document tabs. When you are
displaying overlapping windows, in a maximized database object window, the Minimize,
Maximize/Restore Down, and Close buttons for the object window appear on the right
end of the Ribbon, and the Access icon appears to the left of the Home tab. Clicking the
Access icon opens the control menu, displaying a list of commands related to managing
the active object window: Restore, Move, Size, Minimize, Maximize, and Close. When a
window is not maximized, clicking the object icon at the left end of the object window
title bar displays the control menu.

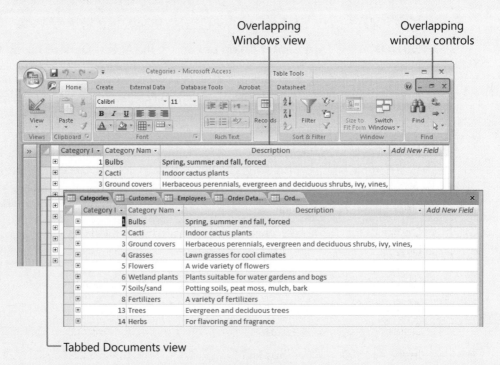

Overlapping
Windows view

Overlapping
window controls

Tabbed Documents view

Every Access object has two or more views. For tables, the most common views are
Datasheet view, in which you can see and modify the table's data, and Design view,
in which you can see and modify the table's structure.

➤ To display objects in the Navigation Pane

1. On the **Navigation Pane** menu, under **Navigate to Category**, click the category of objects you want to display.

2. On the **Navigation Pane** menu, under **Filter By Group**, click the category-specific group of objects you want to display.

   Or

   Click **All Access Objects** to display all groups in the category.

➤ To open a database object

1. In the **Navigation Pane**, display the category of object you want.

2. Expand the category and then double-click the object you want to open.

➤ To open a table in Datasheet view

→ In the **Navigation Pane**, double-click the table name.

→ In the **Navigation Pane**, right-click the table name, and then click **Open**.

➤ To open a table in Design view

→ In the **Navigation Pane**, right-click the table name, and then click **Design View**.

➤ To switch views

→ On the **View** toolbar, click the button for the view you want.

→ On the **Home** tab, in the **Views** group, click the **View** arrow, and then in the list, click the view you want.

➤ To change between tabbed documents and overlapping windows

1. On the **Office** menu, click **Access Options**.

2. Display the **Current Database** page of the **Access Options** dialog box.

3. In the **Application Options** area, under **Document Window Options**, click **Overlapping Windows** or **Tabbed Documents**.

4. If a database is open, close and reopen it for the change to take effect.

➤ To close a tabbed document window

→ Click the **Close Window** button at the right end of the document tab.

Saving in Access

Access saves changes to a database differently depending on whether they are changes to database objects or changes to data.

If you make changes to the design or layout of objects in a database, Access does not save them unless you specifically instruct it to. When you close an object to which you've made changes, Access asks whether you want to save it. When you make changes to data in tables, queries, or forms, Access saves them automatically as soon as you move to another record (or close the form or datasheet). You don't need to explicitly save changes to data.

1 Structuring a Database

The skills tested in this section of the Microsoft Office Specialist exam for Microsoft Office Access 2007 relate to correctly setting up database storage structures to enforce data entry requirements and protect data. Specifically, the following objectives are associated with this set of skills:

1.1 Define data needs and types.
1.2 Define and print table relationships.
1.3 Add, set, change, or remove primary keys.
1.4 Split databases.

Simple database programs store information in only one table. More complex database programs, such as Access, store information in multiple related tables, thereby creating what is known as a *relational database*. You use other database objects, such as forms, queries, and reports, to manage, manipulate, analyze, retrieve, or display the information stored in a table—in other words, to make the information as accessible and therefore as useful as possible. Because this can happen only if the tables are structured correctly, designing a database starts with defining the tables you need and the types of information that can be stored in them. It is also a good idea to identify the primary method of data entry—whether directly into tables, through an input screen, or on a Microsoft SharePoint site—so you can design and save the database in the most appropriate format.

This chapter guides you in studying the principles of database design.

 Important Before you can use the practice files in this chapter, you need to install them from the book's companion CD to their default location. See "Using the Companion CD" at the beginning of this book for more information.

Tip Graphics and operating system–related instructions in this book reflect the Windows Vista user interface. If your computer is running Windows XP and you experience trouble following the instructions as written, refer to the sidebar "If You Are Running Windows XP" in "Working in the Microsoft Office Fluent User Interface" at the beginning of this book.

1.1 Define data needs and types

Strategy It is difficult to test the ability to correctly design a database within the format of the Microsoft Office Specialist exam. However, we recommend that you familiarize yourself with the concepts discussed in the "Database Design" topics in Access Help so that you are prepared for questions on this topic.

Normal Forms

Not many people enjoy typing information into a database table, so an important goal when designing a relational database is to structure the tables in such a way that the database user never has to enter the same information more than once. Equally important is the consideration that if information changes, it should be possible to update it in only one place in the database. Beyond these goals of efficient data entry and ongoing accuracy is the goal of usability. If the database is designed correctly, the information you need can be quickly retrieved in exactly the format in which you need it.

Correct database design involves applying rules that achieve a *Third Normal Form*, or *3NF*, database. A 3NF database includes tables that meet the following criteria:

- **First Normal Form.** In each field of each record, there is only one value that will be manipulated.

- **Second Normal Form.** All the fields in a record can be identified by the primary key field; that is, they are dependent on the primary key. Information that is not dependent on the primary key is stored in a separate table.

  See Also For information about primary keys, see section 1.3, "Add, set, change, or remove primary keys."

- **Third Normal Form.** All the fields in a record are dependent only on the primary key; that is, they are not partially dependent on any other field in the record. Information that is partially dependent on another field is stored in a separate table or calculated in a query.

Data Types

When defining a table, you assign each field the data type that is most appropriate for the type of information you expect the field to contain. The available data types are shown in the following table.

Data type	Holds
Text	General-purpose data up to 255 characters, including letters, numbers, and other characters such as &, %, =, and ?.
Memo	General-purpose data up to 65,535 characters.
Number	Numeric values that can be assigned a Field Size property to restrict their contents.
Date/Time	Dates from January 1, 100 to December 31, 9999, including leap years.
Currency	Numeric values formatted with up to 4 digits to the right of the decimal point and up to 15 to the left. Typically shows negative values in parentheses and is formatted as money.
AutoNumber	Unique sequential or random numeric values automatically assigned by Access to each new record in the table. Cannot be updated.
Yes/No	Boolean data that has only two possible values, such as yes/no or on/off.
OLE Object	A graphic or other object (such as a spreadsheet, audio file, or video file) created with Windows OLE-supporting applications. Can either be linked to the field or embedded in the field.
Hyperlink	A path to a file on your hard disk, a UNC path to a file on your network server, or a URL to an object on the Internet or an intranet.
Attachment	A wide variety of file formats (such as images or spreadsheets). Stores data more efficiently than the OLE Object type.

See Also Most data types are further constrained by field properties. For information about properties, see section 2.4, "Create fields and modify field properties."

Because the data type determines what kind of information can be entered in the field and how Access can work with the information, it is important that you identify the correct data type.

Field Name	Data Type	Description
ProductID	AutoNumber	Number automatically assigned to new product.
ProductName	Text	
SupplierID	Number	Same entry as in Suppliers table.
CategoryID	Number	Same entry as in Categories table.
QuantityPerUnit	Text	(e.g., 1 ea., 25 lb bag, 3 per pkg, etc.)
UnitPrice	Currency	
UnitsInStock	Number	
UnitsOnOrder	Number	
ReorderLevel	Number	Minimum units to maintain in stock.
Discontinued	Yes/No	Yes means item is no longer available.

➤ **To set the data type for a selected field**

→ In **Datasheet** view, click the data type in the **Data Type** list.

Table Analyzer

After you enter data in a table or import a table from an external source, you can run the Table Analyzer Wizard to evaluate whether any of the fields should be moved to separate tables to improve the database design. If the wizard identifies problems, you can have the wizard fix them or you can create new tables and move fields manually.

Tip When you import a table from another program, the last page of the Import Wizard includes an option to run the Table Analyzer.

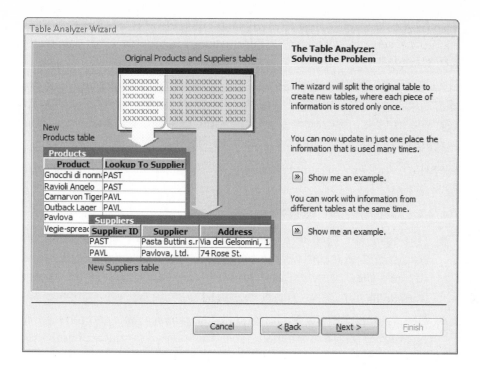

➤ **To analyze table design**

1. On the **Database Tools** tab, in the **Analyze** group, click the **Analyze Table** button.

2. Follow the instructions of the **Table Analyzer Wizard**.

Practice Tasks

The practice file for these tasks is located in the *Documents\Microsoft Press\MCAS\ Access2007\Objective01* folder.

● Open the *Design* database, and delete any fields in the Orders table that should be included in a separate table. Then delete any fields in the Order Details table that should be calculated in a query instead of stored in the table.

● In the *Design* database, assign each of the fields in the Products table to its appropriate data type.

1.2   Define and print table relationships

Relationships

In Access, a relationship is an association between the primary key field in one table and the same field in another table. (In the other table, the field is called the *foreign key*.) You use this association to link one table to another so that you can use a query or report to extract information from both tables.

See Also For information about primary keys, see section 1.3, "Add, set, change, or remove primary keys."

There are three types of relationships:

- **One-to-many.** Each record is unique in the primary table and can have many corresponding records in the other table. The Indexed property of the primary key field allows no duplicates, and the Indexed property of the foreign key field does allow duplicates. This is the most common type of relationship.

- **One-to-one.** Each record is unique in the primary table and can have one and only one related record in the other table. The Indexed property of both the primary key and foreign key fields allows no duplicates. This type of relationship isn't common because it is usually easier to put all the fields in one table. However, you might use two related tables instead of one to break up a table with many fields, or to track information that applies to only some of the records in the first table.

- **Many-to-many.** Each record is unique in the primary table and can have many corresponding records in the other table, and vice versa. This relationship is really two one-to-many relationships tied together through a third table, called a *junction table*.

Access uses the Indexed property of the primary key and foreign key fields to determine the type of relationship.

See Also For information about properties, see section 2.4, "Create fields and modify field properties."

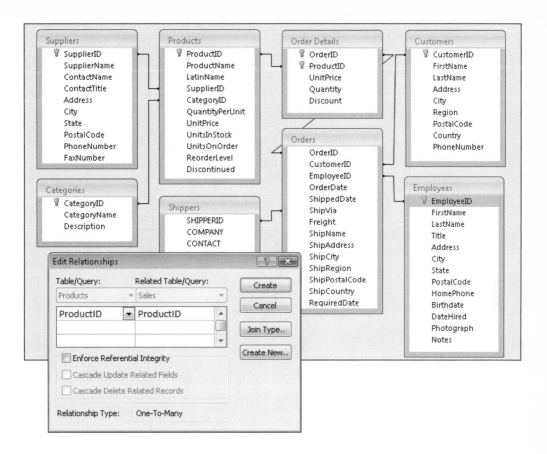

➤ **To create a one-to-many relationship**

1. On the **Database Tools** tab, in the **Show/Hide** group, click the **Relationships** button to display the **Relationship** window.

2. On the **Design** tab, in the **Relationships** group, click the **Show Table** button. Then in the **Show Table** dialog box, select one or more tables or queries, click **Add**, and click **Close**.

3. Drag a primary key field from one table to the foreign key field of another table.

4. In the **Edit Relationships** dialog box, click **Create**.

Referential Integrity

Access uses referential integrity to ensure that the tables in a relationship have at least one field and one value in that field in common. The field definitions and values must match exactly; if they don't, Access will not allow you to create the relationship with referential integrity in effect.

When you turn on referential integrity for a relationship, you also have the option of cascading updates and deletions to related fields, meaning that updating or deleting a record in the primary table will update or delete corresponding records in the related table.

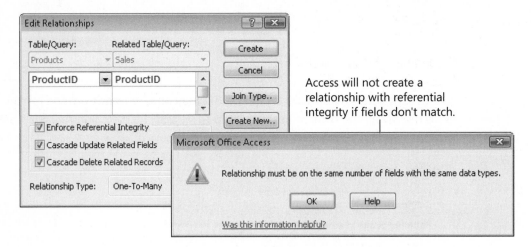

Access will not create a relationship with referential integrity if fields don't match.

➤ **To enforce referential integrity for a new relationship**

1. When the **Edit Relationships** dialog box appears, select the **Enforce Referential Integrity** check box.

2. If you want, select the **Cascade Update Related Fields** and **Cascade Delete Related Records** check boxes.

3. Click **OK**.

➤ **To enforce referential integrity for an existing relationship**

1. Display the **Relationships** window, and click the join line of the relationship you want to change.

2. On the **Design** tab, in the **Tools** group, click the **Edit Relationships** button.

3. In the **Edit Relationships** dialog box, select the **Enforce Referential Integrity** check box

4. If you want, select the **Cascade Update Related Fields** and **Cascade Delete Related Records** check boxes.

5. Click **OK**.

Join Types

By default, running a query against related tables displays only the records where fields in both tables match. You can change the join type of the relationship to display all the records in the primary table and the matching records from the related table, or to display all the records in the related table and the matching records from the primary table.

See Also For more information about joins, see section 4.2, "Modify queries."

➤ **To change the join type**

1. Display the **Edit Relationships** dialog box for a relationship, and then click **Join Type**.

2. In the **Join Properties** dialog box, select one of the options, and then click **OK**.

Relationship Report

When you are designing a database, it is often useful to be able to look at a printout of the relationships you have created. Access provides a ready-made report that documents the relationships in a printable format.

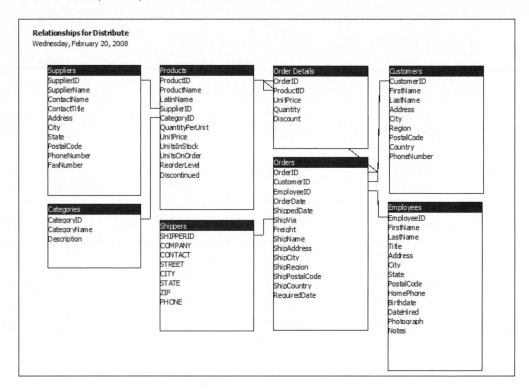

➤ To print relationships

1. Display the **Relationships** window. Then on the **Design** tab, in the **Tools** group, click the **Relationship Report** button.

2. On the **Print Preview** toolbar, click **Print**, and then click **OK** in the **Print** dialog box.

3. Close **Print Preview**, and then close the **Report** window, saving or discarding the report as necessary.

Practice Tasks

The practice files for these tasks are located in the *Documents\Microsoft Press\ MCAS\Access2007\Objective01* folder.

- Open the *Relationships* database, and create a one-to-many relationship between the CustomerID fields in the Customers and Orders tables. Then create a one-to-many relationship between the ProductID fields in the Products and Order Details tables.

- In the *Relationships* database, enforce referential integrity for the Customer ID relationship without cascading either updates or deletes.

- Create a printable report of the relationships in the *Report* database, saving it as *My Relationship Report*.

1.3   Add, set, change, or remove primary keys

The primary key designates the field in a table that is used to uniquely identify each record. When a table has a primary key, no two records in the primary key field can have the same value. If you know the value in the primary key field of a record, you can have Access extract the value from any other field in that record.

You can set, change, and remove the primary key at any time. The primary key field is indicated in Design view by a key icon in the field selector to the left of the field.

Tip If you create a new table in Datasheet view and then enter data, Access automatically adds a primary key field to the table with the AutoNumber data type. You cannot see this field unless you switch to Design view.

➤ **To set the primary key**

1. Open the table in Design view, and click the field you want to define as the primary key.

   Tip To select multiple fields as the primary key, hold down Ctrl and then click the selector for each field.

2. On the **Design** tab, in the **Tools** group, click the **Primary Key** button.

➤ **To remove the primary key**

→ Click the primary key field, and then in the **Tools** group, click the **Primary Key** button.

   Tip You cannot remove the primary key from a field that is part of a relationship without first removing the relationship.

➤ To set an AutoNumber primary key

→ Create a new table in Datasheet view.

Or

1. Create a table in Design view, and then save the table.

2. When prompted to create a primary key, click **Yes** to add an AutoNumber field to the table or use an existing AutoNumber field as the primary key.

   Tip After you enter data into a table you cannot change the data type of *any* existing field to AutoNumber, regardless of whether data has been entered into that field.

Practice Tasks

The practice files for these tasks are located in the *Documents\Microsoft Press\ MCAS\Access2007\Objective01* folder.

● Open the *Keys* database, and in the Products table, set the ProductID field as the primary key.

● In the *Keys* database, in the Orders table, set the OrderID and the EmployeeID fields as the primary keys.

● Open the *Changing* database, and in the Employees table, change the primary key to the Birthdate field.

● In the *Changing* database, remove the primary key from the Categories table without setting a new one.

1.4   Split databases

If a database will be used by multiple people at the same time, processing over the network can be slow. You can use the Database Splitter Wizard to split the database into a front-end database consisting of all the forms, reports, and queries, and a back-end database consisting of all the tables.

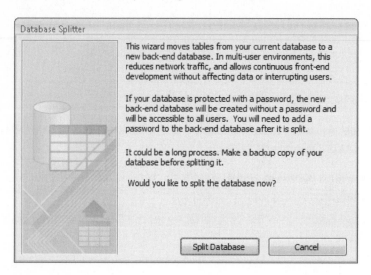

Because the front-end database resides on users' computers, Access needs to move only the data stored in the back-end database over the network, which speeds up processing. Other advantages include greater security and less possibility of data corruption, as well as the smaller file size of the back-end file, and the ability of users to customize their own front-end file.

➤ To split a database

1. Make a copy of the database on your computer, and then open it.

2. On the **Database Tools** tab, in the **Move Data** group, click the **Access Database** button.

3. In the **Database Splitter** wizard, click **Split Database**.

4. In the **Create Back-end Database** dialog box, specify a name and storage location for the back-end database, and then click **Split**.

5. Click **OK** in the message box telling you that the split was successful.

6. Distribute the front-end file (the one you started with) to the database users. (It will automatically connect to the back-end file in the location you specified in step 4.)

Practice Tasks

The practice file for this task is located in the *Documents\Microsoft Press\MCAS\ Access2007\Objective01* folder.

- Open a copy of the *Split* database, and create a back-end database named *Split Back*.

Objective Review

Before finishing this chapter, ensure that you have mastered the following skills:

1.1 Define data needs and types.

1.2 Define and print table relationships.

1.3 Add, set, change, or remove primary keys.

1.4 Split databases.

2 Creating and Formatting Database Elements

The skills tested in this section of the Microsoft Office Specialist exam for Microsoft Office Access 2007 relate to creating and modifying databases and database objects. Specifically, the following objectives are associated with this set of skills:

2.1 Create databases.

2.2 Create tables.

2.3 Modify tables.

2.4 Create fields and modify field properties.

2.5 Create forms.

2.6 Create reports.

2.7 Modify the design of reports and forms.

In many computer applications, each document or object you work with is a separate file. An Access 2007 database, by contrast, is a single .accdb file that can store many different database objects

An Access database can include the types of database objects shown in this table.

Object	Use to
Table	Store and view data.
Query	Organize, combine, and filter data.
Form	View and edit data in a custom format.
Report	Print data in a custom format.

Tip A database can also include macros and modules. Because there are no exam objectives targeted at these objects, we do not discuss them in this book.

Tables are the core database objects. Their purpose is to store information. The purpose of every other database object is to interact in some manner with one or more tables.

This chapter guides you in studying the processes of creating and modifying databases, tables, forms, PivotCharts and PivotTables, and reports.

Important Before you can use the practice files in this chapter, you need to install them from the book's companion CD to their default location. See "Using the Companion CD" at the beginning of this book for more information.

Tip Graphics and operating system–related instructions in this book reflect the Windows Vista user interface. If your computer is running Windows XP and you experience trouble following the instructions as written, refer to the sidebar "If You Are Running Windows XP" in "Working in the Microsoft Office Fluent User Interface" at the beginning of this book.

2.1 Create databases

Creating a database structure used to be a lot of work, and after you created it and entered data, making changes could be difficult. Templates have changed this process. Committing yourself to a particular database structure is no longer the big decision it once was. By using pre-packaged templates, you can create a dozen database applications in less time than it used to take to sketch the design of one on paper. Access templates might not create exactly the database application you want, but they can quickly create something very close that you can tweak to fit your needs.

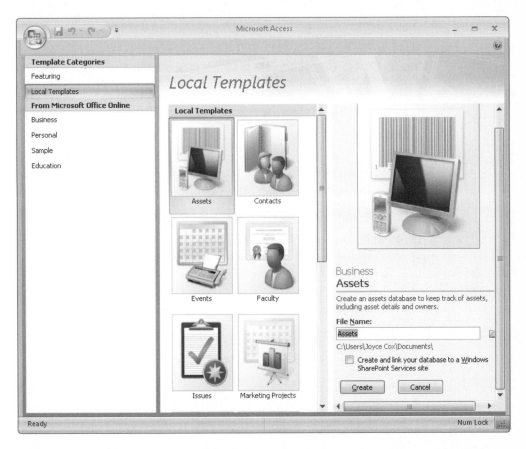

If none of the database templates meets your needs, you can create a new blank database and then create the database structure from scratch. This might be the preferable method if you plan to import or link most of the tables.

➤ To create a database by using a template

1. On the **Getting Started with Microsoft Office Access** page, in the **Template Categories** list, click a category.

2. Click the template icon for the template you want to open.

3. In the **File Name** box, type a new name for the database.

   Tip Naming conventions for Access database files follow those for Microsoft Windows files. A file name, including its path, can contain up to 260 characters, including spaces, but creating a file name that long is not recommended. File names cannot contain the following characters: \ / : * ? " < > |.

4. If you want to change the default location, click the **Browse for a location** button, specify the storage location, and then click **OK**.

   Tip To change the default save location, click the Microsoft Office Button, click Access Options, and then on the Popular page, under Creating Databases, click the Browse button. In the Default Database Path dialog box, browse to the folder you want to select as the default database folder. Then click OK in each of the open dialog boxes.

5. Click **Create**.

➤ To create a blank database

1. On the **Getting Started with Microsoft Access** page, click **Blank Database**.

2. In the **File Name** box, type the name for the database.

3. If you want to change the default location, click the **Browse for a location** button, specify the storage location, and then click **OK**.

4. Click **Create**.

Practice Tasks

There are no practice files for these tasks.

● Create a database application based on the Contacts template in the Local Templates category. Name it *My Contacts*, and store it in the default location. Then open and explore the database.

● Create a new blank database called *My Blank Database* in the *Documents\ Microsoft Press\MCAS\Access2007\Objective02* folder.

2.2 Create tables

You can create simple default tables in Datasheet view, but because most tables require modification in Design view, it is often easier to start there first. You cannot save a table created in Design view without defining at least one field.

See Also For information about fields, see section 2.4, "Create fields and modify field properties."

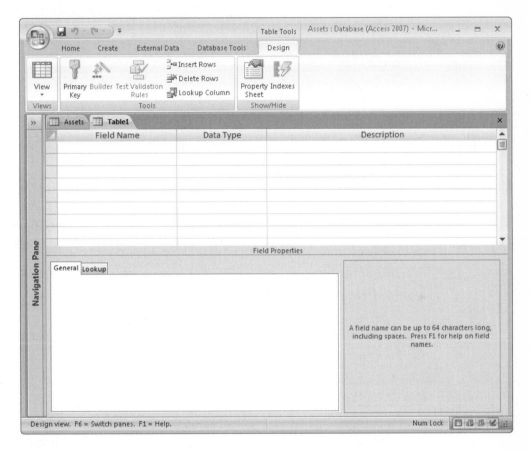

Although manually creating a table is relatively easy, if one of the available table templates is close to what you want, using it might save you a little time and effort.

If you need to create two similar tables, you can define one and duplicate its structure as the basis for the other. Then you can customize the structure for the second table.

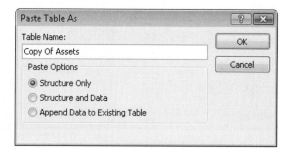

➤ To create a table in Datasheet view

1. On the **Create** tab, in the **Tables** group, click the **Table** button.

2. Save the table with the name you want.

   Tip You must save a new table for it to become part of the database.

➤ To create a table in Design view

1. On the **Create** tab, in the **Tables** group, click the **Table Design** button.

2. Enter at least one field name, and specify its data type.

   See Also For information about data types, see section 1.1, "Define data needs and types."

3. Save the table with the name you want.

   Tip If you try to close the table without saving it, Access will prompt you to save.

➤ **To create a table from a template**

1. On the **Create** tab, in the **Tables** group, click the **Table Templates** button.

2. Click the type of table you want in the list.

3. Save the table with the name you want.

➤ **To duplicate the structure of a table**

1. In the **Navigation Pane**, right-click the table you want to use as the basis for the new table, and click **Copy**.

2. On the **Home** tab, in the **Clipboard** group, click the **Paste** button.

3. In the **Paste Table As** dialog box, name the new table, click **Structure Only**, and then click **OK**.

Practice Tasks

If you worked through the previous tasks, the practice file for these tasks is *My Blank Database* located in the *Documents\Microsoft Press\MCAS\Access2007\ Objective02* folder. Otherwise, work with a new blank database.

● Open the blank database you created in the previous tasks, and add a new table in Datasheet view named *Datasheet*.

● In your database, add a new table in Design view with an AutoNumber primary key field named *ProjectID*. Save the table with the name *Design*.

● In your database, add a table based on the Assets template, and save it with the name *Template*.

● In your database, duplicate the structure of the Template table, naming the new table *Duplicate*.

2.3   Modify tables

After creating a table, you can modify the table as a whole in various ways. You can rename it at any time. You can also change various properties that affect the way the table looks and behaves by changing settings in the table's Property Sheet.

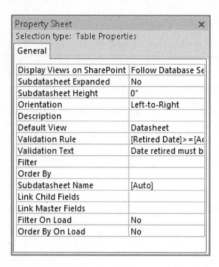

New in Access 2007 is the ability to perform simple calculations in tables that contain numeric data. Instead of having to create a query, you can add a Totals row to the datasheet and then perform aggregate functions, such as sum, average, and count, depending on the data type of the field.

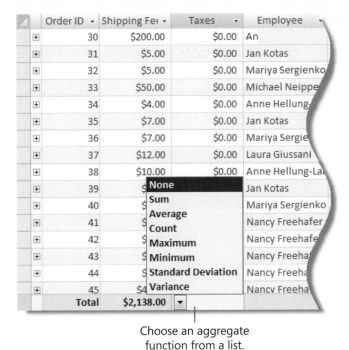

Choose an aggregate
function from a list.

If you create a table and then no longer need it, you should delete the table rather than leaving it to clutter up the database.

➤ To rename a table

1. Make sure the table is closed. Then in the **Navigation Pane**, right-click the table, and click **Rename**.

2. With the old name highlighted for editing in the **Navigation Pane**, type the new name, and press **Enter**.

➤ To modify table properties

1. Display the table in Design view.

2. On the **Design** tab, in the **Show/Hide** group, click the **Property Sheet** button.

3. On the **General** tab, click the box of the property you want to change, and then either enter a new setting or click a list option.

4. Save the table.

➤ To add a Totals row to a table

1. Display the table in Datasheet view.

2. On the **Home** tab, in the **Records** group, click the **Totals** button.

3. In the **Totals** row, click the column on which you want to perform an aggregate calculation, and then click the function you want in the list.

➤ To delete a table

→ Make sure the table is closed. Then in the **Navigation Pane**, right-click the table, and click **Delete**.

Practice Tasks

The practice files for these tasks are located in the *Documents\Microsoft Press\ MCAS\Access2007\Objective02* folder.

- Open the *ModifyTables* database, and rename the Employees table as *Associates*.

- In the *ModifyTables* database, modify the Products table so that when you open it, the records are sorted alphabetically by product name.

- Open the *Totals* database, and in the Orders table, calculate the total freight charges to date.

- Delete the Sales table from the *Totals* database.

2.4   Create fields and modify field properties

Strategy Structuring fields to make data entry efficient while minimizing the risk of input errors is an important part of database design. We can provide only a brief review of all the field properties that are available for different data types in this section. It is important that you thoroughly understand the effect of these properties and how to use them.

New Fields

With earlier versions of Access, you created and modified fields in Design view. With Access 2007, you can create fields in Datasheet view, but you still have to switch to Design view to refine the definitions.

When a table is displayed in Datasheet view, a blank column appears on the right labeled *Add New Field*. You can use this field to create a default text field. If you want the new field to appear elsewhere in the table, you can click any field and then insert a new default text field to its left. You can change the name and data type of both types of fields in Datasheet view, or you can switch to Design view for more specific customization.

You can quickly create a new field with a preset field name, data type, and appropriate property settings by basing the field on a template.

➤ **To create a field in Design view**

1. In the next available row of the **Field Name** column, type the field name you want, and then press **Tab**.

2. In the **Data Type** list, click the data type you want, and then press **Tab**.

3. If you want, enter a description of the field.

➤ **To create a text field in Datasheet view**

→ At the right end of the table, double-click **Add New Field**, type the field name you want, and press **Enter**.

→ Click the name of the field to the left of which you want to insert the new field, and then on the **Datasheet** tab, in the **Fields & Columns** group, click **Insert**.

➤ **To rename a field in Datasheet view**

→ Double-click the default field name, and type the name you want.

➤ **To change the data type of a selected field in Datasheet view**

→ On the **Datasheet** tab, in the **Data Type & Formatting** group, click the data type you want in the **Data Type** list.

➤ **To create a field from a template**

1. On the **Datasheet** tab, in the **Fields & Columns** group, click the **New Field** button.

2. In the **Field Templates** pane, click the template you want, and then drag it where you want it in the table.

3. Close the **Field Templates** pane, and then save the table.

See Also Clicking a field in the Basic Fields list inserts a new field of the selected data type. For information about data types, see section 1.1, "Define data needs and types."

➤ **To delete a selected field**

1. In Datasheet view, on the **Datasheet** tab, in the **Fields & Columns** group, click the **Delete** button.

2. Click **Yes** to confirm the deletion, and then save the table.

Properties

You can specify a field's data type to restrict the type of information that can be entered in the field. To further define and constrain the data, you can set the properties for the selected field in Design view. (Different properties are available depending on the data type of the selected field.) The following properties can be set:

- **Allow Zero Length.** This property, when set to Yes, allows a "" string value.
- **Append Only.** This property, when set to Yes, adds new text to the field, creating a field value history. This property is especially useful for memo fields.
- **Caption.** This value will be displayed instead of the field name in the datasheet, forms, reports, and queries.
- **Decimal Places.** This number of decimal places will be displayed.
- **Default Value.** This value will be entered in a new record, unless you change it.
- **Field Size.** This maximum size is allowed. (Options are specific to the data type.)
- **Format.** This property designates how the field value will appear by default. (Options are specific to the data type.)
- **IME Mode.** This property is related to East Asian languages.
- **IME Sentence Mode.** This property is related to East Asian languages.
- **Indexed.** This property, when set to Yes, speeds up the searching and sorting of data. Setting the property to Yes (No Duplicates) limits the field to a unique value in each record.
- **Input Mask.** This property specifies that the field value must conform to the pattern set by the mask.
- **New Values.** This property, when set to Increment, increases the value for each new record; setting this property to Random assigns a random value.
- **Required.** This property, when set to Yes, ensures that every record will have a value in this field.
- **Show Date Picker.** This property, when set to For Dates, displays a calendar control when the field is activated for editing. If you use an input mask for a Date/Time field, this control is available, regardless of how you set the property.
- **Smart Tags.** This property allows the Date, Telephone Number, Financial Symbol, and Person Name smart tags to be attached to the field. This property is set by default.
- **Text Align.** This field, when set, controls the default alignment of the value.
- **Text Format.** This property, when set to Plain Text, stores only text; setting the property to Rich Text allows formatting because data is stored in HTML format.

- **Unicode Compression.** This property, when set to Yes, compresses values of fewer than 4096 characters.

- **Validation Rule.** This expression establishes criteria that any new or changed value must meet.

- **Validation Text.** This explanation appears when a value does not meet the corresponding validation rule.

Input Masks

You can use the Input Mask property to control how data is entered in text, number (except ReplicationID), date/time, and currency fields. This property has three sections, separated by semicolons, like the mask for a telephone number, shown here:

!\(000") "000\-0000;1;#

The first section contains characters that are used as placeholders for the information to be typed, as well as characters such as parentheses and hyphens. Together, all these characters control the appearance of the entry. The following table explains the purpose of the most common input mask characters.

Character	Description
0	Required digit (0 through 9).
9	Optional digit or space.
#	Optional digit or space; blank positions are converted to spaces; plus and minus signs are allowed.
L	Required letter (A through Z).
?	Optional letter (A through Z).
A	Required letter or digit.
a	Optional letter or digit.
&	Required character (any kind) or a space.
C	Optional character (any kind) or a space.
<	All characters that follow are converted to lowercase.
>	All characters that follow are converted to uppercase.
!	Characters typed into the mask fill it from left to right. You can include the exclamation point anywhere in the input mask.
\	Character that follows is displayed as a literal character.
"Literal Text"	Access treats the string enclosed in double quotation marks as a literal string.
Password	Creates a password entry box. Any character typed in the box is stored as the character but displayed as an asterisk (*).

If you use any characters not included in this list in the mask (for example, parentheses and hyphens), they will be displayed in the field as literal characters. If you want to use one of the special characters in this list as a literal character, precede it with the \ (backslash) character.

The second and third sections of the input mask are optional. Including a 1 in the second section or leaving it blank tells Access to store only the characters entered; including a 0 tells it to store both the characters entered and the mask characters. Entering a character in the third section causes Access to display that character as a placeholder for each of the characters to be typed; leaving it blank displays an underscore as the placeholder.

The input mask *!\(000") "000\-0000;1;#* creates this display in a field in Datasheet view:

(###) ###-####

In this example, you are restricting the entry to ten digits—no more and no less. The database user does not enter the parentheses, space, or dash, nor does Access store those characters. Access stores only the ten digits.

You can enter input masks manually for text, number, date, or currency fields, but for standard types of masks in text and date fields, it is easier to use the Input Mask Wizard.

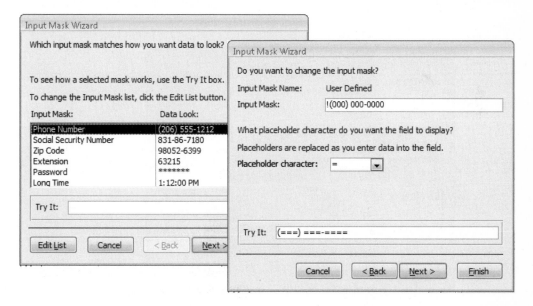

➤ **To define an input mask for a selected field**

1. In the **Field Properties** area, click the **Input Mask** box, and then click the **Build** button to start the **Input Mask Wizard**.

2. Select a type of mask in the **Input Mask** list, and then click **Next**.

3. In the **Input Mask** and **Placeholder character** boxes, make any changes you want, and then click **Next**.

4. Choose whether to store the data with the symbols, and then click **Finish**.

   Tip When you move away from the Input Mask property, the Property Update Options button appears to the left of the input mask. Clicking this button displays a list of options. In this case, the only options are to apply the input mask everywhere the active field is used and to provide help. This button disappears when you edit any other property or change to a different field.

5. Save the table.

Validation Rules

A validation rule is an expression that precisely defines the information that will be accepted in a field. If an entry doesn't satisfy the rule, Access rejects the entry and displays a message explaining why. You can type validation rules by hand, or you can use the Expression Builder to create them.

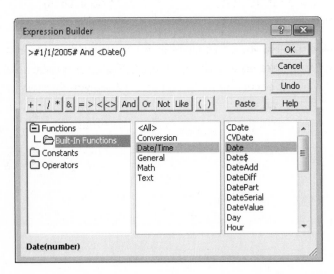

➤ To set a validation rule for a selected field

1. In the **Field Properties** area, click the **Validation Rule** box, and then click the **Build** button.

2. In the **Expression Builder** dialog box, use the contents of the **Functions**, **Constants**, and **Operations** folders and the operator buttons to build an expression that any value entered in the field must meet. Then click **OK**.

   Tip If the text "*<<Expr>>*" appears in the body of your expression in the Expression Builder dialog box, select and delete it.

3. In the **Validation Text** box, type instructions that will help users understand what data must be entered in the field.

4. In the **Field Properties** area, click the **Caption** box and enter a name that will display instead of the field name.

5. Save the table.

Lookup Lists and Multivalued Fields

Minor inconsistencies in the way data is entered might not seem important, but if you tell Access to extract the records of everyone living in *AZ*, the results won't include anyone whose state was entered as *Arizona*. You can limit the options for entering information in a field by providing a lookup list. You can create the list by hand in Design view, or you can use the Lookup Wizard in either Design view or Datasheet view.

When you create the lookup list, you can specify whether the field should allow multiple values. This is useful, for example, if you have more than one person assigned to a project, or if the same event occurs on multiple dates. When you display this type of list in Datasheet view, you can select the check boxes of the values you want, and Access will display them all the in the field, separated by commas.

Tip Although multivalued fields seem to contradict a primary rule of good database design (see section 1.1, "Define data needs and types"), in fact Access maintains hidden tables behind the scenes that comply with the rule. Nevertheless, multivalued fields should not be used if a database is likely to be exported to another database program such as Microsoft SQL Server.

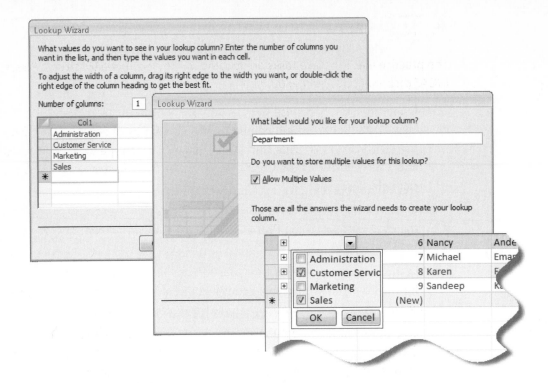

➤ To create a multivalued field by using the Lookup Wizard

1. In Datasheet view, on the **Datasheet** tab, in the **Fields & Columns** group, click the **Lookup Column** button.

   Or

   In Design view, on the **Design** tab, in the **Tools** group, click the **Lookup Column** button.

2. Complete the first two pages of the wizard, either by entering a list of values by hand or by specifying an existing table or query that contains the values.

3. On the wizard's last page, name the field and select the **Allow Multiple Values** check box. Then click **Finish**.

Practice Tasks

The practice files for these tasks are located in the *Documents\Microsoft Press\ MCAS\Access2007\Objective02* folder.

● Open the blank database you created in the previous tasks, and in Datasheet view add a new text field named *MyText* to the Datasheet table. Add a second text field named *MyDate*, and then change its data type to Date/Time. Finally, add a field based on the Condition template in the Assets category to the left of the MyText field.

● Open the *FieldProperty* database, and in the Employees table, specify that the display name of the PostalCode field should be *ZIP* (without changing the field name).

● In the Employees table of the *FieldProperty* database, specify an input mask for the PostalCode field that prompts the user to input an optional four-digit extension. Use the pound sign (#) as the digit placeholder.

● Open the *Validation* database, and in the PhoneNumber field of the Customers table, set a validation rule that will accept only the 206 or 425 area codes. Display the message *Area code must be 206 or 425* if the user enters the wrong code.

● In the Employees table of the *Validation* database, add a multivalued lookup field named *Department* that allows the user to select from a list of these four values: Administration, Customer Support, Marketing, and Sales.

2.5   Create forms

Form Tools

Before you begin creating a form, you need to know which database table or query to base it on and have an idea of how the form will be used. After making these decisions, you can create a form in several ways. The quickest way is use the Form tool, which creates a simple form that uses all the fields in the table or query and opens it in Layout view.

If you want to be able to see the datasheet while you are entering data in a form, you can create a split form. The two views of the data are always synchronized; selecting or changing data in one part of the form simultaneously selects or changes it in the other.

See Also You can turn a regular form into a split form by changing the Default View property on the Form's property sheet to Split Form. For information about form properties, see section 2.7, "Modify the design of reports and forms."

If you want to be able to see more than one record at a time in the form, you can create a multiple item form. This type of form provides the information density of a datasheet but is more flexible in that its design can be easily modified in Layout or Design view.

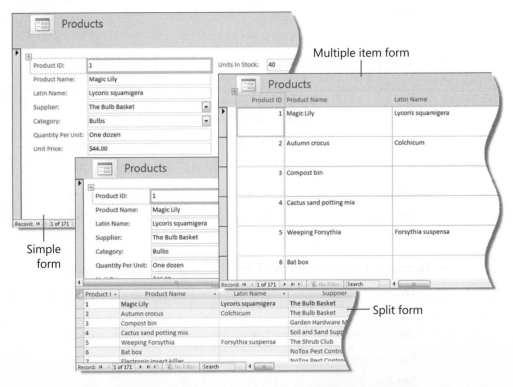

If you use the Form tool to create a form based on a table that has a one-to-many relationship with one (and only one) other table in the database, the Form tool adds a datasheet called a *subform* to the main form. The subform displays all the records in the related table that pertain to the record currently displayed in the main form.

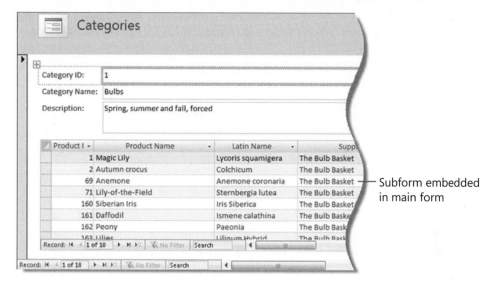

Subform embedded in main form

See Also   For information about relationships, see section 1.2, "Define and print table relationships."

> ► **To create a simple form for the active table or query**

> → On the **Create** tab, in the **Forms** group, click the **Form** button. Then save the form.

> ► **To create a split form for the active table or query**

> → On the **Create** tab, in the **Forms** group, click the **Split Form** button. Then save the form.

> ► **To create a multiple item form for the active table or query**

> → On the **Create** tab, in the **Forms** group, click the **Multiple Items** button. Then save the form.

> ► **To create a form with a subform for the active table or query**

> 1. Ensure that a one-to-many relationship exists between the primary table and the table you want to display in the subform.

> 2. On the **Create** tab, in the **Forms** group, click the **Form** button.

> 3. Save the form.

>   **See Also**   You can use a control wizard to add a Subform/Subreport control to an existing form in Design view. For information about adding controls, see section 2.7, "Modify the design of reports and forms."

Form Wizard

When you want to create a form that includes only some of the fields in a table or tables, the easiest method is to use the Form Wizard, which walks you through the steps of selecting the fields and laying them out.

See Also For information about relationships, see section 1.2, "Define and print table relationships."

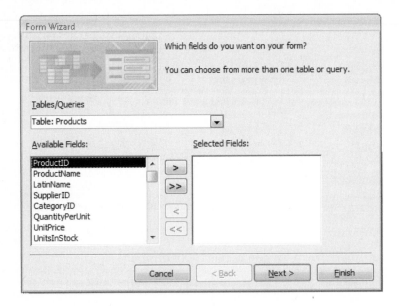

➤ **To create a form for the active table by using the Form Wizard**

1. On the **Create** tab, in the **Forms** group, click the **More Forms** button, and then click **Form Wizard**.

2. In the **Available Fields** list, double-click the fields you want to appear in the form, and then click **Next**.

   Tip You can make the fields of additional tables available by clicking the table you want in the Tables/Queries list. In that case, the wizard asks you to specify how you want to view the data in the form.

3. Follow the wizard's instructions to choose a layout and style for the form.

4. On the wizard's last page, name the form, and then click **Finish**.

Manual Forms

Strategy   It is unlikely that you will be asked to create a new form in Design view on the certification exam. However, you do need to be familiar with the techniques for manipulating a form in Design view. See section 2.7, "Modify the design of reports and forms."

Layout view is a hybrid that combines the visual display of Form view with the form building capabilities of Design view. Starting with a blank form in this view, you can choose fields from the Field List and then arrange and format them as you want.

You can use this method to create forms that can be used to enter records in more than one table at a time. The tables must be related by common fields. If a relationship does not already exist, you are asked to create it while building the form.

See Also   For information about relationships, see section 1.2, "Define and print table relationships."

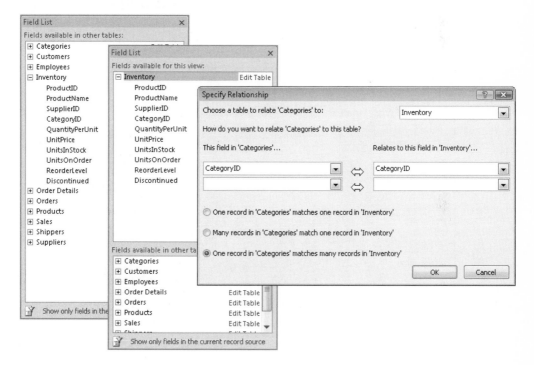

➤ To create a form in Layout view

1. On the **Create** tab, in the **Forms** group, click the **Blank Form** button.

2. In the **Field List**, expand the table or query whose fields you want to use in the form, and then drag fields from the list to the form.

3. To use a field from a different table or query, expand that table or query in the **Fields available in other tables** list, and drag the field you want to the form.

4. If the **Specify Relationship** dialog box appears, indicate the relationship between the primary table or query and this table or query, and click **OK**.

5. When you have finished adding fields, close the **Field List**, and then save the form.

PivotCharts and PivotTables

Used primarily with the results of queries, PivotCharts and PivotTables present datasheet information in dynamic tables and charts that can be viewed in various ways to facilitate data analysis. In Access, you create these tools in forms.

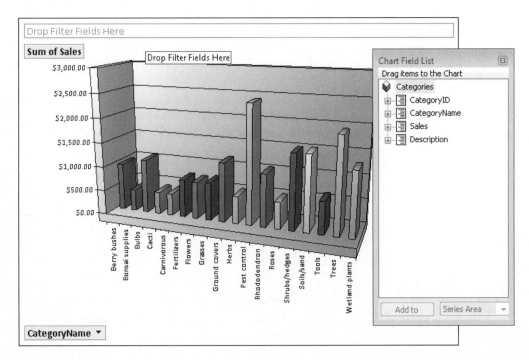

➤ **To create a PivotChart for the selected table or query**

1. On the **Create** tab, in the **Forms** group, click the **PivotChart** button.

   Tip To create a PivotTable, click the More Forms button, and then click PivotTable.

2. In the **Chart Field List**, drag the field you want represented on the category (x) axis to the **Drop Category Fields Here** box at the bottom of the form.

   Tip If the Chart Field List box is not visible, click the Field List button in the Show/Hide group on the design tab until it appears.

3. Drag the field you want plotted as data points in the chart to the **Drop Data Fields Here** box above the chart on the form.

4. Click the plot area, and then on the **Design** tab, in the **Type** group, click the **Change Chart Type** button.

5. On the **Type** tab of the **Properties** dialog box, click the category and layout you want.

6. Close the **Properties** sheet and the **Chart Field List**, and then save the form.

Practice Tasks

The practice files for these tasks are located in the *Documents\Microsoft Press\ MCAS\Access2007\Objective02* folder.

- Open the *CreateFormReport* database, and use the quickest method to create a form based on the Employees table. Then create a split form based on the Products table, a multiple item form based on the Shippers table, and a form with a subform based on the Customers table.

- Open the *Wizard* database, and create a form based on the Inventory table that includes only the Product Name and Discontinued fields. Use a columnar layout and the Trek style.

- Open the *Manually* database, and create a form from scratch that includes the Product Name and Discontinued fields from the Inventory table.

- Open the *PivotChart* database, and create a PivotChart based on the Category table that shows the sales per category name plotted as a 3D Column Clustered chart.

2.6   **Create reports**

Report Tool

When creating reports, you should first consider the end result you want and what information you need to include in the report to achieve that result. If all you need is a simple report that includes all the fields from one table, you can use the Report tool.

After creating the report, you can add a grouping level. When you group the information in a report based on the data in a field, Access first sorts the table based on that field and creates a group header each time the field value changes. You can also sort the records within the group based on a different field. You can add subsequent grouping and sorting levels to refine the display to meet your needs.

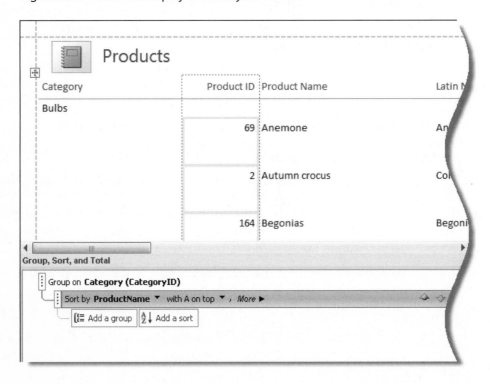

You can also add aggregate functions to the report that perform common calculations, such as totaling, averaging, or counting records. If you add an aggregate function to a report with a grouping level, Access performs the function for each group.

➤ **To create a simple report for the active table or query**

→ On the **Create** tab, in the **Reports** group, click the **Report** button. Then save the report.

➤ **To define the grouping level and sort order for a report**

1. On the **Format** tab, in the **Grouping & Totals** group, click the **Group & Sort** button.

2. In the **Group, Sort, and Total** pane, click **Add a group**, and in the list, click the field you want.

3. Click **Add a sort**, and in the list, click the field you want.

   Tip You can change the grouping field and the type of grouping by clicking the Group on entry in the Group, Sort, And Total section, clicking the arrow, and choosing a different option in the list. Similarly, you can change the sorting field and order.

4. Close the **Group, Sort, and Total** pane, and then save the report.

➤ **To add an aggregate function to a report**

→ On the **Format** tab, in the **Grouping & Totals** group, click the **Totals** button, and then click the function you want.

Report Wizard

If you want anything more complex than a simple listing, you can use the Report Wizard. This wizard guides you through the process of selecting fields from one or more tables or queries, grouping and sorting them, and then choosing a layout and style.

When you include more than one table in a report, the wizard evaluates the relationships between the tables and offers to group the records in any logical manner available. If relationships between tables aren't already established in the Relationships window, you have to cancel the wizard and establish them before continuing; you cannot do it from within the wizard.

See Also For information about relationships, see section 1.2, "Define and print table relationships."

When you use the Report Wizard, you can group the information on multiple fields and you can sort it on up to four fields, each in ascending or descending order. You can also instruct Access to summarize numeric fields by displaying the sum, average, minimum, or maximum value for the field in the report.

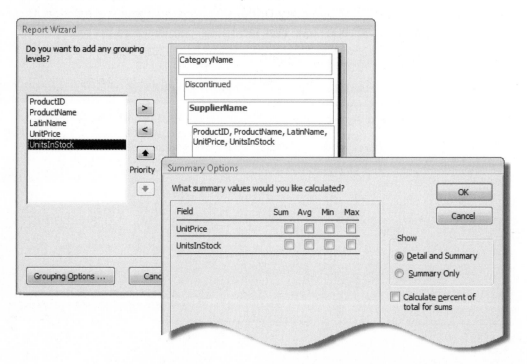

➤ **To create a report by using the Report Wizard**

1. On the **Create** tab, in the **Reports** group, click the **Report Wizard** button.

2. On the first page, click the table or query you want in the **Tables/Queries** list, and then in the **Available Fields** list, double-click the fields you want to move to the **Selected Fields** list.

   Tip Fields appear in a report in the same order that they appear in the Selected Fields list unless you change the order by grouping and sorting.

3. To select fields from additional tables or queries, repeat step 2. Then click **Next**.

4. On the grouping page, select the field on which you want to group the data, and then click **Next**.

5. On the next page, add up to four grouping levels by double-clicking fields to move them to the top of the preview pane. Then click **Next**.

   Tip Clicking Grouping Options displays the Grouping Intervals dialog box, where you can specify a grouping interval for each field.

6. On the next page, specify up to four fields on which you want to sort the data. If you want, click **Summary Options**, and specify aggregate functions to be applied to numeric fields. Then click **Next**.

7. Specify the layout, orientation, and style of the report.

8. On the last page, name the report, and with **Preview the report** selected, click **Finish**.

Manual Reports

Strategy It is unlikely that you will be asked to create a report in Design view on the certification exam. However, you do need to be familiar with the techniques for manipulating a report in Design view. See section 2.7, "Modify the design of reports and forms."

As with forms, you can create reports from scratch in Layout view. Starting with a blank report in this view, you can choose fields from the Field List and then arrange and format them as you want.

➤ **To create a report in Layout view**

1. On the **Create** tab, in the **Reports** group, click the **Blank Report** button.

2. In the **Field List**, expand the table or query whose fields you want to use in the form, and then drag fields from the list to the form.

3. To use a field from a different table or query, expand that table or query in the **Fields available in other tables** list, and drag the field you want to the form.

4. If the **Specify Relationship** dialog box appears, indicate the relationship between the primary table or query and this table or query, and click **OK**.

5. When you have finished adding fields, close the **Field List**, and then specify on which fields the report should be grouped and sorted.

6. Save the report.

Printing

Reports are output documents that could potentially be printed. You need to pay attention to the way your reports are laid out to ensure that the information fits neatly on the printed page. You can get a good idea of what it will look like in Layout view, where you can also refine the layout. For example, you can make columns wider or narrower, and you can control whether groups of data are allowed to break across pages.

You can also scrutinize a report and change its page settings in Print Preview.

Tip Because error checking is turned on, on the Object Designers page of the Access Options dialog box, Access identifies common errors in forms and reports and gives you a chance to fix them.

➤ **To adjust the width of columns in a report**

1. On the **View** toolbar, click the **Layout View** button.

2. Click any field in the column you want to make wider or narrower.

3. Point to the right border, and drag to the left or right.

➤ **To keep grouped data together in a printed report**

1. In Layout view, on the **Format** tab, in the **Grouping & Totals** group, click the **Group & Sort** button.

2. In the **Group, Sort, and Total** pane, click the header for the group you want to keep together, and then click **More**.

3. Click the **do not keep group together on one page** arrow, and in the list, click the option you want.

4. Close the **Group, Sort, and Total** pane.

➤ **To change print settings**

1. On the View toolbar, click the **Print Preview** button.

2. Move the pointer over the report, and click once to display the entire page.

   Tip When the pointer appears as a plus sign, clicking it zooms in on (magnifies) the report. When it appears as a minus sign, clicking it decreases magnification.

3. In the page navigator, click the **Next Page** and **Previous Page** buttons to page through the document.

4. On the **Print Preview** tab, in the **Page Layout** group, select options to change the page size, orientation, and margins.

   Tip You can set custom margins in the Page Setup dialog box.

5. Page through the report again to ensure that it will print efficiently, and then save the report.

Label Wizard

Databases often store information that needs to be extracted from a table to create labels for bulk mailings. Access provides a wizard to take the hard work out of setting up a report from which you can easily print labels.

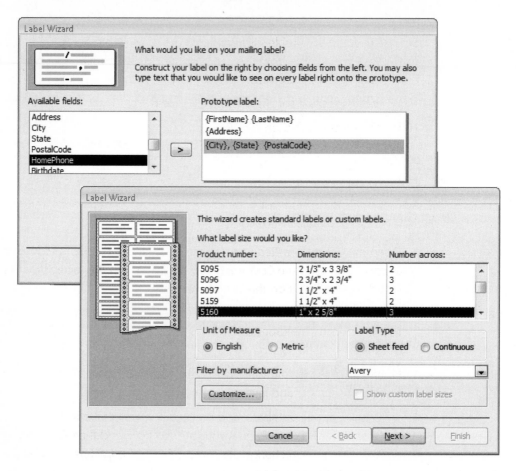

➤ **To create labels from the active table by using the Label Wizard**

1. On the **Create** tab, in the **Reports** group, click **Labels**.

2. On the first page of the Label Wizard, specify the product number of the labels you will use or define a custom label size, and then click **Next**.

3. Specify the font, size, weight, and color of the text, and click **Next**.

4. Set up the label by double-clicking fields in the **Available fields** list to move them to the **Prototype label** box. You can type spaces and punctuation characters to set up the label the way you want it. Click **Next**.

5. If you want, specify a sort field. Then click **Next**.

6. Name the report, and then click **Finish**.

Practice Tasks

The practice files for these tasks are located in the *Documents\Microsoft Press\MCAS\Access2007\Objective02* folder.

- Open the *CreateFormReport* database, and use the quickest method to create a report based on the Customers table. Then group the records by the Region field and sort based on the Last Name field.

- Open the *Wizard* database, and use the Report Wizard to create a report that displays an alphabetical list of product names from the Products table, organized by category names from the Categories table.

- Open the *Manually* database, and create a report based on the Employees table that lists first and last names and phone numbers.

- Open the *Printing* database, and then open the Alphabetical List Of Products report in Print Preview. Page through the report, and then set all the margins to 0.75 inches. Then change the setting that keeps groups together so that they will break across pages.

- Open the *Wizard* database, and use the Label Wizard to create a set of Avery 5160 mailing labels based on the Employees table.

2.7   Modify the design of reports and forms

Strategy To prepare for the exam, you should familiarize yourself with the basic techniques for working in Design view. You should know the purpose of different form and report sections and how to display, hide, and size them. You should also know how to select and manipulate controls and their labels simultaneously and independently.

Controls

When you use the Form or Report tool or a wizard to create a form or report, Access adds a set of controls for each field that you select from the underlying table to the Detail section. It might also add information to the Header and Footer sections. Although labels and text box controls are the most common controls in forms and reports, you can enhance both with other types of controls. For example, in forms you might add option buttons, check boxes, or list boxes to present people with choices instead of having them type entries in text boxes. In both forms and reports, you might add pictures, lines, or titles. All the controls are located on the Design tab in the Controls group.

Tip If a section is empty, Access collapses it, but you can resize the section by dragging the selector to its left.

When you create a simple form or report based on a table, every field is represented by a text box control and its associated label control. These controls are linked, or *bound*, to that specific field in the table. The table is the record source, and the field is the control source. Controls can also be *unbound*. These controls are the ones you create to make a form easier to use or a report easier to interpret. You can add and delete bound or unbound controls in Design view.

See Also Controls can also be calculated. These controls use an expression as their data source rather than a field. For information about creating expressions, see section 4.2, "Modify queries."

Strategy Create a blank form or report and experiment with adding both bound and unbound controls to familiarize yourself with the steps for creating each type of control.

➤ **To delete a control**

→ In Design view, click the control, and press the **Delete** key.

➤ To add a bound control

1. On the **Design** tab, in the **Tools** group, click the **Add Existing Fields** button.

2. In the **Field List**, expand the table containing the field you want, and drag the field to the section of the form or report where you want the control to appear. Then close the **Field List**.

3. If you want, change the default label by double-clicking it and typing the new one.

4. Save the form or report.

   Tip Access assigns a number to each control when it is created and identifies the control internally by this number, not by the name in the control or its label.

➤ To add an unbound control

1. On the **Design** contextual tab, in the right part of the **Controls** group, click the **Use Control Wizards** button to activate it.

2. In the center part of the **Controls** group, click the button of the control you want to add.

3. Move the pointer to the section of the form or report where you want the control to appear, and then drag to create the initial area for the control.

4. If a wizard is associated with the control you clicked, follow the wizard's instructions, and then click **Finish**. Otherwise, complete the setup specific to the control.

5. Save the form or report.

➤ To bind a control

→ In Design or Layout view, display the control's **Property Sheet**, and on the **Data** tab, click the field you want in the **Control Source** list.

➤ To insert a picture in a form or report

1. On the **Design** contextual tab, in the center part of the **Controls** group, click the **Image** button, and then drag a rectangle in the section where you want the picture to appear.

   Tip You can use the Logo control in the Controls group to insert a logo in the upper-left corner of the Header section.

2. In the **Insert Picture** dialog box, locate and double-click the image file.

Layout

After adding controls to a form or report, you can size, move, align, and anchor them. You can manipulate one control, a group of controls, or all the controls on the form or report, and you can manipulate a control and its label simultaneously or independently. (If a selected label or text box can be moved independently, it has a large handle in its upper-left corner.) For simple forms or reports, you can arrange controls in Layout view. But for more precise control over placement, you will want to work in Design view, which has a background grid and rulers to guide you.

Access provides two standard control layouts that it applies automatically to forms and reports you create with the Form, Blank Form, Report, or Blank Report tools. You can apply these layouts to any set of controls on a form or report:

- **Tabular.** Arranges records horizontally, with the controls in one section and their labels in the section above.

- **Stacked.** Arranges records vertically, with the controls to the right of their labels.

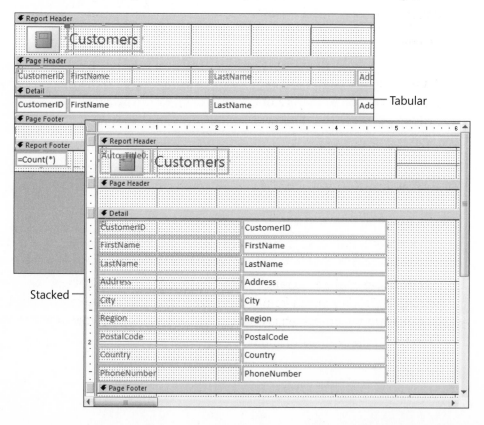

You can add controls to a layout and have more than one layout in the same form or report. However, although these layouts take a lot of the effort out of aligning and evenly spacing controls to make them look pretty, they restrict you to regimented control arrangements. While one of these layouts is applied to a set of controls, you cannot move a control outside of the layout, and sizing one control almost always affects the size or position of other controls in the layout. Removing the layout gives you more options for arranging the controls.

Tip If you want to be able to manipulate a set of controls as a unit, you can group them without applying a layout.

You can move and size specific controls or control groups in the following ways:

- By dragging
- By pressing keyboard keys
- By setting measurements in the control's Property Sheet

You can also arrange controls in relation to each other by using the commands in the Control Alignment, Position, and Size groups on the Arrange tab.

Strategy Explore these commands on your own so that you understand in which order you should select the controls to achieve the effect you want.

If a form will be viewed onscreen and you want a control to change its size dynamically in proportion to the size of the form in the Access window, you can use the new Anchoring feature. This is particularly useful for large controls such as those that are bound to memo fields.

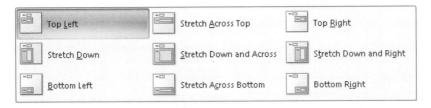

After you have finished rearranging controls on a form, you might want to check that pressing the Tab key moves from one control to the next in a logical order. If it doesn't, you can adjust the order manually or tell Access to adjust the order to reflect the position of the controls on the form.

➤ To apply a layout to a selected set of controls

→ Select all the controls to which you want to apply the layout, and then on the **Arrange** tab, in the **Control Layout** group, click the **Tabular** or **Stacked** button.

➤ To remove a layout

→ Select all the controls in the layout, and then on the **Arrange** tab, in the **Control Layout** group, click the **Remove** button.

Tip You can select all the controls in a form, including those in the header and footer, by pressing Ctrl+A.

➤ To group and ungroup controls

→ Select all the controls you want to be part of the group, and then on the **Arrange** tab, in the **Control Layout** group, click the **Group** button (just to the left of the **Snap to Grid** button).

→ Select the group, and then on the **Arrange** tab, in the **Control Layout** group, click the **Ungroup** button.

➤ To size a selected control

→ Point to the middle of the control's border, and then drag to the left or right.

→ Fine-tune the size by holding down the **Shift** key while pressing the **Up Arrow, Down Arrow, Left Arrow,** or **Right Arrow** key.

→ Display the control's **Property Sheet**, and on the **Format** tab, change the **Width** and **Height** settings to the size you want.

➤ To size a selected label control to fit its contents

→ On the **Arrange** tab, in the **Size** group, click the **Size to Fit** button.

➤ To make a control adjust its size to fit a form window

1. Arrange the controls of the form so that they fit compactly in the upper-left area of the form, and then size the form so that it is just big enough to fit its controls. (Drag the right borders of the design grid, which represents the form.)

2. Select the control whose size you want to be dynamic.

3. On the **Arrange** tab, in the **Size** group, click the **Anchoring** button, and then click the option representing the growth path you want.

4. Switch to Form view, size the Access window to test the anchoring setting, and then save the form.

➤ To position a control

→ Point to the control's border (but not the middle), and then drag the control and its label to its new location.

Tip Controls that are part of groups or layouts affect other controls when they are moved.

→ Point to the large handle in the upper-left corner of the control, and then drag to move the control but not its label.

→ Fine-tune the position by pressing the **Up Arrow, Down Arrow, Left Arrow,** or **Right Arrow** key. To move the control smaller distances, hold down the **Ctrl** key while pressing the arrow key.

Tip You might need to turn off the Snap To Grid command in the Control Layout group to be able to move the control precisely where you want it.

→ Display the control's **Property Sheet**, and on the **Format** tab, change the **Top** and **Left** settings to the coordinates you want.

➤ To align selected controls relative to each other

→ On the **Arrange** tab, in the **Control Alignment** group, click the **Left, Right, Top,** or **Bottom** button.

➤ To change the tab order of controls

1. On the **Arrange** tab, in the **Control Layout** group, click the **Tab Order** button.

2. In the **Tab Order** dialog box, arrange the rows in the order you want.

   Or

   Click **Auto Order** to have Access determine the order.

3. Click **OK**.

Formatting

Each control on a form or report has a number of formatting properties—such as font, font size, alignment, fill color, and border—that determine the appearance of the form or report. In either Layout view or Design view, you can change the formatting properties of an individual control, a multi-control selection, or a group; and you can change the background of a section.

Tip The order in which you make formatting changes can have an impact on the results. If you don't see the expected results, click the Undo button on the Quick Access Toolbar, or press Ctrl+Z.

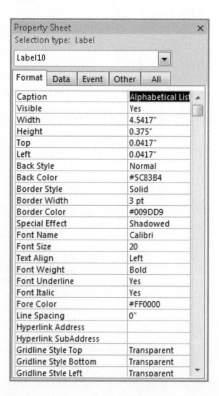

If you select a bound control or controls, you can apply conditional formatting that changes the weight and color of the text and the color of the control so that it stands out in the form or report.

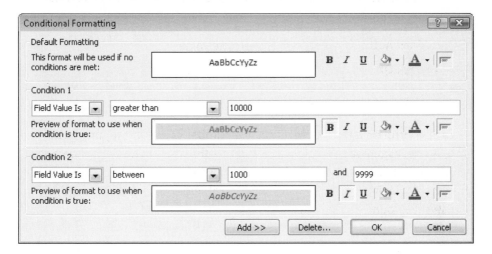

If you select one or more bound controls that contain numeric data in Layout view, you can change the formatting of the data in various ways.

➤ To change the character formatting of selected controls

→ Use the commands in the **Font** group of the **Format** tab or the **Design** tab as you would in any other Microsoft Office program.

→ Display the **Property Sheet**, and change the **Font Name**, **Font Size**, **Font Weight**, **Font Underline**, **Font Italic**, and **Fore Color** settings as necessary.

Tip The Fore Color property controls the color of the font.

➤ To change the color of text in selected controls

1. On the **Format** tab or the **Design** tab, in the **Font** group, click the **Font Color** arrow, and then click a color in the palette.

2. If you don't see the color you need in the palette, click the **More Colors** button, click a color on the **Standard** or **Custom** tab, and then click **OK**.

Or

1. Display the **Property Sheet**, and click a color in the **Fore Color** list.

2. If you don't see the color you need in the list, click the **Color Builder** button, and then click a color in the palette.

➤ **To change the color of selected controls**

1. On the **Format** tab or the **Design** tab, in the **Font** group, click the **Fill/Back Color** arrow, and then click a color in the palette.

2. If you don't see the color you need in the palette, click the **More Colors** button, click a color on the **Standard** or **Custom** tab, and then click **OK**.

   Or

1. Display the **Property Sheet**, and click a color in the **Back Color** list.

2. If you don't see the color you need in the list, click the **Color Builder** button, and then click a color in the palette.

➤ **To make selected controls transparent**

→ On the **Format** tab or the **Design** tab, in the **Font** group, click the **Fill/Back Color** arrow, and then click **Transparent** in the palette.

→ Display the **Property Sheet**, and in the **Back Style** list, click **Transparent**.

➤ **To change the background color of a section**

1. In Design view, display the **Property Sheet**, click the **Back Color** box, and then click a color in the list.

2. If you don't see the color you need in the list, click the **Color Builder** button, and then click a color in the palette.

➤ **To add a special effect to a control or section**

→ On the **Design** tab, in the **Controls** group, click an effect in the **Special Effect** list.

   Tip Not all effects listed are valid for sections.

→ Display the **Property Sheet** for the control or section, and click an effect in the **Special Effect** list.

➤ **To apply conditional formatting to a control**

1. On the **Format** tab or the **Design** tab, in the **Font** group, click the **Conditional** button.

2. In the **Conditional Formatting** dialog box, set up the conditions and formatting you want, and then click **OK**.

   Tip To add more conditions, click Add. To delete a condition, click Delete, select the check box of the condition you want to remove, and then click OK.

➤ **To change the formatting of numeric data in a control**

→ On the **Format** tab in Layout view, in the **Formatting** group, click the command that will achieve the effect you want.

AutoFormats

In Design view, you can use a built-in AutoFormat to apply a set of sophisticated formats to the entire form or report. Each AutoFormat includes font, color, and border specifications. You can choose to use one, two, or all three sets of specifications.

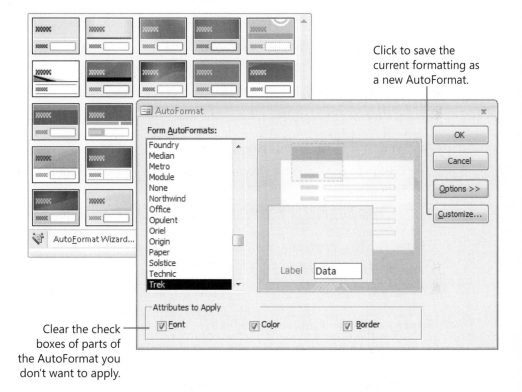

Click to save the current formatting as a new AutoFormat.

Clear the check boxes of parts of the AutoFormat you don't want to apply.

If none of the AutoFormats provided by Access meets your needs, you can format the open form or report and then use the AutoFormat Wizard to create a new AutoFormat based on that formatting. The new AutoFormat will then be available to apply to any form or report in any database you work with on this computer.

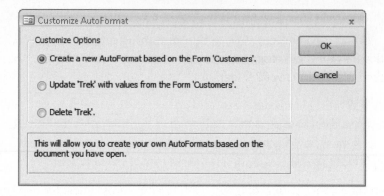

➤ **To apply an AutoFormat to a form or report**

1. In Design view, click the **Form Selector** or **Report Selector**.

2. On the **Arrange** tab, in the **AutoFormat** group, click the **AutoFormat** button.

3. In the **AutoFormat** gallery, click the format you want to apply to your form or report.

   Or

1. Display the **AutoFormat** gallery, and click **AutoFormat Wizard**.

2. On the wizard's only page, click the format you want in the **Form AutoFormats** list, and then click **Options**.

3. In the expanded **Attributes to Apply** area, clear the check boxes of any attributes you don't want to apply.

4. Click **OK**.

➤ **To create an AutoFormat based on a form or report**

1. Start the **AutoFormat** wizard, and click **Customize**.

2. In the **Customize AutoFormat** dialog box, select **Create a new AutoFormat based on the Form '<form>'**, and then click **OK**.

3. In the **New Style Name** dialog box, type the name you want in the **Style Name** box, and then click **OK**.

4. In the **AutoFormat** wizard, click **OK**.

Practice Tasks

The practice files for these tasks are located in the *Documents\Microsoft Press\ MCAS\Access2007\Objective02* folder.

● Open the *AddControls* database, and replace the logo and caption in the Customers form with a control that displays the *Logo* graphic.

● In the Detail section of the Products report in the *AddControls* database, add a text box control that is bound to the SupplierName field in the Suppliers table.

● Open the *RefineControls* database, and open the Customers form in Design view. Enlarge the Detail section, and then move all the controls on the right side of the form below the City label. Resize each control, and then arrange them in logical groupings on the form.

● In the Customers form of the *RefineControls* database, change the formatting of all the controls and labels in the Detail section to 8-point bold MS Sans Serif with a normal yellow background (Back Style and Back Color). Make the background of all the sections pale yellow with the sunken special effect.

● Open the *AutoFormat* database, and apply only the font and color of the Office AutoFormat to the Categories report.

Objective Review

Before finishing this chapter, ensure that you have mastered the following skills:

2.1 Create databases.

2.2 Create tables.

2.3 Modify tables.

2.4 Create fields and modify field properties.

2.5 Create forms.

2.6 Create reports.

2.7 Modify the design of reports and forms.

3 Entering and Modifying Data

The skills tested in this section of the Microsoft Office Specialist exam for Microsoft Office Access 2007 relate to working with data in tables. Specifically, the following objectives are associated with this set of skills:

3.1 Enter, edit, and delete records.
3.2 Navigate among records.
3.3 Find and replace data.
3.4 Attach documents to and detach from records.
3.5 Import data.

The number of records each table in an Access database can contain is limited more by the space available on the storage device than by anything else. Most of the information stored in a database table is in text format; however, Access 2007 also supports attachment fields in which you can attach one or more files to a record.

You can enter data into a table directly, through a form, or by importing or linking to it. However you collect the data, you will likely need to be able to efficiently view and locate information within the table. When a table includes many fields or records, it can be difficult to locate information by scrolling. You can use commands on the record navigation bar to move among records or jump to a specific record. Using the Find and Replace commands that are similar to those in other Microsoft Office programs, you can easily search for specific data and conduct table-wide replacement operations.

This chapter guides you in studying the processes of entering, editing, and deleting records; navigating among records in a table and optimizing the display of records; and finding and replacing data in a table. You will study ways of incorporating additional information by attaching files to a table and then viewing, saving, and removing file attachments. Finally, you will look at the processes of importing or linking to data from another source.

Important Before you can use the practice files in this chapter, you need to install them from the book's companion CD to their default location. See "Using the Companion CD" at the beginning of this book for more information.

Tip Graphics and operating system–related instructions in this book reflect the Windows Vista user interface. If your computer is running Windows XP and you experience trouble following the instructions as written, refer to the sidebar "If You Are Running Windows XP" in "Working in the Microsoft Office Fluent User Interface" at the beginning of this book.

3.1   Enter, edit, and delete records

Entering and Editing

You can enter and edit records either directly in a table or in a form. In a table, you enter each new record in the row indicated by the asterisk. When you start typing in the first field of the record, the asterisk changes to a pencil, indicating that the record has changed but is not saved. Access saves the record as soon as you move to a different record.

In both a table and a form, pressing Tab after you enter the last field value in a new record saves the record and moves you to a new one.

To quickly enter new records in a table, you can copy values from one field to another. You can also copy entire records, but if the table contains a primary key field that requires a unique value, you must edit the primary key field of the new record before Access will allow you to move away from it.

You can double-click a field value to select it for editing and then use the same editing techniques you would use in other Office programs.

➤ **To enter a new record**

1. In a table or form, move to the first field in a new blank record, type the field value, and then press **Tab**.

2. Continue entering field values and pressing **Tab** until you move to a new blank record.

➤ **To copy the value of the same field in the preceding record**

➜ Press **Ctrl+'** (single quotation mark).

➤ To copy most of the fields of a record

1. Click the record selector at the left end of the record, and then on the **Home** tab, in the **Clipboard** group, click the **Copy** button.

2. Click the new record at the bottom of the table, and then in the **Clipboard** group, click **Paste Append** in the **Paste** list.

3. If the table contains a primary key field, change the value in that field.

4. Replace any other field values as necessary. Then click away from the new record to save it.

➤ To edit a record

→ Double-click or drag through a field value to select it, and then make your changes.

Deleting

To maintain an efficient database, you should delete obsolete records. You can't recover deleted records, so it is a good idea to back up your database first. Access warns you before deleting records to give you an opportunity to change your mind. If the table from which you are deleting records is related to another table and the Cascade Delete Related Records option for that relationship is selected, records in the second table will also be deleted. Access warns you before cascading the deletion.

See Also If the records you want to delete have something in common, such as a name or date, you might want to create a query to delete them. For information about queries, see section 4.1, "Create queries."

➤ **To delete a selected record from a table**

→ Press the **Delete** key.

→ Right-click the selected record, click **Delete Record**, and then click **Yes**.

→ On the **Home** tab, in the **Records** group, click the **Delete** button.

Practice Tasks

The practice files for these tasks are located in the *Documents\Microsoft Press\ MCAS\Access2007\Objective03* folder.

- Open the *EnterRecords* database, and enter and save a new record in the Shippers table with the following field values:

SHIPPERID	COMPANY	CONTACT	PHONE
5	Big Things Freight	John Woods	(805) 555-0154

- In the *EnterRecords* database, complete the Big Things Freight record of the Shippers table by copying the STREET, CITY, STATE, and ZIP field values of the preceding record.

- In the *EnterRecords* database, edit the STREET field value in the Big Things Freight record of the Shippers table so that it reads *11095 S.E. 37th Pl.*

- In the Shippers table of the *EnterRecords* database, delete the record you created in the previous tasks.

- Open the *DuplicateRecords* database, and at the bottom of the Customers table, create a duplicate of the last record. Edit the primary key field in the new record so that Access will allow you to save it.

3.2   Navigate among records

You can use normal scrolling and keyboard methods to move around in a table. In both tables and forms, you can click buttons in the record navigator bar to move to the first or last record, the previous or next record, or the new record. If you know the number of the record you want, you can jump straight to that record.

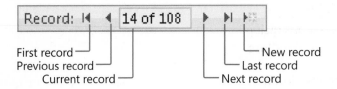

First record ⎯
Previous record ⎯
Current record ⎯   ⎯ New record
                                    ⎯ Last record
                                    ⎯ Next record

See Also You can also jump to a specific record by searching for its value. For information about finding specific records, see section 3.3, "Find and replace data."

You can hide and freeze columns to make moving around in a large table easier. Frozen columns move to the left end of the table, and you can then scroll the remaining columns while the frozen columns remain in view. You can unfreeze and then manually move the columns back to their regular places to continue working on the table, or you can close the table without saving to restore its pre-freeze state.

➤ **To move to the previous or next record**

→ On the **record navigation bar**, click the **Previous record** or **Next record** button.

→ Press the **Up Arrow** or **Down Arrow** key.

Tip You can move one screenful of records at a time by pressing the Page Up or the Page Down key.

➤ **To move to the first or last record**

→ On the **record navigation bar**, click the **First record** or the **Last record** button.

→ Press **Ctrl+Home** or **Ctrl+End**.

➤ **To move to the new record**

→ On the **record navigation bar**, click the **New (blank) record** button.

➤ **To move to a specific record**

→ On the **record navigation bar**, click the **Current record** indicator, and then type the number of the record you want.

➤ **To hide a selected column**

→ On the **Home** tab, in the **Records** group, click the **More** button, and then in the list, click **Hide Columns**.

➤ **To redisplay a hidden column**

1. On the **Home** tab, in the **Records** group, click the **More** button, and then in the list, click **Unhide Columns**.

2. In the **Unhide Columns** dialog box, select the check box of the column you want to redisplay, and then click **Close**.

➤ **To freeze a selected column**

→ On the **Home** tab, in the **Records** group, click the **More** button, and then in the list, click **Freeze**.

➤ **To unfreeze a column**

1. On the **Home** tab, in the **Records** group, click the **More** button, and then in the list, click **Unfreeze**.

2. If you want, move the column back to its original position by selecting it and then dragging its field name. Release the mouse button when the black bar is in the location you want.

Practice Tasks

The practice files for these tasks are located in the *Documents\Microsoft Press\ MCAS\Access2007\Objective03* folder.

● Open the *Navigate* database, and then open the Products table. Move to the last record in the table, and then move back through the preceding five records. Move to the fiftieth record, and then move to the first record. Finally, move to the new record.

● Open the *HideColumns* database, and then open the Customers table. Hide the Address, City, Region, PostalCode, and Country columns. Then unhide the City and Region columns.

● Open the *FreezeColumns* database, and then open the Customers table. Freeze the FirstName and LastName fields. Then scroll the database horizontally until the PhoneNumber field comes into view.

3.3 Find and replace data

Finding

If you want to locate a record or field containing a specific value, you can use the new Search feature. As you type characters, Access jumps to the next field containing those characters in the order you typed them.

If you want to find all the instances of a set of characters, you can use the Find command. This command locates the first field value containing the characters, and you can then jump forward or backward in the table to subsequent occurrences of the same set. You can refine the search by specifying the part of the field you want to find and whether you have typed the precise uppercase and lowercase characters.

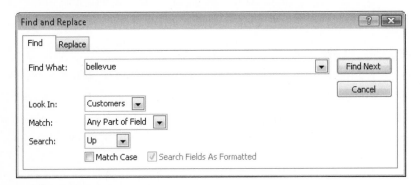

► **To search for a field value**

→ In the **Search** box to the right of the record navigator bar, type characters in the field value until you find the one you want.

Or

1. On the **Home** tab, in the **Find** group, click the **Find** button.

2. In the **Find and Replace** dialog box, type the value or part of the value in the **Find What** box.

3. In the **Match** list, click **Any Part of Field**, **Whole Field**, or **Start of Field**.

4. If you have typed the case of the value exactly as you want to find it, select the **Match Case** check box.

5. Click **Find Next** until you find the value.

See Also You can narrow the range of records in which to conduct a search by filtering the table. For information about filtering, see section 5.2, "Filter data." You can also search for records by using criteria in a query. For information about creating queries, see section 4.1, "Create queries."

Wildcards

If you want to find a specific value but aren't sure of all the characters, or if you want to find all the variations of a value, you can include one or more wildcard characters in the search term you enter in the Find What box of the Find And Replace dialog box. The most common wildcards are:

- *** (asterisk).** Represents any number of characters.
- **? (question mark).** Represents any single alphabetic character.
- **# (number sign).** Represents any single numeric character.

Strategy You can use wildcards with square brackets and various Match settings to achieve different results. Search Access Help for *wildcards* and read the topic "Use the Find and Replace dialog box to change data" to get an idea of all the possibilities.

➤ To find a value by using a wildcard

→ In the **Find What** box of the **Find and Replace** dialog box, type the value you want to look for, replacing the unknown or variable part with a wildcard character.

Replacing

If you want to replace multiple instances of the same word or phrase, you can use the Replace tab of the Find And Replace dialog box. As with the same feature in other Office programs, you can replace individual occurrences or all occurrences.

Tip You cannot use the Replace command to change values that have been entered from a lookup list.

➤ **To replace data**

1. On the **Home** tab, in the **Find** group, click the **Replace** button.

2. In the **Find and Replace** dialog box, type the value or part of the value you want to find in the **Find What** box and the value you want to replace it with in the **Replace With** box.

   Tip You can use a wildcard to find data but not to replace it. If you use a wildcard in the Replace With box, the replacement text will include the wildcard, not the characters it stands for.

3. In the **Match** list, click **Any Part of Field**, **Whole Field**, or **Start of Field**.

4. If you have typed the case of the value exactly as you want to find it, select the **Match Case** check box.

5. Click **Find Next**. until you find an occurrence you want to change, and then click **Replace**.

   Or

   To replace all occurrences, click **Replace All**.

See Also You can perform more sophisticated replace operations with a query. For information about queries, see section 4.1, "Create queries."

Practice Tasks

The practice files for these tasks are located in the *Documents\Microsoft Press\ MCAS\Access2007\Objective03* folder.

● Open the *FindAndReplace* database, and then open the Customers table or the Customers form. Find and step through all Customer records for which the FirstName is *Chris*.

● In the *FindAndReplace* database, open the Products table. Using wildcard characters, find and step through all Products for which Quantity Per Unit is measured by the bag.

● In the *FindAndReplace* database, open the Customers form. Step through all customer records where Region is *or*. Replace all instances of *or* with *OR*—the first three instances individually and all remaining occurrences at one time. Then open the Customers table to check the results.

3.4 Attach documents to and detach from records

When you first create a new field, you have the option of assigning it the Attachment data type; you cannot change the data type of an existing field to Attachment. The field's sole purpose is to hold a file; consequently, the only properties you can set for this type of field are Caption and Required.

In Datasheet view, an attachment field is designated by a paperclip icon with the number of attachments in parentheses. Double-clicking the field opens the Attachments dialog box where you can specify the file to be attached to the record.

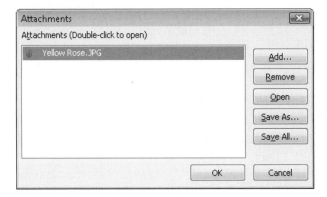

Double-clicking an attachment in this dialog box displays the contents of the attached file. You can also detach files and save an individual attachment or all the attachments as independent files.

Tip If you export an Access database to Microsoft Office Excel or to a text file, attachments are not included in the exported file.

➤ **To attach a file to an attachment field**

1. Double-click the attachment field to open the **Attachments** dialog box, and then click **Add**.

2. In the **Choose File** dialog box, locate and double-click the file you want to attach to the field.

3. Click **OK**.

➤ **To view an attachment**

→ Display the **Attachments** dialog box, and double-click the file you want to view.

➤ **To remove an attachment**

1. Display the **Attachments** dialog box, click the attachment in the list, and then click **Remove**.

2. Click **OK**.

➤ **To save an attachment as a file**

1. Display the **Attachments** dialog box, click the file you want to save, and then click **Save As**.

2. In the **Save Attachment** dialog box, browse to the folder where you want to save the file, and then click **Save**.

3. Click **OK** to close the **Attachments** dialog box.

   Or

1. Display the **Attachments** dialog box, and click **Save All**.

2. In the **Save Attachments** dialog box, browse to the folder where you want to save the files, and then click **Select**.

3. Click **OK** to close the **Attachments** dialog box.

Practice Tasks

The practice files for these tasks are located in the *Documents\Microsoft Press\ MCAS\Access2007\Objective03* folder.

- Open the *Attachments* database, and add an attachment field named *Photos* at the right end of the Products table. Then attach the *YellowRose* photo to the record for ProductID 12.

- In the *Attachments* database, view the *YellowRose* photo attached to the ProductID 12 record in the Products table. Then save the photo as an independent file in a location of your choosing.

3.5   Import data

Importing

Part of designing a database is determining the source of the information you intend to store in its tables. If the information already exists in another database or in a file such as an Excel workbook, you can save time and effort by importing the information rather than retyping it.

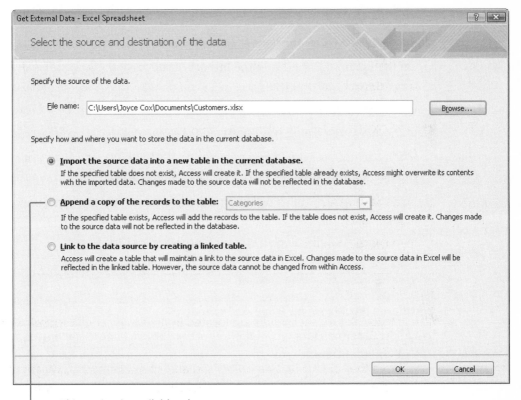

This option is available when you import an Excel spreadsheet.

You can import any of the standard Access database objects. When importing a table, you have the option of importing only the table definition (the structure that you see in Design view), or both the definition and the data. When importing a query, you can import it as a query, or you can import the results of the query as a table.

When you import an Access object, the entire object is imported as an object of the same name. You don't have the option of importing selected fields or records. If the active database already has an object of the same name, Access imports the new object with a number appended to the end of its name.

Tip If you need only some of the fields or records from a table in another database, you can create a query in the other database to select only the information you need and then import the results of the query as a table. Alternatively, you can import the entire table and then edit it. If you want to add records from a table in another database to a table in your database, use an append query. For more information about queries, see section 4.1, "Create queries."

> ### To import data from another Access database

1. On the **External Data** tab, in the **Import** group, click the **Access** button to start the **Get External Data** wizard.

2. On the **Select the source and destination of the data** page, click **Browse**.

3. In the **File Open** dialog box, locate and click the database, and then click **Open**.

4. On the **Select the source and destination of the data** page, with **Import tables, queries, forms, reports, macros, and modules into the current database** selected, click **OK**.

5. In the **Import Objects** dialog box, click the tables you want, and then click **OK**.

6. If you want, save the import steps; otherwise, click **Close**.

   See Also For information about saving and running import specifications, see "Import Specifications" later in this section.

> ### To import data from an Excel worksheet

1. On the **External Data** tab, in the **Import** group, click the **Excel** button to start the **Get External Data** wizard.

2. Browse to and open the Excel workbook.

3. On the **Select the source and destination of the data** page, with **Import the source data into a new table in the current database** selected, click **OK**.

   Tip If you want, you can add the information to an existing table, by clicking Append A Copy Of The Records To The Table and then clicking the table you want in the list.

4. In the **Import Spreadsheet Wizard**, click the sheet or range you want, and then click **Next**.

5. Follow the wizard's instructions, clicking **Next** to move from page to page.

6. On the wizard's last page, name the table, and click **Finish** to import the worksheet.

➤ To import data from a text file

1. On the **External Data** tab, in the **Import** group, click the **Text File** button to start the **Get External Data** wizard.

2. Browse to and open the file.

3. On the **Select the source and destination of the data** page, with **Import the source data into a new table in the current database** selected, click **OK**.

4. In the **Import Text Wizard**, specify whether the data is delimited or fixed width, and then click **Next**.

5. Follow the wizard's instructions, clicking **Next** to move from page to page.

6. On the wizard's last page, name the table, and click **Finish** to import the data.

Linking

If the information you need is being actively maintained elsewhere and you want to bring it into the current database to analyze it or create reports, you can link to the existing information in its original program rather than importing the information. When you link to data in another program, you can view and edit it in both programs, and what you see in your database is always up to date. Access indicates a linked table by an arrow to the left of the table icon.

Tip You can import but not link to data stored in Lotus 1-2-3 and XML files. Data from nontabular sources must be in comma-delimited or fixed-width format.

You can view and modify most types of linked data; the exception is data linked to an Excel worksheet, which can be modified only from Excel.

➤ To link to data in an external source

→ Follow the steps for importing a table, but on the **Select the source and destination of the data** page of the **Get External Data** wizard, click **Link to the data source by creating a linked table**.

Tip If you link to a file on a local area network (LAN), be sure to use a universal naming convention (UNC) path, rather than a mapped network drive. A UNC path includes the computer name as well as the share and folder names, so it is less likely to change.

Import Specifications

After running the Import Wizard, you are given the opportunity to save the import steps so that you can repeat them with the same or a different source file. (You can also save some export specifications, but you cannot save linking steps.)

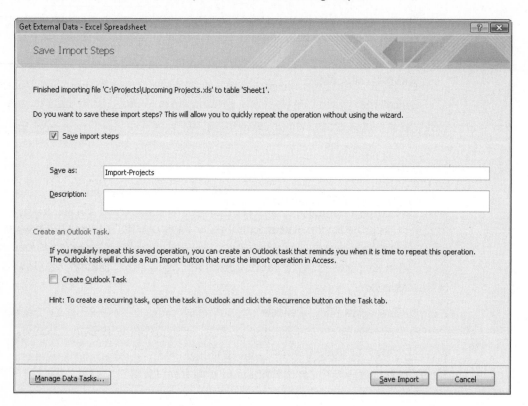

> ➤ **To save the import specification**

1. Complete the steps of the **Import Wizard**. After clicking **Finish**, on the **Save Import Steps** page, select the **Save import steps** check box.

2. On the expanded page, assign a name for the specification in the **Save as** box, and if you want, enter a description.

   Tip If you want to be reminded about running this specification in the future, you can create a Microsoft Office Outlook task. Selecting the Create Outlook task check box opens a task window where you can enter task details.

3. Click **Save Import**.

➤ **To run a saved import specification**

1. On the **External Data** tab, in the **Import** group, click the **Saved Imports** button.

2. In the **Manage Data Tasks** dialog box, on the **Saved Imports** tab, click the saved specification you want to run.

3. To run the specification with a different source file, click the path, make your changes, and then press **Enter**.

4. Click **Run**.

5. Click **OK** in the message confirming that the import operation was successful. Then click **Close**.

Practice Tasks

The practice files for these tasks are located in the *Documents\Microsoft Press\ MCAS\Access2007\Objective03* folder.

● Open the *ImportAccess* database, and import the Products table from the *Products* database. Then append the data from the *Products* worksheet to the existing Products table, saving the import specification with the name *Import-Products*.

● In the *ImportAccess* database, run the Import-Products import specification.

● Link the information in the Employees table of the *Products* database to a new Employees table in the *ImportAccess* database.

Objective Review

Before finishing this chapter, ensure that you have mastered the following skills:

3.1 Enter, edit, and delete records.

3.2 Navigate among records.

3.3 Find and replace data.

3.4 Attach documents to and detach from records.

3.5 Import data.

4 Creating and Modifying Queries

The skills tested in this section of the Microsoft Office Specialist exam for Microsoft Office Access 2007 relate to queries. Specifically, the following objectives are associated with this set of skills:

4.1 Create queries.

4.2 Modify queries.

You can locate information stored in a table or multiple tables by creating a query specifying the parameters of the information you want to find. Some types of query can also change the information in specific ways. Running a query (also called *querying the database*) displays a datasheet containing the records that fit your search criteria. You can use the query results as the basis for further analysis, create other Access objects (such as reports) from the results, or export the results to another format, such as a Microsoft Office Excel spreadsheet or a Microsoft SharePoint list. You can save the query so that you can run it again from the Queries section of the Navigation Pane.

This chapter guides you in studying ways of creating and modifying queries of various types, setting up the criteria Access uses to match records, and using calculations in queries.

 Important Before you can use the practice files in this chapter, you need to install them from the book's companion CD to their default location. See "Using the Companion CD" at the beginning of this book for more information.

Tip Graphics and operating system–related instructions in this book reflect the Windows Vista user interface. If your computer is running Windows XP and you experience trouble following the instructions as written, refer to the sidebar "If You Are Running Windows XP" in "Working in the Microsoft Office Fluent User Interface" at the beginning of this book.

4.1   Create queries

Strategy Because queries are the most powerful method of extracting information from a database, you should be thoroughly familiar with the different types of queries. It is important that you have hands-on experience with setting up the appropriate type of query for achieving the desired results and that you know how to modify queries in Design view.

Select Queries

When you want to do nothing more than find the records in a database that match a set of criteria, you use a select query. You display in the query window the field list of the table or tables from which you want to extract information and then specify the criteria for the search in a query grid. To extract information from more than one table, you must ensure that there are established relationships between them. These relationships must be created prior to using the Query Wizard, but their creation can be done on the fly in Query Design view.

See Also For information about relationships, see section 1.2, "Define and print table relationships."

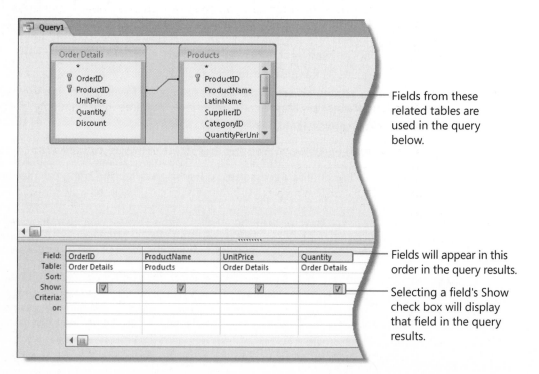

The field list boxes contain the fields that can be included in this query. The line connecting the boxes indicates that they are related by virtue of a common field. The Field row of the grid below contains the names of the fields actually included in the query, and the Table row shows which table each field belongs to. The Sort row indicates whether the query results will be sorted on this field. A selected check box in the Show row means that the field will be displayed in the results datasheet. (If the check box isn't selected, the field can be used to determine the query results, but it won't be displayed. The Show check box is not available in crosstab queries.) The Criteria row contains criteria that determine which records will be displayed, and the Or row sets up alternate criteria.

You can create queries from scratch in Design view, but it is often simplest to start by using a wizard to set up the query. You can then refine the query in Design view. Access provides four wizards:

- **Simple Query.** Locates records and displays information from the fields you specify in one or more sources.

- **Crosstab Query.** Locates records and displays information from the fields you specify in a worksheet format. You can use a crosstab query to calculate a sum, average, count, or other type of total for data that is grouped by two types of information—one down the left side of the datasheet and one across the top. The cell at the junction of each row and column displays the results of the query's calculation.

- **Find Duplicates.** Locates records that have the same information in one or more fields in a single table.

- **Find Unmatched Query.** Locates records in one table that have no matched records in another table.

Regardless of how you create a query, when you run it, the matching records are displayed in a new datasheet.

Tip If you apply a filter to a table to locate records and might need to use the same filter again, you can save it as a query so that you can run it at any time. Display the Save As dialog box, enter a name, select Query as the object type, and then click OK.

➤ **To create a simple query**

1. On the **Create** tab, in the **Other** group, click the **Query Wizard**.

2. In the **New Query** dialog box, double-click **Simple Query Wizard**.

3. In the **Tables/Queries** list, click the table you want to use, and then in the **Available Fields** list, double-click the fields you want to move to the **Selected Fields** list.

   Tip To move all the fields, click the >> button.

4. Repeat step 3 to add fields from other tables to the **Selected Fields** list, and then click **Next**.

   See Also If any of the selected fields contain data that supports aggregate functions, you are asked if you want so see the field details or a summary. For information about summary calculations, see section 4.2, "Modify queries."

5. Name the query. If you want to run it, leave **Open the query to view information** selected. If you want to add conditions to the query, click **Modify the query design**. Then click **Finish**.

➤ **To create a crosstab query**

1. Display the **New Query** dialog box, and double-click **Crosstab Query Wizard**.

2. Click the table you want to use, and then click **Next**.

   Tip To create a crosstab query from more than one table, first create a simple query to gather the fields in one datasheet, and then create a crosstab query based on the query results.

3. In the **Available Fields** list, double-click up to three fields whose values you will use as row headings, and then click **Next**.

4. Select the field whose values you want to use as column headings, and then click **Next**.

5. In the **Fields** list, click a field, and in the **Functions** list, click the function to use to calculate summary values. If you want to include row sums, select the **Yes, include row sums** check box. Then click **Next**.

6. Name the query. If you want to run it, leave **View the query** selected. If you want to refine the query, click **Modify the design**. Then click **Finish**.

➤ **To check a table for duplicate field values**

1. Display the **New Query** dialog box, and then double-click **Find Duplicates Query Wizard**.

2. Select the table you want to check, and then click **Next**.

3. In the **Available fields** list, double-click the fields that might have duplicate values to move them to the **Duplicate-value fields** list. Then click **Next**.

4. In the next **Available fields** list, double-click any other fields you want to display in the query results to move them to the **Additional query fields** list. Then click **Next**.

5. Name the query. If you want to run it, leave **View the results** selected. If you want to refine the query, click **Modify the design**. Then click **Finish**.

➤ **To find unmatched records**

1. Display the **New Query** dialog box, and then double-click **Find Unmatched Query Wizard**.

2. Click the table that contains unmatched records, and then click **Next**.

3. Click the related table, and then click **Next**.

4. If the wizard has not already identified the matching fields, click a field in each table, click the **<=>** button, and then click **Next**.

5. In the **Available fields** list, double-click the fields you want to see in the results to move them to the **Selected fields** list. Then click **Next**.

6. Name the query. If you want to run it, leave **View the results** selected. If you want to refine the query, click **Modify the design**. Then click **Finish**.

➤ **To make fields available in Design view**

1. On the **Design** tab, in the **Query Setup** group, click the **Show Table** button.

2. In the **Show Table** dialog box, double-click the table you want to add to the query window, and then click **Close**.

   Tip You can add the fields used in existing queries to the query window from the Queries tab of the Show Table dialog box.

➤ **To add fields to a query in Design view**

→ Double-click a field from its field list to move it to the next blank column in the query grid.

→ Drag a field from its field list to a specific column in the query grid.

→ Double-click the field list title bar to select all the fields, and then drag the selection to the grid to add all the fields in order.

→ Drag the asterisk at the top of the list to the grid to add all the fields, and then individually drag any field you want to sort or add criteria for.

See Also If two tables have fields with the same name, Access creates an alias by prepending the table name to the field name; for example, Customers_LastName: LastName or Employees_LastName: LastName. For more information, see section 4.2, "Modify Queries."

➤ **To specify a sort order in Design view**

→ In the query grid, in the column of the field on which you want to base the sort, click **Ascending** or **Descending** in the **Sort** row list.

➤ **To specify in Design view whether to include a field in query results**

→ In the field's column in the query grid, select or clear the **Show** check box.

➤ **To run a query**

→ On the **Design** tab, in the **Results** group, click the **Run** button.

Criteria

To identify the records you want a query to select, you can add the following types of criteria to the Criteria row of the query grid:

- Specific field values
- Approximate field values that include wildcards such as ? (one character) or * (multiple characters)
- Expressions that include comparison operators such as = (equal to), < (less than), and > (greater than)
- Expressions that include logical and special operators such as And, Or, Not, Like, and Null

You can use a query to select records that meet more than one criterion in more than one field by combining criteria in the Criteria and Or rows. You can also find records that don't meet a criterion and records that have no value in a specific field.

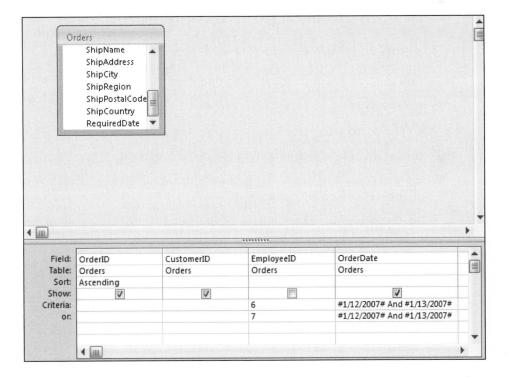

➤ **To select all records that match a field value**

→ In the query grid, in the **Criteria** row of the field, type the value you want to find.

➤ To select all records that do not match a field value

→ In the query grid, in the **Criteria** row of the field, type the value you want to find preceded by the word *NOT*.

➤ To select all records that contain no value in a field

→ In the query grid, in the **Criteria** row of the field, type *NULL*.

Tip When you press Enter or move away from the field, Access converts the entry to "Is Null."

➤ To use wildcards in selection criteria

→ In the query grid, in the **Criteria** row of the field, type the value you want to find with a wildcard character replacing the unknown or variable parts.

Tip When you press Enter or move away from the field, Access precedes the criterion you typed with the word *Like*.

➤ To use comparison operators in selection criteria

→ In the query grid, in the **Criteria** row of the field, type the comparison operator followed by the value you want to find.

➤ To find records in which more than one field meets a criterion

→ In the query grid, in the **Criteria** row of each field, enter the value you want to find for each field.

➤ To find records in which one field meets two criteria

→ In the query grid, in the **Criteria** row of the field, enter the values you want to find separated by the **And** operator.

Tip This type of criterion is often used to find values that fall in a range (both more than one value And less than another).

➤ To find records in which one field meets either of two criteria

→ In the query grid, enter one of the values you want to find in the **Criteria** row of the field, and enter the other value in the **or** row.

Tip If you have more than two alternatives, you can enter them in the rows below the Or row.

➤ To find records meeting one criterion in a set of criteria

→ In the query grid, enter one of the values you want to find in the **Criteria** row of one field, and enter the other value in the **or** row of the other field.

Action Queries

Sometimes you want to do nothing more than find the records; at other times, you will want to extend the query to do something with the matched records. You can create the following types of action queries to perform an action on the results of the selection process:

- **Append.** Adds records from one or more tables to the end of the table you specify in the Append dialog box.

- **Delete.** Deletes records from one or more tables. Access adds a Delete row to the table to allow you to specify the criteria for the deletion. If you don't enter at least one criterion, all the records will be deleted.

- **Make Table.** Creates a new table by copying field values from one or more tables. The new table, which you name in the Make Table dialog box, has the same structure as the source tables.

- **Update.** Changes values in one or more tables. Access adds an Update To row to the design grid to allow you to specify the value that should replace the one in the Criteria row. If you don't enter these values, this field will be unchanged in all the records.

  See Also You can update values by entering calculations in the Update To row. For example, you could increase the retail price of selected products by 2 percent. For information, see section 4.2, "Modify queries."

You can create action queries by setting up the part that selects the records as usual and then adding the action you want in Design view.

Tip Two additional types of action queries involve building criteria using Structured Query Language (SQL) commands: Pass-through queries perform SQL processing on a database server; and Union queries use SQL commands to combine the results of two or more select queries.

➤ To add records to the end of a table by using a query

1. Create a query that selects the records you want to copy to another table, and open it in Design view.

2. On the **Design** tab, in the **Query Type** group, click the **Append** button.

3. In the **Append** dialog box, enter the name of the table to which you want to add the records in the **Table Name** box, and click **OK**.

4. Run the query.

5. In the message box stating that you are about to append the selected records to the table, click **Yes**.

➤ To delete records by using a query

1. Create a query that selects the records you want to delete, and open it in Design view.

2. On the **Design** tab, in the **Query Type** group, click the **Delete** button.

3. Ensure that at least one field has a selection criterion in the **Criteria** row.

4. Run the query.

5. In the message box stating that you are about to delete the selected records, check that the number of records reported is logical, and then click **Yes**.

   Tip It's important to check the message before authorizing the delete operation. It cannot be undone. If an error message appears, stating that some or all of the records could not be deleted due to a key violation, it is probably because the records are part of a relationship with another table. For example, this error will appear if you attempt to delete a record from the Products table for which a related record exists in the Order Details table.

➤ To use a query to create a table

1. Create a query that selects the records you want to copy to a new table, and then open it in Design view.

2. On the **Design** tab, in the **Query Type** group, click the **Make Table** button.

3. In the **Make Table** dialog box, enter a name for the table in the **Table Name** box, and then click **OK**.

4. Run the query.

5. In the message box stating that you are about to paste the selected records into a new table, click **Yes**.

   Tip If you rerun a make table query, Access warns you that the existing table will be deleted, deletes it based on your confirmation, and then returns you to step 5.

➤ **To update fields in a table by using a query**

1. Create a query that selects the records you want to update, and open it in Design view.

2. On the **Design** tab, in the **Query Type** group, click the **Update** button.

3. Ensure that at least one field has a value in both the **Update To** row and the **Criteria** row.

4. Run the query.

5. In the message box stating that you are about to update the selected records, check that the number of records reported is logical, and then click **Yes**.

   Tip It's important to check the message before authorizing the update operation. It cannot be undone.

Subqueries

When you want to use the results of one query as a field in another query, you can use a subquery. The name assigned to the subquery is called a *field alias*, and it appears as the name of the field in the main query's results. A subquery that you use as a field alias cannot include more than one field in its results. You can also enter a subquery as a criterion in the Criteria row. In either case, the subquery is a SQL expression that you enter in a magnified representation of the selected query-grid cell called the *Zoom box*.

Strategy Subqueries can be complex structures, and you need hands-on experience to be able to construct them. However, anyone can copy a SQL expression into the Zoom box and run the resulting subquery. If you want, practice using the examples given in Access Help so that you understand how subqueries work.

➤ **To display the Zoom box used to create a subquery**

→ With the main query displayed in Design view, right click the **Field** row of a blank column for which you want to use a subquery as a field alias, or the **Criteria** row of a field for which you want to use a subquery as a criterion.

Practice Tasks

The practice files for these tasks are located in the *Documents\Microsoft Press\MCAS\Access2007\Objective04* folder.

- Open the *SelectQuery* database, and create a query that lists the ProductID, ProductName, and Discontinued fields from the Products table together with the SupplierName and PhoneNumber fields from the Suppliers table. Name the query *Discontinued Products*. In the results, display the records in which the Discontinued field value is Yes, but don't display the Discontinued field value.

- Open the *CrossTab* database, and create a query from the Orders table that lists the EmployeeID field as the row headings and the ShipRegion field as the column headings. Count the ShipCity field values for each column and row intersection. Name the query *SalesByRegion*. Change the field alias of the Total Of ShipCity field to *Total Orders*. Then run the query.

- Open the *Unmatched* database, and identify the records in the Products table that have no value in the Orders Details table. Display the ProductName and UnitPrice in the query results. Accept the suggested query name, and run the query.

- Open the *Update* database, and create a query that will change the PostalCode value in the Customers table from 88053 to 88052. Name the query *ZipCodeUpdate*, and run the query.

- Open the *MakeTable* database, and create a query that will copy the discontinued products from the Products table to a new *Discontinued Products* table. Accept the suggested query name, and run the query.

- Open the *Append* database. Create a query based on the Customers and Orders tables that will identify all customers who have not placed an order since 2/1/2007, and append these records to the CustomersWithoutOrders table. Name the query *AppendCustomers*.

- Open the *Delete* database, and create a query named *DeleteProducts* that will delete all the discontinued products from the Products table.

4.2   Modify queries

Table Changes

You can add new tables to a query at any time. Sometimes you might need to add a table that has relationship with two other tables only so that you can provide a link between the two other tables. If you aren't using a table any more, you can remove it to avoid clutter.

➤ **To add a table to an existing query**

→ In Design view, drag the table object from the **Navigation Pane** to the Table window.

Or

1. In Design view, in the **Query Setup** group, click the **Show Table** button.

2. In the **Show Table** dialog box, double-click a table to add it to the query, and then click **Close**.

   Tip You can use this method to add a second copy of a table to the query window. The copy is designated in the query by *_1* appended to the table name.

➤ **To remove a table from a query in Design view**

→ Right-click the table, and then click **Remove Table**.

→ Select the table in the Table window, and then press the **Delete** key.

Parameters

If you frequently run a query against the same table and the same field but with a different criterion each time, you can save the query once and ask for the criterion to be supplied each time the query is run.

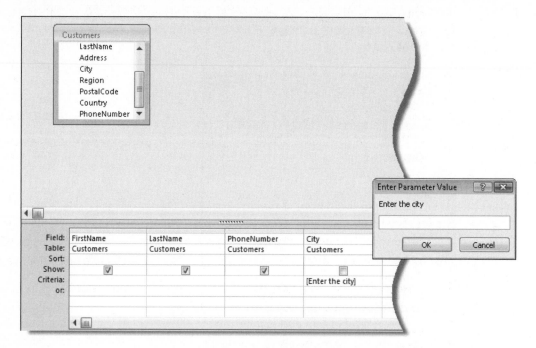

You can use wildcards in a parameter prompt to allow the person running the query to enter a partial field value. You can also specify the data type that must be entered.

Tip If you specify a data type other than text and the user enters the wrong type, Access displays an error message explaining what type of data is required.

➤ **To allow the user to enter a criterion when running a query**

→ In the **Criteria** row of the field for which you want to specify a parameter, type the criterion prompt enclosed in square brackets.

Tip You can't use a period or an exclamation point in the prompt.

➤ **To allow the user to enter part of a criterion when running a query**

1. In the **Criteria** row of the field for which you want to specify a parameter, type the criterion prompt enclosed in square brackets.

2. Precede the prompt with the word *Like* and a space.

3. Follow the prompt with &"*" (an ampersand followed by an asterisk enclosed in quotation marks).

➤ **To specify the data type that must be entered**

1. In Design view, on the **Design** tab, in the **Show/Hide** group, click the **Parameters** button.

2. In the **Query Parameters** dialog box, enter the parameter text (matching the user criteria in the expression) enclosed in brackets, click the type of data in the **Data Type** list, and then click **OK**.

   Tip You also have to enter the parameter in the Criteria row.

➤ **To run a parameter query**

1. Open the query from the **Navigation Pane**, or run the query in Design view.

2. In the **Enter Parameter Value** dialog box, enter the value as prompted, and then click **OK**.

Joins

The join type between two tables is determined by Access when you create a permanent table relationship, or you can specify a join type between tables that do not have an existing table relationship during query design. The following join types are available:

- **Inner.** Represents the SQL INNER clause, which combines only the matching records from two joined tables.

- **Left.** Represents the SQL LEFT clause, which combines all records from the Left table with their matching records from the Right table.

- **Right.** Represents the SQL RIGHT clause, which combines all records from the Right table with their matching records from the Left table.

If the tables you are querying have an existing join that will not produce the query result you want, you can change the join type while creating the query.

➤ **To change the join type of two tables for a query**

1. In Design view, double-click the join line between two related tables.

2. In the **Join Properties** dialog box, verify the table and column names. Then select **1** to create an inner join, **2** to create a left join, or **3** to create a right join.

3. Click **OK**.

Calculations

In addition to using crosstab queries to summarize information in a datasheet format, you can enter aggregate functions in the Total row of a select query to produce the sum, average, count, and other summaries of values. Access queries support the following aggregate functions in the Total row:

- **Sum.** Totals the values in a field.
- **Avg.** Averages the values in a field.
- **Count.** Counts the number of values in a field, not including Null (blank) values.
- **Min.** Identifies the lowest value in a field.
- **Max.** Identifies the highest value in a field.
- **StDev.** Calculates the standard deviation of the values in a field.
- **Var.** Calculates the variance of the values in a field.
- **First.** Returns the oldest date in the field.
- **Last.** Returns the latest date in the field.

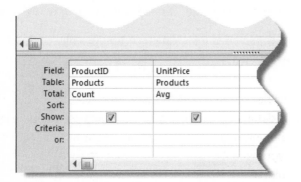

See Also You can add a Total row to a datasheet to perform aggregate functions on all the data in a field. For information, see section 2.3, "Modify tables."

You can also use calculations as criteria in the query grid. You can enter simple calculations directly in either the Criteria row or the Zoom box, or you can use the Expression Builder to create more complex expressions. You can use the +, -, *, and / arithmetic operators in these calculations. To include the value in a field in a calculation, enclose the field name in square brackets.

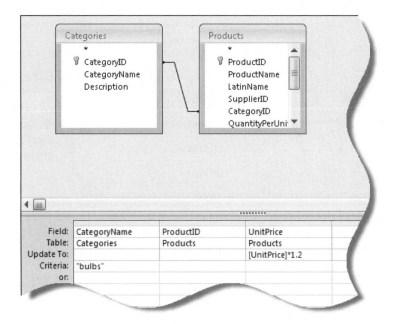

Calculations can also be used to derive the values of a new field from the values in existing fields. One of the rules of good database design is that you should not store information that can be calculated from other information in the database, but you should instead perform the calculation when you need it in a query. That way, you avoid inflating the size of the database file and the maintenance costs associated with updating the calculated information if the base information changes. This type of calculation creates a new field to contain the calculated values. You name the new field by including a field alias in the calculation expression. As with calculated criteria, you can enter the calculation directly in either the Field row or the Zoom box, or you can use the Expression Builder.

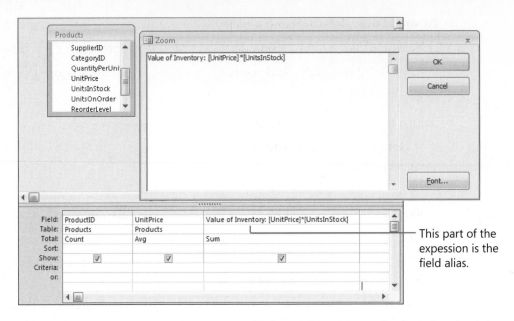

This part of the expression is the field alias.

Tip You can widen a column of the query grid to see all its contents by dragging the right border of the gray selection bar above the column. You can quickly make any column as wide as its contents by double-clicking the border.

In addition to being used to represent a field name or expression in a query Field row, an alias can also be used to clarify the source of data for a field (for example, "Customers_LastName: LastName" where Customers_LastName is the alias referring to the LastName field in the Customers table). If you do not assign a required alias, Access assigns the alias *Expr* for you. The syntax of an alias is as follows:

alias name: expression or field name

When you run the query, the alias becomes the column name in the datasheet.

Tip If the Caption property value of a field is set at the table level, it overrides the Alias name in the query result.

If the same field name appears in two tables and you want to be sure the query uses the correct field, precede the field name with the table name enclosed in square brackets and an exclamation point, as in the following example:

ExtendedPrice: CCur([Order Details]![UnitPrice][Quantity]*(1-[Discount]))*

Here, [Order Details]![UnitPrice] clarifies which UnitPrice field is to be used in the calculation.

➤ **To summarize data by using a query**

  1. In Design view, on the **Design** tab, in the **Show/Hide** group, click the **Totals** button.

  2. In the **Total** row of the field you want to summarize, click the aggregate function you want in the list.

➤ **To use a calculation as a criterion in a query**

  1. In Design view, in the **Criteria** row, click the field for which you want to enter a calculated criterion.

     Or

     Right-click the field, and then click **Zoom** to display the **Zoom** dialog box.

     Or

     Click the field, and then on the **Design** tab, in the **Query Setup** group, click the **Builder** button to display the **Expression Builder** dialog box.

  2. Type or build the expression, and then either click away from the **Criteria** row or click **OK** to close the dialog box.

➤ **To create a calculated field by using a query**

  1. In Design view, in the **Field** row, click the next blank column in the query grid.

     Or

     Right-click the **Field** row of the next blank column, and then click **Zoom** to display the **Zoom** dialog box.

     Or

     Click the **Field** row of the next blank column, and then on the **Design** tab, in the **Query Setup** group, click the **Builder** button to display the **Expression Builder** dialog box.

  2. Type or build the expression, preceding it with the field alias representing the name of the calculated field, followed by a colon.

     Tip The Expression Builder will automatically precede the expression with the Expr1 field alias. Replace this term with the field alias you want.

  3. Either click away from the **Field** row or click **OK** to close the dialog box.

Practice Tasks

The practice files for these tasks are located in the *Documents\Microsoft Press\ MCAS\Access2007\Objective04* folder.

● Open the *AddTable* database, and then display the CheckByCity query, which finds customers who live in the city of Seattle. To this query, add a criterion so that the query finds only customers who live in Seattle and who have no orders in the Orders table.

● In the *AddTable* database, add a parameter to the CheckByCity query that allows you to specify the city at runtime.

● Open the *Calculate* database, and create a query based on the Products table that counts the number of records that have a value in the ProductID field and averages the values in the UnitPrice field. Name the query *Aggregate*, and then run the query.

● In the *Calculate* database, change the Products By Category query so that it includes a NewUnitPrice field reflecting the fact that the unit price of the products in the Bulbs category will be increasing by 2 percent (that is, they will be multiplied by 1.02).

● In the *Calculate* database, add to the Aggregate query a field named *Value of Inventory* that calculates inventory valuation by multiplying the unit price of each product by the number of units in stock. Do not display the ProductID field.

Objective Review

Before finishing this chapter, ensure that you have mastered the following skills:

4.1 Create queries.

4.2 Modify queries.

5 Presenting and Sharing Data

The skills tested in this section of the Microsoft Office Specialist exam for Microsoft Office Access 2007 relate to extracting and sharing data. Specifically, the following objectives are associated with this set of skills:

5.1 Sort data.

5.2 Filter data.

5.3 Create and modify charts.

5.4 Export data.

5.5 Save database objects as other file types.

5.6 Print database objects.

A database is a repository for information. It might contain only a few records or thousands of records, stored in one table or multiple tables. No matter how much information a database contains, it is useful only if people can locate the information they need in the format in which they need it. Access 2007 provides tools you can use to organize the display of information stored in a database, to locate specific items of information, and to make database information available in a variety of way.

This chapter guides you in studying how to sort and filter information and locate and display records that match multiple criteria. You will also study how to export and save database information, and finally, how to print it.

 Important Before you can use the practice files in this chapter, you need to install them from the book's companion CD to their default location. See "Using the Companion CD" at the beginning of this book for more information.

Tip Graphics and operating system–related instructions in this book reflect the Windows Vista user interface. If your computer is running Windows XP and you experience trouble following the instructions as written, refer to the sidebar "If You Are Running Windows XP" in "Working in the Microsoft Office Fluent User Interface" at the beginning of this book.

5.1   Sort data

Text vs. Numbers

The concept of sorting seems quite intuitive, but it is complicated by the fact that numbers can be treated as text or as numerals. Because of the spaces, hyphens, and punctuation typically used in a phone number or postal code, numbers in these fields are usually treated as text. Numbers in a price or quantity field, on the other hand, are usually treated as numerals.

When Access sorts text, it sorts first on the first character in the selected field in every record, then on the next character, then on the next, and so on—until it runs out of characters. When Access sorts numbers, it treats the contents of each field as one value and sorts the records based on that value. This tactic can result in seemingly strange sort orders. For example, sorting the numbers in the first list as text produces the second list, whereas sorting the first list as numerals produces the third list:

1	1	1
1234	11	3
23	12	4
3	1234	11
11	22	12
22	23	22
12	3	23
4	4	1234

If a text field contains numbers, you can sort the field numerically by padding the numbers with leading zeros so that all entries are the same length. For example, 001, 011, and 101 sort correctly even if the numbers are defined as text.

Tables and Forms

You can sort the values in one or more fields in a table in Datasheet view or a form in Form view, in either ascending or descending order. To correctly sort on multiple fields, you have to know the order in which you want the records to be sorted. For example, if you want to sort the records in a Customer table by Region, then by City, and then by LastName, you would specify the sort for the LastName field (the innermost field), then the sort for the City (one step further out), and finally the sort for the Region (the outermost field).

Region	City	LastName	CustomerID	FirstName
WA	Bellevue	Ackerman	ACKPI	Pilar
BC	Vancouver	Adams	ADATE	Terry
BC	Vancouver	Allen	ALLMI	Michael
WA	Redmond	Ashton	ASHCH	Chris
WA	Woodinville	Bankov	BANMA	Martin
WA	Oak Harbor	Bento	BENPA	Paula
WA	Kirkland	Berry	BERJO	Jo
WA	Yakima	Berg	BERKA	Karen
MT	Butte	Boseman	BOSRA	Randall
OR	Beaverton	Bremer	BRETE	Ted
WA	Seattle	Browne	BROKE	Kevin F.
CA	San Francisco	Campbell	CAMDA	David
CA	Palo Alto	Cannon	CANCH	Chris
BC	Sidney	Charney	CHANE	Neil
BC	Sidney	Clark	CLAMO	Molly
WA	Seattle	Coleman	COLPA	Pat
WA	Bellevue	Cornejo	CORCE	Cecilia
ID	Moscow	Cox	COXBR	Brian
WA	Seattle	Culp	CULSC	Scott
WA	Seattle	Danseglio	DANMI	Mike

The selected fields are arranged in outermost to innermost order.

After sorting a table or form, you can save the sort order so that the next time you open that object, the fields are sorted the same way.

➤ To sort a table on one field in Datasheet view

→ Click the arrow in the field name of the field to be sorted, and then click the ascending or descending option.

→ Click the field name of the field to be sorted, and then on the **Home** tab, in the **Sort & Filter** group, click the **Ascending** or **Descending** button.

➤ To sort a table on more than one field in Datasheet view

1. Click the arrow in the field name of the innermost field to be sorted, and then click the ascending or descending option.

2. Sort the next innermost field, and then the next, sorting the outermost field last. Or

1. Arrange the fields in the order you want to sort them, with the outermost field on the left and the innermost on the right.

   Tip You can move a column by clicking its field name and then dragging the field name to the left or right..

2. Select the adjacent columns you want to sort, and then on the .**Home** tab, in the **Sort & Filter** group, click the **Ascending** or **Descending** button.

➤ To sort field values in a form in Form view

→ Right-click the field to be sorted, and then click the ascending or descending option.

→ Click the field to be sorted, and then on the **Home** tab, in the **Sort & Filter** group, click the **Ascending** or **Descending** button.

➤ To save a sort order for a table

1. In Design view, press **F4** to display the **Property Sheet** for the table.

2. On the **General** tab, set the **Order By On Load** property to **Yes.**

➤ To save a sort order for a form

1. In Design view, click the form selector, and display the **Property Sheet** for the form.

2. On the **Data** tab, et the **Order By On Load** property to **Yes.**

➤ To remove a sort order from a table or form

→ On the **Home** tab, in the **Sort & Filter** group, click the **Clear All Sorts** button.

Queries

You sort the results of a query the same way you sort a table. To display query results already sorted on one or more fields, you specify the sort order in the Sort row of the query grid. To sort multiple fields, you must arrange the fields from left to right in the grid in outermost to innermost order.

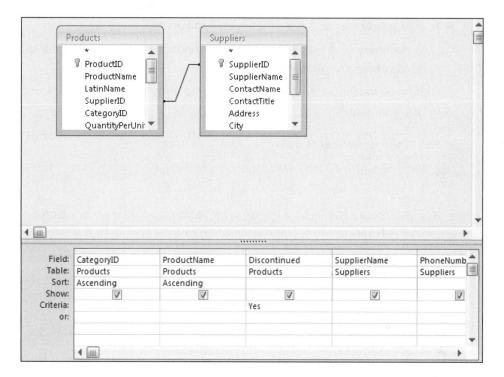

After sorting on a field, you can specify that the query results should show only the highest values (for an ascending sort) or lowest values (for a descending sort).

➤ To have a query sort its results on one field

→ In the Design view, in the **Sort** row, click the field on which you want to sort the results, and then click the sort order you want in the list.

➤ To have a query sort its results on more than one field

1. If the fields on which you want to sort are not already in left to right, outermost to innermost order, put the fields in that order by dragging their selectors.

2. In the **Sort** row, click each field on which you want to sort the results, and then click the sort order you want in the list.

➤ To have a query show the highest or lowest values in a field

1. In the query grid, specify the sort order you want (ascending for highest values and descending for lowest values.)

2. On the **Design** tab, in the **Query Setup** group, in the **Return** list, click the number or percentage of records you want to display in the results.

➤ To set the default sort order for query results

→ In the Design view, on the **Design** tab, display the **Property Sheet** for the query, and set the **Order By On Load** property to **Yes.**

See Also For information about sorting in reports, see section 2.6, "Create reports."

Practice Tasks

The practice files for these tasks are located in the *Documents\Microsoft Press\ MCAS\Access2007\Objective05* folder.

● Open the *Sort* database, and sort the Customers form by Region and then by City in ascending order. Then in the Products table, rearrange the fields so that with one command, you can sort the table by Supplier and then by Product Name.

● In the *Sort* database, save the sort order of the form so that in the future, the form will open with the records sorted by Region and then by City.

● In the *Sort* database, modify the Customers Query so that its results display matching records sorted by City and then by LastName.

5.2   Filter data

Simple Filters

Sorting organizes data in a logical manner, but does not locate specific records. To locate records containing (or not containing) specific field values without first creating a query, you can apply simple filters while viewing a table, a form, query results, or a report. To filter by multiple criteria, you can apply additional filters to the results of the first one.

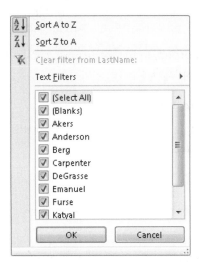

➤ To display records containing a specific field value

1. Click the field you want to filter, and then on the **Home** tab, in the **Sort & Filter** group, click the **Filter** button.
    Or

    In a table or in query results, click the field name arrow.

2. In the field value list, click **Select All** to clear all the check boxes.

3. Select the check box(es) of the field value(s) you want to display, and then click **OK**.

➤ To temporarily remove the filter from a table, report, or query result

→ On the **Home** tab, in the **Sort & Filter** group, click the **Toggle Filter** button (the ScreenTip is **Remove Filter**). Click the button again (the ScreenTip changes to **Apply Filter**) to reapply the filter

→ To the right of the record navigator bar, (in tables and query results only), click **Filtered.** Click the setting again (it changes to **Unfiltered**) to reapply the filter.

➤ **To permanently remove a filter**

1. On the **Home** tab, in the **Sort & Filter** group, click the **Filter** button.
Or

In a table or in query results, click the field name filter icon.

2. Click **Clear filter from** *<field>*.

Common Filters

In addition to filtering on entire field values, you can use ready-made filters to locate records that meet certain criteria. The criteria vary depending on the data type of the field.

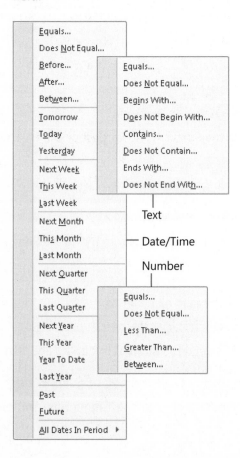

Strategy Take the time to familiarize yourself with the wide range of ready-made filters and the kinds of criteria you can create with them. Experiment with criteria that include and don't include a specific value. Be sure to thoroughly explore the criteria available for the Date/Time data type, which vary depending on the range of dates in the field.

➤ To apply a common filtering criterion

1. Click the field you want to filter, and then on the **Home** tab, in the **Sort & Filter** group, click the **Filter** button.
Or

   In a table or in query results, click the field name arrow.

2. Point to *<data type>* **Filters**, and then click the criterion you want to filter by..

3. In the **Custom Filter** dialog box, enter the value that completes the criterion, and then click **OK**.

➤ To display records containing numbers or dates within a range

1. Display the filter list.

2. Point to *<data type>* **Filters**, and then click **Between**.

3. In the **Between** dialog box, enter the **Smallest** and **Largest** or **Oldest** and **Newest** values, and then click **OK**.

Tip In a date field, you can click All Dates In Period to display all date values in a particular quarter or month.

Filter by Selection

You can quickly filter records based on a current selection in a field. The criteria available vary with the data type of the field.

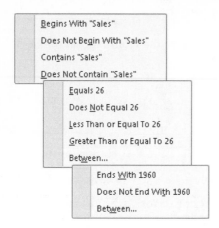

> ➤ **To display records matching the selection**

1. Select the field value or part of the value that you want to use as a filter.
2. On the **Home** tab, in the **Sort & Filter** group, click the **Selection** button.
3. Click the criterion you want to filter by.

Filter by Form

In a table, query results, or a form, you can quickly filter records based on the values in several fields by using the Filter By Form command. This command displays a filtering datasheet or form that looks empty. However, each blank field is actually a combo box containing a list of all the entries in that field. You can select a value from the list or enter a new one.

Using Filter By Form on a table that has only a few fields is easy. But using it on a table that has a few dozen fields gets a bit cumbersome, and it is simpler to find information by using the Filter By Form command with the form version of the table.

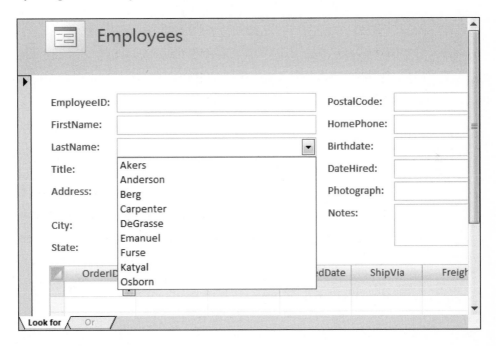

Applying the filter displays the records containing the specified values. In a filtered form, you move between records by clicking the buttons in the record navigation bar.

Tip Because defining the filter is sometimes easier in a form and viewing the results is sometimes easier in a table, you might consider creating a form based on the table, filtering the data within the form, and then switching to Datasheet view to display the results.

➤ **To select multiple field values for filtering from lists**

1. On the **Home** tab, in the **Sort & Filter** group, click the **Advanced Filter Options** button, and then click **Filter By Form.**

2. On the **Look for** tab of the **Filter By Form** template, click the field you want to filter, and then click the value you want in the list.

3. Repeat step 2 for any other fields you want to filter.

4. On the **Home** tab, in the **Sort & Filter** group, click the **Advanced** button, and then in the list, click **Apply Filter/Sort.**

   Tip Use the Or tab to select all field values that meet any of two or more criteria.

Practice Tasks

The practice files for these tasks are located in the *Documents\Microsoft Press\MCAS\ Access2007\Objective05* folder.

● Open the *Filter* database, and filter the Alphabetical List Of Products report to display only the records in the Trees category.

● In the *Filter* database, filter the Customers form to display the three customers who live in Washington state (WA) and whose last names begin with the letter *S*.

● In the *Filter* database, remove the saved filter from the Employees table.

● In the *Filter* database, display only the products in the Products table that have the word *fertilizer* in their name.

● In the *Filter* database, use Filter By Form to display the orders in the Order Details table for product number 37 that were sold at full price (no discount).

5.3   **Create and modify charts**

Strategy Charts don't work as well in Access as they do in other 2007 Microsoft Office programs. You need to experiment with them to be able to predict the outcome of plotting different types of charts and formatting them in various ways.

When you want to display visual representations of numeric data from a table or query in a form or report, you can add a chart control in Design view. After you create the chart, dummy data is plotted in Design view but you see your own data when you switch to Form view or Report view.

In Design view, you can size and move the chart just like any other control. You can change the chart type, modify various chart options such as the title, gridlines, and legend; and format the border and background of the chart area.

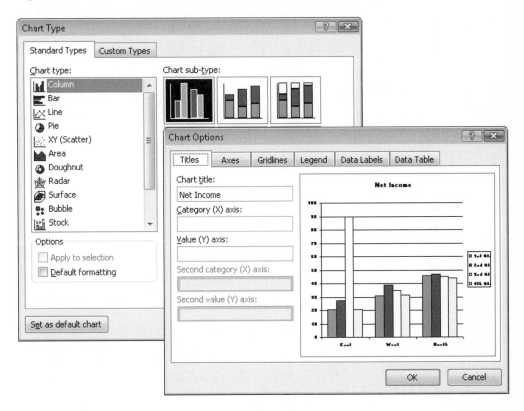

See Also A more straightforward way of creating a chart on a form is to create a PivotChart. For information about creating forms with PivotCharts, see section 2.5, "Create Forms."

➤ **To add a chart to a form or report**

1. Open a form or report in Design view, and on the **Design** tab, in the **Controls** group, click the **Insert Chart**

2. Click a blank area of the design grid to create an area for the chart.

3. On the first page of the **Chart Wizard**, click the table or query on which you want to base the chart, and then click **Next**.

4. Select the fields that contain the data you want to be plotted in the chart, and then click **Next**.

5. Click the icon for the type of chart you want to create, and then click **Next**.

6. If necessary, adjust the way the data series are plotted, and then click **Next**.

7. If necessary, select the **Form** and **Chart** fields.

8. Type a title for the chart, specify whether a legend should be included, and then click **Finish**.

➤ **To change the chart type**

1. Double-click the chart to open it, and close the datasheet.

2. On the **Chart** menu, click **Chart Type**.

3. In the **Chart Type** dialog box, click the category you want in the **Chart Type** list. Then in the **Chart sub-type** area, click the type you want, and click **OK**.

➤ **To change elements of a chart**

1. Double-click the chart to open it, and close the datasheet.

2. On the **Chart** menu, click **Chart Options.**

3. Make any changes you want on the tabs of the **Chart Options** dialog box, and then click **OK.**

4. Click outside the chart area to return to the form or report in Design view.

➤ **To format a chart**

1. Double-click the chart to open it, and close the datasheet.

2. Right-click an area of the chart, and then click **Format Chart Area.**

3. In the **Format Chart Area** dialog box, make any formatting changes for the area you clicked, and then click **OK..**

4. Click outside the chart area to return to the form.

Practice Tasks

There are no practice tasks for this objective. Experiment on your own with the type of data that lends itself to being plotted, such as monthly sales or expenses.

5.4   Export data

You can export Access database objects in a variety of formats by using the Export wizard. Any database object can be exported to another, existing Access database. You can also export certain objects to common formats such as a Microsoft Office Excel workbook (or other spreadsheet program), a Microsoft SharePoint list, a Rich Text Format (RTF) file, or a text file. The specific formats available depend on the object you are trying to export, as shown in the following table.

Database object	Valid export formats
Table	ACCDB, XLS, XLSB, XLSX, SharePoint List, PDF, XPS, RTF, TXT, XML, ODBC, HTML, dBASE, Paradox, Lotus 1-2-3, Word Merge
Query	ACCDB, XLS, XLSB, XLSX, SharePoint List, PDF, XPS, RTF, TXT, XML, ODBC , HTML, dBASE, Paradox, Lotus 1-2-3, Word Merge
Form	ACCDB, XLS, XLSB, XLSX, PDF, XPS, RTF, TXT, XML, HTML
Report	ACCDB, PDF, XPS, RTF, TXT, XML, Snapshot, HTML
Macro	ACCDB
Module	ACCDB, TXT

Tip To display a list of valid export file formats for a specific Access object, right-click the object in the Navigation Pane, and then point to Export.

You can export a table, form, or query results from an Access 2007 database to an Excel workbook.

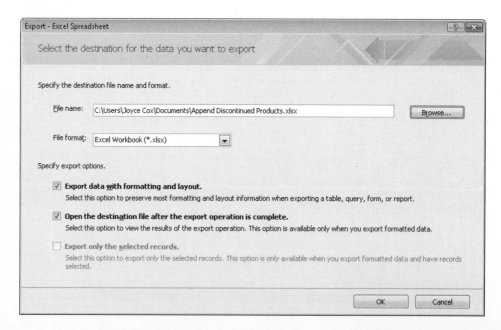

Tip When you export a table or form that contains a subdatasheet or subform, Access exports only the main datasheet or form. To export a subdatasheet or subform, you must perform an export operation on each object.

After running the Export wizard, you are given the opportunity to save the export steps so that you can repeat them with the same or a different destination file. You can then run the export operation at any time.

➤ **To export an object to another Access database**

1. In the **Navigation Pane**, select the object you want to export. On the **External Data** tab, in the **Export** group, click the **More** button, and then in the list, click **Access Database**

2. In the **Export – Access Database** wizard, click **Browse.**

3. In the **File Save** dialog box, locate and double-click the database into which you want to export the table.

4. Click **OK.**

5. In the **Export** dialog box, assign a name to the table, **Definition and Data** or **Definition Only,** and then click **OK**

6. Unless you want to save the export steps, click **Close.**

➤ **To export a table, a form, or query results to an Excel worksheet**

1. With the object selected in the **Navigation Pane**, on the **External Data** tab, in the **Export** group, click the **Excel** button

   Tip To export only some of the records in a table, open the table and select the records before beginning the export operation. Then in the Export wizard, select Export Only The Selected Records. If you need only some of the fields, create a query to select only the information you need and then export the query results.

2. In the **Export – Excel Spreadsheet** wizard, if you want to change the default name and location, click **Browse**. Then in the **File Save** dialog box, name the workbook, navigate to the folder where you want to save the table, and click **Save.**.

   Tip If the workbook does not exist, it will be created. If it does exist, a new worksheet will be created for tables or query results saved without formatting, but the workbook will be overwritten for forms or formatted data.

3. In the **Export – Excel Spreadsheet** wizard, select the check boxes of any export options you want.

4. With **Excel Workbook** selected in the **File format** list, click **OK.**

5. Unless you want to save the export steps, click **Close.**

➤ **To save an export specification**

1. Complete the steps of the **Export** wizard. After clicking **OK**, on the **Save Export Steps** page, select the **Save export steps** check box.

2. On the expanded page, assign a name for the specification in the **Save as** box, and if you want, enter a description.

   Tip If you want to be reminded about running this specification in the future, you can create a Microsoft Office Outlook task. Selecting the Create Outlook Task check box opens a task window where you can enter task details.

3. Click **Save Export**.

➤ **To run a saved export specification**

1. On the **External Data** tab, in the **Import** group, click the **Saved Exports** button.

2. In the **Manage Data Tasks** dialog box, click the saved specification you want to run.

3. To run the specification with a different destination file, click the path, make your changes, and then press **Enter.**

4. Click **Run.**

5. Click **OK** in the message confirming that the export operation was successful. Then click **Close.**

Practice Tasks

The practice file for these tasks is located in the *Documents\Microsoft Press\MCAS\ Access2007\Objective05* folder.

- Open the *ExportExcel* database, and export the Suppliers table to a new Suppliers workbook, saving the export specification with the name *Export Suppliers*.

- In the *ExportExcel* database, run the Export Suppliers specification, but this time, export the Suppliers table to a workbook named *Contacts*.

5.5   Save database objects as other file types

Earlier Access Formats

If a database will be used on a computer on which Access has not been upgraded to the 2007 version, after developing the database, you can save it in a format that is compatible with the appropriate version of Access.

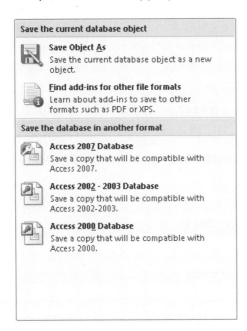

➤ **To save a database for use with an earlier version of Access**

1. Close all database objects. Then click the **Microsoft Office Button**, point to **Save As** on the **Office** menu, and in the **Save the database in another format** area, click the Access format you want.

2. In the **Save As** dialog box, name the new version of the database in the **File name** box, browse to the location where you want to save the file, and then click **Save**.

XPS Format

When publishing a report, you might need to ensure that the appearance of the content is the same no matter what computer it is displayed on. You can download an add-in from Microsoft that enables you to export information from 2007 Office system programs to the following formats:

- **Portable Document Format (PDF).** A widely used format developed by Adobe Systems.

- **XML Paper Specification (XPS).** A relatively new format developed by Microsoft.

Tip You can learn more about the XPS format and download several XPS viewers by visiting *www.microsoft.com/whdc/xps/* or by pointing to Save As on the Office menu, and then clicking Find Add-Ins For Other File Formats. To view a PDF document, install Adobe Reader from *www.adobe.com*.

The export process follows the same steps as exporting to other formats, except that you are "publishing" the exported file rather than "saving" it.

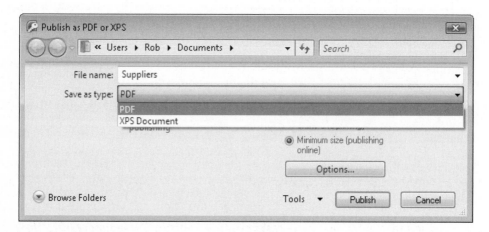

➤ To save a database object as an XPS file

1. Open the table or report, or select it in the **Navigation Pane**. On the **Office** menu, point to **Save As**, and then click **PDF or XPS**.

2. In the **Publish as PDF or XPS** dialog box, browse to the folder where you want to save the file, and click **XPS Document (*.xps)** in the **Save as type** list.

3. Click **Publish**.

Database Objects

You can save individual tables, queries, and forms as a different type of object in the same database, as follows:

- **Table.** As a table, query, form, or report
- **Query.** As a query, form, or report
- **Form.** As a form or report

You cannot save a report as another object.

> **To save a copy of a database object as a different type of object**

1. With the object you want to copy selected in the **Navigation Pane**, point to **Save As** on the **Office** menu, and then click **Save Object As**.

2. In the **Save As** dialog box, type a name for the new object in the **Save to** box, click the object type in the **As** list, and then click **OK**.

Practice Tasks

The practice files for these tasks are located in the *Documents\Microsoft Press\ MCAS\Access2007\Objective05* folder.

- Open the *OtherFileTypes* database, and save it so that it can be used on a computer on which Microsoft Office Access 2003 is installed.
- In the *OtherFileTypes* database, save a copy of the Customers table in XPS format.
- Open the *Objects* database, and save the Order Details table as a query, a form, and a report.

5.6   **Print database objects**

Because Access is a Windows application, it interacts with your printer through standard Windows dialog boxes and drivers. This means that any printer that you can use from other programs can be used from Access, and any special features of that printer, such as color printing or duplex printing, are available in Access. The print-related commands are available from the Office menu or on the Ribbon when their use would be appropriate, which is determined by the object displayed and the current view of that object.

See Also For information about printing complete documentation for a database or a database object, see section 6.2, "Manage databases."

➤ To preview a database object

1. On the **Office** menu, point to **Print**, and then click **Print Preview**.

2. In the **Print Preview** window, do any of the following:

   - Click the preview document to zoom in, and click again to zoom out.

   - At the bottom of the **Print Preview** window, click the **Next Page** or **Previous Page** button to page through the document.

   - On the **Print Preview** tab, in the **Page Layout** group, click the **Size** button to change the page size; click the **Landscape** or **Portrait** button to change the orientation; and click the **Margins** or **Page Setup** button to change the margins.

3. When you finish, click the **Close Print Preview** button.

➤ To print an entire database object

1. On the **Office** menu, click **Print**.

2. In the **Print** dialog box, adjust the settings as you want, and then click **OK**.

➤ **To print a selected part of a database object**

1. On the **Office** menu, click **Print**.

2. In the **Print** dialog box, in the **Print Range** area, click **Selected Record(s)**, and then click **OK.**.

   Tip This print option is available only if the object is open and records are selected.

Practice Tasks

The practice file for these tasks is located in the *Documents\Microsoft Press\MCAS\ Access2007\Objective05* folder.

- Open the *Print* database, and preview the Company Info tab of the Employees form. Change the layout settings of the form so that three records fit on each page, and then print the form.

- In the *Print* database, print the Orders table records for 1/12/2007.

Objective Review

Before finishing this chapter, ensure that you have mastered the following skills:

5.1 Sort data.

5.2 Filter data.

5.3 Create and modify charts.

5.4 Export data.

5.5 Save database objects as other file types.

5.6 Print database objects.

6 Managing and Maintaining Databases

The skills tested in this section of the Microsoft Office Specialist exam for Microsoft Office Access 2007 relate to keeping a database running smoothly and preventing problems. Specifically, the following objectives are associated with this set of skills:

6.1 Perform routine database operations.

6.2 Manage databases.

A useful relational database will contain many database objects—tables, forms, queries, and reports—that interact with and depend on each other. A problem with one object can create havoc throughout the database. Access provides a variety of tools to help you keep your database healthy.

This chapter guides you in studying some of the routine maintenance operations that can help you detect and fix problems. You will also look at ways to avoid problems by restricting who can open the database and what authorized users can do with the data and the database structure. Finally, you will look at sources of information about the database that can assist in its management.

 Important Before you can use the practice files in this chapter, you need to install them from the book's companion CD to their default location. See "Using the Companion CD" at the beginning of this book for more information.

Tip Graphics and operating system–related instructions in this book reflect the Windows Vista user interface. If your computer is running Windows XP and you experience trouble following the instructions as written, refer to the sidebar "If You Are Running Windows XP" in "Working in the Microsoft Office Fluent User Interface" at the beginning of this book.

6.1   Perform routine database operations

Exclusive Use

If you are working with other people on a network, when you open a database from a network location by double-clicking it in Windows Explorer or by clicking Open in the Open dialog box, the database is opened for shared access. You can work with any record in the database that no other users are working with. When you want to perform maintenance on the database, you must first open the database for exclusive use, meaning that no one else can open the database.

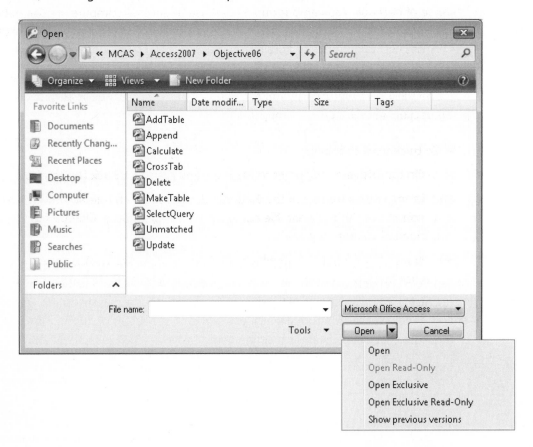

➤ **To open a database exclusively**

1. Click the **Microsoft Office Button**, and then click **Open**.

2. In the **Open** dialog box, navigate to the folder where the database is located, and then click the database to select it.

3. Click the **Open** arrow, and in the list, click **Open Exclusive**.

Backing Up

Your first line of defense against damage or corruption in any kind of file is the maintenance of backups. You can back up a database to another computer on the network or to removable media such as a USB flash drive or a tape drive. From there, you can burn a CD or DVD if you want to store a copy off site.

If the original database becomes corrupted, you can restore an entire database. If you accidentally delete an object, you can restore specific objects by importing them from the backup (see section 3.5, "Import data").

➤ **To back up a database**

1. On the **Office** menu, point to **Manage**, and then click **Back Up Database**.

2. In the **File name** box of the **Save As** dialog box, the name Access suggests consists of the database file name plus the current date. Change the file name if you want.

3. Navigate to the folder in which you want to store the backup, and then click **Save**.

See Also If you are working with a split database, you need to back up the front-end and back-end databases separately. For more information, see section 1.4, "Split databases."

Problem Prevention

In the day-to-day use of an Access database—such as adding and deleting records and modifying forms and reports—various problems can develop. This is especially true if the database is stored on a network, rather than on a local drive, and is accessed by multiple users. Access monitors the condition of database files as you open and work with them. If a problem develops, Access attempts to fix it. If Access can't fix the problem, it usually provides additional information that might help you to find a solution.

In spite of this behind-the-scenes maintenance, you might notice database performance slowing down or becoming erratic. Even if no actual errors occur, normal database use causes the internal structure of a database to become fragmented, resulting in a bloated file and inefficient use of disk space. You can use the following Access utilities to keep your database running smoothly:

- **Compact And Repair Database.** This utility first optimizes performance by re-arranging how the file is stored on your hard disk, and then attempts to repair corruption in tables, forms, reports, and modules.

- **Performance Analyzer.** This utility analyzes the objects in your database and offers three types of feedback. You can instruct Access to optimize the file by following through on any of the suggestions or recommendations.

Tip If a problem persists, you can run the Microsoft Office Diagnostics utility from the Resources page of the Access Options dialog box. Be careful with this utility, because it might change files and registry settings that affect all Office programs.

> **To manually compact and repair a database**

1. On the **Office** menu, point to **Manage**, and then click **Compact and Repair Database**.

2. Acknowledge the safety warning if prompted to do so.

   Tip If you don't have enough space on your hard disk to store a temporary copy of the database, you don't have appropriate permissions, or another user also has the database open, the Compact And Repair Database utility will not run.

> **To automatically compact and repair a database when closing it**

1. On the **Office** menu, click **Access Options**.

2. On the **Current Database** page, in the **Application Options** area, select the **Compact on Close** check box.

3. Click **OK**.

> **To analyze the performance of a database**

1. On the **Database Tools** tab, in the **Analyze** group, click the **Analyze Performance** button.

2. In the **Performance Analyzer** dialog box, on the **All Object Types** tab, click **Select All**, and then click **OK**.

3. Click each result in the **Analysis Results** box to display more information about that result in the **Analysis Notes** area.

4. Select any results you want to fix, and then click **Optimize**.

5. Click **Close**.

Link Repair

If a database contains a linked table and the source file for the table is moved, you might need to use the Linked Table Manager to repair the link.

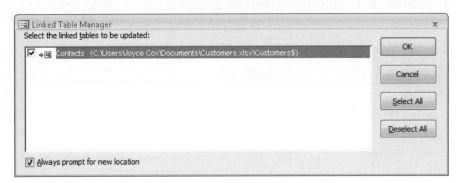

> ➤ **To repair a table link**

1. On the **Database Tools** tab, in the **Database Tools** group, click the **Linked Table Manager** button.

2. In the **Linked Table Manager** dialog box, select the check box of the table whose link needs to be repaired, and then click **OK**.

3. In the **Select New Location of** *<table>* dialog box, locate and double-click the source file.

4. Click **OK** in the message box to acknowledge that the link has been refreshed, and then click **Close** in the **Linked Table Manager** dialog box.

Practice Tasks

The practice files for these tasks are located in the *Documents\Microsoft Press\ MCAS\Access2007\Objective06* folder.

● Open the *Routine* database, and back it up to a file stored in the same folder.

● Run the Performance Analyzer on all the objects in the *Routine* database. Note the recommendations, suggestions and ideas, and then tell Access to implement all the recommendations and suggestions.

● Open the *Compact* database, and run the Compact And Repair Database utility to improve storage efficiency and fix problems.

6.2   **Manage databases**

Passwords and Encryption

You can prevent unauthorized users from opening a database by assigning it a password. To assign or remove a password, you must first open the database for exclusive use so that you can ensure that nobody else is using it.

Not only does assigning a password keep out people who might open the file in Access; it also prevents people who don't have Access from being able to scan and perhaps make sense of the data in your file. An Access database is a binary file, and theoretically its contents can be exposed. When you assign a password, your database is encrypted to make it unreadable. It is then automatically encrypted each time it is closed and decrypted when someone provides the correct password to open it.

➤ To encrypt a database by using a password

1. On the **Database Tools** tab, in the **Database Tools** group, click the **Encrypt with Password** button.

2. In the **Password** box of the **Set Database Password** dialog box, type a password.

3. In the **Verify** box, type the same password. Then click **OK**.

➤ To open an encrypted database

1. Open the database from the **Open** dialog box or from Windows Explorer.

2. In the **Password Required** dialog box, in the **Enter database password** box, type the password, and then click **OK**.

➤ **To remove a password**

1. On the **Database Tools** tab, in the **Database Tools** group, click the **Decrypt Database** button.

2. In the **Password** box of the **Unset Database Password** dialog box, type the password, and then click **OK**.

Database Options

Strategy Many of the settings in the Access Options dialog box can be used to control the database environment. This discussion highlights only a few of them. You should explore the others on your own to become familiar with these settings and their effects.

If a database will be used by people with little or no experience with Access, you might want to limit their ability to cause the database to become unstable or corrupted. In the Access Options dialog box, you can set the following options to reduce these risks:

- Specify the startup form (such as the primary data input form or a switchboard linked to several input forms).
- Turn off the ability to change table design in Datasheet view.
- Turn off the Navigation Pane.
- Disable Ribbon tabs except for the Home tab, and disable shortcut menus.
- Ensure that error checking is turned on. By default, Access checks entries and alerts the user if an entry might cause errors.

Tip When the Use Access Special Keys check box is selected, a number of special key combinations are available. These options are handy to have available while developing a database, but you might want to disable them before you make the database available to other users.

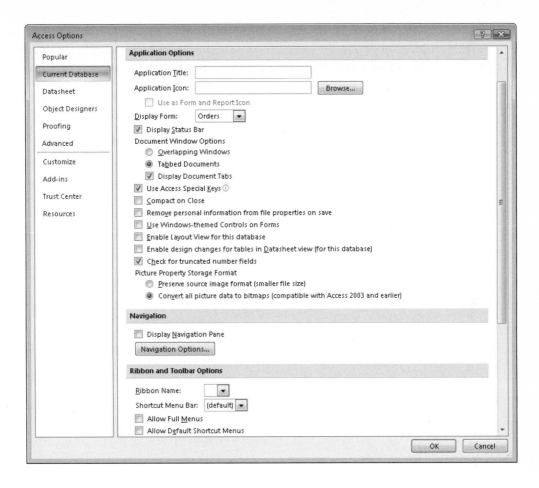

➤ **To specify the form displayed when the database is opened**

1. On the **Office** menu, click **Access Options**.

2. In the **Access Options** dialog box, display the **Current Database** page.

3. In the **Application Options** area, click the form you want in the **Display Form** list, and then click **OK**.

➤ **To limit what users can do in the database**

1. In the **Access Options** dialog box, display the **Current Database** page.

2. To prevent design changes, in the **Application Options** area, clear the **Enable Layout View for this database** and **Enable design changes for tables in Datasheet view** check boxes.

3. To hide the Navigation Pane, in the **Navigation** area, clear the **Display Navigation Pane** check box.

4. To hide most Ribbon tabs and shortcut menus, in the **Ribbon and Toolbar Options** area, clear the **Allow Full Menus** and **Allow Default Shortcut Menus** check boxes.

5. Click **OK**.

➤ **To have Access check input for errors**

1. In the **Access Options** dialog box, display the **Object Designers** page.

2. In the **Error checking** area, select check boxes of the options you want, and then click **OK**.

Tip Holding down the Shift key while you open a database bypasses all the startup options, so the database starts the same way it did before you set those options. The only way to prevent a user from bypassing your startup options is to write and run a Microsoft Visual Basic for Applications (VBA) procedure that creates the AllowByPassKey property and sets it to *False*. There is no way to set this property through Access. For information about how to do this, search for *AllowByPassKey* in the Visual Basic Editor Help file.

Database Information

To help you manage your database, you can use the following sources of information:

● **Properties.** You can specify information about the database, also known as *metadata*, that helps identify the database file and makes it easier to find. You enter standard details in the Properties dialog box. You can also create special-purpose properties.

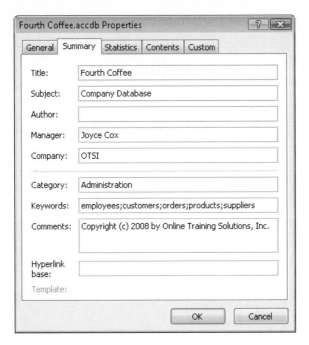

- **Object Dependencies.** You can find out whether any objects depend on a selected object before deleting it or changing its design. You can also ensure that if you copy or move an object to another database, you also copy or move the objects it depends on.

- **Database Documenter.** This utility produces a detailed report, about the entire database or about specific database objects, containing enough information to rebuild the database structure if that were ever necessary. You can view, print, or export the report generated by the Documenter, but you can't save it as a database object.

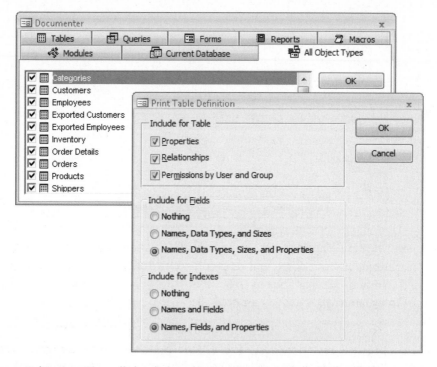

A report documenting all database objects can run to hundreds of pages, so you probably don't want to print it. However, it is a good idea to create and save a report such as this for your critical databases.

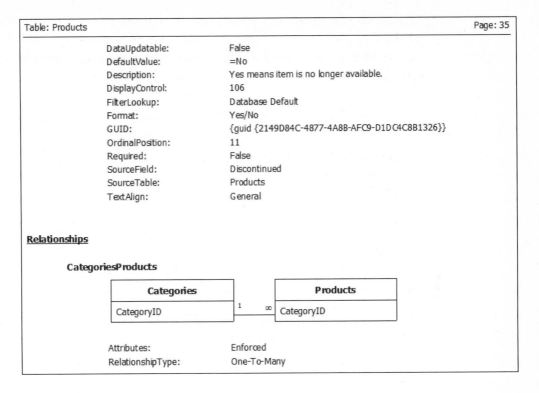

> ### To enter properties for a database

1. On the **Office** menu, point to **Manage**, and then click **Database Properties**.

2. In the **Properties** dialog box for the database, on the **Summary** tab, enter information that will allow the database to be quickly identified.

3. Click **OK**.

> ### To create a custom property for a database

1. In the **Properties** dialog box, click the **Custom** tab.

2. Specify a name and type for the property.

3. In the **Value** box, type a value for the property you just created, and then click **Add**.

4. In the **Properties** dialog box, click **OK**.

➤ **To identify object dependencies**

1. In the **Navigation Pane**, click the object whose dependencies you want to see.

2. On the **Database Tools** tab, in the **Show/Hide** group, click the **Object Dependencies** button.

3. In the **Object Dependencies** pane, click plus signs to expand dependent objects so that you can trace their dependencies. Click minus signs to hide dependencies.

4. To see the objects that the selected object depends on as sources of its data, click **Objects that I depend on**.

5. When you have finished viewing dependencies, close the **Object Dependencies** pane.

➤ **To document an entire database**

1. On the **Database Tools** tab, in the **Analyze** group, click the **Database Documenter** button.

2. In the **Documenter** dialog box, click the **All Object Types** tab, click **Select All**, and then click **Options**.

3. In the **Print Table Definition** dialog box, specify the information you want to display for each class of information, and then click **OK**.

4. Click **OK** in the **Documenter** dialog box, and then, if necessary, click **OK** in the message box prompting you to close open tables.

5. On the **Print Preview** tab of the **Object Definition** report, change the page layout settings if you want, and then print the report, view it on-screen, or export it to a file.

   Tip Page through the report by clicking the Next Page, Previous Page, First Page, and Last Page buttons in the lower-left corner of the report window. Scroll an individual page by using the vertical scroll bar on the right side of the window.

➤ **To document specific database objects**

1. On the **Database Tools** tab, in the **Analyze** group, click the **Database Documenter** button.

2. In the **Documenter** dialog box, click the **Tables**, **Queries**, **Forms**, **Reports**, or **Macros** tab. On the tab, select the check box for each database object you want to document, or click **Select All**. Then click **Options**, specify the report scope for this type of database object, and click **OK**.

3. Repeat step 2 for each type of object you want to document. Then in the **Documenter** dialog box, click **OK**.

   Tip To document modules, properties, or relationships, display the Modules or Current Database tab.

4. On the **Print Preview** tab of the **Object Definition** report, change the page layout settings if you want, and then print the report, view it on-screen, or export it to a file.

Practice Tasks

The practice files for these tasks are located in the *Documents\Microsoft Press\ MCAS\Access2007\Objective06* folder.

- Open the *Password* database, and assign the password *P@$$w0rd* to the database. Then close the database, open it again, and remove the password.

- Open the *Startup* database, and specify that the Switchboard form should be displayed when the database is opened. Then turn off the Navigation Pane and all the Ribbon tabs except the Home tab.

- Open the *Information* database, and enter your company name as the Title property of the database. Then display the dependencies of the Categories table. Finally, use the Database Documenter to produce a report of only the Categories table.

Objective Review

Before finishing this chapter, ensure that you have mastered the following skills:

6.1 Perform routine database operations.

6.2 Manage databases.

Index

Numbers

E

About the Authors

Joyce Cox

Joyce has 25 years' experience in the development of training materials about technical subjects for non-technical audiences, and is the author of dozens of books about Microsoft Office and Windows technologies. She is the Vice President of Online Training Solutions, Inc. (OTSI). She was President of and principal author for Online Press, where she developed the *Quick Course* series of computer training books for beginning and intermediate adult learners. She was also the first managing editor of Microsoft Press, an editor for Sybex, and an editor for the University of California.

Joyce and her husband, Ted, live in downtown Bellevue, Washington, and escape as often as they can to their tiny, offline cabin in the Cascade foothills.

Joan Preppernau

Joan has worked in the training and certification industry for 12 years. As President of OTSI, Joan is responsible for guiding the translation of technical information and requirements into useful, relevant, and measurable training, learning, and certification deliverables. Joan is a Microsoft Certified Professional and Microsoft Certified Application Specialist, and the author or co-author of more than a dozen books about Windows and Office.

Joan has lived and worked in New Zealand, Sweden, Denmark, and various locations in the U.S. during the past two decades, and is now happily ensconced in America's Finest City—San Diego, California—with her husband, Barry, and their daughter, Trinity, who truly believes that "working on chapters" is what all mommies do at night.

The Team

This book would not exist without the support of these hard-working members of the OTSI publishing team:

- Susie Bayers
- Jan Bednarczuk
- RJ Cadranell
- Rob Carr
- Jeanne Craver
- Kathy Krause
- Marlene Lambert
- Jaime Odell
- Barry Preppernau
- Jean Trenary
- Lisa Van Every

We are especially thankful to the support staff at home who make it possible for our team members to devote their time and attention to these projects.

Maria Gargiulo, Juliana Aldous, Sandra Haynes, and Bill Teel provided invaluable support on behalf of Microsoft Press.

Online Training Solutions, Inc. (OTSI)

 OTSI specializes in the design, creation, and production of Office and Windows training products for information workers and home computer users. For more information about OTSI, visit:

www.otsi.com

Special Offer from Certiport for Microsoft Press Users:

Save 25% on the MOS exam and get the Microsoft Official Learning Plan Assessment for FREE!!

By earning the MOS credential, you will prove your expertise using the latest Microsoft Office programs. Certification can help you differentiate yourself in today's competitive job market, broaden your employment opportunities, and garner greater earning potential. In your current job, certification can help you advance, while the greater skills mastery can also lead to increased job satisfaction. Research indicates that Office-certified individuals have increased competence and productivity with Microsoft Office programs as well as increased credibility with their employers, co-workers, and clients.

ACT NOW!

You can purchase a Microsoft Office Specialist exam voucher for 25% off the regular price and receive a Microsoft Official Learning Plan Assessment voucher for free.

Go to **www.certiport.com/mspressoffer** to redeem this offer, purchase your discounted exam, and get your learning plan assessment.

Microsoft Official Learning Plan Assessment

The Microsoft Official Learning Plan Assessment is a tool to help you identify your level of skill on 2007 Microsoft Office programs or Windows Vista. Taken online, you can receive a custom learning path with recommendations for training, Microsoft E-Learning, and Microsoft Press *Step by Step* books to help prepare for the certification exams.

Microsoft Office Specialist certification exam

Microsoft Office Specialist certifications are primarily for office workers who use Microsoft Office programs as a vital part of their job functions. These certifications cover the core Microsoft Office suite, encompassing: Word, PowerPoint, Excel, Outlook, and Access, as well as Windows Vista.

What do you think of this book?

We want to hear from you!

To participate in a brief online survey, please visit:

microsoft.com/learning/booksurvey

Tell us how well this book meets your needs—what works effectively, and what we can do better. Your feedback will help us continually improve our books and learning resources for you.

Thank you in advance for your input!

Microsoft®
Press